Finland

a travel survival kit

Markus Lehtipuu

Virpi Mäkelä

Finland – a travel survival kit

1st edition

Published by
    Lonely Planet Publications
    Head Office: PO Box 617, Hawthorn, Vic 3122, Australia
    Branches: PO Box 2001A, Berkeley, CA 94702, USA and London, UK

Printed by
    Colorcraft Ltd, Hong Kong
    Printed in China

Photographs by
    Markus Lehtipuu (ML)
    Virpi Mäkelä (VM)

    Front cover: Saame traditional shoes crafted by Petteri Laiti (Greg Videon)

First Published
    January 1993

Although the authors and publisher have tried to make the information as
accurate as possible, they accept no responsibility for any loss, injury or
inconvenience sustained by any person using this book.

National Library of Australia Cataloguing in Publication Data

Lehtipuu, Markus
    Finland, a travel survival kit.

    1st ed.
    Includes index.
    ISBN 0 86442 156 7.

    1. Finland – Guide-books.
    I. Mäkelä, Virpi II. Title. (Series: Lonely Planet travel survival kit).

914.8970434

Markus Lehtipuu

After learning to hitchhike in South Finland and trek in Lapland, Markus started his world exploration from India in 1982. After an extensive Asian tour in 1986, he has tried to return to Asia almost every year, and cover other parts of the planet when possible, including working spells in Sweden, Norway and Canada. When not travelling, he has tried to pass as many exams as possible at the Helsinki University and to write articles for local magazines. He has also authored half a dozen 'Finnish Guidebooks', including country guides for Morocco, Thailand, Malaysia and Singapore. Finally he found the time to go home and see his own country. Markus researched the sections on central and eastern Finland, Ostrobothnia and East Lapland and most of the Helsinki chapter for this edition. With much information on disk, he left Finland for South-East Asia, where he put the entire book together with his worn-out lap-top computer. He has recently joined the Helsinki-based OPAS Travel Magazine as a coeditor.

Virpi Mäkelä

Virpi was born in Helsinki. She started her travels by exploring Eastern Europe during school holidays. Since then, she has travelled on five continents. After graduating from high school, Virpi began studying for a Master's degree in economics. In summer 1986, she arranged trips to various parts of Finland for foreign students with summer jobs in Finland. Virpi is currently working as a management consultant for a well-known international firm. She researched the South Finland, Turku, Åland, South Häme and West Lapland sections of this book.

Acknowledgments It would be impossible to name all those who have helped to get this book together. Some of the local tourist staff drove us around the attractions; others checked the accuracy of our manuscripts. Some of the people we want to thank are Maija-Liisa Aho, Tuula Alanen, Jyrki Heiskanen, Jyrki Hukka, Leena Julku, Tiina Jäppinen, Pentti Järvinen, Hilkka Kangastie, Pekka Koivisto, Ulla Kortelainen, Irma Lehtipuu, Timo-Pekka Lehtipuu, Kaisu Mattila, Tim Morgan, Veikko Mäkelä, Aija Muhonen, Juhani Nurmi, Jouni Ortju, Mari Palosaari, Markku Pesonen, Reijo Pihlajaharju, Leena Pitkänen, Tuula Poutanen, Juha Rantala, Maritta Ryhänen, Tuija Rytkönen, Kaija Siitonen, Teijo Siponen, Mikko Timonen, Paavo Tuononen, Pekka Virkkunen, Pertti Väänänen and Leena Waismaa-Matsi.

From the Publisher

Alison White edited this book. It was proofed by Diana Saad, Tom Smallman, Kristin Odijk and Peter Turner, while Peter saw the book through production. Tracey O'Mara and Rachel Black drew the maps, and Tracey also did the layout, design and cover design.

Warning & Request

Things change – prices go up, schedules change, good places go bad and bad places go bankrupt – nothing stays the same. So if you find things better or worse, recently opened or long since closed, please write and tell us and help make the next edition better.

Your letters will be used to help update future editions and, where possible, important changes will also be included in a Stop Press section in reprints.

We greatly appreciate all information that is sent to us by travellers. Back at Lonely Planet we employ a hard-working readers' letters team to sort through the many letters we receive. The best ones will be rewarded with a free copy of the next edition or another Lonely Planet guide if you prefer. We give away lots of books, but, unfortunately, not every letter/postcard receives one.

Contents

TURKU..126

ÅLAND ISLANDS..139

HÄME...156

CENTRAL FINLAND 188

WEST COAST 197

SAVO 230

Map Legend

BOUNDARIES

━ ･ ━ ･ ━ ･ ━	........International Boundary
━ ･ ━ ･ ━ ･ ━	................Internal Boundary
+++++++++++++	....National Park or Reserve
-------------	........................The Equator
....	........................The Tropics

SYMBOLS

◉	NEW DELHI	.........................National Capital
●	BOMBAY	.........Provincial or State Capital
●	Pune	...............................Major Town
●	Barsi	................................Minor Town
■		...........................Places to Stay
▼		...........................Places to Eat
✉		.................................Post Office
✈		....Airport
i		......................Tourist Information
⊖		............Bus Station or Terminal
66		............Highway Route Number
☪ ✝ ⌂ ⛪		......Mosque, Church, Cathedral
∴		...........................Temple or Ruin
✚		....Hospital
✳		....Lookout
⚑		...........................Camping Area
⊼		................................Picnic Area
⌂		............................Hut or Chalet
▲		..........................Mountain or Hill
┝━┿┥		...........................Railway Station
═		...............................Road Bridge
+++++		...........................Railway Bridge
⇒ ⇐		...............................Road Tunnel
→→ ←←		...........................Railway Tunnel
⌒⌒		.....................Escarpment or Cliff
‿		....Pass
⌐⌐⌐		.............Ancient or Historic Wall

ROUTES

━━━━	........Major Road or Highway
------------	.........Unsealed Major Road
━━━━	........................Sealed Road
- - - - - - -	.....Unsealed Road or Track
═══	............................City Street
+++++++++++++	.................................Railway
●━━◉━━●	................................Subway
....	.......................Walking Track
- - - - - - -	.............................Ferry Route
++-++-++-++-++	........Cable Car or Chair Lift

HYDROGRAPHIC FEATURES

	.....................River or Creek
	..............Intermittent Stream
	........Lake, Intermittent Lake
	...........................Coast Line
	....Spring
	...............................Waterfall
	...............................Swamp
	................Salt Lake or Reef
	....................................Glacier

OTHER FEATURES

	Park, Garden or National Park
	........................Built Up Area
	... Market or Pedestrian Mall
	.........Plaza or Town Square
	...............................Cemetery

Note: not all symbols displayed above appear in this book

Introduction

With 800 years of dominance by either Sweden or Russia, or both, Finland retains much of its unique Finno-Ugric culture and combines the Western Lutheran and the Eastern Russian Orthodox influences in an interesting way. It is a developed welfare state, yet you won't see high-rise buildings anywhere. As negotiations for a full membership in the European Community (EC) are underway, Finland remains something of a backwater – quiet, rural and wild. With over 188,000 lakes and 75,000 km of roads, you'll have some choices to make!

If you want to see medieval castles and stone churches, 18th century church paintings or modern architecture, Finland has them. If you want to cover some of the best trekking areas in Europe, try canoeing routes, bicycle on little-travelled roads or do some free island-hopping in the beautiful archipelago, staying in wilderness huts for free or taking advantage of other services provided by the municipalities, Finland is the place to go. Visit Finland in summer and you'll have the midnight sun, hot saunas waiting for you at lakeside, 100-year-old steamers plying blue lakes, plenty of cottages and youth hostels available at US$10 per person, or less, and any of the 50 Finland Festivals (which offer anything from opera and jazz to folk music and dance). Or go in winter to see the other side of Finland, with busy cultural life in cities and towns, and plenty of possibilities for skiing, both cross-country and downhill.

Finland's Top 20

There are so many things to do in Finland, it

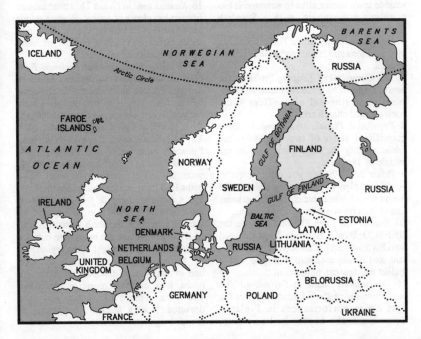

9

is hard to choose a top 20, but we've come up with this one:

1. *Passenger ferries between Finland & Sweden* The most luxurious passenger ferries anywhere, these offer a very relaxing way to enter Finland. With discounts available for students and rail-pass holders, this is an experience not to be missed.

2. *The island of Suomenlinna off Helsinki* With several museums, galleries, dark bunkers and isolated spots, this island is now on the UNESCO World Heritage List.

3. *A bicycle tour on the island of Åland* See the oldest churches in Finland, some castles and unusual flora while cycling on narrow roads. Do some island-hopping on free passenger ferries.

4. *Historical Turku* Modern Finland started in Turku, and a castle, a cathedral and a large open-air museum remain.

5. *Tammisaari Old Town* This attractive seaside town comes alive in summer. It has a unique atmosphere, with a Swedish flavour.

6. *Aulanko in Hämeenlinna* This old park has nice pavilions and accommodation in all categories.

7. *The Cathedral of Tampere* Probably the best example of National Romantic architecture, the cathedral also offers some controversial church art.

8. *Pyynikki & Pispala area, Tampere* Enjoy magnificent views of two beautiful lakes while visiting the large park right in the middle of Tampere.

9. *Route 66* Whether you drive or cycle, you'll find plenty of interesting sights in the Ruovesi and Virrat areas, including some fine church paintings in nearby Keuruu.

10. *Rauma Old Town* The first entry on the UNESCO World Heritage List, this old wooden township has attractive houses, artisans and a unique culture, complete with a dialect that few can understand.

11. *Olavinlinna Castle in Savonlinna* The most dramatic castle in Finland features the best opera performances in Finland. Savonlinna is also a centre for lake cruises,

which give you the chance to see the castle from a different angle.

12. *Lappeenranta Fort* Visit the several interesting museums and handicraft workshops in what is called the summer capital of South Karelia.

13. *Lake steamship trips* The 100-year-old steamers sail the Finnish lakeland, carrying passengers through lakes, straits and canals. You can bring your bicycle to combine other means of travelling with old steamers.

14. *Monasteries & canals in Heinävesi area* Probably Finland's most interesting set of attractions, including Orthodox monasteries, canals, and pleasant places to stay in the most beautiful lakeland of Savo, make Heinävesi an area you should explore.

15. *Orthodox Museum of Kuopio* A priceless collection of old icons, textiles, and gold and silver artefacts, saved from the Soviet-occupied Orthodox monasteries, make this museum one of the most interesting in Finland.

16. *Ruunaa area in Lieksa* The entire eastern frontier has plenty of appeal. Ruunaa stands out because of its variety; you can fish, trek, shoot rapids and visit a number of more distant attractions from here.

17. *Trekking in Saariselkä National Park* One of the largest wilderness areas in Europe, the park has an incredible choice of free accommodation in well-equipped huts, but you'll need a week to visit any number of them, as well as a good map and a compass.

18. *Karhunkierros Trek in Kuusamo* Finland's most established trekking route will take you to rugged landscape, roaming waterfalls and unusual flora and fauna. Good paths lead from one free hut to another.

19. *Kilpisjärvi lakes & fells* The highest mountains in Finland can be reached by starting a trek from the north-western village of Kilpisjärvi. There are many free huts for trekkers staying overnight in the region.

20. *Any major summer music festival* Attend one of the Finland festivals. Whether it's opera, jazz, chamber music or accordion, you'll have more of it than you ever dreamed, from a weekend happening to month-long cultural events.

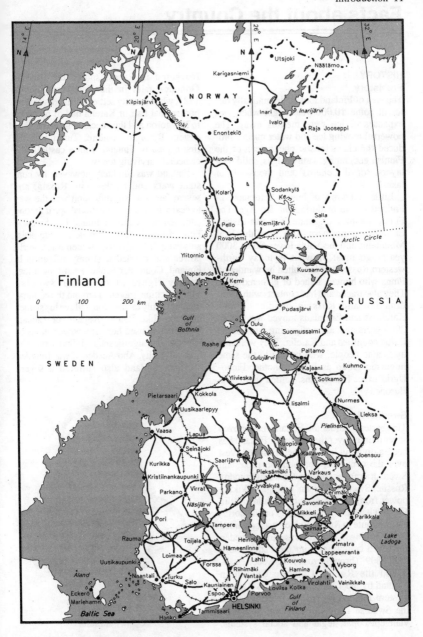

Facts about the Country

HISTORY
Prehistory

The area of Finland looked dramatically different some 10,000 years ago, when vast expanses of ice were melting away. The powerful moving ice and water masses produced the characteristic phenomena of the Finnish geography: sandy ridges, solid rock layers, 'devil's churns' and thousands of lakes.

Little is known of human settlement in Finland before or during the Ice Age. The Finnic peoples originate in north-eastern Europe and northern Asia near the Ural Mountains and the Volga River. Some 3000 years ago most of what is today northwestern Russia was inhabited by wandering Finns who hunted, fished or gathered food. They also traded and had contacts with Scandinavian and Russian peoples. Finns, Karelians and Estonians moved west about 2000 years ago, after migrating through the Baltic countries and Karelia. They were met by Saame people, who belong to the same linguistic group as Finns. Another Finno-Ugric tribe, Hungarians, settled in Central Europe.

Swedish Rule

The eastern border of Finland has moved several times over the centuries. Finland has been a dividing line between East and West over the centuries, between the protestant Swedish empire and the Eastern Orthodox Russia. Sweden was an emerging Viking power from the 9th century, with interest in Finland because of its position on the north-eastern route to Russia (which was so named by the Vikings). Finland was part of Sweden for seven centuries, from the 12th century until 1809. Through crusades, Sweden established the Roman Catholic Church in Finland by the 12th century, and as a result, western Finland became an integral part of the Swedish kingdom, adopting Scandinavian episcopal, legal and social systems.

Novgorod in Russia spread the Russian Orthodox faith in the Karelia region. In 1323, when a treaty settled Finland's eastern border, that half of Karelia had to be ceded to Novgorod and thus became influenced by eastern Byzantine culture. Turku was the first capital of Finland, with a castle and a cathedral surviving today.

Finland was blighted, however, by constant wars and battles with Russia, and severe famines. Swedification was the way to deal with the rising national spirit among educated and cultured Finns. For Swedes, Finland remained a backwater, where peasants lived. In the 1600s, Sweden was a world power and exerted a strong influence in Finland. Count Per Brahe, even now a legendary figure of the local Swedish administration, travelled around the country, founded many towns. You will see his statues in places like Raahe, Kajaani or Lieksa. Sweden also used her superpower status to increase the significance of Swedish. The first university, Åbo Academy, was founded in 1640. Finland also suffered a severe

Count Per Brahe

12

famine in 1696-97 when almost a third of the population died.

The 1700s saw two bitter wars against Russia. In 1714 Russia occupied Finland, and the following period is still referred to as the Great Wrath, lasting until 1721, when south-east Finland was ceded to Russia. In 1741-43, the Swedish-Finnish army was again defeated. Russia again occupied Finland, for a period called the Lesser Wrath, and the border was pushed further west.

Only after the 1740s did the Swedish government try to improve Finland's socioeconomic situation. Defences were strengthened by the building of the fortress Sveaborg (now called Suomenlinna) off the coast of Helsinki, and many new towns were founded. With the emergence of Peter the Great and his foundation of St Petersburg, the Swedish empire declined, and was to lose Finland to Russia.

Russian Rule

After the Treaty of Tilsit was signed by the Russian tsar (Alexander 1) and Napoleon, Russia attacked Finland in 1807. Sweden ceded Finland to Russia as an autonomous grand duchy, which could have its own Senate and the Diet of the Four Estates, but all major decisions had to be approved by the tsar. At first, Finland benefited from the annexation and was loyal to the tsar, who encouraged Finns to develop the country in many ways. There followed a surge of nationalistic aspirations, during the National Romantic era of the latter half of the 19th century. The researcher Elias Lönnrot compiled the national epic *Kalevala*, and the poet J L Runeberg wrote the words of the present Finnish national anthem. Mr Snellman, the statesperson, fought successfully for the equality of Finnish language with the Swedish language, as there were constant disputes between the Fennomans and Svecomans.

Another figure of that time, Mr Arwidsson, uttered the much-quoted sentence: 'Swedes we are not, Russians we will not become, so let us be Finns'. However, the rise of Pan-Slavonic ideas in Russia after 1880 was followed by oppression and Russification, resulting in various illegal measures from the Russian government. After the general strike in Finland in 1905, the new unicameral parliament was introduced with universal and equal suffrage. Finland was the first country in Europe to grant women full political rights (second in the world after New Zealand). Yet, new oppression and Russifying actions followed, which made Finns emotionally ripe for independence.

Independence

The downfall of the tsar of Russia, and the Communist revolution in 1917, made it possible for the Finnish senate to declare independence on 6 December 1917. Finland was first recognised by Soviet Russia one month later. Independence was no easier for Finns than for any other nation. Russian soldiers remained, and the nation was still in the making. A bloody civil war emerged from bitter class differences. The Reds, the rising working class, aspired to follow the Russian-style socialist revolution yet retain independence, whereas the nationalistic Whites dreamed of monarchy and sought models from Germany. A German prince was actually chosen as the king of Finland; his crown is now on display in the Gemstone Gallery in Kemi.

Whites eventually gained victory under Lieutenant General Gustaf Mannerheim, with help from Germany, whereas Finnish underground activists, *Jääkärit*, had secretly undergone military training under the pseudonym *Jägers* or 'hunters'. The bloody and devastating war ended in May 1918. A year later, Finland's status was established, and relations with the Soviet Union were normalised in the Tartto peace settlement of 1920. The defeat of imperial Germany made Finland choose a republican state model, and the first president was K J Ståhlberg. Finland soon gained fame as a brave new nation, as the only country to pay its debts to the USA, and as a sporting nation. One of several Finnish long-distance runners, Paavo Nurmi, won six gold medals in three

Finland's Changing Borders

1323-1617

1323 – Peace of Pähkinäsaari. South-west Finland becomes Swedish territory, and the north and Karelia becomes part of Novgorod.

1595 – Peace of Täyssinä. After a war between Sweden and Russia, Kainuu and Lapland are annexed by Sweden.

1617 – The Peace of Stolbova, after a Swedo-Russian war, sees Sweden gain control of Karelia and areas around the Gulf of Finland.

1809 – Sweden loses Finland to Russia, while Finland becomes an autonomous state within Russia. Borders are defined along rivers in the north and north-west. Finland's territory enlarges in 1812, 1826 and 1833 to include the present territory, Karelia and the Salla Kuusamo region.

1920 – Peace of Tartto. The new Bolshevik empire of the Soviet Union gives the 'left arm' of Petsamo to Finland, and Finland gives up some minor areas. Finland is at its largest.

1809-1920

WW II

1944 – During WW II, Finland loses territory to the USSR along its eastern frontier. In the Scolt region in the north, Saame refugees cross into Finland. Russia gains rich nickel deposits, which have become the main source of pollution in north-east Lapland.

Finland also loses some of its most scenic territory around Lake Paanajäru, made famous by the painter, Gallén-Kallela.

In the south-east Finland loses the important town of Viipuri, and 400,000 refugees are uprooted twice during WW II.

Olympic Games and became a national figure. With continuing Finnish success in athletics, Helsinki was chosen to host the Olympic Games in 1940 (but these were postponed until 1952, due to WW II).

WW II

During the relatively prosperous years of the 1930s, Finland had developed close ties with the emerging Nazi Germany. Relations remained warm with the newly independent Estonia, and suspicious towards the newborn communist Soviet Union. Finally, as war approached, the Soviet Union presented territorial claims to Finland, feeling its security threatened from the Finnish territory of south-eastern Karelia. J K Paasikivi (the president after the war) visited Moscow for negotiations (or dictations) on the ceding of the Karelian Isthmus to the Soviet Union. Paasikivi disregarded the threats, with the result that the Russians fired shots from their territory at the Finnish village of Mainila, and accused Finland of violating peace agreements. It was a few days later, early on the morning of 30 November 1939, that the 'Winter War' began. Finland had little chance in its fight against a world power, but the soldiers nevertheless endured. It was an uniquely harsh winter, with temperatures reaching -40°C, and soldiers died in their thousands. The war lasted a full 100 days and ended in the victory of the Red Army. Consequently Finland had to give up the Karelian Isthmus and settle a large number of refugees. The Soviet army occupied the Hanko Peninsula for use as a military base.

The Soviet Union continued to pressure Finland, even after the Moscow peace treaty was signed in March 1940. After the annexation of the Baltic States to the Soviet Union, the Soviets started making plans to occupy Åland. The Red Army primarily feared the Swedes, who were planning a union with Finland which would have increased Finland's power considerably. Finland was quite aware of the danger of losing the western islands to the USSR, so the islands were even offered to Nazi Germany as a buffer against the USSR. Germany refused, however.

The second, 'Continuation War' between Finland and the Red Army started in June 1941. Finland, isolated from Western allies, joined Germany for help. Again, the war started successfully for Finland. One of the dramatic moments occurred when Finnish soldiers advanced over the old border to the Russian Karelia, inhabited by linguistic relatives of the Finns. Finns believed much of what the Nazis fed to them, and started to dream of the Greater Finland which would span the entire Karelia. This move was criticised as a violation of justice; supposedly, the only reason for the war was to regain territories lost during the winter war. People were moving back to the once-lost Karelia, and everyone expected Karelia to remain a Finnish territory. Only during the summer of 1944 was the Soviet Union able to launch an enormous counterattack, to force Finland into peace negotiations. Finland did remain independent, but at a price: Finland was to cede territories and pay heavy war reparations. The Porkkala Peninsula was 'leased' to the Soviet Union for 50 years (but was returned in 1956). The final bitter phase of the war took place in Lapland, when Finland had to drive Germans out of the country. Before leaving, the Germans burned everything to which they had access.

In all, Finland's war experience was an enormous defeat, not only territorially but also financially, materially, politically and (most of all) emotionally. Even these days in Helsinki, some old drunkards, many of them war veterans, curse the Russians.

From Ashes to Prosperity

The peace agreement in 1947 was tough. The Karelian Isthmus was ceded to the Soviet Union, as well as the eastern Salla/Kuusamo region and the 'left arm' of Finland in the Kola Peninsula. Half a million Karelian refugees had to be resettled, again, and heavy war reparations were paid to the Soviet Union.

Although there was never a foreign military presence in Finland after the war, the conflict had continuing political repercussions. In 1948 Finland was to sign a *yya* agreement, or Treaty of Friendship, Cooperation & Mutual Assistance, with the Soviet Union. This agreement was seen as an inevitable solution to an uneasy coexistence. The agreement practically drew the two countries into an awkward semimilitary relationship, in spite of the Finland's claim of neutrality. The agreement remained valid until 1992, when it was replaced by a new loose agreement with Russia without any reference to military aspects.

Finland was a typical Third World country immediately after the war, with almost everything rationed, widespread poverty and the vast majority of the population engaged in agriculture. War reparations played a central role in laying foundations for the heavy engineering industry which transformed Finland's trade patterns and stabilised Finland's internal position. They also started the phase of joint projects and profitable trade agreements with the USSR. Things changed quickly over the following decades, and domestic migration from the north to the south was especially strong in the 1960s and 1970s, with new suburbs appearing almost overnight in and around Helsinki. However, many people have had difficulty adjusting to urban life.

In Finland the political parties largely followed the same foreign policy line, known as the 'Paasikivi-Kekkonen line'. This pragmatic approach to geopolitics was also referred to as Finlandisation, which hinted at subservience to pressure from a stronger state, but it included, in fact, a unique formula for survival in a difficult geographical situation.

One of the great leaders of his age, and the main brain behind this tightrope-walking foreign policy, U K Kekkonen (president from 1956 to 1981) gained fame abroad as an eccentric and witty president. He was also well know for his role as host of the initial Conference on Security & Cooperation in Europe (CSCE) meeting, in Helsinki in 1975. On the home front, however, things weren't all that good. Democracy reached an all-time low during his reign when, in 1974, a vast majority of delegates from all major parties decided to postpone presidential elections and to extend Mr Kekkonen's term by four years. Kekkonen 'advised' opponents quite strongly by sending his then-famous letters, and political nominations were submitted to Moscow for approval within the framework of 'friendly coexistence'.

Any status within the Finno-Soviet protocol was regarded as a gain. As recently as the late 1980s, the Soviet Communist Party exercised cold-war tactics by infiltrating Finnish politics, aiming to reduce US influence in Finland and trying to prevent Finnish membership of the EC. Even the acknowledgement of an Estonian national identity was considered taboo for a while. When Kekkonen finally became unfit to fulfil his job as president, his true state of health was carefully kept secret. He spent his last years virtually caged in Tamminiemi House, which is now a museum open to tourists.

As a balance to all this, relations with Scandinavia were always extremely important. If there were some doubtful aspects to the situation in the east, Finland, as a member state of the Nordic Council (the other members are Denmark, Iceland, Norway and Sweden), was to nurture old contacts, pursuing a similar social welfare programme to Scandinavia and enjoying the benefits of the free movement of labour, a passport-free area, and even common research and educational programmes with western neighbours. In fact, much of the rural population fleeing from the north bought one-way tickets all the way to Sweden, which at that time welcomed foreign labourers with open arms, thus providing Finland with a valve for the inevitable pressures of the drastic social transformation from a rural country to modern Finland.

Finland has always kept a low profile in almost everything, and has tried to make friends all over the world. It now faces new challenges in relation to the mighty EC and to the tumbling former Soviet Union across the border. Most of all, Finland may have to redefine its true identity now that its southern neighbour and closest ethnic relative,

Estonia, is an independent state and (Russian) Karelia, just across the border, is seeking new forms of cooperation with Finland. Some voices in the autonomous Karelia call for a union with Finland, which currently shows little interest in altering international borders, having learned the lessons of history, it seems.

GEOGRAPHY

With an area of 338,000 sq km, Finland is the seventh largest country in Europe. The southernmost point, the town of Hanko, lies at the same latitude as Oslo in Norway, as well as Greenland's southernmost tip and Anchorage in Alaska. The shape of Finland has been compared to that of a female, holding her right arm up (the 'left arm' was lost to the former Soviet Union after WW II). Finland is situated between Sweden and Russia, with which it shares a 1269-km border. With Norway, Finland shares a 716-km land border in the far north. The Gulf of Finland separates South Finland from Estonia. Some 70% of Finland is covered by forests. The Finnish bedrock is stable, with few earthquakes ever recorded. Much of the country is lakeland. There are few, if any,

mountains, rather, there are sandy ridges and wooded hills. The highest hills, or *tunturi*, are in Lapland, which borders the mountainous areas of northern Norway and Sweden. The highest point, the Halti, rises 1328 metres above sea level.

There are 188,000 lakes in Finland, and together with marshes and bogs, water covers about 10% of the country. Finland is a country shaped by water: lakes and ponds, rivers and creeks, rapids and small waterfalls, islands and islets, bays, capes and straits, and the large archipelago outside Turku, Åland, Helsinki and Vaasa.

CLIMATE

Finland enjoys four seasons. The climate is bearable, and excellent in summer. Because of its inland waters, the Baltic Sea and the mild winds from the Gulf Stream along the Norwegian coast, Finland's climate is, on average, much warmer than in other places of similar latitude (Siberia, Greenland and Alaska). Winters *are* cold, but the cold is dry. The last couple of winters have been unusually mild, however, with little snow in the south. Whether or not this is an indication of global warming remains to be seen. To travel

Average Rainfall & Temperature

City	Precipitation (mm)			Temperature (°C)		
	Annual	Jan	July	Annual	Jan	July
Helsinki	622	49	58	5.3	-5.5	17.4
Mariehamn	536	41	49	5.4	-3.2	16.1
Joensuu	606	42	74	2.4	-10.9	16.5
Oulu	474	29	64	2.2	-9.9	16.3
Utsjoki	400	26	56	-0.9	-11.5	12.0

Winter Gloom & Midnight Sun

Place	Hours of Winter Gloom Darkness at 22 Dec	Hours of Midnight Sun Daylight at 22 June	Starts	Ends
Helsinki	16h 15min	22h 40min	–	–
Oulu	17h 30min	24h	–	–
Kuusamo	NA	24h	12 Jun	30 June
Rovaniemi	NA	24h	6 Jun	7 July
Ivalo	NA	24h	22 May	21 July
Kilpisjärvi	NA	24h	20 May	23 July
Utsjok	19h 47min	24h	16 May	27 July

in Finland in winter, you will need fur-lined boots and mittens, woollen caps, overcoats, quilted jackets, thermal suits and parkas to keep warm, but you can also stay indoors. Houses are well insulated, with triple windows, and are well heated in winter.

Weather in Finland changes from day to day and depends largely on winds, often dry from the east, cold from the north, rainy from the west and warm and humid from the south. It is not unusual to have temperatures of 5°C in January or to get hailstorms or soil frost in June, but yearly averages follow a logical curve: the shorter the nights, the warmer the days, and vice versa. Summer sees hot spells and weeks of little rain, but the temperatures can be as low as 10°C at any time in summer.

FLORA & FAUNA

Finnish flora is surprisingly rich and varied during the dynamic period between late May and September. Some low-lying valleys in the south, with creeks flowing through, resemble real jungle by late July.

There are several unique or rare species which have been preserved in national parks and natural reserves around the country. The three main types of forest are pine, spruce and birch. Each type has a typical flora. Pine grows generally on dry ground and sand ridges, and there is little vegetation. Spruce forests are dark and dense, whereas deciduous forests, birch being the typical tree, are the most varied in terms of flora.

You will come across few mammals in Finnish forests. The largest is the brown bear, which was once so feared that even mentioning its name *(karhu)* was taboo.

Other mammals include elks, foxes, lynxes, wolves and wolverines, and there are plenty of small animals such as lemmings, hedgehogs, muskrats, martens, otters and hares. Beavers are also quite common. Reindeer *(poro)* abound in north Finland. Elk *(hirvi)* are hunted every year on licences, because they cause severe road accidents and hunting is supposed to keep the stock stable. Lynxes *(ilves)*, Häme's 'national' animal, used to be very rare but numbers are increas-

Flowers of Finland

ing. There are practically no domestic wolves left in Finland, but plenty of them cross the border regularly from Russia. Hatred for the wolf *(susi)* is so deep-rooted in eastern Finland that whenever wolves are sighted, friends are alerted by cellular phone, and within a few hours the poor animals are rounded up by 4WD vehicles and shot dead. The viper is the commonest poisonous snake, with antivenins readily available in pharmacies.

There are over 300 species of birds to be seen in Finland. Large species include black grouse, capercaillies, whooper swans and birds of prey, such as ospreys. Chaffinches and willow warblers are the two most common species in forests, and sparrows are very common in inhabited areas. Black woodpeckers, black-throated divers, ravens and many owls are supposed to be 'wilderness birds'. The Siberian jay, on the other hand, is a common sight in Lapland because it follows people, as does the lumberjack, its close relative in North America. Bird life in winter is also of interest, with bullfinches and waxwings flying around. Birds only sing from March to the end of June. Finns who watch migratory birds arriving from the south have a saying on how to determine when summer will come: it is one month from skylark, half a month from chaffinch, just a little from white wagtail and not a single day from swiftlet.

Less popular creatures include bugs, mosquitoes, horseflies, wasps, gnats and the rest of the nasties. June and July are the most active months for these little devils, whereas August can be quite mosquito-free when trekking in Lapland. Some *ohvi* (the 'Off' brand) will help a great deal, but few of the insects are really harmful.

GOVERNMENT

Finland is a democratic republic with a president elected to six-year terms by a two-stage vote. Presidential duties include overseeing foreign policy, appointing cabinet ministers and acting as the commander in chief of the Finnish army. Legislative powers rest with the unicameral parliament, or Eduskunta,

which has 200 members elected to four-year terms. The president has the right to veto a bill. Executive functions are performed by the prime minister and a coalition government of ministers, who are normally elected members of the parliament. Every citizen over 18 years of age has the right to vote.

Major political parties *(puolue)* represented in Finland include the agrarian-oriented Centre Party, or Keskusta (24.8%), the Social Democratic Party (22.1%), the conservative National Coalition Party, or Kokoomus (19.3%), the ex-communist Left-wing Alliance, or Vasemmistoliitto (10.1%), the Greens, or Vihreä liitto (6.8%), the Swedish People's Party, or Svenska folkpartiet (5.5%), the agrarian Rural Party, or Suomen Maaseudun Puolue (4.8%), and the Christian League, or Kristillinen Liitto (3.0%). Left-wing parties have lost a significant share of the vote in the last couple of years, which is just one indication of the changes that are expected to occur in Finnish politics in the 1990s.

Dr Mauno Koivisto, a Social Democrat, has been the elected president since 1982. The term of office is six years. Since 1919 there have been 10 presidents in Finland, with the next election due in 1994. For local administration, the country is divided into 12 provinces *(lääni)* and approximately 470 municipalities *(kunta)* or 85 towns *(kaupunki)*.

ECONOMY

Finland is a prosperous welfare state. Forestry products are the main source of income, employment, pollution and environmental debate, but metal mining and engineering contribute an equally large share of export income. There is much scientific research in several fields, and over 600 companies are based in 'high-tech villages' in Oulu, Espoo, Turku, Lappeenranta, Tampere, Kuopio and Jyväskylä; there are over 20 industrial villages around Finland where companies are granted special privileges. Hydroelectric power is available, mostly from the Kemijoki River in Lapland, and there are four nuclear power plants.

NORWAY

SWEDEN

RUSSIA

Gulf of Bothnia

Finland
Provinces

LAPIN LÄÄNI
(Lappi Province)

OULUN LÄÄNI
(Oulu Province)

KUOPION
LÄÄNI
(Kuopio
Province)

POHJOIS-
KARJALAN
LÄÄNI
(North Karelia
Province)

VAASAN LÄÄNI
(Vaasa Province)

KESKI-
SUOMEN
LÄÄNI
(Central
Finland
Province)

MIKKELIN LÄÄNI
(Mikkeli Province)

TURUN JA
PORIN
LÄÄNI
(Turku &
Pori
Province)

HÄMEEN
LÄÄNI
(Häme
Province)

KYMEN
LÄÄNI
(Kymi
Province)

UUDENMAAN
LÄÄNI
(Uusimaa Province)

ÅLAND
PROVINCE

ST PETERSBURG

The 1980s saw an economic boom, caused by monetary liberalisation and speculation created in the overheated stock exchange. The Bank of Finland lifted most currency restrictions but, at the same time, regulated the markka's external value. This, together with high interest rates, resulted in an overvaluation of the currency. It soon became obvious that enjoying cheap imports and holidays while regularly increasing salaries through lengthy strikes was impossible; export-oriented companies faced difficulties in selling their products and high interest rates stifled investment. Finland became the most expensive country in the world and was announced the fourth richest, measured by GNP per capita. The central bank ruled out devaluation but insisted on the centralised reduction of all wages. The government tried to negotiate this with Finland's powerful trade unions, which boast over one million members, but long discussions proved useless. To maintain financial confidence, the Finance Minister, in a national TV interview in November 1991, bet 1000 mk that there would be no devaluation; the very same evening, in panic, the markka was devalued when foreign reserves stood at US$500 million. The recession in the 1990s has seen record unemployment, the collapse of trade with the former Soviet Union, plenty of bankruptcies and huge bank losses, but the lowest inflation in decades.

The future of the welfare economy is discussed widely, as are the huge farming subsidies. There is overproduction of grain, butter, cheese and eggs, and the prices of most farm products are centrally fixed at an artificially high level. To make things worse, some people exercise their consumer power by visiting Sweden just to buy cheap butter. The system assures that all production is paid for, but to 'save money', the government also pays farmers to have their fields lie fallow or to transform fields into forests. Even exporting food costs Finland money, as farmers expect to earn the predetermined prices, which are much higher than world prices. Some farmers have shown militancy in the face of Finland's future EC membership, which is expected to lower food prices in the long run.

Forestry

Forests are administered by local forest rangers, who mark stands of trees for cutting. These days, logging sites (called *savotta* in Finnish) are taken care of by multipurpose machines, and only a few down-to-earth lumberjacks still work by hand. Some forests still disappear through clear felling, but professionals are more likely to talk about 'forest improvement', trimming or silviculture, and they even point out that 'forests rot unless you cut'. Nevertheless, Finland lives out of its forests, and for each area felled, a similar area is planted with small saplings. As you tour the country, you can see forests of all ages, young and old. Forests are either private or owned by large timber companies. Timber sales have been based on predetermined prices (some of the highest in the world), but these days there is more pressure for price fluctuations. Paper and pulp industries bring work to thousands but also cause environmental hazards which are easily seen in areas surrounding factories. To keep everyone happy, the National Board of Forestry maintains magnificent trekking and fishing areas, with free accommodation available to anyone.

POPULATION

Finland's population is currently five million, with an annual growth rate of 0.3%. The average household size is 2.4 people. Finland has gone through typical demographic phases in its development; 10 children in a family was not uncommon just 50 years ago. In 1800 the population stood at 800,000; in 1900 it was about two million. Large numbers of Finns have emigrated to other countries: some 250,000 to Sweden, 280,000 to the USA, 20,000 to Canada and 10,000 to Australia. At the time of writing, there is a possibility of population growth through immigration from countries of the former Soviet Union, but Finns don't seem to be attracted to this idea. Approximately 75% of the population lives in towns. Over half of Finns live in the three south-western provinces (around Helsinki, Turku and Tampere), which have 15% of the total land area. The Greater Helsinki area, including Espoo, Vantaa and several municipalities, houses one million people, or 20% of the total. Other large towns include Tampere, Turku, Oulu, Lahti, Kuopio, Pori and Jyväskylä.

More facts and figures: the average working week is 39 hours, 73% of women go to work and the unemployment rate is 13%. In 1991, men earned an average of US$2380 per month, women US$1910. Less than 10% of the population earns a living from agriculture, 32% from industries and 58% from services.

PEOPLE

Nearly 99.5% of all people living in Finland today were born in Finland. There were just 34,000 foreigners living in Finland in 1991, or 0.7% of the population. This is the lowest percentage in any country in Europe. The main minority groups include the 300,000 Swedish-speaking Finns (called *Finlandssvensk*, or 'Finland's Swede'), the 4000 Saame people of Lapland and the 5000 Gypsies. Finns can also be divided into several historical 'tribes', but this distinction has lost some of its significance, to the point that you can now only tell the difference by a person's dialect. In the old days, Savonian people were considered talkative and easy-going but clever, Karelians friendly and hospitable, people of Häme the most reserved and introverted, and Ostrobothnians (people living around the flat West Coast) proud, cool and sometimes willing to fight. Some of these characteristics can still be observed.

There is no exact evidence of where the original Finns came from. The early Finno-Ugrians were nomadic tribespeople who inhabited much of North Russia. North Asia or the Ural Mountains are generally considered to be 'homes' for the Finno-Ugrians, and there are still small Finnic groups living in that area. Linguistic comparisons have found some similarities to Korean grammar,

and Hungarian is definitely a language related to Finnish, though very few similar words remain. Estonians and Karelians are very close relatives to Finns. During the centuries, however, a substantial Indo-European influence has affected the population of Finland, to the extent that many Finns look very Scandinavian, Baltic or Russian (or vice versa), even though the language is different. Another approach maintains that Finns, Balts and even Czechs may be racially close but linguistically distant. You may also see hints of (East) Asian character in some faces in Finland.

EDUCATION

The literacy rate in Finland is practically 100%, and the number of newspapers and books printed per capita is one of the highest in the world. This is partly due to the high education standards in Finland. The nine-year comprehensive school *(peruskoulu)* is one of the most 'equal' systems in the world, which means that tuition, books, meals, and commuting to/from school are free. However, it also means that the most talented pupils have few chances to excel above others. All Finns learn Swedish and English in school, and many also study German or French.

The three-year secondary school *(lukio)* attracts some 30,000 students every year and serves as a stepping stone to universities in Helsinki, Turku, Tampere, Oulu, Jyväskylä, Joensuu, Kuopio, Rovaniemi and Vaasa. Approximately 18,000 new university students start every year.

The first university in Finland was founded in Turku in 1640 and transferred to Helsinki, where it now has some 26,000 students. More than half of the undergraduates are women. Universities are state-owned and there are practically no fees. State grants and state-guaranteed low-interest loans, and subsidised health care, meals and student hostels are available for most students. With these benefits, Finnish students stay an average of seven to eight years in their universities.

In addition to higher education, there are

several educational institutes, from vocational schools to those specialising in an individual subject or just in 'how to live a happy life'.

ARTS

Architecture

The high reputation of modern Finnish architecture was established through works by Alvar Aalto and Eliel Saarinen. Many people interested in architecture make pilgrimages to Finland to see remarkable examples of modern architecture in Helsinki and Espoo, Turku, Tampere, Jyväskylä, Seinäjoki and Oulu. Unfortunately, much of the superb Finnish architecture is overshadowed by supermarkets and other concrete blocks that dominate in towns and villages.

The oldest architectural monuments include medieval castles and 75 stone churches, scattered around villages in South Finland, such as Lohja, Sipoo and Hattula. In these Catholic churches, Gothic ideals were emulated but with little success, and as a result, an original Finnish style emerged.

Wood has been the dominant building material in Finland. In the late 17th century, Protestant churches adopted cruciform in conjunction with Swedish patterns. Some of the best early examples of wooden architecture include churches on Finland's West Coast. Interesting belfries can be found in Ruokolahti in the east and Tornio in West Lapland.

Eastern influences date back to 1812, when Finland became an autonomous grand duchy under Russian rule and Helsinki was made the new capital. The magnificent city centre was created by C L Engel, a German-born architect, who combined neoclassical and Petersburg features in designing the cathedral, the university and other buildings around Senate Square. Engel also designed a large number of churches in Finland. After the 1850s, National Romanticism emerged in response to pressure from the Russians. The Art Nouveau period, which reached its climax by the turn of the century, combined Karelian ideals with rich ornamentation. Materials were wood and grey granite. The best examples of this style are Hvitträsk and the National Museum (Eliel Saarinen) and the Cathedral of Tampere (Lars Sonck).

After independence was achieved in 1917, rationalism and functionalism emerged with Alvar Aalto's sanatorium in Paimio. Aalto's latter works are to be seen in Säynätsalo, Jyväskylä, Helsinki (Finlandia Hall), Seinäjoki and Rovaniemi. Since the 1950s, architects such as Viljo Revell, Aarno Ervi, Heikki Siren, Toivo Korhonen, Timo Penttilä, Aarno Ruusuvuori, Erkki Kairamo and Kristian Gullichsen, Timo and Tuomo Suomalainen (Rock Church in Helsinki), Raili and Reima Pietilä (Dipoli in Espoo, Library of Tampere) and Juha Leiviskä (St Thomas Church in Oulu) have designed notable buildings.

Design

Finns have created their own design idioms in their craft tradition, use of natural materials (wood, glass, ceramics, fabric and metal) and simple but pure forms. Stylistically they combined colourful geometrically ornamented Karelian (originally Byzantine) design with a more European Western style. Traditional textile art, such as woven *ryijy* rugs and *raanus*, and national costumes, as well as wooden furniture and everyday utensils and implements, can be seen in various museums, but this common heritage is still clearly visible in the works of modern designers.

The products of some early designers, such as Louis Sparre, Gallén-Kallela and Eliel Saarinen, reflected the ideas of Karelianism, National Romanticism and Art Nouveau. In the 1930s Alvar Aalto, the architect, invented wooden furniture made of bent and laminated plywood, and his famous Savoy vases, today promoted by Artek. Aalto got a prize for his furniture in the Milan Triennale in 1933.

After WW II, the 'Golden Age of Applied Art' began, and in 1951 in Milan, Finland received 25 prizes for various designer products. Tapio Wirkkala, Kaj Franck, Timo Sarpaneva, Eero Aarnio and Yrjö Kukkapuro were the most notable designers of that time.

Unfortunately the high quality of Finnish design suffered during the turbulent years of the 1970s, and it has had difficulties recovering. Iittala, Nuutajärvi and Arabia are still some of the best brands of Finnish glassware and porcelain, and Pentik is a more recent brand. Aarikka is famous for wooden products, and Kalevala Koru for silver designs.

Painting

Of the prehistoric rock paintings to be found in several places across Finland, those of Hossa and Ristiina are the most famous. Medieval churches in Åland and in South Finland have frescoes, and several 18th century wooden churches have interesting paintings by Mikael Toppelius or others, most notably in Paltaniemi, Keuruu and in several villages near Oulu, especially in Haukipudas. Some of the best-known Finnish classical painters include the three von Wright brothers (photo-like landscapes and birds) and Werner Holmberg (landscape). Albert Edelfelt is one of the most appreciated, and Akseli Gallén-Kallela created Kalevala-inspired National Romantic paintings. Other names worth remembering include Eero Järnefelt, Pekka Halonen, Magnus Enckell, Hugo Simberg and Helene Schjerfbeck. The Ateneum in Helsinki has the best collection of Finnish art, and should not be missed.

Dance

Dance is one of the serious arts nurtured in Finland. The Finnish National Opera has its own ballet school, and there are a handful of small dance groups in Helsinki and a few other large towns. Mr Jorma Uotinen, director of the Finnish National Ballet, is currently the most interesting figure in contemporary dance in Finland. You should try to attend the annual Kuopio Dance & Music Festival to see the latest trends. Few traditional folk dances (*kansantanssit*) remain, but they can be seen on some ceremonial occasions.

In summer you may come across a noisy dance stage in the middle of nowhere, to experience *lavatanssit*, where local singers

and their bands play pop music, and people dance. If the participants are older people, the music is *humppa* or *tango*, and instruments include accordion and violin. Younger people demand a contemporary band, so the *lava* ('stage') is almost like a disco. The lavatanssit is a traditional rural dating system, still alive across the country. You may be interested in a *naistentanssi*, or 'women's dance', where women propose a dance. This arrangement is generally valid once a week in many local dance restaurants.

Literature

Written Finnish was created by Mikael Agricola (1510-57) who wrote the first Finnish alphabet and who also covered traditional Finnish culture and religion in his writings. Because Finnish remained a language of education rather than of literature, the earliest fiction was written in Swedish.

Some of the 19th century writers include J L Runeberg (*Tales of the Ensign Ståhl*), fairy-tale writer Zacharias Topelius, and Aleksis Kivi, who founded modern Finnish literature with *Seven Brothers*, a story of brothers who try to escape education and civilisation to the forests. Other notable writers include Minna Canth, Juhani Aho, Teuvo Pakkala, and Eino Leino, the poet.

In the 20th century, Mika Waltari gained fame through his famous *The Egyptian*, and F E Sillanpää received the Nobel Prize for literature in 1939. The national bestseller in the postwar period was *The Unknown Soldier* by Väinö Linna, and the nearly endless series of autobiographical novels by Kalle Päätalo and the witty short stories by Veikko Huovinen are also very popular in Finland. Another internationally famous author is Tove Jansson, whose books on the Moomin family have much to offer adult readers, too.

Kalevala The most famous of all 19th century writers was Elias Lönnrot, who trekked in eastern Finland on a scholarship in order to collect poems, oral runes, folk legends and stories. The *Kalevala*, the national epic of Finland, was the result, and it became the foundation of Finnish culture, literature and history. The first version appeared in 1833, another version in 1835 and yet another, *Uusi-Kalevala*, or 'New Kalevala', in 1849.

The main story concentrates on the mutual life of two imaginary countries, Pohjola ('The North', a mythical place of evil) and Kalevala. The *Kalevala* has been translated into almost 40 languages, but as with the Koran, it should really be read in the language of origin. You'll find an interesting Kalevala theme park in Kuhmo, and a Kalevala exhibition in Parppeinvaara in Ilomantsi. The most notable Kalevala-inspired paintings are to be found in the Ateneum art museum and in the national museum in Helsinki. It may be useful to know some of the main characters of the *Kalevala*:

Elias Lönnrot

Aino – The bride of Väinämöinen and sister of Joukahainen, who had drowned

Antero Vipunen – A shaman. Väinämöinen is looking for the Right Words and ends up into Antero's belly. Eventually, Antero Vipunen has to let him go and give him the Words.

Ilmarinen – One of the main characters of the *Kalevala* and the husband of the Daughter of Pohjola. He is a smith who makes the mystical Sampo, probably a machine of sorts.

Joukahainen – A youngster who is about to drown in a wet swamp by the singing of Väinämöinen. To be saved, he must promise his sister Aino to Väinämöinen.

Kalervo – The father of Kullervo.

Kullervo – The main character of the Kullervo poems, who suffers under a curse.

Lemminkäinen – Lönnrot added several characters of the spoken tradition and created one of the heroes of the *Kalevala* epic.

Louhi – The matron of Pohjola, also called Pohjan Akka or Pohjolan emäntä, the leader of Pohjola.

Pohjolan tytär – The daughter of Pohjola.

Väinämöinen – The main character of the *Kalevala*. He was a bard and probably a shaman, a Santa Claus-type old man and a strong personality.

Music

Jean Sibelius is the greatest composer Finland has ever produced, and he may be the greatest in the whole of Scandinavia. Born on 8 December 1865 in Hämeenlinna, he became a composer who wrote music for the glorification of his own people and in defiance of the oppressor, Russia. His most famous composition, *Finlandia*, has become a strong expression of Finnish patriotism and pride. He can also be said to have composed the *Kalevala* saga, as Gallén-Kallela painted it. Sibelius' work can be best understood in terms of Finnish nature. Many Finns can hear in Sibelius' music a sunrise in summer, the energetic days of springtime or the dark spruce forest before a rainstorm. If you take a Walkman into the wilderness and listen to Sibelius there, you may be able to get the picture. Sibelius' music is dark, almost depressing, but then you should listen to the almost pop-like *Alla Marcia* from the *Karelia Suite*.

After Sibelius, nothing can quite compare. Fredrik Pacius composed the song that is currently the national anthem of both Finland and the newly independent Estonia. There are plenty of popular Finnish songs from the early 1990s, which are sung in summer or at Christmas time. Even though Finnish music has always taken examples from abroad, it has its own aspects, melancholia being the most notable one. These days musical life is very active, from classical music to jazz, pop and rock. Karelian-type folk music is gaining in popularity across the country, and you should try to hear the music of a group called Värttinä, preferably live.

Cinema

Try to see a movie made by either of the Kaurismäki brothers.

CULTURE

For Finns, life becomes a juhla when you leave Stadi for your mökki in the middle of a metsä at a järvi, drink some viina after the sauna and then watch the kisat on TV and drink lots of kahvi and maito. To understand Finnish culture, there are a number of five-letter words you should know:

Juhla – Party. With long, dark, cold winters, a history of several less-than-victorious wars and the main guidance of the rugged and blunt Lutheran faith (which emphasises individualism), Finland is not a likely country for interesting celebrations and festivals. This is true: Finns take partying very seriously. Yet, there are juhlas on every occasion: when schools end, on birthdays, on name days and on national holidays. When it's official, people dress properly, act muted and look serious. When it's religious, they dress properly, act muted and look serious. When it's unofficial, they dress casually, act light-heartedly and look serious.

Järvi – Lake. Finns have built their towns and villages, factories and hydroelectric plants, transportation systems and timber-floating routes, bridges and road networks, and have formed their distinctive sports and recreational habits, in close relation to their lake-island-river system. Lakes provide fish and drinking water, and you can cross them by boat to reach other villages. The lake geography has several other extremely important features, such as *saari* (island), *ranta* (lakeshore), *niemi* (cape), *lahti* (bay), *koski* (rapids), *virta* (stream) and *joki* (river). Incidentally, all these words, and especially Järvinen, Saarinen, Rantanen, Nieminen, Lahtinen, Koskinen, Virtanen and Jokinen, are some of the most common Finnish family names.

Kahvi – Coffee. Finns consume, on average, nine cups of coffee each day – the world record. It sounds like addiction, which it is, but coffee is much more than just a hot drink. You will seldom visit a house without being served coffee. Traditionally you were supposed to say 'no' three times

and then accept, by saying 'OK, just half a cup', which then turned out to be four or five; even now, taking a few long coffee breaks in the office is a must. Coffee is one of the few things whose price has actually come down over the last couple of decades. Coffee has been so important that during WW II a substitute was invented to keep people happy. You pour your kahvi into a *kuppi* and usually eat some *pulla* (wheat bun) with it. After the first cup, you'll have eight more to go.

Kisat – Games. Finns are serious about spectator sports. Success in *Olympiakisat* (Olympic Games) is about the best thing any Finn can dream of; a gold medal means a visit to the President's Palace (actually the whole team goes there) and innumerable centrefold posters and front-cover photos in magazines, but even the smallest rowing boat competitions are treated with much enthusiasm. Indeed, 'sport' in Finnish translates roughly as 'heroism'. Even the smallest villages have sports fields, indoor halls, swimming pools, tennis courts, downhill slopes and jogging and skiing tracks, and at least Lahti and Kuopio are currently dreaming of hosting the Winter Olympic Games one day. And, of course, all Finns love to talk about a football or ice-hockey *matsi* (match).

Maito – Milk. The main drink with lunch and dinner, milk has been so important that grocery stores have been called *maitokauppa*, or 'milk store'. Milk was once the basic nourishing ingredient of all Finnish food, and it is now being promoted because of overproduction, the result of large farm subsidies and the *sisu* character of Finnish farmers. Maito comes naturally from the *lehmä* (cow), which the current agricultural policy treats as holy.

Metsä – Forest. Finns are characteristically forest people who like to listen to winds humming in trees, either *mänty* or *honka* (pine), *kuusi* (spruce) or *koivu* (birch). Deciduous forests, where *lehti* (leaf) dropping trees dominate, are called *lehto*, whereas real wilderness is *korpi* or *kaira*. Again, Mäntynen, Honkanen, Kuusinen, Koivunen, Lehtinen, Lehtonen and Korpinen are all fairly typical Finnish family names, with or without the *-nen* appendix. Other useful metsä words include *marja* (berry), *sieni* (mushroom), *eläin* (animal), *hirvi* (elk) and *lintu* (bird).

Mökki – Cottage. The *kesämökki*, or 'summer cottage', is an important part of summer life in Finland. Even if people demand modern amenities in their regular home, the mökki should be basic and definitely in the middle of nowhere. Mökki requirements include a *takka* (fireplace), and a sauna at the ranta of a järvi. In summer, after a proper sauna bath, you go to the pier at the waterfront, drink some *kalja* (beer) and relax, listen to birds singing and watch the midnight sun approaching the horizon, and then you're a Finn.

Sauna – If you didn't already know, the sauna is a Finnish invention. There are 1.2 million saunas in Finland, which means that practically all Finns have access to a sauna. Usually it's on Saturday evenings that families bathe in their own sauna. It is the ancient *savusauna*, or 'smoke sauna', that has helped to keep the tradition alive and popular; the modern electric sauna stoves don't produce the pleasant *löyly* (steam) you should expect. In towns and in many hotels, you will bathe in an electric sauna, but in the countryside you'll bathe in a log-heated lakeside sauna. Look for a savusauna and check the price first. Try to test one before leaving Finland. The sauna was originally a place to bathe, to meditate and even to give birth, but it is not (and never has been) used for making babies; Finns are quite strict about the nonsexual character of the sauna bath, and this point should be respected. These days people go to a sauna to relax, to small-talk and to talk seriously (Finns always talk seriously). For your sauna, you'll use a *kauha* to throw water on the *kiuas*, which then gives off the löyly. At this point, at least in summer in the countryside, you'll take the *vihta* or *vasta* (a bunch of fresh koivu twigs) and hit yourself. This improves your circulation and gives your skin a pleasant smell. After this, you'll go out to the *ranta* of a *järvi* to swim.

Stadi – Helsinki. The word stadi is derived from the Swedish *staden*, for 'city'. Although Stadi has just 10% of the entire Finnish population, to the people of Stadi it represents about 99% of the country. The *lande*, or countryside, is the place where you spend the Midsummer weekend. Stadi ends at the *susiraja*, or 'wolf frontier', which is at the Vantaa border, according to the most recent definition.

Viina – Aquavit. Finns drink a lot. The expensive bottle of viina is typically purchased in the nearest Alko store on Fridays after work. Yes, yuppies sip their expensive *viini* (wine), and much kalja is brewed and consumed, but viina characterises the entire hopeless drinking pattern of some Finns; you drink until you pass out. An old man from Lapland once summed it all up on a local radio programme: 'You basically travel abroad to buy cheap viina.'

RELIGION
Old Finnish Religion
In the past, Finns lived in close harmony with nature and made a simple living by fishing, hunting and cultivating land. There were few gods, as Finns generally preferred spirits that inhabited both forests *(haltija)* and back yards *(tonttu)*. These spirits were offered gifts to keep them happy. Deceased relatives were treated with respect. Finns believed that the dead wandered around, especially during festival seasons. The *kalmisto* (graveyard) was the place for offerings, and conspicuous trees and stones had great significance for local cults. With the arrival of Catholicism, the animist religion was soon influenced by 'new gods', but a handful of old shamans kept the traditions alive for decades.

Some of the old Finnish gods include *Ahti* (god of waters and fish), *Ilmarinen* (god of winds and storms), *Tapio* (god of forests) and *Ukko* (god of growth, rain and thunderstorms).

Christianity
The Christian faith was brought to Finland by the Roman Catholic Bishop Henry from England, who arrived in mainland Finland in about 1155 and stayed to tend the church. He met a tragic death on the ice of Lake Köyliö at the hands of a jealous Finnish peasant named Lalli. There were even earlier crusades to Åland, where the oldest churches in Finland are to be found. The Catholic Church was gradually displaced by the Reformation of Martin Luther, which reflected the rugged individualism that is typical of Finns. Finland's own reformer was Mikael Agricola, who also created the written Finnish language. The whole Bible appeared in Finnish in 1642. Old stone churches, decorations and objects, the bishops' official signs, and popular saints' names and name days are remnants of the Catholic era. The Eastern (Greek or Russian) Orthodox Church is evident in eastern provinces, but there are small chapels (called *tsasouna* in Finnish) in many western towns, as many refugees from the Soviet-annexed Karelia settled in these towns after WW II. Yet, only 1% of Finns belong to the Orthodox Church, which is noted for its beautiful church architecture, old icons and the two monasteries in the municipality of Heinävesi.

Approximately 88% of Finns belong to the national church, the Evangelical-

Lutheran Church of Finland. Within the Church there are large revivalist groups, such as the Pietists, the Evangelicals and the Laestadians, who all have their large summer convents, with some 20,000 participants in open-air gatherings. One of the most interesting modern evangelical movements in Finland is the 'People's Bible Society' (Kansan Raamattuseura), should you want to learn more about current spiritual trends.

The two 'official' churches (Lutheran and Orthodox) still register births, but already 10% of the population belong to the civil register. Some of them are opposed to paying the church taxes, and many women left the church in protest when the battle over women's priesthood was at its fiercest. There are now female priests in the Lutheran Church.

Religious instruction is given in schools, and there are state-supported offices for chaplains serving in the army, hospitals and prisons. Parliament opens and closes its sessions with a church service. However, services have proved unpopular, and only 5% of members attend them regularly. The Church has tried to be active in building new clubrooms, rooms for hobbies and sports, and family guidance centres, in running holiday courses and in arranging gospel concerts for young people, but with limited success. Evangelical free churches abound. They represent rather outlandish charismatic movements, most of which derive from America. The largest group is the Pentecostals (Helluntaiseurakunta).

Mormons' churches are called Myöhempien Aikojen Pyhien Jeesuksen Kristuksen Kirkko, and Jehovah's Witness Halls are called Jehovan Todistajain valtakunnansali, in case you were wondering.

LANGUAGE

Finland is officially a bilingual country, with 6% of the population speaking Swedish. Finnish, a Finno-Ugric language, is considered to be difficult. There are 15 cases for nouns, and at least 160 conjugations and personal forms for verbs. There are no arti-cles and no gender, but the word 'no' also conjugates. There are words borrowed from English, Swedish, Russian, German and Baltic languages, yet *puhelin* is telephone and *sähkö* is electricity. Note that *ä* is pronounced as 'a', as in the American 'can't', and *ö* is pronounced 'er', as in 'number'. These letters are the last two in the Finnish alphabet.

Swedish is one of the Scandinavian languages that belong to the Indo-European group of languages that was separated from the original Germanic some 3000 years ago. *Finlandssvenska*, or 'Finland's Swedish', is very similar to the language spoken in Sweden, but local dialects have many Finnish words, so if you have learned Swedish in Sweden, you'll have some more learning to do!

Lonely Planet also publishes a *Scandinavian Phrasebook*, which is a handy pocket-sized introduction to Finnish, Swedish and other languages of the region.

Essentials

The following phrases should see you through most basic situations:

Please write it down	*Voitko kirjoittaa sen*
Please show me (on the map)	*Näytä minulle (kartalta)*
I understand	*Ymmärrän*
I don't understand	*En ymmärrä*
Does anyone speak English?	*Puhuuko kukaan englantia?*
Where are you from?	*Mistä olet kotoisin?*
I am from...	*Olen...-sta*
Age?/How old are you?	*Ikä?/Kuinka vanha olet?*
I am...years old	*Olen...-vuotias*
Surname	*Sukunimi*
Given names	*Etunimet*
Date of birth/place of birth	*Syntymäaika/syntymä paikka*
Nationality	*Kansallisuus*
Male/female	*Mies/nainen*
Passport	*Passi*

Help! *Apua!*
Go away! *Mene pois!*
Call a doctor/the *Kutsu lääkäri/poliisi*
police
I'm allergic to peni- *Olen allerginen*
cillin/antibiotics *penisilliinille/*
antibiooteille

Entrance *Sisään*
Exit *Ulos*
Open/closed *Avoinna/suljettu*
Prohibited *Kielletty*
Toilets *WC*

Greetings & Civilities

Hello *Hei*
Goodbye *Näkemiin*
Good morning *Huomenta*
Good evening *Iltaa*
Thank you (very *Kiitos (paljon)*
much)
You're welcome *Ole hyvä*
Yes *Kyllä*
No *Ei*
Maybe *Ehkä*
Excuse me *Anteeksi*
I am sorry (forgive *Olen pahoillani*
me) *(anna anteeksi)*
How are you? *Mitä kuuluu?*
I'm fine, thanks *Kiitos hyvää*

Small Talk

What is your name? *Mikä sinun nimi*
on?)
My name is... *Minun nimeni on...*
(Mun nimi on...)
I'm a tourist/student *Olen turisti/*
opiskelija

Are you married? *Oletko naimisissa?*
Do you like...? *Pidätkö...?*
I like it very much *Pidän siitä paljon*
I don't like... *En pidä...*
Just a minute *Pieni hetki*
May I? *Saanko?*
How do you *Miten sanotaan...*
say...(in Finnish)? *(suomeksi)?*

Getting Around

I want to go to... *Haluan mennä...*

What time *Mihin aikaan*
does...leave/arrive? *lähtee/saapuu...?*
Where does...leave *Mistä...lähtee?*
from?
it *se*
the bus/tram *bussi/raitsikka*
the train *juna*
the boat/ferry *vene/lautta*
the airplane *lentokone*
How long does the *Kauanko matka*
trip take? *kestää?*
The train is *Juna on*
delayed/cancelled/ *myöhässä/peruttu/*
on time *ajoissa*
Do I need to *Täytyykö minun*
change? *vaihtaa?*
left-luggage locker *säilytyslokero*
one-way (ticket) *yhdensuuntainen*
(lippu)
platform *laituri*
return *menopaluu (lippu)*
station *asema*
ticket *lippu*
ticket office *lipputoimisto*
timetable *aikataulu*

I'd like to hire a... *Haluaisin vuokrata*
bicycle *polkupyörän*
car *auton*
canoe *kanootin*
rowing boat *soutuveneen*
guide *oppaan*

Directions

How do I get to...? *Miten pääsen...*
Where is...? *Missä on...?*
Is it near/far? *Onko se*
lähellä/kaukana
What...is this? *Mikä...tämä on?*
street/road *katu/tie*
street number *kadunnumero*
suburb *kaupunginosa*
town *kaupunki*

(Go) straight ahead *(Kulje) suoraan*
eteenpäin
(Turn) left *(Käänny) vas-*
empaan

(Turn) right — *(Käänny) oikeaan*
at the traffic lights — *liikennevaloissa*
at the next/second/ — *seuraavassa/toisessa*
  third corner — */kolmannessa*
    risteyksessä

up/down — *ylös/alas*
behind/opposite — *takana/vastapäätä*
east/west — *itä/länsi*
here/there — *täällä/siellä*
north/south — *pohjoinen/etelä*

Accommodation

I'm looking for... — *Etsin...*
the youth hostel — *retkeilymajaa*
the camping ground — *leirintäaluetta*
a hotel — *hotellia*
a guesthouse — *matkustajakotia*
the manager — *johtajaa*
What is the address? — *Mikä on osoite?*

Do you have — *Onko teillä...?*
  a...available?
  bed — *sänkyä*
  cheap room — *halpaa huonetta*
  single/double — *yhden/kahden*
  room — *hengen huonetta*

  for one night/two — *yhdeksi yöksi/*
    nights — *kahdeksi yöksi*
How much is it per — *Paljonko on yöltä/*
  night/per person? — *henkilöltä*
Does that include — *Sisältyykö hintaan*
  breakfast/sheets? — *aamiainen/lakanat?*
Can I see the room? — *Voinko nähdä*
  huoneen?

Where is the toilet? — *Missä on vessa?*
It is very dirty/ — *Se on hyvin likainen/*
  noisy/expensive — *meluisa/kallis*
I am/we are leaving — *Olen/olemme*
  now — *lähdössä nyt*

Do you have...? — *Onko teillä...?*
  a clean sheet — *puhtaat lakanat*
  hot water — *kuumaa vettä*
  a key — *avain*
  a shower — *suihku*
  sauna — *sauna*

Around Town

Where is the/a...? — *Missä on...?*
  bank — *pankki*
  town centre — *keskusta*
  embassy — *suurlähetystö*
  entrance/exit — *sisäänkäynti/*
    uloskäynti
  hospital — *sairaala*
  market — *tori*
  police — *poliisi*
  post office — *posti*
  public toilet — *yleinen käymälä*
  restaurant — *ravintola*
  telephone office — *Tele-toimisto*
  tourist informa- — *matkailutoimisto*
    tion office

I want to make a — *Haluaisin soittaa*
  telephone call — *puhelimella*
I'd like to change — *Haluaisin vaihtaa...*
  some...
  money/travellers' — *rahaa/matkashek-*
  cheques — *kejä*

Food

I am hungry/thirsty — *Minulla on nälkä/*
  jano
breakfast — *aamiainen*
lunch — *lounas*
buffet — *seisova pöytä*
dinner — *päivällinen*
grocery store — *ruokakauppa*
market — *tori*
restaurant — *ravintola*
food stall — *grilli*
café — *kahvila*
I would like some... — *Haluaisin...*
I don't eat... — *En syö...*

Baltic herring — *silakka*
beef — *naudan-*
beer — *olut, kalja*
bread — *leipä*
bread roll — *sämpylä*
cabbage — *kaali*
carrot — *porkkana*
cheese — *juusto*
chicken — *kana*
coffee — *kahvi*
drinking water — *juomavesi*

egg	*kananmuna*	clothing	*vaatteita*
filled bread	*kukko*	souvenirs	*matkamuistoja*
fish	*kala*	Do you take	*Voiko maksaa*
herring	*silli*	travellers'	*matkashekeillä*
ham	*kinkku*	cheques?	
liver	*maksa*	Do you have	*Onko muuta*
meat	*liha*	another	*väriä/kokoa?*
milk	*maito*	colour/size?	
minced meat	*jauheliha*	big/bigger	*iso/isompi*
mushroom	*sieni*	small/smaller	*pieni/pienempi*
oats	*kaura*	more/less	*enemmän/vähemmän*
omelette	*munakas*	cheap/cheaper	*halpa/halvempi*
open sandwich	*voileipä*		
onion	*sipuli*	**Time & Dates**	
pea	*herne*	When?	*Milloin?*
pepper	*pippuri*	today	*tänään*
pie	*piiras*	tonight	*tänä iltana*
pork	*porsaan-*	tomorrow	*huomenna*
porridge	*puuro*	the day after tomor-	*ylihuomenna*
potato	*peruna*	row	
reindeer	*poron-*	yesterday	*eilen*
rice	*riisi*	all day/every day	*koko päivän/joka*
rye	*ruis*		*päivä*
salad	*salaatti*		
salmon	*lohi*	Monday	*maanantai*
salt	*suola*	Tuesday	*tiistai*
sauce	*kastike*	Wednesday	*keskiviikko*
sausage	*makkara*	Thursday	*torstai*
soup	*keitto*	Friday	*perjantai*
steak	*pihvi*	Saturday	*lauantai*
stew	*laatikko*	Sunday	*sunnuntai*
sugar	*sokeri*		
swede	*lanttu*	January	*tammikuu*
tea	*tee*	February	*helmikuu*
vegetable	*vihannes*	March	*maaliskuu*
vegetarian	*kasvis-*	April	*huhtikuu*
water	*vesi*	May	*toukokuu*
		June	*kesäkuu*
		July	*heinäkuu*
Shopping		August	*elokuu*
How much does it	*Mitä se maksaa?*	September	*syyskuu*
cost?		October	*lokakuu*
I would like to buy	*Haluan ostaa sen*	November	*marraskuu*
it		December	*joulukuu*
It's too expensive	*Se on liian kallis*		
for me	*minulle*	What time is it?	*Mitä kello on?*
Can I look at it?	*Voinko katsoa sitä?*	It's...o'clock	*Kello on...*
I'm just looking	*Mä vain katselen*	in the morning	*aamulla*
I'm looking for...	*Etsin...*	in the evening	*illalla*
the chemist	*kemikaalikauppaa*	1.15	*vartin yli yksi*

1.30	*puoli kaksi*	21	*kaksikymmentäyksi*
1.45	*varttia vaille kaksi*	30	*kolmekymmentä*
		40	*neljäkymmentä*
Numbers		50	*viisikymmentä*
one	*yksi*	60	*kuusikymmentä*
two	*kaksi*	70	*seitsemänkymmentä*
three	*kolme*	80	*kahdeksankymmentä*
four	*neljä*	90	*yhdeksänkymmentä*
five	*viisi*	100	*sata*
six	*kuusi*	1000	*tuhat*
seven	*seitsemän*	one million	*miljoona*
eight	*kahdeksan*	half	*puoli*
nine	*yhdeksän*		
10	*kymmenen*		

Numbers

one	*yksi*
two	*kaksi*
three	*kolme*
four	*neljä*
five	*viisi*
six	*kuusi*
seven	*seitsemän*
eight	*kahdeksan*
nine	*yhdeksän*
10	*kymmenen*
11	*yksitoista*
12	*kaksitoista*
13	*kolmetoista*
14	*neljätoista*
15	*viisitoista*
16	*kuusitoista*
17	*seitsemäntoista*
18	*kahdeksantoista*
19	*yhdeksäntoista*
20	*kaksikymmentä*

Map Words

Some common words you should know in Finnish include: *-asema* (station), *-järvi* (lake), *-joki* (river), *-katu* (street), *-koski* (rapids), *-kylä* (village), *-lahti* (bay), *-lääni* (province), *-maa* (land, area), *-museo* (museum), *-mäki* (hill), *-niemi* (cape), *-ranta* (shore), *-saari* (island), *-salmi* (strait), *-salo* (island), *-selkä* (lake), *-suo* (marshland), *-talo* (house), *-tie* (road), *-tori* (market or square), *-tunturi* (fell) and *-vuori* (mountain).

Facts for the Visitor

VISAS & EMBASSIES
Passports
Citizens of Denmark, Iceland, Sweden and Norway do not need a passport to enter Finland. A British Visitor's Passport is accepted as a passport in Finland. Finland also accepts valid identity cards issued by the officials of Austria, Belgium, Germany, France, Liechtenstein, Luxembourg and Switzerland to citizens of their country. All other nationalities require a valid passport.

Visas
The following nationalities can stay in Finland for three months, without requiring an entry visa: Andorra, Argentina, Australia, Austria, Bahamas, Barbados, Belgium, Belize, Bolivia, Botswana, Brazil, Canada, Chile, Colombia, Costa Rica, Cyprus, Czechoslovakia, Denmark, Dominican Republic, Ecuador, El Salvador, Fiji, France, Gambia, Germany, Greece, Grenada, Guatemala, Honduras, Hungary, Iceland, Ireland, Israel, Italy, Ivory Coast, Jamaica, Japan, Kenya, Korea, Lesotho, Liechtenstein, Luxembourg, Malawi, Malaysia, Malta, Mauritius, Mexico, Monaco, Netherlands, New Zealand, Nicaragua, Niger, Norway, Panama, Peru, Portugal, San Marino, Seychelles, Singapore, Spain, St Vincent and Grenadines, Surinam, Swaziland, Sweden, Switzerland, Tanzania, Trinidad and Tobago, Uganda, United Kingdom, USA, Uruguay, Vatican City, Yugoslavia and Zambia.

Russian Visas Russian visas are obtainable at the former Soviet Union embassy (☎ 90-661 876) at Tehtaankatu 1B, 00140 Helsinki (entrance on Vuorimiehenkatu). As rules and regulations are changing fast, consult the Russian embassy in your own country first. Allow eight working days for visa processing.

Finnish Embassies
Visas and information can be obtained at Finnish diplomatic missions, including:

Australia
    10 Darwin Ave, Yarralumla, Canberra, ACT 2600 (☎ 062-733 800)
Belgium
    489 Ave Louise, 1050 Brussels (☎ 02-648 8484)
Canada
    55 Metcalfe St, Suite 850, Ottawa, Ontario K1P 6L5 (☎ 613-236 2389)
    1176 West Georgia St, Suite 1100, Vancouver BC V6E 4A2 (☎ 604-688 4483)
China
    Tayuan Diplomatic Office Building 1-10-1, Liangmahe nanlu 14, Beijing 100600 (☎ 01-532 1806)
Denmark
    Sankt Annas Plads 24, 1250 Copenhagen K (☎ 3313 4214)
Estonia
    Liivalaia 12, EE0001, Tallinn (☎ 449 522)
France
    2 rue Fabert, 75007 Paris (☎ 01-4705 3545)
Germany
    Friesdorferstrasse 1, 5300 Bonn (☎ 0228-382 980)
India
    Nyaya Marg 5, Chanakyapuri, New Delhi 110021 (☎ 011-605 409)
Indonesia
    Bina Mulia Building, Jalan H R Rasuna Said Kav 10, Jakarta 12950 (☎ 021-520 7408)
Israel
    Beth Eliahu, 8th floor, 2 Rehov Ibn Gvirol 64077 Tel Aviv, (☎ 03-695 0528)
Italy
    via Lisbona 4, 00198 Rome (☎ 06-854 8329)
Japan
    3-5-39 Minami-Azabu, Minato-ku, Tokyo 106, (☎ 03-3442 2231)
Malaysia
    15th floor, Plaza MBF, Jalan Ampang, 50450 Kuala Lumpur (☎ 03-261 1088)
Mexico
    Monte Pelvoux 111, piso 4, Lomas de Chapultepec, Delegacion Miguel Hidalgo, 11000 Mexico DF (☎ 05-540 6036)
Netherlands
    Groot Hertoginnelaan 16, 2517 KH The Hague (☎ 070-346 9754)

Norway
Drammensveien 40, 0255 Oslo 2 (☎ 02-430 400)
Philippines
BPI Building, 14th floor, Ayala Ave, corner Paseo de Roxas, Makati, Metro Manila (☎ 02-816 2105)
Singapore
101 Thomson Rd 21-03, United Square, Singapore 1130 (☎ 254 4042)
Sweden
Jacobsgatan 6, 6tr, 11152 Stockholm (☎ 08-676 6700)
Thailand
16th floor, Amarin Plaza, 500 Ploen Chit Rd, Bangkok 10330 (☎ 02-256 9306)
UK
32 Grosvenor Gardens, London SW1W ODH, (☎ 071-235 9531)
USA
3216 New Mexico Ave NW, Washington DC 20016 (☎ 202-363 2430)
1900 Ave of the Stars, Suite 1025, Los Angeles, CA 90067 (☎ 213-203 9903)
Finland House, 380 Madison Ave, New York, NY 10022, (☎ 212-573 6007)

Foreign Embassies in Finland

This is a full listing of representatives of foreign governments in Helsinki:

Argentina
Bulevardi 10A 14 (☎ 90-607 630)
Austria
Eteläesplanadi 18 (☎ 90-171 322)
Belgium
Kalliolinnantie 5 (☎ 90-170 412)
Brazil
Mariankatu 7A 4 (☎ 90-177 922)
Bulgaria
Itäinen Puistotie 10 (☎ 90-661 707)
Canada
Pohjoisesplanadi 25B (☎ 90-171 141)
China
Vanha kelkkamäki 11 (☎ 90-684 8976)
Columbia
Fredrikinkatu 61 (☎ 90-693 1255)
Cuba
Paasivuorenkatu 3 (☎ 90-766 199)
Czechoslovakia
Armfeltintie 14 (☎ 90-171 051)
Denmark
2nd floor, Yrjönkatu 9 (☎ 90-641 948)
Egypt
Stenbäckinkatu 22A (☎ 90-413 288)
Estonia
Fabianinkatu 13A (☎ 90-179 719)
France
Itäinen Puistotie 13 (☎ 90-171 521)

Germany
Fredrikinkatu 61 (☎ 90-694 3355)
Greece
Lönnrotinkatu 15C 26 (☎ 90-645 202)
Hungary
Kuusisaarenkuja 6 (☎ 90-484 144)
India
Satamakatu 2A 8 (☎ 90-608 927)
Indonesia
Eerikinkatu 37 (☎ 90-694 7816)
Iran
Bertel-Jungin tie 4 (☎ 90-684 7133)
Iraq
Lars Sonckin tie 2 (☎ 90-684 9177)
Israel
Vironkatu 5A (☎ 90-135 6177)
Italy
Fabianinkatu 29C 4 (☎ 90-175 144)
Japan
Lönnrotinkatu 4 (☎ 90-644 206)
Korea
Mannerheimintie 76A 7 (☎ 90-498 955)
Latvia
Bulevardi 5A (☎ 90-605 640)
Mexico
Fredrikinkatu 51-53A (☎ 90-640 637)
Netherlands
Raatimiehenkatu 2A 7 (☎ 90-661 737)
North Korea
Kulosaaren puistotie 32 (☎ 90-684 8195)
Norway
Rehbinderintie 17 (☎ 90-171 234)
Poland
Armas Lindgrenin tie 21 (☎ 90-684 8077)
Portugal
Itäinen Puistotie 11B (☎ 90-171 717)
Romania
Stenbäckinkatu 24 (☎ 90-413 624)
Russia
Vuorimiehenkatu 6 (☎ 90-661 449)
Yugoslavia
Kulosaarentie 36 (☎ 90-684 7466)
South Africa
Rahapajankatu 1A 5 (☎ 90-658 288)
Spain
Bulevardi 10A 8 (☎ 90-647 351)
Sweden
Pohjoisesplanadi 7B (☎ 90-651 255)
Switzerland
Uudenmaankatu 16A (☎ 90-649 422)
Turkey
Topeliuksenkatu 3b A 1-2 (☎ 90-406 058)
Venezuela
Mannerheimintie 14A (☎ 90-641 522)
UK
Uudenmaankatu 16-20 (☎ 90-647 922)
USA
Itäinen Puistotie 14A (☎ 90-171 931)

CUSTOMS

You can bring 200 cigarettes or 250 grams of tobacco into Finland, plus either two litres of beer and two litres of wine, or two litres of beer, one litre of wine and one litre of spirits. Fines for violators are severe.

MONEY

Currency

The Finnish unit of currency is the *markka* (MAHRK-kah, plural markkaa, often abbreviated as mk), which is equal to 100 *penniä*. Paper currency comes in denominations of 10, 50, 100, 500 and 1000 markkaa. Coins include 10 and 50 penniä pieces and 1, 5 and 10 mk coins. New coins in all denominations have been introduced in the early 1990s, and old coins have disappeared fast. Five mk is often called *vitonen*, 10 mk *kymppi* and 100 mk *satanen*. The currency fluctuates freely within a 6% 'tunnel', which is pegged to the European Currency Unit *ecu*.

Exchange Rates

The following table shows the exchange rates:

A$1	=	2.86 mk
C$1	=	3.32 mk
DM1	=	2.75 mk
HK$1	=	0.52 mk
NZ$1	=	2.15 mk
SIN$1	=	2.50 mk
UK£1	=	7.68 mk
US$1	=	3.97 mk

Costs

Finland was declared the world's most expensive country in 1990, right before it plunged into a deep recession. After the November 1991 devaluation and a continuing recession, it seems that the prices are levelling off to European averages. Food and drink, in particular, can still be prohibitively expensive in places, so care with the budget is essential at all times.

High prices are the result of high labour and transport costs, agricultural policies and cartels in many industries. It is generally possible to stay overnight in a comfortable hotel for 200 mk per person. A good set lunch goes for 30 to 40 mk, and a local bus trip costs 8 mk. A train trip of 100 km costs 45 mk, and the same trip by bus costs 55 mk. A discounted return flight within Finland costs 270 to 630 mk.

Budget travellers should be able to get by on 100 mk per day if they really keep watch on their expenses. This estimate includes youth hostel accommodation, self-catering food and/or lunch specials. To save on drinks, you can use tap water for drinking; bottled drinks are expensive and alcohol is very expensive. The price tags on some food items include a 'per kg' price, which enables price comparisons. Free accommodation is available along most trekking routes, and hitchhiking is easy, especially in summer, when there are nearly 24 hours of daylight each day.

Fifteen Free Things in Finland To really keep your costs down, consider taking advantage of some of the free things in Finland. Here are 15 of them:

1. Accommodation in wilderness huts in North Finland
2. Accommodation in shelters and at camp sites along trekking routes all over Finland
3. Firewood and garbage services along all established trekking routes
4. Free rental bicycles in Pori and Tampere
5. Easy hitchhiking across the country
6. Abandoned vegetables at many markets in Helsinki after 2 pm
7. English books and magazines in most public libraries
8. Excellent town maps of most towns and villages
9. Use of all roads, and *lossi* ferries across waterways
10. Route ferries to/between coastal islands, including Åland, for island-hopping
11. Rock concerts in summer in Helsinki
12. Church concerts, in most cases
13. Berries and mushrooms in all Finnish forests
14. Concerts and fun at markets
15. Free fishing for anyone under 18 years of age

Bargains Here are 10 of Finland's best bargains:

1. Ferries to/from Sweden (transport only), including free transport of bicycles
2. Suomenlinna ferry, or the 3T tram in Helsinki's HKL transport system
3. Student restaurants/cafés in all university towns
4. Sauna and swimming in public indoor swimming pools
5. Special discount return flight from Helsinki to Ivalo
6. Health care
7. Camping at camp sites on Åland
8. Many youth hostels around Finland
9. Student discount tickets for museums and concerts in large towns
10. Buffet breakfast in most top-end hotels

Tipping

Tipping is generally not necessary in Finland. You will pay service charges in restaurants as percentages, and they are generally included in the quoted menu price. You may ask the taxi driver to keep the change *(pidä loput)*. One of the strange habits in Finland is giving a few coins to the 'gorilla' who has done his best to bar your entry and freeze you to death on winter evenings outside the restaurant. Even though this may make you feel unwelcome, afterwards you feel so happy to have finally been able to warm up after some two hours' standing in -20°C, that you tip the door attendant, perhaps hoping to be given quicker access next time.

Bargaining

All prices in shops are fixed and clearly displayed. There is no bargaining in supermarkets and similar establishments. When buying electrical appliances, trekking equipment or used bicycles and similar products in small specialist shops, bargaining is useful and recommended. Many shops can easily drop 10% to 20% off the normal price. For best results, bargaining should be done in a subtle and friendly manner.

Consumer Taxes

Finnish sales tax is currently 22% and is included in marked prices. It is possible to avoid paying this tax by making purchases in designated shops, which will provide you with a tax payment slip. If your purchases are over 200 mk, you will be refunded the tax (actually just part of it) on presentation of the slip and the merchandise at your point of departure (ie airport transit halls, on board major ferries or at overland border crossings).

WHEN TO GO

You should visit Finland in summer. Any time from May to September is OK, though late autumn may become too rainy, cold and dark to amuse anyone. There are several reasons why summer is the best season: it is the time of the midnight sun, high temperatures and the freshness of nature, and the only time when many youth hostels, camp sites, museums and attractions are open. It's also when the steamboats ply the Finnish lakes. The dark winter is something quite different. Don't plan to cross Siberia in a heated Russian railway carriage, then appear at the Helsinki railway station on a dark weekend afternoon in January when there's nowhere to cash your travellers' cheques and everyone seems to be drunk, depressed or ready to kill you. Nevertheless, winter offers some fine opportunities for extensive cross-country skiing treks in national parks, and every town has illuminated skiing tracks in the town area. Winter is also quite good for meeting up with local people, who can be really friendly and talkative once you get out of the cold. Cultural life is active in winter. In fact, Helsinki gets quieter in summer, when many offices are closed, especially in July. Winter is the busiest time for theatre, films and exhibitions. The following list should give you an idea of what to expect of the various months in Finland:

January – Cold, dark and depressing everywhere. The *kaamos* in Lapland may be of interest if you don't want to see the sun at all.

February – Still cold and dark all over Finland

March – Towards the end of March, the days become longer than the nights. In the south, this is the spring thaw, but there is still snow and ice everywhere. The first migratory birds arrive.

April – Snow disappears in most places around South Finland. Many migratory birds return in April, and forests are full of birdsong. In Lapland, this is the best skiing season: long days and warm sunshine, yet plenty of snow everywhere.

May – Trees get foliage, and all migratory birds have returned by the end of May. Many lakes still have ice in early May, but snow can only be found in Lapland. The ground is still wet everywhere. Some attractions open in May for the summer season.

June – This month sees the longest hours of daylight. The ground dries, and snow melts in Lapland. Birds sing everywhere, the vegetation grows rapidly and flowers bloom. Many youth hostels and open-air museums open on 1 June, and school holidays start, which results in fewer buses on some routes.

July – Another light month, with no darkness at all in North Finland. Birds no longer sing, but the growing vegetation has reached its zenith and Finland is at its greenest. Lapland is experiencing its short but hectic summer, and the number of mosquitoes is reaching an unpleasant level. All tourist attractions around the country are open in July.

August – The nights get shorter but vegetation is still growing. Some trees turn yellow towards the end of the month, and birds start to move about. Many youth hostels and open-air museums close on 15 or 31 August. Schools resume by mid-August, with many changes occurring in bus timetables.

September – Day and night are the same length. Temperatures reach freezing point, but can still be pleasant in the south. Rain is not uncommon, and the ground is generally wet. Most trees turn yellow and start dropping leaves. Birds start their migration to the south.

October – You can still feel the summer in South Finland, but temperatures are getting crisper and snow is not uncommon in North Finland. All migratory birds have left, and trees no longer have leaves. It often rains, and days become shorter.

November – This is the least popular of all months among Finns. It is dark and cold. The wet snow seldom stays, so everything is grey, muddy and depressing.

December – The darkest month may see heavy snowfall all over Finland, which makes the landscape more attractive, and it is not so dark. Temperatures range from freezing point down to - 30°C.

WHAT TO BRING

Bring along most of what you think you will need. Buying such items as soap or shampoo may be more expensive in Finland than in your country, so you can save a bit by bringing them along. Taking sheets will save you a lot of money at youth hostels and in cottages. Bring a sleeping bag for trekking and camping. You won't need one if you stay indoors, as all houses have heating and blankets to keep you warm. Finnish houses in winter must be among the warmest in Europe at that time! If you travel in winter, you'll need plenty of clothes.

TOURIST OFFICES
Local Tourist Offices

Local tourist information offices are very helpful and useful. Apart from some less touristed municipalities, all cities, towns and municipal centres have a tourist office (sometimes several). They are open during office hours; in summer they are also open in the evenings and on weekends. Surprisingly, the Finnish Tourist Board is not at all active at the grass-roots level, whereas local offices will provide you with all imaginable information, from local history and attractions to the seating capacity of petrol station cafés and activities in nearby farmhouses, mostly in Finnish but increasingly in English. Visitors are generally greeted with enthusiasm, and staff will go out of their way to help meet your needs. With this in mind, leaving your travel plans to the last minute is not a bad idea, as tourist offices do have quite a range of suggestions to offer.

Finnish Tourist Board Offices Abroad

The Finnish Tourist Board has offices in the following countries:

Denmark
Vester Farimagsgade 3, 1606 Copenhagen V (☎ 3313 1362, fax 3332 0501)
France
13 rue Auber, 75009 Paris (☎ 01-4266 4013, fax 01-4742 8722)
Germany
Darmstädter Landstrasse 180, 6000 Frankfurt (☎ 069-961 2360, fax 069-686 860)
Italy
Via Larga 4, 20122 Milano (☎ 02-8646 4914, fax 02-7202 2590)
Japan
Imperial Hotel M2, I-I-I Uchisaiwaicho/Chiyoda-ku, Tokyo 100 (☎ 03-3501 5207, fax 03-3580 9205)
Netherlands
Stadhouderskade 69, 1072 AD Amsterdam (☎ 020-6719 876, fax 020-675 0359)
Norway
Lille Grensen 7, 0159 Oslo 1 (☎ 02-411 070, fax 02-334 082)
Sweden
Kungsgatan 4 a 6 tr, 11143 Stockholm (☎ 08-236 875, fax 08-249 594)
Switzerland
Schweizergasse 6, 8001 Zürich (☎ 01-211 1340, fax 01-211 1119)
UK
66/68 Haymarket, London SW1Y 4RF (☎ 071-839 4048, fax 071-321 0696)
USA
655 Third Ave, New York, NY 10017 (☎ 0212-949 2333, fax 0212-983 5260)

BUSINESS HOURS

Banks are open from 9.15 am to 4.15 pm Monday to Friday, and office hours are 9 am to 5 pm Monday to Friday. People choose their own lunch time, but in many companies coffee and lunch breaks may amount to quite a long time, so reaching people at their offices may be a bit of a problem. Shop hours are somewhat variable, but generally you can visit department stores and supermarkets from 9 am to 8 pm Monday to Friday and from 9 am to 6 pm on Saturdays. Sunday is still generally considered inappropriate for retail business. Few places are open at night, except some petrol stations. Specialised shops generally stay open until 5 pm Monday to Friday and until 1 or 2 pm on Saturdays.

HOLIDAYS & FESTIVALS

These days, the term 'festivals' in Finland commonly refers to cultural events that are generally arranged annually and which concentrate on a certain theme, such as opera in Savonlinna, chamber music in Kuhmo or contemporary music in Viitasaari. You should refer to each town section for details of individual festivals.

The following days are either public holidays or other important events:

January

New Year's Day – Public holiday.
Loppiainen – 'The end of Christmas' on 6 January is a public holiday.

February

Runeberg Day – On 5 February, people eat 'Runeberg cakes', available in all shops, to commemorate the national poet.
Penkinpainajaiset – The last day of school for secondary school students, who dress in funny clothes, stand in the back of decorated trucks and drive around town, throwing candies to children. This event, known as 'penkkarit', generally takes place on the third Thursday in February.
Laskiainen – Seven weeks before Easter, this two-day event (Sunday and the next Tuesday) is devoted to downhill skiing and other winter sports in the countryside and in schools. People eat *laskiaispulla*, a wheat bun with whipped cream and hot milk.

April

Pääsiäinen – Easter is celebrated over several days. Thursday evening has church concerts, Good Friday is a public holiday, and on Sunday, people go to church or paint eggs and eat *mämmi* with sugar and milk. Mämmi is made of rye and malt; it looks and tastes weird. The following Monday is a public holiday.

May

Vappu – May Day is traditionally a festival of students and workers, but it also marks the beginning of summer, and is celebrated with plenty of alcohol and merrymaking. The 'official' celebration starts on 30 April at 6 pm, especially in Helsinki, where people gather in the Esplanade Park, around the 'Manta' statue, which receives a white 'student cap'. On 1 May everyone comes out onto the streets. People drink *sima* mead and eat *tippaleipä* cookies.

Äitienpäivä – Mothers' Day sees buffet lunch settings in all restaurants, where families go to eat so that mothers don't have to prepare food at home.

Naisten kymppi – This extremely popular jogging event in Helsinki, held towards the end of May, attracts thousands of women, who form teams to run 10 km. There are similar events in other towns, too.

June

Juhannus – Midsummer is the most important annual event for Finns. People leave cities and towns for summer cottages to celebrate the longest day of the year. It is also the day of the Finnish flag, as well as the day of John the Baptist. Bonfires are lit on the waterfront, and people swim and row boats. In many cases, lots of alcohol is consumed (to the point that, every Midsummer, several people are drowned). Juhannus is celebrated on the Saturday between 20 and 26 June, but the most important time is the Friday night.

Praasniekka – These Orthodox celebrations are day-long religious and folk festivals held in North Karelia and in other eastern provinces between May and September, most notably at the end of June.

July

Kalas – Stundars, in the municipality of Korsholm, holds an old-fashioned feast twice in July.

Sleepyhead Day – On 27 July the laziest person in the towns of Naantali and Hanko is thrown into the sea.

August

Venetian Nights – The end of the summer cottage season is celebrated on the west coast at the end of August. There are bonfires, fireworks, concerts and exhibitions.

Taiteiden yö – This night of art is held in Helsinki and some other towns by the end of August. It features a whole series of street performances, fringe art, open book stores and...no alcohol!

November

All Soul's Day – On the first Saturday in November, people visit the graves of deceased friends and relatives.

December

Itsenäisyyspäivä – Finland celebrates independence on 6 December, which is typically a cold, dark day. There are illuminated windows, students march in procession carrying burning torches, and in some towns there are fireworks. Churches have concerts and ordinary people watch TV to see what kind of clothes the rich and famous wear on this visit to the President's Castle. This is a public holiday.

Pikkujoulu – During 'Little Christmas', companies and schools organise private parties. In the month of December, much alcohol is consumed and much questionable conduct occurs. Foreign visitors are often welcomed, to experience something wild.

Joulu – Christmas is a public holiday. All traffic comes to a halt on Christmas Eve and resumes only on 26 December, or *Tapaninpäivä*. Families get together and stay together over the holidays.

New Year's Eve – Offices and shops are open till early afternoon. The night sees fireworks and much celebration.

POST & TELECOMMUNICATIONS

Post offices are open from 9 am to 5 pm Monday to Friday but main offices in large towns often have extended opening hours. *Posti* in Finnish and *Post* in Swedish, they sell packing material of various sizes, and often provide you with tape and wrapping material free of charge if you ask politely.

Postal Rates

Any letter or postcard weighing less than 50 grams can be sent within Finland or to Scandinavia for a little over 2 mk (price hikes generally take place on 1 January every year). To other countries, a weight limit of 20 grams applies, and sending a letter to

Europe costs approximately 3 mk; to countries outside Europe, postage is 3 mk for postcards and 3.50 mk for letters. All post offices display price lists for all types of mail.

Sending Mail

The Finnish postal system is both reliable and efficient. Letters posted before 5 pm Monday to Friday will reach their destination in Finland the next working day. Letters to Scandinavia take a few days, to Australia less than a week, and to North America almost two weeks.

Receiving Mail

There are poste restante services in all main post offices. The best kind of address to write on an envelope is as follows:

Name
Poste restante
Postcode and town

The postcodes are five-digit numbers that follow this logic: the first two numbers indicate towns and areas, the next two identify

the post office in the town or area, and the last number is always zero, except when you are sending mail to a post office box or poste restante, when the last number is one. The main post office is always '10' in all large towns, so the postcode for the main office in Helsinki is 00101, for Tampere 33101, for Turku 20101 and for Savonlinna 57101.

Telephone

You can use any telephone booth to make domestic or international calls. Use 5 mk coins for international calls. Most booths have a minimum 2 mk fee these days, so dial carefully! Telephone companies know how to make money; generally you can talk locally for approximately one minute per mk, which makes phone conversations an expensive hobby. Many post offices and separate Tele offices have comfortable phone booths, where a service charge of 4 mk applies, so use them only for long-distance conversations. It is cheapest to call Europe, North America or Australia between 10 pm and 8 am (Finnish time). At other times, a one-minute call to Europe costs 3.50 mk, to North America and Australia 5.40 mk and to other countries 9.10 mk per minute.

All phone numbers in this book include the area code, which is naturally dropped when calling from within the respective area. Finland area codes currently start with '9' (dropped when dialled from abroad), but this may change during the 1990s. When calling abroad from Finland, dial 990 for the International Access Code. When calling from abroad, dial 358 for Finland's country code.

Fax, Telex & Telegraph

Tele offices also have telefax, telegram and telex services.

TIME

Finnish time is two hours ahead of GMT/UTC in winter. Daylight Saving Time is in effect from late March to late September, when Finnish time is three hours ahead of GMT. Noon in Finland is 2 am in Los Angeles, 5 am in New York, 10 am in London and 8 pm in Sydney.

ELECTRICITY

Outlets in Finland are 220 volts, 50 cycles AC, so North American and Japanese appliances will require an adapter. All plugs are of the two-pin Continental European type, so take appropriate conversion plugs if you're bringing any electrical equipment with you. There is electricity in almost every house, including most private summer cottages, but not in wilderness huts along trekking routes.

LAUNDRY

There are no self-service launderettes available, except for the odd overpriced rip-off place in each town, meant for company laundry rather than individual travellers' jeans and underwear. Nor are there that many automated washing machines in youth hostels, not to mention hotels. Hotel laundry price lists could be good jokes if they were not true. This unhappy situation forces the traveller to use laundry machines when available and to do laundry manually at other times. To make things more difficult, shops don't have small packs of laundry powder available, so you either have to waste most of the pack or carry the open pack around with you.

WEIGHTS & MEASURES

Finland uses all the standard metric weights and measures (see the conversion table at the back of this book).

BOOKS & MAPS

Even though Finland produces quite a lot of serious literature, there is not an enormous supply available in English. The number of translations is increasing, and you should see what is currently available at Akateeminen or Suomalainen bookshops in Helsinki, in their 'Fennica' sections. Naturally you'll see a selection of glossy coffee-table books with magnificent nature photography and prohibitive prices. The most renowned classical literature dates back to the 19th century. The *Kalevala*, the national epic translated by Keith Bosley, is available in soft cover from Oxford University Press, as is *The Kanteletar*, a new title printed in 1992. The WSOY publishing company has produced several hard-cover translations of the works of notable Finnish authors, such as *The Egyptian* and *The Dark Angel* by Mika Waltari, and *The Unknown Soldier* by Väinö Linna. These books cost around 150 mk.

History

Finnish history is constantly unfolding, especially with the opening of Russian archives dating to the postwar decades of the Soviet Union era. If you want to read about general history, you should find *A Short History of Finland* by F Singleton, or *A Brief History of Finland* and *Let Us Be Finns* by Matti Klinge, of interest. The books of Mr Klinge give quite a reliable insight into the forces that were behind the growth of the Finnish nation. *Finland: Myth and Reality* by Max Jacobson deals with postwar history. *Blood, Sweat and Bears* by Lasse Lehtinen is a parody of a war novel, and it deals with Soviet relations.

Travel Guides

Apart from the 'official' presentations, it is hard to find good guidebooks on Finland. A recommended book is the annual *Finland Handbook*, which contains plenty of useful information, from current hotel prices to the addresses of tour operators around Finland. It really is only a handbook, though; little information on local attractions or hotels is revealed, and its price is quite high. From a different point of view, *Facts about Finland* contains plenty of background information on the history, economy and society of Finland. This book comes in several languages and costs around 100 mk.

Timetables

There is plenty of free travel information available, but if you want just one book which contains accurate details of every train, bus, flight and ferry route in Finland, you should invest approximately 70 mk for *Suomen kulkuneuvot*, which is published four times a year. The summer edition is generally referred to as *Kesäturisti*. It is probably one of the most complicated timetables to use, but in some areas buses are so few and far between that you'll have plenty of time to learn! It is all in Finnish, but there are summaries in English and a few other languages.

Maps

There are excellent maps in various scales available for every region in Finland. Free maps are handed out with a smile in all tourist offices around Finland, so town maps, some regional maps and most local bus maps will cost you nothing. For extensive treks, for canoeing or sailing tours and for driving and bicycling, however, you should buy a map. Karttakeskus (☎ 90-154 3102) at Opastinsilta 12B in the Pasila suburb of Helsinki produces and/or sells the largest variety of maps for Finland.

Road Maps There are 19 'GT' maps covering all Finland, available in a scale of 1:200,000. These maps are very clear and show practically all the places that you could be interested in, including youth hostels and wilderness huts. Each sheet costs 46 mk.

Outdoor Maps Karttakeskus has produced approximately 40 titles for trekking areas, including walking-track presentations of town areas (in 1:25,000 to 1:50,000 scale) and national park maps (1:50,000 to 1:100,000). Prices are usually 47 mk per map.

Field Maps For more detail and accuracy, there are 1:20,000 maps available covering all Finland, a full 3730 sheets in all. They cost a hefty 45 mk per sheet. If you don't feel secure about trekking, you could buy enough of these maps, though you can also consult them in public libraries, especially in provincial capitals. The complicated numbering system will take you some time to master! These maps also come in a scale of 1:50,000, with several sheets printed in one, available at 65 mk per sheet.

Sailing Maps Accurate coastal maps cost

187 mk per series, and maps for lakes and waterways are approximately 50 mk each.

Historical Maps Karttakeskus has published several regional and town maps from the 1930s of the Soviet-annexed Karelia, as well as maps from the 19th century. These souvenir maps are available for about 80 mk per sheet.

MEDIA
Newspapers & Magazines

At the time of writing, there are no locally edited English papers or magazines in Finland. Imported papers are widely available in Helsinki and other cities.

Radio & TV

There are four national radio stations and several local radio stations. Radio Mafia plays pop music and a wide variety of 'world music'. Local radio stations often have long talk shows. In Helsinki, Radio City (96.2 mHz) plays rock, while Radio Ykkönen/Ettan (91.1 mHz) often plays more mature American pop music.

There are currently three national TV channels. TV1 and TV2 are government channels. They have no commercials and show a fairly good number of English films and series (with Finnish subtitles). TV3 shows advertisements and many English programmes. There is one Finnish cable channel, which offers local programmes in some of the larger towns. In Helsinki it's called PTV, and it shows lots of American series. Many hotels and hostels are connected to the local cable network, and you can watch Super Channel, MTV and EuroSport.

FILM & PHOTOGRAPHY

North Finland offers 24 hours of sunshine around Midsummer, and there are beautiful summer days all over Finland. Shadows are very long in the mornings and evenings, as well as at any time in winter. In summer you can take photos all day. Taking photos in Finnish forests is much easier than in tropical forests, but there are tricky shadows and reflections which may result in bad photos.

Film prices vary considerably between shops, so shop around. Anttila department stores have generally lower prices than most others, and there are small companies selling cheap film when bought in bulk, such as Hertell in Tampere. Processing film is not too expensive and can be done in all towns.

HEALTH

You will not be likely to have health problems in Finland unless you engage in endurance tests in the wilderness. There is one dangerous snake and a few poisonous mushrooms, berries and plants in Finnish forests.

Predeparture Preparations

Health Insurance A travel insurance policy to cover theft, loss and medical problems is a wise idea. There is a wide variety of policies, and your travel agent will have recommendations. Some policies offer lower and higher medical expenses options, but the higher one is chiefly for countries like the USA, which have extremely high medical costs. Check the small print:

1. Some policies specifically exclude 'dangerous activities', which can include scuba diving, motorcycling or even trekking. If such activities are on your agenda, you don't want that sort of policy.
2. You may prefer a policy which pays doctors or hospitals direct (rather than you having to pay on the spot and claim later). If you do have to claim later, make sure you keep all documentation. Some policies ask you to telephone (reverse charges) a centre in your home country, where an immediate assessment of your problem is made.
3. Check whether the policy covers ambulances or an emergency flight home. If you have to stretch out on an aeroplane, you will need two seats, and somebody has to pay for them!

Medical Kit A small, straightforward medical kit is a wise thing to carry. A possible kit list includes:

1. Aspirin or Panadol – For pain or fever.
2. Antihistamine (such as Benadryl) – Useful as a decongestant for colds or allergies, to ease the itch from insect bites or stings and to help prevent motion sickness.
3. Antibiotics – Useful if you're travelling well off the beaten track, but they must be prescribed and you should carry the prescription with you.
4. Kaolin preparation (Pepto-Bismol), Imodium or Lomotil – For stomach upsets.
5. Rehydration mixture – For treatment of severe diarrhoea, and particularly important if travelling with children.
6. Antiseptic, mercurochrome and antibiotic powder or similar 'dry' spray – For cuts and grazes.
7. Calamine lotion – To ease irritation from bites or stings.
8. Bandages and Band-aids – For minor injuries.
9. Scissors, tweezers and a thermometer (note that mercury thermometers are prohibited by airlines).
10. Insect repellent, sunscreen, suntan lotion, chap stick and water purification tablets.

Ideally antibiotics should be administered only under medical supervision and should never be taken indiscriminately. Overuse of antibiotics can weaken your body's ability to deal with infections naturally and can reduce the drug's efficacy on a future occasion. Take only the recommended dose at the prescribed intervals and continue using the antibiotic for the prescribed period, even if the illness seems to be cured earlier. Antibiotics are quite specific to the infections they can treat, so stop taking them immediately if there are any serious reactions and don't use them at all unless you are sure you have the correct one.

Health Preparations Make sure you're healthy before you start travelling. If you are embarking on a long trip, make sure your teeth are OK; there are lots of places where a visit to the dentist would be the last thing you'd want to do.

If you wear glasses, take a spare pair and your prescription. Losing your glasses can be a real problem, although you can get new spectacles made up quickly and competently. However, new spectacles are not cheap in Finland.

If you require a particular medication, take an adequate supply, as it may not be available locally. Take the prescription, with the generic rather than the brand name (which may not be locally available), as it will make getting replacements easier. It's a wise idea to have the prescription with you to show that you legally use the medication – it's surprising how often over-the-counter drugs from one place are illegal without a prescription, or even banned, in another.

Water You can drink the tap water in all Finnish towns and villages, but it is not always very tasty. In Lapland and in many places in the eastern provinces, the water in lakes and rivers is fresh and pure, and most trekkers end up relying on it. Note that the brownish colour of water in lakes does not necessarily indicate pollution.

Mushrooms & Berries Eat only blueberries, lingonberries, cloudberries and cranberries in forests. Some attractive red berries can cause you stomach problems, so it's advisable to avoid berries you don't know. Don't pick mushrooms you don't know, and get yourself a mushroom guidebook.

Everyday Health A normal body temperature is 98.6°F or 37°C; more than 2°C higher is a 'high' fever. A normal adult pulse rate is 60 to 80 beats per minute (children 80 to 100, babies 100 to 140). You should know how to take a temperature and a pulse rate. As a general rule the pulse increases about 20 beats per minute for each °C rise in fever.

Respiration (breathing) rate is also an indicator of illness. Count the number of breaths per minute: between 12 and 20 is normal for adults and older children (up to 30 for younger children, 40 for babies). People with a high fever or serious respiratory illness (like pneumonia) breathe more quickly than normal. More than 40 shallow breaths a minute usually means pneumonia.

Many health problems can be avoided by taking care of yourself. Wash your hands frequently – it's quite easy to contaminate your own food. Clean your teeth with purified water rather than water straight from the tap. Avoid climatic extremes: keep out of the sun when it's hot and dress warmly when it's cold. Wear footwear that is appropriate to the activity and the terrain. You can avoid insect bites by covering bare skin when insects are around, by screening windows or beds and by using insect repellents. Seek local advice: if you're told the water is unsafe for swimming, don't go in. In situations where there is no information, discretion is the better part of valour.

Medical Problems & Treatment

Potential medical problems can be broken down into several areas. First there are the climatic and geographical considerations – problems caused by extremes of temperature, altitude or motion. Then there are diseases and illnesses caused by poor sanitation, insect bites or stings, and animal or human contact. Simple cuts, bites or scratches can also cause problems.

Self-diagnosis and treatment can be risky, so wherever possible, seek qualified help. Although we do give treatment dosages in this section, they are for emergency use only. Medical advice should be sought before administering any drugs.

Cold Too much cold is just as dangerous as too much heat, particularly if it leads to hypothermia. You should always be prepared for cold, wet or windy conditions, even if you're just out walking or hitchhiking.

Hypothermia occurs when the body loses heat faster than it can produce it and the core temperature of the body falls. It is surprisingly easy to progress from very cold to dangerously cold due to a combination of wind, wet clothing, fatigue and hunger, even if the air temperature is above freezing. It is best to dress in layers; silk, wool and some of the new artificial fibres are all good insulating materials. A hat is important, as a lot of heat is lost through the head. Keeping dry is vital, so a strong, waterproof outer layer is essential. Carry basic supplies, including food containing simple sugars (to generate heat quickly) and lots of fluid to drink.

Symptoms of hypothermia are exhaustion, numb skin (particularly toes and fingers), shivering, slurred speech, irrational or violent behaviour, lethargy, stumbling, dizzy spells, muscle cramps and violent bursts of energy. Irrationality may take the form of sufferers claiming they are warm and trying to take off their clothes.

To treat hypothermia, first get the patient out of the wind and/or rain. If their clothing is wet, remove it and replace it with dry, warm clothing. Give them hot liquids – not alcohol – and some high-kilojoule, easily digestible food. This should be enough for the early stages of hypothermia, but if it has gone further, it may be necessary to place victims in warm sleeping bags and get in with them. Do not rub patients, place them near a fire or remove their wet clothes in the wind. If possible, place a sufferer in a warm (not hot) bath.

Motion Sickness Eating lightly before and during a trip will reduce the chances of motion sickness. If you are prone to motion sickness, try to find a place that minimises disturbance – near the wing on aircraft, close to midships on boats, near the centre on buses. Fresh air usually helps; reading or cigarette smoke doesn't. Commercial anti-motion-sickness preparations, which can cause drowsiness, have to be taken before starting the trip; when you're feeling sick it's too late. Ginger is a natural preventative and is available in capsule form.

Sexually Transmitted Diseases Sexual contact with an infected sexual partner spreads these diseases. While abstinence is the only 100% preventative, using condoms is also effective. Gonorrhoea and syphilis are the most common of these diseases; sores, blisters or rashes around the genitals, discharges or pain when urinating are common symptoms. Symptoms may be less marked or not observed at all in women. Syphilis symptoms eventually disappear completely but the disease continues and can cause severe problems in later years. The treatment of gonorrhoea and syphilis is by antibiotics.

There are numerous other sexually transmitted diseases, for most of which effective treatment is available. However, there is no cure for herpes and there is also currently no cure for AIDS. Using condoms is the most effective preventative.

Snakes The *kyy* (viper) is the only dangerous snake in Finland. Antivenins are readily available in pharmacies; just ask for *kyypakkaus*.

Women's Health

Gynaecological Problems Poor diet, lowered resistance due to the use of antibiotics for stomach upsets and even contraceptive pills can lead to vaginal infections when travelling in hot climates. Keeping the genital area clean, and wearing skirts or loose-fitting trousers and cotton underwear will help to prevent infections.

Yeast infections, characterised by a rash, itch and discharge, can be treated with a vinegar or even lemon-juice douche or with yoghurt. Nystatin suppositories are the usual medical prescription. Trichomonas is a more serious infection; symptoms are a discharge and a burning sensation when urinating. Male sexual partners must also be treated, and if a vinegar-water douche is not effective, medical attention should be sought. Flagyl is the prescribed drug.

Pregnancy Most miscarriages occur during the first three months of pregnancy, so this is the most risky time to travel. The last three months should also be spent within reasonable distance of good medical care, as quite serious problems can develop at this time. Pregnant women should avoid all unnecessary medication, but vaccinations and malarial prophylactics should still be taken where possible. Additional care should be taken to prevent illness and particular attention should be paid to diet and nutrition.

WOMEN TRAVELLERS

Finland is a relatively easy country for women travellers to negotiate. Most Finnish women would consider themselves to be 'liberated', and the country as a whole is sexually tolerant (though not particularly sexually active) and liberal. Nevertheless, women hitchhiking should take the usual precautions.

DANGERS & ANNOYANCES

Finland is generally a very safe country for visitors. Lately, however, the social and political changes in Eastern Europe have contributed to a rise in Finland's crime rate. Higher levels of unemployment have also driven more Finns into criminal activity. Ordinary travellers are unlikely to be affected by this, though the usual care should be taken of money, belongings, passport and so on.

The only real annoyance likely to be encountered by the visitor to Finland's cities is drunks. Finland has something of an alcohol problem (which, incidentally, generates significant revenue for the government, which derives up to 9% of its income from alcohol taxes). There are many drunkards in Helsinki, most of them homeless, but they are not generally beggars nor do they behave in a particularly offensive manner. In fact, they can be talkative and amusing, and many speak good English.

For the trekker, mosquitoes can be a real problem. In Finland, the mosquito breeding season is very short (about six weeks in July/August), but the mosquitoes make good use of the time. Insect repellent is absolutely essential.

WORK

There are active work exchange organisations in many universities around Finland. Enquire through student organisations such as AIESEC (economics and commerce), IAESTE (technology and engineering) or ELSA (law). Getting a short-term job is rather difficult because there is chronic unemployment, but getting a low-paid job as a dishwasher might be possible in big towns if you try hard and shop around. To stay on the legal side, some institutions have working-holiday schemes for travellers, most notably in the Valamo monastery in Heinävesi or strawberry picking in Savo. For any serious career-oriented work, a work permit must be obtained beforehand from the Finnish embassy that normally handles business with your country.

Busking in Finland Tim Morgan of England has written to us to say that if you have a good voice and/or a musical instrument and are a bit short of cash, you should seriously consider doing some busking in Finland. Tim says that Finland is undoubtedly one of the best countries in Europe in which to play – even a moderate talent can bring in several hundred markkaa a day here. There are good places to play in most of the major towns – Rovaniemi, Oulu, Tampere, Turku and Helsinki, for example – but even better are some of the smaller places, where buskers are rarer and the novelty value greater. It is simply not the case that the more people there are, the more money you will make – a quiet pedestrian street in somewhere like Tammisaari, for example, will probably be far better than a bustling market in a big town, and you will also be spared any hassle from the police about licences etc (although, in practice, you certainly shouldn't worry about these, even in the larger places, if you are only playing for a day or two – no-one seems to mind much, provided the shopkeepers or market stall holders around you are happy for you to play there). Lunch times and Saturday mornings are the best times to play, and English songs go down very well, especially those of The Beatles. If you have a modicum of talent, gather your courage and give it a go!

TREKKING

Trekking in Finnish forests and wilderness areas requires a map and a compass, good preparations and all-weather trekking gear. In exchange, you'll get much freedom and good facilities. Nights are short or nonexistent in summer, so you can walk at any hour if you don't find a suitable place to sleep. Water is abundant everywhere, and you can camp practically anywhere (though some national parks have restrictions).

You will have to carry all food. Plan a nutritionally well-balanced daily food allowance and ration it with a strict discipline. Buy oats, macaroni, *jälkiuunileipä* rye bread slices, raisins, peanuts, chocolate, sugar and other dry food of your choice, plus some salami and Olympia soft cheese. Look for Blå Band's trekkers' food packs in sports shops. If you plan to walk from one wilderness hut to another, you will not need a cooking kit, but for unexpected situations it's good to have something to boil water in.

A sheath knife will be essential for making a campfire, but a saw and axe are not necessary. Lighting a campfire is a common-sense issue on dry summer days, though in practice, fires will be forbidden on such days. Don't light campfires away from the lakefront, and preferably use only established campfire places *(nuotiopaikka* in Finnish).

Finnish wilderness areas are essentially open to anyone. No guides or porters are available, so you'll have to be able to survive on your own. In Lapland the recommendation is to avoid trekking alone, but Markus trekked solo for five days, all the way to the Russian border, and there's really no problem, as long as you know what you are doing and are careful. For those going solo, it is obligatory to sign up in the trekkers' book as you depart, write your name and next destination in each hut you visit and finally announce the completion of your trek. Without these arrangements, no-one will be aware of your whereabouts.

Everyman's Right Finland grants trekkers more freedom than most other countries. The 'everyman's right' gives you the right to walk, ski and cycle anywhere in forests, and to travel on lakes in summer, or on ice in winter. You can rest and swim anywhere, and pitch a tent for one night, as long as it's not on private property. You can pick wild berries and mushrooms wherever you go. Fishing is also possible everywhere (see 'Fishing'). Restrictions apply to snowmobiles (their use is allowed on established routes only) and fire (no campfires on private land, and when you do light fires, be very careful). Felling trees is forbidden (gather fallen wood for your campfire), and hunting is not allowed unless you have a licence.

Fishing

Finnish waters are teeming with fish, and the best fishing waters have been established as 'Government Fishing Areas'. The National Board of Forestry farms tonnes of fish every year in these waters. Fishing with a rod or lure always requires a permit. In addition to a local permit, which has time and fish limits (say, two salmon per day and an unrestricted amount of other species), you will need a national fishing permit, which is available from all post offices.

This system is enforced by permit checkers, who sneak around the fishing areas. Markus was once picked up by one while hitchhiking, and he found out that fishers without permits are caught regularly. You always wonder whether anyone actually goes and checks these things! Well, they do in Finland.

ACCOMMODATION

Accommodation in Finland doesn't necessarily have to be expensive for a shoestring traveller. During a one-month trip you may well spend a week for free in various wilderness huts, a few nights in trains and, if you hitchhike or cycle, a few unlucky nights in the isolated barns or abandoned farmhouses that are dotted around the countryside. Youth hostels are probably a bit cheaper than the US or Western Europe average, and several people can share cottages at camping grounds. With some planning, you won't pay more than US$10 per night anywhere.

Camping

The 'everyman's right' grants you legal permission to temporarily pitch your tent anywhere, except on private property (near houses or summer cottages). Few travellers are known to have taken advantage of this unrestricted possibility, but as you consider the geography of Finland, there are no limits on where and how you can stay overnight for free, as long as you keep a low profile and stay discreet. If you ask permission from the landowner, you will be able to stay longer than one night. There are restrictions on the lighting of campfires, though.

The 360 official camping grounds generally cater more to caravans than to those carrying their own tents. Except for some cheap places on Åland, camping fees can be anything from 35 mk per person to 75 mk per family per night, but then all facilities can be used.

Cottages

What makes camping grounds so recommendable is the availability of pleasant cottages and bungalows. If you have a group of two to six people, prices are comparable to youth hostels, typically starting from 100 mk for two-bed cottages and 150 mk for four-bed cottages. Amenities vary widely, but a kitchen, toilet and shower are not uncommon. Some even have microwave ovens and TV sets. There are far more possibilities than we can record in this book, so you should always enquire about the availability of vacant cottages when you see a camping ground sign.

Wilderness Huts

There is a large network of huts throughout Lapland. Most of them have open doors, simple bunks, cooking facilities, leftover dry food, a pile of dry firewood and even a wilderness telephone. You should always leave the hut as it was – replace the used firewood and clean the place. The 'wilderness rule' states that the last one to arrive will

be given the best place to sleep. The tendency at the National Board of Forestry, which maintains most of the huts, is to increase the number of locked huts, which must be reserved beforehand (and which cost money), but most of the huts are still open to a tired trekker, at no cost. Most huts are shown on maps, even on the 1:200,000 GT maps. Finding them might be difficult without a 1:50,000 map, however. Huts have several names, and they all have slightly different meanings:

Autiotupa – A general word for 'desolate hut'. Doors are open and facilities are meagre. You may cook inside and sleep on hard bunks.

Kammi – A traditional Lappish hut (that is, made out of earth, wood and branches). It is very basic but will provide shelter for one or two people. A kammi may be hard to find.

Kämppä – This word means simply 'a hut'. Kämpät are used by Saame reindeer keepers as a shelter, and are always open and uninhabited. They provide shelter for one to six people. In the south, kämpät are often private and locked.

Rajavartioston tupa – A small hut built for the use of border guards. Most of them have unlocked doors, and sheltering overnight is legal. Keep a low profile, however, as the ordinary users have a serious mission.

Tunturitupa – A 'fell hut'. It has open doors and typical facilities.

Varaustupa – 'A hut to be reserved'. This kind of hut always has a locked door. Some have an 'open' side, too. The reservable side has mattresses and better facilities.

Yksityiskämppä – A private hut. It should not be used for any purpose other than as an emergency shelter when everything else fails. Remember: the 'everyman's right' never gives permission to go into private property.

Other names – Indicate private property. Names given to houses in the wilderness mean that they are out of bounds to the trekker.

Shelters

Outside Lapland, trekking routes generally have no free houses to stay in, but you may find a simple log shelter, called *laavu* in Finnish. Although the original laavu was a handmade shelter made of fresh spruce branches, what you are likely to come by these days is made of solid logs and good timber. A warm fire outside the laavu makes the inside warmer and keeps mosquitoes away, yet the smoke will not disturb you. You will still need insect repellent and a sleeping bag.

Youth Hostels

There are over 150 youth hostels in Finland, yet you won't find two that are similar. Youth hostels offer good value for money. Many are cheap yet attractive, they are seldom full and in some places you can really get away from it all. Hostels are run by the Finnish Youth Hostel Association (SRM), which classifies *retkeilymajat* (youth hostels) as either basic two-star hostels or 'standard' three-star hostels. Summer Hotels & Hostels are 'superior' hostels, now associated with SRM. They tend to be occupied by students during term, and consequently are open for travellers in summer only. Finnhostels are superior hostels, and may be open all year round or only in summer. In towns they resemble hotels, and in the countryside they may be farmhouses.

All youth hostels are open to anyone. However, you should purchase a membership card, as it gives a 15 mk discount in all hostels (we quote discounted prices throughout this book). You should also bring your own sheets, as sheets cost 15 mk extra in most hostels. Breakfast is generally not included in the price, but it is available for 25 mk or so (not so cheap compared to breakfast buffets in hotels).

Top 15 Youth Hostels We ranked all youth hostels in Finland in terms of friendly management, relaxed atmosphere and a good price/quality ratio to produce a top 15. Most of them are of the 'off the beaten track' variety, but we concluded that by staying in these hostels, you could relax, get away from all the hustle and bustle, and find some activities, too. We're not sure whether we should give the first prize to the Heinävesi or the Rauma hostel, but here is our list, in alphabetical order:

Dragsfjärd
Heinävesi (Pohjataipale)

Kaskinen
Kerimäki (Korkeamäki)
Kittilä (Sillankorva)
Koli
Kotka (Kärkisaari)
Liljendal
Nurmes (Hyvärilä)
Outokumpu
Porvoo
Rauma
Ruotsinpyhtää
Turku (Turku Town Hostel)
Vuonislahti (Herraniemi)

Guesthouses

Guesthouses in Finland are called *matkustajakoti*. They are usually slightly run-down establishments meant for travelling salespeople and other dubious types. Some are exceptionally clean and offer pleasant, homey accommodation in old wooden houses. Guesthouses are to be found in town centres and/or near railway stations. In this book they are listed under the 'middle' category.

Private Cottages

Finnvacations features 1000 private cottages around Finland in its excellent *Finnvacations* brochure. Cottages house two to eight people and are rented by the week all year round. Prices range from as low as 500 mk per week in low season to 4500 mk per week in high season. The high season is from mid-June to the end of July. Contact the Lomarengas organisation (☎ 90-3516 1321, fax 90-3516 1370) at Malminkaari 23, 00700 Helsinki well in advance for further information.

Farm Holidays

As some of the best youth hostels are in old farmhouses, it is true to say that the most interesting accommodation available in Finland is to be found in farmhouses. Some farm holiday schemes are promoted by Suomen 4H-Liitto (☎ 90-642 233, fax 90-642 274) at Abrahaminkatu 7, 00180 Helsinki, which represents quite a number of farms scattered around Finland. The minimum stay is two days, from about 230 mk per person full board, 190 mk half-board. Prices include food, accommodation, sheets and sauna. The company charges 60 mk for each reservation. There is an English brochure available.

In addition to the farms represented by this organisation, there are hundreds of farms offering accommodation, board and plenty of activities to visitors, often at lower prices. Advance bookings are not necessary. Local tourist offices will have information on individual farms, and their prices and services.

Hotels

There are apparently fewer hotels than museums in Finland, and among travellers, hotels are not at all the most popular places to sleep. As a result, hotels have to work hard to attract guests: facilities are luxurious, service tends to be good and hotel restaurants have become popular with locals. Prices remain high, but compared to hotels of the same quality around Europe, they are not overpriced. List prices are definitely out of reach for most budget travellers, but there are often summer discounts available (in winter, hotels are used by business people). A special bargain available in practically all Finnish hotels is the buffet breakfast. Because of some taxation regulations, this delightful breakfast offer is available to anyone, even though hotels are a bit reluctant to feed masses of starving travellers at this low price. It should be no problem, though, if you keep a low profile and ask politely.

Finncheque The Finncheque scheme, available in most chain hotels, allows accommodation in designated luxury hotels around Finland at a discounted price. This works out at US$40 per person in double rooms, or approximately US$60 in singles (there is a single supplement). This price reduction may come in handy if you compare these prices to the ordinary price of a double (US$100 to US$150).

The system is simple to use. You purchase coupons in advance in your country, or in Finland, and use them as a means of payment. All supplements have to be paid in the hotel, so you won't have to make any strict plans beforehand. In 1992 each Finncheque cost 165 mk. Enquire at your travel agent or at agents in Finland. Hotels are classified into three categories in relation to the Finncheque system. In I Class, you pay 75 mk extra for each guest, and a 75 mk supplement for single occupancy. There is no supplement in II Class, except for singles. In III Class, lunch is included in the price. Most hotels are II Class.

Note In summer most hotels have discounted prices anyway. Check special offers before wasting your Finncheques in discounted hotel rooms. There may be better deals elsewhere.

Rental

If you are planning to stay in Finland for more than just a few months, you could try renting an apartment. Just a few years ago, this was difficult, but there are now vacant apartments available, though the prices advertised in daily newspapers are quite high, starting at something like 2000 mk per month, including utilities. If you are enrolled at the university or some other institution, you might be able to gain access to student apartments. The rent may be as low as 500 mk per month, including utilities, for a *solu* room with a common kitchen and bathroom. Many apartment houses have laundry facilities and other common utensils.

FOOD

Typically, inexpensive meals in Finland are pizzas, hamburgers, kebabs or *grilli makkara* (grilled sausages), just like anywhere else in the world. Large towns have international restaurants, with Russian, Chinese, Italian, Vietnamese, Turkish or French food available. Finnish food is generally served as 'home-made' at most restaurants, available as an inexpensive lunch. Finnish food also has elements of both Swedish and Russian cuisines, but with a lot of variations and local specialities.

There are specialities for Christmas and

Easter, for other festivals and for each of the four seasons. Originally, Finnish food was designed to nourish a peasant population who did open-air manual work in cold weather. Consequently it was heavy and fatty, but made of pure, natural ingredients: fish, game, meat, milk and dairy products, oats, barley and dark rye in the form of porridges and bread, with few spices other than salt and pepper. Vegetables were more rarely used in everyday meals, except in the form of casseroles. Potato is the staple food, served with various fish or meat sauces. Soups such as pea soup, meat soup, cabbage soup or fish soup are common. Hot and heavy dishes, including liver, Baltic herring, turnip and cabbage, and even carrot casseroles, are served as the main course or as part of it. Typical fish dishes are prepared from whitefish, pikeperch, pike, perch, bream, vendace, Baltic herring and salmon, or trout.

Typical Food

Some traditional meals include game: try snow grouse *(riekko)*, reindeer stew *(poronkäristys)*, glowfired salmon *(loimulohi)* or raw pickled salmon *(graavi lohi)*. One of the most typical fish species is *muikku*, or *Coregonus albula*, a small whitefish.

Kaalikääryleet is cabbage with minced-meat stuffing. *Metsästäjänpihvi*, or 'hunter's steak', is minced meat with mushroom sauce. *Lihamureke* is seasoned minced meat

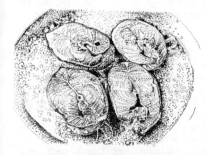

Salmon Cutlets

prepared in the oven, and *lihapullat* are meatballs. *Kesäkeitto*, or 'summer soup', is a popular vegetable soup.

In the east, you'll be able to taste *karjalanpiirakka* (rye pie with rice, barley or potato filling) and *lörtsy* (a thin pancake-shaped doughnut with apple or meat filling), or one of the several *-kukko* varieties. This large rye bread loaf is stuffed with pork and either vegetables, such as swede *(lanttukukko)* and potato *(perunakukko)*, or fish *(kalakukko)*, specifically small whitefish *(muikkukukko)* or perch *(ahvenkukko)*.

Western provinces have more of a Swedish influence, with such meals as *janssonin kiusaus* (Janssons frestelse in Swedish), potato and herring prepared in the oven, and *pyttipannu* (pytt-i-panna), which is ham and potatoes fried in butter.

Milk is often served with meals, and much *voileipä* (literally 'butter bread') is eaten. This is bread slices with butter and cheese or salami. Brown rye bread *(ruisleipä* or *jälkiuunileipä)* is very popular in Finland; try some with butter and cheese, and some cold milk.

For interpreting menu lists, refer to the Language section of this book.

Fruit, Berries & Mushrooms

The 'everyman's right' gives you the right to pick berries and mushrooms anywhere in Finland, except on private property or in restricted nature parks. Every August, billions of kg of edible berries and mushrooms rot in forests because there is no-one to pick them. Some berries can be found by the bucketful, and they generally contain many vitamins.

Mustikka – Blueberry. Widely available from late July onwards.
Puolukka – Lingonberry. Less sweet, but a sweetened purée with some milk is quite OK.
Hilla or *lakka* – Cloudberry. The most appreciated and expensive berry in Finland, but you need to preserve it first with some alcohol to make it delicious. The 'Lakka liquor' is a Finnish speciality.

Berries

Karpalo – Cranberry. Can be found in bogs and marshland, and tastes best after the first night frost, so it is still edible the following spring.

Cultivated berries include blackcurrant, gooseberry, raspberry, redcurrant and strawberry. They can be purchased in most markets from July onwards. Apples are grown in private gardens in South Finland. Apple season is September.

Edible mushrooms are numerous, as are the poisonous ones. Some of them must be boiled first to make them edible. Unless you already know everything about mushrooms, you should buy a *sieniopas* (mushroom guidebook) and learn such words as *myrkyllinen* (poisonous), *keitettävä* (has to be boiled first) and *syötävä* (edible).

Breakfast

Whether or not you stay in top-end hotels, you should check the buffet breakfast, available in almost all of them. At 20 to 25 mk, it is one of the real bargains in Finland.

Lunch

Almost everywhere in Finland, there are economical set lunch offers in hotels, restaurants, department store cafés and even petrol stations. Typically, you'll find a hot meal, a salad buffet, a few slices of bread, a drink (milk, water or malt drink) and sometimes coffee available at self-service counters for 25 to 45 mk. Prices, quality and the number of extras vary considerably, but because à la carte prices are so high, you should always look for lunch specials for some substantial eating at lunch time.

Self-Catering

Each town and municipality has several supermarkets with regular special discounts on selected food items. These vary daily or weekly, but as the Finnish retail business is very centralised, daily discounted items are sometimes the same in all shops. The main retail chains include K-Kauppa, T-Market and S-Market, but these also tend to be the most expensive ones. Usually each large village centre has at least one competing discount store. These offer fixed prices, and they include Alepa, Misto, Rabatti, Siwa and Säästäri.

Surprisingly, food produced in Finland is often very expensive in Finnish shops. (This may change if Finland becomes part of the EC). Again, this is a result of the no-competition pricing policy of primary production as well as the high profit margins of the retail stores. Shopping at discount stores, keeping your eyes open for special discounts and buying imported food, such as canned tuna fish, pineapple slices, sardines and bananas, are options to stretch the budget. Relatively cheap Finnish food that makes a simple meal includes fresh potatoes, yoghurt, eggs, fresh or smoked fish and canned pea soup *(hernekeitto)*, and in late summer, any market vegetables. Salmon can be bought at reasonable prices if you shop around. Cheese, salami, meat and bread are expensive.

DRINKS
Nonalcoholic Drinks

Buying soft drinks or even water can easily take a large share of your budget if you are not careful. Half a litre of soda water costs the equivalent of US$3 in railway station booths, and bottles of mineral water cost over US$3. This is not the whole picture, though. All tap water is safe to drink (if not very tasty), and in Lapland, water in rivers is pure and fresh. Supermarkets often have special prices for soft drinks in one-litre glass bottles (say, under US$2). You pay a deposit for each glass bottle of locally bottled soft drink and beer; when you return them to any store, your deposit is refunded. You can also easily make a few markkaa by picking up empty bottles. In some stores, there are even machines to take empty bottles. The deposit slips can be cashed at cashiers. Local soft drinks include Jaffa, Aurinko, Frisco and Pommac, but international brands are also widely available.

Alcohol

Beer, wine and spirits are available from

licensed bars and restaurants. There is a state monopoly on alcohol retail sales. Coupled with strict import regulations, this makes alcohol prices prohibitively high. Many travellers bring the allowed quota of alcohol from abroad (plan ahead, as Sweden and Norway are equally expensive), and some make a profit by selling their imports (which, naturally, is illegal). Apart from light beer, retail alcohol is sold exclusively at Alko liquor stores.

Beer Beer is very popular. There are several breweries, and the variety is staggering. The strongest beer is called IVA, or *nelos olut*, with some 5% alcohol content. It can only be purchased in Alko stores or in restaurants. Widely available in supermarkets are the lighter types of beer, the III Beer (called *keski kalja, keskari, kepu, kolmonen* or *kolmos olut)*, and the I Beer (called *Mieto Olut, ykkös olut* or *pilsneri*), which is less than 2% alcohol. Equally popular is a product named Gin Long Drink, also called *lonkero*. It is readily available in Alko stores and in restaurants.

Wine Alko bottles cheap wine, which provides a budget option (say, under 30 mk per bottle) for self-catering meals. Alko's supply of high-quality wines reaches gourmet standards, and prices are sky-high. Wine drinking in restaurants, despite its cost, has become more popular in Finland. Restaurants have long wine lists, but even 120 cc of red wine can cost 20 mk in many restaurants.

THINGS TO BUY

Finland is not the world's most exciting country for shopping, but there is plenty of interesting glassware, handicrafts, wooden items, jewellery, designer household utensils and pottery available in various local styles. Woven wall-hangings (raanu or ryijy) and embroidery are also examples of local handicrafts. Objects made of birch bark reflect a very old tradition, and the Lappish *kuksa* cup is quite an original item to take home. Colourful mittens *(lapaset)* or woollen hats *(myssy* or *pipo)* are necessary for winter travel. An impressive sheath knife *(puukko* or *leuku)*, available in many local designs, is essential for treks.

If you don't care for other people's work, contact the nearest *Käsityöasema* (there are hundreds of them in Finland) and create your own handicrafts. These places preserve cottage industries and provide free advice. You pay only for the material, plus a small fee for rental of the equipment.

Getting There & Away

AIR

Fewer airlines fly to Finland than to many other European countries, but most European international operators will fly you to Helsinki after a stopover in their respective hub. From outside Europe, you will find that prices are similar for flights to any European city, including Helsinki. In Europe, there is more variety in fares, depending on which city you want to fly from.

Finnair is the Finnish national carrier, with flights from Bangkok, Beijing, Istanbul, New York, Singapore and Tokyo, as well as Amsterdam, Athens, Berlin, Brussels, Budapest, Copenhagen, Düsseldorf, Frankfurt, Geneva, Gothenburg, Hamburg, Hanover, Lisbon, London (Heathrow), Madrid, Milan, Moscow, Munich, Oslo, Paris, Prague, Riga, Rome, St Petersburg, Stockholm, Stuttgart, Tallinn, Vienna, Warsaw and Zürich.

To/From North America

Finnair no longer flies from Toronto or the US west coast, so you'll need to check other airlines for the most convenient routing. Delta now flies the former Pan Am routes to Helsinki.

To/From the USA

Finnair and Delta fly from New York to Helsinki nonstop, and Delta has a wide range of connecting flights from other cities around the USA. IATA prices tend to be fairly high (US$1130/2260 one-way/return). APEX return fares (for seven to 90 days) are US$1058 on weekends, US$998 on weekdays. You should also check the discounted trans-Atlantic fares, and the prices of connecting flights to Helsinki, which tend to be relatively low.

The *New York Times*, *LA Times*, *Chicago Tribune* and *San Francisco Chronicle Examiner* all produce weekly travel sections in which you'll find any number of travel agency ads. Council Travel and STA Travel have offices in major cities across the USA. The *Travel Unlimited* newsletter (PO Box 1058, Allston, MA 02134) publishes details of the cheapest airfares and courier opportunities from the USA to destinations all over the world.

From Helsinki, you can fly to New York (1480 mk one-way) or Los Angeles (2080 mk one-way). Prices are for students and people under 26 years of age for summer 1992, as quoted by Kilroy (the main student travel agent in Finland and Scandinavia).

To/From Canada

Finnair no longer flies from Toronto to Helsinki, but you will find any number of North American and European airlines with connecting flights all the way to Helsinki. Most airlines will fly you over Greenland on the way. Travel CUTS has offices in all major cities. The *Globe & Mail* and *Vancouver Sun* carry travel agency ads. You will also find the magazine *Great Expeditions* (PO Box 8000-411, Abbotsford BC V2S 6H1) useful when looking for airfare information.

To/From the UK

IATA economy fares to Helsinki are £250/500 one-way/return. Three-month return flights from London cost £330 to £340, when purchased 14 days in advance. For people under 25 years of age, a special price (£164/328 one-way/return) applies. You may be able to find cheaper options. Local travel agencies offer flights to Finland – look for listings in the magazines *Time Out* and *City Limits* for the most attractive prices. Check the ads in the Sunday papers and in *Exchange & Mart*, and look out for the free magazines widely available in London (outside the main railway station, in the city, etc).

Most British travel agents are registered with ABTA (Association of British Travel Agents). If you have paid for your flight through an ABTA-registered agent who then goes out of business, ABTA will guarantee a refund or an alternative. Unregistered bucket shops are riskier but sometimes cheaper.

Athens	1110 mk
Stockholm	395 mk
Zurïch	1050 mk

To/From Europe

Helsinki is well connected by a number of airlines to most European capitals and major cities. From Paris, for example, you can get an advance-purchase return flight for FF 2780, and ordinary tickets for FF 4015/8030 one-way/return. For people under 25, a one-way ticket can be purchased for FF 1390.

If you live in Europe, you will probably know how to find your way to Finland, but if not, you will find busy flight markets in cities such as Amsterdam, Athens, Berlin and Paris. In other towns, consult local telephone directories first. (Travel agency is *reisebüro* in German, *agence de voyages* in French, *reisbureau* in Dutch and *rejsebureau* in Danish.) In Amsterdam, most inexpensive travel agencies, such as Malibu Travel and NBBS, are to be found along Damrak. In Athens, there are many agents near Syntagma Square. In Berlin, consult the magazines *Zitty* and *TIP* for travel agency ads. In Paris, there are several discount travel agencies on Avenue de l'Opéra, as well as around the Latin Quarter, including the large agency Nouvelles Frontieres.

From Helsinki, Kilroy (the student travel bureau) offers return flights to London (1795 mk), Brussels (1650 mk), Frankfurt (1620 mk), Rome (2750 mk), Athens (2295 mk), Copenhagen (990 mk), Paris (1795 mk), Amsterdam (1650 mk) and Zurïch (2195 mk). These prices apply from 19 June to 16 August 1992 and are available to anyone. (Fares are apparently lower in summer than in winter.) For one-way flights from Helsinki to European cities, Kilroy quotes the following summer 1992 prices for students and people under 26 years of age:

Destination	Price
Amsterdam	995 mk
Frankfurt	1205 mk
Copenhagen	655 mk
London	935 mk
Paris	895 mk

To/From Russia & Estonia

Finnair and Aeroflot fly daily between Helsinki and St Petersburg and Moscow. Finnair, Estonian Air and Aeroflot fly twice a day from Tallinn to Helsinki. There are also flights to Helsinki from Riga and Kiev.

To/From Asia

Aeroflot, Lot and other Eastern European airlines have traditionally been the budget options for ticket purchase in Bangkok and other Asian cities. Agents on Khao San Rd and Soi Ngam Duphli offer the best prices.

Flights from Asia to Europe tend to be cheaper than flights in the other direction, so it's worth purchasing the return flight in places like Bangkok, Penang (Malaysia), Hong Kong, New Delhi or even Kathmandu. In Hong Kong, the *South China Morning Post* carries travel agency prices, but in most other cities, you will have to shop around. As you will soon find out, it makes little difference whether you want to fly to Helsinki or Paris – most airlines will sell a standard 'European' fare, regardless of the distance flown from the first stop. But then again, it's worth shopping around first. Aeroflot (via Moscow), Lot (via Warsaw) and CSA (via Prague) are among the cheapest airlines offering the general European fare, but some airlines (such as Thai or SAS) will sometimes promote special fares for students or young people.

Finnair flies to Helsinki from Singapore, Bangkok, Tokyo and Beijing. Its prices are no cheaper than other West European airlines but flights are generally nonstop and convenient. From Helsinki, there are flights to several Asian cities, including Bangkok (2945 mk one-way) and Tokyo (3305 mk one-way). Prices are for students and people under 26.

To/From Australia

Flying from Australia is (at least) a two-stage journey, with likely stopovers in either Singapore or Bangkok, or cities in Europe. Qantas flies to Frankfurt, and British Airways, KLM, Lufthansa and a few other European airlines fly to Helsinki from Australia via London, Amsterdam, Frankfurt, or other cities, respectively. In Australia, STA and Flight Centres International are major dealers in cheap air tickets. Check the travel agency ads in the Yellow Pages and shop around.

To/From New Zealand

Air New Zealand flies to London and Frankfurt, and British Airways, Lufthansa and the French airline UTA will fly you to Europe, with frequent connections available to Helsinki. The cheapest way to visit Finland from New Zealand, on the opposite side of the globe, might be an inexpensive round-the-world ticket which allows you to stop in Helsinki.

As in Australia, STA and Flight Centres International are popular travel agencies.

Round-the-World Tickets

Round-the-world (RTW) tickets have become popular in the last couple of years. Many of the RTW tickets are real bargains, and can work out being even cheaper than an ordinary return ticket. Prices start at about UK£850, A$1800 or US$1300, depending on the season.

The official RTW tickets offered by the airlines are usually put together by two airlines, and permit you to fly anywhere you want on their route systems, as long as you don't backtrack. Another restriction is that you (usually) must book the first sector in advance, and cancellation penalties then apply. There may also be restrictions on how many stops you are permitted. The tickets are usually valid for between 90 days and a year. Finnair has combination routes with Qantas, Cathay Pacific and United. An alternative type of RTW ticket is put together by a travel agency, using a combination of discounted tickets.

Buying a Plane Ticket

The plane ticket will probably be the single most expensive item in your travel budget, and buying it can be an intimidating business. There is likely to be a multitude of airlines and travel agents hoping to separate you from your money, and it is always worth putting aside a few hours to research the current state of the market. Start early: some of the cheapest tickets have to be bought months in advance, and some popular flights sell out early. Talk to other recent travellers – they may be able to stop you making some of the same old mistakes. Look at the ads in newspapers and magazines, consult reference books and watch for special offers. Then phone around travel agencies for bargains. Find out the fare, the route, the duration of the journey and any restrictions on the ticket. Then sit back and decide which is best for you.

Use the fares quoted in this book as a guide only. They are approximate and are based on the rates advertised by travel agencies at the time of going to press. Quoted airfares do not necessarily constitute a recommendation for the carrier.

Once you have your ticket, write down the ticket number, together with the flight number and other details, and keep the information somewhere separate. If the ticket is lost or stolen, this will help you get a replacement.

It's also sensible to buy travel insurance as early as possible. If you buy it the week before you fly, you may find, for example, that you're not covered for delays to your flight caused by strikes or other industrial action.

LAND
To/From Sweden

There are six bridges over the Muonio and Tornio rivers that mark the border between Finland and Sweden. Locals constantly cross the border, which must be one of the most peaceful land borders in the world. The border stations are in Karesuando, Muonio, Kolari, Pello, Övertorneå and Haparanda. See the West Lapland chapter for further details.

Bus Buses along the Swedish east coast drive from Stockholm to Haparanda, and further north along the border. Get off at any of the six crossing points and walk to Finland.

Train The typical route to Finland from any point in Europe goes via Denmark to the Swedish town of Helsingborg, from where there are regular trains to Stockholm. This journey is probably the most boring train trip in the whole of Europe. Once you get to Stockholm, you should transfer to the Tunnelbana underground train, which will take you to Ropsten for Silja Line, or to Slussen for Viking Line. There are free shuttle buses from both these Tunnelbana stations to all ferries. Silja Line traditionally gives a complimentary ferry ride to anyone in possession of an Eurail ticket. If you want to sail to Finland from Kapellskär, there are buses to Kapellskär from the central bus terminal, adjacent to the Stockholm railway station.

There are also discounts available for those carrying Inter-Rail or Eurail passes or an International Student Identity Card (ISIC) or Youth International Educational Exchange (YIEE) card, for Wasa Line and Jacob Lines ferries to Finland from Sundsvall, Örnsköldsvik, Umeå and Skellefteå.

If you don't like the idea of paying for a ferry ride, you can continue by train to the Swedish town of Haparanda in the far north, and transfer there to the bus to Tornio.

To/From Norway

There are six border crossings from the Norwegian Finnmark to Finnish Lapland. This is a real no-hassle border, with no formalities performed in normal cases. In fact, some border stations actually close in the early evening, after which you can cross the border with no control at all. The stations are in Kilpisjärvi near Skibotn, in Kivilompolo near Kautokeino, in Karigasniemi near Karasjok, in Utsjoki near Levajok, in Nuorgam near Polmak, and in Näätämö near Neiden.

Bus Buses between Hammerfest and Kirkenes are very useful because they will drop you off at Karasjok, Levajok, Skipagurra and Neiden, with further connections to Finland available. There are several daily buses from Kirkenes to Neiden, but you may have to hitchhike on to Näätämö, stay there overnight, and catch the morning post bus to Ivalo via Sevettijärvi. For Nuorgam, you can catch the nightly bus from Skipagurra via Polmak. There are also Norwegian buses from Vadsø to Nuorgam at 10.20 am; you can catch the morning bus from Kirkenes and change in Varangerbotn to these buses. There are also two daily departures from Polmak for Rovaniemi. From Lakselv, there are buses to Karigasniemi and Ivalo daily from 10 June to 20 August, and several buses from Karasjok to Ivalo, via Karigasniemi. For Kilpisjärvi (the 'arm of Finland'), there are buses from Skibotn daily from 15 June to 15 August, with very early departures on weekdays. You can reach Skibotn daily from Tromsø. For Kivilompolo and Enontekiö, catch the bus from Kautokeino; there are four buses per week. To get to Kautokeino, you have a choice of buses from Alta or Karasjok.

To/From Russia

Bus/Vehicle Crossing to Finland from Russia along the 1269-km border used to be really tricky, but these days new border stations are opening, so you should enquire in advance about all new possibilities. From the south, there are the busy border stations in Vaalimaa and Nuijamaa, for road traffic from St Petersburg and Vyborg. Further up, there's a new crossing open in the municipality of Kitee. At the time of writing, there is no other place to cross until you reach the municipality of Salla in Lapland, and the relatively busy crossing point in Raja-Jooseppi, just north of the Saariselkä region, which will take you to Murmansk in north-west Russia.

Train There are two trains a day between St Petersburg and Helsinki, and a daily train to/from Moscow.

To/From Hong Kong & China

The popular trans-Siberian train route is still going strong, but its pricing policy, a long-time case of inequality in world travelling, may soon change as the new Russian economy develops. It used to be ridiculously cheap to purchase a train ticket through the Chungking Mansion noticeboard in Hong Kong, at Hong Kong travel agents, at the train station in Beijing or at the China International Travel Service (CITS) (though CITS rarely has tickets). One-way tickets from Beijing to Moscow would trade at US$100 or less, and a further train ride to Helsinki could be arranged for a little extra. Nowadays, buying a one-way train ticket to Moscow costs around US$280. Helsinki to Beijing costs at least 1500 mk (over US$300), and reservations are extremely hard to come by, as there are only a few seats for each departure. Enquire in Stockholm before arriving in Finland, as there may be more seats available there.

SEA

To/From Sweden

Stockholm is the main gateway to Finland, due to the incredibly luxurious passenger ferries that travel regularly between Stockholm and Turku/Helsinki. Before you get confused, remember that Åbo is the Swedish word for Turku. Many travellers have left Stockholm for Åbo, only to find out the next morning that they have actually arrived in Turku. It is the same place.

There are several reasons for the high quality of the ferries. To attract customers, operators have to make ferries suitable for luxurious cruises to and fro, yet keep ticket prices low. There are two competing operators, Silja Line (white ferries) and Viking Line (red ferries). Silja has been considered better in overall performance, but its listed prices are also slightly higher, though Silja does give some attractive discounts. Viking used to be the budget option, but its present fleet is as superb as that of Silja, and Viking has a monopoly on Åland and Kapellskär-Naantali routes.

Another reason for low prices is that the major source of income for these two companies is actually tax-free sales; with high sales taxes in both Sweden and Finland, especially for alcohol and cigarettes, ferry operators offer some of the leading tax-free shops in the whole world, though prices for alcohol on board are much higher than those in the supermarkets of central Europe. Silja recently introduced 'the longest shopping arcade between Helsinki and Stockholm', which spans the entire MS *Serenade* and MS *Symphony*. People dress in their best clothes to stroll past shops and gourmet restaurants, though there may be arctic winds and snow-storms outside.

Food is a feature of the Silja ferries, with a complimentary buffet breakfast for all passengers. Silja also introduced the first 'cabin for everyone' system. With appropriate discounts, ferries are one of the best bargains in Finland.

From Stockholm Silja ferries depart daily from Värtan (free shuttle bus from Ropsten, or walk from Gärdet) in Stockholm at 6 pm for Helsinki, and at 7.45 am and 8.15 pm for Turku. Viking departs for Helsinki from the Statsgården pier (bus No 45 from Slussen, free of charge) daily at 6 pm, and at 5 pm on Tuesdays, Thursdays and Saturdays. Departures for Turku are at 8.10 am and 8.15 pm. The morning ferry stops at Mariehamn on Åland at 2.25 pm. Birka Line's MS *Birka Princess* leaves the Statsgården pier in Stockholm for Mariehamn each afternoon from Monday to Saturday. The trip takes six hours and costs about 30 mk. If you have up to four people in a car, the MS *Sea Wind* is the best value, with transport, cabins and breakfast for 540 mk one-way. You should call ahead toll-free (☎ 020-795 331 in Sweden, 9800-6800 in Finland) for reservations.

From Kapellskär Viking Line has departures from Kapellskär at 10 am and 8 pm for Naantali via Åland. To catch these ferries, take the bus from Stockholm at 8.15 am and 6.15 pm, respectively. The MS *Ålandsfärjan* sails between Kapellskär and Mariehamn twice a day, leaving Kapellskär at 9 am and 3 pm. At US$7 return, this is a cheap route.

From Grisslehamn Even cheaper are the Eckerö Line ferries from the small town of Grisslehamn to Eckerö in western Åland. In summer there are five departures daily, at 10 and 11.30 am and 3, 5 and 9 pm. The trip takes two hours and costs 20 mk (one-way or return).

From Sundsvall Wasa Line operates the MS *Fennia* between Vaasa and the Swedish town of Sundsvall. There are daily departures in summer, at 8.30 pm from Sundsvall and at 12.30 pm from Vaasa.

From Örnsköldsvik Wasa Line's ferries from the Swedish town of Örnsköldsvik depart daily at noon from 24 June to 11 August. There are extra weekend departures from June to August.

From Umeå Wasa Line departs daily at 9 am and 1 and 6.30 pm from Umeå for Vaasa. The trip takes four hours. There are also daily departures from Umeå to Pietarsaari/Jacobstad on Jacob Lines ferries.

From Skellefteå Jacob Lines operates daily ferries between Skellefteå in Sweden and Pietarsaari and/or Kokkola in Finland.

To/From Poland

The MS *Pomerania* sails all year round from the Polish town of Gdansk to Helsinki. In the summer high season, from 24 May to 26 September, there are departures at 9 pm on Sundays, sailing via Öxelösund in Sweden, and at 1.30 pm on Thursdays. At other times,

the ferry departs from Gdansk at 10 pm on Sundays and at 7 pm on Thursdays. High-season tickets are 360 mk one-way (240 mk for ISIC or Interrail pass holders) and low-season tickets are 230 mk (180 mk for pass holders). In the low season, you'll need to buy a cabin (from 100 mk up) or an aeroplane-style chair (50 mk).

To/From Germany

Silja Line sails a few times a week from the Skandinavienkaj in the German town of Travemünde to Helsinki on the MS *Finnjet*, reputedly the longest passenger ferry in the world. There are nine to 12 departures each month, and one-way prices start at DEM 260 in the low season. Small discounts are available for students.

To/From Estonia

With the independence of the Baltic States, the trans-Baltic route may become more popular as a transit route from Western Europe to Finland. In practice, you have to enter Lithuania from Poland, and follow the main roads from Kaunas to Riga to Pärnu and Tallinn, then continue on one of the ferries. At the time of writing, petrol can only be bought with hard currencies in the Baltic States. There are several ferry operators covering the 80 km between Tallinn and Helsinki. Estonian New Line is by far the cheapest, at 50 mk per person and 150 mk per vehicle. There are morning departures from Tallinn, and from Helsinki at 8 pm. Slightly more expensive is Tallink, with departures from Tallinn at 9 am and from Helsinki at 3 pm. Check current departure times before making any detailed plans.

Getting Around

AIR

Finland can offer some of the cheapest domestic flights in Europe if you are eligible for the discounts available. The best deal is the discounted return between Helsinki and Ivalo, which makes it cheaper to fly than to take trains or buses.

There are five domestic airlines in Finland. Finnair (AY) flies DC-9s, Finnaviation (FA) has 34-seater SAABs and Karair (KR) has 66-seater Aeritalia ATR-72s. These three airlines all belong to the same company, in which the government has a majority stake. Usage of various aeroplanes (and airlines) is determined by the demand – on those routes that have few passengers, you are likely to be using Finnaviation planes. There are also two private airlines: Air Botnia (KF) and Polarwing (WO). Prices and discounts are the same for the three major companies, and for most KF and WO flights, too.

Discounts

There are four price categories. A normal price applies to anyone, and especially to the Blue Flights, which run during the most popular times. *Lento & Säästö* is a return flight with a 40% discount; you must reserve both legs of the flight at the same time and pay for the flight within three days of making your reservation. For a discounted *one-way* flight under this scheme, you have to be a pensioner, or under 25 years of age, or a student under 29 years of age. There are further reductions for children under 11 years of age. *Lento & Erikoissäästö* is a return flight with a 60% discount; reservations and payment must be made at least seven days before departure. There are some restrictions in terms of the date of the return, but these are waived for pensioners, youngsters and students. There are additional reductions for children under 11 years of age. For group discounts etc, enquire at the nearest Finnair office.

Air Passes

The *Finnair Holiday Ticket* allows unlimited air travel within Finland for 15 days. The ticket costs US$300 and is valid for all flights except 'blue routes'. The *Finnair Youth Holiday Ticket* is available to persons between 12 and 24 years of age for US$250. Some restrictions apply.

Domestic Airline Offices

Finnair is the main internal air carrier, with two other companies operating within the same system. There are offices in many Finnish towns:

Helsinki
    Töölönkatu 21 (☎ 90-818 7670)
    Asema-aukio 3 (☎ 90-818 7980)
    Aleksanterinkatu 17 (☎ 90-818 7750)
    Mannerheimintie 102 (☎ 90-818 8360)
Enontekiö
    Tunturikuva Ky (☎ 9696-51399)
Ivalo
    Ivalontie 38 (☎ 9697-21502)
Joensuu
    Kirkkokatu 25 (☎ 973-120 921)
Jyväskylä
    Väinönkatu 3 (☎ 941-212 411)
Kajaani
    Pohjolankatu 33 (☎ 986-131 440)
Kemi
    Airport (☎ 9698-23344)
Kittilä
    Valtatie 41 (☎ 9694-12072)
Kokkola
    Isokatu 15 (☎ 968-13444)
Kuopio
    Asemakatu 22-24 (☎ 971-125 544)
Kuusamo
    Kitkantie 15 (☎ 989-852 1395)
Lappeenranta
    Airport (☎ 953-13302)
Maarianhamina
    Skarpansvägen 24 (☎ 928-11522)
Mikkeli
    Porrassalmenkatu 23 (☎ 955-367 333)
Oulu
    Hallituskatu 21 (☎ 981-223 644)
Pietarsaari
    Raatihuoneenkatu 7 (☎ 967-231 100)
Pori
    Mikonkatu 7 (☎ 939-326 255)

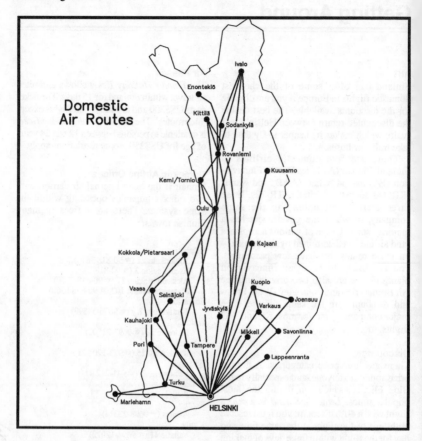

Domestic Air Routes

Ivalo
Enontekiö
Kittilä
Sodankylä
Rovaniemi
Kuusamo
Kemi/Tornio
Oulu
Kajaani
Kokkola/Pietarsaari
Kuopio
Vaasa
Seinäjoki
Joensuu
Varkaus
Jyväskylä
Kauhajoki
Mikkeli
Savonlinna
Pori
Tampere
Lappeenranta
Turku
Mariehamn
HELSINKI

Rovaniemi
    Koskikatu 1 (☎ 960-22916)
Savonlinna
    Airport (☎ 957-523 206)
Tampere
    Kyttälänkatu 2 (☎ 931-233 440)
Turku
    Eerikinkatu 4 (☎ 921-513 600)
Vaasa
    Hovioikeudenpuistikko 21 (☎ 961-179 666)
Varkaus
    Ahlströminkatu 8 (☎ 972-26952)

BUS

Buses in Finland run efficiently and on

schedule. There are public buses in towns and cities and a variety of private buses on the longer trips. Surprisingly, buses cover some 90% of all public roads, but on some routes there is only one bus per week. Long-distance buses stop at blue-white stops. In larger towns, yellow-black stops are for regional or local buses. Express buses stop only at *pikavuoro* stops.

Each town and municipal centre has a bus terminal *(linja-autoasema* in Finnish), with timetables displayed. Bus terminals are run by Matkahuolto, another sign to look for. Express buses generally operate on the long rips between major towns but always stop n towns and in some villages along the route. Regional buses mainly serve commuting workers and, in more isolated regions, school children. Schools are closed from 1 June to mid-August ('summer'), so there are generally fewer buses available then. Most buses run Monday to Friday, hourly between major towns; there is little bus traffic on Sundays. Check times and days in advance to avoid disappointment. We have seen few full buses, and sometimes buses are almost empty.

Costs

All bus prices are centrally determined according to the distance travelled. Express buses charge a flat 10 mk supplement. Bicycles are transported for 10 mk if there is space available. There are regular price hikes, but to give you an idea of the price structure, here are some approximate fares:

6 km	8 mk
10 km	10 mk
30 km	20 mk
50 km	30 mk
100 km	55 mk
200 km	100 mk
300 km	140 mk
500 km	230 mk
700 km	310 mk

Coach Holiday Ticket

For those on a budget, Matkahuolto has introduced a discount pass, available at most bus terminals and travel agents in Finland. It is valid on all buses, and entitles you to cover 1000 km for 300 mk (in 1992), which means a discount of at least 35%. The pass has coupons for trips of various lengths, in 'denominations' of 250 km, 100 km, 50 km or 10 km, so you use the appropriate combination of coupons for each journey. You will need to calculate carefully, however, because there's a catch: they don't give change. If you have few coupons left and the journey is, say, 220 km, you will have to use the 250-km coupon and lose 30 km worth of travelling. But if you then take several short journeys and don't 'lose' too many kilometres, your

total saving will approach 50%. This makes bus travel much cheaper than buying individual train tickets.

TRAIN

Trains of the State Railways of Finland, or Valtion Rautatiet (VR), are clean and right on schedule. There are three main electric rail lines: the Ostrobothnian line runs between Helsinki and Oulu, and continues to Kemijärvi in Lapland, the Karelian route runs from Helsinki to Joensuu, and continues to Oulu via Kainuu, and the Savonian route runs from Kouvola in the south to Iisalmi in the north, continuing to Kajaani. One of the most popular routes for travellers in a hurry is the triangle between Turku, Helsinki and Tampere. There are several side routes, notably between Tampere and Pori, Seinäjoki and Vaasa, Ylivieska and Iisalmi, Parikkala and Savonlinna, Turku and Joensuu, and Seinäjoki and Jyväskylä. VR operates passenger trains in two classes – 1st and 2nd. Most carriages are open 2nd-class carriages with soft chairs. Many trains have just one 1st-class carriage, containing small sections, each with seats for six passengers. Practically every long-distance train has a restaurant carriage, with expensive snacks but reasonably priced coffee and beer. Some trains transport cars from the south to Oulu, Rovaniemi and Kittilä for approximately 500 mk. Finland uses broad gauges, similar to those in Russia, so there are regular trains to/from Russia. At the time of writing, there is a daily train to/from Moscow and two trains a day to/from St Petersburg. Tickets for these trains are sold at the Helsinki railway station.

Bookings

There are few trains where you must have a reservation. You should book for all intercity (IC) trains and some special express (EP) trains. On all other long-distance trains, you can reserve a seat if you wish. The conductor does not mark a reserved seat, so you may have to ask someone to move if your seat is already taken. On the other hand, if you don't have a reservation, you can take any free seat ◆

but will have to be prepared to give it up if someone with a reservation shows up. Having paid for the seat, they seldom let you stay. Seats can be reserved up to the departure time. The new 'Duetto' reservation system makes it possible to reserve seats in special carriages. These include video carriages, children's carriages and handicapped persons carriages.

Train Passes

Several discounted train passes are available for train travel in Finland. Both Inter-Rail and Eurail passes give unlimited travel in Finland for Europeans and non-Europeans, respectively. For travel within Scandinavia, the Pohjola Junalla rail pass is valid for 21 days and can be purchased in any Scandinavian country. For Finnish trains, the Finnrail pass is valid for eight, 15 or 22 days. It is available on arrival, or at major train stations in Finland, and costs:

duration	2nd class	1st class
8 days	470 mk	705 mk
15 days	730 mk	1095 mk
22 days	920 mk	1380 mk

Charges & Surcharges

Train tickets are perhaps slightly cheaper in Finland than in Sweden or Norway. A one-way ticket for a 100-km train journey costs approximately 45 mk in 2nd class, 65 mk in 1st class. Return fares for the same journey are 80 mk and 120 mk, respectively (there's a 5% discount). For a journey of 500 km, fares are 170/250 mk one-way and 315/470 mk return. On the overnight trains, sleeping berths are available in one-bed, two-bed and three-bed cabins. The fare system is quite complicated, but for 100 mk you'll be able to get a bed in a three-bed cabin.

As far as discounts are concerned, most of them apply only to Finnish citizens, but then many travellers carry discount passes. Surcharges are compulsory on certain EP and IC trains, as well as on some special 'weekend trains'. The surcharge depends on the distance travelled, as shown below:

train type	1-75 km	76-200 km	>200 km
EP train	12 mk	20 mk	25 mk
IC 1st class	50 mk	60 mk	70 mk
IC 2nd class	15 mk	25 mk	30 mk
weekend train	15 mk	25 mk	30 mk

Cargo & Bicycles

Normal long-distance trains do carry cargo; IC trains don't. Most large railway stations have a cargo office which takes luggage in advance. Sending cargo anywhere in Finland costs 20 mk. Transporting a bicycle costs 40 mk. You can take your bicycle directly to the cargo carriage *(Konduktöörivaunu)*, or leave it at the cargo office. Our experience is that the self-service system is faster, more pleasant and cheaper. When you leave Finland by train from almost any point in Europe, you can send your luggage at a very low price to the station at your destination. It's worth checking current rates while in Finland.

Station Services

VR Matkapalvelu is a travel agency and ticket vendor, whereas VR Lippupalvelu is a normal ticket office which also sells some special products, such as train-bus tickets to Lapland. Left-luggage service generally costs 10 mk per day, but several stations still have 3 mk lockers available. For complete national timetables, buy the *Taskuaikataulu* booklet for 5 mk at the nearest railway station. For individual routes, there are small pocket timetables available, and every station displays all departures in the yellow and white tables, as is typical for all European railway stations.

TAXI

Taxis in Finland are luxurious, expensive and equipped with all kinds of gadgets. In Espoo's taxis, incoming calls are displayed on LCDs and printed on a piece of paper by a small fax-like machine. You will feel like the rich and famous, and pay like the rich and famous. Flagfall is 12 mk in the daytime, 19 mk in the evenings and 25 mk at night, then 4.80 mk for each km if there are one or two passengers. For three people, it's 5.70 mk per km. If you call a cab, the meter starts ticking when the taxi starts. Taxis are easy to recog-

A	D
B	
C	E

A: Raasepori Castle near Tammisari (VM), B: An old villa, Hanko Town (VM),
C: Children's playhouse in a Valkeakoski farm (VM),
D: The Old Church, Maakalla Islet (ML), E: Windmill, Keuruu (ML)

A: Fly Agaric Mushrooms (ML), B: Autumn colours, Kuusamo (ML),
C: Autumn colours (ML), D: Santa, near Rovaniemi (VM), E: Lily of the Valley (ML),
F: Squirrel (VM), G: Reindeer (VM)

nise and there are plenty of them in most places, the exception often being Helsinki at night.

There is no shared taxi transport available in Finland, the only possible exceptions being some off-the-beaten-track routes in Lapland. However, if you have a group of four people and want to cover a lengthy distance 'in the middle of nowhere', you should be able to negotiate with taxi drivers and end up with an attractive price.

CAR & MOTORBIKE

In Finland, vehicles drive on the right-hand side of the road. Traffic is orderly, and regulations are strict and should always be adhered to. Police checks are frequent and tickets include unpleasant figures. The wearing of seat belts is compulsory, in front seats and in the back, and there is a blood alcohol limit of 0.05%. Always drive with your headlights on; even though it's not compulsory in towns, it's easy to forget to turn them back on as you leave inhabited areas. Note that the excellent highway-type roads around Helsinki have speed limits of 70 km per hour, whereas on some narrow dirt roads in other parts of Finland, the limit may be 80 km per hour.

Parking in Helsinki is extremely difficult, except between Midsummer and the end of July, when most locals are out of town on holidays. In central Helsinki, one-hour parking costs 8 mk. In other towns, parking is rarely a problem, and is much cheaper than parking in Helsinki. Free parking is always possible in small towns. There are no tow-away zones in Finland.

Petrol is much more expensive than in the USA, but the price is generally about average, compared to other European countries (currently around 4 mk per litre). The major motoring organisation in Finland is Autoliitto (☎ 90-694 0022, fax 90-693 2578), at Kansakoulunkatu 10 in Helsinki. The postal address is PL 568, 00101 Helsinki.

Major car rental agencies in Finland include Ansa, Avis, Budget, Hertz, Inter-Rent-Europcar and Scandia Rent, but there are also local operators, especially in Helsinki. See the Yellow Pages, under the heading 'Autonvuokraamoja', for addresses and telephone numbers. Rates are quoted by the day, with an additional mileage charge, and range from 180 to 550 mk per day plus 2 to 5 mk per km. Special weekend and weekly unlimited-mileage rates are available on request. Don't plan on buying a car in Finland, as it's simply too expensive.

A final word of warning to motorists: you must always give way to elk and reindeer. Elk are dangerous on the roads, because of their size. In Lapland, reindeer can make motoring somewhat slow and/or hazardous. Expect them to appear at any time.

BICYCLE

Riding a bicycle in Finland is recommended in summer. There are practically no mountains in Finland, main roads are excellent and minor roads have little traffic. Bicycle tours are further facilitated by the liberal camping regulations and the nearly 24 hours of daylight in June and July. Temperatures can easily exceed 20°C during summer, and on sunny days, all you have to worry about is not burning your skin.

Main roads can be pretty boring and slightly dangerous, as trucks pass by fast. Narrow secondary roads offer by far the best views, and they often follow historical walking routes. Most farmhouses are along these roads.

Carry enough water, as there are few places to fill up on extra supplies along some roads. Weather can be unpredictable, so have a raincoat available. Note that there are still small milk-gathering stations along many roads, and they make excellent shelters during occasional rainstorms.

In most towns bicycles can be hired for around 20 to 50 mk per day. Bicycles can be carried on long-distance buses for 10 mk if there is space available (and there usually is), and on trains (except IC trains) for 40 mk.

HITCHHIKING

Finland is reputedly an easy country in which to hitchhike, and it is likely to remain so. You should look nice and tidy, stand up and stand out. Relatively few Finns like picking up hitchhikers but the few friendly ones do it with passion. The best time to hitchhike is Monday to Friday, when lonely travelling salespeople are on the road. They generally like to talk. Most drivers ask *Minne matka?* ('Where are you going?'), so you just tell them your destination. Standing and hitchhiking on motorways is forbidden, but there are relatively few motorways in Finland. Quiet roads are not really bad, as drivers seem to be more willing to stop than on busy roads.

WALKING

Finland is a superb country for extensive walking tours, as there are no high mountains and the paths are clearly marked and serviced with care. In the north and east of Finland, the countryside is unpolluted and water from lakes or rivers along the way can generally be used for drinking, although boiling the water can prevent problems. There are several established walking routes (see regional sections for details). They include *Pirkan taival* in North Häme, *Maakuntaura* in Central Finland, *Suden taival* in Ilomantsi, *Karhun polku* in Lieksa, *UKK Reitti* in Kainuu, and *Karhunkierros* in Kuusamo.

In addition to these lengthy and demanding routes, there is an almost endless choice of route possibilities in national parks such as Patvinsuo, Seitseminen, Lemmenjoki, Saariselkä, Pyhätunturi, Pallastunturi and Kevo. Free rock-bottom accommodation is available along all established walking routes, including most 'recreational areas'.

BOAT
Passenger Ship

Finland has 187,888 lakes, 179,584 islands and 647 rivers. There are also several historical canals that serve as piers along passenger routes. Canals connect separate lakes, so that even Nurmes can be reached by yachts from international waters. Not visiting the Finnish lakeland is like missing the pyramids in Egypt. Before the road network was constructed, lake steamers and 'church longboats' took care of passenger transport in much of Finland. They disappeared until the 1970s, but since then quite a few of them have been brought back into service. Apart from two-hour cruises starting from Kuopio, Savonlinna, Tampere, Nurmes, Mikkeli and other towns, you can actually cover half of Finland on scheduled boat routes. Many of the steamers now in use were built around the early 1900s, and they do have a lot of character. Most ships take bicycles, and short-distance travel is also possible.

Ferries only run in summer (June to August). The main lakes that do have important traffic include Saimaa (in Savo), Pielinen (in North Karelia), Päijänne (in Central Finland), and Pyhäjärvi and Näsijärvi (in Häme). There is detailed information in regional chapters.

Ferries on the Coast

There are three kinds of ferries operating between various islands on the coast, and between the islands and the mainland. First, there are the free *lossi* ferries. They are part of the public road system, and run to a schedule or just continuously, connecting important inhabited islands to the mainland. These simple ferries take all kinds of vehicles, as well as bicycles and even pedestrians. For example, the island of Hailuoto near Oulu is connected to the mainland, over six km away, by a lossi that runs every half hour in the high season. Second, there are ferries that run between several islands to support the livelihood of the small fishing villages that can be found especially near Turku and in the province of Åland. Some of these ferries are also free of charge to those who stay overnight on one of the islands, making it possible to island-hop from the mainland to Åland free of charge. Third, there are several cruise companies that run express boats to interesting islands on the coast. From Kalajoki you can visit the historical island of Maakalla, from Kokkola the island of Tankari, and from Helsinki the foremost tour is the short trip to Suomenlinna, to name just a few.

LOCAL TRANSPORT

Most big towns have a local bus network, with departures every 10 to 15 minutes in Helsinki and other large towns, and every half hour in smaller towns. Fares are centrally determined for all Finland, and they are something like 8 mk per ride. The Coach Holiday Ticket coupons are valid for local buses, except in the Helsinki region, Tampere and Turku. There are useful local train routes in the Helsinki area. Taxis seem to have a fare cartel, so they are always expensive.

TOURS

Many local tourist offices arrange daily or weekly sightseeing tours around their towns in summer, which may be useful and good value. In addition to regular tours, there is a large number of small tour operators taking groups into the wilderness, on treks, on white-water rafting expeditions and for all imaginable activities. Local tourist offices will provide you with practical information on how to reach these operators. Finnair offers several package tours for those arriving in Finland on Finnair flights.

Helsinki

Helsinki, the capital and the centre of cultural, financial and economic activity in Finland, is also the rainiest and windiest place in the country. With its green parks and waterways, Helsinki truly represents Finland: it is surrounded by water on all sides. It is a pleasant place to visit in summer, with fresh sea winds, seagulls flying over the busy fish market and many open-air cafés. Summer is also the best time to visit the islands; bring some food and go for the day if the weather is fine.

HISTORY

Helsinki was founded in 1550 at the mouth of the Vantaa River. For over 200 years it remained a sleepy market town with wooden houses scattered around the rocky peninsula. When Russia annexed Finland from the decaying Swedish empire in 1808, a capital closer to St Petersburg was needed, to keep a better watch on Finland's domestic politics. Helsinki was chosen, and in 1812 Turku lost its long-standing status as Finland's premier town, something the people of Turku still haven't forgiven.

To give the new capital a proper look, work soon started on the monumental buildings of what is now known as Senate Square. The square had been the town centre for over a century, but wars and fire had destroyed all wooden buildings there. The square's oldest surviving building, Sederholm House (1757), is made of brick. Carl Ludvig Engel, a native of Berlin, was invited to design the new centre. He had earlier worked in St Petersburg, so what you see today in Helsinki looks quite Russian (which may explain why Helsinki has been used by Hollywood to shoot 'Russian scenes' in *Reds*, *White Nights* and *Gorky Park*) when in fact C L Engel was German! In 1828 the University of Turku was transferred to Helsinki. The statue in the middle of the square, cast in 1894, is of Tsar Alexander II, and symbol-

ises the strong Russian influence in 19th century Helsinki.

Over the following decades, Helsinki grew rapidly in all directions. The fine railway station, finished in 1919, was designed by Eliel Saarinen, who also created an impressive town plan for the entire city of Helsinki. It was never implemented, and was replaced by the somewhat messy town plan of Töölö, built in the 1930s. At that time, Helsinki was the only place in Finland to have an intellectual elite and a high society, something that died away during WW II when Helsinki was bombed by the Russian air force.

The postwar years saw continuing division between the 'haves' and 'have-nots', with the short bridge (Pitkäsilta or 'Long Bridge') between Helsinki proper and the suburb of Kallio representing the demarcation line. Helsinki rose, however, to host the Olympic Games in 1952, probably the last noncommercial Games held.

In the 1970s, many new suburbs were built around Helsinki, and in 1975 Helsinki enhanced its international reputation when it hosted the Conference on Security and Cooperation in Europe (CSCE). The 'Helsinki Spirit' emerged, a term used for Cold War détente. Since then, Helsinki has officially been an international meeting

>int on numerous occasions, but the reality
always surprising: no high-rise buildings
d the fish market still surrounded by 19th
entury architecture. By population,
.elsinki remains a clearly Finnish town
including the Swedish-speaking popula-
on), with relatively few foreign residents.

)RIENTATION
Ielsinki was built on a windy peninsula,
/ith pretty much everything within walking
distance of the railway station (or the nearby
>us terminal). The main streets include
Aleksanterinkatu (department stores and
»anks), Esplanadi (designer shops and a nice
>ark) and especially Mannerheimintie,
which takes you from the town centre all the
way through Helsinki to the north. The business centre is near the railway station.

The southern suburbs, Eira and
Kaivopuisto, are the 'posh' quarters, with
villas, embassies and wealthy residents, as is
Kruunuhaka with its many historical buildings. Katajanokka is an island to the west,
connected to the mainland by several
bridges, with some interesting architecture.
Kallio and Töölö are densely populated residential areas offering relatively little of
interest, and very much the same applies to
all outlying suburbs. Pasila to the north is the
'New Helsinki', with ugly box-like office
buildings and the busy train station.
Itäkeskus in the east has probably the largest
cluster of supermarkets, shopping centres
and boutiques in the whole of Scandinavia,
while the nearby areas of Marjaniemi and
Vuosaari offer possibilities for seaside
walking or bicycle tours. Kumpula and
Käpylä have large areas of refurbished
wooden villas, and you should tour the area
by bicycle if the weather is fine. Finally,
Meilahti will give you access to the museum
island of Seurasaari, and afterwards, you can
make an attractive scenic loop from Meilahti
through Kuusisaari, Lehtisaari and
Lauttasaari, and back to the centre.

INFORMATION
Helsinki has all the services you would
expect of a major European capital.

Tourist Offices
The city tourist information office (☎ 90-169
3757) at Pohjoisesplanadi 19 is probably the
busiest and the most helpful tourist office in
Finland (we've heard of 2000 visitors per
day in summer). The office will give you an
updated city map, and lists of events, restaurants, nightclubs and much more. You can
also buy a Helsinki Card here (see the
'Helsinki Card' details later in the
'Information' section). The office is open
daily in summer from 8.30 am to 6 pm
Monday to Friday and from 8 am to 1 pm on
Saturdays. In winter, opening hours are 8.30
am to 4 pm Monday to Friday.

Just opposite, across the Esplanade park,
is another useful office to visit – the Finnish
Tourist Board (☎ 90-174 631) at
Eteläesplanadi 4. Here you'll find brochures
dealing with attractions all over the country.
The office is open from 9 am to 4 pm
Monday to Friday.

Money
All banks have similar opening hours, from
9 am to 4.15 pm Monday to Friday. At other
times, cashing your travellers' cheques is
more difficult. If you arrive by aeroplane
outside office hours, you should change
enough money at the airport, where banks
are open daily from 6.30 am to 11 pm. In the
city centre, the Viking Line ferry terminal
has an exchange booth open from 9 am to 6
pm Monday to Friday; on weekends it is
open in the mornings and from 3.45 to 6 pm.
Forum and Kluuvi shopping centres have
cash exchange machines that take foreign
cash in several currencies. Hotels serve only
their customers, and rates are lousy. There is
no black market, nor are there any private
exchange booths at this time. There is no
exchange service at the railway station,
either.

Post & Telecommunications
There are approximately 80 post offices in
the Helsinki area. The main post office
(☎ 90-195 5117) is the large building
between the railway station and the bus terminal on Mannerheimintie. Office hours are

9 am to 5 pm Monday to Friday, but the poste restante in the same building (Entrance 'F'), opposite the railway station, is open from 8 am to 9 pm Monday to Friday, 9 am to 6 pm on Saturdays and 11 am to 9 pm on Sundays. The main telephone office is in the same building, at Mannerheimintie 11B. Here you can use telephone booths from 8 am to 10 pm Monday to Friday, and until 9 pm on weekends.

Cultural Centres

The British Council (☎ 90-640 505) at Erottajankatu 7B has a library and is open from 10.30 am. The American Center Library (☎ 90-176 599) is on the 4th floor, Kaivokatu 10A, just opposite the railway station. It's a good place to find magazines, books and videos. The Goethe Institute (☎ 90-641 614) is at Mannerheimintie 20A, and the French Cultural Centre (☎ 90-694 6244) is at Ruoholahdenkatu 23.

Libraries

Helsinki has several public libraries. The most central, at Rikhardinkatu 3, is open from 9.30 am to 8 pm Monday to Friday and from 9.30 am to 3 pm on Saturdays. The main library is actually in Pasila, and there is another good branch in Kallio. The well-stocked parliament library (☎ 90-4321) is at Aurorankatu 6 – you'll have to sign up and check-in your bags to get in. The Statistics Library, or *Tilastokirjasto* (☎ 90-17341), 2nd floor, Annankatu 44, has every imaginable official publication from all over the world.

Travellers' Centres

There is a travellers' café called the International Meeting Point (☎ 90-169 3698) at Linnakatu 10.

Travel Agencies

Helsinki is not known for its variety of budget travel agencies, but a few agencies stand out for their reasonable prices. Kilroy Travels (☎ 90-624 101) at Mannerheimintie 5 is the former Travela, the student travel bureau. It has the lowest prices for Aeroflot

and other airlines. In summer the office packed, so service can be slow at times. T Indian-owned Intia-Keskus (☎ 90-651 06 at Yrjönkatu 8-10 also has cheap fligh Matkantekijät (☎ 90-640 944) at Annanka 16B represents Iberia and Malaysian, ar they have a listing of cheap flights. Suom Seuran Matkatoimisto (☎ 90-625 155) Mariankatu 8 sells flights to Australia ar North America.

Agencies specialising in travel to th former Soviet Union come and go. You ca easily arrange trips to the Baltic State (Russian) Karelia, St Petersburg and beyon Consult the 'Matkailu' pages of the dail *Helsingin Sanomat* for listings. Estonia i *Viro*, St Petersburg is *Pietari*, and Karelia i *Karjala* in Finnish. Agencies includ Etumatkat (☎ 90-18261) at Keskuskatu 1 & 5, LS-Matkat (☎ 90-685 1520) a Salomonkatu 5A, Matka RE-KA (☎ 90-65! 052) at Mikonkatu 13G, and Matk Kapsekki (☎ 90-177 177) at Laivurinkat 43. Intourist (☎ 90-631 875) at Mikonkat 15 is the official tourism representative of th former Soviet Union.

Books & Maps

Akateeminen Kirjakauppa at Keskuskatu 1 is the largest bookshop in Scandinavia. It has an extensive selection of English, German and French magazines, paperbacks and guidebooks, but prices are quite high. The best map selection in Finland is available at Karttakeskus at Opastinsilta 12B in Pasila, but maps are also sold in most bookshops. Associated with the Student Union, Libri Academici at Vuorikatu 5 imports academic English books and sells them slightly cheaper than larger bookshops. Valtikka sells 'official' publications, some of them in English, at Annankatu 4 (☎ 90-1734 2012) and Eteläesplanadi 4 (☎ 90-662 801).

Medical Services

Medical services in Helsinki are efficient, but exactly where you will be taken for medical services and how long you will have to wait depends on the current situation; at some times, hospitals are very congested.

or serious injuries or other medical emergencies, call the Helsinki University Central Hospital (☎ 4711), which will then redirect you to the appropriate hospital. To obtain treatment for serious injuries, go to the Töölön sairaala (Töölö Hospital) at Töölönkatu 40. For cases of poisoning, go to the Meilahti Hospital at Haartmaninkatu 4.

For less urgent medical problems, contact the nearest Terveysasema clinic. For opening times and other information ☎ 10023. The most convenient clinic, with access to a wheelchair, is in Kallio, at Eläintarhantie 3D (the round building just off Hakaniemi Square). To get there, take the metro to Hakaniemi or catch tram Nos 1, 2, 3T, 3B, 6 or 7. In addition to normal opening hours, this clinic is open from 8 to 11 pm on weekdays, 2 to 11 pm on Saturdays and 8 am to 11 pm on Sundays and public holidays. At more inconvenient hours, go to the Kivelä Hospital at Sibeliuksenkatu 12-14 (a short walk from tram Nos 3B, 3T and 8). It's open 24 hours a day on weekends, as well as from 3.30 pm right through to 8 am on weekdays.

Foreign visitors pay no more than approximately 120 mk per day for hospital treatment. Because most travellers carry medical insurance, there has been much debate over whether foreign patients should be charged the real cost of their treatment (which is about 3000 mk per day), but at the time of writing, hospital treatment remains very cheap for travellers in Finland. Visiting a clinic costs no more than 50 mk (and, often, is free).

Pharmacy is *apteekki* in Finnish, and you'll find one at Mannerheimintie 5 (☎ 90-179 092), right in the city centre, open daily from 7 am to midnight. A pharmacy (☎ 90-415 778) at Mannerheimintie 96 is open 24 hours a day.

Emergency
Call ☎ 112 for emergencies (ambulance, fire brigade or search and rescue). For police, call ☎ 10022. For strictly medical problems, there is a 24-hour information service at ☎ 10023.

Helsinki Card
This card will give you free travel on all local transport in Helsinki, Espoo and Vantaa, free admission to 48 museums and a number of other attractions, a free sightseeing tour, and some discounts and free gifts. If you keep busy, Helsinki Card is definitely good value at 80/105/125 mk for one/two/three days. It is available from local tourist information offices, the railway station, some travel agencies and most hotels.

THINGS TO SEE
Museums
The Helsinki Card gives free admission to all of the following museums. You will have to sign in on arrival at the museums when carrying the Helsinki Card.

Amos Anderson Art Museum The collection of Mr Anderson, one of the wealthiest Finns of his time, includes Finnish and European paintings and sculptures. The permanent exhibitions are on the 4th to 6th floors at Yrjönkatu 27, and a large gallery on the bottom floor has temporary exhibitions. It's open from 11 am to 6 pm Monday to Friday, and until 4 pm on weekends. Entry is 20 mk for adults, 10 mk for students.

Museum of Applied Arts If you are interested in Finnish design, this museum has much to offer. It's located at Korkeavuorenkatu 23, adjacent to the architectural museum. It's open daily (except Mondays) from noon to 4 pm, and until 6 pm on Wednesdays. Admission is 7 mk.

Arabia's Museum This porcelain factory museum (☎ 90-393 9326) is rather bleakly located on the 9th floor of a suburban factory at Hämeentie 135. Most visitors come for the factory sales downstairs. There are special offers and three price categories, of which the test production series offers the most economical buys. To get there, take tram No 6 to the terminus and walk 200 metres. The factory museum is open daily. There is a nominal admission fee, with a student discount available. Hours are 10 am to 8 pm on

Mondays, 10 am to 5 pm Tuesday to Friday, and 9 am to 3 pm on weekends. Factory tours are available on request.

Ateneum This is the most notable art museum in Finland. Its list of painters reads like a 'Who's Who' of Finnish art. Even the building itself is a masterpiece of, well, renovation, which was successfully completed in 1991. The most notable classical paintings are the Kalevala-inspired works of Gallén-Kallela, works by Edelfelt and Schjerfbeck, and the collection of paintings of the brothers von Wright. Note also the paintings of Mr Holmberg, which beautifully depict quiet life in Finnish forests in the 19th century. Upstairs are more recent works at the-**Museum of Contemporary Art.**

The Ateneum and is open daily (except Mondays). Hours are 9 am to 5 pm on Tuesdays and Fridays, 9 am to 9 pm on Wednesdays and Thursdays, and 11 am to 5 pm on weekends. Tickets cost 10 mk.

Cygnaeus Gallery This attractive wooden building in Kaivopuisto has 19th century paintings. It's open from 11 am to 4 pm Wednesday to Sunday and from 6 to 8 pm on Wednesdays. Admission is 6 mk.

Gallén-Kallela Museum This magnificent studio of one of the most notable Finnish painters should not be missed. It's in Tarvaspää, just across the Helsinki-Espoo border. The building itself is of Jugend style and was designed by the artist. There are paintings and temporary exhibitions, and just having a cup of coffee in the garden is attractive. To get there, you can take tram No 4 to its terminus and walk the two-km seaside path, or catch bus No 33, which runs morning and afternoon, Monday to Friday. HKL buses won't take you all the way to the museum, as it's in the municipal area of Espoo. The museum is open in summer from 10 am to 8 pm Monday to Thursday, and until 5 pm Friday to Sunday. In winter, it's open from 10 am to 4 pm Tuesday to Sunday. Admission is 25 mk, but with the Helsinki Card you won't pay anything.

Helsinki City Museum This old villa oppo site the National Museum has a larg miniature model of historic Helsinki, givin a glimpse of a life from the past. Sometime the temporary exhibition is more interestin than the regular one. The museum is ope daily (except Saturdays) from noon to 4 pm and until 8 pm on Thursdays. Entry costs 5 mk, 2 mk for students.

Helsinki City Art Museum There are temporary exhibitions in this modern building at Tamminiementie 6, not far from the museum island of Seurasaari. It's open all year round from 11 am to 6.30 pm Wednesday to Sunday. Admission is 10 mk.

Helsinki Art Hall Large temporary exhibitions can be seen at Nervanderinkatu 3. In summer, the hall is open daily (except Saturdays) from 11 am to 5 pm; at other times, it's open until 6 pm Tuesday to Sunday. Admission is 15 mk.

Hotel & Restaurant Museum This museum is at Itämerenkatu 23A in Ruoholahti; catch tram No 8. It's open from noon to 5 pm Tuesday to Friday. Admission is free.

Missionary Museum An attractive collection of Chinese and African artefacts, including a history of Finnish missionary work in Namibia, can be seen on Sundays at Tähtitorninkatu 16. To get there, catch the southbound tram No 10 to its terminus, or walk. The museum is open from noon to 3 pm. Admission is 5 mk.

Museum of Medical History This unusual museum at Hämeentie 153C (catch bus Nos 71, 74 or 76) is open from noon to 3 pm on Tuesdays and Fridays and from 3 to 6 pm on Thursdays. Admission is 4 mk.

Mannerheim Museum The interesting home museum of C G Mannerheim, former president and marshal of Finland, is at Kalliolinnantie 14 in the Kaivopuisto quarters. It is open from 11 am to 3 pm Friday to Sunday. Admission is 15 mk.

National Museum This notable building deserves a close look for its National Romantic design and for the Kalevala-inspired frescos on the ceiling of its main hall. The museum is less successful in drawing Finnish history into an interesting exhibition, but there are a number of reasons why this museum should not be missed. The oldest artefacts are in the main hall. Room No 6 has religious objects of Catholic Finland. Notable historical pieces include a throne of Tsar Alexander I dating from 1809, when Finland was incorporated into Russia, and the 1899 painting *Attack* in room No 31, which dramatically symbolises nationalist opposition to the Pan-Slavistic movement. Entry to the Finno-Ugric (ethnographic) exhibition in the basement is from room No 46. The museum is open all year round. Hours are 11 am to 3 pm daily, until 4 pm on Sundays and in summer. On Tuesdays, it is also open from 6 to 9 pm. Admission is 10 mk, free on Tuesdays.

Co-operative Bank Museum One of the several bank museums in Helsinki, this one has the most convenient opening hours: 10 am to 3 pm Monday to Friday. It's located at Arkadiankatu 23, and admission is free.

Postal Museum This undervisited museum has interesting historical exhibitions and an extensive collection of Finnish and foreign stamps. It's open from 11 am to 5 pm Tuesday to Friday. Admission is 4 mk.

Collection of Reitz Foundation A home museum at Apollonkatu 23B 64 has Finnish art from the 19th century. It's open all year round, except July, from 3 to 5 pm on Wednesdays and Sundays. Admission is free.

Burgher's House This attractive small house is the oldest surviving wooden building in Helsinki, dating from 1818. Your visit will be more interesting if you ask questions. The house is located in Kruunuhaka, at Kristianinkatu 12. It's open all year round daily (except Saturdays) from noon to 4 pm,

and until 8 pm on Thursdays. Admission is 5 mk.

Sinebrychoff Museum of Foreign Art The largest collection of Italian, Dutch and Flemish paintings in Finland can be found on the premises of the Koff brewery at Bulevardi 40 (catch tram No 6). It's open daily from 9 am to 7 pm. Admission is free.

Military Museum This extensive collection of Finnish army paraphernalia has plenty of character. The museum is in Kruunuhaka, at Maurinkatu 1, and is open daily (except Saturdays) from 11 am to 3 pm. Admission is 5 mk.

Museum of Finnish Architecture This large exhibition of Finnish architecture is at Kasarmikatu 24. It's open daily (except Mondays) from 10 am to 4 pm, and until 7 pm on Wednesdays. Admission is free.

Sport Museum of Finland The Olympic Stadium houses Finland's 'sporting hall of fame'. It's open from 11 am to 5 pm Monday to Friday and from noon to 4 pm on weekends. Admission is 10 mk. Tram Nos 3B, 3T, 4, 7A, 7B and 10 will get you to the stadium. For nice views from the tower, catch a lift to the top between 9 am and 8 pm Monday to Friday, and 9 am to 6 pm on weekends, for 5 mk (free with a Helsinki Card).

Photographic Museum of Finland This centrally located photo museum at Keskuskatu 6 features temporary exhibitions. Take a lift from opposite the Ateneum building. The photographic museum is open from 11 am to 7 pm Monday to Friday, and until 4 pm on weekends. Admission is 5 mk.

Tuomarinkylä Museum The Tuomarinkylä manor dates back to 1790. It is a branch of the Helsinki City Museum, and features paintings and exhibitions. It's open daily (except Saturdays) from noon to 4 pm, and until 8 pm on Thursdays. To get there, catch bus No 64 from the railway square, then walk

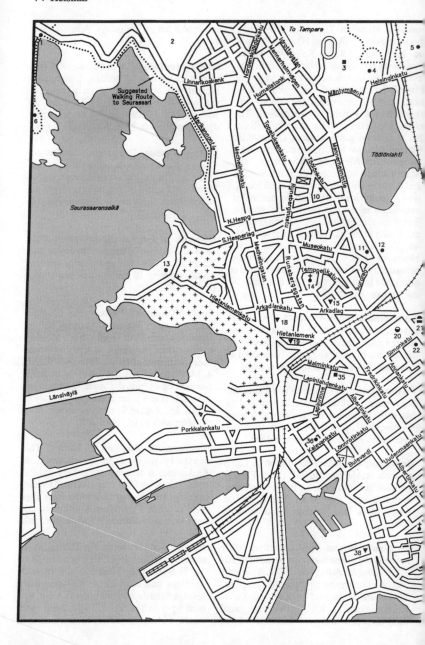

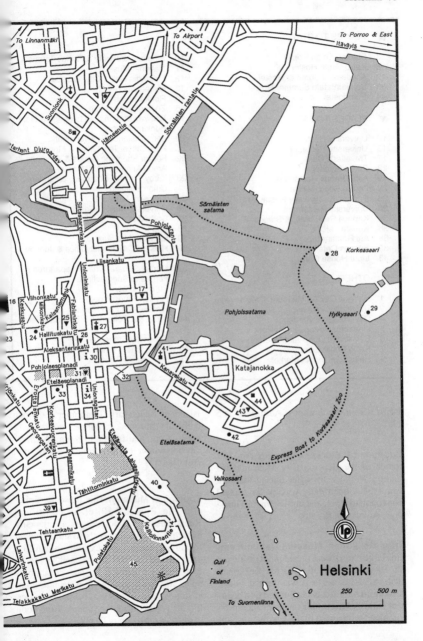

one km from the terminus. Admission is 5 mk.

Museum of Worker Housing Another branch of the Helsinki City Museum, this features workers' lifestyles during the 20th century. It's open daily (except Saturdays) from noon to 4 pm, and until 8 pm on Thursdays. Admission is 5 mk.

Urho Kekkonen Museum Tamminiemi This large house was a presidential residence for 30 years, right up until Mr Kekkonen died. After his death it was turned into a museum. The house is surrounded by a beautiful park. A visit to this museum should be combined with a visit to the nearby museum island of Seurasaari. Tamminiemi is open daily all year round. In summer, hours are 11 am to 4 pm, and from 6 to 8 pm on Thursdays; in winter it's open from 11 am to 3 pm. Admission is 10 mk.

Zoological Museum This museum, opposite the Ramada Hotel at Pohjoinen Rautatienkatu 13, doubles as a university department, and there is also a small student restaurant there. The exhibits of stuffed animals are on three floors, and include a two-headed mutant calf. The museum is open Monday to Friday, from 9 am to 2 pm in summer and from 9 am to 3 pm in winter. It is also open on winter Sundays from noon to 4 pm. Admission is 10 mk.

Churches

There are evangelical interdenominational services every Sunday at 10 am in the Mission Church on Tähtitorninkatu, and at 2 pm in the Rock Church.

Cathedral This Helsinki landmark is surprisingly uninteresting inside – climb the staircase for a good view over old Helsinki. The church is open daily in summer.

Rock Church The Temppeliaukio, or Taivallahti church, designed by Timo and Tuomo Suomalainen and built into solid rock, remains one of Helsinki's foremost attractions. It has a peaceful atmosphere, and there are always 'summer musicians' giving concerts for visitors. Some of the most popular church concerts, both gospel and classical, are given here. The English-language afternoon service at 2 pm on Sundays is followed by an informal coffee hour. The church is in Töölö, with the entrance at the end of Frederikinkatu.

Uspensky Cathedral This very photogenic red brick church, built in 1868, is one of the foremost Orthodox churches in Finland. It is just off the fish market and is open from 9.30 am to 4 pm Tuesday to Friday, 9 am to noon on Saturdays and noon to 3 pm on Sundays.

St Henrik's Church The main Catholic church in Helsinki is at Puistokatu 1. It has English services at 10 am on Sundays. This pleasant small church keeps its doors open even in winter, unlike Lutheran churches.

Korkeasaari

The main zoo in Finland is on an attractive island. Opened in 1889, it has a large variety of animals from Finland and around the world. There are regular express boats from the fish market, as well as from the pier at the Hotel Strand in Hakaniemi. You can also catch bus No 16 to Kulosaari, and walk 1.5 km through the island of Mustikkamaa. The zoo is open daily from May to September from 10 am to 8 pm. Admission is 18 mk, free with a Helsinki Card.

National Maritime Museum of Finland

You can reach this interesting cluster of exhibitions only via Korkeasaari. The main building has four floors of exhibits, and there's the MS *Kemi* and two boat shelters to be seen. The museum is open daily from May to September from 11 am to 5 pm. Admission is 6 mk.

Seurasaari

The large museum island of Seurasaari is a pleasant place to walk around, visiting the old houses that have been gathered here from around Finland. There's also the 17th century church from Karuna. Most houses have exhibits, and inside are guides in national costumes. There are folk dances on Tuesday, Thursday, Saturday and Sunday evenings at 7 pm, but you should check actual times (☎ 90-484 234). Admission to the dances is 20 mk, free with a Helsinki Card. To get to Seurasaari, catch bus No 24 to its terminus. Opening hours are June to August daily from 11 am to 5 pm; in May and September from 9 am to 3 pm Monday to Friday, and 11 am to 5 pm on weekends.

ACTIVITIES
Saunas & Swimming

Helsinki has several public indoor swimming pools, with inexpensive admission fees. The sauna on Yrjönkatu, adjacent to the Forum, has nude swimming (and consequently, separate hours for men and women). There are swimming pools in Kallio on Helsinginkatu, and a very large sports complex in Pirkkola in the Keskuspuisto park. You can get there by jogging or cycling along the popular tracks that crisscross the forests, but be warned: the park's forests are home to some of Helsinki's more desperate individuals. For some authentic bathing in a smoke sauna, catch bus No 20 to Vaskiniemi, on the island of Lauttasaari. The Finnish Sauna Society (☎ 90-678 677) has male sauna on Tuesdays, Wednesdays and Fridays from 2 to 8 pm, and on Saturdays from noon to 5 pm, all year round (except July). For women, hours are 1 to 8 pm on Thursdays.

Check the times first. Admission is a hefty 70 mk.

Cruises

When strolling in the fish market in summer, you will not have to look for cruises – the boat companies advertise through loudspeakers. There are several companies that will take you around the Helsinki area. Tickets cost around 50 mk. Don't miss the cheapest cruise in Helsinki, to the island of Suomenlinna. You can visit the island of Kaunissaari on a day trip, leaving the fish market daily at 10.30 am and returning some time after 4 pm. One-way tickets cost around 50 mk.

Language Courses

Helsinki University, Fabianinkatu 33 offers regular full-term courses in Finnish, starting mid-September. As a rule, you should be enrolled in the university to qualify for free education. The Helsinki Summer University (☎ 90-135 4577) at Liisankatu 16A, open all year round from 9 am to 3 pm Monday to Friday, will give Finnish lessons in summer. Expect to pay a few hundred markkaa for a summer course.

Organised Tours

Use your Helsinki Card for a complimentary sightseeing tour, which otherwise costs 60 mk. The tour takes 1½ hours and starts between the railway station and the post office. There are daily departures at 11 am and 1 pm from June to August, and one departure at 11 am on Tuesdays, Thursdays and Sundays in May and September. At other times, it's every Sunday at 11 am. There are also several walking tours arranged in summer, but there is usually only one each week, so enquire about the next one once you reach Helsinki.

Festivals

Helsinki may sometimes seem quite sleepy in summer, as many locals are touring Finland for summer festivals. But there is always something going on in Helsinki in summer: concerts, performances and much

more. Ask for details at the tourist information office, which regularly produces a list of all events. A few years ago, details of street music were published in morning papers (because you had to arrange a permit beforehand to play in a designated place).

The most notable event is the Helsinki Festival, held from late August to early September, but there are related concerts all summer. Kaivopuisto Park sees the immensely popular free rock concerts on Sundays in July, from 2 pm.

PLACES TO STAY – BOTTOM END

Cheap accommodation in Helsinki can be hard to come by in summer, even though capacity is on the increase. No private-home accommodation schemes are available, so it's dormitories for those on a budget.

Camping

You could pitch your tent anywhere in the large 'Central Park' (Keskuspuisto), if you are discreet; in other places, with the landowner's permission, it certainly won't be a problem either. Camping in public parks or on the islands of Suomenlinna or Seurasaari is not possible. *Rastila Camping* (☎ 90-316 551) charges 25 mk per person for camping, or 50 mk per tent if there is more than one person. It is open from 15 May to 5 September. To get there, take the metro to Itäkeskus and change to bus Nos 90, 90A, 96, 96S or 98. At night, if metros are not running, bus Nos 90N or 96N from the city centre will take you there.

Hostels

The busiest, but probably the least attractive youth hostel in Finland, the *Stadionin retkeilymaja* (☎ 90-496 071) is situated inside the Olympic stadium at Pohjoinen Stadionintie 3B. It is a quiet location, though, and there are several walks in the vicinity. The hostel is open all year round and offers accommodation from 40 mk. There are 200 beds in large dormitories. To get there, walk through the parks, or take tram Nos 3T, 3B, 7A or 7B.

The *Kallio youth hostel* (☎ 90-7099 2590)

at Porthaninkatu 2 is generally open only in summer, from 15 May to 31 August. There is space for 15 males and 15 females in concrete rooms. Dormitory beds cost 50 mk (including sheets). There is a TV room, a kitchen and a laundry room. If you don't feel like walking to Kallio, take the metro to Hakaniemi, or tram Nos 1, 2, 3B or 3T.

Independent dormitories come and go, but you could check the *Oranssi* (☎ 90-419 502) at Paciuksenkatu 23, open in July and August, which has beds from 35 mk, and the *Interpoint* (☎ 90-557 849) at Raumantie 5 (40 mk per night, but you first need to purchase a membership card for 16 mk).

PLACES TO STAY – MIDDLE
Hostels
The *Eurohostel* (☎ 90-664 452) at Linnankatu 9 in Katajanokka is associated with SRM (the Finnish Youth Hostel Association). There are 135 rooms, and singles/doubles/triples are 145/200/240 mk for members (15 mk per person more for nonmembers). There are kitchens available on each floor, and a self-service launderette. Reception is open 24 hours a day. To get there, take tram Nos 4 or 2.

The *Academica* (☎ 90-402 0206) at Hietaniemenkatu 14, a student apartment building in winter, is open for travellers from 1 June to 1 September. A renovation is expected, after which it will supposedly be good value, with singles/doubles at 185/240 mk.

The *Satakunnantalo* (☎ 90-695 851) at Lapinrinne 1A is also a student apartment building. It has singles/doubles for 200/290 mk and is open from 1 June to 31 August.

For something more distant and informal, try the *Bed & Breakfast* (☎ 90-519 519) at Gallén-Kallelantie 7, where private lodging is available from 100 mk per person.

Guesthouses
There is a cluster of guesthouses near the railway station. These places defy the typical 'cheap hotels near the station' definition, charging something like 200 mk for a single and 200 to 350 mk for a double. It is certainly

cheaper to stay in these than in hotels, but facilities are quite basic.

The *Matkustajakoti Clairet* (☎ 90-656 695), with singles/doubles at 210/250 mk, and the slightly more expensive *Matkustajakoti Omapohja* (☎ 90-666 211) are both at Itäinen Teatterikuja 3. The nearby *Matkustajakoti Irmala-Pilvilinna-Terminus* (☎ 90-607 072) has singles for 190 to 225 mk and doubles for 200 to 350 mk. Also near is the *Matkustajakoti Mekka* (☎ 90-630 265) at Vuorikatu 8B. The *Kongressikoti* (☎ 90-135 6839) at Snelmanninkatu 15 has just 10 rooms; singles are 170 to 220 mk and doubles are 280 mk. The *Pensionat Regina* (☎ 90-656 937) at Puistokatu 9 has singles/doubles at 200/300 mk. Other guesthouses include the *Matkustajakoti Erottajanpuisto* (☎ 90-642 169) at Uudenmaankatu 9 (singles/doubles at 200/250 mk), the *Matkustajakoti Lönnrot* (☎ 90-693 2590) at Lönnrotinkatu 16 (singles/doubles at 210/290 mk) and the *Matkustajakoti Tarmo* (☎ 90-701 4735) at Siltasaarenkatu 11B.

Hotels
Some of the cheaper hotels include the *Finn* (☎ 90-640 904) at Kalevankatu 3, where singles/doubles start at 250/300 mk, and the *Finnapartments Fenno* (☎ 90-773 1661) at Franzéninkatu 26 in the suburb of Kallio, where singles/doubles cost from 240/480 mk.

PLACES TO STAY – TOP END
There are apparently plenty of empty rooms in Helsinki hotels these days, but this is not necessarily reflected in special discounts. There are, however, attractive summer prices available, and many hotels accept Finncheques. For all reservations, including some hostels, contact the Hotel Booking Centre (☎ 90-171 133) near the railway station. From 1 June to 31 August, it's open from 9 am to 7 pm Monday to Saturday and from 10 am to 6 pm on Sundays. At other times, hours are 9 am to 5 pm Monday to Friday.

The noteworthy top-end hotels in Helsinki include:

Hotel Anna (☎ 90-648 011), Annankatu 1. Singles/doubles cost 330/450 mk in summer (Finncheques accepted).

Hotel Aurora (☎ 90-717400), Helsinginkatu 50. Singles/doubles cost 350/410 mk in summer (Finncheques accepted).

Hotel Cumulus Kaisaniemi (☎ 90-172 881), Kaisaniemenkatu 7. This place is central but has a noisy location. Singles/doubles are 540/670 mk or more (Finncheques OK), with weekend discounts available.

Hotel Grand Marina (☎ 90-16661), Katajanokanlaituri 7. The hotel is in an old (renovated) harbour building and opened in 1992. It has 462 rooms and charges 370/440 mk for singles/doubles in summer (Finncheques OK, with a supplement).

Hotel Helka (☎ 90-578 581), Pohjoinen Rautatiekatu 23. Singles/doubles are 490/620 mk (Finncheques accepted).

Hotel Helsinki (☎ 90-131 401), Hallituskatu 12. Singles/doubles at this centrally located hotel are 350/450 mk in summer (Finncheques OK).

Hotel Hesperia (☎ 90-43101), Mannerheimintie 50. This is supposedly the best hotel in Helsinki, but many would disagree. Singles/doubles are 780/1020 mk (Finncheques OK, with a supplement).

Hotel Hospiz (☎ 90-173 441), Vuorikatu 17. Singles/doubles cost 390/500 mk, less on weekends (Finncheques OK).

Hotel Inter-Continental (☎ 90-40551), Mannerheimintie 46. With 555 rooms, this is one of the most notable international hotels in Helsinki. Singles/doubles are 890/990 mk (Finncheques OK, with a supplement), with 50% discounts on weekends. Traffic can be a bit noisy, though.

Hotel Kalastajatorppa (☎ 90-45811), Kalastajatorpantie 1. Many official visitors have stayed at this legendary hotel, outside the town centre. Singles/doubles are 345/430 mk in summer (Finncheques OK, with a supplement).

Hotel Klaus Kurki (☎ 90-618 911), Bulevardi 2. One of the pleasant hotels in the town centre, the Klaus Kurki has singles/doubles for 680/840 mk (Finncheques OK, with a supplement). Lower weekend rates are also available.

Hotel Marski (☎ 90-68061), Mannerheimintie 10. This traditionally appreciated city hotel has singles/doubles for 790/890 mk (Finncheques accepted, with a supplement), with lower weekend prices available.

Marttahotelli (☎ 90-646 211), Uudenmaankatu 24. Singles/doubles at this pleasant small hotel are 300/380 mk in summer (Finncheques OK).

Merihotelli Cumulus (☎ 90-708 711), just off Hakaniemi Square. Singles/doubles are 330/420 mk in summer (Finncheques OK, with a supplement).

Hotel Palace (☎ 90-134 561), Eteläranta. The Palace offers good views of the harbour. Singles/doubles are 780/920 mk (Finncheques OK, with a supplement), with a 50% discount on weekends.

Hotel Ramada Presidentti (☎ 90-6911), Eteläinen Rautatienkatu. The centrally located Ramada Presidentti has 495 rooms and a casino. Singles/doubles are 295/440 mk in summer, 800/920 mk at other times (Finncheques OK, with a supplement).

SAS Royal Hotel (☎ 90-69580), Runeberginkatu 2. This is one of the finest and most expensive hotels in Helsinki. Singles/doubles are 860/960 mk, with a discount of approximately 50% on weekends.

Hotel Seurahuone Socis (☎ 90-170 441), Kaivokatu 12. This place just opposite the railway station has a lot of style and class. Singles/doubles are 650/850 mk (Finncheques OK, with a supplement). Weekend rates are lower.

Hotel Strand Inter-Continental (☎ 90-39351), John Stenbergin ranta 4. This hotel near Hakaniemi Square is one of Helsinki's newer hotels, and the most expensive. Singles/doubles are 990/1140 mk, 450/500 mk on weekends (Finncheques OK, with a supplement).

Hotel Torni (☎ 90-131 131), Yrjönkatu. Torni translates as 'tower', and for a long time this hotel was the highest building in the city centre. Singles/doubles are 660/790 mk (Finncheques OK, with a supplement).

Hotel Vaakuna (☎ 90-131 181), Asema-aukio 2. This hotel opposite the railway station has singles/doubles at 670/880 mk (Finncheques OK, with a supplement).

PLACES TO EAT

The bottom floor of the Forum shopping centre has the only food centre in Helsinki, with several pleasant restaurants in one spot. Prices are not especially low, but the *kebab restaurant* at the back offers a good-value meal.

Fast Food

When restaurants close or the last movies end, people queue for hamburgers or makkara (sausage) at numerous grillis, snägäri or nakkikioski scattered around Helsinki. These are true junk-food outlets, offering little nutritious value, but a salty sausage with mustard tastes excellent late at night. The *Jaskan Grilli* on Töölönkatu, behind the National Museum, is the best grilli in Helsinki, but there are several others.

The *Tepan Grilli* on Hakaniemi Square stays open till 3 am, with good garlic hamburgers available. Avoid the overpriced stalls at the railway station. These days you will find several simple kebab restaurants, a few taco bars and several local Carrols hamburger restaurants in the centre of Helsinki, but prices are high compared to prices of similar products in other countries. Also in the budget category, several stalls in market halls on Eteläranta, Hakaniemi Square and Hietalahti Square serve simple food at friendly prices.

University Places

Local students pay between 10 and 15 mk for discounted meals, available in a dozen *Uni* restaurants around central Helsinki. You will have to say 'Ei oo korttia' *(AY OOH KORT-ti-ah)*, meaning 'I don't have a card', and pay the ordinary price of 15 to 20 mk. The price includes three slices of bread, milk and some salad. Coffee and snacks are also inexpensive. The most pleasant place to eat is the *Alibi/Domus* at Hietaniemenkatu 14. It closes at 4 pm, then opens again in the evenings as a student bar, often with live music. Opposite the Ramada Hotel, the *Eläinmuseo*, Pohjoinen Rautatiekatu 13, is in the Zoological Museum building. The *Porthania* serves good food at Hallituskatu 11-13, and many foreign students eat there. The *main building* at Fabianinkatu 33 looks quite depressing but has lots of historical value, as one of the old houses designed by Mr Engel. Finally, the *Taukotupa* at Fabianinkatu 39 is the restaurant of the Forestry Department.

Lunch Eateries

Most restaurants around Helsinki offer lunch specials from about 30 mk. The meal usually includes salad, bread, milk or malt drink and sometimes coffee; shop around and ask first. The *Lähetysruokala* on Alppikatu, in the Kallio district, is the cheapest place to eat lunch, at under 30 mk. Also very cheap is the nearby *Alppimaa* at Castréninkatu 3. The *Suola ja pippuri* ('Salt & Pepper') on Vironkatu is open for lunch only, with cheap meals between 2 and 3 pm. The nearby

Kolme Kruunua at Liisankatu 5 is a relic of the 1930s, and is famous for its lihapullat (meatballs), which can be had for under 40 mk. Lunch is 45 mk.

For an à la carte meal, the *Hyvä Ystävä* restaurants have slightly lower prices than others but still can't beat the lunch specials. *Sam's* at Annankatu 22 is not particularly expensive and has very good food.

Smorgasbords

The *Konstan Möljä* at Hietalahdenkatu 14 is one of the most attractive restaurants in Helsinki, and one of the few to offer genuine Finnish food buffets. Its interior reflects an old Karelian fishing culture from the island of Uuras, annexed by the former Soviet Union in 1944. An 'all you can eat' lunch costs 42 mk on weekdays, 48 to 59 mk on weekends. Excellent soups are the speciality, and freshly brewed coffee is available at bargain prices. The place is normally full at noon. Lunch is served from 11 am to 4 pm daily, except on Sundays, when the hours are noon to 5.30 pm. To get there, take tram No 6 to the end of Bulevardi.

The *Cantina West* is quite an authentic Tex-Mex bar and restaurant at Kasarminkatu 23. A Mexican-style buffet lunch is available upstairs for a little over 40 mk. The colourful menu has nachos from 27 mk, but beware of expensive extras. In the evenings, the bar is often full.

The *Ani* at Telakkakatu 2 has the best Turkish buffet in town, at 38 mk. There is belly-dancing in the evenings (Monday to Friday), and it is often full then. Finding a table is no problem at other times. A similar place is the *Persepolis* at Pieni Roobertinkatu 2, where kebabs and vegetarian food are available.

Vegetarian

The *Green Way* at Kaisaniemenkatu 4 is a strictly vegetarian restaurant where all food is served uncooked. The *Kasvisravintola* at Korkeavuorenkatu 3 is a simple, informal place with an understanding of vegetarian philosophy. There are free vegetables available for the quick and brave at Kauppatori,

Töölöntori and Hakaniementori markets soon after 2 pm, when the sellers leave. Vegetables not picked up by anyone will be thrown away.

International Food

Surprisingly, the best Russian food available can be found outside Russia, and Helsinki is not a bad place to try some. The *Šašlik* (☎ 90-170 544) at Neitsytpolku 12 is the top Russian restaurant in Helsinki. Also very good is the *Bellevue* (☎ 90-179 560) at Rahapajankatu 3 in Katajanokka. The *Kosmos* (☎ 90-647 255) at Kalevankatu 3, a regular haunt of local artists, also serves Russian blini.

Reputedly, the best Indian cuisine is available at the *Namaskaar* (☎ 90-477 1960) at Mannerheimintie 100, but this is also one of the most expensive restaurants in Helsinki. Expect to pay 100 mk for a decent thali.

Of the Italian restaurants, *La Vista* (☎ 90-134 561) at Eteläranta 10 has been a local favourite for years. The *König* (☎ 90-171 271) at Mikonkatu 4 is one of the most appreciated à la carte restaurants. The *Svenska Klubben* at Maurinkatu 17 is an expensive restaurant but has plenty of charm and historical value. In summer, you can eat at the *Margona* (☎ 90-666 411), a boat restaurant at the fish market.

Cafés

Locals have developed a sophisticated taste for pleasant cafés, where you can also have snacks and small meals. The *Café Ekberg* at Bulevardi 9 is probably the oldest café in Finland, known in 1861 by the name 'The Pit'. There are good pastries; pay first and have them brought to your table. Another historical café is the *Fazer*, Kluuvikatu 3. Founded in 1891, it now serves excellent but costly pastries.

Currently the most popular café for huge and inexpensive korvapuusti (cinnamon buns) is the *Café Succes* at Korkeavuorenkatu 2. A favourite café among foreigners, especially Mediterranean tourists, is the *Socis*, just opposite the railway station. Prices are very high, but it is a particularly

attractive old café. Another popular place to meet people is the nearby *Piccadilly*, a modern café and restaurant; you often hear live music here, and the staff is exceptionally friendly.

For historical views, the *Café Engel* at Senate Square is recommended. Quite different is the café at the fish market. You'll see pictures of the kings and presidents who have visited this simple tent café over the 100 years it has been there, under the ownership of the same family. Near the island of Seurasaari is the *Tamminiementien kahvila*, Tamminiementie 8. This manor, dating back to the 17th century, retains its old ambience.

The night cafés in Helsinki are the Socis (cover charge 15 mk), and the *Miina* at Hakaniemi Square. Visiting the Miina at night is a peaceful experience, and you can sometimes bump into interesting people there.

Bars

The *Elite* at Eteläinen Hesperiankatu 22, with its Art Nouveau décor, is a popular open-air bar in summer. You'll also see quite a number of others in the city centre, including the *Café Kappeli*, the *Kaisaniemi*, and the *Pikkuparlamentti*. Other names to keep in mind include the *Bier-Akademie* at Pohjoinen Rautatiekatu 21, the Cantina West and the König, but none can beat the *Kaarle XII*; it always has long queues outside, and the regulars seem to have first access!

Self-Catering

Alepa, Rabatti and Säästäri are the cheapest food chains, with several stores scattered around Helsinki. The most central Alepa store can be found in Asematunneli, below the railway station, and is open daily till 10 pm. Check special discount prices, available regularly on selected items in all food stores in Helsinki.

ENTERTAINMENT
Cinemas

Most cinemas hand out weekly cinema programmes, with a listing in English. Go to the central Forum for a choice of seven cinemas and for the programmes. There are free films on Helsinki at 2 pm on Tuesdays and Thursdays in Amanda, at Sofiankatu 4, just off the fish market.

Nightclubs
The Kaivohuone, the Hesperia, the Fizzi, the Inter-Continental and the RAY Casino in the Ramada Hotel offer some interesting nightlife. Locals know which place is currently 'in', so ask around.

Music
Daily concerts are held in several locations in Helsinki. The tourist information office publishes an excellent leaflet, *Clubs, Gigs & Music Bars*, with daily programmes for individual clubs and music bars, and a calendar of events. Rock concerts are regularly held at the Tavastia, the Botta, the Vanha and the Savoy, to name just a few. The Jumo Jazz Club features local and foreign ensembles.

Theatre
Theatres in Helsinki have shows in Finnish, but there is opera and ballet, too. You can get programmes in Lippupalvelu ticket offices or at the tourist information office.

THINGS TO BUY
Helsinki has the largest variety of shops in Finland, but prices are generally higher than in most other large towns in Finland. The largest single area for discount shopping would be the eastern suburb of Itäkeskus, which you can reach by Metro. In the centre, you'll find Stockmann, the oldest and largest department store in Finland, and Forum and Kluuvi, the two modern shopping centres. Senate Centre, opposite the cathedral, is worth a visit even if you're not interested in handicrafts and souvenirs. The notable shopping streets are Mannerheimintie, Aleksanterinkatu, Pohjoisesplanadi (designer shops and galleries) and Frederikinkatu (boutiques). Mariankatu has many antiques shops, and Iso-Roobertinkatu is a pedestrian street. For exhibits on Finnish design, visit the Design Forum Finland at Eteläesplanadi

8, open from 11 to 5 pm Monday to Friday and from noon to 6 pm on Saturdays.

Markets
The famous fish market is a must for anyone visiting Helsinki. Fish, strawberries and makkara (sausages) are on sale, but you'll also find any number of stalls selling hand-painted stones and Nepali caps, Saame dolls (made in Hong Kong?) and fur hats. Another place that should not be missed is the Hietalahti market (catch tram No 6), where all sellers are ordinary local people who generally set up a stall for one week (this is an official restriction). This is the main second-hand centre in Helsinki: you'll find anything from used clothes to broken electronic goods. Bargain hard, and for really low prices, go a little before 2 pm, when the market closes. New people and new goods arrive in the evening.

There are also some interesting indoor markets, near the fish market and in Hakaniemi and Hietalahti.

GETTING THERE & AWAY
Air
Helsinki is served by several airlines from the USA and Europe, and Finnair connects Helsinki to all major cities and towns around Finland. Here is a list of airline companies in Helsinki:

Aeroflot
    Mannerheimintie 5 (☎ 90-659 655)
Air France
    Pohjoisesplanadi 27C (☎ 90-625 862)
Alitalia
    Erottajankatu 19 (☎ 90-680 1168)
American Airlines
    Mikonkatu 8 (☎ 90-661 544)
Austrian Airlines
    Mikonkatu 7 (☎ 90-171 311)
Balkan Bulgarian Airlines
    Annankatu 9 (☎ 90-647 752)
British Airways
    7th floor, Keskuskatu 7 (☎ 90-650 677)
Cheskolovenské Aerolinie
    Uudenmaankatu 6B (☎ 90-647 786)
Delta Airlines
    (☎ 90-796 9400)
El Al Israel Airlines
    Rikhardinkatu 4B (☎ 90-669 390)

Finnair
(☎ 90-81881)
Mannerheimintie 102
Aleksanterinkatu 17
Asema-aukio 3
Töölönkatu 21
Airport (☎ 90-81851)
Reservations (☎ 90-818 800)
Iberia
Annankatu 16B (☎ 90-640 944)
JAL Japan Airlines
Iso-Roobertinkatu 20-22 74A (☎ 90-612 1828)
KLM Royal Dutch Airlines
Mannerheimintie 14B (☎ 90-646 645)
LOT Polish Airlines
Keskuskatu 6 (☎ 90-660 400)
Lufthansa
Yrjönkatu 29A (☎ 90-694 9900)
Malaysian
Annankatu 16B (☎ 90-640 944)
Malév
Yrjönkatu 25 (☎ 90-646 116)
Qantas Airways
Museokatu 25B (☎ 90-447 522)
Royal Nepal Airlines Corporation (RNAC)
(☎ 90-651 066)
SABENA World Airlines
Mannerheimintie 20A (☎ 90-693 5833)
SAS Scandinavian Airlines
4th floor, Keskuskatu 7 (☎ 90-175 611)
Singapore Airlines (SIA)
Mannerheimintie 20A (☎ 90-693 5834)
Swissair
Mikonkatu 7 (☎ 90-175 300)
THAI International Airways
Keskuskatu 4 (☎ 90-602 044)
THY Turk Hava Yollari
(☎ 90-628 199)
United Airlines
Laajalahdentie 16 (☎ 90-484 1991)
USAir
(☎ 90-254 242)
Varig
(☎ 90-490 649)

Bus

The bus terminal is located between Mannerheimintie and the Kamppi metro station. Long-distance buses depart from between the white building on Mannerheimintie and the main bus station. Buses from the larger square are local or regional buses for western parts of Helsinki, Espoo and Vantaa.

Train

The railway station is right in the middle of Helsinki. All trains also stop at the Pasila station, three km to the north. Helsinki is the terminus for three main railway lines, with regular trains from Turku to the west, Tampere to the north and Lahti to the northeast.

Ferry

All international ferries arrive just off the central fish market: Viking and Silja from Sweden, Polferries from Poland, Tallink and Estonian New Line from Estonia, Finnjet from Germany and a few companies from Russia. An attractive way of leaving or entering Helsinki is on the MS *J L Runeberg*, a former steamship. Catch it from the fish market, to Porvoo, Loviisa or Hanko. There are departures almost daily – check timetables at Ageba (☎ 90-625 944).

The best places to purchase a ferry ticket are the harbour check-in offices. If you need timetable details or other information, ferry companies do have offices in Helsinki, and travel agents also sell tickets. Companies dealing with states of the former Soviet Union include Baltic Express Line (☎ 90-665 755) at Kluuvikatu 6, Kristina Cruises (☎ 90-629 968) at Korkeavuorenkatu 45, Saimaa Lines (☎ 90-43051) at Fabianinkatu 14, Tallink (☎ 90-602 822) at Kalevankatu 12, and Estonian New Line (☎ 90-624 434) at Fabianinkatu 12. These offices should be able to give you information on trips to Estonia or to Russia.

GETTING AROUND
To/From the Airport

There are two bus companies serving the airport. Finnair buses are more expensive, at 18 mk; they generally depart every 15 minutes from the Finnair terminal near the railway station, picking up passengers at the Hotel Inter-Continental bus stop. The local bus No 615 is somewhat slower but also several markkaa cheaper. There are also Airport Express minibuses that will take you to any place in Helsinki for a flat fee of 50 mk. Taxis charge approximately 120 mk for a ride between central Helsinki and the airport.

City Transport System

The city transport system, Helsingin Kaupungin Liikennelaitos (HKL), operates buses, metro trains, trams and local trains, and a ferry to the island of Suomenlinna. There are frequent departures on all routes; timetables and route maps are available free of charge from HKL ticket offices, one of which is located in the central Rautatientori metro station. A single journey costs something under 10 mk (price hikes are frequent), and you can change transport an unlimited number of times in the (exactly) 69 minutes from the time stamped on your ticket. Bus and tram drivers sell tickets, which you will have to stamp by yourself. For the metro and local trains, you should use the automatic ticket-vending machines. You can easily get on a tram, a metro train, a local train or the Suomenlinna ferry without a ticket, but there are frequent ticket checks. The penalty for a ticketless ride may be over 200 mk by now. As far as we know, acting dumb or playing the helpless foreigner won't help. There are one to three-day travel cards available, and a Helsinki Card gives you unlimited access to all HKL transport, including buses and trains to Espoo and Vantaa.

Bus

Most blue HKL buses leave from one of two locations in central Helsinki: the large open area behind the main bus terminal, and Rautatientori (railway square). There are also bus stops near both these places where you can catch other buses. You will need the free bus route map to find your way.

Train

The red or grey local trains all depart from the main railway station. If you travel within the municipal area of Helsinki, you can use the HKL ticket. All local trains have cars where you can buy tickets, and cars where you can't.

Tram

The green-yellow or red trams offer slow but pleasant transport in Helsinki. A very popular 'tourist tram' is 3T (or 3B, which goes in the opposite direction). The route takes you past several tourist attractions.

Underground

The Metro has just one line: from Ruoholahti in the west to Mellunmäki in the east. Trains run every five minutes from Monday to Saturday, but in the evenings and on Sundays they only run every 10 minutes. In summer there are also fewer trains. The last train leaves the centre at 11.20 pm.

Taxi

A vacant taxi can be hard to come by at certain times. If you need one, join a queue at any of the several taxi stands. All taxis are luxurious, expensive and equipped with all kinds of gadgets. Prices are fixed in Helsinki.

Car & Motorbike

Cars can be rented at the airport or in the city centre. Some of the more economical rental companies include Lacara (☎ 90-719 062) at Hämeentie 12 and Transvell (☎ 90-351 3300) at Ormuspellontie 5. These offices are outside the city centre. Motorbike rental is not common in Helsinki, and information on rental is not published. You could check the local telephone directory (under the heading 'Moottoripyöria') for shops that may have secondhand bikes that could be rented. It may also be possible to buy such a bike and sell it before departure.

Bicycle

There are several bicycle rental places in and around Helsinki. The Stadionin Maja youth hostel and the stall behind the Finlandia Hall are among the most convenient.

Around Helsinki

SUOMENLINNA

Suomenlinna is a quiet island cluster just

south of Helsinki fish market. It is an old Swedish fortress called Sveaborg, or 'Swedish fortress' (in Finnish, nationalistically, 'fortress of Finland'). There is plenty to do and see in this still relatively untouched place, a picnic spot for locals. When you return to the ferry, you may be surprised at how quickly the boat fills up – you might not have seen another person while in Suomenlinna! Allow at least five hours to explore properly. If you plan a picnic or a few beers, go for the whole day. Be sure not to miss the sight when the Silja and Viking ferries pass Suomenlinna at 6.15 pm. The strait next to the restaurant is one of the narrowest along the ferry route. There are always dozens of people waving – and more on the ferries.

History

The greatest fortress of the Swedish empire was founded in 1748 to protect the eastern part of the empire against Russian attacks. In 1808, during the War of Finland, Sveaborg had to surrender to the Russians. British troops bombed Sveaborg in 1855, during the Crimean War, but the fortress remained Russian until Finland gained independence in 1917. It continued to have military significance until 1983. These days it houses a number of inhabitants, in former barracks and recently built residential houses. In 1991 Suomenlinna was placed on the UNESCO World Heritage List, making it the most recognised historical landmark in South Finland.

Information

There is an information booth between the two major islands, which are connected by a beautiful bridge. The office is open daily from 5 May to 31 August between 10 am and 5 pm. There is also a telephone booth.

Things to See

Nordic Art Centre Temporary exhibitions by Finnish and Scandinavian artists are held in old barracks adjacent to a small café opposite the HKL ferry pier. Exhibitions are open daily (except Mondays) from 11 am to 6 pm. Admission is free.

Ehrensvärd Museum Old furniture, paintings, maps and weaponry are displayed in this attractive old museum. It's open daily from 1 May to 30 September and on weekends in October and November. Hours are 10 am to 5 pm in summer, 10 am to 3.30 pm in September and 11 am to 3 pm on autumn weekends. Entry is 6 mk.

Armfelt Museum Furniture and exhibits for this museum were brought here from Joensuu Manor in south-west Finland. The Armfelt family was an important family, closely linked to the tsars of Russia. The museum displays family portraits and fine pottery. It's open daily from 15 May to 31 August, and on September weekends, from 11 am to 5.30 pm. Entry is 6 mk.

Military Museum This building contains an aeroplane, a tank and other heavy machinery. Opening hours are similar to those of the Ehrensvärd Museum. Entry is 5 mk.

Coastal Defence Museum There is coastal defence equipment in this bunker-style exhibition. It's open daily from 10 am to 5 pm from 12 May to 31 August, and from 11 am to 3 pm in September. Admission is 5 mk.

Submarine Vesikko Because Finland was forbidden by the 1947 Paris Peace Conference to be in possession of submarines, this is the only submarine in Finland. It dates back to WW II, and is open daily from 10 am to 5 pm from 12 May to 31 August, and from 11 am to 3 pm in September. Admission is 5 mk.

Bunkers There are kilometres of old bunkers and caves all over the place. It is not quite certain whether anyone really knows how many there are or their locations. Bring a torch and enter – it is free adventure. After crossing the bridge and passing the information booth, you can start on either side of the fort. The more you explore, the more likely you are to find one that seems to be

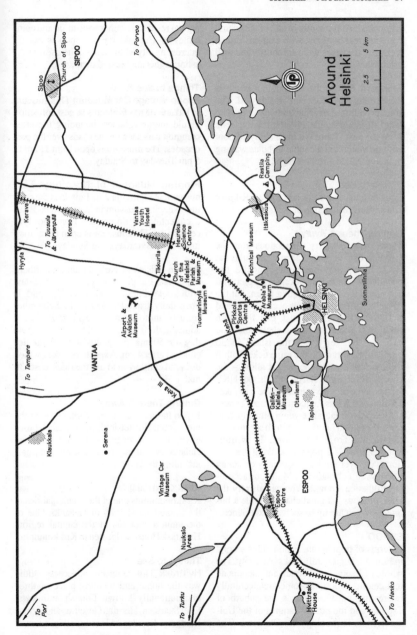

Around Helsinki

0   2.5   5 km

untouched. At the southern end of the island, there are real bunkers, with cannons and so forth, but the caves there are shorter and well established.

Shipyard Before the information booth is the entrance to a cooperative shipyard. The sign prohibits entry but nobody seems to mind. It is a dilapidated yet charming relic from the past. There is a huge shipyard pool with no water and a couple of boats waiting to be renovated – quite a sight.

Places to Eat
Suomenlinna has a food store, an R-kiosk and several restaurants or cafés.

Getting There & Away
There are a few ferry connections from the Helsinki fish harbour. The most useful is the HKL ferry, leaving from opposite the president's house. Buy tickets at the pier; you can board the ferry without a ticket, but the 'blue ladies' control tickets occasionally, and ticketless travellers must pay the high penalty. If you have only a short time, you can take the ferry, see the island in 30 minutes and return on the same ticket within the 69 minutes that the tickets allow – the cheapest cruise you can do in Helsinki! HKL ferries run every 35 minutes. The trip takes 15 minutes. A less frequent and more expensive express boat takes you a bit further, to the information booth, but you'll see more of the island from the shore. In winter, Suomenlinna is a popular walking destination (yes, over the ice), especially on sunny Sundays in February and March, or according to the ice strength. You can also try the HKL minibus – a good chance to ride a bus on ice, if you are up to such an experience.

ESPOO
In terms of population, Espoo ranks second in Finland, but it hardly looks like a city. The whole of Espoo is suburban, and there is no real centre. Espoo has some architecturally interesting places, such as the suburb of Tapiola, and the nearby campus of the University of Technology in Otaniemi. The

typical resident is rather well-to-do and commutes to Helsinki daily. Espoo is not an interesting city as such, but quite a few interesting sights are located there.

Things to See & Do
Espoo Vintage Car Museum This museum in Pakankylä has Finland's largest collection of old motor vehicles, including the most common cars seen on the roads over the past decades. The museum is open from 11 am to 5 pm Tuesday to Sunday.

Finnish Museum of Horology This museum at Opinkuja 2 in Tapiola is the only time-keeping museum in Scandinavia. It has a collection of timepieces from the 17th century on. The museum is open from noon to 4 pm on Saturdays and Sundays.

Serena This water park in Lahnus, northern Espoo is a fun place on a nice summer day, with a selection of water slides. The park is open daily from 15 May to 15 September from 10 am to 8 pm. Tickets cost 70 mk for adults and 60 mk for children for a whole day, or 50 mk for adults and 40 mk for children after 4 pm. A spectator ticket, which does not entitle you to use the rides, costs 30 mk.

Getting There & Away
Espoo has a local bus network, and near the bus terminal in Helsinki, you can catch buses to various parts of Espoo. Local trains from Helsinki will drop you off at several stations, including the central Espoo station.

KIRKKONUMMI
Kirkkonummi is one of the municipalities in the immediate vicinity of Helsinki. One of the main attractions of the capital region, Hvitträsk House, is located in Kirkkonummi.

Things to See
Hvitträsk This fantastic wilderness studio was the home and working place of three internationally known Finnish architects: Eliel Saarinen, Herman Gesellius and Armas Lindgren. Besides its location, this is one of

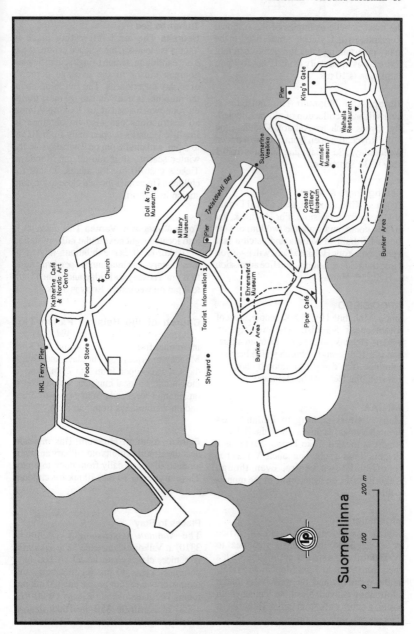

King's Gate

Pier

Walhalla Restaurant

Armfelt Museum

Coastal Artillery Museum

Submarine Vesikko

Doll & Toy Museum

Tykistölahti Bay

Military Museum

Pier

Bunker Area

Church

Ehrensvärd Museum

Katherine Café & Nordic Art Centre

Tourist Information

Piper Café

Bunker Area

HKL Ferry Pier

Food Store

Shipyard

Suomenlinna

0   100   200 m

the most notable examples of the National Romantic style. If you have time, listen to the many entertaining tales the guides can tell. Hvitträsk is open daily from 10 am to 7 pm; admission is 10 mk.

Vintage Car Museum This museum at Svartvik has a collection of old cars, including names such as Auburn, Cadillac and Rolls Royce. It's open from noon to 4 pm on Wednesdays, Saturdays and Sundays from 1 May to 30 September.

Getting There & Away
To get to Kirkkonummi, take a local L-train or U-train from Helsinki. For Hvitträsk, get off in Luoma, and walk the two km, or take the fast S-train to Masala and catch a taxi from there. Your Helsinki Card will give you a free train ride to Luoma, and free admission to Hvitträsk House.

SIPOO/SIBBO
Sipoo is inhabited by 14,800 people, most of whom speak Swedish. The municipality borders Helsinki to the east. Its main attraction is a 15th century church which has fine paintings. You can get to Sipoo by taking a bus from the Helsinki bus terminal.

VANTAA
Many visitors coming to Finland pass through Vantaa, as this is where the Helsinki airport is located. Like Espoo, Vantaa is a city, but it has a suburban touch. Vantaa has no official town centre, even though Tikkurila is the de facto centre of the municipality.

Information
Vantaa has a tourist information office (☎ 90-839 3134) in Tikkurila, right next to the Tikkurila train station, at Unikkotie 2. It's open from 9 am to 5 pm Monday to Friday. In the evenings and on weekends, tourist information is available at the Vantaa youth hostel, a short walk from either Tikkurila or Hiekkaharju train station.

Things to See
Heureka The most interesting place in Vantaa is Heureka, the science centre. It has a big exhibition, which brings scientific phenomena closer to the average person's everyday experiences. The fun thing about the museum is that you can try most things on your own, instead of just looking. Almost all instructions can also be obtained in English. Heureka is open daily from 10 am to 6 pm, and until 8 pm on Thursdays. In the winter season, it is closed on Mondays. Tickets cost 40 mk for adults, 25 mk for children. Heureka is located close to the train station in Tikkurila.

Town Museum of Vantaa This museum is also located right next to the railway station in Tikkurila. It has exhibitions related to local history. The museum is open from noon to 6 pm Tuesday to Friday and from 11 am to 4 pm on weekends. Entry is 5 mk.

Church of the Helsinki Parish This greystone church dates from 1494. It's open in summer from 9 am to noon and 1 to 3 pm Monday to Friday; on Tuesdays and Thursdays, it's also open from 3 to 7 pm. Next to the church is a local museum, which is open on summer weekends from 11 am to 3 pm and on Wednesdays from 5 to 8 pm.

Finnish Aviation Museum This museum near the airport exhibits old military and civil aircraft. It's open daily from noon to 6 pm. The entry fee is 20 mk, 10 mk for children and students.

Places to Stay
The *Vantaan Retkeilyhotelli* (☎ 90-839 3310) at Valkoisenlähteentie 52 in Tikkurila is a nice, clean youth hostel. A bed in a dormitory costs 30 mk for members, and rooms for two to four people are 300 mk per room. The *Asuntohotelli Kuriiri* (☎ 90-873 4822) at Kuriiritie 35B in Tikkurila has homely singles/doubles for 220/270 mk.

Getting There & Away

Local trains and Vantaa buses are by far the most convenient means of transport from Helsinki to Vantaa (just make sure you catch the right train). Most local trains stop in Tikkurila, but not the long-distance ones.

South Finland

South Finland is known less for its scenic beauty than for its historic landmarks. This area has always been on an important transport route from Turku to Helsinki and on to Vyborg and St Petersburg. Consequently, many old churches, castles and fortresses are to be found here.

South Finland consists of the provinces of Uusimaa and Kymi, with special areas such as Hanko Peninsula in the western part of Uusimaa, and South Karelia, a border area in the south-eastern corner of Finland, between Lake Saimaa and Russia. South Karelia only acquired its present borders after WW II, when the Karelian Isthmus was annexed by the Soviet Union. Administratively, South Karelia is part of the Province of Kymi.

Central Uusimaa

HYVINKÄÄ

Hyvinkää has a number of attractions to offer the visitor. This relatively small town is located midway between Helsinki and Hämeenlinna. When the railway was built between these two towns, it also passed through Hyvinkää. The railway from Hyvinkää to Hanko was finished in 1873. Hyvinkää is also known for a recreational area called Sveitsi (Finnish for 'Switzerland').

Information

The tourist information office (☎ 914-251 275) is at Hämeenkatu 3D.

Things to See

Railway Museum This is Hyvinkää's best-known museum, at Hyvinkäänkatu 9. Its exhibits include renovated locomotives and carriages, including an Imperial train from Russia and a carriage that used to belong to the Finnish president. The railway museum is open from 11 am to 4 pm Tuesday to

Sunday from 2 May to 31 August. From 1 September to 30 April, it's open from noon to 3 pm Tuesday to Friday and from noon to 4 pm on weekends. Entry is 10 mk, 5 mk for children.

Hyvinkää Art Museum This museum at Hämeenkatu 3D hosts changing art exhibitions and has a permanent collection of Yrjö Saarinen's works. It's open from 11 am to 7 pm Tuesday to Friday, 10 am to 3 pm on Saturdays and 11 am to 5 pm on Sundays. Entry is 5 mk.

Hyvinkää Church This modern triangular building at Hämeenkatu 16 is is open daily from 9 am to 4 pm.

Einola House There are art exhibitions in this building at Hyvinkäänkatu 11. It's open in summer from 1 to 7 pm Tuesday to Friday and from 11 am to 5 pm on weekends. Entry is 5 mk.

Promenadigalleria You'll find free art exhibitions at Vaiveronkatu 10. The gallery is open from 1 to 6 pm Tuesday to Friday and on Sundays, and from noon to 3 pm on Saturdays.

Hyvinkää Gallery This art gallery at Vaiveronkatu 12-14 is open from 1 to 6 pm Tuesday to

Friday and from noon to 4 pm on weekends. Entry is free.

Art Centre for Children & Youth

This unusual gallery at Siltakatu 6 has changing exhibitions, such as international collections of children's paintings. The centre is open from 1 to 4 pm on Tuesdays, Thursdays and Fridays, 1 to 7 pm on Wednesdays and noon to 4 pm on weekends.

Places to Stay & Eat

The *Finnhostel Sveitsin maja* (☎ 914-86747) is a nice, clean youth hostel, located inside the Sveitsi park. It's open all year round. Dormitory beds cost 70 mk, sheets included.

The *Top-Kapi* is a popular place for Turkish food.

Getting There & Away

In addition to regular buses from Helsinki and surrounding towns, all Riihimäki-bound local R-trains and H-trains stop in Hyvinkää.

JÄRVENPÄÄ

Jean Sibelius, the most famous Finnish composer, lived in Järvenpää. Sibelius's home, **Ainola**, is now a museum. The building was

Sibelius

designed by Lars Sonck, and built on this beautiful site in 1904. Ainola is open from May to September on Tuesdays, Wednesdays, Saturdays and Sundays from 11 am to 5 pm. Entry is 15 mk. The **Järvenpää Church** is open from 15 May to 15 August from 10 am to 6 pm Tuesday to Saturday and from 1 to 3 pm on Sundays. All Riihimäki-bound local R-trains and H-trains stop in Järvenpää.

KERAVA

Kerava is a modern suburban town, best known for its Garlic Festival in late August. Kerava's modern architecture has been awarded many prizes. The **Kerava Museum** is open from 1 May to 30 September from 1 to 5 pm on Sundays and from 2 to 7 pm on Wednesdays. To get to Kerava, catch any local R-, H- or K-train from Helsinki.

NURMIJÄRVI

Nurmijärvi was the home of Aleksis Kivi, the famous Finnish writer and the author of 'Seven Brothers'. **Aleksis Kivi's home** in the village of Palojoki is open from 1 May to 31 August, Tuesday to Sunday. In the village of Rajamäki, there is a **House Museum**, which is open from 1 May to 15 July from 9 am to 3 pm Wednesday to Sunday. A **School Museum** in the village of Nukari is open in May, from 10 am to 6 pm Monday to Friday. To get to Nurmijärvi, take one of the buses from the Helsinki bus terminal.

TUUSULA

The municipality of Tuusula, just north of Vantaa, has a number of interesting sights scattered through the countryside. Having a car is certainly of benefit, but you can also reach many of the attractions using local buses.

Things to See

Halosenniemi The studio of Pekka Halonen, one of the most famous Finnish painters, is Tuusula's most interesting sight. It's located on the museum road (Rantatie), and is open from 2 May to 30 August from 11 am to 5 pm on Tuesdays, Thursdays and

Fridays, noon to 8 pm on Wednesdays and 11 am to 6 pm on weekends. From 1 September to 15 December, it is open from 11 am to 3 pm Tuesday to Friday and from 11 am to 5 pm on weekends. Entry is 10 mk.

Aleksis Kivi's Cottage Aleksis Kivi, the famous 19th century author, died in this small cottage, also located on Rantatie. From 2 May to 30 August, it has similar opening hours to Halosenniemi. From 1 September to 10 October, it is open from 11 am to 3 pm Tuesday to Friday and from 11 am to 5 pm on weekends. Admission is 5 mk.

Klaavolan Museo This local museum in the village of Hyrylä is an old estate dating back to the 1880s. The opening hours are similar to those of Aleksis Kivi's cottage.

Air Raid Defence Museum Located on Klaavolantie in Hyrylä, the Air Raid Defence Museum is open from 1 May to 15 September from noon to 6 pm Tuesday to Sunday. Entry is 5 mk.

Tuusula Church This wooden church dates back to 1734, but its current interior was designed by Pekka Halonen. The church is open daily (except Saturdays) in June and July from noon to 8 pm, and in August from noon to 6 pm.

Getting There & Away
Ventoniemi and a few other companies run regular buses via Hyrylä and other Tuusula locations.

Eastern Uusimaa

PORVOO
Porvoo is the second oldest town in Finland. It has officially been a town since 1346, but even before that, Porvoo was an important trading centre. Porvoo's old town is exceptionally large and well preserved, which makes it one of the most popular places for travellers to visit from Helsinki, just 50 km

away. For those who have more time, Porvoo is an excellent first stop on the way to eastern parts of Finland.

Orientation
Porvoo has been built close to the sea, on both sides of the Porvoo River. The old centre is in the hills just north of the river, mostly west of the main street, Mannerheiminkatu.

Information
The tourist information office (☎ 915-580 145) is located at Rauhankatu 20.

Things to See
Cathedral The medieval church on Kirkkotori has been an important place in Finnish history: this is where the first Diet of Finland assembled in 1809, after Finland had become an autonomous part of tsarist Russia. It's open from 1 May to 30 September from 10 am to 6 pm Monday to Friday, 10 am to 2 pm on Saturdays and 10 am to 5 pm on Sundays. From 1 October to 30 April, opening hours are 10 am to 2 pm Tuesday to Saturday and 2 to 4 pm on Sundays.

Home of Johan Ludvig Runeberg The house of the national poet of Finland is located at Aleksanterinkatu 3. It is one of the best-preserved buildings in the Empire part of the town centre. The interior has been preserved as it was when Runeberg lived in the house. This charming house is open from 1 May to 30 September from 9.30 am to 4 pm Monday to Saturday and from 10.30 am to 5 pm on Sundays. From 1 October to 30 April, it's open from 10 am to 4 pm Wednesday to Saturday and from 11 am to 5 pm on Sundays.

Walther Runeberg Sculpture Museum Next door to Runeberg's home, at Aleksanterinkatu 5, there is a collection of 150 of the sculptures of Walther Runeberg, J L Runeberg's eldest son. Opening hours are similar to those of Runeberg's home.

Porvoo Historical Museum This attractive

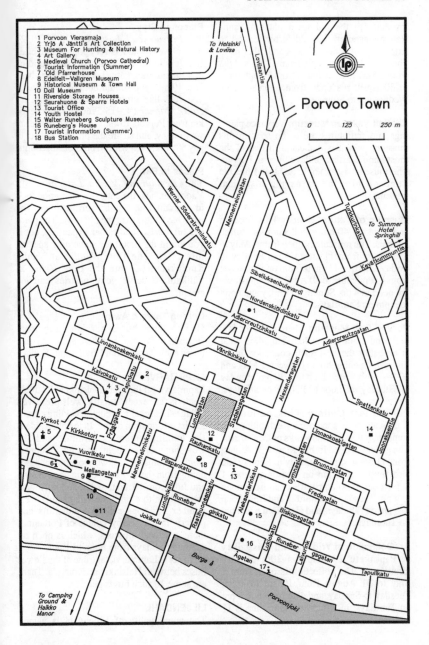

1 Porvoon Vierasmaja
2 Yrjö A Jäntti's Art Collection
3 Museum For Hunting & Natural History
4 Art Gallery
5 Medieval Church (Porvoo Cathedral)
6 Tourist Information (Summer)
7 'Old Pfarrerhouse'
8 Edelfelt–Vallgren Museum
9 Historical Museum & Town Hall
10 Doll Museum
11 Riverside Storage Houses
12 Seurahuone & Sparre Hotels
13 Tourist Office
14 Youth Hostel
15 Walter Runeberg Sculpture Museum
16 Runeberg's House
17 Tourist Information (Summer)
18 Bus Station

Porvoo Town

0   125   250 m

To Helsinki & Loviisa

To Summer Hotel Springhill

museum, in the old town hall on Vanha Raatihuoneentori, has old furniture, and an extensive collection of keys and other paraphernalia. It's open daily from 11 am to 4 pm from 1 May to 31 August; from 1 September to 30 April, it's open from noon to 4 pm Wednesday to Sunday.

Edelfelt-Vallgren Museum Very nice paintings and sculptures are to be seen in this museum, which is dedicated to two of the most famous artists to have lived in Porvoo. The museum is at Völikatu 11 and has the same opening hours as the historical museum.

Museum of Natural History This museum at Kaivokatu 40 has a collection of stuffed animals. The museum is open from 1 May to 31 August from 11 am to 4 pm Sunday to Friday and from 11 am to 3 pm on Saturdays; from 1 September to 30 April, opening hours are noon to 4 pm Sunday to Friday and noon to 3 pm on Saturdays.

Porvoo Doll Museum There are over 800 dolls and other toys at Jokikatu 14, in what is probably the best such collection in all Finland. Opening hours between 1 May and 30 September are 11 am to 3.30 pm Monday to Saturday and noon to 3.30 pm on Sundays.

Porvoo Art Gallery This gallery at Kaivokatu 40 has temporary exhibitions. In summer, it displays the works of local artists. The gallery is open from 1 May to 31 August from 11 am to 4 pm Tuesday to Sunday and also from 6 to 8 pm on Tuesdays; from 1 September to 30 April, it's open from noon to 4 pm Tuesday to Saturday and from noon to 5 pm on Sundays, and also from 6 to 8 pm on Tuesdays.

Art Collection of Yrjö A Jäntti This gallery at Papinkatu 19 displays 20th century Finnish art. The collection is open from 1 May to 31 August from 10 am to 4 pm Tuesday to Sunday, and also from 6 to 8 pm on Tuesdays; in winter, opening time is 11 am.

Places to Stay
The *Porvoo youth hostel* (☎ 915-130 012), open all year round, is very popular and often full. It is located in a nice wooden building at Linnankoskenkatu 1-3. Dormitory beds cost 40 mk; you should book in advance. If you feel like giving yourself a treat, try *Haikko Manor* (☎ 915-57601), some seven km from Porvoo. Rooms in the old house are very classy, and so are the prices – expect to pay 500 mk, even with all possible discounts.

Places to Eat
The *Restaurang Vanha Laamanni* on Vuorikatu, near the cathedral, has good food in pleasant 18th century surroundings. The patio has a view over the old town. The place is a bit touristy and rather expensive, but if you are in the mood for something special, this is it. The *Café Natalia* at Vanha Kuninkaantie 2 and the *Café Helmi* at Välikatu 7 serve good pastries and ice cream.

Getting There & Away
One to three buses per hour run from Helsinki to Porvoo, and there are six to nine buses each day to/from Loviisa and Kotka.

LAPINJÄRVI
Lapinjärvi, off the main Helsinki to Kouvola road, is an exceptionally well-preserved village. The local museum, Kycklings, has a tourist information office. In the old residential building, there is furniture and the workshops of a shoemaker and a coppersmith. Lapinjärvi has two wooden churches dating from the 1700s. They are open in June and July from 10 am to 6 pm, and in August from 10 am to 4 pm. The village also has a number of shops selling handicrafts and pottery. In the nearby village of Porlammi, there is a local museum, which is open on summer Sundays from noon to 1 pm.

To get to Lapinjärvi, take one of the slower buses between Helsinki and Kouvola. There are some 10 such buses per day.

LILJENDAHL
The municipality of Liljendahl is named

Top: Kaivopuisto Park, Helsinki (ML)
Bottom: The Cathedral, Helsinki (ML)

Top: Porvoo riverfront, Porvoo (ML)
Bottom: Serena Water Park, near Espoo Town (VM)

after the Liljendahl mansion that was run by Gertrud von Ungern in the 1630s. There is an excellent youth hostel (☎ 915-66354) in Embom, two km off the No 6 Helsinki to Kouvola road. The owners are very friendly, and the hostel is pleasantly located close to a river. You'll pay just 35 mk for dormitory beds in the old wooden villa, which is open all year round.

LOVIISA

Loviisa is a charming small town some 90 km east of Helsinki. It was established in 1745 and named after the Swedish Queen Lovisa Ulrika. In the 18th century, it was one of the three towns in Finland allowed to engage in foreign trade. In the 19th century, Loviisa became an important port for sailing ships, and a spa town. The population is currently 20,000.

Orientation

The main buildings of Loviisa lie on either side of the main street, Mannerheiminkatu. The town centre is rather compact, and all places of interest are within walking distance. The bus station is on Mannerheiminkatu.

Information

The tourist information office (☎ 915-555315) at Aleksanterinkatu 1 has information on Loviisa and the surrounding areas. It's open from 9 am to 4 pm Monday to Friday; from 1 June to 30 August, it's also open on Saturdays from 9 am to 2 pm. You can hire bicycles here.

Things to See & Do

Loviisa Old Town The old town of Loviisa, south of Mannerheiminkatu, is what is left of the oldest parts of Loviisa. These buildings were saved from the disastrous fire of 1855.

Loviisa Church This impressive neogothic church at the western end of Mannerheiminkatu is one of the few churches of its kind in Finland.

Sibelius House The house at Sibeliuksenkatu 10 was the summer home of the family of Jean Sibelius, the composer. Today it hosts art exhibitions in summer.

Ungern & Rosen These two fortresses just off the eastern end of Mannerheiminkatu were built in the 18th century to guard the road between Vyborg and Turku. The ruins of the fortresses can be visited at any time, free of charge.

Svartholm This sea fortress lies on an island 10 km from the town centre. The tourist information office arranges boat tours to the fortress on Sundays in June, July and August. Tours take 2½ hours, with departures at 10 am and 2 pm. Guides on the morning tour speak Finnish and Swedish.

Nuclear Plant Tour If you are interested in nuclear power stations, you'll have a chance to visit one in Loviisa. The operator, Imatran Voima, arranges two-hour tours for the public on summer Sundays. A bus leaves at 12.30 pm from the bus terminal.

Places to Stay & Eat

Loviisa has two hotels, neither of which is especially cheap. The nicer one, the *Hotel Skandinavia* (☎ 915-531 725) at Karlskrona-bulevardi 9-11, has singles/doubles at 300/400 mk. You can also try *Guesthouse Helgas* (☎ 915-531 576) at Sibeliuksenkatu 6.

The *Degerby Gille* (☎ 915-531 529) at Sepänkuja 4 is the most famous restaurant in Loviisa. It is located in a 17th century building on the Degerby estate and is considered to be something worth seeing.

For smaller dishes, try the excellent *cafeteria* at Aleksanterinkatu 2, just opposite the tourist office.

Getting There & Away

There are six to nine buses a day to/from Kotka, Helsinki and Porvoo, and two buses a day from Lahti and Tampere.

Map legend:
1 Town Museum
2 Land Fortresses Ungern & Rosen
3 Hospital
4 Orthodox Church
5 Public Library
6 Sibelius House & Guesthouse Helgas
7 Market Square
8 Hotel Zilton
9 Old Town
10 Degerby Estate
11 Neo—Gothic Church
12 Tourist Information Office
13 Hotel Skandinavia
14 Hotel Degerby

Loviisa

MYRSKYLÄ

For Finns, Myrskylä is best known as the home of Lasse Viren, a long-distance runner who won four gold medals at the Olympic Games in Munich and Montreal. The church was built in 1803 and is open from 1 June to 31 August from 11.30 am to 2 pm. The local museum next to the church is open on summer Sundays from 11.30 am to 2 pm. To get to Myrskylä, take a bus from Helsinki or Kouvola. There are three buses a day from Helsinki and three from Kouvola.

ORIMATTILA

The name of this municipality refers to the horses for which it is famous. Orimattila's sights relate to local history.

Things to See

Museums The local museum on Sairaantie displays old farm buildings and objects used on the farm. The museum is open from 1 June to 15 September from 6 to 8 pm on Wednesdays and from noon to 4 pm on Sundays. The Orimattila Bottle Museum must have the shortest opening hours of any museum in Finland. It is open just once a year, on 1 May. The museum is located at Rantatie 6B 13, and entry costs 10 mk.

Handicrafts Hyyttärin perinnetalo (Hyyttäri Tradition House) at Heinämaa exhibits traditional handicrafts, especially laces. It is open between April and August from noon to 4 pm on Sundays only. Käkelän Sipilä at Heinämaa is an artists' shop where you can see and buy laces, ceramics and textiles. The shop is open every day in July from noon to 7 pm.

Other The Municipal Art Collections are kept in the town hall, where they can be seen in June and July from noon to 6 pm Monday to Friday, 10 am to 2 pm on Saturdays and noon to 5 pm on Sundays. Another attraction is the Orimattila Church, open daily in summer from 9 am to 6 pm.

Getting There & Away
To get to Orimattila, take a bus from Helsinki or Lahti. There are some 10 buses a day from Helsinki, with even more frequent connections from Lahti.

PERNAJA/PERNÅ
Pernaja is a primarily Swedish-speaking municipality between Porvoo and Loviisa. There are a few interesting sights, and a boat youth hostel in Kabböle.

Things to See
Pernaja Church The old medieval church is very beautiful. It's open from 15 May to 15 August from noon to 3 pm Monday to Friday.

Archipelago Museum This museum in Rönnes has exhibits relating to the history of the archipelago and to boat-building. The museum is open from the beginning of June to mid-August from noon to 5 pm Wednesday to Sunday.

Horse Carriage Museum You can find this museum in Suur-Sarvilahti. It is open from 2 to 4 pm on Sundays in June and July.

Places to Stay
The youth hostel (☎ 915-35643, 949-302 525) is superbly located in Kabböle, at the southernmost tip of Pernaja. It is in an old *Katarina* boat. The hostel is open from 1 May to 30 September, and bunk beds cost 50 mk per person.

PUKKILA
The wooden Pukkila Church was built in 1814. In summer it is open from 9 am to 4 pm. The Art Café Koivulinna arranges art exhibitions in summer, and Nauha Atelje Leena Hyytiä offers handicrafts, especially handmade custom jewellery. The studio is open daily from 1 to 6 pm in June, July and December. To get to Pukkila, take a bus from Helsinki or Porvoo. There are two to five buses a day from Helsinki and half a dozen from Porvoo.

RUOTSINPYHTÄÄ
Ruotsinpyhtää is the easternmost municipality in the Province of Uusimaa. The long name means 'Pyhtää of Sweden', as the nearby village of Pyhtää was predominantly Finnish-speaking. Ruotsinpyhtää has a very interesting old industrial milieu: the Strömfors ironworks area from the 1700s, whose many attractions make it a popular spot with tourists.

Things to See & Do
The Workshop Museum consists of an old smith's workshop and equipment. It's open from 1 June to 15 August from 10 am to 7 pm daily. The octagonal wooden church dates from 1770; its altarpiece was painted by Helene Schjerfbeck, a famous Finnish painter. The ironworks area has several craft workshops. You can find a pottery maker, a silversmith, textile makers and painters. One of the buildings serves as an art gallery in summer.

Places to Stay
Two buildings in the ironworks area have been renovated as youth hostels (☎ 915-78474). Both hostels are open all year round. Accommodation in small dormitories costs

45 mk in the *Lukkarinkäki youth hostel* and 70 mk in the *Krouvinmäki youth hostel*; doubles are also available. The hostels are in good shape and are close to hotel standard.

Getting There & Away
To get to Ruotsinpyhtää, take a bus from Helsinki, Loviisa or Kouvola. There are one or two connections a day from Helsinki via Porvoo, three to five from Loviisa and one to three from Kouvola.

Western Uusimaa

HANKO
Hanko is the southernmost town in Finland. Even before Hanko was founded, in 1874, the peninsula on which the town lies had been an important anchorage for travellers between East and West. Hanko has also been a major point of departure from Finland: between 1881 and 1931, approximately half a million Finns left for the USA and Canada via the Hanko harbour. At that time, the town expanded rapidly, becoming an industrial centre and a bathing resort, both of which remain characteristics of the town today. When Finland was a part of tsarist Russia, Hanko was especially popular among Russian bathing guests, who returned year after year. Many of the beautiful seaside villas date from that time. During WW II, Hanko was annexed by the Soviet Union for a year.

For tourists, Hanko is very much a summer town. Its population is said to double in summer when all guests come. Many of them arrive by boat; the guest harbour of Hanko is the largest in Finland. Hanko has a population of 11,600. These days 52% of Hanko's population speaks Finnish. Swedish speakers used to constitute a majority, and when the situation changed, Finnish speakers demanded that all the official signs in the town be changed so that the Finnish text was above the Swedish. As a result, every street sign in the town was promptly removed and changed.

Orientation
Hanko is divided into two parts by a railway line. The town centre is squeezed between the railway in the north, the sea in the south and the western harbour. The main streets are Bulevardi on the southern side of the railway line and Esplanadi on the northern side.

Information
There are two tourist information offices in Hanko. The main office (☎ 911-85617) at Bulevardi 15 is open from 9 am to 5 pm Monday to Friday. The harbour information booth (☎ 911-803 411) is open from 9 am to 6 pm every day, and from 21 June to 31 July, opening hours are an astonishing 7 am to midnight.

The free *Coast Media* comes in Finnish and Swedish, with one of the best maps of Hanko that we have seen.

Things to See & Do
According to the tourist information office, there are over 900 events in Hanko annually. Information about them can be obtained from a special brochure, which you can order from the tourist office free of charge.

Hanko Museum This museum on the eastern harbour has several different exhibitions every year. The museum is open from 1 May to 31 August from 11 am to 4 pm Tuesday to Sunday, and also from 6 to 7 pm on Thursdays. In winter, it's open on Wednesdays, Thursdays, Saturdays and Sundays. Admission is 5 mk.

Churches The church on Vartiovuori was originally completed in 1892 but, after being badly damaged in WW II, was thoroughly renovated in 1953, from which time the exterior dates. The interior got its current look in 1972 to 1974, when the church was renovated again. Note the handwoven altarpiece, which pictures a extraordinarily happy Christ. In summer, the church is open from 10 am to 2 pm Monday to Saturday and from 1 to 3 pm on Sundays. The nearby water tower is open from 1 June to 31 August from

10 am to noon and from 3 to 5 pm. Admission is 5 mk.

On Täktomintie, there is also a beautiful wooden Orthodox church, which was built in 1895 by the Russian merchants living in Hanko. This church is open only during services.

Hanko Regatta Hanko's most important event is the annual Hanko Regatta, with over 200 boats competing every year. The regatta always takes place on the first weekend of July and attracts thousands of viewers. Usually the whole regatta turns out to be a carnival, with masses of people partying in the restaurants and on the roads and beaches of Hanko. Many just come for the party, and some are even blissfully unaware of the fact that there is a sailing competition going on. If you like civilised festivals, skip this one, as you are unlikely to see more than a handful of sober persons during the whole weekend. However, the regatta can be great fun, if you don't mind the excessive drinking. If you come by car, be extremely careful about drinking: there are a lot of police around and they breath test most drivers. If you get caught, you may go to jail, or even worse, you could have a serious accident on the winding road out of Hanko. During the regatta, many places raise their prices, so don't be surprised if you have to pay more for accommodation than the rates quoted in this book.

Eastern Harbour On summer Wednesdays at 6 pm, there is a programme at the eastern harbour (☎ 911-83541), which everyone can watch free of charge. On Wednesdays and Fridays from 5 to 8 pm, a market is held at the harbour; you can purchase fruit and berries, antiques, junk, clothes and much more.

Hauensuoli Perhaps the most interesting thing to see in Hanko is the narrow strait between the islands of Tullisaari and Kobben, called Hauensuoli (Pike's Gut). It was once used as a protected natural harbour, and many of the visitors who passed through

it wanted to leave their mark in the place. About 600 carvings display the names of the visitors, their coats of arms, the years of their visit, owner's marks and even short stories. Most of these date back to the 16th and 17th centuries and have been made by travellers from Finland, Sweden, Germany and other countries. Hauensuoli can only be reached by sea, so to get there, take a cruise on the MS *Marina*. Between 15 June and 15 August, you can catch the boat from the eastern harbour at 1 pm Monday to Friday and at noon and 2.30 pm on weekends. The cruise costs 40 mk.

House of the Four Winds This café along the coast, 1½ km east of the town centre, is famous for its strawberry cakes. It was built in 1910. During the Finnish prohibition (1919-32), it was called Café Africa and so-called hard tea was served there. Field Marshal Mannerheim, who later became president of Finland, had his summer cottage next door. He found the merry parties disturbing, and solved the problem by buying the whole place and turning it into the current House of the Four Winds in 1926. The town of Hanko leases the place to an entrepreneur. The café is open from 12 May to 18 August.

Places to Stay – bottom end
Unfortunately Hanko has no place to stay that could be considered really cheap. The traditional pensionates are the most economical and possess a lot of 'old charm', but they do lack some of the modern comforts.

The only cheap accommodation in Hanko is camping. The *Silversand* camping ground (☎ 911-85500) is excellent, with a lot of services and a long beach. The price per family or group is 70 mk, 35 mk if you travel alone. Cottages for four to eight people cost 320 mk and caravans for three people are 220 mk. During the regatta and at Midsummer, the prices are considerably higher.

Probably the best value for money can be obtained by staying at the old villas in the town centre. The villas *Tellina*, *Thalatta*, *Maija* and *Eva* have a common reception at

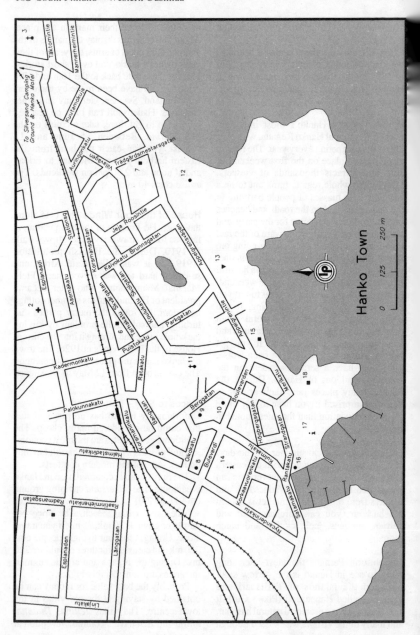

Hanko Town

0   125   250 m

1	Tourists' Home Evangelica
2	Hospital
3	Orthodox Church
4	Railway Station
5	Shopping Centre
6	Gasthaus Hanko
7	Villa Doris
8	Market Square & Post Office
9	Public Library
10	Town Hall & Police
11	Church & Water Tower
12	Beach
13	Casino Summer Restaurant
14	Tourist Information Office
15	Beach & Pension Tellina-Thalatta
16	Eastern Harbour, Evening Market & Museum
17	Tourist Information Booth
18	Hotel Regatta & Beach

Appelgrenintie 2 (☎ 911-86356) at the end of Bulevardi, at the seaside. All these buildings are old and incredibly beautiful. Some have been renovated, others haven't yet, but all give you a feel for how Hanko was 100 years ago. Singles/doubles cost 180/300 mk. There is a 50 mk surcharge for rooms with a shower and toilet. For other rooms, the perfectly modern showers and toilets are in the corridors. Breakfast is included in the room rates. If you are looking for cheaper accommodation, it is worth asking whether one of their most modest rooms is vacant – you may be able to stay there for as little as 90 mk. The villas are open from 1 June to 20 August.

Another nice and charmingly old-fashioned pensional, *Villa Doris* (☎ 911-81228), is further down, at Appelgrenintie 23. The rooms have old furniture from various decades, and the facilities are in the corridors. This place is open all year round. Prices in summer (15 May to 15 August) are 125 to 145 mk for singles and 240 to 270 mk for doubles. In winter, singles cost 85 to 100 mk and doubles are 170 to 200 mk. Prices are negotiable for longer stays.

It is also possible to stay with local families. You can arrange this only at the town tourist information office (☎ 911-803 411). Rooms cost 70 to 130 mk per day, plus the booking fee of 20 mk charged by the tourist office.

Places to Stay – middle

The *Tourists' Home Evangelica* (☎ 911-86923) at Esplanadi 61, on the northern side of the tracks, is an evangelical college in winter. The surroundings are nice, but if you intend to have wild parties, it might be wise to choose another place to stay. Some rooms have toilets and showers. Singles/doubles with facilities cost 200/400 mk, and those without a bathroom are 150/200 mk.

At Korsmaninkatu 46, there is the *Gasthaus Hanko* (☎ 911-84165). The rooms are small, but neat and clean. This guesthouse has no special character and, as it is next to the railway tracks, can get noisy at times. Toilets and showers are in the corridors. Singles/doubles cost 220/350 mk, but winter prices are slightly lower.

Places to Stay – top end

The only real hotel in Hanko is the *Hotel Regatta* (☎ 911-86491) at Merikatu 1. What seemed cute in the pensionales just seems old-fashioned in this hotel. Singles cost 380 to 500 mk and doubles are 550 to 750 mk. Higher prices apply for rooms with a view of the sea.

Next to the Silversand camping ground, off the road to Helsinki, is the *Hanko Motel* (☎ 911-82881), three km from the centre of Hanko. Singles/doubles in this typical motel are 300/350 mk. There is a swimming pool, and the sea is only a few steps away.

Places to Eat

There are several places to eat in the central part of town. The best choice for reasonably priced food is the *Satamaruokala* on Satamakatu, with home-made dishes at 20 to 40 mk. The place caters mainly to the harbour workers and is open from 6.30 am to 5 pm Monday to Friday.

If you only want to have a light meal, the *Café Elsa* at Bulevardi 3 is ideal. They serve delicious crêpes and pies with salad for 20 mk a smallish portion. The setting, in an old building, is so nice that you should at least pop by for a cup of coffee.

If you are looking for a good meal in an interesting place, go to the *Origo* at the eastern harbour. The restaurant is an almost cave-like cellar (sounds weird but the setting is very tasteful) and is famous for its excellent fish. Meals cost 45 to 100 mk. The Origo is open from 30 April to 30 September.

The summer restaurant *Casino* is the most famous nightspot in Hanko. The place is huge, with dancing and a roulette table. The cover charge is 25 to 30 mk, depending on the day, and the food is good but expensive.

Getting There & Away
Bus Hanko is 132 km from Helsinki, and express buses cover the distance in just over two hours. Ordinary buses take more than three hours.

Train You can catch a train from Tammisaari, or change trains in Karjaa; there are five to seven trains a day from Helsinki or Turku.

Getting Around
Hanko is small, so you can get to all places on foot. Bicycles can be rented at the eastern harbour, and at Paul Feldt's bicycle shop at Tarhakatu 4. Paul's shop is cheaper and will hire out three-speed bikes without a surcharge. Paul charges 20 mk per day, 30 mk per 24 hours or 150 mk per week.

LOHJA/LOJO
The areas around Lohja have been inhabited for the past 9000 years. Since 1542, Lohja has been known as a mining town. In the beginning, there were a few small iron mines, but since 1897, limestone has been the most important product. The Tytyri Mining Museum just north of the town centre traces the history of mining in and around Lohja. It is also possible to go down the mines, with tours at 6 pm daily in summer and 6 pm on Fridays from 1 September to 31 May.

Things to See
Building of the impressive Lohja Church started in the 1300s, and the whole interior is painted with rich murals. It's open daily in summer from 9 am to 6 pm and in winter from 10 am to 3 pm. The local museum next door has a historical exhibition in 11 buildings. It's open from noon to 4 pm Tuesday to Sunday and from noon to 7 pm on Wednesdays.

Getting There & Away
Lohjan Liikenne and Siuntion Linja run regular buses to Lohja from the Helsinki bus terminal. The 60-km ride takes one hour.

POHJA/POJO
The municipality of Pohja has two interesting old industrial areas: Fiskars and Billnäs. Both are old ironworks areas, which have today become popular tourist attractions. The tourist information office (☎ 911-37041) is in Fiskars and is open from 1 May to 31 August from 10.30 am to 6 pm.

Fiskars
In Fiskars, you can get to know the history of the area by visiting the local museum, open daily from 1 May to 30 September from 11 am to 4 pm. Entry costs 7 mk. In the same area, there is the Gallery Expohja, open daily from May to August from 11 am to 7 pm. Admission is 30 mk. The Fiskars area also has a host of shops selling souvenirs and handicrafts. To get to Fiskars, take the hourly bus from Tammisaari or Karjaa. There are also a few direct buses from Helsinki.

Billnäs
In this village, you will find the Billnäs Ironworks. Founded in 1641, they have been important for the development of a metal industry in Finland. The Power Generating Museum is really a museum power plant, complete with a turbine house and meter boards. It's open daily from 10 am to 6 pm. The Axe Museum next door exhibits axes and other tools manufactured at Billnäs. It's open from 10 am to 7 pm Monday to Friday, 11 am to 4 pm on Saturdays and 11 am to 7 pm on Sundays. If you're hungry after all those sights, try the Café Old Mill. It's open

for lunch only (34 mk), from 11 am to 3 pm daily. Buses going to Fiskars also pass Billnäs.

Skarpkulla

The local museum in the village of Skarpkulla specialises in old farm equipment. It's open from 15 May to 31 August from 2 to 5 pm on Saturdays and Sundays; in July, it's also open on weekdays from 2 to 5 pm.

TAMMISAARI/EKENÄS

Tammisaari (population 11,300) is one of the most interesting towns in Finland. The locals say it is the most beautiful town on the southern coast, and they may be right. There are two things that make Tammisaari very attractive: the well-preserved old buildings and the beautiful countryside, especially the archipelago. Parts of the archipelago around Tammisaari have recently been declared a national park, and there are restrictions on the recreational use of this area.

Tammisaari is one of the oldest towns in Finland. There was a fishing village on the site of modern-day Tammisaari for a long time, and in 1546 Tammisaari was declared a town by King Gustafus Vasa of Sweden. The majority of people here speak Swedish, with Finnish the native language of only 17% of the population. Tammisaari is also the home of the only Swedish-speaking army unit in Finland, stationed at Dragsvik.

Orientation

Tammisaari is situated on a peninsula, along the road from Helsinki to Hanko. The bus terminal and the railway station are opposite each other on the same road, Rautatienkatu, in the northern part of the town centre. The town is small, so everything is within walking distance. The most interesting old buildings are on a little peninsula called Barckenin niemi, in the western part of the town. Ramsholmen and Högholmen islands and the Hagen peninsula form the Ramsholmen natural park.

Information

The tourist information office (☎ 911-711 955) at Town Hall Square is open from 8 am to 6 pm Monday to Friday and from 10 am to 2 pm on summer Saturdays. In winter, it's open from 8 am to 4 pm Monday to Friday. The office has a lot of useful brochures and a very helpful staff. Another office, at the harbour, is open daily in summer from 10 am to 10 pm.

Things to See

Tammisaari Museum Located at Kustaa Vaasan katu 13, the museum has two parts: an old house and an art exhibition. The house belonged to a wealthy artisan family in the 1800s, and the interior has been kept as it was at that time. The guides can give you many interesting details about the items displayed. The art museum has temporary exhibitions. The museum is open daily from 15 May to 31 July from 11 am to 4 pm Tuesday to Sunday. At other times, it's open only during art exhibitions – from 6 to 8 pm Tuesday to Thursday and from noon to 4 pm Friday to Sunday. Admission is 10 mk, students and children 5 mk.

Tammisaari Artisans' House This house near the museum displays the works of amateur artists and local artisans from 1 to 6 pm daily (except Mondays). The pieces are for sale and there is no admission charge. The quality of works varies, but this small exhibition is of some interest.

Church The tower of the church can be seen from most parts of town. It was originally built in 1651-80 and was last renovated in 1990. The oldest object in the church is the frame of the altar painting: the original painting was destroyed with the rest of the church in a fire in 1821 – only the frame could be saved. The church is open from 10 am to 8 pm Monday to Friday, every day in summer.

Old Town The old town of Tammisaari is worth exploring. Its narrow streets are named after the hatters, combmakers, weavers and other artisans who once worked

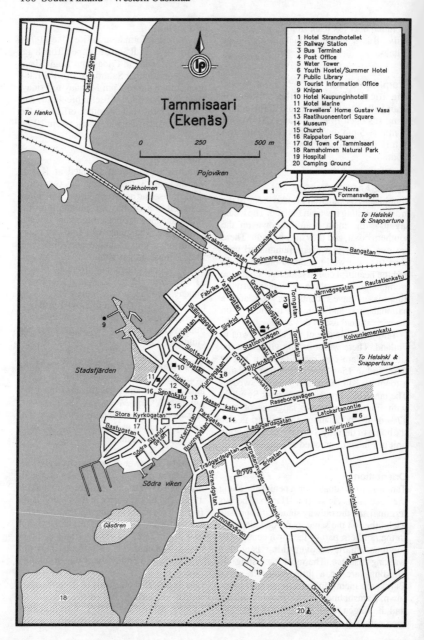

Tammisaari
(Ekenäs)

0   250   500 m

1 Hotel Strandhotellet
2 Railway Station
3 Bus Terminal
4 Post Office
5 Water Tower
6 Youth Hostel/Summer Hotel
7 Public Library
8 Tourist Information Office
9 Knipan
10 Hotel Kaupunginhotelll
11 Motel Marine
12 Travellers' Home Gustav Vasa
13 Raatihuoneentori Square
14 Museum
15 Church
16 Raippatori Square
17 Old Town of Tammisaari
18 Ramsholmen Natural Park
19 Hospital
20 Camping Ground

there. The buildings date back to the 16th and 17th centuries, and the whole area has been preserved, with no modern buildings allowed. Remember that this is not a museum: people live here.

Ramsholmen Natural Park This area consists of the two islands of Ramsholmen and Högholmen, and the peninsula of Hagen. It is a nice area to visit for those attracted by the outdoors and is of particular interest to bird-watchers. The area features unusually fresh forests in summer. Free maps are available at the tourist information office at Town Hall Square.

Cruises
The archipelago around Tammisaari is extremely beautiful. You can explore it by boat, but note that there are restrictions on where you can go, because there are nature conservation areas and military areas around. Get information about this at the tourist office.

The easiest way to see some of the archipelago is to take a boat tour. The MS *Marina* operates from 15 June to 15 August, departing from the northern harbour. Tours lasting 1½ hours start at 3 pm on Saturdays and noon on Sundays, and at 6 pm on Tuesdays in July, and cost 30 mk per person. The three-hour tours start at noon on Saturdays and 2 pm on Sundays, and at 6 pm on Thursdays in July, and cost 50 mk.

If you would rather go on your own, you can rent a boat at the camping ground. A rowing boat or a canoe costs 20 mk for the first hour and 8 mk for each subsequent hour; a motor boat costs 40 mk per hour.

Places to Stay – bottom end
Tammisaari is no paradise for the budget traveller, as most accommodation is rather expensive. The cheapest place to stay is the *Ekenäs Vandrarhem*, or youth hostel (☎ 911-16393), at Höijerintie 10. It's open from 16 May to 23 August. The rooms are neat and modern and most of them are singles or doubles. The few triples are usually given to families, but you can ask for them, even if

you travel alone. The only difference between the youth hostel rooms and the hotel rooms is that in the hotel rooms, the bedclothes are provided. For YHA members, a bed costs 40 to 50 mk, and singles are 90 mk. As a summer hotel, the place charges 130/240 mk for singles/doubles. Breakfast is included in the hotel prices.

Places to Stay – middle
The *camping ground* in Tammisaari is excellently located at the seaside, next to the Ramsholmen natural park. Camping costs 50 mk per tent or 25 mk per individual traveller. During Midsummer, the whole weekend costs 150 mk per person. There are also four-bed cottages at 200 mk, or doubles at 150 mk in a big cottage. The camping ground has boats and bicycles for hire.

At the *Travellers' Home Gustav Vaasa* (☎ 911-711 551) on Raatihuoneentori, right in the town centre, singles/doubles cost 160/240 mk. The room decoration is old-fashioned and slightly worn out; whether you like it or not is a matter of taste – I found it very cute and somehow romantic. The toilets and showers are in the corridors. The *Motelli Marine* (☎ 911-13833) at Kammantekijänkatu 4-6 is a typical motel. Rooms are neat, and cost 170 to 270 mk for singles, 280 to 450 mk for doubles. Cheaper rooms have no showers.

Places to Stay – top end
There are two hotels in Tammisaari; both are rather expensive and neither accept Finncheques. The *Kaupunginhotelli* (☎ 911-713 131) at Pohjoinen Rantakatu 1, in the town centre, has singles/doubles for 350/480 mk. The *Strandhotellet* (☎ 911-61500) at Pohjankatu 2 has singles/doubles for 380/480 mk.

Places to Eat
Fanny's, a little café and restaurant at Kustaa Vaasankatu 6, serves home-made food for 30 to 35 mk. It also has a nice garden. Fanny's is open from 9 am to 5 pm Monday to Friday, 9 am to 3 pm on Saturdays and noon to 4 pm on Sundays.

At the *Alfa Salaattibaari* at Pitkäkatu 14, in the Kungsen shopping centre, an 'all you can eat' salad bar and a soup will cost you 27 mk. For an extra 8 mk, you can add a vegetarian main course. It's open from 9 am to 5 pm Monday to Friday and from 9 am to 4 pm on Saturdays.

At the harbour, you can buy hamburgers with salad for 20 mk. The *Knipan* is a summer restaurant built on a pier at the harbour. It serves good (but expensive) food at 65 to 120 mk a meal. It is open from 26 April to 1 September but is closed on Mondays in May and August.

Another place to eat good food is the *Svenska Klubben* at Panimonkatu 9, which has been built in an old brewery. There is a smorgasbord for 65 mk (75 mk on weekends) and meals for 40 to 140 mk. This is a peaceful place, with quiet music but no dancing.

Entertainment

The Knipan is definitely the number one place for entertainment in Tammisaari, with a live band from Tuesday to Saturday, and also on Sundays in July. There is an age limit of 18 years, and a cover charge of 25 mk on Fridays and 30 mk on Saturdays.

Getting There & Away

Bus There are 10 buses a day from Hanko, six from Helsinki and five from Turku. Tammisaari is 94 km and 1½ hours from Helsinki.

Train To get to Tammisaari by rail, you'll have to change trains in Karjaa. There are five to seven trains a day from Helsinki and/or Hanko.

Getting Around

Tammisaari is small enough to be explored on foot. There are bicycles for hire at the camping ground; rates are 10 mk for the first hour plus 5 mk for each subsequent hour, 30 mk per day or 150 mk per week. You can also rent bicycles at the harbour.

AROUND TAMMISAARI

Snappertuna

Snappertuna, within the municipality of Tammisaari, has several places of interest to visitors. There in no public transport, so come on foot, by bicycle or in a car. Take road No 53 towards Helsinki and Karjaa, then follow the 'Raaseporin linna' signs.

Raasepori The ruins of an old castle at Raasepori are the most interesting sight in Snappertuna. It is not known exactly when the castle was built, but it is estimated that the oldest parts date from the 13th century. The castle was of great strategic importance in the 15th century, when it protected the town of Tuna, an important trading place. By the mid-1500s, its importance declined, and the castle was left empty for over 300 years. All the walls of the castle still stand, but the interior is in ruins. The castle area is never really closed, so you can enter at any time. When the cafeteria is open (1 May to 31 August from 10 am to 10 pm), tickets should be purchased; they cost 5 mk. From 1 June to 31 August at 3 pm on Wednesdays, Saturdays and Sundays, there are free guided tours (guides speak Finnish, Swedish and English).

Snappertuna House Museum Close to the castle, 300 metres along a forest path called the Path of Love, this museum consists of several old houses and other buildings collected from various parts of the province. The museum is open from 1 June to 31 July from 4 to 8 pm on Wednesdays and from noon to 4 pm Thursday to Sunday. Admission is 3 mk.

Snappertuna Church A short walk from the house museum is the Snappertuna Church, which was built in 1688. It's open daily in summer from 9 am to 6 pm.

Tenhola/Tenala

Tenhola is a small municipality north-west of Tammisaari. In the village of Tenhola is a very beautiful old church. The village of Bromarv has a local museum, open on Saturdays from 10 am to 3 pm from 1 June to 31 August. There is a slightly run-down youth hostel some four km from the village. The hostel is usually rather quiet, as it is hard to reach without a car. The nearest bus stop is in the village. To get to Tenhola, take a bus from Tammisaari or Hanko.

Western Province of Kymi

ELIMÄKI
Elimäki is a rural municipality along road No 6, some 110 km east of Helsinki and 25 km west of Kouvola. Many visitors stop there to see the Arboretum Mustila and other sights.

Things to See
Arboretum Mustila The arboretum was founded in 1902 when State Secretary A F Tigerstedt planted the first foreign trees in the area, and in the 1920s both woody and perennial ornaments were introduced. The original idea of the arboretum was to gain information about the economic value of exotic tree species in the Finnish climate. In 1981, Arboretum Mustila became a national conservation area so that its unique collection of trees and shrubs would be preserved. The arboretum is at its most beautiful in June, when literally thousands of rhododendrons blossom, and in September during the *ruska* period. There are walking routes of 1.5, 2.5 and three km in the arboretum area. Until recently the arboretum was open only to researchers, but now, all visitors are welcome. The entry fee of 10 mk can be paid in the cafeteria. All fees are used for the upkeep and development of the arboretum. Mustila is located on road No 6. Mustila Mansion, in the immediate vicinity of the arboretum, is privately owned, and the residents don't seem to want visitors.

Elimäki Homestead Museum The museum in Elimäki village, half a km west of road No 6, consists of old farm buildings and items used on a farm. It's open in summer from 3 to 7 pm Monday to Friday, 1 to 5 pm on Saturdays and noon to 7 pm on Sundays. A school museum, which is located on the opposite side of the road, has the same opening hours. The Elimäki Church, built in 1638, is one of the oldest wooden churches in Finland still in regular use. There is also a church museum.

Places to Eat
There are two places on road No 6 to eat and buy things: the *Alppiruusu* serves food and sells handicrafts, while the smaller *Piika ja Renki*, on the opposite side, is a café with a handicrafts shop and an art exhibition. Piika ja Renki has been built in an old grain magazine.

HAMINA
Hamina was founded in 1653, when Finland was a part of Sweden. In 1722, work began on fortifications, and the town's unique circular plan and the ramparts date from that time. The Russian period in Hamina began as early as 1742. Since then, the town has been an important garrison town. The cadet school of imperial Finland was here, and today, Hamina is known as the home of the Finnish Reserve Officer School. For a visitor, Hamina is interesting because of its unique town plan and its pleasant small-town atmosphere.

As Hamina is close to the eastern border of Finland, it has become a favourite place for Russians to visit. Many of them earn convertible currency by selling things at the Hamina market square.

Orientation
The central parts of Hamina are around Raatihuoneentori. The two main streets, Pikkuympyrä and Isoympyrä (the 'small circle' and the 'great circle'), are around the square, and around them are the walls of the fortification. The town itself is on a peninsula between Lake Kirkkojärvi and the sea. The railway station is out of the town centre.

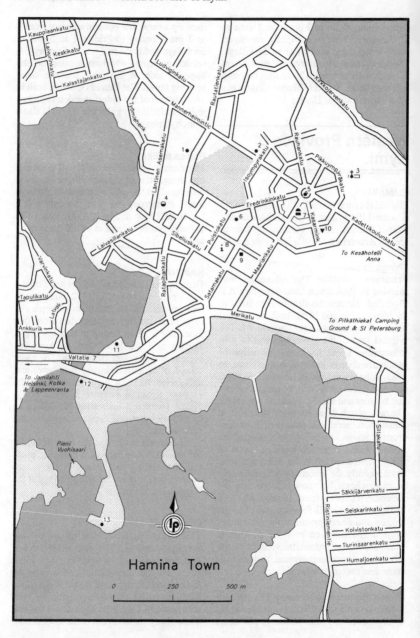

Hamina Town

0   250   500 m

1 Public Library
2 Reserve Officers' School Museum &
  Gallery Ruutikellari
3 Vehkalahti Church
4 Bus Terminal
5 Raatihuoneentori (Town Hall,
  Hamina Church,
  Peter-Paul's Orthodox Church,
  & Town Museum)
6 Market Square
7 Post Office
8 Flag Tower Tourist Office
9 Hotel Gasthaus
10 Kauppiaantalo Museum &
  Resenkov's Bun Bakery
11 Guest Harbour
12 Tervasaari Harbour & Museum
  Ships
13 Beach

Information

The main tourist information office (☎ 952-495 520) is at Pikkuympyräkatu 5. It's open from 8 am to 4 pm Monday to Friday, closing at 3 pm from 27 May to 26 August. Get a copy of *Walking in Old Hamina*, available free of charge. There is another tourist information office (☎ 952-495 252) in the Flag Tower, opposite the market square on Kaivokatu. A slide show can be seen on the 2nd floor. From 20 to 31 May and from 12 to 25 August, the office is open from 9 am to 1 pm; from 1 June to 11 August, it's open from 9 am to 5 pm.

Things to See

Churches Hamina Church, built in neoclassical style, is on Raatihuoneentori. It's open daily in June, July and August from 9 am to 3 pm. The nearby Vehkalahti Church at Pikkuympyräkatu 34 is the oldest building in the Province of Kymi. It's open in summer from 9 am to 6 pm. On Raatihuoneentori, Peter-Paul's Orthodox Church is brilliantly decorated with gold and icons. It's open from 4 June to 31 August from 11 am to 6 pm Tuesday to Sunday.

Town Museum of Hamina There are old restored rooms and local history exhibits at

Kadettikoulunkatu 2. King Gustafus III of Sweden and Tsarina Catarina II of Russia held negotiations in one of the rooms in 1783. The museum is open from 11 am to 3 pm Tuesday to Saturday and from noon to 5 pm on Sundays. Admission is 4 mk.

Kauppiaantalo Museum A former merchant's store and residence at Kasarminkatu 6, this is one of the best house museums in Finland. The shop itself is full of interesting details, and all the storehouses, sheds and stables are also part of the museum. Kauppiaantalo Museum has similar opening hours and entry fees to the Town Museum.

Reserve Officers' School Museum This museum at Mannerheimintie 7B is in a building that used to be the main guardhouse of the fortress. On display are military uniforms and weapons. It's open from 14 May to 1 September from 11 am to 3 pm Tuesday to Sunday. Admission is 4 mk.

Gallery Ruutikellari An ancient gunpowder warehouse on Roopertinkatu has been renovated into an art gallery. It's open from noon to 6 pm Tuesday to Sunday.

Resenkov's Bun Bakery The Resenkovs came from Russia. They still run this bakery at Kasarminkatu 8, which has a 100-year tradition in the bakery business. The building was erected at the beginning of the 20th century.

Museum Ships At the Tervasaari harbour are two museum ships: the SS *Hyöky* and the MS *Merikarhu*, a harbour icebreaker. They are open daily from 9 am to 10 pm from April to October. Admission is 10 mk. The museum ships serve coffee and beer in the cafeteria and offer cabins for accommodation.

Places to Stay

Pitkäthiekat Camping, six km east of Hamina, is open from 1 June to 25 August. Pitching a tent costs 50 mk per family or 25

mk per person. Cottages cost 160 to 350 mk. On the western side of Haminanlahti, the *Jamilahden kansanopisto*, two km from the town centre, offers accommodation in summer. The place is an old mansion and is beautifully located by the sea. Rooms in the main building are more romantic than the new dormitory rooms, but have no facilities. Rooms cost 100 to 180 mk, less if you have your own bedclothes. The *Kesähotelli Anna* at Annankatu 1 is open from 1 June to 15 August and has singles/doubles for 190/280 mk. Singles/doubles cost 300/400 mk at the *Hotel Gasthaus* (☎ 952-41434) at Kaivokatu 4. The entrance, through a restaurant, looks horrible, but the rooms are OK. The SS *Hyöky* has cabins for 150 mk. Accommodation may not be the most comfortable possible, but the boat has some style!

Places to Eat
The *Café Mimosa* at Puistokatu 8 is a pleasant place to eat lunch for 25 to 38 mk. Also on offer are salads and bakery products. The *Café Varvara* at Puistokatu 2 offers good home-baked buns and cakes, as well as snacks and beer. The *Restaurant Poppeli* at Isoympyräkatu 15 has pizzas from 40 mk upwards.

The *Restaurant Gasthaus* at Kaivokatu 4 is a popular nightspot, with dancing. The *Restaurant Messi* (☎ 952-42384) at Vallikatu 2 is more of a pub, where people go to drink beer and sing karaoke. On summer weekends, the *Pursiravintola Vantti*, on the island of Pieni Vuohisaari, is the place to go for dining and dancing to live music. To get to the island, take one of the special boats from Tervasaari harbour (5 mk per person).

Getting There & Away
You can reach Hamina hourly from Kotka, 26 km away. Express buses from Helsinki make the 153-km trip in less than three hours; ordinary buses take 3½ hours.

IITTI
The municipality of Iitti (population 8000) is on the main Lahti to Kouvola road No 12.

The municipal centre is in the village of Kausala. The village of Iitti has just 100 inhabitants. It was elected the best-kept village in Finland in 1990, and in 1991 it won fourth prize in a Europe-wide competition. Iitti is indeed a pleasant little village, but don't expect too much – it doesn't look all that different from other villages.

Information
The Iitti Summer Café also functions as a tourist information office. It's open between 10 May and 8 September from 10 am to 8 pm Sunday to Friday and from 10 am to 3 pm on Saturdays.

Things to See
Church The 450-year-old church is the pride of Iitti. It is among the oldest surviving wooden churches in Finland. The church is open from 1 June to 11 August from 11 am to 6 pm Monday to Friday and from 11 am to 9 pm on weekends.

Local Houses The buildings of Iitti village date from the 19th and early 20th centuries. Some of the villagers have given permission for visitors to enter their yards to look at the houses. A map of these houses can be obtained at the Iitti Summer Café.

Museum The museum in the village of Iitti has been built in an old grain magazine, and has some interesting items, including a church chandelier. The museum is open from 1 June to 25 August from 11 am to 7 pm on weekdays and on Sundays, and from 11 am to 3 pm on Saturdays. Admission is 5 mk.

Places to Stay & Eat
The *Mansion Hotel Radansuu* is located five km north of Kausala, the municipal centre. It is a quiet lakeside place and offers accommodation for 85 to 195 mk per person. The cheapest accommodation is in the old mansion, where rooms do not have facilities.

There are no restaurants in the village itself, but there are a few cafés, including the *Kahvila Iitin Tiltu*. In the nearby village of Kausala, you will find the *Ravintola Ten-*

sikka at Kauppakatu 13, as well as a number of grillis and cafés.

Getting There & Away

The Sipoon Liikenne bus company runs three buses a day from Helsinki to Kouvola, via Iitti. Iitti is 42 km from Helsinki and 28 km from Kouvola.

JAALA

Jaala is a rural municipality to the north of Kouvola. Information about Jaala can be obtained from the local Union petrol station and from the Kelopirtti, both along road No 60 between Kuusankoski and Heinola.

Things to See & Do

Verla Factory Museum This old cardboard factory in a beautiful location by the river is the area's most interesting attraction. The museum is open from 15 May to 30 August from 11 am to 4 pm Tuesday to Sunday. Admission is 7 mk. To get there, take road No 60 south from Jaala, then turn east on road No 369 and follow the signs to Verla.

Trekking There is a 50-km trekking route around Jaala, starting and finishing behind the Kelopirtti restaurant or at the Ruhmasjärvi camping ground. The route is marked.

KOTKA

Kotka is Finland's most important port and is sometimes called 'the Sea Town'. For a traveller, Kotka has a lot to offer – interesting museums, small islands on the Gulf of Finland and one of the most pleasant youth hostels in the country.

Orientation

The town of Kotka has two main parts: the old town of Kotka, and Karhula, which used to be an independent municipality. The town centre is at the tip of a narrow peninsula, the western banks of which are occupied by the Port of Kotka. West of the town centre is Mussalo Island, which has a port and recreational areas. Karhula is located on another peninsula, east of old Kotka.

Information

The tourist information office (☎ 952-274 424) at Keskuskatu 17 is open from 9 am to 4 pm Monday to Friday and from 9 am to 1 pm on Saturdays. Get a copy of *Walking Tours in Kotka*. If you are interested in visiting some of the islands, get the boat timetables as well.

Things to See

Langinkoski Imperial Fishing Lodge This is the most interesting building in Kotka. It was built in 1889 for Tsar Alexander III, who stayed there frequently. It has been said that the tsar came to Langinkoski to be able to live like the common people – newspapers reported, to everyone's astonishment, that the tsarina cooked meals for the family and the tsar carried firewood and water. The lodge is big for a summer residence, but in comparison to the tsarist palaces in St Petersburg, it is just a small hut. Most of the furniture has been retained, so the rooms look as they did at the turn of the century. The area around the lodge has been declared a national park. The lodge is open daily from 1 May to 30 September from 10 am to 7 pm. In October, it's open on weekends from 11 am to 4 pm. Admission is 8 mk.

Kymenlaakso Provincial Museum This museum at Kotkankatu 13 is open from noon to 6 pm Tuesday to Friday and from noon to 4 pm on weekends. Admission is 2 mk.

Stevedoring Museum This museum at Vuorikatu 2 has exhibits relating to the history of stevedoring and to the way work was conducted at the Port of Kotka before the age of modern technology. The museum is open from 15 May to 16 September from noon to 6 pm Tuesday to Friday and from noon to 4 pm on weekends. Admission is 5 mk, free on Sundays.

Church of St Nicholas Kotka's Orthodox church is the town's oldest building. When all of Kotka (then called Ruotsinsalmi) was destroyed in the Crimean War in 1855, the church was the only building to survive.

According to legend, this was due to the courageous actions of a 100-year-old lady, Maria Feodorovna Purpur, a colonel's widow. Most of the church treasures were taken to Hamina, where some of them remain. The church is located in the middle of Isopuisto Park and is open daily (except Mondays) from May to August between noon and 3 pm.

Kotka Church This Lutheran church is one of the few churches in Finland built in the Gothic style. The altarpiece was painted by the famous Pekka Halonen.

Fort Elisabet This fort on Varissaari was built by the Russians as part of a fortification to defend the coast against the Swedes. When Russia took over the rest of Finland, shifting Russia's western border to the Gulf of Bothnia, the fort lost its military significance. Since the end of the 19th century, Fort Elisabet has been used for nonmilitary purposes. It is a popular venue for festivals, dances and open-air performances, and a favourite picnic spot. If you do not wish to bring a picnic, there is also a restaurant.

From May to August, there is an hourly boat connection between Varissaari and Sapokanlahti in Kotka. Return tickets cost 18 mk. The boat trip takes only a few minutes.

Haukkavuori Observation Tower The tower, at the western end of Keskuskatu, gives a good view over Kotka and the surrounding islands. It's open from 1 May to 31 August, and the entry fee is 2 mk.

Activities
Island Cruises The island of **Lehmäsaari** has beautiful beaches. There are three to four boat connections between Sapokka and Lehmäsaari each day. Boats operate daily in July and four days a week in June and August. One-way tickets for the half-hour trip cost 15 mk.

There is a fishing village and a local museum on the island of **Kaunissaari**, a one-hour boat trip from Kotka. There are one

to three connections a day between Sapokka and Kaunissaari (30 mk one-way). There is a restaurant on Kaunissaari, and you can stay overnight in a cottage.

Furthest away of those islands with regular boat connections is **Haapasaari**, where the great outdoors is somewhat less hospitable than on other islands. The island's little church is open from noon to 2 pm on Wednesdays, Saturdays and Sundays. There are one or two boat connections per day between Sapokka and Haapasaari. The trip takes 1½ hours and costs 30 mk.

Fishing If you want to emulate Tsar Alexander III and go fishing, you can do this in the Kymijoki River near Munkkisaaren maja. A daily permit costs 50 mk and can be obtained at the Restaurant Munkkisaaren maja.

Festivals
The biggest event in Kotka is the Kotkan meripäivät, or Kotka Maritime Festival, which is held annually at the beginning of August. Events include boat racing, concerts, cruises and a market.

Places to Stay – bottom end
The *Kärkisaari youth hostel* (☎ 952-604 215), at the northern end of the island of Mussalo, must be one of the nicest hostels in Finland. It is an old wooden building located on a small island, and there are no neighbours. Guests can use the small seaside sauna, swim or have a barbecue on the terrace. The Kärkisaari hostel is open from 2 May to 30 September and is often fully booked by groups, or rented out for special occasions, so it is wise to make reservations in advance. There are a few doubles (80 mk per person) and two big dormitories (55 mk per person). New guests must arrive between 10 am and 6 pm. You can hire bicycles and boats here for 10 mk per three hours or 40 mk per day. To get to Kärkisaari, take bus Nos 12, 13, 14 or 27. There is an 800-metre walk from the bus stop to the hostel.

The *Kotkansaari youth hostel* (☎ 952-186 603) at Puistotie 9-11, in the sports centre, is not nearly as romantic as the Kärkisaari but

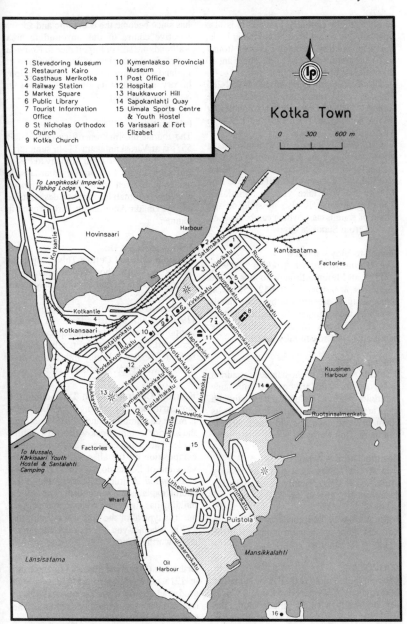

Kotka Town

1 Stevedoring Museum
2 Restaurant Kairo
3 Gasthaus Merikotka
4 Railway Station
5 Market Square
6 Public Library
7 Tourist Information Office
8 St Nicholas Orthodox Church
9 Kotka Church
10 Kymenlaakso Provincial Museum
11 Post Office
12 Hospital
13 Haukkavuori Hill
14 Sapokanlahti Quay
15 Uimala Sports Centre & Youth Hostel
16 Varissaari & Fort Elizabet

0   300   600 m

is much more centrally located. It is also open all year round. Rooms are rather basic, but clean and tidy. Reception is open from 7 to 10 am and from 4 to 11 pm. There are 10 dormitories; beds cost 45 mk.

The *Koskisoppi youth hostel* (☎ 952-285 555) at Keisarinmajantie 4, close to the Imperial Fishing Lodge, has six doubles, at 50 mk per person. It's open from 1 May to 31 August.

Santalahti Camping in Mussalo has a good location by the sea. Camping costs 70 mk per family or 35 mk per person. There are also four-bed cottages for 350 mk. Bus Nos 13 and 14 will take you to Santalahti. Camping in tents is also possible on the island of Kaunissaari, which can be reached by boat from Sapokka Quay.

Places to Stay – middle
The Huoneistohotelli Ankkuri (☎ 952-16051) at Merenkulkijankatu 6 and the *Gasthaus Merikotka* (☎ 952-15222) at Satamakatu 9 are modest but nice hotels owned by the same people. Singles/doubles are 280/320 mk in either place. The Merikotka is more centrally located.

Places to Eat
The *Kairo* is by far the most fabled restaurant in Kotka. Its walls are covered with nude paintings (to attract sailors), and even though there are more tourists than sailors among its clientele these days, the old atmosphere is still there. Don't miss it.

Getting There & Away
Bus Kotka serves as a base for visiting south-east Finland. Hourly buses make the 45-minute trip to Hamina, 26 km away.

Train A railway line connects Kotka with Kouvola. Four to six trains a day cover the 50 km in 40 minutes.

KOUVOLA
Kouvola (population 32,000) is the capital of the Province of Kymi. Founded in 1875, it was originally a small village along the Riihimäki to St Petersburg railway line but

has since become the economic and administrative centre of the surrounding area. Railroads are still of importance to Kouvola, which is the busiest railway junction in Finland. The town does not have a long history, so most of its attractions are of the rather modern kind.

Information
The tourist information office (☎ 951-296 557) is at Varuskuntakatu 11. In summer, it is open from 8 am to 6 pm Monday to Friday and from 11 am to 3 pm on Saturdays. In winter, it is open from 8 am to 4 pm on weekdays. A small information desk outside the Tykkimäki Amusement Park is open in summer.

Things to See & Do
Kouvola Cultural Centre This complex at Varuskuntakatu 11 houses the Kouvola Art Museum, a concert hall and the tourist information office. The Art Museum has a permanent exhibition of contemporary (1960 to 1990) Finnish art, as well as other temporary exhibitions, and specialises in textile art. The museum is open from 11 am to 6 pm Tuesday to Friday and from noon to 5 pm on weekends. Admission is free.

Kouvola Central Church This building is modern to the point of being ugly. The façade is made of aluminium and painted steel, and the interior features brick walls and a ceiling made of steel and concrete units. The metal composition on the altar wall is a modern variation of Leonardo da Vinci's *The Holy Communion*. A little leaflet available in the church explains the symbolism. The church building has always been very controversial, but it is typical of the time it was built: the 1970s. Whether you like it or not, the building is worth seeing.

Orthodox Church of the Holy Cross Built in 1915 for the Russian army, it was long used as a Lutheran church – only in 1982 was it turned back into an Orthodox church. The icons are beautiful. The church is open from

18 June to 4 August from 11 am to 3 pm Tuesday to Sunday.

Pharmacy Museum This museum at Varuskuntakatu 9 recreates the interior of an old pharmacy. It's open on Wednesdays from 1 to 7 pm and on Sundays from noon to 5 pm. There is no entry fee. The surrounding area of Kaunisnurmi will be developed as a centre for museums, artists and artisans. The Pharmacy Museum, opened in 1991, was the first museum in this area.

Puolakka Folk Museum Along the main Kouvola to Kotka road, just south of Kouvola, there is an open-air museum consisting of an old farmhouse and its storage buildings. It's open from 1 June to 31 August from 1 to 6 pm Tuesday to Friday, noon to 4 pm on Saturdays and 1 to 6 pm on Sundays.

Tykkimäki Amusement Park This place, five km east of the town centre, has the rides and games typical of amusement parks, as well as a terrarium with snakes, crocodiles and turtles. Tykkimäki has an excellent ticket system – you can either buy a pass that is valid for an unlimited number of rides or you can pay a small entry fee and buy tickets for individual rides. The passes cost 60 mk for both adults and children. Entry costs 8 mk for adults and 4 mk for children, and individual tickets for rides are also 8 mk for adults and 4 mk for children. Between 15 June and 15 August, Tykkimäki is open from noon to 8 pm daily. From 1 May to 1 September, it's open on weekends.

Places to Stay
Käyrälahti Camping, five km east of the town centre along road No 6, is pleasant and well kept. It is also close to the Tykkimäki Amusement Park. The camping fee is 60 mk per family or 30 mk per person. Four-bed cottages cost 190 mk. There are tennis courts, and you can rent boats and canoes. The *Kouvonpesä youth hostel* (☎ 951-254 771) at Sippolankatu 3B is open from 1 June to 11 August. Beds cost 120 mk in single rooms, 85 mk in double rooms and 65 mk in

triple rooms. There are no smaller dormitories. The *Hotel Cumulus* (☎ 951-28991) at Valtakatu 11 is centrally located and has nice rooms. Singles/doubles are 270/390 mk on weekends and 425/570 mk on weekdays.

Getting There & Away
Bus Most eastbound buses from Helsinki stop at the Kouvola bus terminal, which is right in the centre of town. Buses from the east will take you to Kouvola.

Train Kouvola is one of the busiest railway junctions in Finland, and there are hourly trains from Helsinki, Riihimäki and Lahti. The journey from Helsinki generally takes less than two hours.

South Karelia

LAPPEENRANTA
Lappeenranta (population 55,000) is the capital of South Karelia. It is an old spa and garrison town situated at the southern end of Lake Saimaa. Thanks to its interesting sights, beautiful location and friendly people, Lappeenranta is one of the most frequently visited cities in Finland.

Orientation
Lappeenranta is a long, narrow town between Lake Saimaa in the north and road No 6 in the south. Kauppakatu and Valtakatu are the main streets. The bus terminal is at the southern end of the town centre, and the railway station is approximately one km further south along Kauppakatu. The university area and most cheap places to stay are in the western part of town.

Information
Lappeenranta has excellent municipal tourist information services. The main tourist information office (☎ 953-560 860) is at the bus terminal, on the 2nd level of the complex. The staff hands out brochures, makes hotel reservations and arranges sightseeing tours. In June and August, the office is open from

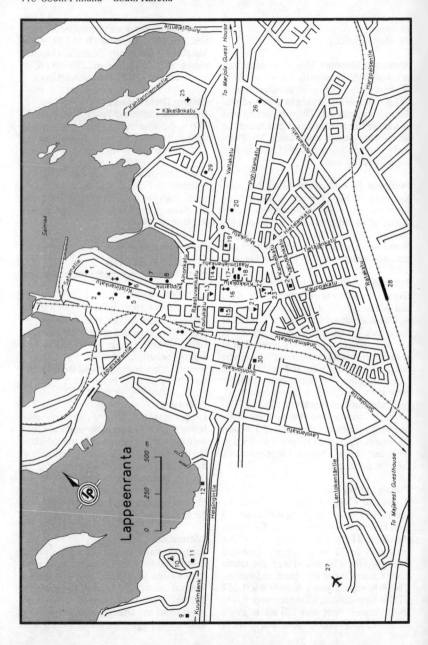

1   South Karelia Museum
2   Kristina Workshops
3   Art Museum
4   Orthodox Church
5   Cavalry Museum
6   Café Majurska
7   Passenger Quay
8   Prinsessa Armaada
9   Summer Hotel Karelia-Park
10 Huhtiniemi Camping
11 Finnhostel Lappeenranta
12 Hotel Carelia Congress
13 Café Galleria
14 Pifferia
15 Hotel Cumulus
16 Lappee Church
17 Post Office & Tele
18 Police
19 Library
20 Water Tower
21 Pink Burger
22 Bus Cafeteria
23 Bus Station & Tourist Office
24 Matkahovi Guesthouse
25 Hospital
26 Medical Centre
27 Airport
28 Railway Station
29 Laura Korpikaivo-Tamminen Handi-
    craft Museum
30 Kesä-LOAS Summer Hotel

8 am to 6 pm Monday to Friday and from 9 am to 1 pm on Saturdays. In July, it's open from 8 am to 8 pm Monday to Friday, 9 am to 3 pm on Saturdays and 10 am to 3 pm on Sundays. A smaller office at the harbour is open daily, from 9 am to 8 pm between 3 June and 26 June and from 9 am to 9 pm between 26 June and 15 August. There is also an information booth on road No 6, open daily from 3 June to 15 August from 9 am to 8 pm.

Get a copy of the *Lappeenranta Summer* brochure, which has a wealth of information in English.

Things to See

Fortress The old town of Lappeenranta (the Fortress) was built when Finland was part of tsarist Russia. Many museums and handicrafts workshops can be found in this fascinating part of town. Take your time,

walk around in the area and be sure to visit Café Majurska, probably the most beautifully decorated café in Finland.

On summer Sundays, guided walking tours of the Fortress depart from the Fortress gate at noon and take two hours. The Fortress has many cosy workshops and boutiques selling ceramics, art and handknitted garments. Shops are also open on Sundays.

Cavalry Museum The cavalry tradition is cherished in Lappeenranta. The town's oldest building, a former guardhouse in the Fortress area, houses the Cavalry Museum. The exhibits in the museum tell the history of the Finnish cavalry since the Thirty Years' War. The Cavalry Museum is open from 1 June to 31 August from 10 am to 6 pm Monday to Friday and from 11 am to 5 pm on weekends. In winter, it's open on Sundays from 11 am to 5 pm. Admission is 10 mk, 5 mk for students. The red trousers and skeleton jackets of the cavalry, which could be seen on the streets from the 1920s to the 1940s, reappear every summer: from 1 June to 17 August, cavalrymen on horseback ride around the harbour and the Fortress area for three hours every day (except Sundays and Mondays).

South Karelian Museum The historical museum at the northern end of the fortress is the provincial museum of South Karelia. Exhibits include Karelian national costumes. The most interesting part of the museum is the Vyborg section. Before the war, Vyborg was the capital of Karelia and the second biggest town in Finland. A detailed model of the old Vyborg has been constructed in the museum. If you intend to visit Vyborg, be sure to see this model first, so you can see how things changed under the Soviets. The museum is open from 1 June to 31 August from 10 am to 6 pm Monday to Friday and from 11 am to 5 pm on weekends. In winter, it's open from 11 am to 5 pm daily (except Mondays). Admission is 10 mk, 5 mk for students. The same ticket is valid for the South Karelian Art Museum and for the Cavalry Museum.

South Karelian Art Museum The museum has a permanent collection of paintings, as well as temporary exhibitions. The opening hours and ticket prices are the same as for the South Karelian Museum.

Churches The oldest Orthodox church in Finland, built in 1785 by Russian soldiers, can be found in the Fortress. The church is open from 1 June to 15 August from 10 am to 6 pm daily (except Mondays). The Lappee Church in the middle of town was built in 1794. It's open to the public from 1 June to 15 August between noon and 5 pm daily.

Laura Korpikaivo-Tamminen Museum This museum at Kantokatu 1 exhibits textile handicrafts, including a permanent collection of over 2000 pieces of handmade textiles. It's open in June, July and August from 10 am to 6 pm Monday to Friday and from 11 am to 5 pm on weekends. In winter, opening hours are 11 am to 5 pm daily (except Mondays). Admission is 10 mk.

Observation Tower The tower, near the intersection of Valtakatu and Myllykatu, has a collection of old radios and also holds art exhibitions. It's open daily, from 10 am to 4 pm in May, 11 am to 7 pm in June and July and 10 am to 4 pm in August. Admission is 5 mk.

Activities
Swimming & Sauna The public sauna at Myllysaari beach, 1.5 km north-east of the town centre, is open for women on Wednesdays and Fridays and for men on Tuesdays and Thurdays, from 3 to 8 pm. The sauna fee is 10 mk per person.

Canoeing Lake Saimaa offers excellent boating. Huhtiniemi Camping (☎ 953-11888) rents kayaks for 70 to 100 mk per day or 350 to 400 mk per week, and Saimaan Kanoottikeskus (☎ 953-17772) at Kirkkokatu 10 has canoes for 90 mk per day or 490 mk per week.

Harbour Cruises In summer, the harbour is one of the centres of Lappeenranta. It is the scene of various events, and many people just go there to have waffles and coffee from one of the coffee stands. The numerous scheduled and charter cruises start at the harbour. During the high season, there are daily departures for the Saimaa Canal, the nearby archipelago and Vyborg, on the Russian side of Karelia. Shorter cruises cost 50 to 60 mk, and cruises to Vyborg are 240 to 360 mk per person.

Saimaa Canal, a 43-km waterway with eight locks from Lake Saimaa to the Gulf of Finland, is a local sight in its own right.

Organised Tours
Sightseeing tours on a very special bus (it has flowers on the windows) depart from the harbour three times a day in summer, at 11 am, noon and 1 pm. The tour takes one hour and costs 15 mk.

Places to Stay
The most inexpensive youth hostel in Lappeenranta is the *Huhtiniemi youth hostel* (☎ 953-11888) at Kuusimäenkatu 18, in front of the camping ground. Accommodation in small dormitories costs 40 mk. Singles/doubles are considerably more expensive, at 230/280 mk. The youth hostel is only open until 31 August. The Huhtiniemi also has also a well-kept camping ground. Camping costs 58 mk per family or 30 mk per person. Two/four-bed cottages cost 170/190 mk. A more exotic alternative is staying in a cottage on the island of Nuottasaari. Four/six-bed cottages cost 200/220 mk, and prices include the use of a rowing boat and a sauna. The cottages have cooking facilities.

The *Summer Hotel Karelia-Park* (☎ 953-5521) at Korpraalinkuja 1 is a comfortable, hostel-type establishment, open from 1 June to 31 August. Singles/doubles are 160/210 mk. The hotel also has some youth hostel rooms, with beds at 50 mk. From 1 June to 31 August, the *Kesä-LOAS* at the Technical University offers accommodation for travellers. Singles/doubles are 160/190 mk.

In the upper price bracket, the *Grand*

Hotel Patria (☎ 953-5751) at Kauppakatu 21 is the best hotel in Lappeenranta. In July and on weekends, singles/doubles are 310/420 mk. The regular prices are about 200 mk higher. Finncheques are accepted, with a supplement.

Places to Eat

The favourite way to eat out in Lappeenranta is to literally eat out! Stands in the market square and at the harbour sell fast food and coffee, including some interesting local specialities. At the harbour, try sweet or savoury waffles filled with jam, whipped cream, cheese or ham. *Martat* has the tastiest ones. At the market square, the favourite dishes are vety and atomi (meat pies with different fillings), at 15 to 20 mk a piece.

Another local speciality is lemin särä – mutton roasted in a wooden trough in an oven. It is served at the *Restaurant Kippurasarvi* on Rantatie. The dish has to be ordered two days prior to the dinner.

The *Café Marjuska* at Kristiinankatu 1, in the Fortress, should be visited for its atmosphere alone. The building used to be the Young Officers' House. The Marjuska serves coffee and tea with home-baked buns and cakes. It is open daily from 10 am to 6 pm.

If you really want to rough it, go to the *Technical University cafeteria* at the end of Skinnarilankatu. A warm meal costs only 15 to 20 mk, but don't expect culinary delights. The *Aitiopaikka* at Kauppakatu 41 has a lunch bargain: soup, main course and a dessert for 34 mk between 11 am and 2.30 pm. The place is on the 5th floor and can be a little hard to find. The *Hullu Hanhi*, in the Hotel Cumulus at Valtakatu 31, has tasty food at standard prices. You can get a meal for 40 to 60 mk.

Entertainment

The Dancing Club Kleopatra, a disco at Valtakatu 41, is a favourite nightspot on Saturdays. There is a cover charge of 25 to 30 mk. The Disco Willimies at Kauppakatu 39 is popular in the evenings among 18 to 20-year-olds. There is also dancing from 2 to 6 pm, but the people are older. The Doris, in the Hotel Lappee at Brahenkatu 1, is perhaps the most popular disco in town. Cover charges can be up to 40 mk.

Getting There & Away

Air Some of the smaller airlines operate several flights between Helsinki and Lappeenranta each weekday. The cheapest return ticket is currently 310 mk.

Bus All buses along the eastern route, between Helsinki and Joensuu, stop in Lappeenranta. Buses run hourly from Lappeenranta to Imatra, 37 km away.

Train Seven to eight trains a day between Helsinki and Joensuu will take you to Lappeenranta. The trip from Helsinki takes a bit more than 2½ hours.

Ferry In July, you can catch the weekly MS *Kristina Brahe* between Savonlinna and Lappeenranta. A one-way ticket is approximately 150 mk; for an extra 150 mk, you can sleep in the cabin in Savonlinna before departure.

Getting Around

Bicycles can be hired at Pyörä-Expert (☎ 953-18710), Valtakatu 64, for 30 mk per day or 110 mk for five days, and at the Finnhostel (☎ 953-15555), Kuusimäenkatu 18, for 20 mk per hour or 50 mk per day.

IMATRA

Imatra (population 34,000) is an industrial town, which has grown along the Vuoksi River and Lake Saimaa. One of the highest waterfalls in Finland, the Imatra Rapids, is used for power generation. Parts of the town are in the border zone between Finland and Russia, and there is a checkpoint there.

Orientation

Imatra has four centres: Imatrankoski, Mansikkala, Tainionkoski and Vuoksenniska. Imatrankoski, the oldest of the four, is where you'll find the town's main shopping street: Lappeentie. Mansikkala is a new commercial centre to the south of the

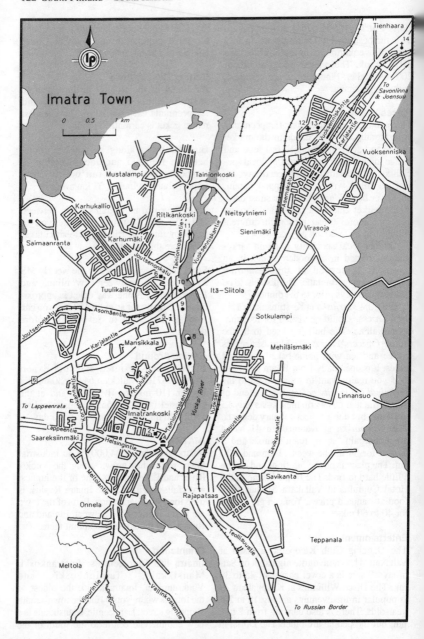

Imatra Town

0   0.5   1 km

Tienhaara

14

To Savonlinna & Joensuu

Vuoksenniska

12 13

Vuoksenniskantie

Karjalantie

Asemakatu

Mustalampi

Tainionkoski

Karhukallio

Ritikankoski

Neitsytniemi

1

Sienimäki

Virasoja

Saimaanranta

Karhumäki

Joutsenonkatu

Tainionkoskentie

Vuoksenniskantie

Tuulikallio

6

3

10

11

Itä–Siitola

9

Asomäentie

5

Sotkulampi

Karjalantie

Mansikkala

8

Mehiläismäki

7

Joutsenonkatu

6

Kannankatu

Koulukatu

Tainionkoskentie

Vuoksi River

Vuoksentie

Teollisuustie

Linnansuo

To Lappeenrata

Imatrankoski

Savikannantie

Lappeentie

2

Saareksiinmäki

Helsingintie

3

Savikanta

Meltolantie

Onnela

Rajapatsas

Teppanala

Meltola

Teollisuustie

Viipurintie

Vallinkoskentie

To Russian Border

central station (a combined train and bus station). Tainionkoski is a smaller centre, north of the central station, and Vuoksenniska is the community centre of a former municipality, now part of Imatra.

Information
The tourist information office operates from the Mansikkapaikka shopping centre in Mansikkala. It's open from 9 am to 7 pm in June, July and August, and from 8 am to 4 pm at other times.

Things to See & Do
Imatra Rapids This is one of the highest waterfalls in Finland. The water flow is restricted because the rapids are used for power generation. However, in summer the water is allowed to flow free every day for travellers and locals to admire. This takes place at 7 pm on weekdays and at 3 pm on Sundays and holidays. In August, there are special displays, in which a blazing raft is lowered into the torrent. Crown Park, Finland oldest natural park, is located near the rapids. There is a marked path through the park.

Church of the Three Crosses This church, on Ruokolahdentie in Vuoksenniska, was designed by Alvar Aalto, the most famous Finnish architect. As an interesting detail, only two of the 103 windows of the church are identical. The church is open from 9 am to 8 pm.

Karelian Farmhouse Museum The museum, a restored 19th century farmhouse, is open from May to August from 10 am to 6 pm, closed on Mondays. It is located in Mansikkala, on the bank of the Vuoksi River.

Industrial Workers' Housing Museum This museum in Tainionkoski portrays the housing conditions of industrial workers in the 1890s. It's open between May and August from 10 am to 6 pm, closed on Mondays.

Imatra Art Museum Located in the premises of a school in Vuoksenniska, this art museum is supposed to have the most extensive collection of art in the Province of Kymi. The museum is open from noon to 6 pm Tuesday to Friday and from 2 to 6 pm on weekends. Admission is 5 mk for adults, 2 mk for children.

Valtionhotelli The most famous building in Imatra must be the castle-like Hotel Valtionhotelli, right next to the rapids. It was originally built in 1902 to replace a burnt-down wooden hotel that stood in the same place. The new hotel was built in Art Nouveau style and called 'The Grand Hotel Cascade'. It was a favourite spot of the St Petersburg aristocracy – every day, 14 trains brought people to admire the waterfall and to have an outing. Tsar Nicholas II visited the place several times. The flow of tourists, as well as the habit of romantically committing suicide by jumping into the waterfall, continued until the beginning of WW I. After WW II, the hotel was completely refurbished. In 1982, the Finnish alcohol monopoly, Alko, bought the property and, in honour of the company's 50th anniversary, restored Valtionhotelli to its original glory.

Border Zone You can reach the Finnish border by taking Teollisuustie all the way to the checkpoint, about seven km from Imatrankoski. You cannot get further than the checkpoint without having a visa for Russia or special permission to enter the border zone. At the border, you will find the studio of an artist who makes wooden sculptures. The studio can be visited whenever the owner is at home.

Fishing The Vuoksi Fishing Park (☎ 954-23123) is located along the Vuoksi River, on Varpasaari in Mansikkala. Spike and salmon can be caught here. One-day permits cost 15 mk, and one-week permits are 35 mk. The park is open from 1 May to 31 August from 10 am to 9 pm. Fishing equipment can be rented for 5 to 20 mk per day.

Places to Stay
Imatra Camping at Leiritie 1, in the Imatra Leisure Centre, is open from 1 June to 11 August, but camping is still possible after that – showers are open, but there is no service and no-one to collect camping fees. The cheapest place in town is the *Ukonlinna youth hostel* (☎ 954-21270), also located in the leisure centre. It is run-down and a little hard to reach without a car. Accommodation in small rooms costs 30 to 35 mk. The *Summer Hotel Mansikkala* (☎ 954-2091) at Rastaankatu 3 is open from 1 June to 11 August. It is located close to the train station. The *Hotel Martina* (☎ 954-63555) at Lappeentie 3 has singles for 200 to 300 mk and doubles for 360 to 470 mk. The lower prices apply on weekends and in summer.

The *Valtionhotelli* (☎ 954-68881) at Torkkelinkatu 2 is the most impressive place to stay. If you want to invest in a good hotel once during your trip to Finland, this is the place. Singles/doubles in the castle hotel cost 500/680 mk. Also on the new side, rooms at the *Congress Hotel* cost 430/520 mk. If there are any discounts on these prices in summer, they are likely to be in the less romantic Congress Hotel, where Finncheques are accepted (with a supplement).

Places to Eat
A number of places offer good lunch prices. Locally popular is the *Hotelli Vuoksenhovi* (☎ 954-25011) at Siitolankatu 2, where there is live music, on occasion. Special lunch prices are available from Monday to Saturday. Also offering lunch specials is the *Park Hotel Imatra* (☎ 954-4734300) at Torikatu 4. The *Ristorante Bella* (☎ 954-31287) at Vuoksenniskantie 82, in the suburb of Vuoksenniska, has pizzas, steaks and small meals, as well as attractive lunch prices. The *Piz Pepiitto* (☎ 954-66166) at Tainionkoskentie 10 is an Italian restaurant, serving pizza, pasta, steaks and hamburgers. Lunch prices are attractive. The *Smuggler* (☎ 954-63811) at Helsingintie 1, not far from the rapids, serves steaks, salads and pizzas, and has a good lunch offer.

For something a little different, try the *Kankaan Kievari* (☎ 954-33075) at Kaukopäänkatu 8, in the suburb of Kaukopää. Near main road No 6, it's built in Lappish style, of pine. An inexpensive buffet is available from 11 am to 7 pm daily. The *Valtionhotelli* (☎ 954-68881) at Torkkelinkatu 2 serves à la carte meals (breakfast, lunch and dinner). It's not cheap but it is licensed.

Then there is the *Buttenhoff* restaurant near the rapids. It is the most legendary restaurant in Imatra, with a 100-year old history.

Entertainment
The Cellar of Valtionhotelli is a popular nightspot. It is rather expensive, and you should be well dressed to get in. The Restaurant Smuggler, at Helsingintie 1 in Imatrankoski, is a rock pub, popular among young people.

Getting There & Away
Imatra is well served by all eastbound trains and buses from Helsinki, and by hourly buses from Lappeenranta. There are seven trains a day from Helsinki to Imatra.

YLÄMAA
Ylämaa is a rural municipality of 1800

inhabitants, best known for the gemstone spectrolite, a special kind of labradorite found only here. Spectrolite is a dark stone which glitters in all the colours of the spectrum.

Things to See

Church The Ylämaa Church, in the municipal centre, was built in 1931. Its façade is made of spectrolite. The church is open daily in June, July and August from 9 am to 5 pm.

Jewel Village This village on the No 387 Lappeenranta to Vaalimaa road is Ylämaa's main attraction. The village consists of two stone grinderies, a goldsmith's workshop and a gem museum. There is also a cafeteria and a tourist information desk, which is connected to the museum. The gem museum has a collection of spectrolites and other precious stones. Admission is a hefty 15 mk. The museum is open daily from 1 June to 31 August from 10 am to 6 pm. The shops in the area have similar opening hours.

Places to Stay & Eat

Ylämaa has nowhere to stay. It does, however, have a couple of eateries, both down-to-earth bars. The *Korupirtti Kahvila* is a café which serves meals, while the *Rosita Baari* offers beer and meals.

Getting There & Away

Saimaan Liikenne runs regular afternoon school buses from Lappeenranta, 21 km away. In summer, catch the afternoon bus from Lappenranta, which runs Monday to Friday only.

Turku

Turku and its surroundings are often called 'Finland Proper', a description that may well derive from the viewpoint of early Swedish settlers. Once you've toured Finland, you may decide that the *real* Finland is nowhere near Turku. Whatever you think, Turku is where modern Finland started, so it's quite a logical place to start exploring the country. This is the most historic part of Finland, with medieval stone churches in every other village. The Turku area, along with Åland, also has some of Finland's most beautiful islands. You will not only be able to do some of the finest island-hopping in Europe, but it may all be free. Many of the ferries that link inhabited islands are supposed to be part of the free-of-charge road system (it would not be fair if the locals had to pay to go shopping, would it?). Locals always have priority access to ferries, but if there is space, and if you stay overnight on one of the islands, you should have no trouble getting aboard. Not all ferries are free, though. The authority in charge of archipelago traffic (☎ 921-512 600) will give details on ferries.

Turku/Åbo

Turku (Åbo in Swedish) is by far the most popular gateway to Finland, due to the inexpensive ferries (free with some rail passes) from Sweden. The historic capital of Finland, and the capital of what is generally called 'Finland Proper', it has much to offer the visitor.

The Turku area has been inhabited for several thousand years. It is the oldest town in Finland and was Finland's first capital. The early Catholic church, as well as the Swedish administration, ran the country from Turku, and Count per Brahe had his castle here. Fire destroyed Turku several times over the centuries, but the transfer of the capital to Helsinki was the main blow to

the town. Today, Turku is a substantial city with fine attractions, though locals sometimes joke that after Turku spread culture to the rest of Finland, it never returned.

Orientation

The Turku harbour is a few km from the city centre, accessible by train from each arriving ferry. There are also local buses. The city centre is on both shores of the Aurajoki River, and everything is well within walking distance.

Information

The main tourist information office (☎ 921-233 6366) at Käsityöläiskatu 3 is open Monday to Friday, from 8 am to 4 pm in summer and from 8.30 am to 4 pm in winter. The helpful staff hands out useful brochures. The free map booklet includes bus routes and maps of the city centre and the surrounding area. There is also a bicycle map, and a brochure called *Two Walking Tours in Turku*. Another tourist office branch (☎ 921-315 262), at Aurakatu 4 in the city centre, is open from 8.30 am to 7.30 pm Monday to Friday and from 8.30 am to 4 pm on weekends.

An Interrail centre (☎ 921-304 551) for train travellers has recently been opened at Läntinen Rantakatu 47. It offers a meeting place, a left-luggage service and somewhere to take a shower. The centre is open daily from Midsummer to mid-August from 8 am to 10 pm. Bicycles can be hired for 10 mk per day. The youth hostel will also provide you with some very useful information.

Things to See
Most places in Turku will give discounts to students, children and pensioners, so keep your card readily available.

Turku Castle The castle, near the Viking and Silja Line ferry terminals, is a must for everyone visiting Turku. It houses an interesting historical museum, and the castle itself has a long history. Founded in 1280 at the mouth of the Aurajoki River, the castle has been growing ever since, with recent renovations making it the most notable historic building in Finland. It's open daily from 2 May to 30 September from 10 am to 8 pm, and from 1 October to 30 April from 10 am to 3 pm. Admission is 15 mk.

Luostarinmäki This open-air handicrafts museum on the southern slopes of Vartiovuori Hill is worth a visit. Many carpenters, stonemasons, board carriers and other workers bought plots in the area after 1779, when the first plots were allotted. When the great fire of 1827 destroyed most of Turku, the settlement in Luostarinmäki survived. Since 1940, it has served as a museum. There are about 30 workshops altogether, representing different trades, and you can always find people working in the houses. On weekends, there is more action. The museum is open from 2 May to 30 September from 10 am to 6 pm daily. Admission is 15 mk; discounted tickets are 7 mk.

Turku Cathedral This medieval cathedral, the mightiest of all Finnish churches, is the national shrine of the Evangelical-Lutheran Church of Finland. Its oldest parts date back to the 13th century, and in the Middle Ages, the cathedral was extended by the addition of side chapels. Important people, including Catherine Månsdotter, Queen of Sweden and Finland, have been buried here. At noon on Christmas Eve, outside this church, the message of Christmas peace is declared for the city of Turku and for all Finland. This declaration has traditionally been broadcast on Finnish TV and radio, and in recent years has even been aired abroad. The cathedral museum displays models showing different stages of the cathedral's construction, wooden sculptures and other religious paraphernalia.

The cathedral is open from 1 June to 31 August from 9 am to 7 pm Monday to Friday, 9 am to 3 pm on Saturdays and from the end of the service until 4.30 pm on Sundays. From 1 September to 31 May, it's open from 10 am to 4 pm Monday to Friday, 10 am to 3 pm on Saturdays and 2.30 to 4.30 pm on Sundays. Admission to the museum is 5 mk.

Pharmacy Museum This cute riverside museum at Läntinen Rantakatu 13 is located in the oldest wooden house in Turku. It's open daily from 2 May to 30 September from 10 am to 6 pm, and from 1 October to 30 April from 10 am to 3 pm. Admission is 7 mk.

Biological Museum Here you will see 13 landscapes from various parts of Finland, including 136 stuffed birds and 29 mammals displayed in their natural settings. The museum is on Neitsytpolku, and has similar opening hours and admission fees to the Pharmacy Museum.

Maritime Museum This museum on Vartiovuori Hill is in an observatory building designed by Mr Engel, the architect. On display are scale models of ships, paintings of ships and navigation equipment. There is also a good view from the 2nd floor. Opening hours are the same as for the Pharmacy Museum, and entry costs 7 mk.

Sibelius Museum For anyone interested in the most famous Finnish composer, Jean Sibelius, this museum is the place to go. It is in an ugly modern building at Piispankatu 17, behind the cathedral. In addition to the

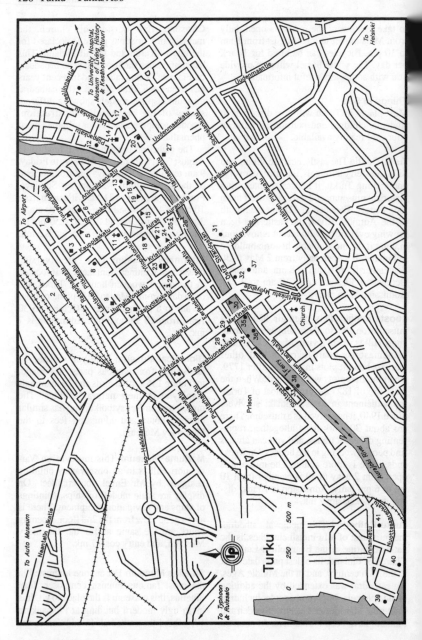

■ PLACES TO STAY

3 Matkakievari
9 Aura Hostel
10 Turisti Aula
15 Hamburger Börs
27 Kåren Hostel
29 Turku City Youth Hostel

▼ PLACES TO EAT

4 Amir Kebab
5 Kasperi
15 Fransmanni & Bärsin puisto
16 Verso Vegetarian Restaurant
17 Al Amir
18 Hesburger & Foija
19 Michelangelo Pizzeria
21 Myllärimatti &Indoor Market
24 Ristorante Dennis
30 Le Pirate Boat Restaurant

OTHER

1 Bus Terminal
2 Central Railway Station
6 Naantali Buses
7 University
8 Art Museum
11 Orthodox Church
12 Sibelius Museum
13 Finnair
14 Cathedral
20 Åbo Academy
22 Tourist Office
23 General Post Office
25 Tourist Information & Town Hall
26 Tourist Association, Pharmacy
   Museum & Waterbus pier
28 Police
31 Swimming Centre
32 Wäinoä Aaltonen Museum
33 Inter-Rail Centre
34 SS *Ukkopekka* & Cruise Boat Pier
35 *Suomen Joutsen* Ship
36 *Sigyn* Museum Ship
37 Windmill
38 Marina
39 Silja Line & Seawind Line
40 Viking Line
41 Turku Castle

spring and autumn, there are concerts on Wednesdays and occasionally on Sundays. The museum is open daily (except Mondays) from 11 am to 3 pm. Admission is 10 mk.

Ett Hem The name of this museum means 'a home'. Ett Hem features a wealthy 18th century home at Piispankatu 14. It's open daily (except Mondays) from noon to 3 pm. Admission is 10 mk.

Rettig Palace This walled mansion, standing in a garden on Hämeenkatu, was a private home for over 60 years. Now owned by a local bank, it houses temporary art exhibitions. The mansion is open only during exhibitions; enquire at the tourist information office.

Museum Ship *Sigyn* This ship is the world's only surviving barque-rigged, wooden, ocean-going cargo vessel. Launched in the Swedish town of Gothenburg in 1887, it has sailed all over the world. The ship can be found at Itäinen Rantakatu 48, and is open from 10 May to 31 August from 10 am to 3 pm Sunday to Friday and from 10 am to 5 pm on Saturdays. Admission is 10 mk, with a 50% discount for children and students.

Suomen Joutsen The 'Swan of Finland', the white ship next to the *Sigyn*, was originally built in 1902. The Finnish navy bought the ship in 1930 to use as a training ship. During WW II, it served as a mother ship for submarines and as a hospital. After the war it became a training school for sailors, until 1988. You can visit the *Suomen Joutsen* daily from 15 May to 15 August from 10 am to 6 pm. Admission is 10 mk.

Art Museum The collection of the Turku Art Society is at Aurakatu 26. The second-largest art collection in Finland, it exhibits Finnish art, as well as works from other Nordic countries. It's open from 10 am to 4 pm Monday to Saturday and from 10 am to 6 pm on Sundays, and also from 6 to 8 pm on Thurs-

interesting collection of instruments from all over the world, a special room is devoted to exhibits on the life and works of Sibelius, and you can listen to his music on record. In days. Admission is 15 mk for adults, with 5 mk discounts available.

Wäinö Aaltonen Museum This museum at Itäinen Rantakatu 38 exhibits works by Wäinö Aaltonen, a famous Finnish sculptor of the National Romantic era. It also has contemporary Finnish art and changing exhibitions. The museum is open daily from 19 June to 1 September from 10 am to 6 pm. At other times of the year, it's open from 10 am to 4 pm and 6 to 8 pm Monday to Friday, 10 am to 4 pm on Saturdays and 10 am to 6 pm on Sundays.

Matti Koivurinta Gallery On the 3rd floor at Pitkämäenkatu 13, this gallery has a collection of modern art representing various significant trends. It's open on Wednesdays and Sundays from 2 to 5 pm, and admission is 10 mk. You can get there on bus No 20.

Scout Museum Supposedly the oldest scout museum in Europe, the Turku Scout Museum is near the Kaarina Church (take bus No 50). The museum has a large collection of camping and hiking equipment, uniforms and literature. It's open on Sundays from noon to 4 pm.

Ruissalo The large island of Ruissalo, just outside Turku, has a large number of attractive old wooden villas with restaurants and cafés, signposted walking tracks and large botanical gardens. It is a nice area to explore with a bicycle or a vehicle, or take bus No 8 to the camping ground and walk back through the forest.

Organised Tours

The tourist information office organises sightseeing bus tours between 15 June and 31 August. Tours start at 1 pm from Aurakatu 4 and take about two hours. The price is a steep 50 mk per person.

Festivals

There are two international 'Finland Festivals' in Turku in summer, which you should consider attending. The Turku Music

Festival, in the second week of August, offers traditional classical music performed by Finnish and foreign orchestras and choirs. Quite different is the very popular Ruisrock, probably the oldest annual rock festival, held since 1969. Both Finnish and international bands play, during the last weekend of June, in the Ruissalo park, near the town centre. For further information on both festivals, contact the Turku Music Festival Foundation (☎ 921-511 162, fax 921-313 316), Uudenmaankatu 1, 20500 Turku.

Places to Stay – bottom end

Ruissalo Camping is a high-quality camping ground on a peninsula in the farthest corner of the island of Ruissalo. The camping fee is 50 mk per family or 25 mk per individual. Bus No 8 will take you to Ruissalo.

Turku has one of the best-kept youth hostels in Finland. The *Turku Town Hostel* (☎ 921-316 578) is close to the Aurajoki River, at Linnankatu 39, and is open all year round. The staff is friendly, and there are all kinds of services for the traveller, including free use of laundry machines. To get to the youth hostel, take bus No 1 from the ferry terminal. Beds cost 35 mk in dormitories, 45 mk in smaller rooms and 55 mk in doubles. There is another youth hostel (☎ 921-320 421) at Hämeenkatu 22, which is only open from June to August. It is not as nice, but rooms are smaller. Dormitory beds cost 45 mk for members.

Places to Stay – middle

The *Birgittalaisluostarin vieraskoti* (☎ 921-501 910) at Ursininkatu 15A is a guesthouse kept by nuns. Clean singles/doubles are a very reasonable 180/280 mk, but you have to respect the lifestyle of the nunnery. The *Summer Hotel Ikituuri* (☎ 921-376 111) at Pispalantie 7 is open from June to August. Singles/doubles are 200/270 mk.

Places to Stay – top end

Most hotels in Turku will give you accommodation on presentation of Finncheques. Here are some of the most central hotels in Turku. The prices listed are approximate winter prices, but most hotels offer lower rates in summer:

Hotel Astro (☎ 921-511 800), Humalistonkatu 18. Singles/doubles are 250/350 mk (no Finncheques)

Hotel Aura (☎ 921-651 111), Humalistonkatu 7. Singles/doubles are 300/600 mk (no Finncheques)

Hotel Cumulus (☎ 921-638 211), Eerikinkatu 28. Singles/doubles cost 455/600 mk

Hotel Hamburger Börs (☎ 921-637 381), Kauppiaskatu 6. The oldest in town. All rooms are 450 mk

Hotel Hansa (☎ 921-617 000), Kristiinankatu 9. Singles/doubles are 460/600 mk

Hotel Julia (☎ 921-651 311), Eerikinkatu 4. Singles/doubles start at 490/660 mk

Hotel Kantri (☎ 921-320 921), Yliopistonkatu 29A. Singles/doubles are 290/350 mk (Finncheques not accepted)

Keskushotelli (☎ 921-337 333), Yliopistonkatu 12A. Singles/doubles are 315/395 mk

Hotel Marina Palace (☎ 921-336 300), Linnankatu 32. Singles/doubles cost 700/900 mk (Finncheques OK, with a supplement)

Park Hotel (☎ 921-519 666), Rauhankatu 1. Singles/doubles are 600/800 mk (Finncheques OK, with a supplement)

Hotel Ruissalo Spa (☎ 921-605 511) in Ruissalo. Singles/doubles are 535/680 mk (no Finncheques)

Scandic Hotel Turku (☎ 921-302 600). This hotel at the harbour has singles/doubles for 340/440 mk

Hotel Seurahuone (☎ 921-637 301), Humalistonkatu 2. Singles/doubles are 350/690 mk

Places to Eat

Turku is a university city, so it is always possible to get a lunch for 15 mk at one of the university cafeterias. The *Restaurant Pinella* on Porthaninpuisto has good food at affordable prices. The pleasant surroundings, in an old wooden building, are an added benefit. You can get a meal for 35 to 40 mk. The *Restaurant Vanha Ratikka* at Yliopistonkatu 9B serves an excellent lunch for 34 mk. The *Foija* at Aurakatu 10 is a very popular place. Food is good, portions are big and prices are OK at 40 to 60 mk. Turku is the home of the *Hesburger*, a local hamburger chain that has become more popular than the big international chains because of the quality of its products. Prices are similar to those of other hamburger restaurants in

Finland. The *Börsin puisto* at Kauppiaskatu 6, right in the town centre, is a popular outdoor restaurant. The *Olavin krouvi* at Hämeenkatu 30, a popular student bar, has live music.

Getting There & Away

Air There are seven weekday flights and four to five weekend flights from Helsinki to Turku. The cheapest return flight from Helsinki currently costs 280 mk. There are also flights to/from Vaasa.

Bus The bus terminal has regular departures to all towns and villages around Turku, and several express buses a day to towns in South Finland. It's 143 km and two hours to Pori, 113 km and 1¾ hours to Vammala, 95 km and three hours to Houtskär, and 149 km and three hours to Hanko. Each destination has its own platform.

Train Turku harbour is the terminus for the south-eastern railway line, and there are regular trains from the city railway station to Helsinki, Uusikaupunki and Tampere, and beyond.

Ferry Turku is the major gateway to mainland Finland from Sweden and Åland. Both Silja Line and Viking Line operate night and day ferries from Stockholm, and Viking Line also calls at Mariehamn harbour. Several discounts apply to these ferries, including the complimentary ride granted by Silja Line to those producing an Inter-Rail/Eurail train pass. The harbour is served by trains and buses, which meet each arriving ferry. The MS *Seawind*, a car ferry between Stockholm and Turku, operates daily in summer and five times a week at other times of year. Only car passengers are allowed on the *Seawind*, but its total prices are generally lower than those of the other companies. In summer, there are also express boats along the coast, from Naantali and other places.

Getting Around

Local buses will take you to most places – timetables can be obtained from the tourist information office. A one-day tourist ticket costs 20 mk.

Around Turku

NAANTALI

Naantali is an idyllic port town 13 km north of Turku. Regular Viking Line ferries from the Swedish town of Kapellskär arrive here. Naantali, a popular day trip from Turku, is a typical summer town, lively from June to mid-August and very quiet for the rest of the year. Only 11,000 people live here.

History

Naantali grew around a Catholic convent, the Convent of the Order of Saint Birgitta, which was founded in 1443. After Finland became Protestant, the convent was dissolved and Naantali had to struggle for its existence; the convent had been important not only spiritually but also economically. When the pilgrims no longer came to town, people had to find other means of making a living, notably by knitting socks, which became Naantali's main export.

Orientation

Naantali sprawls on both sides of the channel Naantalinsalmi. The town centre is on the mainland, on the north-eastern side of the channel. The island of Luonnonmaa is on the western side. The modern town centre is around the bus terminal, but the old part of Naantali, one km to the west, is by far the most interesting place to visit. Naantali's guest harbour is very centrally located in the heart of the old town.

Information

The tourist information office (☎ 921-850 850) is at Kaivotori 2, at the guest harbour. It is more commercially orientated than most municipal tourist offices, but you should be able to get some leaflets free of charge.

Things to See & Do

Old Town The old town of Naantali is like a big open-air museum. The town grew around the convent, without any regular town plan, and new buildings were always built on the sites of older ones. Thus, the medieval town plan can still be seen in Naantali. Only old windmills and storehouses along the shore have been replaced by the modern guest harbour.

Convent Church The massive church dominates the harbour area. The church was completed in 1462 and the tower in 1797. Until this century, the wooden clock face had painted hands, which always showed 11.30. People used to say that the end of the world would come when the clock of Naantali Church struck 12. On summer evenings at 8 pm, vespers are played by a trumpet from the church tower. The church is open from 2 May to 15 August from noon to 7 pm daily, and from 16 to 30 April and from 16 August to 30 September from noon to 3 pm daily. At other times, the church is only open on Sundays and holidays, from noon to 3 pm.

Kultaranta The summer residence of the president of Finland is across the channel. The 56-hectare estate, with its large rose gardens, can be visited at any time with a guide (book at the tourist office); on Fridays from 8 am to 8 pm, you don't need to be with a guide.

Naantali Museum The museum's exhibition on local history dates back to the 17th century.

Kailo To the west of the harbour is the island of Kailo, which is the main recreational area of Naantali. It can be reached by a footbridge. Kailo has a beach, and facilities for tennis and other games. It also provides a stage for many open-air concerts and theatre performances.

Farm Museum of Käkölä The speciality of this museum, on the island of Luonnonmaa, is a collection of woodwork made with a chainsaw. It's open on Sundays from noon to 6 pm, and entry is free.

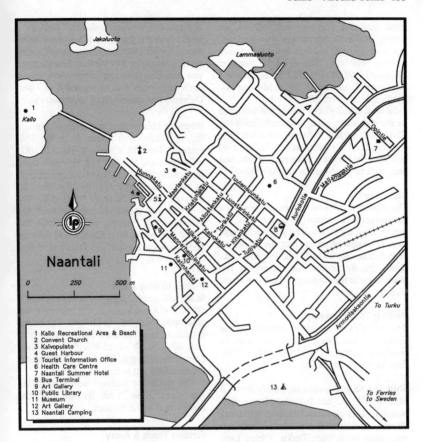

1 Kailo Recreational Area & Beach
2 Convent Church
3 Kalvopuisto
4 Guest Harbour
5 Tourist Information Office
6 Health Care Centre
7 Naantali Summer Hotel
8 Bus Terminal
9 Art Gallery
10 Public Library
11 Museum
12 Art Gallery
13 Naantali Camping

Spa Naantali's spa traditions go back as far as 1723, when people began taking health-giving waters from a spring in Viluluoto. In 1863, Naantali's spa was opened, and at the turn of the century, the town was well known as a resort. The new spa was opened in 1984. It is much like other spas found around Finland.

Festivals

Sleepyhead Day (27 July) has become a local festival in Naantali. The annual tradition involves the townspeople waking early in the morning to select a well-known person as the 'sleepyhead', who is then woken up by being thrown into the sea. If this doesn't make any sense to you, you could always be there, well awake, to see for yourself.

The Naantali Music Festival, held in June, features chamber music.

Places to Stay

Naantali Camping (☎ 921-850 855), on top of Kuparivuori Hill ('Copper Mountain'), is 800 metres from the town centre, between Naantali centre and the Viking Line ferry terminal. This is an exceptionally pleasant camping ground, with a superb location and good facilities. Camping costs 69 mk per family or 34 mk per person. Two-bed cottages are 160 mk, and four-bed cottages cost 210 to 420 mk. The modern *Naantali Summer Hotel* (☎ 921-850 850) at Opintie 1 is open from June to mid-August. Singles/doubles are 200/290 mk.

Several small places to stay can be found in the old town, along Mannerheiminkatu. They all have few beds and are often fully booked. The *Villa Antonius* (☎ 921-751 938) at Mannerheiminkatu 9 is a particularly nice one, with singles/doubles for 300/380 mk.

Places to Eat

The *Restaurant Merisali* in the harbour area has an excellent bargain fish buffet, salad and main course for 40 mk. The popular *Restaurant Torintupa* at the market square serves tasty lunches for 28 to 38 mk. For entertainment, the *Restaurant Kaivohuone* is the place to go in the evenings. There is a cover charge.

Getting There & Away

Bus Virtually all routes to Naantali go via Turku, 13 km away. There are buses to Naantali every 10 to 15 minutes from Aninkaistentori in Turku.

Ship The SS *Ukkopekka* sails daily from 16 June to 11 August between Turku and Naantali. This pleasant three-hour trip costs 80 mk one-way, 100 mk return. There are also other boats from Turku. Viking Line operates several ferries a day in summer between Kapellskär in Sweden and Naantali. These ferries are one of the cheapest ways to reach Finland from Sweden. Catch a bus for Kapellskär from the central Cityterminalen in Stockholm.

DRAGSFJÄRD

With an excellent youth hostel and some unusual villages, Dragsfjärd (population 4000) is a nice place to visit.

Things to See

Dalsbruk This lovely seaside village in southern Dragsfjärd is an old industrial site, and some of the early industrial areas have been preserved. Dalsbruk is a popular destination for sailboats but is also worth a visit by bicycle, car or bus. At the guest harbour, you will find a tourist information office, open daily from 9 to 10 am and 6 to 7 pm. Dalsbruk has a museum of local history.

Högsåra This isolated island features an old fishing village with houses from the 18th century. The MS *Falkö* (☎ 949-320 097) sails between Kasnäs and Högsåra three times a day from Monday to Friday and once or twice on weekends. The trip takes 20 minutes. The MS *Satava* (☎ 949-320 094) will take you around the other islands. On Mondays and Fridays, you can reach the island of Högsåra from Kasnäs, and the boat sails between Kasnäs and Dalsbruk a few times a week.

Places to Stay & Eat

In the village of Dragsfjärd is a *youth hostel* (☎ 925-4553) that gives you probably the best value for money in Finland. The hostel is really of hotel standard, but the rooms cost only 40 to 60 mk – even less if you stay in a dormitory. Virpi paid 30 mk for a 'dormitory' which turned out to be a single room.

The restaurant *Stallcafé* serves delicious lunches for 20 to 30 mk. Be sure to try the bakery next to the harbour.

Getting There & Away

To get to Dragsfjärd and Dalsbruk, take a bus from Turku or Kimito. There are two to four buses a day.

HOUTSKÄR

A cluster of islands off Turku, this municipality of 750 inhabitants offers some interesting scenery, and an old church on the island of Houtskär. To get there, catch one of the two daily buses from Turku, via Pargas, Nagu and Korpo. This interesting route takes three hours. Once there, you can do some island-hopping (☎ 921-512 600 for route information) on the MS *Bastö*, which sails between islands from 1 June to 15 August.

INIÖ

The isolated island world of Iniö, a municipality of 260 inhabitants, offers some of the most desolate archipelago scenery. The ferry *Klara* sails from Turku on Wednesdays and/or Saturdays between the end of May and mid-August, calling at several islands. The MS *Jurmo II* sails twice a day between the inhabited islands. There is a museum café on the main island.

KIMITO/KEMIÖ

The Sagalund (☎ 925-1738) in Kimito is an exceptionally interesting museum of local history. If possible, get a guide to tell you some of the stories about the buildings and objects – they are very entertaining. To get to Kimito, take one of the three to five buses a day from Turku. Some 3400 people live in Kimito.

KORPO/KORPPOO

Korpo is the most distant island that can be reached without a long ferry trip. Korpo, with a population of 1150, is connected to Nagu by a car ferry, which operates continuously, without a timetable. You can then take other ferries to Houtskär and even Åland. If you come by car, avoid Friday and Sunday nights in summer, when you may have to wait in the ferry queue for a long time. The ferry ride is free. Korpo does not offer the tourist many sights, but it is a nice place to stay a while for fishing, swimming and relaxation. There is a youth hostel (☎ 926-43799), open from 1 May to 30 September, with dormitory beds for 32 mk. To get to Korpo, take a bus from Turku. There are four to 11 buses per day, travelling via Parainen and Nagu.

NAGU/NAUVO

Nagu (population 1430) is an idyllic island between Parainen and Korpo. It is connected to both by free ferries, which run continuously, without a timetable. Nagu Church dates back to the 14th century. It is open from 1 June to 15 August from 10 am to 6 pm, and from 16 to 30 August from 10 am to 4 pm. Nagu village has an excellent French restaurant called *l'Escale*. It is not cheap, but the food is worth the expense. The restaurant is open all year round. Downstairs, you can get meals for 60 to 90 mk; upstairs, in the 'posh' section, meals are 120 to 140 mk. To get to Nagu, take a bus from Turku. There are four to 11 buses a day, all via Parainen.

NOUSIAINEN

Nousiainen Church, built in the 1300s and restored in the 1960s, is where the first (Catholic) bishop of Finland, St Henrik, lies buried. His sarcophagus was made in Flanders in 1430. The church is a triple-aisled hall church, with chalk murals from the early 15th century. Nousiainen is 21 km north of Turku, and there are buses almost every hour.

PARAINEN/PARGAS

Parainen (population 11,900) is sometimes called 'the capital of the archipelago'. It has 740 km of coastline, including islands in the area. To get further out in the archipelago, you will pass through Parainen.

Information

The tourist information office (☎ 921-889 480) at Rantakatu 14 has a lot of useful information about Parainen and the surrounding islands. If you intend to travel around, this is the place to go. Get a copy of a ferry timetable – it is essential, and can be hard to find in other places. The office is open from 9 am to 4 pm Monday to Friday.

Things to See

In the old town of Parainen, there is a 14th century church. The nearby chapel houses a church museum. Parainen is known for its limestone. Visitors can go and see the biggest limestone quarries in Scandinavia, at Partek's site, almost in the middle of Parainen.

Places to Stay

There is a nice *camping ground* located 1.5 km from the town centre, in Solliden, with four/six-bed cottages for 190/220 mk. Next to the camping ground is a *youth hostel* (☎ 921-745 255). It is rather basic, but beds

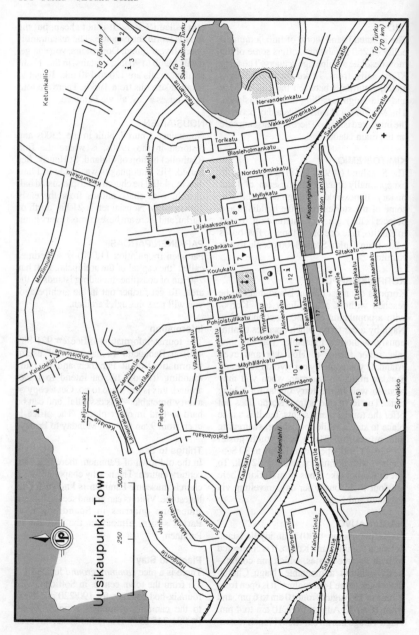

Uusikaupunki Town

1	Camping Ground
2	Hotel Lännentie
3	Tourist Information Office
4	Vocational School
5	Myllymäki Park
6	New Church
7	Gasthaus Pooki
8	Cultural Museum
9	Market Place & Bus Terminal
10	Pilot Museum
11	Old Church
12	Tourist Information Office & Public Library
13	Guest Harbour
14	Restaurant Rantamakasiinit
15	Hotel Aquarius
16	Hospital
17	Railway Station

cost only 30 mk in dormitories and 50 mk per person in doubles.

Places to Eat
The restaurant boat *Selma*, just out of the town centre, is open whenever weather permits. You can see it from the bridge that leads to the mainland. At the seaside, close to the centre, you can find the *Hesburger* hamburger kiosk, which serves excellent fast food for 20 to 30 mk.

Getting There & Away
There are one to three buses an hour from Turku to Parainen, and five to six buses a day from Helsinki.

UUSIKAUPUNKI
Uusikaupunki (population 15,000) is an idyllic seaside town to the north of Turku. It is best known for its windmills and its car factories. The name translates as 'New Town'. Incidentally, Uusikaupunki is one of the oldest towns in Finland, having been founded in 1617 by Gustavus II Adolf, the king of Sweden.

Orientation
Uusikaupunki has been built beside the sea, with its centre located on both sides of the narrow Kaupunginlahti Bay. The town

centre is on the northern side of the bay, and the market square is the centre point.

Information
The tourist information office (☎ 922-21225) at Alinenkatu 34 is open in summer from 9.30 am to 12.30 pm and 1 to 5 pm Monday to Friday, 9 am to 2 pm on Saturdays and 11 am to 3 pm on Sundays. At other times, the town hall at Levysepänkatu 4, 3rd floor, north-west of the town centre, will provide you with information. It is open from 8.30 am to 3.15 pm Monday to Friday.

Things to See
Windmill Hill Myllymäki Hill has four windmills, the sole survivors of the dozens of windmills that used to be found in Uusikaupunki. There is also a water tower, which serves as an observation tower.

Church The old church at Kirkkokatu 2 was finished in 1629. The roof was raised in the 1730s, when the current vaulted roof was also built. The church is open from 1 June to 15 August from 11 am to 3 pm Monday to Saturday and from noon to 4 pm on Sundays.

Cultural Museum of Uusikaupunki This museum at Ylinenkatu 11 is in a house built by a powerful shipowner and tobacco manufacturer. Part of the museum is furnished in the style of a wealthy 19th century home. The exhibits include a collection of textiles, coins, ceramics, glassware and weapons, as well as objects related to seafaring. The museum is open from 1 June to 15 August from 10 am to 5 pm Tuesday to Friday and from noon to 3 pm on weekends.

Pilot Museum The museum on Vallimäki Hill, behind the old church, used to be a pilot's cottage. In addition to the original furniture, the museum exhibits an old telescope and the library of another pilot station. It is open from 1 May to 31 August from noon to 3 pm. Between 1 June and 15 August, it is also open from 11 am to 3 pm Tuesday to Friday.

Saab-Valmet The Saab-Valmet car factory is the biggest employer in Uusikaupunki. It welcomes visitors on Tuesdays and Thursdays from noon to 7 pm (except in July, which is the holiday month). In the vicinity of the car factory is a car museum, which specialises in old Saabs. The Saab museum is open from noon to 6 pm on Tuesdays, Wednesdays, Saturdays and Sundays.

Pyhämaa Church In the nearby village of Pyhämaa, you can find a very special church. It looks modest outside, but the interior is richly decorated with paintings. The church is open on Sundays, after the service.

Places to Stay

For a cheap place to stay, try *Santtionranta Camping* (☎ 922-23862), or the *Pirkholma* (☎ 922-41737) for cottages. The *Hotel Lännentie* (☎ 922-12636) at Levysepänkatu 1 provides basic, inexpensive hotel accommodation in neat singles/doubles for 350/450 mk (250/320 mk in summer and on

weekends). Accommodation in the adjacent motel is slightly cheaper. Hotel guests can use the bowling alley connected to the hotel.

Places to Eat

The *Gasthaus Pooki* at Ylinenkatu 21 serves nice meals at reasonable prices. You can also sit on the pleasant terrace and have a beer or two. In the evenings, the Pooki has dancing to live music. Other places worth checking include the *Sualaspuar* at Sorvakon rantatie and the *Veijon Baari* at the bus terminal.

Getting There & Away

Bus Buses from Turku, 74 km away, run once or twice per hour on weekdays, with fewer buses on weekends. There are five to eight buses per day from Rauma. Buses from Helsinki run via Turku.

Train Probably the shortest train in Finland runs between Uusikaupunki and Turku: it usually has only one carriage. There are one to three trains a day.

Åland Islands

Åland, or 'Ahvenanmaa' in Finnish, the smallest province of Finland, has special autonomous status. The population is entirely Swedish-speaking. Åland is also the name of the main island.

This beautiful island world is perfect for bicycle tours. Regular ferries connect Åland to both Sweden and Finland, and free transport is provided by inter-island ferries, for those interested in island-hopping.

ACTIVITIES
Bicycling
Bicycling is *the* thing to do on Åland. A large proportion of all travellers move around by bicycle, and Åland is indeed ideal for bicycling: distances are short, services are good and the main routes are clearly marked with special signs. Many camping grounds and small cottages can be found around the island. You can travel from island to island on car ferries, which are free. Only the small ferries carrying cyclists and trekkers charge a fee. Some of the most popular routes are:

Mariehamn-Godby-Kastelholm-Bomarsund-Prästö-
(bicycle ferry)-Långnäs-Lemland-Mariehamn
Mariehamn-Hammarland-(Eckerö)-Skarpnåtö-
(bicycle ferry)-Hällö-Geta-Godby-Mariehamn
Galtby (in Korpo, mainland Finland)-Kökar-
Sottunga-Överö-Degerby-Svinö-Mariehamn
Mariehamn-Prästö-Töftö-Hummelvik-Enklinge-
Kumlinge-Lappo-Torsholma-Åva-Osnäs (in
Kustavi, mainland Finland)

Mariehamn

Mariehamn, the only town on Åland, is sometimes called the 'town of a thousand linden trees'. It is hectic here in summer, when Mariehamn becomes the town of a thousand tourists, but in winter the town is quiet, with a population of only 10,300. Mariehamn was founded in 1861 by Tsar Alexander II, who named the town after his

wife, Tsarina Maria. Today, Mariehamn is the administrative and economic centre of Åland. It is the seat of the *landsting* and *landskapsstyrelse*, the legislative and executive bodies of Åland. Educational and training facilities, foreign consulates, culture and commerce are also centred in Mariehamn. Besides tourism, the most important industries are shipping and trade.

Mariehamn is a charming little town, and you should take a day or two to explore it. However, be sure to visit the countryside as well – visiting only Mariehamn does not show you much of Åland.

Orientation
Mariehamn lies on a long, narrow peninsula between the busy East and West harbours (Östra Hamnen and Västra Hamnen). The two harbours are connected by a one-km 'linden avenue', Storagatan/Norra Esplanaden. Storagatan, Ålandsvägen and Torggatan are the main streets. Most tourists will arrive in Mariehamn by ferry. The main ferry terminals are at the Västra Hamnen, only a short walk from the town centre. The airport is north-west of the centre.

Information
Tourist Office The Mariehamn tourist information office (☎ 928-27300) at Storagatan 11, not far from the ferry terminals, has material about the whole of Åland. Although

the staff is very helpful, the place is so busy that you may have to wait a while for service. Many of the brochures are in Swedish only, but there is enough information in English to get by. Be sure to pick up the free maps of Mariehamn and Åland. If you intend to travel to smaller islands, get a copy of the ferry timetable, too – it is essential and can be hard to find in other places. The tourist office is open daily, from 10 am to 4 pm between September and January and from 9 am to 6 pm in June, July and August.

The 'Frida' (☎ 15050) is an automatic telephone answering machine which gives information on places and happenings of interest to travellers. Dial and listen to the English-language message.

Post & Telephone The post office at Torggatan 4, open from 10 am to 4 pm, sells Åland stamps, issued since 1984. Don't think they make a good investment; the number of each issue printed may well be one million, for a province of 20,000 people!

Foreign Consulates There are a number of foreign consulates in Mariehamn:

Denmark
    Skräddargränd 4A (☎ 928-22024)
France
    Neptunigatan 34B (☎ 928-13431)
Germany
    Storagatan 2 (☎ 928-16270)
Iceland
    Skarpansvägen 23B (☎ 928-11845)
Norway
    Norra Esplanadgatan 9 (☎ 928-26050)
Russia
    Esplanadgatan 11 (☎ 928-11524)
Sweden
    Norragatan 44 (☎ 928-11624)
The Netherlands
    Torggatan 2 (☎ 928-16200)
UK
    Södragatan 16B 4 (☎ 928-16620)

Travel Agencies The Ålandsresor (☎ 928-28040) at Storgatan 9 is a travel agency which specialises in arranging tours to Åland and in renting out summer cottages. If you intend to stay here longer and want to rent a cottage for a week, this is the place to contact.

Library The light-blue modern building at the Östra Hamnen is the Mariehamn Municipal Library. It is worth a visit because of its architectural interest and because it subscribes to a fair number of foreign newspapers. The library is open from 11 am to 8 pm Monday to Friday, and the reading room is open from 9 am.

Things to See & Do
St Göran's Church This church in central Mariehamn was designed by the architect Lars Sonck. It is open from 10 am to 3 pm Monday to Friday. Services are held at 11 am on Sundays.

Åland Museum The Åland Museum is well worth a visit. It covers the history of Åland from prehistoric times to the present, and received the 1982 Council of Europe Award for the best new museum. The exhibits are unusually lively and well presented. The museum is open from 1 May to 31 August from 10 am to 4 pm. At other times of year, it's open from 11 am to 4 pm daily (except Mondays). Admission is 7 mk for adults, 4 mk for children. The same ticket is valid for the Åland Art Museum.

Åland Art Museum Located in the same building as the Åland Museum, the Art Museum has a permanent collection of art from Åland, as well as temporary exhibitions. Opening hours and ticket prices are the same as those of the Åland Museum.

Åland Maritime Museum This museum (☎ 928-19930) on Hamngatan is considered to have one of the best presentations of sailing ships in the world. The museum is open from 10 am to 4 pm daily, all year round. It stays open until 5 pm in June and August, and until 7 pm in July. Admission is 13 mk for adults, 7 mk for children.

Pommern The museum ship *Pommern* (☎ 928-531 421), behind the Maritime

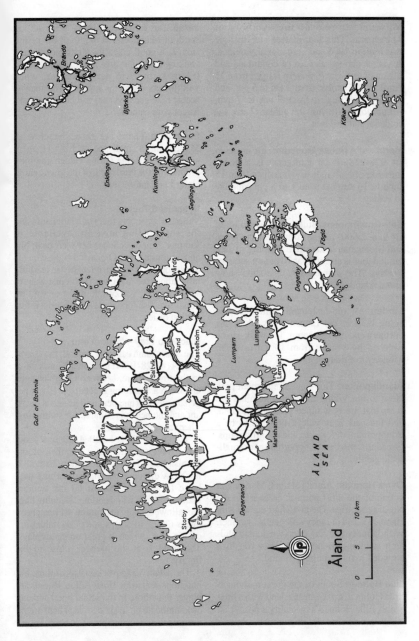

Museum, is one of the symbols of Mariehamn. This four-masted steel barque was built in 1903 and is supposedly unique. A visitor can get an idea of conditions and life on board. The *Pommern* is open from 15 April to 20 October from 9 am to 5 pm, and in July and August from 9 am to 7 pm. Admission is 13 mk for adults, 7 mk for students and children.

Merchant's House Museum This museum (☎ 928-23866) on Parkgatan is a house museum of craft industry. It is open from 15 June to 15 August from 1 to 3 pm Monday to Friday.

Self-Government Building This building (☎ 928-25000) on the corner of Österleden and Storagatan is an office building. A free guided tour is arranged at 10 pm on summer Fridays. The tour ends with a slide show about Åland.

Linden An old-fashioned sailing ship is being built at the Linden shipyard, at the northern end of Österhamn. The work can be watched by visitors from 10 am to 4 pm Monday to Friday.

Ålandsparken This small amusement park close to the Viking Line ferry terminal has rides that are best suited to small children, and the park may indeed turn out to be a disappointment for older kids or grown-ups. For adults, there is the opportunity for small-scale gambling.

Östra Hamnen Among sailors, Mariehamn is one of the most popular harbours in the Nordic countries. The guest harbour in Östra Hamnen is full of fancy sailboats all summer. With laundry hanging everywhere and children running around, it reminds you of a crowded luxury camping ground.

Lilla Holmen South of the guest harbour is Lilla Holmen, a park on an island with a little beach. Lilla Holmen's speciality is peacocks, which can be seen walking around.

Järsö The Järsö recreational area, 12 km south of Mariehamn at the tip of the peninsula, is a good place for short bicycle and walking tours. The area is at its most beautiful in spring and early summer, when wildflowers cover the ground. The narrow scenic road goes over several bridges. Don't forget your camera.

Swimming There are three beaches in Mariehamn: a small one on Lilla Holmen, another next to the Gröna Udden camping ground and the third north of the town centre, along Lemlandsvägen.

Organised Tours
Various sightseeing tours of Mariehamn and the surrounding area are available in summer. You can choose between boat, bus and minitrain tours. Organised sightseeing is a good option if you are interested in learning more about the town, but if you just want to see the sights, you can do it just as well on your own. Ask for details at the tourist information office.

Places to Stay – bottom end
The Mariehamn camping ground, the *Gröna Udden* (☎ 928-19041), is conveniently close to the town centre, between Österäsvägen and the sea. Camping is cheap, at 10 mk per person, per tent and per car. The site is pleasant and the beach is suitable for swimming. There are no cottages.

The 'botel' (boat hotel) *Alida* is a youth hostel but is no longer a member of the Finnish Youth Hostel Association, so there is no YHA discount. Rooms are cabins with basic facilities. Beds cost 60 mk without bedding, 90 mk with bedding. Sleeping bags are allowed. The restaurant serves cheap meals (30 to 40 mk); some of the tables are on the deck, which is great on sunny days. The botel is at the harbour, close to the library.

The *Adlon Sleepover* consists of three old buildings next to the Hotel Adlon. Rooms are bigger than those in the actual hotel and can accommodate up to six people. There are no dormitories, so you pay for each room.

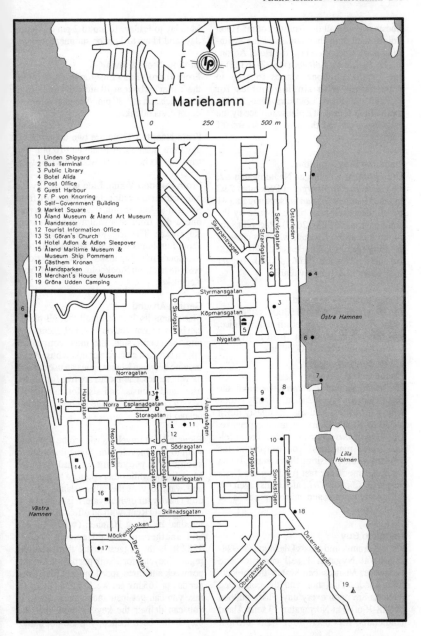

Mariehamn

0   250   500 m

1 Linden Shipyard
2 Bus Terminal
3 Public Library
4 Botel Alida
5 Post Office
6 Guest Harbour
7 F P von Knorring
8 Self–Government Building
9 Market Square
10 Åland Museum & Åland Art Museum
11 Ålandsresor
12 Tourist Information Office
13 St Göran's Church
14 Hotel Adlon & Adlon Sleepover
15 Åland Maritime Museum &
   Museum Ship Pommern
16 Gästhem Kronan
17 Ålandsparken
18 Merchant's House Museum
19 Gröna Udden Camping

Österleden
Servicegatan
Strandgatan
Skarpansvägen
Styrmansgatan
Köpmansgatan
Nygatan
O Skogatan
Norragatan
Havsgatan
Norra Esplanadgatan
Storagatan
Neptungatan
Södragatan
V Esplanadgatan
Mariegatan
Skillnadsgatan
Ålandsvägen
Torggatan
Sonckslägen
Parkgatan
Möckelöbrinken
Berggatan
Östergvägen
Österhåsvägen

Östra Hamnen
Västra Hamnen
Lilla Holmen

Guests may use all the facilities of the Hotel Adlon, including the sauna and the swimming pool. Reception is at the Hotel Adlon.

The *Pensionat Solhem* (☎ 928-16322) is one of the cheaper places to stay in Mariehamn, with singles/doubles for 135/240 mk. It is on Lökskärsvägen, 2.5 km south of the centre, at a pleasant place by the sea. Guests can use the rowing boats free of charge.

Places to Stay – middle

The *Gästhem Kronan* at Neptunigatan 52, the *Gästhem Kvarnberget* at Parkgatan 28C and the *Gästhem Neptun* at Neptunigatan 41 are all nice, well-kept places owned by the same person (☎ 928-12617). Reception for all three is at the Kronan, which is close to the ferry terminal. Singles cost 180 to 200 mk and doubles are 265 to 300 mk. Bigger family rooms are also available.

Places to Stay – top end

The *Hotel Adlon* (☎ 928-15300) is right next to the Viking Line ferry terminal. It is a nice, ordinary place with hotel prices. Singles/doubles cost 440/550 mk.

Places to Eat

The boat restaurant *F P von Knorring* in the Östra Hamnen is a pleasant, slightly exotic setting for meals. You can get a tasty lunch for 30 to 40 mk. Dinner is more expensive. The *Ålands Museum cafeteria* serves excellent Åland pancakes. You can eat at the cafeteria without visiting the museum. If you are in the mood for fast food, try the *Dixie Burger & Chicken Grill* at Ålandsvägen 40. It has tasty burgers and chicken portions for 20 to 30 mk.

Things to Buy

Jussis Keramik and Jussis Glashytta (☎ 928-13606) at Nygatan 1 sell ceramics and glassware. Visitors can watch the objects being made. The shop and the connected cafeteria are open every day. Fäktargubben (☎ 928-19603) at Norragatan 13 sells Åland handicrafts. It is open from 9 am to 5 pm

Monday to Friday, 10 am to 2 pm on Saturdays and 11 am to 2 pm on summer Sundays.

Getting There & Away

From Turku Viking Line ferries depart from the Turku harbour at 10 am daily and arrive in Mariehamn at 3.20 pm. A regular one-way ticket costs 60 mk.

From Naantali There are two departures a day from Naantali, at 10 am and 10 pm. The trip takes six hours and costs 45 mk one-way.

From Sweden Viking Line is currently the only carrier operating ferry transport from Sweden to Mariehamn. There is one departure a day from Stockholm and two from Kapellskär. The trip to Mariehamn takes about four hours from Stockholm and about two hours from Kapellskär. A one-way ticket costs 48 mk from Stockholm and 27 mk from Kapellskär.

Getting Around

Mariehamn itself is so small that all places can be easily reached on foot. For excursions into the countryside, the most convenient option is to rent a bicycle or take a bus. When moving between islands, you can use car and bicycle ferries. Car ferries are free for pedestrians and cyclists, and also for cars, under certain conditions (see the section on archipelago traffic).

Bicycle Most travellers who come to Åland want to do a bicycle tour. Some just want to spend a day cycling in and around Mariehamn, while others prefer a longer tour and want to visit the outer islands. If you don't have your own bicycle, it is easy to hire one. RO-NO Rent, with an office at the ferry terminal in Västra Hamnen (☎ 928-12821) and another in Östra Hamnen (☎ 928-12820), is the biggest rental firm. It rents regular bicycles for 25 mk per day or 125 mk per week and three-speed models for 33 mk per day or 165 mk per week. For an extra 10 mk, you can get insurance against theft: if you can deliver the key to show that the bicycle has been locked, you are not liable.

RO-NO Rent is open from 1 June to 31 August from 9 am to noon and 1 to 7 pm. At other times, arrangements can be made by phone. RO-NO Rent also rents boating and windsurfing equipment.

Around Åland

ECKERÖ

Eckerö (population 800) is the westernmost municipality in Finland, just a two-hour ferry ride from mainland Sweden. As the name indicates, it is on an island *(ö* in Swedish). Eckerö has long been popular among tourists, having been a well-known holiday spot in the 1800s. Today most of the tourists come from Sweden, partly because of the chance for tax-free shopping on the ferry. The distance from Mariehamn to Eckerö (40 km) makes this a suitable day trip by bicycle. Eckerö has two main centres: the area around the church and Storby (the centre for tourist activities, near the ferry terminals). Storby has some beautiful 19th century wooden buildings.

Things to See & Do

Post & Customs House The number one sight in Eckerö is the old post and customs office, near the harbour. It was completed in 1828, during the era of Tsar Alexander I of Russia. The building was designed by the famous architect Engel, who also designed parts of the centre of Helsinki. The building was meant to be an outpost against the West and, for that reason, is far more grandiose than a post office in a small village should be. Today the building is used as a holiday centre for employees of Posti Tele (the Finnish post and telecommunications company).

Postrota Museum In the post and customs office area, there is the Postrota Museum. The communication link across the Baltic has passed through Åland since Viking times. In 1638, the farmers of Eckerö were divided into 'rotas', groups of eight men,

which were responsible for maintaining mail services between Eckerö and mainland Sweden. Mail was transported in rowboats and iceboats until 1910, and the voyages were dangerous. Over the 350 years that the post rota system operated, more than 200 men lost their lives. This museum exhibits objects used in the post rota service, including a mail boat. A video film on the mail services and a slide show about the geography and history of Eckerö are also available. The museum is open daily (except Mondays) from 1 June to 15 August from 1 to 4 pm. Admission is 5 mk.

St Lars Church The church of Eckerö, some five km west of the harbour, dates from the 13th century. The church is small and beautifully decorated. One of the most interesting objects is a 14th century madonna sculpture. The church is open from 10 am to 8 pm Monday to Friday, 10 am to 6 pm on Saturdays and noon to 6 pm on Sundays. Services are held at 11 am on Sundays.

Local Museum The local open-air museum, called Labbas, is a group of old archipelago buildings in the middle of Storby. It is open from 1 June to 15 August from 4 to 5.30 pm daily (except Mondays).

Peters Krukmakeri This shop in Storby sells pottery and is open from 9 am to 4 pm Monday to Friday.

Swimming Eckerö has by far the best beach in Åland. Degersand, approximately nine km south of Storby, has long sand dunes and is certainly worth the extra bicycle trip.

Festivals

Every other year, on the second Saturday in June, a Post Boat Festival is held. Old-fashioned boats are rowed to Eckerö from Grisslehamn in Sweden.

Places to Stay

Notviken Camping (☎ 928-38429), two km south of the church village, charges 9 mk per person, per tent and per car. Two-bed cottages cost 140 mk and four-bed ones are 200 to 330 mk. The camping ground also rents boats and fishing equipment. The other camping ground in the area, *Kärinsund Camping* in Kärinsundby, has nice four-bed cottages for 150 mk.

Places to Eat

The *Café Lugn & Ro* at Post & Customs House serves sandwiches and hamburgers in historic surroundings. The restaurant *Käringsund* at Käringsundsby offers lunch for 50 mk per person.

Getting There & Away

From Mariehamn Road No 2 runs from Mariehamn to Eckerö. If you use public transport, take bus No 1. The trip takes 40 minutes and costs 21 mk.

From Sweden Eckerö Lines has five connections a day from Grisslehamn during the high season and three during the low season. Most of the tours have a bus connection to/from Stockholm and Mariehamn. The boat trip takes two hours, and a trip from Stockholm to Mariehamn takes five hours altogether. Tickets are ridiculously cheap: a regular one-way ticket costs 20 mk from Grisslehamn and 26 mk from Stockholm. Return tickets are even cheaper. Ordinary passenger cars are transported free of charge.

FINSTRÖM

Finström (population 2180) is the most centrally located municipality in Åland and home of the second-biggest centre on the island: Godby. Godby has schools and a big, well-stocked shopping centre. Attraction-wise, Finström has few interesting things to offer, but most visitors will travel through it anyway, on the way to other parts of the island.

Things to See & Do

Finström's beautiful church, St Mikael's, is in a valley some five km north-east of Godby. Untypically, there is no village around it. The exact age of the building is not known – estimates vary from 550 to 850

years. Inside the church are a lot of wooden sculptures from the Middle Ages. The church is open from 10 am to 4 pm Monday to Friday. Services are held at 11 am on Sundays.

Svartsmara This village approximately three km south of St Mikael's Church is considered to be one of the best-preserved old villages in Åland.

Walking The Café Uffe på Berget, just before the bridge to Sund, is a good lookout spot. The view from the bridge is great as well. In the immediate vicinity there is the Godby Arboretum, which has both domestic and foreign trees. A walk along the marked trail takes half an hour.

Places to Stay & Eat

The *Godby Kongresshotelli* (☎ 928-41170), an old hospital turned into a hotel, is pleasantly located near the arboretum. Singles cost 200 to 320 mk and doubles are 300 to 420 mk. The place is popular with groups, so phone to check that there are vacant rooms.

The *Grillsnäckan servering*, on the opposite side of the road from the shopping centre in Godby, serves tasty hamburgers and other fast food. You should be able to get a fast-food meal for under 30 mk. The *Café Uffe på Berget* is a popular place, due to its magnificent view over the island. Turn off the main road just before the bridge to Sund.

Getting There & Away

Road No 2 from Mariehamn takes you to Godby. Bus Nos 2, 3 and 4 from Mariehamn all go via Godby. The trip takes 25 minutes and costs 12 mk. To get to other parts of Finström, use bus No 6.

GETA

The municipality of Geta (population 460) boasts the high 'mountain', Mt Geta.

Things to See & Do

St Görans Church The church of Geta was probably built in the 1460s. A cemetery from the pre-Christian era can be found about one km south of the church. The church is open from 10 am to 6 pm, and services are held at 10 am on Sundays.

Mt Geta The Getabergen is Geta's main attraction. The highest peak is 98 metres above sea level – not much, but enough to give a good view. At the top you can follow the two-km path to the caves of Getabergen. The path is marked by white arrows. The caves are not much to see, but visiting them is a good excuse for a nice walk.

Dånö Museum This open-air museum at the end of the road to Dånö is a quiet little place, with well-preserved old buildings. The museum is in an old house that used to belong to a sailor.

Places to Stay & Eat

The *Granqvist Allservice* has a group of cottages on the opposite side of the road from the Geta church. Clean two/four-bed cottages are 160/210 mk. The *Soltuna stugor*, at the top of the Getabergen, is a pleasant, well-located group of cottages. Accommodation costs 170/220 mk in two/four-bed cottages. This is a popular place among cyclists. Breakfast is available at the nearby restaurant for 25 mk.

The restaurant/café at top of the Getabergen serves breakfast, lunch and dinner. Lunch starts at 30 mk, and hamburgers cost 15 to 25 mk. The restaurant side is supposed to have very good chefs. The kiosk at the Granqvist Allservice, opposite the church, sells hamburgers and sausages for 10 to 20 mk.

Getting There & Away

Road Nos 2 and 4 from Mariehamn via Godby take you to Geta. A daily bicycle ferry connects Hällö in Geta to Skarpnåtö in Hammarland (see the Hammarland section for the schedule). To get to Geta from Mariehamn, take bus No 2. The trip to the last stop in Hällö takes 50 minutes and costs 27 mk.

HAMMARLAND

The western parts of mainland Åland form Hammarland (population 1200). To the west is the island of Eckerö and to the east is Jomala. From Skarpnotö in the north of Hammarland, you can take a bicycle ferry over to Geta.

Things to See & Do

Sta Catharina Church This attractive church in the village of Kattby was probably built in the 12th century. Unfortunately, few old objects have been preserved – one of the exceptions is a baptismal bowl from the 1250s. The church is open daily from 15 May to 31 August from 9 am to 4 pm.

Mörby At Mörby, some 1.5 km north off road No 1 to Eckerö, there is a wool spinnery called Ålands Ullprodukter. It sells home-spun yarn and woollen garments. The shop is open from 15 June to 15 August from noon to 3 pm Monday to Saturday.

Lillbostad In this village, four km to the north along the road to Skarpnåtö, there is a ceramics shop, Lugnet Keramik. All products are handmade. The shop is open from 11 am to 6 pm Monday to Thursday and from 11 am to 3 pm on Saturdays.

Bovik To the west of the Mörby to Skarpnåtö road is this lively village harbour of some 30 buildings. Bovik is also suitable for swimming.

Skarpnåtö All activities in Skarpnåtö centre around the Södergård estate (☎ 928-37212/27). The old main building has been converted into a museum, and one of the other buildings is used as a handicrafts shop. The environment is so well preserved that it was chosen as the setting for the TV series *Myrskyluodon Maija*, which depicts life in the archipelago in the 1800s. The handicrafts shop is open from 11 am to 3 pm Tuesday to Saturday and from noon to 3 pm on Sundays. The museum has no regular opening hours, but the collection will be shown by the personnel, on request. The museum fee is 4 mk. The owners of the estate also run the bicycle ferry and have some cottages and boats to rent. For fishing, hire a rowboat for 50 mk per day or 30 mk an evening. If you have time, stay a while – they are nice people.

Places to Stay
In Kattnäs, two km south of road No 1, there is a pleasant camping ground by the sea. Camping is cheap, at 6 mk per person, per tent and per car. The camping ground also has cottages. At Skarpnåtö you can rent a two/four-bed cottage for 180/230 mk. If you use the bicycle ferry, you can camp in the area free of charge.

Getting There & Away
Bus Bus No 1 from Mariehamn to Eckerö runs through Hammarland. A single ticket costs 12 to 20 mk.

Ferry In June, July and August, bicycle ferries (☎ 928-37212) run regularly between Skarpnåtö and Hällö in Geta, leaving at noon and 4.30 pm from Skarpnåtö and at 12.30 and 5 pm from Hällö. The trip takes 25 minutes and costs 25 mk one-way. No advance booking is necessary for the scheduled tours. If you want to travel at another time, phone the ferry operators and make arrangements.

JOMALA
Jomala, a municipality of 3000 inhabitants, lies to the north of and around Mariehamn. After Mariehamn, it is Åland's biggest municipality. Jomala has two centres: the village of Jomala, near the church, and Gottby, a typical Åland village. All places in Jomala are within a short day trip of Mariehamn.

Things to See & Do
St Olof's Church The church of Jomala is the oldest in Åland, and parts of it were built in the 12th century. A sculpture in the shape of a lion's head probably dates from 1175 to 1200. At the time of writing, the church was closed for repair.

Ramsholmen The nature conservation area of Ramsholmen, approximately five km east

of Mariehamn, is only 12 hectares in size but has a rich and varied vegetation. Follow the path around the area and have lunch at one of the picnic tables. Ramsholmen is at its best in spring, when the wood anemones blossom.

Lemström Canal The Lemström canal is located five km west of Mariehamn along road No 3. It was built at the end of the 19th century by prisoners of war. The canal is still in use, although today, the main user group is holiday-makers, not traders or warships. On a beautiful summer day, the bridge may be opened as many as 40 times.

Önningeby On the southern side of the canal, in Önningeby, the well-known painter Victor Westerholm had his summer house. A group of other painters followed him there, and for two decades around the turn of the century, the area was known as the 'Önningeby colony' of painters.

Getting There & Away
From Mariehamn, you can catch bus No 3 to Jomala church, bus No 5 to Önningeby and bus No 1 to Gottby. A one-way ticket to these places costs 8 to 9 mk.

LEMLAND
Lemland is located between Lumparland and the Lemström canal, and despite the fact that it is surrounded by water, it is considered part of mainland Åland.

Things to See
Lembóte Here, on the southern side of road No 3, just past the canal, there is an old chapel in the middle of the woods. The chapel is not open to the public, but the peaceful place is worth a visit.

Sta Birgitta Church The church of Lemland, along the main road, is another 12th century church. It is open from noon to 4 pm Monday to Friday.

Herrön This place at the southernmost tip of

Lemland is a popular picnic spot. There is a small observation tower for sighting birds.

Getting There & Away
To get to Lemland from Mariehamn, take bus No 5. Tickets cost 10 to 15 mk, depending on the distance travelled.

LUMPARLAND
The municipality of Lumparland in south-east Åland does not have many sights of note. Despite that, many travellers pass through Lumparland, as it is on several popular bicycle routes.

Things to See & Do
St Andreas Church Built in 1720, St Andreas Church is one of the newer churches of Åland. This little wooden church, in a beautiful spot at the seaside, is open from noon to 4 pm.

Bicycle Tours Bicycle routes to Sund, Föglö and Kumlinge all pass through Lumparland.

Places to Stay
The cottages at Långnäsby (π 928-35557), next to the ferry terminal, are a convenient place to stay overnight. Two/four-bed cottages cost 170/220 mk. Another possibility is the cottages in Svinö, in the southern part of Lumparland. The site is just off the main road. Two-bed cottages are reasonably priced at 120 mk and four-bed cottages cost 200 mk.

Getting There & Away
From Mariehamn Take bus No 5. The trip to Långnäs takes 45 minutes. The bus goes via Svinö, with a connection to the ferry to Föglö, and tickets cost 15 to 19 mk.

From Sund There is a daily bicycle ferry service between Prästö in Sund and Långnäs in Lumparland. The trip takes 40 minutes and costs 40 mk.

From Kumlinge There are one to three ferries a day from Snäckö in Kumlinge to Långnäs in Lumparland. Some of the ferries

also call at Överö in Föglö. The trip from Kumlinge takes two hours.

From Föglö Two ferry lines travel to Föglö, one from Svinö to Degerby and the other from Långnäs to Överö. Departures on the first route are much more frequent – 13 a day in each direction. On the latter route, ferries depart only once or twice a day. If you want to go to/from Överö, you have to order the ferry (π 949- 229 263). The Svinö to Degerby trip takes half an hour and the Långnäs to Överö trip takes an hour.

SALTVIK
The municipality of Saltvik, in the north-east corner of Åland, is known for the highest 'mountain' in Åland, which also offers free accommodation for visitors.

Things to See & Do
Sta Maria Church This church, located in Kvarnbo, is probably over 800 years old. Some of the objects in the church date from the 13th century. Services are held at 11 am on Sundays.

Borgboda Castle The ruins of the ancient castle of Borgboda can be found 600 metres south of the road from Kvarnbo to Björby. The bicycle road passes close to the ruins. Built at the end of the Iron Age (400-1000 AD), Borgboda was the biggest castle in Åland during the Viking era. Some ruins of the stone parts can be seen today, but all wooden parts decayed long ago.

Orrdahlsklint This is the highest mountain in Åland, a full 128 metres above sea level! The view is magnificent. To find your way, take the road from Kvarnbo towards Långbergsöda and then follow the signs to Orrdahl or Orrdahlsklint. Take the stairs all the way up. On the mountain is a wilderness hut with four beds, which anyone can use for free. There is no tap and no well, so bring your own drinking water.

Places to Stay
The cottage at the top of the Orrdahlsklint is

definitely the cheapest and most scenic place to stay. This experience is strongly recommended!

Getting There & Away

Bus No 3 runs to Saltvik from Mariehamn. The journey costs 19 mk.

SUND

Sund, at the eastern end of mainland Åland, is one of the most interesting municipalities for travellers. The three places not to be missed are in Sund: Kastelholm Castle, the ruins of the Bomarsund Fortress and the Jan Karlsgården Museum. Sund is 30 km from Mariehamn, which makes it an ideal first overnight stop on a slow-pace bicycle tour.

Things to See

Kastelholm Castle This impressive castle, 23 km from Mariehamn along road No 2, is one of the most interesting places in Åland. Its exact age is not known, but it was mentioned in writings as early as 1388. Parts of the castle have since been rebuilt. Kastelholm was of strategic importance during the 16th and 17th centuries, and members of the Swedish royal family governed it at that time. In 1634, the legal position of Åland was changed, and the importance of the castle declined. The castle has been under renovation since 1980, but many think that, because of lack of funds, the work will never be finished. It is not possible to visit the castle on your own, but there are several guided tours a day in summer. Tours cost 6 to 10 mk per person, and tickets are sold at the gate to the Jan Karlsgården Museum.

Vita Björn Jail Museum In the castle area, close to the entrance to the Jan Karlsgården Museum, there is a jail museum called Vita Björn. This little museum is certainly worth a visit. The building was used as a jail from 1784 to 1974, and the exhibition shows how jails have changed over time. The museum is open from 1 May to 30 September from 10 am to 5 pm daily. Entry is free.

Jan Karlsgården Museum This magnificent open-air museum is in the immediate vicinity of Kastelholm Castle, on the other side of a little hill. The area consists of traditional buildings from the archipelago. In summer there is often some event going on in the museum area. The museum is open daily from 1 May to 30 September from 9 am to 9 pm, and entry is free.

Bomarsund Fortress The ruins of Bomarsund Fortress are a memorial to the time when Åland, together with the rest of Finland, was under Russian rule. Åland was of strategic importance to the Russians, and after the war of 1809, Russian troops were sent to Åland. The Russians started to build Bomarsund, a strong fortress against the Swedes. Later, during the Napoleonic Wars, Russia allied with England and Sweden against France, and building of the fortress was discontinued until 1829. The fortress was designed for 5000 men and 500 cannons. The main fortress, finished in 1842, was big enough to house 2500 men. Before the fortress was finished, however, it was destroyed by the French and the English during the Crimean War. Bomarsund survived the bombing, but after the Russians surrendered, the fortress was blown up. The fortress was never rebuilt, and the remaining stones were used to build houses. The ruins of Bomarsund can be seen on both sides of road No 2, between Kastelholm and Prästö. The most impressive area is just before the bridge to Prästö. On the Prästö side of the bridge, in a little white house, there is a museum devoted to the history of Bomarsund. It is open from 1 May to 31 August from 10 am to 3 pm Tuesday to Sunday.

Prästö Graveyards There are six old graveyards on the island of Prästö. If you turn right after the Prästö Turistservice, you can find an old Greek Orthodox graveyard. Further out in the woods are Jewish and Muslim graveyards, side by side.

Djävulsberget This hill to the north of the

road, half a km before the Bomarsund bridge, is an excellent lookout and picnic spot. The hilltop can be reached by passenger car.

St Johannes Church The church of Sund is the biggest church on Åland. It is 800 years old and has beautiful paintings. Note the stone cross with the text 'Wenni E'. According to researchers, it was erected in memory of the Hamburg bishop Wenni, who died on a crusade in 936 AD.

Golf Åland's only golf course is in Sund, across the bay from Kastelholm Castle. It is considered one of the best courses in the Nordic countries. Regular golf rules are followed, so you have to have a green card to be allowed to play.

Places to Stay
Puttes Camping (☎ 928-44036), right next to the Bomarsund area, is the more pleasant of Sund's two camping grounds. The *Prästö turistservice* on the tiny island of Prästö has a camping ground and cottages. Two/four-bed cottages cost 170/220 mk. The *Kastelholma Gästhem* (☎ 928-43841), a guesthouse, gives good value for money. It has a main building and an old henhouse, which has been converted into hotel rooms. If there is room in the main building, stay there – the rooms are excellent. At 105/180 mk for singles/doubles, the price is right. Even bigger rooms are available. For an extra 25 mk, you can have a good breakfast brought to your room.

Places to Eat
The restaurant at the Jan Karlsgården Museum serves both light snacks and real meals. The cafeteria side is cheaper than the actual restaurant.

Getting There & Away
Road No 2 from Mariehamn takes you to Sund. A bicycle ferry from Prästö to Långnäs in Lumparland departs at noon every day from 1 June to 15 August. The trip takes 40 minutes and costs 40 mk. To get to Sund from

Mariehamn, take bus No 4. It goes via Kastelholm, Svensböle and Prästö. Tickets cost 15 to 21 mk, depending on the distance.

VÅRDÖ
The island of Vårdö (population 380), just off the main island, has several attractions. The island roads offer plenty of scenic value for visitors, and there are also a few good swimming places. The old mail route from Sweden to Finland passed through Vårdö, and some of the old 'milestones' have been put up again.

Things to See & Do
St Mathias Church The church of Vårdö dates from the 15th century. The priest's house is made of stones taken from the ruins of Bomarsund Castle. The church is open from 10 am to 6 pm, and services are held at 11 am on Sundays.

Lövö The village of Lövö was once the setting for a peace conference between Carl XII of Sweden and Tsar Peter of Russia. The conference was opened on 20 May 1718. Fine buildings were erected for the occasion but were torn down the following year. Few monuments remain in the village today.

Simskäla The tiny island of Simskäla is known as the home of Anni Blomqvist, author of *Myrskyluodon Maija*. She died in 1990, and her home is now open once a week to visitors. The tourist information office will provide you with further details.

Canoeing The archipelago offers an excellent setting for canoeing. The owner of Sandösund Camping will give advice on good routes and places to stay. He also rents canoes and cayaks for 90 to 125 mk per day or 60 to 90 mk for five hours, and rowing boats for 60 mk per day or 25 mk for two hours.

Places to Stay
Sandösunds Camping has a beautiful seaside location, a large camping ground and pleasant cottages. Camping costs 9 mk per person,

per tent and per car, and two/four-bed cottages are 165/215 mk. This place is highly recommended.

Getting There & Away
From Mariehamn Take bus No 4 via Sund. The trip, including a ferry ride from Sund, takes one hour and costs 27 mk.

From Sund There is a ferry between Prästö in Sund and Töftö in Vårdö. It has no schedule, making the short trip whenever needed (except for two half-hour breaks, at 11.30 am and 7 pm).

From Sandö to Simskäla There are 14 ferries a day each way. Some of the trips are made only on request, if someone has phoned the ferry reservation centre (☎ 928-25155, 928-47520). The trip takes 15 minutes.

From Kumlinge & Enklinge There are three ferries a day to/from Kumlinge and Enklinge to Hummelvik, Vårdö. The trip from Enklinge takes an hour, and the trip from Kumlinge 1½ hours.

Other Islands

BRÄNDÖ
The municipality of Brändö (population 530) consists of a group of 1180 islands, the most important of which are connected by bridges. Of the villages in the area, Lappo, Asterholma and Jurmo can be reached only by ferry. The special shape of the main island makes it an interesting bicycling region – no matter where you go, you will always ride by the sea.

Things to See
Ahvenanmaan Elävän Ravinnon Instituutti This institute (☎ 928-56285) on the island of Fiskö teaches people how to prepare uncooked vegetarian food. You can take courses there or just visit for lunch, but only if you make arrangements beforehand.

St Jakobs Church This wooden church in Brändö was built in 1893. It's open every day, and services are held at 11 am on Sundays.

Getting There & Away
From Lappo, Kumlinge, Enklinge & Vårdö There are three connections a day from Vårdö to Torsholma in southern Brändö. The trip all the way from Vårdö takes three hours.

From Mainland Finland There are five connections a day from Osnäs in Kustavi to Åva in the northern part of Brändö all year round, and a few more in summer time. The trip takes half an hour.

FÖGLÖ
The name Föglö denotes a place with a lot of birds. The island was first mentioned in 1241 by a Danish bishop when he wrote about his trip to Tallinn. An inn was founded in 1745 at Föglö, on the Enigheten estate. The local population lived from fishing and farming, and were subject to the taxes and demands of two governments, Swedish and Russian.

The population now numbers 600. Föglö is a barren but beautiful island. It is a popular holiday spot, so the population triples in summer, when the tourists and cottage owners arrive. A popular biking route goes from Överö to Degerby. At both ends of the route, there is a ferry service to mainland Åland, and from Överö you can continue to the island of Kumlinge.

Things to See
Degerby The village of Degerby, which is the 'capital' of Föglö, has many interesting old buildings. Most of the inhabitants have traditionally been civil servants, not farmers, so the houses stand close to each other. Some of them have been built in Jugend or Empire styles instead of the traditional archipelago style. In the red building right at the harbour, you will find the local museum. It is open daily (except Mondays) in June, July and August from noon to 2.30 pm and 3.30 to 7

pm. Admission is 5 mk; children under 12 are admitted free.

Sta Maria Magdalena Church The church of Föglö was probably built in the 14th century. The little bells date from the 16th century. The church is open from 15 June to 15 August from noon to 3 pm Monday to Friday. Services are held at 10 am on Sundays.

Enigheten This old farmhouse and inn is the only place to stay on Föglö and is also one of the most interesting places to visit. The buildings, and especially the interior decorations, are worth seeing. The old buildings were restored in 1984 to 1985, and since then, the Enigheten Inn has been run by a local cooperative. The oldest surviving parts of the buildings are from the 18th century. In 1822, the last death sentence on Ahvenanmaa, for murdering an unwanted child, was read in the main building. Note the pictures on the living-room walls; they are of King Fredrik I of Sweden, his wife Ulrika Eleonora and a high-ranking civil servant.

Places to Stay
The *Enigheten Inn* (☎ 928-50310) in Degerby is the only place in Föglö to stay overnight. It is a very romantic place, and even Mauno Koivisto, the president of Finland, has stayed at the Enigheten. The buildings are old and have been kept as they have always been, so there are no toilets or showers in the rooms. The modern facilities are in another building, a few metres from the sleeping quarters. Most of the guests come from the Nordic countries, and the innkeeper does not understand much English. Try your basic Swedish or Finnish instead. The inn is open in summer. Single rooms cost 90 to 140 mk, doubles are 180 to 220 mk and booking beforehand is essential. The good breakfast costs 20 mk. To get to Enigheten, turn left after the Degerby ferry terminal and walk one km. You can pitch your tent in the back yard of the Enigheten, if you ask; check beforehand.

Getting There & Away
From Lumparland Thirteen ferries a day make the one-hour trip between Svinö and Degerby. They can be very crowded during the high season. From Långnäs, there are one or two ferries a day, which continue on to Kumlinge. They stop at Överö only on request (☎ 949-229 263); call from any normal telephone or from a special phone at the harbour.

From Kumlinge One or two ferries a day from Kumlinge stop at Överö, on request, and then continue on to Långnäs.

KUMLINGE
The municipality of Kumlinge (population 470) has four main islands: Kumlinge, Enklinge, Seglinge and Björkö.

Things to See
Seglinge The main attraction of this charming little island is its moor-like natural beauty. Be sure to take the two-km walking route to see the 'devil's churns'. In themselves, they are not all that special, but the walk across the empty island is magnificent. There are some picnic tables on the way and at the end.

Sta Anna Church This church in Kumlinge, some two km north of the actual village, looks like any other church from the outside, but the interior is covered with 500-year-old, Franciscan-type paintings.

Hermas Open-Air Museum Unlike many other open-air museums, this old estate in Enklinge (☎ 928- 55334) is not a collection of buildings from various places. Rather, it is a small farm that has been opened as a small museum. It has no regular opening hours, but if you would like to see it, phone ahead to get someone to open the doors.

Places to Stay & Eat
Kumlinge has a few places to stay, but none is especially attractive. *Kumlinge Camping*, near the Snäckö harbour, is a rather badly kept place. Camping costs 10 mk per person,

per tent and per car. The *Värdshuset Remmaren* is the only pensionat in Kumlinge. The décor is old-fashioned in an unpleasant way and the place is often fully booked by groups. Singles/doubles are 300/395 mk, which is a lot of money for the quality you get. The Remmaren has the only restaurant on the island. The dinner buffet costs 55 mk and, as Remmaren does not serve meals à la carte, is the only alternative.

The best thing to do, if you need to stay overnight in the area, is to take the ferry over to Seglinge. The *Remmarina stugor* cottages, approximately four km north of the ferry terminal, are the only cottages in Kumlinge. They are spacious but, at 215/280 mk for two/four-bed cottages, rather expensive.

Getting There & Away
From Enklinge The ferries between Hummelvik and Torsholma are the only connection between Kumlinge and Enklinge.

From Seglinge Ferries go from Snäckö in Kumlinge to Seglinge, without a schedule, whenever needed. The daily breaks are 11 to 11.30 am and 6.30 to 7 pm.

From Lumparland One or two ferries a day go from Långnäs in Lumparland to Snäckö in Kumlinge, via Överö on the island of Föglö. The trip takes two hours.

From Vårdö, Lappo & Torsholma Three ferries a day go from Hummelvik in Vårdö to Enklinge and the northern end of Kumlinge. They then continue on to Lappo and Torsholma. The trip to Enklinge takes an hour, and to Kumlinge 1½ hours.

From Sottunga There are ferry connections on Fridays, Saturdays and Sundays.

KÖKAR
This small island has a population of 280 people.

Things to See
Sta Anna Church The church of Kökar was built on the ruins of a Franciscan monastery. Building began in the 14th century and finished in 1784. Beside the church is the chapel of St Franciskus. The church is open from 9 am to 9 pm; the chapel is always open. Services are held in the church at 11 am on Sundays, and from 25 June to 13 August, there is also an evening prayer session in the chapel on Tuesdays and Thursdays.

Kökar Museum This museum is in an old school building in Hellsö. Its exhibitions relate to local history. The museum in open from mid-June to mid-August from 1 to 5 pm daily.

Places to Stay
The *Antons Gästhem* near the harbour is open from 1 June to 15 August. It has singles/doubles without facilities for 130/220 mk. Breakfast costs 25 mk extra.

Getting There & Away
From Mainland Finland There are one or two connections a day from Galtby in Korpo to Kökar. The trip takes two hours.

From Sottunga, Föglö & Långnäs There are three to five connections a day from Långnäs to Kökar, via Överö (on Föglö) and Sottunga. Travel time is 2½ hours from Långnäs, two hours from Föglö and 1½ hours from Sottunga.

SOTTUNGA
Sottunga is the smallest municipality in Finland, with only 140 inhabitants. The first thing that strikes you is that there are more cows than people on the island. There is not much to see, but many travel here just to 'visit the smallest place in Finland'. Despite the small population, the island has its own post office, bank, shop, school, health care centre, library and church.

Things to See & Do
The wooden Sta Maria Magdalena Church

in Sottunga was built in 1661 and renovated in 1974. It's open from 10 am to 6 pm, and services are held at 11 am on Sundays. The village harbour is at the northern end of Sottunga. A short walking route starts from the harbour.

Places to Stay

An island of this size obviously doesn't have too many hotels. Two-bed cottages at the *HE-övernattningsstugor*, the only place to stay in Sottunga, cost 170 mk per night.

Häme

The historic area of Häme, or 'Tavastland' in Swedish, is a place of contrast, from the busy towns of Lahti or Tampere to the old villages of Hattula or Kangasala, from the wilderness of North Häme to the flat farmland of the south. This is where the coastal inhabitants started their conquest of the hinterland, and where the native inhabitants covered large distances on foot, hunting wildlife. In addition to the wealth of historic places and interesting towns and villages, Häme offers many opportunities for trekking, canoeing and lake travel.

Note that our area division is slightly different from the present provincial division. We include all municipalities traditionally considered part of Häme, which is historically a tribal and cultural definition rather than an administrative one. These days, for example, Kuhmoinen belongs to the Province of Central Finland, Ikaalinen to the Province of Turku & Pori and Hartola to the Province of Mikkeli. Häme itself has been divided into several areas. The Tampere area is generally called Pirkanmaa ('land of Pirkka'), and we call it Central Häme. East Häme is actually called Päijät-Häme (Häme in the Lake Päijänne region) and South Häme is sometimes called Kanta-Häme (the 'actual' Häme).

ACTIVITIES
Lake Cruises

Regular ferries operate in summer between Tampere and Hämeenlinna on Lake Pyhäjärvi, and between Tampere and Virrat on Lake Näsijärvi. There are ferries between Lahti and Heinola on Lake Päijänne and some smaller lakes, as well as between Lahti and Jyväskylä, in central Finland. You can cross Lake Päijänne on the MS *Linta* from Kuhmoinen to Sysmä. Bring your bicycle and tour the entire area, taking lake tours and cycling in between.

Trekking

There is some 330 km of marked walking track in North Häme. Together, the tracks are called Pirkan taival, or 'trail of Pirkka'. This 'off the beaten track' route was created in the 1950s by Mr Tuomas Vinha, who trekked from house to house asking for permission to mark trees with orange triangles. These marks remain, along with the new red circles. There are clear signs where the path forks. As a present to Tuomas Vinha on his 80th birthday, the Ruovesi leg of the path was named Tuomaan taival ('trail of Tuomas'). Pirkan taival runs between Parkano and Ähtäri, via Seitseminen, Kuru, Ruovesi, Helvetinjärvi and Virrat. Get a copy of the Pirkan taival topographical sheet, which is sold in the Tampere tourist information office for 25 mk. It shows all accommodation options along the tracks.

Canoeing

With its abundance of waters, North Häme offers many places for canoeing.

Pihlajavesi Route There are rivers, lakes and rapids along this route from Lake Pihlajavesi to Lake Tarjanne. Mr Tapio Vaali of Viva Company (☎ 934-55875) in Virrat rents canoes and organises tours. You can also arrange this tour through a company called Järvisuomen Toimintamatkat (☎ 934-44743, 949-233 319) at Kertuntie 1 in the village of Vilppula. Before you go, contact Pirkanmaan Matkailu in the Tampere tourist office for maps, information and other assistance.

Ikaalinen Routes There are canoes for hire at the Ikaalinen tourist information office (☎ 933-450 1221). Three routes end in Lake Kyrösjärvi, and you can easily paddle across the lake to the village of Ikaalinen:

Sipsiönjoki River – Start from Lake Liesjärvi, inside Seitseminen National Park. Beware of the Vaho rapids under the railway tracks (carry the canoe).
Aurejoki River – First paddle right across Lake Aurejärvi. The Kallikoski rapids are very tricky, so carry the canoe unless you're experienced.
Parkano Route – Start this route from the town of Parkano, or further north in Kihniö. Even though road No 3 is just a few hundred metres away, this is a very quiet route. It is mostly narrow lakes, with no difficult rapids.

Ruovesi Routes The Ruovesi area features beautiful wilderness and picturesque waterways. Canoe rentals have to be arranged at least one week in advance through Ruoveden Matkailu (☎ 934-761 388) at the Haapasaari Holiday Village. Charges are 140 mk per canoe per day, and transportation costs are approximately 150 mk per 100 km:

Haukkajoki – The route starts from Lake Haukkajärvi in Helvetinjärvi National Park and ends near the village of Kuru
Kovero – This gorge lake route connects two gorge lakes, Lake Luoma and Lake Kovero, but you may have to carry the canoe in between

Driving
Klaus Kurjen Tie This historic route is entirely within the municipal area of Vesilahti.

Route 66 The Finnish version of the popular jazz song has lyrics that follow the scenic road from Orivesi to Virrat and beyond. Many of North Häme's attractions can be reached from this road.

South Häme

HÄMEENLINNA
Hämeenlinna (population 42,500) is the capital of the Province of Häme and one of the oldest towns in Finland. In the 9th century, there was already a trading settlement at Lake Vanajavesi. Häme Castle was built during the 13th century by Swedes who made a crusade to Finland. Later, Hämeenlinna developed into an administrative, educational and garrison town. Much of this image remains.

These days Hämeenlinna is a popular place to visit, with its many attractions and its proximity to Helsinki.

Orientation
Hämeenlinna is built on both sides of Lake Vanajavesi. The town centre is a compact area between the lake in the south and east, the main Helsinki to Tampere road in the west and the garrison in the north. Häme Castle is in the northern part of the town centre. Raatihuoneenkatu is the main street, part of which has been turned into a pedestrian mall. The market square is the most central point in Hämeenlinna, with the church and many administrative buildings around it.

Information
The tourist information office (☎ 917-202 388), 2nd floor, Palokunnankatu 11, hands out a useful leaflet describing a walking tour in the town centre. The office is open in June, July and August from 9 am to 6 pm Monday to Friday and from 9 am to 2 pm on Saturdays. At other times of the year, it's open from 9 am to 5 pm Monday to Friday.

Things to See & Do
Many museums give discounts to children or students.

Häme Castle The castle is a must for every-

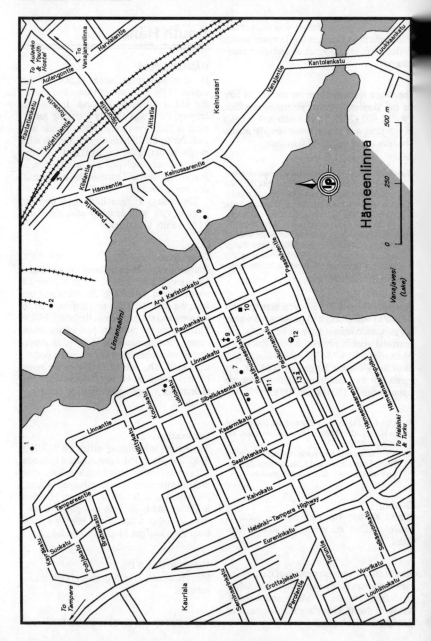

1 Häme Castle
2 Varikonniemi
3 Railway Station
4 Historical Museum
5 Harbour
6 Sibelius Museum
7 Market Square
8 Church
9 Art Museum
10 Hotel Kaupunginhotelli
11 Hotel Emilia
12 Bus Terminal
13 Tourist Office

one visiting Hämeenlinna. Its construction was started during the 1260s by Swedes, who wanted to establish a military base in Häme. The construction work actually took 700 years, since changes have been made throughout the centuries. A major change took place in 1837, when the castle was turned into a jail. The last prisoners were moved away in the 1980s. Renovation of the castle started in 1956 and was finally completed 35 years later, in 1991. Today the castle is a popular tourist site and also a venue for exhibitions, concerts, festive dinners and local weddings. The Varikonniemi area opposite the castle, across a narrow channel, has had an urbanised trading settlement since the 7th century. European merchants sailed here to trade furs. The castle is open daily from May to August from 10 am to 6 pm; from September to April, it's open from 10 am to 4 pm. Admission is 14 mk.

Aulanko Silk House Next to the Hotel Aulanko is a unique silk exhibition. It is open daily from 1 June to 15 August from 11 am to 7 pm. The rest of the year, it's open from 11 am to 3 pm on weekends and from 4 to 7 pm on Tuesdays, Wednesdays and Thursdays. Admission is free.

Vanajanlinna This hunting mansion in Harviala, 10 km from the town centre towards Lahti, was built in 1919 to 1924. Many of the rooms are richly decorated.

Vanajanlinna was long used as the school of the Finnish Communist Party. It can be visited on weekdays, from 8 am to 3 am in summer and from 8 am to 4 pm in winter.

Sibelius Museum Jean Sibelius, the most famous Finnish composer, was born in Hämeenlinna and went to school here. His first home, at Hallituskatu 11, has been converted into a small museum (☎ 917-25698). It is open daily from 1 May to 31 August from 10 am to 4 pm, and from 1 September to 30 April from noon to 4 pm. Admission is 3 mk.

Historical Museum This museum at Lukiokatu 6 has temporary exhibitions and a permanent collection of items relating to local history. It is open from noon to 4 pm Monday to Saturday and from noon to 6 pm on Sundays, all year round. Admission is 3 mk.

Hämeenlinna Art Museum There is an interesting collection of Finnish art from the 19th and 20th centuries, including some well-known works, at Viipurintie 2. There are also temporary exhibitions. The museum is open from noon to 6 pm Tuesday to Sunday, until 8 pm on Thursdays. Admission is 5 mk, free for students and children.

Car Museum The oldest car museum in Finland is next to the Ahvenisto Motor Racing Track, at Poltinahontie 45. It is open daily from May to August from 10 am to 6 pm, and on Saturdays and Sundays from 10 am to 6 pm in September. Admission is 12 mk.

Aulanko Park This beautiful park was founded early in the 20th century by Mr Hugo Standertskjöld, who dreamed of a Central European-style park with small ponds and pavilions. He spent a fortune to achieve his goal, and the result was Aulanko, with its exotic trees, swannery, observation tower and little houses. In 1930, it was declared a nature conservation area. A quarter of a million people visit the park annually. The best way to move around it is on foot, along the beautiful forest paths. The observation tower is open in May from 9 am to 5 pm Monday to Friday and 11 am to 7 pm on weekends, and daily in June, July and August from 11 am to 7 pm. Admission is 6 mk. There are many recreational choices in the Aulanko area. You can swim in the lake, play golf, ride horses and, in winter, go cross-country skiing. There is also a hotel, a camping ground and a youth hostel.

Festivals

The Aulangon Satuteatteri (Aulanko fairy-tale theatre) plays familiar tales every summer. All actors are children, some of them quite young. The open-air site is at the ruins of an old fortress close to the Hotel Aulanko. Performances are in Finnish, but the theatre is worth the experience anyhow. Tickets cost 25 mk. The Children's Cultural Festival (☎ 917-142 590) is held at the castle every August. The festival includes theatre performances, concerts, workshops and films. The Giants of the Rock is a big heavy-rock concert which takes place in July at the Ahvenisto Motor Racing Track.

Places to Stay – bottom end

The cheapest accommodation in Hämeenlinna is at the Kuusisto youth hostel (☎ 917-28560) in Aulanko. Open from 29 May to 16 August, it offers accommodation for YHA members in doubles and triples at 60 mk per person, sheets included. The Summer Hotel Amis (☎ 917-25621) at Lahdensivuntie 25 is open in June and July. Doubles cost 190 mk.

Places to Stay – middle

The Vanajanlinna (☎ 917-19561) in Harviala, 10 km from the town centre, is a fascinating place to stay. Rooms do not have facilities, but the setting is superb. Singles cost 190 to 330 mk and doubles are 380 to 480 mk. The Hotel Emilia (☎ 917-122 106) at Raatihuoneenkatu 23, in the very heart of town, has nice rooms, even if the crowd in the bar does not look particularly attractive. Singles/doubles cost 280/350 mk from

Monday to Friday, 250/300 mk in summer. Finncheques are accepted. The Kaupungin-hotelli (☎ 917-23561) at Rauhankatu 3 is a bit worn but has reasonable prices. Ask for newly renovated rooms – they are much nicer than the older ones. Singles/doubles cost 240/300 mk on weekdays and in summer, 200/260 mk on weekends.

Places to Stay – top end

The Hotel Aulanko (☎ 917-58801) has a long tradition and is considered the best hotel in town. Its lakeside location, near all the attractions of Aulanko, could not be better. Singles/doubles are 610/760 mk, 395/490 mk on weekends. From mid-June to mid-August, doubles cost 390 mk. The hotel also accepts Finncheques.

Places to Eat

The Linnankatu Pauliina is such a popular lunch place that you can hardly fit in at lunch time. The food is good and you can eat lunch for 34 mk. The Piparkakkutalo behind the church has an old-fashioned décor. The food is good but expensive at 60 to 100 mk per portion. Williams Pub has a good salad buffet, which can be enjoyed as a full meal or eaten as an entree. A lunch costs 30 to 40 mk and a dinner 60 to 100 mk. The Café Janne serves pies, salads and soup in addition to the regular pastries. You can get a piece of a pie and a cup of tea for 15 to 20 mk. Lunch costs 20 to 30 mk. At the Nylander bakery, a window separates the café from the bakery part, so you can see the bakers working. The Café Kaneli is a cosy place in an old building by the river. It is supposed to have the best buns and gingerbread in town. The Laurell is another good, traditional café.

Entertainment

To meet up with 20 to 30-year-olds, go to the Tiffany disco. The Kolibri has dancing to live music from Monday to Friday. The music varies from the traditional Finnish humppa to rock. On weekends, when the place is a disco, it is popular among 20-year-olds. The cover charge depends on the band, and can be anything from 30 to 70 mk. The

Top: The Beach, Hanko (VM)
Bottom: Tammisaari (VM)

Top: Luostarinmäki Museum Area, Turku (VM)
Bottom: The Hämeenlinna Castle (VM)

Marlon, at the Hotel Vaakuna, is a popular nightclub. It's open until 4 am and has a cover charge of 30 to 40 mk.

Getting There & Away
Bus The bus terminal is right in the town centre. There are hourly buses between Helsinki and Tampere, and they all stop in Hämeenlinna. From Turku, there are eight buses a day.

Train The railway station is one km from the town centre. All trains between Helsinki and Tampere stop at Hämeenlinna. From Turku, you will have to change trains in Toijala.

Getting Around
Bicycles can be rented at the Hotel Vaakuna for 40 mk per day, and at the Aulangon ulkoilukeskus for 10 mk per hour.

HATTULA
Hattula is a small municipality north of Hämeenlinna. 'Hattu' is Finnish for hat, but exactly how Hattula got its name is unclear. There are a few interesting places to visit.

Things to See
Church of the Holy Cross The Pyhän Ristin kirkko was built in the 14th century. It is one of the oldest churches in mainland Finland, with beautiful paintings and plenty of historical value. The church is on road No 62, just five km north of Hämeenlinna. It is open from 9 am to 5 pm in May, 10 am to 5 pm from 1 June to 15 August and noon to 4 pm from 15 August to 30 September. English-speaking guides are available.

Beekeeping Museum This unusual museum, in an old grain storage close to the old church, is open irregularly from mid-May to the end of August.

Tank Museum Many Finnish men are familiar with Parola, a big garrison area in Hattula. Travellers are welcome to visit the museum, which is open in summer.

Getting There & Away
To get to Hattula and Parola, you can take local bus Nos 5 or 6 from Hämeenlinna.

IITTALA
Iittala is a village situated 20 km north of Hämeenlinna along the main Helsinki to Tampere road. It is best known for its glass factory, which also markets its products under the brand 'Iittala'. The main attraction of Iittala, the Glass Centre, is well worth a visit.

Things to See
Glass Centre Directly opposite the bus terminal, you will find the Glass Centre. From May to August, it is open daily from 9 am to 8 pm, and at other times it is open from 9 am to 6 pm. The interesting glass museum exhibits objects designed and manufactured locally. It also gives an insight into an important part of the history of Finnish design. Admission is free. On weekdays (except in July), there are free guided tours of the glass factory at 11 am and 1 and 3 pm. From mid-June to mid-August, there is an art exhibition. Tickets are 25 mk, 20 mk for students. In the back room of the restaurant, you can watch the craftspeople blowing glassware. It is very impressive to see them make a bird or a flower out of a glowing hot mass of glass.

Things to Buy
If you have a sweet tooth, visit the little chocolate factory, which also sells its products. This is a good chance to see a different type of manufacturing. There are several shops in the area, the most interesting of which is the glass shop, where you can buy second-grade products at 35% below normal price. Sometimes it is hard to see what the defects are, so this can be considered a good bargain. If you mail your purchases outside the Nordic countries, you will get an additional 17% discount.

Getting There & Away
You can get to Iittala by driving or hitchhiking along main road No 3. Buses from

Hämeenlinna run four to 10 times a day. The fast trains do not stop at Iittala, but one of the four or five daily local trains from either Hämeenlinna or Tampere will take you there.

JANAKKALA

The municipality of Janakkala has four centres: the administrative centre of Turenki, the villages of Tervakoski (with its paper mill) and Leppäkoski, and the old village of Janakkala. The population of the entire municipality is 15,000.

Things to See & Do

Puuhamaa The name of this place in the village of Tervakoski translates roughly as 'Action World', and it offers a host of activities for children, including water slides, bowling, minigolf, video games, bicycles and minicars. The Puuhamaa attracts lots of Finnish children and is open from 15 May to 15 August. Tickets cost 50 mk per person.

Jussis Keramik Tervakoski's other attraction is an old mansion at Kartanontie 1. Here you can watch artisans blowing glass, and making crystal and ceramics. It is open from 1 June to 15 August from 9 am to 8 pm, and from 16 August to 31 May from 10 am to 6 pm.

Janakkala Village In the old village of Janakkala, there is a medieval church, open from 1 to 7 pm Monday to Thursday, 1 to 6 pm on Fridays and 11 am to 6 pm on Sundays. The Laurinmäen torpparimuseo (local museum) in the village is open on summer weekends from noon to 6 pm.

Getting There & Away

Most buses between Helsinki and Hämeenlinna stop at Tervakoski. To get to the village of Janakkala, take a bus from Hämeenlinna.

JOKIOINEN

Jokioinen is a small municipality along the main Turku to Hämeenlinna road.

Things to See & Do

Jokioinen's most interesting feature is its museum railway. Trains used to run between Forssa and Humppila, and these days you can travel the six-km railroad track between Jokioinen and Minkiö in an old train. The trip takes 20 minutes one-way and the trains run four times each Sunday from June to August.

The old wooden church, built in 1631, is open in summer from 7 am to 3 pm Monday to Friday and from 1 to 5 pm on weekends. The nearby vicarage museum is open in summer from noon to 5 pm.

Getting There & Away

There are one to three buses a day from Helsinki to Jokioinen. Some of the buses between Tampere and Turku also stop in Jokioinen.

RIIHIMÄKI

The town of Riihimäki (population 25,000) has grown around a major railway junction. Located in the very south of the Province of Häme, it is known for its glassware.

Orientation

Most of Riihimäki's interesting sights are out of the town centre, along the main Helsinki to Hämeenlinna road. The centre is located to the west of the railway station. Hämeenkatu and Keskuskatu are the main streets.

Information

The tourist information office (☎ 914-741 225) at Kalevankatu 1 is open from 11 am to 3 pm Monday to Thursday and from 11 am to 2.30 pm on Fridays.

Things to See

Finnish Glass Museum An interesting museum in the former Riihimäki Glass Factory at Tehtaankatu 23, just off the main road, has an exhibition of Finnish glassware since the 17th century, as well as tools and a small collection of foreign glassware. Tapio Wirkkala, the architect, designed the interior. The museum is open daily from April to September from 10 am to 6 pm. From

October to March, it is open from Tuesday to Sunday. The museum is closed in January.

Hunting Museum This museum, located next to the Glass Museum, has a historical exhibition on hunting methods and equipment. It has the same opening times as the Glass Museum.

Hyttikortteli The 'Cabin Quarters', half a km from the museums, used to be the accommodation area for workers in the glass factory. Now restored, it houses artists and artisans. You will find attractive shops selling glassware and dolls, and there is a shop museum there.

Workers' Clubhouse Museum This museum on Elomaankatu is open from noon to 4 pm on Sundays from May to October.

Signal Museum The Signal Museum in the nearby garrison area has objects and equipment connected with the signal operations of the Finnish army. It is open from 1 to 3 pm on Saturdays and from 1 to 4 pm on Sundays.

Riihimäki Town Museum The local museum at Öllerinkatu 3 has historical objects from the area and from the community of Antrea in Karelia, annexed by the former Soviet Union during WW II. The museum is open on Wednesdays and Sundays from noon to 6 pm.

Places to Stay
The *Riihimäki youth hostel* (☎ 914-741 471) at Merkuriuksenkatu 7 is outside of the town centre, some 300 metres from the railway station. It is open from 25 May to 7 August. Dormitory beds cost 60 mk, and singles/doubles are 140/180 mk for YHA members. The *Teatterihotelli Rivoli* (☎ 914-7721) at Hämeenaukio 1 is in the same building as the theatre. It is a pleasant, if rather expensive hotel. Doubles cost 380 mk in July; at other times, singles/doubles are 490/620 mk. Finncheques yield handy discounts here.

Getting There & Away
Bus Most buses between Helsinki and Hämeenlinna stop in Riihimäki. There are three or four buses a day from Turku.

Train Riihimäki must be the easiest place in Finland to reach by train. Practically all northbound and eastbound trains from Helsinki stop here. It is also the last stop for some local trains from Helsinki.

TAMMELA
The scenery in the Saari park, in the municipality of Tammela, inspired many painters during the National Romantic era. For the best view, climb the 20-metre observation tower. You can get the keys from the restaurant Lounais-Hämeen Pirtti, which is in the park area. The old church in the village of Tammela dates from the 15th century.

VALKEAKOSKI
Valkeakoski, an industrial town between Hämeenlinna and Tampere, is probably best known for its bad smell, which is caused by the pulp and paper industries. The locals will tell you that what smells here is money: the factory is the most important employer in town. There are some interesting places to visit, and beautiful lake scenery on the outskirts of town.

Orientation
Valkeakoski is divided into two parts by a canal between lakes Mallasvesi and Vanajavesi. The town centre is in the northern part of town. There are two bridges over the canal, and you can have nice walks along the canal banks.

Information
The tourist information office (☎ 937-46997) is at Valtakatu 20, in the main street.

Things to See
Kauppilanmäki An open-air museum on Kauppilankatu features old Finnish buildings. It's open daily (except Mondays) from 2 June to 15 August from noon to 5 pm.

Admission is 4 mk. At 2 pm every Sunday in summer, special events are held there.

Myllykoski Museum This small museum next to the main bridge displays Valkeakoski's development from a village to an industrial town. It's open from 11 am to 6 pm Monday to Thursday and from noon to 4 pm on Sundays. Admission costs 4 mk.

Sääksmäki This area is several km south of Valkeakoski along the main road. The **Voipaala Art Centre**, on the premises of an old manor, specialises in children's culture. It's open daily (except Mondays) from noon to 7 pm. Admission is 6 mk, with student discounts available. The ancient fortification on **Rapola Hill** is right next to the art centre. From 400 to 1000 AD, it was the centre of defence in Häme. Apart from piled stones, little remains, but it is still worth visiting; take the marked walking track around the area, starting at the parking area of the Voipaala Centre. The **stone church** of Sääksmäki was built at the end of the 15th century and reconstructed in 1933. In addition to the interesting paintings inside, there is a small church museum there.

Visuvuori Once the studio of Emil Wicström, a sculptor from the National Romantic era, this is the best-known sight in the Valkeakoski area. This house dates back to the early 20th century, and since 1967, it has been a museum. Some 600 sculptures and sketches are exhibited at Visavuori. Another exhibition of works by Kari Suomalainen, the most famous political cartoonist in Finland, is displayed in Visavuori. Mr Suomalainen has received an award from the US National Cartoonist Society for his daring cartoons on communists. Mr Suomalainen is Emil Wickström's grandson. The museum is open daily from 1 May to 30 September from 11 am to 7 pm, closing at 5 pm on Mondays. From 1 October to 30 April, it's open from 1 to 7 pm daily (except Mondays). Admission costs 30 mk, 20 mk for students. Visavuori is one km from the main Helsinki to Tampere road. There are also ferries from Tampere, Hämeenlinna and Valkeakoski in summer. The daily ferry between Tampere and Hämeenlinna will give you approximately one hour to explore the area. The fare is 132 mk from Hämeenlinna (182 mk return) and 60 mk from Valkeakoski.

Places to Stay

Valkeakoski has few places to stay, and the best accommodation is actually outside the town centre. The camping ground (☎ 937-42441) on Apiankatu, approximately one km from the bus terminal, has four-bed cottages for 130 to 200 mk. It costs 65 mk to pitch a tent. The cheapest place is the youth hostel (☎ 937-721 405) at Apiankatu 43, open from 1 June to 15 August. Basic dormitory beds cost 65 mk and singles/doubles are 120/165 mk for YHA members.

Ilola Farm (☎ 937-89027) offers the best value for money. You can stay there for 140 mk in summer, 120 mk in winter, and breakfast is included in the price. Accommodation is in old farm buildings, which have been fully renovated. Let them know before you arrive. The family speaks English. The farm is in Metsäkansa, seven km from road No 3 along the road to Toijala. Buses between Toijala and Valkeakoski stop approximately 400 metres from the Ilola house.

The only hotel in Valkeakoski, the *Hotel Waltikka* (☎ 937-7711), is beautifully located on the northern bank of the canal, close to the town centre. The hotel is nice and clean but there is nothing special about it. Singles/doubles are 295/350 mk, and you can use Finncheques here.

Getting There & Away

There are over 20 buses from Hämeenlinna, and most buses between Helsinki and Tampere stop in Valkeakoski. You can also catch a connecting bus from the Toijala railway station.

East Häme

ASIKKALA

Vääksy Canal, in the municipality of Asikkala, is the busiest in Finland – over 15,000 vessels pass through it every summer. There is a **water-mill museum** near the canal. Here you can catch one of the boats which sail between Lahti and Heinola in summer. It's 30 mk to Lahti and 45 mk to Heinola on the MS *Tehi*. **Urajärvi Manor** (☎ 918-667 191) is worth a look if you have a vehicle. This old house is surrounded by a nice park and is open daily from 15 May to 31 August from 11 am to 5 pm.

HARTOLA

This sleepy village to the north of Lahti has proclaimed itself a kingdom. This is not a secessionist movement – more a promotional stunt to attract visitors. The reason for this is the special rights granted to Hartola by a king during the Swedish era. Hartola has a tourist information office (☎ 918-161 311), on the main road, and the **Itä-Hämeen Museo** (East Häme Museum), located in the 18th century Koskipää Manor, with several exhibitions and a cluster of old buildings. The museum is open from 9 August to 10 May from noon to 4 pm daily. At other times of the year, it's open from 11 am to 6 pm. Admission is 7 mk. Hartola is on the eastern Lahti to Jyväskylä road, and there are several express buses every day.

HEINOLA

Heinola has a scenic waterfront setting, with the Jyrängönvirta River flowing through the small town. The place is not particularly interesting but it serves as a starting point for scenic summer lake cruises.

Places to Stay

Heinäsaaren Camping (☎ 918-153 083) on the island of Heinäsaari, 1.5 km from the town centre, has cottages from 150 mk. The youth hostel (☎ 918-152 683) at Opintie 1 is open from 1 June to 2 August and has doubles at 60 mk per person for YHA members. The *Gasthaus Puistola* (☎ 918-143 585) at Maaherrankatu 5 has singles/doubles for 140/240 mk.

Getting There & Away

Bus All buses heading north-east from Lahti will take you to Heinola.

Ferry The PRH Ferries from Jyväskylä and Lahti, including the legendary SS *Suomi*, sail occasionally to Heinola in summer. A trip from Lahti takes 4½ hours and costs 90 mk. On Tuesdays, Wednesdays and Thursdays from 24 June to 5 August, you can catch the MS *Tehi* at 9 am in Lahti or at 2.30 pm in Heinola for a pleasant cruise on Lake Päijänne. The one-way trip takes nearly four hours and costs 55 mk. On Saturdays in July, the *Tehi* leaves Padasjoki at 9.30 am and Heinola at 2 pm for the 2½-hour journey, which costs 50 mk one-way.

HOLLOLA

The interesting **Hollola Church** was finished in 1480. It's open daily from 15 May to 16 August from 10 am to 6 pm. The **Hollola open-air museum** features old buildings, and objects found in the area. It is open daily from 1 June to 16 August from 11 am to 6 pm. Entry costs 5 mk. **Pyhäniemi Manor**, dubbed the 'Hollywood of Hollola' in the 1930s, when many films were staged here, houses art exhibitions in summer. It is open daily from 17 May to 16 August from 11 am to 6 pm. Admission is 35 mk.

KUHMOINEN

Kuhmoinen is quite a popular summer retreat among people from big cities, yet it still has surprisingly few services for travellers. There are rocky hills, beautiful forest lakes and some interesting wildlife. The village is a base for visits to Isojärvi National Park, in the northern corner of the municipality, which is a pleasant trekking region. Kuhmoinen village has hardly anything of interest, other than an old village road, across the main road from the bus terminal, and the Päijänne lakeside. The main street, Toritie, has a few banks, a post office and some shops, which serve the population of 3500 people. There are a few restaurants along Toritie. The café at the bus terminal serves simple meals from 25 mk.

Getting There & Away
Catch a Jyväskylä-bound pikavuoro bus from Helsinki or Lahti, or one of the several daily buses from Tampere. The MS *Linta* car ferry crosses Lake Päijänne daily from early June to mid-August, leaving Sysmä at 9 am and 12.40 and 4.20 pm. It costs 45 mk one-way, plus 40 mk for a car.

ISOJÄRVI NATIONAL PARK
Isojärvi gets few visitors, other than vacationing Finns, but it is well worth the effort if you want to stay a day or two in a quiet, picturesque forest and experience the setting of Finland's traditional logging culture. The park was established in 1982, and facilities have been provided. Come in the middle of the week, when you may have most of the park to yourself.

Information
Heretty House, on the main gravel road, serves as a tourist information office in summer. You can pick up a free map and guide at any time from the shelter behind the main building.

Things to See & Do
Huhtala Huhtala House preserves an 18th century rural farm. It is an open-air museum consisting of several farmhouses. If the main building is open, check the *tupa* room. Some 1.5 km from Huhtala is a parking area, and a quick one-km hike to your left brings you to the shore of Lake Isojärvi. One of the three boats there can be used, if you get the key from Heretty House.

Trekking There are a number of possible walking routes in the Isojärvi area, with good paths, marked in blue, and sufficient route information along the way. Most people head first for Lake Lortikka, which has a sauna, a camp site and two houses offering accom-

modation. Take the red-marked nature trail to Lortikka Hill, near the southern end of Lake Lortikka. There are other trails in Latokuusikko and near Heretty. You can see a lot of birds and hear the mighty cry of the black-throated diver in the night, and occasionally you can even spot elks. Picking berries and mushrooms is allowed. Expect a lot of blueberries in July and the excellent cloudberries in August, if you are lucky enough to be the first to find them.

Places to Stay
There are camp sites in Kuorejärvi and Lortikka. Lortikka also has a cabin with 15 beds (☎ 941-211 455), which you'll have to reserve in advance; the key is available at Heretty House. Avoid weekends. There are also other buildings where some trekkers stay overnight for free.

Getting There & Away
There is no bus service. Hitchhiking could be a possibility, but don't count on it here. If you drive, Isojärvi is most easily reached from the main Tampere to Jyväskylä road. Turn south at Länkipohja and take the gravel road to your left two km further. If you want to see Huhtala House first, follow the sign a few km from there. If you have taken a taxi from Länkipohja to Huhtala, it would be advisable to trek from there to Lortikka. From the Huhtala fork, it is another seven km to Heretty. It is 18 km from Kuhmoinen to Lortikka. Cross the main road from the Kuhmoinen bus terminal, drive two km and turn left.

LAHTI
The people of Lahti like to call their town 'Business City', but it is really best known as a sports city. It is the main venue for winter sports in Finland and has hosted five World Championships in Nordic skiing. Lahti's location, by Lake Vesijärvi, with a connection to Lake Päijänne, makes it a good place to start a ferry trip on Lake Päijänne. Lahti is relatively young, having been incorporated as a town only in 1905, and consequently has few old buildings.

Orientation

The compact town centre is situated around the main street, Aleksanterinkatu. The famous Sport Centre is just to the west of the town centre. Mukkula and Messilä, two recreational areas, are by Lake Vesijärvi, Mukkula some three km to the north and Messilä eight km to the north-west. The bus terminal is at the west end of Aleksanterinkatu, the main street. The railway station is a few blocks south of the town centre.

Information

Tourist Office The tourist information office (☎ 918-818 2580) is on the 2nd floor at Torikatu 3B, near the market. The office stocks useful leaflets and the staff will assist in planning sightseeing tours. It's open from 1 June to 31 August from 8 am to 5 pm Monday to Friday and from 10 am to 2 pm on weekends. From 1 September to 31 May, it is open from 8 am to 4 pm Monday to Friday. In summer, there are additional information desks, at the Sport Centre (open from 9 am to 5 pm Monday to Friday and from 10 am to 3 pm on weekends) and at the market square (open from 9 am to 3 pm Monday to Friday). The tourist office publishes a monthly leaflet listing all events. You can also listen to a recorded English-language message (☎ 058).

Library The public library at Kirkkokatu 31 is open from 10 am to 8 pm (until 7 pm in summertime) Monday to Friday and from 10 am to 3 pm on Saturdays. The newspaper room is also open on Sundays from noon to 4 pm.

Things to See

Skiing Museum The only museum in Finland specialising in winter sports is at the Sport Centre. Its permanent exhibition traces the development of cross-country skiing and ski jumping from ancient times to the present day. The exhibits include the first Olympic medals won by Finns, a small functioning snow cannon, and a short, entertaining video about the development of ski-jumping styles

over the years. There are also temporary exhibitions. The centre is open from 10 am to 5 pm daily. Admission is 10 mk.

Historical Museum This museum at Lahdenkatu 4 is in a most beautiful building, which used to be a private mansion. If the building is impressive, so are the collections, displayed on three floors. In addition to objects from nearby areas, exhibits include the Klaus Holma collection of French and Italian furniture and medieval and Renaissance art. The coin collection is also interesting. Parts of the collections of the former Historical Museum of Vyborg were moved here after Vyborg was annexed by the former Soviet Union. The museum is open daily from 10 am to 5 pm. Admission is 10 mk, free on Fridays.

Lahti Art Museum The collection of the former Vyborg Art Museum is displayed at Vesijärvenkatu 11, where there are also temporary exhibitions. The museum is open daily from 10 am to 5 pm. Admission is 10 mk, free on Fridays. The same ticket is valid for the Poster Museum.

Poster Museum There are temporary exhibitions, posters and furniture on the 6th floor of the Art Museum building. Opening hours and tickets are the same as for the Art Museum.

Radio Museum This museum on Radiomäki Hill, between Mannerheimintie and Harjukatu, is the old broadcasting station of Lahti. Its collection includes old radios, and there's a working broadcasting studio from the 1950s. The museum is open from 1 to 4 pm on Sundays. Admission is free.

Museum of Military Medicine This surprising museum at the Hennala garrison is open from 1 June to 15 August from noon to 5 pm Tuesday to Friday and from 11 am to 3 pm on weekends. In May and from 16 August to 30 September, it's open from 11 am to 3 pm on Thursdays, Saturdays and Sundays.

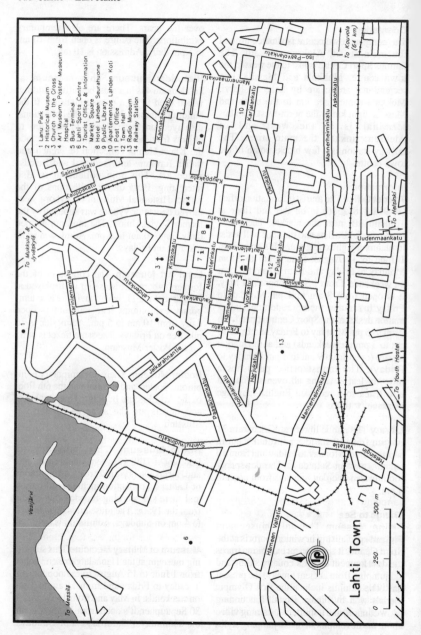

1 Lanu Park
2 Historical Museum
3 Church of the Cross
4 Art Museum, Poster Museum &
   Hospital
5 Bus Terminal
6 Lahti Sports Centre
7 Tourist Office & Information
8 Market Square
9 Hotel Lahden Seurahuone
10 Apartements Lahden Koti
11 Public Library
12 Post Office
13 Town Hall
14 Radio Museum
14 Railway Station

Lahti Town

Admission is 5 mk, 1 mk for children. Enter the garrison area through the main gate.

Church of the Cross This church at Kirkkokatu 4, designed by Alvar Aalto, is very modern in style. It is open from 10 am to 3 pm daily.

Town Hall Designed by another famous Finnish architect, Eliel Saarinen, this building at Harjukatu 31 is open to the public on Fridays. There are guided tours from 2 to 3 pm.

Activities
Lahti Sport Centre This is the biggest winter sports centre in the country and is best known for its ski jumps. The tallest ski jump serves as an observation tower in summer. Starting at the Sport Centre, there is a total of 145 km of ski tracks, 35 km of which is illuminated. Skiing equipment can be rented in the main building for 50 mk per day (25 mk without ski boots) or 160 mk per week. In summer, there are two open-air pools in the ski-jump pit; admission is 12 mk. The Sport Centre also has a ski museum.

Messilä This recreational centre 11 km north-west of Lahti has been built around a mansion. It has downhill skiing slopes (the longest of which is 800 metres long), as well as artisans' shops, a hotel and restaurants. The area, with its 19th century Art Nouveau buildings, is worth seeing. Lift tickets cost 90 mk per day or 60 mk for three hours. Equipment can be rented for 80 mk per day or 50 mk per half day.

Canoeing Canoes can be rented at Kahvisaari for 45 mk a day.

Organised Tours The tourist information office organises sightseeing bus tours. Tours take two hours and cost 25 mk per person.

Festivals
The annual Lahti Poster Biennale is one of the world's most important poster exhibitions. The posters can be seen almost all summer long. Another important cultural event is the Mukkula Writers Forum, which takes place every summer, attracting authors from all over the world. The Salpausselän kisat (Lahti Ski Games) are held every winter, in February to March. The Mukkula Writers Reunion is held every second summer.

Places to Stay – bottom end
In Mukkula, on a peninsula in Lake Vesijärvi, the camping ground has cottages for 195 to 350 mk. Camping costs 65 mk per family, or 30 to 35 mk per person. The youth hostel (☎ 918-826 324) is at Kivikatu 1 in Keijupuisto, three km south of the town centre. It consists of ugly, barrack-type buildings, and the location, behind tall apartment buildings, is not that great either. At 50 mk for YHA members, prices are rather high for what you get.

Places to Stay – middle
The *Mukkula Mansion Hotel* in Mukkula, four km north of Lahti, has singles for 210 to 370 mk and doubles for 285 to 550 mk. The lakeside location is superb and the old mansion is a romantic place to stay. Less romantic is the dormitory-looking *Mukkula Summer Hotel*, with singles/doubles at 170/240 mk.

The *Apartementos Lahden Koti* (☎ 918-522 173) at Karjalankatu 6 definitely gives you the best value for money. It is a totally renovated apartment building, which has been converted into a hotel. Most of the apartments are singles, but there are some doubles as well. All apartments are tastefully decorated and come with a well-equipped kitchen and a bathroom. Studios cost 250 mk per person or 310 mk for two people. Two-room apartments cost 380 mk for one to two people, 480 mk for three to four. From Midsummer to early August, prices are 60 to 70 mk lower for studios. It is advisable to book beforehand, as this place is very popular.

Places to Stay – top end
At the top end of the scale, the *Lahden Seurahuone* (☎ 918-57711) at Aleksanterin-

katu 14, right in the town centre, is reputedly the best hotel in Lahti. Singles/doubles are 575/680 mk, 290/380 mk on weekends. There are special prices in summer.

Places to Eat

The *Café Sinuhe* at Mariankatu serves lunch for 29 to 35 mk. It is a pleasant, street café-type place in the very centre of town. The pastries are fantastic. The *Café Faarao* at Aleksanterinkatu 16 is where many young people go to eat salad. Lunch costs 35 mk. The *Charles Café* (☎ 918-520 225) at Rautatienkatu 23 is a popular place to eat, both at lunch and dinner time. Lunch is 32 to 37 mk and dinner 25 to 90 mk. The *Kantakrouvi* at Aleksanterinkatu 10 has good pizzas and salads for 20 to 75 mk. The *Café Catalina* at Rauhankatu 14 serves lunch from 33 mk. The *Old Fashion*, 2nd floor, Aleksanterinkatu 9, has a choice of three lunch dishes for 35 mk. For good food in a slightly more classy environment, try the *Grand Paradise* at Kauppakatu 7 or the *Lahden Seurahuone* at Aleksanterinkatu 14. Both serve meals for 68 to 140 mk. The *Lahden Seurahuone* at Aleksanterinkatu 10 is a very pleasant café. In addition to pastries, it serves salads, soup and sandwiches for 15 to 30 mk.

Entertainment

The *Kauppahotelli Grand* (☎ 918-525 146) at Vapaudenkatu 23 has 'afternoon dancing', starting at 2 pm Wednesday and Sunday, 4 pm Saturday. Generally speaking, people go to afternoon dances to dance, not to drink. The *Aleksander* at Rauhankatu 14 has dancing to live music every day, except Sundays. The place is popular, with a cover charge of up to 45 mk, depending on the band. The *Café Faarao* at Aleksanterinkatu 16 has a disco on Fridays and Saturdays. There is an age limit of 20 for women and 22 for men. The *Amoroso*, at the *Lahden Seurahuone* at Aleksanterinkatu 14, is a classy nightclub with an age limit of 22. The *Cat Club* at Rautatienkatu 21 and the *Nuutti* at Vesijärvenkatu 22 are nightspots favoured by 18 to 20-year-olds.

Getting There & Away

Bus Each day, there are more than 35 buses from Helsinki (102 km), at least 10 buses from Tampere (128 km) and 11 buses from either Jyväskylä (171 km) or Turku (214 km).

Train There are at least 15 direct trains a day from Helsinki, and 23 trains from Riihimäki, where you will have to change trains if you are travelling from Tampere.

Ship In summer, there are scheduled ferries to Lahti from Jyväskylä and Heinola. If you are interested in a shorter cruise, there are boat trips from Lahti to the Vääksy canal and cruises around Lake Vesijärvi. Some have activities such as dancing.

PADASJOKI

The water-mill museum at Vesijako dates from the 18th century and is still used (though for fun only) on summer Sundays from noon to 4 pm, when you can also buy porridge made from the mill flour. The museum is open daily from 21 June to 4 August from 10 am to 8 pm.

SYSMÄ

For those who cross Lake Päijänne on the MS *Linta* from Kuhmoinen, the municipality of Sysmä (population 6000) has a number of attractions.

Things to See & Do

The 15th century stone **church** is open daily from 1 June to 31 August from 8 am to 3 pm Monday to Friday and from 9 am to 6 pm on weekends. The **local museum** is open only on Sundays from 11 am to 2 pm. The **Suvi-Pinx** art exhibition in the village of Suopelto, not far from the car ferry, is open from 13 June to 2 August from 11 am to 6 pm daily. **Kammiovuori Hill** (221 metres) is the highest peak in the region; take the path to the top for a good view.

Places to Stay & Eat

Sysmä Camping (☎ 918-171 386) is good value, at 60 mk per night in two-bed cottages. It's open from 1 June to 31 August. The *Hotelli Uoti* (☎ 918-172 766) has singles/doubles for 200/250 mk.

Getting There & Away

Sysmä is well connected to Helsinki by express buses. The ferry from Kuhmoinen, across Lake Päijänne, arrives at Suopelto, several km from the village.

Tampere

Tampere, a proud city of self-assured people, is the second-largest city in Finland. Long known for its textile industries, it has gone through all the Rostowian development stages, from an industrial town, often called 'the Manchester of Finland', to a service-oriented society.

It remains a relatively undervisited city, though it offers all the attractions of the lakeland as well as its own rich culture. There are several world-class sights, including the Lenin Museum, one of the museums most frequented by foreign visitors to Tampere. Pyynikki Hill and the adjacent Pispala suburb have excellent examples of the sand ridges that are found around Finland. There are good views from the ridges, and the whole area is pleasant for short or long walks.

History

In the Middle Ages, the area around Tampere was inhabited by the Pirkka tribe, who collected taxes all the way to Lapland. Modern Tampere, founded in 1779, started its growth at the rapids (called Tammerfors, 'rapids of Tammer', in Swedish) between the two lakes. With abundant hydroelectric power available, several textile industries soon started operations here, including the British company Finlayson.

Because of Tampere's large working population, the Russian Revolution in 1917 increased local interest in socialism, and Tampere was the capital of the 'Reds' during the civil war that followed Finnish independence. Since then, Tampere has diversified its image. It is now the largest Nordic city without access to the sea.

Orientation

Tampere has a beautiful setting between Lake Pyhäjärvi and Lake Näsijärvi. The Tammerkoski Rapids connect the two lakes. Hämeenkatu, the main street, runs from the railway station to the Aleksanteri Church. The commercial centre sprawls on both sides of Tammerkoski and the railway station.

Information

Tourist Offices The efficient tourist information office (☎ 931-124 488, fax 931-196 463) and the provincial tourist organisation Pirkanmaan Matkailu (☎ 931-124 804) share an office at Verkatehtaankatu 2, round the corner from the Hotel Ilves. The offices have a variety of leaflets, brochures and useful information to hand out, such as *Key to Tampere* and *Blue Lakes Holidays*, and good maps.

Pirkanmaan Matkailu sells trekking maps of North Häme and arranges contacts with private tour operators based elsewhere. In June, July and August, the tourist office is open from 8.30 am to 8 pm Monday to Friday, 8.30 am to 6 pm on Saturdays and 11.30 am to 6 pm on Sundays. At other times of year, it's open from 8.30 am to 5 pm Monday to Friday.

Vuoltsu at Vuolteenkatu 13 offers a number of services for travellers, including left-luggage services, bicycle hire and coffee. It is open from 25 June to 31 August from 4 to 10 pm.

Money All banks have foreign exchange facilities, but only during normal banking hours, Monday to Friday. Outside these hours, you can change money at Sokos and Stockmann department stores, both on Hämeenkatu.

Post & Telecommunications The main post office at Rautatienkatu 21, between the railway station and the cathedral, is open from 8 am to 8 pm Monday to Friday, 10 am to 3 pm on Saturdays and 2 to 8 pm on Sundays. The telegraph service is also open every day. There are a few dozen other post offices scattered around Tampere.

Laundry Call ahead (☎ 931-228 755) to reserve time at the self-service laundromat at Hämeenpuisto 12B, operated by Mr Lehtiö.

Library Don't miss the Tampere City Library at Pirkankatu 2, opposite the Aleksanteri Church. Locals call it 'Metso' (Wood Grouse) because of its unusual architecture, the work of Reima and Raili Pietilä in 1985. There are over half a million books here, and thousands of records can be listened to upstairs. The *käsikirjasto* section has English magazines, 1:20,000 topographical sheets of all of Häme, town and trekking maps, and guidebooks. There are also two museums on the premises. The newspaper reading room at Puutarhankatu, by the river, has magazines in English. It's open daily.

Travel Agencies Kilroy Travel, the student travel agency on Tuomiokirkonkatu, is open from 9 am to 5 pm Monday to Friday.

Bookshops Akateeminen, on Tuomiokirkonkatu, near the railway station, has the widest choice of English books. A large variety of foreign magazines is available at the railway station.

Medical Services The Central Hospital (☎ 931-247 5111), two km east of the railway station, deals with medical emergencies.

Things to See
Churches
The Catholic church (☎ 931-127 280) at Amurinkuja 21 has one or two services every day. Lutheran churches have services on Sundays at 10 am. An English service is given downstairs in the cathedral on the first Sunday of each month.

Tampere Cathedral When Finns wanted to translate the Swedish word *domkyrka*

('cathedral'), they ended up with *tuomiokirkko*, which translates literally as 'church of judgement'. The Tampere Cathedral is one of the most notable examples of National Romantic architecture in Finland, and should not be missed. It is open daily from 10 am to 6 pm in summer and from 11 am to 3 pm in winter.

Orthodox Church This conspicuous church (☎ 931-124 935) near the railway station is open from 1 May to 31 August from 10 am to 3.30 pm Monday to Friday, and at other times on request. There are services on Saturdays at 6 pm and on Sundays at 10 am.

Messukylä Old Church This stone church in the eastern suburb of Messukylä is the oldest in Tampere. It is open from 1 May to 31 August from 9 am to 5 pm daily.

Kaleva Church Many locals consider this modern concrete church ugly, but it is quite impressive once you get inside. It is open in summer from 10 am to 6 pm and in winter from 11 am to 3 pm.

Aleksanteri Church There is nice woodwork in this landmark church at the western end of the main street. It is open in summer from 10 am to 6 pm and in winter from 11 am to 3 pm.

Old Church Another landmark, the old wooden church at the central square, sometimes has gospel concerts on Saturday evenings. It is a simple church, open daily from 10 am to 3 pm in summer and from 11 am to 1 pm in winter.

Museums
Workers' Museum of Amuri The Amurin työläismuseokortteli, an entire block of wooden Amuri workers' quarters, has been preserved while other houses have been demolished to make way for new apartments.

This large museum complex is the most realistic home museum in Finland, and many homes look as if the tenant had just left to go shopping. Ask at the ticket booth for an English guide.

The museum is open from mid-May to mid-September daily (except Mondays) from 10 am to 6 pm. Admission is 10 mk.

Art Museum Just next door at Puutarhakatu 34 is the Taidemuseo, which displays contemporary art. Entry is 10 mk, 3 mk for students.

Lenin Museum Apparently the only surviving Lenin museum in the world, this place at Hämeenpuisto 28 attracts a surprising number of visitors, most of them foreign. Few Russians come here, unlike the old days. Ask for an English leaflet for explanations.

The museum is open from 9 am to 5 pm Monday to Friday and from 11 am to 4 pm on weekends. Admission is 10 mk.

Moominvalley Museum Tove Jansson, the Finnish artist and writer, created her Moomin figures decades ago, but the Japanese TV cartoon has created a new 1990s Moomin boom, judging by the popularity of this small exhibition in the basement of the Tampere City Library. Nearly all the original drawings by Ms Jansson are now displayed here.

The museum is open all year round from 9 am to 5 pm Monday to Friday and from 10 am to 6 pm on weekends. Admission is 10 mk.

Natural Science Museum This small museum next to the Moominvalley Museum is probably not worth the 10 mk admission fee. It's open daily (except Mondays) till 5 pm.

Pyynikinlinna The old furniture in this large manor at Mariankatu 40 is worth a look. There are also a few attractive old paintings, and temporary exhibitions upstairs. It's open from noon to 5 pm on Sundays, and from Tuesday to Sunday during exhibitions. Admission is 10 mk.

Hiekka Art Gallery There are paintings and gold and silver items in this impressive building at Pirkankatu 6. It's open on Wednesdays and Sundays from noon to 3 pm. Admission is 10 mk.

Verkaranta This former factory building by the river, near the tourist office, exhibits and sells handicrafts. For a small fee, you can use the loom upstairs to create something.

City Museum This interesting museum in an old manor in Hatanpää is worth a visit for its room interiors, which depict different styles. The museum is open from 11 am to 5 pm Tuesday to Sunday. Admission is 10 mk. Outside the museum, Arboretum Park has about 350 species of flora. These alluring gardens also offer good views of Lake Pyhäjärvi and Pyynikki Ridge. The park is always open. Bus No 21 runs to the museum every 15 to 30 minutes.

Haihara Dolls Museum Over 3000 dolls are presented in changing exhibitions at the historic Haihara estate, an old manor house with a large park. The place is open daily (except Fridays) from noon to 6 pm in summer. In March-April and September-November it is open Sundays from noon to 4 pm. Admission is 15 mk, 5 mk for students, and the same ticket is valid for all exhibitions. To get there, take the eastbound bus No 15 all the way to its terminus.

Särkänniemi

This large area includes several tourist attractions. You can walk to Särkänniemi via the small Näsinpuisto Park, or catch bus No 4 from the railway station. From mid-May to mid-August, it departs every 20 minutes between 11.30 am and 8 pm. The joint ticket for the area costs 60 mk, which includes entry to four places of your choice.

Amusement Park This park is open in summer, generally from 11 am to 8 pm. There's a 10 mk admission fee, and a 'wristband' for admission to all attractions costs 70 mk per day.

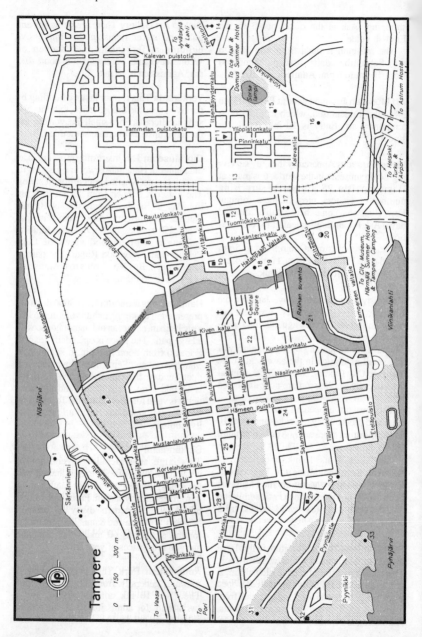

Tampere

To Jyväskylä & Lahti
Teiskontie 14
To Ice Hall & Domus Summer Hotel
To Astrum Hostel
Kalevan puistotie
Itsenäisyydenkatu
Viinikankatu
Sorsa lampi 15
16
Tammelan puistokatu
Yliopistonkatu 11
Pinninkatu
Kalevantie
To Helsinki, Turku & Airport
13
Rautatienkatu
Tuomiokirkonkatu 12
7
8
Rongankatu
Kyttälänkatu
Aleksanterinkatu
Hatanpään Valtatie
17
20
Murikankatu
To City Museum, Härmälä Summer Hotel & Tampere Camping
9
10
18
19
Ratinan suvanto
Tampereen valtatie
Viinikanlahti
Central Square
Aleksis Kiven katu
22
Rafinan suvanto 21
Kuninkaankatu
Näsilinnankatu
Puutarhakatu
Kauppakatu
Hämeenkatu
Hallituskatu
Satakunnankatu
6
Hämeen puisto
24
Eteläpuisto
23
Mustanlahdenkatu
25
Kortelahdenkatu
26
Amurinkatu
Mariank
27
28
Niemikatu
Pirkankatu
Tiiliruukinkatu
Satamakatu
29
30
Näsijärvi
Särkänniemi
1
5
Näsijärvenkatu
Paasikiventie
To Vaasa
To Pori
Sepankatu
Pyynikintie
Pyynikki
31
32
33
Pyhäjärvi

0   150   300 m

■	PLACES TO STAY	13	Railway Station & (Free Bicycle Outlet in Summer)
8	Tampere YWCA Youth Hostel	14	Kaleva Church
9	Grand Hotel Tammer	15	Tampere-talo Concert & Congress Centre
10	Hotel Cumulus & Finnair Terminal		
12	Hotel Tampere	16	University Main Building
19	Hotel Ilves & Koskikeskus Shopping Centre	17	Orthodox Church
		18	Tourist Information Office & Handicrafts Centre
26	Swimming Pool & Uimahallin Maja Youth Hostel/Hotel	19	Koskikeskus Shopping Centre
32	Hotel Rosendahl	20	Bus Terminal
		21	Laukontori Market & Pyhäjärvi Lake Pier (Finnish Silverline)
▼	PLACES TO EAT	22	Indoor Market
11	University Library & Restaurant	23	Public Library 'Metso' & Moominvalley Cartoon Museum
	OTHER	24	Lenin Museum
1	Särkänniemi Amusement Park	25	Hiekka Art Gallery
2	Sara Hildén Art Museum	27	Museum of Workers' Housing
3	Näsinneula Tower & Aquarium & Planetarium	28	Art Museum
		29	Beautiful Villas
4	Dolphinarium & Children's Zoo	30	Pyynikinlinna Art Museum
5	Näsijärvi Boat Pier ('The Poet's Way')	31	Pyynikki Observation Tower
6	Näsinpuisto Park & Häme Museum	33	Pyynikki Open-Air Theatre
7	Cathedral		

Aquarium The aquarium opens at 10 am and closes around 6 pm in summer, a bit earlier in winter. Admission is 20 mk.

Children's Zoo This small zoo is open from 9 May to 30 August from 10 am to 6 or 7 pm daily.

Dolphinarium There are one to five dolphin shows daily from 17 April to 27 September. Admission is 30 mk, 15 mk for children.

Näsinneula Observation Tower This is the highest observation tower in Finland, at 168 metres, and the view is excellent. There is a restaurant and a café up in the tower. It's open daily from 10 am, all year round. Admission is 12 mk.

Planetarium There are hourly presentations in Finnish every day, all year round. Admission is 20 mk.

Sara Hildén Art Museum This modern

building in the Särkänniemi area displays contemporary art in spacious exhibitions. It's open daily from 11 am to 6 pm, and admission is 10 mk. In winter the museum is closed on Modays.

Activities
Saunas & Swimming The newer indoor swimming pool at Joukahaisenkatu 7, behind the Kaleva Church, is open from 6 am to 7.45 pm Monday to Friday and from 10 am to 4.45 pm on weekends. It is closed on Tuesday mornings.

The older *uimahalli*, adjacent to the youth hostel building, is closed in summer and on Wednesdays and Sundays. Both places have proper facilities and good public saunas.

Fishing To fish in the Tammerkoski Rapids in the town centre, you will need a daily or weekly permit, available from the tourist information office.

Walking Not all walks in the town centre are

urban. The first place you visit on foot should be Pyynikki Ridge, which offers spectacular views of both lakes around Tampere. The old observation tower is open daily from 9 am to 8 pm. The protected pine forests stretch to the suburb of Pispala. Long known as a workers' residence, these days it attracts lots of wealthy people, due to the excellent views. You can also take westbound bus No 15 to its terminus and walk back from there along the ridge.

Back in the town centre, you should explore the riverside area on foot. For a long time, the river was surrounded by busy factories, but the area is now a good example of urban planning. In winter, the entire riverside is illuminated.

Lake Cruises Tampere has two beautiful lakes on which to go cruising in summer. If you are short of time, Lake Pyhäjärvi is probably your best bet, but if you have time for just one long trip, you should sail on Lake Näsijärvi. Both cruises are nice, though, so travelling all the way from Virrat in the north to Hämeenlinna in the south, or vice versa, would be the preferred way to go.

Finnish Silverline and The Poet's Way (☎ 931-124 804) are both located in the tourist information office at Verkatehtaankatu 2. The office is open from 9 am to 4 pm Monday to Friday. From 4 June to 16 August, it's open from 8.30 am to 5 pm Monday to Friday and from 8.30 to 1 pm on Saturdays. Silja Line (☎ 931-145 122) is at Keskustori 1 (central square) and Viking Line (☎ 931-140 511) is at Kuninkaankatu 17.

Lake Pyhäjärvi Finnish Silverline operates the MS *Roine*, the MS *Silver Star*, the MS *Silver Swan*, and the MS *Tampere* on routes between Tampere and Hämeenlinna. There are daily departures from 4 June to 15 August. You can go as far as Visavuori, and return the same day on another boat.

The MS *Teemu* and the MS *Ratina* have regular services to Sotkanvirta on Wednesdays and Saturdays and to Nokia on Thursdays, and to Vesilahti, as well as to the

island of Viikinsaari, hourly from 10 am to midnight. If the weather is fine, Viikinsaari is a pleasant place for a picnic.

Lake Näsijärvi The Poet's Way, from Tampere to Virrat, is one of the finest routes in Finland. The SS *Tarjanne* sails in both directions three times a week. For about 100 mk per person, you can sleep in this old boat before or after your trip. A one-way ticket costs approximately 200 mk to Virrat, 150 mk to Ruovesi. The boat transports bicycles for about 30 mk. From 1 June to 18 August, the unusual paddle-wheel MS *Finlandia Queen* has cruises from Särkänniemi, every two hours from noon to 6 pm Tuesday to Sunday. The fare is 50 mk.

Organised Tours In June, July and August, there are daily tours, starting from the tourist office at 2 pm. The 1½-hour tour costs 25 mk.

Festivals
In addition to the lively cultural programme in the concert halls, theatres, galleries and museums, there are three notable annual festivals in Tampere. Usually held in winter, the Tampere Film Festival concentrates on short films. The Pispalan Sottiisi, an international folk-dance festival, takes place in early June. The Tampere Theatre Summer is a six-day theatre event held during the second or third week of August.

Places to Stay – Bottom End
Camping *Camping Härmälä* (☎ 931-651 250) in the suburb of Härmälä, five km from the town centre, has three-bed cottages and is open from 8 May to 23 August. You can get there on bus No 1.

Hostels The *Uimahallin Maja youth hostel* (☎ 931-229 460) at Pirkankatu 10-12 is the oldest of them all. Dormitory beds cost 65 mk, and singles/doubles start at 125/210. Much more pleasant is the *NNKY youth hostel* (☎ 931-225 446) at Tuomiokirkonkatu 12A, a YWCA hostel close to the railway station. Beds in five-bed rooms are

38 mk, and singles/doubles start at 90/110 mk. The *Domus* (☎ 931-550 000) at Pellervonkatu 9 is open only from June to August. Prices range from 55 to 185 mk, depending on whether you stay at the hostel or the Summer Hotel.

Places to Stay – middle
Singles/doubles at the *Sportmotelli* (☎ 931-444 281) at Vuorentaustantie 5 start at 100/200 mk, while the *Uimahallin Maja* has singles/doubles from 125/210 mk. A small hotel with a difficult name to pronounce, the *Yöpylä* (☎ 931-451 821) at Rahtimiehenkatu 3, to the west of the suburb of Pispala, has singles/doubles for 220/320 mk.

Places to Stay – top end
Hotels in Tampere have lower rates in summer (from Midsummer to early August) and on weekends. At other times, expect prices to rise by up to 200 mk. Most hotel prices include breakfast. Summer/weekend prices are quoted in this list:

Cumulus Koskikatu (☎ 931-242 4111), Koskikatu 5. This hotel at the Finnair bus terminal has singles/doubles for 270/390 mk
Hotel Ilves (☎ 931-121 212), Hatanpään valtatie 1. Reputedly the best hotel in Tampere, it charges 400 mk for all its rooms
Lapinniemen kylpylä (☎ 931-597 111), Lapinniemenranta 12. Singles/doubles at this fine spa hotel cost 360/490 mk, and prices include access to the pools
Pinja (☎ 931-241 5111), Satakunnankatu 10. This attractive town hotel near the cathedral has singles/doubles for 250/350 mk
Rantasipi (☎ 931-245 5111), Yliopistonkatu 46. The Rantasipi, between the railway station and the Tampere-Talo Hall, has singles/doubles for 325/390 mk
Rosendahl (☎ 931-244 1111), Pyynikintie 13. This impressive modern hotel below Pyynikki Ridge has singles/doubles for 340/440 mk in July and on weekends, 580/720 mk at other times
Sokos Hotel Tammer (☎ 931-228 111), Satakunnankatu 13. One of the old hotels in Tampere, it charges 350 mk for all rooms
Tampere (☎ 931-244 6111), Hämeenkatu 1. This hotel opposite the railway station has singles/doubles at 300/400 mk in July and on weekends, 470/620 mk at other times

Victoria (☎ 931-242 5111), Itsenäisyydenkatu 1. Also near the railway station, the Victoria has singles/doubles for 240/340 mk
Sokos Hotel Villa (☎ 931-229 111), Sumeliuksenkatu 14. Rooms at this pleasant new hotel adjacent to the Tullintori shopping centre are all 350 mk

Places to Eat
The Tampere speciality is mustamakkara ('black sausage'). It may look disgusting, but it is nutritious and delicious. Locals prefer the original Tapola brand, perfect with a pint of milk. Mustamakkara is sold by the unit (not by weight), and the best places to buy it are Laukontori and the Kauppahalli indoor market. Probably the only mustamakkara fast-food restaurant in the world can be found in the western suburb of Lielahti. To get there, take bus No 11 and get off at the city-market bus stop.

University Places The two most recommendable places to meet up with local students are the *Tampere University main building* and *Attila House*, where substantial meals can be had for less than 20 mk. Coffee and snacks are also inexpensive.

Lunch Eateries Most restaurants in Tampere have special lunch prices. Even department stores such as Anttila serve meals at reasonable prices, starting well below 30 mk. The *Pihvinki* at Hallituskatu 22 and the *Aleksanteri* at Aleksanterinkatu 26 offer a cheap lunch, and the food is good.

The *Pizzeria Ristorante Bellaroma* at Kuninkaankatu 15 is cheap and good, with lunch starting at 27 mk. The *Pizzeria Ravenna* at Suvantokatu 10, near the Orthodox church, is not especially attractive but has good, inexpensive pizzas.

Fairly cheap places in Tampere include the numerous kebab restaurants, of which the *Abu Fuad* is the most established. There are outlets on Hämeenkatu, in Koskikeskus and near Laukontori.

The *Meidän Muori* at Rautatienkatu 16 serves inexpensive salads and soups, and is famous for its kanttarellikeitto (mushroom soup). The *Ohranjyvä* at Näsilinnankatu 15 is frequented by local journalists. A home-made lunch costs 35 mk on weekdays, but this is really a beer-drinking place.

For something cheap yet filling, try the workers' restaurants that can be found outside the town centre. The *St Eleena* at Hatanpään valtatie 22D, in an industrial building not far from the bus station, and the *Näsinranta* at Rantatie 27, below the Pispala area, offer lunch from 25 mk up.

Smorgasbords The *Silakka* in the Koskikeskus shopping complex has an attractive daily fish buffet, including salads and a fish soup, for 49 mk on weekdays and 68 mk on weekends.

International Food The following restaurants are known for their quality in food and service, as well as for their high prices (but check their lunch prices, which are always lower): the *Anatolia* at Verkatehtaankatu 5 for Turkish food, the *El Toro Espanol* at Näsilinnankatu 25, the *Fransmanni* and the *Louisiana* in the Hotel Ilves, the *Katupoika* at Aleksanterinkatu 20, the *Klingendahl* at Hämeenpuisto 44, the *Myllärit* at Åkerlundinkatu 4, the *Salud* at Otavalankatu 10, the *Scuuzi* in the Hotel Tammer, the *Suomalainen Klubi* at Puutarhakatu 13 and the *Tiiliholvi* at Kauppakatu 10.

Self-Catering The cheapest food stores in Tampere are the numerous Vikkula shops, which have a special *tarjous* price on almost anything. There are also other discount chains, such as Rabatti and Alepa. Visit the Kauppahalli market (on Hämeenkatu) and the marketplaces for fresh vegetables and other food.

Entertainment

Cinemas The Nordia at Hallituskatu 16 has four cinemas, presenting mostly American films. The Biobio in the Koskikeskus Shopping Centre also has four cinemas. Other cinemas in the town centre include the Adams at Hämeenkatu 9 and the Hällä at Hämeenkatu 25.

Nightclubs Nightlife in Tampere is vivid but not spectacular. The two best places in town are the Ilves Night Club (in the Hotel Ilves) and Joselin's (carved into the rock in the basement of the Hotel Rosendahl). Both places are open till 3 am Monday to Saturday. Joselin's has a cover charge of 40 mk. On weekends, check the pleasant old Laterna at Puutarhakatu 11, which has live swing music. There are several nightclubs along Hämeenkatu, of which the Hämeensilta, at No 13, offers spectacular views across Tampere. People under 22 are not admitted, and there is a cover charge. Quite special is the Senssi Club at Pirkankatu 8, open daily from 10 pm to 3 am. The Club Mixei at Otavalankatu 3 is a gay club, open Tuesday to Sunday.

Bars The *Salhojankadun pubi* on Salhojankatu is the most traditional pub in Tampere and is well known among travellers. There are several other interesting bars on Hämeenkatu, the main street. The *Pub Leena & Pekka* in the Hotelli Tampere is quite popular, but you have to be over 22 years of age to get in.

Music Tampere is a centre for the performing arts – check the current programme at the tourist office. In summer there are free concerts at 7 pm on Tuesdays and Thursdays, folk dances at 6.30 pm on Wednesdays and rock concerts at 6 pm on Sundays, in the park behind the old church. Sometimes, if the weather is fine, you will come across an amateur group performing in Näsinpuisto Park, or other locations. The Tampere-talo Concert Hall (☎ 931-243 4500) has classical concerts on Fridays, except in summer; tickets are available on the spot. There are popular nightly rock concerts in the Tullikamari, not far from the railway station (an admission fee is charged), and rock or blues concerts are frequently held in the Student House at Kauppakatu 10.

Theatre Tampere is known for its several theatres, but performances are generally in Finnish. Popular plays are presented from 15

June to 16 August in an unusual revolving theatre behind Pyynikki Ridge, at the Lake Pyhäjärvi waterfront. Even if the play is in Finnish, the experience, on a warm summer evening, may well be worth the 100 mk you'll pay for a ticket. Catch bus No 12.

Spectator Sports Tampere has two ice-hockey teams in the national league (Helsinki also has two), and most people living in Tampere identify as fans of either Ilves or Tappara. Political parties may be less divisive factors among locals than these ice-hockey teams! The Hakametsä Ice Hall is the venue for matches, or *peli*, on Thursdays and Sundays from September to March. Take eastbound bus No 25 to its terminus and see for yourself. You'll also find Europe's only ice-hockey museum (☎ 931-124 200) on the premises, open during matches, or at other times on request. Football (soccer) is played in summer at the Ratina stadium.

Things to Buy

Tampere is probably the most interesting Finnish town in which to go shopping: it has a large variety of shops and lacks the unnecessary sophistication that makes Helsinki more expensive.

Discount shops such as Rihkama-Pörssi, Super-Myynti, Vapaa-Valinta and a few others sell glassware and useful items at reasonable prices, and there is an unusually large number of second-hand shops for goods or books, to be found under the signs 'Osto & Myynti', 'Antikva' or 'Divari'.

Probably the cheapest film in Finland, if purchased in bulk, can be found at Hertell on Tuomiokirkonkatu. There are two shopping centres, Koskikeskus and Tullintori, on either side of the railway station. Interesting handicrafts can be found at Kehräsaari, converted from a factory into a shop-cum-office centre, or at Verkaranta, across the Tammerkoski River.

Markets There are several market squares in Tampere. Keskustori, the central market, is busy only on the first Monday of each month, but in summer, there is a weekday evening market. There is a weekday vegetable market at Laukontori, also called *alaranta* ('lower lakeside'), where Lake Pyhäjärvi boats depart. It's open from 6 am to 2 pm. There's also a Saturday market here, open till 1 pm, and one at Tammelantori. The traditional Market Hall at Hämeenkatu 19 is open from 8 am to 5 pm Monday to Friday and from 8 am to 2 pm on Saturdays.

Getting There & Away

Air There are five flights every weekday from Helsinki to Tampere, and a few flights on weekends. Considering the time wasted on airport transport at both ends, it doesn't make much sense to fly, unless you have a connecting flight. The cheapest return ticket is currently 275 mk. There are also daily flights between Tampere and Oulu.

Finnair (931-233 440) is at Kyttälänkatu 2, SAS (☎ 931-230 366) at Vuorikatu 3 and Aeroflot (☎ 931-237 303) at Näsilinnankatu 33.

Bus The bus terminal, 300 metres south of Koskikeskus, serves the entire Province of Häme, with regular departures to outlying towns. Regional buses, run most notably by the Paunu company, are most conveniently caught in Keskustori (central square). Several hourly Pauna buses go to Nokia, Lempäälä, Kangasala and beyond.

Train The railway station is right in the city centre. There are hourly trains from Helsinki during the day, and several trains a day from Turku, Jyväskylä, Pori and Oulu.

Hitchhiking If you're heading for Helsinki or Turku, try hitchhiking at the Viinikka roundabout, not far from the university main building. Most cars won't stop, but you are not allowed to stand at the highway, one km away. For Jyväskylä or Lahti, walk east beyond the Kaleva Church to the large hospital, two km from the railway station. For Vaasa, you'll have to catch westbound bus No 11, then walk a little further, as this is a difficult direction in which to hitchhike.

Getting Around

To/From the Airport The Finnair bus terminal is in the Cumulus Hotel at Koskikatu 5. Each arriving flight is met by a bus to Tampere.

Bus The local bus company TKL offers a 24-hour pass for local buses. It costs 25 mk and can be purchased at the tourist office or from the TKL office at Aleksis Kiven katu 11. Individual tickets cost 7 mk and include a transfer within an hour. A useful route map is available at the TKL office for a few markkaa.

Taxi The luxurious but expensive taxis depart from several locations along Hämeenkatu, including the railway station.

Bicycle Free bicycles are available from four outlets around the city, one of them at the railway station. You will need to sign up to receive the key and will be told where to leave the bicycle. You can also hire bicycles from Urheilu-10 (☎ 931-552 600) at Sammonkatu 13, and from Vuoltsu at Vuolteenkatu 13.

Central Häme

ERÄJÄRVI

Now a part of the municipality of Orivesi, Eräjärvi may have some of the oldest traces of human settlement in the region. Locals maintain that Eräpyhä Hill (159 metres), which offers fine views to Lake Längelmävesi, may have been a holy place for prehistoric hunters and fishers.

Things to See & Do

The Nunnankirkko ('Nun's Church') stone area down at the lakeside, some 10 km from the village of Eräjärvi, has historical significance. In the main village, the Kivimuseo ('Stone Museum') has local rarities on display. It is open from noon to 6 pm daily in July; in June and August, it's open on weekends only.

Several km due west from the village, the abandoned Uiherla mine has fine 'pools' for swimming, if the weather is fine. You have to look for it, as there may not even be a gate left.

Midway between Eräjärvi and Orivesi, the Rönni dance stage has humppa or other public dances on Fridays in summer, and and on Wednesdays in July.

Getting There & Away

There are buses from Orivesi to Eräjärvi, but to reach the attractions, you will need to walk.

HÄMEENKYRÖ

Hämeenkyrö is a wealthy rural municipality that is best known for F E Sillanpää, a Nobel prize winner for literature in 1939. It has a number of attractions, scattered around the beautiful countryside. The village of Hämeenkyrö has banks, restaurants, cafés and supermarkets.

Things to See & Do

Myllykolu This small house is the birthplace of Mr Sillanpää. The setting is very picturesque. Follow the Maisematie road, south of the village of Hämeenkyrö, and turn towards Heinijärvi, then Kierikkala. In summer there are theatre plays by or about Sillanpää. The house is open from 1 June to 16 August from noon to 6 pm Tuesday to Sunday. Follow the Taatan taival track that takes you to the Maisemakahvila café, a beige manor with superb views of the lake below. It is open from 15 June to 15 August from noon to 8 pm daily.

Töllinmäki This simple museum in the village of Heinijärvi is the house where Mr Sillanpää lived as a boy. It is open at the same times as Myllykolu. If you have little time, skip this one.

Other Sights There is a **local museum** in the old red brick building beside the village church. It's open from 1 June to 16 August from 11 am to 6 pm daily. The church has similar opening hours.

The **Frantsilan yrttitarha**, by the river, is a herb garden, and the Kehäkukka café serves home-made herb tea. Docked at the pier, the MS *Purimo* offers cruises for groups. Five km north of Hämeenkyrö is the spectacular **Kyröskoski Waterfall**, which can only be seen at full flow during the spring floods.

Places to Stay

There is no accommodation in the village of Hämeenkyrö. The *Pinsiön majat* (☎ 931-406 074), open all year round, is five km from the Tampere to Vaasa road along the parallel old road. Follow the 'Pinsiö' sign. This gravel road runs through spectacular countryside and is, in fact, a recommended option for reaching Hämeenkyrö. Dormitory beds cost 70 mk for YHA members, and there are boats and bicycles for hire.

Getting There & Away

Hourly buses make the 30-minute, 36-km trip between Tampere and Hämeenkyrö.

IKAALINEN

This small town, surrounded by Lake Kyrösjärvi, is on a peninsula off the main Tampere to Vaasa road. The main street has a number of banks, supermarkets and other businesses.

Information

The tourist information office (☎ 933-450 1221) at Valtakatu 7 is easy to spot. You can hire canoes here and also get assistance with your accommodation arrangements. It's open in summer from 8 am to 4 pm Monday to Friday and from 10 am to 2 pm on Saturdays; in winter, it's open on weekdays only.

Things to See

Vanha Kauppala The 'Old Township' quarters have few remaining wooden houses, but this is still a nice area to walk around. You can get a map of the area from the tourist office, free of charge.

Soitinmuseo The small museum opposite the tourist office on Valtakatu displays old

musical instruments. It is open in June and July from 11 am to 4 pm Tuesday to Sunday.

Other Sights There is a small **Pesäpallo (Baseball) Museum** at Kauppakatu 8. It is open in summer from 10 am to 2 pm. The beautiful **cross-shaped church**, built in 1801, is open in summer from 9 am to 6 pm daily. Right beside the church is a small **local museum**, which is open in summer from 10 am to 1 pm on Wednesdays and from noon to 2 pm on Sundays.

Festivals

Every year in early June, Ikaalinen celebrates accordion music during the Sata-Häme Soi Festival (☎ 933-86991). Another local event, the Midnight Sun Guitar Festival, takes place in early July. For further information, contact the local Cultural Office (☎ 933-450 1249).

Places to Stay

The cheapest accommodation option is *Toivolansaari Camping* (☎ 933-86462), on the small island that is linked to the town by a bridge. Rooms cost 130 to 220 mk. The place is open from 29 May to 16 August. The *Hotelli Ika-Hovi* (☎ 933-86325) at Keturinkatu 1, in the town centre, has singles/doubles for 200/300 mk in summer; winter prices are higher.

The largest spa in Scandinavia, the *Ikaalisten Kylpylä* (☎ 933-4511), is about 10 km north of the town of Ikaalinen. In winter, there is a road across the frozen Lake Kyrösjärvi, cutting the distance to a third. There are five large hotels in the area. The centre of activity is the Maininki, with the Tropiikki spa, several restaurants and sports facilities. Admission to the pool and sauna section costs 50 to 60 mk. Accommodation is available in singles/doubles from 355/490 mk, with discounts available for prebooked rooms.

Places to Eat

Ikaalinen has its fair share of grillis and restaurants to choose from. Discount supermarkets include Siwa and Sale, in the town centre. You can buy fresh bread from the *Kotileipomo* in the village near the main road and the *Myllyn leipä* along the road.

Getting There & Away
Several buses a day make the one-hour trip from Tampere to Ikaalinen and the Kylpylä.

KANGASALA
Geographically, the municipality of Kangasala, to the east of Tampere, is a continuation of the same formation as Pyynikki Ridge. Consequently, Kangasala offers a lot of scenic value for visitors who stop at any of the three ridges that cross Kangasala. Mr Topelius's popular song *Summerday in Kangasala* was written in praise of the scenery.

Things to See
The **old church**, built in 1765, has been carefully renovated. It's open daily in summer. The **local museum** is open daily in summer from 11 am to 5 pm. Several km to the east in Vehoniemi, the **automobile exhibition** includes displays relating to road history. It's open from 1 May to 31 August from 10 am to 8 pm daily, and on weekends in winter from noon to 6 pm. Admission is 30 mk.

Getting There & Away
Regular Paunu buses will take you to Kangasala from Tampere.

KORKEAKOSKI
Literally 'high waterfall', Korkeakoski used to be a busy factory village, because of the ample water energy available from the waterfall. It's a quiet place these days, with a post office, a few banks, several shops and a restaurant.

Things to See
Koskenjalan Museo This museum right at the waterfall has artefacts that relate to the local leather industry. There is also a café and a gallery. The museum is open only in summer.

Juupajoki Gorge Follow the steep path down from the museum to the riverside. It is a nice walk through lush vegetation.

Getting There & Away
Paunu and a few other bus companies service Korkeakoski from Keuruu, Orivesi and Tampere, 59 km away.

LEMPÄÄLÄ
This rural municipality 23 km south of Tampere has an old **stone church**, which is open to the public in summer from 9 am to 6 pm Monday to Friday. The beautiful belfry has a small museum, which is open on summer Sundays around noon. It is a short walk to the church from the railway station. Finnish Silverline ferries call at the Lempäälä canal pier daily during the summer season. Only local trains between Helsinki and Tampere stop at Lempäälä. Paunu buses for Lempäälä depart from Tampere every 30 minutes.

NOKIA
Nokia, Tampere's western neighbour, is the home of Finland's most international company (named after the town). Nokia was part of the strong Pirkkala municipality, which controlled an area from Viiala to Ähtäri from the late 13th century, and whose people collected taxes along the coast all the way to Lapland. Industries grew on the shores of the Nokia River. These days, Nokia is a possible day trip from Tampere.

Information
The tourist information office (☎ 931-423 255) is at Välikatu 18. It is open from 8 am to 4 pm Monday to Friday.

Things to See & Do
Church The wooden church was designed by Mr Engel and was completed in 1838. It is open from 1 June to 15 August from noon to 6 pm.

Hinttala Museum Opposite the church is the large local museum, with the Krouvi café, which provides tourists with information.

Sometimes there are concerts and theatre plays in the museum. The museum is open from 1 June to 31 August from noon to 8 pm.

Swimming & Sauna The modern indoor pool, not far from the museum on the main street, is not a bad place to swim for 11 mk. For more luxury, try the Eden spa on the western Tampere to Turku road. Expect to pay 60 mk for two hours of swimming and bathing.

Places to Stay
Viinikanniemi Camping (☎ 931-413 384) has cottages from 165 mk. It is open from 8 May to 13 September.

Getting There & Away
There is a Paunu bus from Tampere to Nokia every 10 to 30 minutes; the fare is 12 mk.

ORIVESI
There's nothing spectacular in the village of Orivesi, but it is at a major crossroads and is the first stop along the main Tampere to Jyväskylä road. You can get tourist information at the Auvinen handicrafts sales exhibition in the village centre. It is open from 9 am to 5 pm Monday to Friday and till 1 pm on Saturdays.

Things to See
The modern church was controversial when built, one reason being the Kain Tapper woodcarving in the altar. It is open in June and July from 10 am to 5 pm Monday to Friday. The old belfry remains, with its *vaivaisukko* pauper statue.

Places to Stay & Eat
The *Hotelli Orivesi* (☎ 935-40666) has singles/doubles at 300/320 mk. On weekdays, the *Bella*, in the Sokos building, has a set lunch for 34 mk, including drink, bread and coffee. There are three choices, including a vegetarian option.

Getting There & Away
Orivesi is 43 km from Tampere on the main Tampere to Jyväskylä road. Buses run fre-

quently, and the trip costs 25 mk. Trains stop at the small station several km from the village centre.

VESILAHTI
Once an important settlement for Lapps, Vesilahti is now a sleepy but fairly scenic municipality south of Lake Pyhäjärvi. An established 'tourist' route, the Klaus Kurjen Tie (named after a historical character who lived in Laukko Manor, now one of the attractions along this route) is a nice road for cycling, if the weather is fine.

The *Kanteletar* epic tells that Klaus Kurki killed the young girl Elina here. The 'Murder of Elina' is one of the oldest legends in Finland, and in 1992, a new opera based on this legend was presented.

The village of Vesilahti has a number of services, including a tourist information office (☎ 931-738 200). The very old village of Narva is worth a stop; the village restaurant, Voisilmä, has inexpensive snacks. There is also a tiny museum not far from Narva.

Places to Stay
Contact the Tampere tourist office in advance for more information on farm holiday possibilities along the Klaus Kurjen Tie route.

Getting There & Away
Lempäälä is the gateway to Vesilahti, and road No 313 starts a few km south of the Lempäälä railway station. Buses run on this route. In summer, there are also ferries from Tampere to the starting point of the route.

North Häme

KURU
In the tiny village of Kuru, you can visit the old church and the small local museum. Several buses a day run from Tampere to Kuru, but there is little reason to stay here. One of the national parks in Häme,

Seitseminen, is inside the municipal area of Kuru.

Seitseminen National Park

Protected mainly for its virgin forests, Seitseminen is west of the village of Kuru, some 80 km from Tampere. The excellent information centre one km south of the Kuru to Parkano road is open daily from April to October from 10 am to 6 pm; in winter, it's open on weekends only. A café sells drinks, sandwiches and sweets. Free maps of the park are available at the centre, which also features interesting exhibitions.

There are a few attractions that can be reached in a vehicle or by following walking tracks. Kovero House, seven km south of the information centre, has been converted into a museum, open in July only. The Multijärvi trail, a two-km loop around a forested hill, can be congested on weekends.

Places to Stay You can pitch your tent at any of the several camp sites inside the park. Three old houses within the park area can be booked for groups (☎ 933-33236).

Getting There & Away Several unsealed roads lead to the park, but the normal entry point is the tiny village of Länsi-Aure, on the Kuru to Parkano road. There are buses from Tampere via Kuru. Hitchhiking is possible but not very easy.

MÄNTTÄ

There are two reasons to visit the industrial town of Mänttä. One is the regular summer steamer service from Keuruu. The other is the Serlachius Art Museum, which has one of the best art collections in Finland. The museum is open daily (except Mondays) from 1 June to 15 August. There is a restaurant in the same building.

The tourist information booth at the Makos hamburger restaurant on Ratakatu has details of other art galleries in Mänttä.

Places to Stay

The youth hostel (☎ 934-419 641) at

Seppälän puistotie 12 has beds from 55 mk. It is open from 1 June to 9 August.

The two hotels in Mänttä, the *Casa Mia* (☎ 934-47041) at Kauppaneuvoksenkatu 2 and the *Mäntänkoski* (☎ 934-412 214) at Kauppakatu 23, have doubles starting at 400 mk.

Getting There & Away

You can catch the Sunday ferry from Keuruu. Otherwise, there are several buses a day to Mänttä from Tampere, Keuruu or Orivesi.

RUOVESI

Once voted the most beautiful village in Finland, Ruovesi retains much of its charm. There is not much to see or do in the village, but the journey through the wilderness of northern Häme has a lot of scenic appeal for visitors.

Information

Ruoveden Matkailu, the local tourist information office (☎ 934-761 388), is on the island of Haapasaari. Because of the camping activity, the office is open daily, from 8 am to 10 pm in summer and from 8 am to 4 pm in winter.

Things to See

Local Museum This museum features a North Häme house from the 18th century. It is open from 14 June to 9 August from noon to 6 pm. Entry is 5 mk.

Runebergin Lähde The 'Runeberg Spring' does not necessarily have anything to do with the national poet, though it is believed that one of his poems was inspired by this pleasant spring. Located a little to the north of the village centre, it is worth a visit for its unusual vegetation. Bring your water bottle and fill it with fresh, pure water.

Kalela Another celebrity from the National Romantic Era, Mr Gallén-Kallela stayed a long time in this 'wilderness studio', and in fact painted most of his famous Kalevala works here. There are exhibitions every

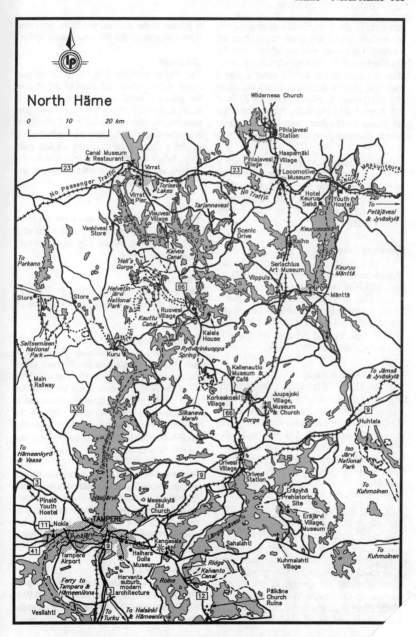

North Häme

0   10   20 km

Wilderness Church

Pihlajavesi Station

Canal Museum & Restaurant

Haapamäki Village

[23]   Virrat   Pihlajavesi Village

No Passenger Traffic

Toriseva Lakes   [23]   Locomotive Museum

Maakuntaura

Virrat Pier   Tarjannevesi   No Traffic   Hotel Keurus Selkä   Youth Hostel

Visuvesi Village   To Petäjävesi & Jyväskylä

Vaskivesi Store   Scenic Drive   Keurusselkä

To Parkano   'Hell's Gorge   Kaivos Canal   Serlachius Art Museum   Rolho   Keurju Mänttä

Helvetin-järvi National Park   Vilppula

Store   Store   Kauttu Canal   Ruovesi Village   Mänttä

Seitsemisen National Park   Kuru   Kalela House   Ryövärinkuoppa Spring

Main Railway   Kallenautio Museum & Café

[330]   To Jämsä & Jyväskylä

Korkeakoski Village   Juupajoki Village, Museum & Church

Siikaneva Marsh   [66]   Gorge   [9]   Huhtala

To Hämeenkyrö & Vaasa   Iso Järvi National Park

Orivesi Village   To Kuhmoinen

[3]   Näsijärvi   Orivesi Station

Pinsiö Youth Hostel   Messukylä Old Church   Eräpyhä Prehistoric Site

[11]   Nokia   TAMPERE   Kangasala   Eräjärvi Village, Museum

[41]   Tampere Airport   Halhara Dolls Museum   Sahalahti   To Kuhmoinen

Ferry to Tampere & Hämeenlinna   Hervanta suburb, modern architecture   Roine   Ridge   Kuhmalahti Village

Vesilahti   [3]   Kaivanto Canal   Pälkäne Church Ruins

To Turku   To Helsinki & Hämeenlinna   [12]

summer. To get there, follow main road No 66 several km south from the village of Ruovesi. Cross the modern bridge over the old Kautun canal, then turn left (east) soon after. It's three km to Kalela along a gravel road. The place is definitely worth the effort of getting there. Kalela is open from 27 June to 9 August till 5 pm daily. Admission is 30 mk, 10 mk for children under 16 years of age. Ferries also stop here on request.

Ryövärin Kuoppa Another spring worth a quick stop, especially if you are thirsty, can be found several km south of Ruovesi. You don't really see where the water comes from, but it is fresh and good. The name means 'thief's ditch'.

Places to Stay
The cheapest place to sleep is the *Haapasaaren lomakylä* (☎ 934-761 388), on the small islet north of the village. It's open from 1 May to 30 September. Rooms start at 95 mk. Of the two small hotels in the village, the *Hotelli Ruovesi* (☎ 934-762 273) has a greater capacity and cheaper rooms, with singles/doubles for 190/270 mk.

Getting There & Away
See the Häme 'Activities' section at the beginning of this chapter for details of ferry transport to and from Ruovesi. Ruovesi is on the famous Route 66, and several buses a day connect Ruovesi with Tampere and other places in the region. There are also direct buses from Helsinki. The village is off the main road, so take that into account if you hitchhike.

AROUND RUOVESI
Helvetinjärvi National Park
The main attraction of this national park, often called 'the Hell' for short, is a narrow gorge, probably created as the ice moved the huge rocks apart some 10,000 years ago. The scene inspired the design of the Finnish pavilion at the Seville World Exhibition in 1992. There are paths to follow, and you can even stay overnight. The only available map

is printed in the *Ruovesi* brochure, provided free of charge by the Ruovesi tourist office.

Siikaneva
The largest marshland in Häme accommodates unusual owls and other birds. Due to the pressure from environmentalists, it is now protected. Staying overnight is neither possible nor recommended, but if you have a vehicle of any kind, it may be worth driving to either starting point of the six-km path loop, which can be walked in a few hours. The entrance is at the 'Varikko' sign on the Orivesi to Ruovesi road.

VIRRAT
The town of Virrat is the end point for ferry trips from Tampere. It is useful to have a bicycle with you, as you may have to travel long distances here.

Information
The tourist information office (☎ 934-512 276) is in the town hall, in the centre of Virrat.

Things to See & Do
Perinnekylä The 'Tradition Village' features four museums, handicrafts sales and a restaurant with a 40 mk buffet lunch (60 mk on weekends). The area is six km from the town centre, at the Herraskoski canal, itself an interesting place to visit. One of the Finnish canal museums is right here. Set aside half a day for this area, and bring some food if the weather is fine.

Toriseva One of the most spectacular gorges in the region includes three lakes, which together constitute a nice five-km walking loop. Start from the small café on the top of the hill, near the parking area, some five km south of the town of Virrat. The café has a map that shows the track.

Places to Stay
The cheapest places to stay are camping grounds. The *Lakarin leirintäalue* (☎ 934-58639) has bungalows from 100 mk, and the *Suvi-Nuuttila* (☎ 934-58634) is not much

dearer. In the town itself, the *Summer Hotel Domus* (☎ 934-54570) at Rantatie 11, open from 1 June to 15 August, has singles/doubles for 165/210 mk. The best hotel is the *Tarjanne* (☎ 934-55454) at Virtaintie 35, with singles/doubles for 280/360 mk.

Getting There & Away

See the Häme and Tampere sections for details of ferry transport to and from Virrat. Several buses a day connect Virrat to other towns in the region.

Central Finland

The Province of Central Finland is not the wealthy flat farmland of Ostrobothnia or the rich and busy south, nor is it true lakeland or hilly Lapland. Yet, Central Finland is a little bit of everything: lonely lakes and low hills, farmhouses and villages, and gravel roads that cross the sparsely populated country-side. You will soon see what Central Finland is made of: forests are everywhere.

This is the most typical landscape of Finland. Here, amidst the might of nature, people struggle to survive, and in summer the *halla* (night frost) can sometimes destroy much of the crop. To those willing to try canoeing routes along scenic rivers, walking tracks through forests or just a ferry cruise on Lake Päijänne, Central Finland will display its subtle beauty, which may be one of the most lasting memories Finland has to offer.

ACTIVITIES
Trekking
The Maakuntaura, literally 'Provincial track', zigzags right through Central Finland. Much of the route is still in the early stage of planning, but walking tracks are marked with blue plastic strings all the way and there are good signs wherever the path forks. With the excellent 1:20,000 topo-graphical sheets, available at cost in local tourist offices, trekking is easy.

Lake Cruises
Some people say Päijänne is the most beau-tiful lake in Finland. In summer, there is daily ferry traffic between Jyväskylä and Lahti, and between the villages of Kuhmoinen and Sysmä.

Canoeing
There are two superb canoeing routes in Central Finland. One starts from the village of Karstula and runs through some scenic countryside and several interesting rapids to the town of Saarijärvi. There are several camp sites along the way, and a few demand-ing rapids, which you should check out beforehand, especially the infamous Kalmukoski (which translates roughly as 'rapids of death').

The second route, the Vanhan Vitosen route, runs from the village of Petäjävesi to the Rasua camping ground (☎ 942-81124), north of the town of Jämsänkoski. There are also several camp sites along this route.

JYVÄSKYLÄ
The town of Jyväskylä (population 67,000), founded in 1837, is the capital of the Prov-ince of Central Finland. It is another water-blessed commercial centre, with a handful of interesting museums. The first thing you may see in Jyväskylä is a cluster of box-like supermarkets, so it might sur-prise you to find that the town is in fact known for its architecture. Alvar Aalto designed quite a number of the buildings for which Jyväskylä is famous.

Orientation
The town centre lies between the train and bus stations, with a lush university campus and most museums to the west.

Information
Tourist Office The tourist information office (☎ 941-624 903, fax 941-214 393) at

Vapaudenkatu 38 stocks a large number of brochures covering attractions all over the country, and an excellent town map.

Post & Telephone The main post office, including the poste restante service, is opposite the church park, at Kilpisenkatu 8. There are a dozen other post offices around Jyväskylä. The Tele office, at Kilpisenkatu 5, is open from 9 am to 5 pm Monday to Friday.

Library The spacious public library has all 1:20,000 topographical sheets of Central Finland, easily seen in drawers on the 3rd floor. The library is open from 11 am to 7 pm Monday to Friday and till 3 pm on Saturdays. Also good is the library of the Jyväskylä University.

Bookshop There is a branch of the Akateeminen in the Torikeskus at Väinön-katu 11.

Things to See & Do
Harju This small hill near the town centre has a tower with a good general view over Jyväskylä and its surroundings. Entry is 5 mk. Every summer, the town council plants beautiful flowers along the staircase to the hill.

Museums Several museums can be seen for free with an ISIC card. Alternatively, for 20 mk, you can get a joint ticket, which is valid for three important museums in Jyväskylä. Museums in Jyväskylä are open from 11 am to 6 pm Tuesday to Sunday.

Museum of Central Finland The Keski-Suomen Museo was reopened in 1991, and it may be 1995 before all exhibitions have been reinstituted. The building was designed by Alvar Aalto.

Alvar Aalto Museum An exhibition of architecture and furniture by possibly the most famous Finnish architect is on display in this important museum. Mr Aalto's talent is greatly appreciated by most Finns, but his works also include less ambitious buildings; here you see photos of them all. For further 'field research', get free leaflets of Jyväskylä's buildings, with a map and English text.

Handicrafts Museum The permanent exhibition has information in English about Finnish handicrafts and their history. There are also temporary displays.

Environmental Information Centre Kammi If you have an interest in environmental questions, this exhibition is worth a look. Catch a local bus to Kuokkalantie 4, across the lake. The centre is open from noon to 6 pm Tuesday to Thursday and on Sundays, and until 4 pm on Fridays and Saturdays. Admission is 30 mk.

Lake Cruises There are cruises available on Lake Päijänne from early June to mid-August. The MS *Kymppi* has daily two-hour cruises (50 mk) at 11.30 am and 3 pm. In addition, there are three-hour evening cruises (65 mk) at 8 pm on Wednesdays and weekends.

Festivals
Jyväskylä always seems to be busy with minor local or international events. The Jyväskylä Arts Festival in early June features concerts, exhibitions, theatre and dance.

Places to Stay
Tuomiojärvi Camping on Taulumäentie has several cottages at 180 mk per night, and they accommodate four people. The cheapest place to stay is the *Laajari youth hostel* (☎ 941-253 355) at Laajavuorentie 15. Dormitory beds cost 30 mk for YHA members. There are also singles/doubles at 160/200 mk, with showers and a kitchen in the hallway. YHA discounts apply.

There are a few top-end hotels opposite the railway station, all of which will accept Finncheques.

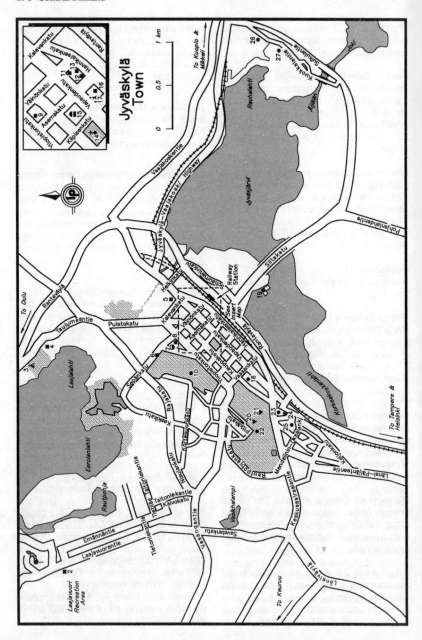

Jyväskylä
Town

To Kuopio &
Mikkeli

To Oulu

To Tampere &
Helsinki

To Keuruu

Laajavuori
Recreation
Area

■ PLACES TO STAY

1 Hotel Rantasipi Laajavuori
2 Laajari Youth Hostel
3 Tuomiojärvi Camping
4 Priimus Hotel
5 Arctia Hotel
6 Amis Summer Hotel
9 Hotel Jyväshovi
11 Cumulus Hotel
12 Areena Hotel
13 Alexandra Hotel
16 Milton Hotel

▼ PLACES TO EAT

20 University Main Building,
Ilokivi Restaurant & Museum
21 Lozzi Restaurant

OTHER

7 Bus Terminal
8 Market
10 Water Tower
14 City Church
15 Post Office
17 Tourist Information Office
18 Finnish Handicraft Museum
19 Jyväskylä Harbour
22 Swimming Pool
23 Museum of Central Finland
(Keski-Suomen Museo)
24 Alvar Aalto Museum
25 Fotokram Photographic Gallery
26 Kammi Environmental Information
Centre
27 Viherlandia Garden Centre

Areena (☎ 941-611 700), Asemakatu 2. Singles/
doubles start at 290/380 mk in summer and on
weekends
Alexandra (☎ 941-651 211), Hannikaisenkatu 35.
Singles/doubles cost 350/450 mk on weekends
and in July
Milton (☎ 941-213 411), opposite the railway station.
Singles/doubles are 290/390 mk, with a discount
of 100 mk on weekends and from 20 June to 31
July

Places to Eat

The cheapest meals in town are available at
university restaurants. The *Ilokivi* in the
Student Union building is actually an ordinary restaurant, with meals a little over 20
mk. There are rock concerts on Wednesday
and Thursday evenings. For cheaper and
more substantial meals, try the *Lozzi*
between the main building and the Ilokivi.
On the 2nd floor of the university library, you
can get cheap soups and snacks.

Most restaurants serve discounted lunch
meals. One of the best deals is the *Pikantti* in
the city market building. There are four
lunch options for 25 to 40 mk, and they
include salad, malt drink, bread and dessert.
Less attractive but slightly cheaper is the
Reimari, opposite the tourist office, where
lunch is available on weekdays only.

Things to Buy

Jyväskylä is quite a good place to look for
things to buy. The market square is busy till
2 pm, and there are handicrafts for sale.
Opposite the bus terminal, Torikeskus has
over 50 shops to choose from.

Getting There & Away

Air There are seven flights from Helsinki to
Jyväskylä each weekday and a few less on
weekends. The cheapest return ticket costs
340 mk.

Bus The bus terminal near the hill serves the
entire southern half of Finland, with several
daily express buses from big cities. The left-
luggage service at the bus terminal is more
expensive than the one at the railway station.

Train The railway station is between the
town and the harbour. There are direct trains
from Helsinki, Turku and Joensuu.

Ferry Lake Päijänne ferries depart from
Lahti and Jyväskylä at 10 am Tuesday to
Saturday, arriving at either end at 8 pm the
same day. Try to catch the SS *Suomi*, one of
the oldest steamers still plying the Finnish
lakes. A one-way ticket costs 190 mk.

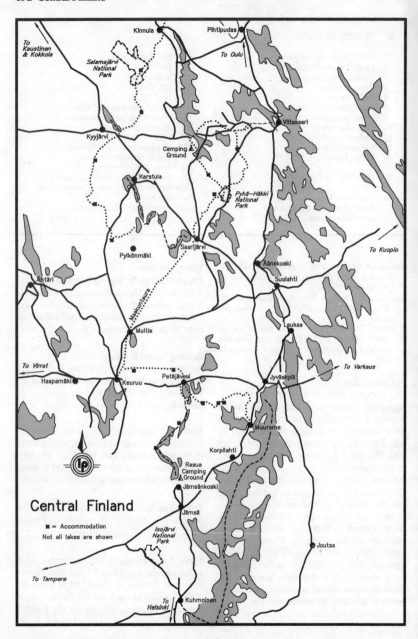

Central Finland

■ = Accommodation
Not all lakes are shown

Top: Jan Karlsgården Museum, Åland Islands (VM)
Left: A frozen windmill, Uusikaupunki (ML)
Right: Sommarstång ('summer pole') in Jomala, Åland Islands (VM)

Top: Locomotive Museum, Haapamäki (ML)
Left: The old church, Keuruu (ML)
Right: A gate, Kristinestad (VM)

Getting Around

To/From the Airport Finnair buses meet each arriving aeroplane.

Bus The most convenient place to catch local buses is at the church park. Timetables are available. Tickets cost 7 mk, or use your 10-km Coach Holiday Pass coupons for individual journeys.

Taxi Luxurious, expensive taxis are available at the bus terminal.

Bicycle Bicycles can be rented at the tourist office and at Retki & Pyöräily. Both places charge 35 mk per day, with weekly rates available at the tourist office.

HAAPAMÄKI

Haapamäki used to be a busy railway junction. When the new track through Parkano was opened, Haapamäki literally ceased to exist – it is now administratively a 'suburb' of the town of Keuruu. A few trains still pass by, and for train buffs, there is the **Höyryveturipuisto** (Steam Locomotive Museum). Old machines can be seen in this delightful collection. In summer, activities are available for children. The museum is officially open from 1 June to 16 August from 10 am to 8 pm, but locomotives can be seen at all times.

Getting There & Away

There are several buses a day from Keuruu, 16 km away, but around noon, buses only run on school days. Trains from Seinäjoki, Jyväskylä and Orivesi stop here several times daily.

JÄMSÄ

One of the most popular downhill skiing slopes, the Himos, is near the town of Jämsä on the main Tampere to Jyväskylä road. It has neither length nor height to boast about but nevertheless attracts people from big cities in South Finland. Several cottages around the slopes and in Jämsä village are available for daily or weekly rent. The local tourist information office Majakka (☎ 942-

14099) at Keskuskatu 10-12 is open from 9 am to 4 pm Monday to Friday. Get the excellent *Himos* brochure here.

KARSTULA

The remote village of Karstula, whose population of 5500 includes inhabitants of the outlying areas, is in a beautiful setting, surrounded by lakes. It is here that one of the most exciting canoeing routes starts. You can rent canoes in Karstula or in Saarijärvi.

Places to Stay

The *Vanhan Tussarin majatalo* (☎ 944-61402) on Koulutie has singles/doubles for 230/330 mk, or use Finncheques. Its rates are slightly lower than those of the *Harkko* (☎ 944-61311) at Keskustie 7, which has rooms from 300 mk.

Getting There & Away

Karstula is a few km off the main Jyväskylä to Kokkola road, and there are express buses that cover the 100 km from Jyväskylä.

KEURUU

The little town of Keuruu is on the northern shore of Lake Keurusselkä. This is where one of the most interesting wooden churches in Finland can be seen. Keuruu is recommended as a place with a lot of scenic value for visitors.

Information

The tourist information office (☎ 943-77144) in the town hall at Multiantie 5 is open in June, July and August from 9 am to 3 pm Monday to Friday. The information booth opposite the old church is open in summer only.

Things to See

Old Church The old wooden church, built in 1758, is one of the greatest places to visit in Central Finland. It has superb portraits of Bible characters, and there are old artefacts on display in the back room. See the photos of old mummified corpses found below the chancel. The church is open from 15 May to 31 August from 10 am to 5 pm daily, with a lunch break at noon. At other times of year, contact the Lutheran congregation for entry. Admission is 5 mk.

Ulkomuseo This open-air museum behind the new church contains several old buildings, complete with local tools and paraphernalia. The museum is open in June, July and August from 10 am to 6 pm daily. Entry is 4 mk.

Activities

Trekking Keuruu is one of the jumping-off points to the Maakuntaura tracks that zigzag through the Province of Central Finland. See the Central Finland trekking information for details of maps and trail marking. You can walk the 36-km track to Petäjävesi or the 84-km leg to Saarijärvi via Multia.

Keuruu to Petäjävesi It is nine km to the Veikkola (☎ 943-45815), where you can cook food. Further to the east, there is a laavu at Lake Haukinen. Proceed two km and cross the road to Rahikkala Farm (☎ 943-45415), which provides food by appointment. There is a small museum and a historical chapel in the vicinity. Some nine km before Petäjävesi, the Riihelän kämppä (☎ 943-77201) has accommodation and a sauna. Heading due east from here, you soon hit the railway track that leads to the village of Petäjävesi.

A few km north of Veikkola House is the rural Korpi-Jukolan Tila (☎ 943-45849), which has meals and accommodation from 120 mk, breakfast included. The Maakuntaura skiing track is maintained in winter, from 20 January to 20 March, and there are short skiing tracks around Keuruu and the Hotel Keurusselkä.

Lake Cruises From 6 June to 16 August, the MS *Elias Lönnrot* sails daily (except Mondays) from Keuruu to the Hotel Keurusselkä and back. Departure times are noon and 2 pm (in July, also 4 pm) Monday to Saturday, 11 am and 1 pm on Sundays. A ticket costs 40 mk one-way, 60 mk return. The departure at 1 pm on Sundays continues on to Mänttä.

Places to Stay

An economical option for groups is *Camping Nyyssänniemi* (☎ 943-20480), open from 5 June to 9 August. Bungalows cost 120 to 250 mk. The cheapest accommodation in Keuruu is the new youth hostel (☎ 943-72719) at Kivilouhoksentie 3, not far from the camping ground. It's open from 1 June to 16 August. It is two km from the railway station, along the Mänttä road. Dormitory beds cost 60 mk, and there are singles/doubles for 120/160 mk. Each room has a kitchen, a laundry is available and a sauna can be rented for about 20 mk per person. Doors are closed from 10 am to 6 pm. The top-end *Hotelli Keurusselkä* (☎ 943-80800), 10 km from the town centre, has singles/doubles for 370/430 mk.

Getting There & Away

Buses to Keuruu can be caught from Jyväskylä or even Tampere. There are several trains a day from Jyväskylä and Haapamäki.

MUURAME

If you are driving along the main Tampere to Jyväskylä road, you may want to stop in Muurame, 13 km south of Jyväskylä, to have a look at the Saunakylä (Sauna Village). This open-air museum (of sorts!), open daily in summer from 9 am to 9 pm, has various types of old saunas, but you can't bathe there.

PETÄJÄVESI

Petäjävesi Church, a cross-shaped wooden church, may be the third of Finland's attractions to be placed on the UNESCO World Heritage List. Built in 1764, it is considered the most notable example of the architecture of its time. The church has not been used since 1879, when the new church was opened.

Getting There & Away

Unless you trek along the Maakuntaura, you will need to catch an express bus between Tampere and Jyväskylä via Keuruu, or the Töysän Linja bus which runs almost hourly between Jyväskylä and Petäjävesi. It is a 33-km trip.

PIHLAJAVESI
The sleepy little village of Pihlajavesi is now part of the Keuruu municipality. All shops, banks, the post office and the public library are near the railway station.

Things to See
Pihlajavesi has an old wilderness church, built in 1780, which is fairly similar to the one in Inari in Lapland. The two-km gravel road starts between the new church and the station area, and the road signs read 'Vanha kirkko'. A guide is available on Saturdays and Sundays from noon to 7 pm in summer; at other times, use the old key which hangs above the door. The 'new' church, built in 1870, is a few km west of the railway station, and there is a small local museum there.

Getting There & Away
There are three trains a day between Seinäjoki and Haapamäki, and many of them stop at Pihlajavesi on request.

SAARIJÄRVI
The small town of Saarijärvi, home of 10,000 people, is where the Karstula to Saarijärvi canoeing route ends.

Things to See
Saarijärvi has a few attractions you may want to visit, such as the local museum, and the Upper-Class Residence, where Finland's national poet J L Runeberg worked in the 1820s, open daily from noon to 6 pm in summer. The Stone Age Village on the island of Summasaari is a reconstruction of a pre-historic habitation.

Trekking
The Maakuntaura tracks run via Saarijärvi, so at least two treks are possible from here. The northern route takes you to Pyhä-Häkki National Park, with accommodation at the Tiilikan kämppä (☎ 944-2911) and the Haarajärven kämppä (☎ 944-51551).

Walking tracks to the south will take you eventually to Keuruu, 84 km away.

Places to Stay
The *Hotelli Menninkäinen* (☎ 944-39711) has rooms from 380 mk, and there are canoes for rent. A little cheaper is the *Seurahuone* (☎ 944-21951), which has singles from 250 mk.

Getting There & Away
Many of the westbound buses from Jyväskylä will take you to Saarijärvi.

PYHÄ-HÄKKI NATIONAL PARK
The virgin forest of Pyhä-Häkki has been protected since 1912, and became a national park in 1956. Much of the park is marshland. Old trees remain the main attraction, as little wildlife can be seen, but with some luck, you'll see hole-nesting birds, some owls and even a few elk. The highlight, a bit off the shorter walking track, is the **Iso puu**, a big tree that is over 500 years old.

Information
Get a free leaflet and map at the wooden information shelter. There are two educational nature trails, with explanations in the guide. The shorter route takes you through the deep forests. The longer one passes Lake Iso Kotajärvi. You can light a campfire there, but there is no place to stay overnight.

Getting There & Away
The narrow road between Saarijärvi and Viitasaari runs through Pyhä-Häkki. It is worth driving through the park, even if you don't have time to stop. Probably the most interesting way to enter Pyhä-Häkki is to follow the Maakuntaura hiking trails from Saarijärvi.

SÄYNÄTSALO
The large Säynätsalo Civic Centre is one of the most famous works of architect Alvar Aalto. Regular buses from Jyväskylä will take you there.

VIITASAARI

Midway between Oulu and Tampere is Viitasaari. There is not much to see in the village itself, except for its scenic setting. Viitasaari is known for its taste in different art and music.

Things to See

Art Port There is an exhibition of modern art in two school buildings off the main road. It's open daily in summer till 8 pm. Entry is 30 mk, 20 mk for students.

Punainen Paja There is another exhibition worth seeing in the Wiikin kartano, 15 km north of the village of Viitasaari.

Festivals

Viitasaari is known for its 'Time of Music' Summer Festival. With modern, experimental music, it is definitely outside the mainstream. Further information is available from Time of Music (☎ 946-23195, fax 946-23438), Keskitie 10, 44500 Viitasaari.

Places to Stay & Eat

Viitasaari doesn't have much accommodation to boast about. Singles/doubles at the *Pihkuri* (☎ 946-21440) at Kappelintie 5 are expensive, at 360/470 mk. The *Ruuppo* (☎ 946-21480), several km away in Ruuponsaari, has cottages from 145 mk. The *Wiikin kartano* (☎ 946-42240) is a really an old mansion, but its stone-walled hotel rooms are in a magnificently renovated cowshed. Singles/doubles are 200/270 mk. There are also small bungalows for 200 mk. The set lunch, served from 11 am to 7 pm, starts at 42 mk and includes salad, bread and dessert. The place is close to the main Jyväskylä to Oulu road, some 15 km north of Viitasaari village.

Getting There & Away

Viitasaari is well connected by express and normal bus routes to all major towns in Central Finland.

ÄHTÄRI

Ähtäri is a success story in attracting families by means of commercial tourism. It features a zoo, the 'Mini-Finland' park and a Western Village, as well as hotels and restaurants. Admission charges are high, but this is not a bad place if you have 80 mk to spend on such things. Much more interesting is the Vehicle Museum between the village and the zoo. It houses a good collection of vintage cars, old radios and other paraphernalia.

Places to Stay & Eat

The cheapest place to stay in the village of Ähtäri is the *Gasthaus Hankola* (☎ 965-30198) at Hankolantie 17, where accommodation costs 100 mk per person. Across the lake, five km from the village, the *Hyvölän Talo* (☎ 965-30071) has beds from 80 mk, breakfast included. For information on private cottages and other accommodation, contact the Ähtärin Matkailu (☎ 965-31754, fax 965-31998) at Ostolantie 4. It's open from 1 June to 8 August from 8 am to 6 pm Monday to Friday and from 10 am to 4 pm on Saturdays. The rest of the year, it's open from 8 am to 4 pm Monday to Friday.

Getting There & Away

Trains heading east from Seinäjoki stop at Ähtäri and at the zoo (on request, though). There are three or four trains a day. Bus connections from around the region are also excellent.

West Coast

For many travellers, staring in apathy through the dusty train window, the flat Ostrobothnia may be the ugliest part of the planet they have ever seen. This first impression is a pity, because the West Coast has some of the most interesting historical places in Finland, from colourful old Catholic churches to more recent wooden towns that have been surprisingly well preserved. The West Coast also has a unique, Swedish-speaking population whose customs are quite different from those of other Finns, and from those of the Swedes themselves! You can forget about the flat plains, but missing the coastal towns altogether, from Rauma in the south to Raahe in the north, would be a serious mistake for anyone wanting to get a full picture of Finland.

ACTIVITIES
Canoeing
Although nature is not at its best in the flat Ostrobothnia, the Kyrönjoki River is good for canoeing. The entire length of the river is 205 km, but you can also do shorter trips down the river from Kauhajoki, Kurikka or Ilmajoki. Several historical points of interest are along this route. Get a copy of the *Kyrönjoen Melontareitti* leaflet for further information.

Trekking
Some shorter walks can be done in the two national parks situated between Seinäjoki and Kaskinen: Lauhanvuori park (26 sq km) and the nearby Kauhaneva & Pohjankangas National Park (32 sq km). Facilities are rather meagre, but some rewarding day trips are possible.

South-West Coast

KASKINEN/KASKÖ
If you want to visit a really small and quiet town, Kaskinen is the place to go – it is Finland's smallest town, with a population of 1800. The old centre, with its wooden buildings, is very beautiful.

Information
Kaskinen is on an island, and two bridges connect the town to the mainland. The town centre is small, so everything is within easy walking distance. There is no tourist information office, but you can get advice and brochures from the town hall (☎ 962-27711) at Raatihuoneenkatu 34 from 8 am to 3 pm Monday to Friday. You can also get information at the youth hostel.

Things to See
Museum There is a museum exhibiting old buildings and other items at Raatihuoneenkatu 48. It's open in summer from 2 to 5 pm on Sundays and Wednesdays.

Fishing Museum Fishing has traditionally been the main industry in Kaskinen, and this museum at Kalaranta displays objects related to fishing. It's open on summer Sundays from 2 to 4 pm. The old boat sheds at Kalaranta are also worth a look.

Places to Stay & Eat
The camping ground (☎ 962-27589) is small, but pleasantly located at the seaside,

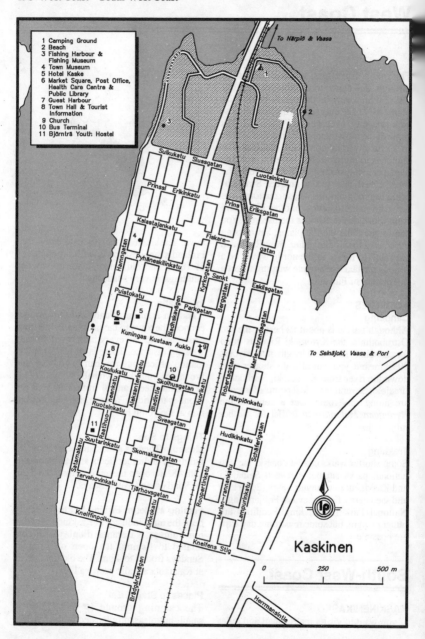

1 Camping Ground
2 Beach
3 Fishing Harbour &
  Fishing Museum
4 Town Museum
5 Hotel Kaske
6 Market Square, Post Office,
  Health Care Centre &
  Public Library
7 Guest Harbour
8 Town Hall & Tourist
  Information
9 Church
10 Bus Terminal
11 Björnträ Youth Hostel

To Närpiö & Vaasa

To Seinäjoki, Vaasa & Pori

Kaskinen

0   250   500 m

right next to the local beach. Camping costs 50 mk per family, 25 mk for single travellers. Four-bed cottages cost 110 to 125 mk. Regardless of your budget, the very nice *Björnträ youth hostel* (☎ 962-27007) at Raatihuoneenkatu 22 can be recommended. The rooms are almost of hotel standard and cost only 40 to 60 mk for members. If you want to have breakfast, an arrangement with the nearby hotel allows you to dine in the hotel breakfast room. There is also a kitchen for guests.

The only restaurant in town is connected with the *Hotel Kaske* at Raatihuoneenkatu 41-43. It has pizzas for 30 to 40 mk and lunch for 48 mk. On Wednesdays, Fridays and Saturdays, there is live music, with a cover charge of 20 mk.

Getting There & Away

There is a daily bus between Kaskinen and Vaasa. The trip takes two hours and you have to change buses in Närpiö. One of the daily buses between Pori and Vaasa goes via Kaskinen. This bus will also take you from Kristinestad to Kaskinen.

KRISTINESTAD/KRISTIINANKAUPUNKI

Kristinestad (population 9000) is one of the small, idyllic towns along the West Coast of Finland. Like other towns in the area, it is bilingual. Some 58% of the population speak Swedish.

History

Kristinestad was founded in 1649 by Count Per Brahe, and was named after his wife and the Queen Christina of Sweden. By the 1850s, the town was one of the main ports in Finland, and an important centre for shipbuilding. With the arrival of steamships, Kristinestad's importance declined and many of its inhabitants moved to Sweden. The immigration came to an end only in the 1970s, when the opening of several industrial plants provided the long-needed stimulus for the town.

Orientation

The land area of the municipality of Kristinestad is large, and in addition to the town itself, there are several smaller villages in the area. The charming wooden town centre is on the western coast of a bay. The most important places are close to the market square, but to see the nicest areas you have to get slightly out of the square – unfortunately, some of the old buildings along the market square have been replaced by (uglier) new ones.

Information

From the beginning of June to mid-August, there is a special tourist information office (☎ 962-12200) on Aitakatu, in an old customs house next to Ulrika Eleonora's Church. It's open from 10 am to 5 pm Monday to Friday and from 10 am to 2 pm on Saturdays. There are some useful leaflets covering both Kristinestad and the surrounding towns; ask for the leaflet with maps for interesting walks in the old town.

Things to See

The most interesting thing to see in Kristinestad is the town itself, where relics of old customs still survive. In the old times, every traveller entering the town had to pay customs duty, which was collected at one of two houses: the one housing the tourist information office dates from 1720, and the other one, at the northern end of the town, from 1680.

Catwhipper's Lane The narrowest street in town, Kissanpiiskaajankuja is only 299 cm wide, and one of the narrowest streets in Finland. In the 1880s the town had employed a catcatcher, whose job was to kill sick cats in order to prevent the spreading of plague, hence the name of the street.

Lebell Trader's House This house museum (☎ 962-12159) at Rantakatu 51 was once a wealthy home, dating from the beginning of the 19th century. Ask for the English-language brochure. The museum is open daily (except Mondays) from noon to 4 pm. Admission is 5 mk.

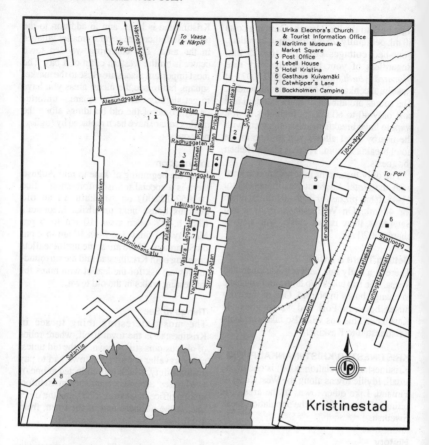

Kristinestad

Maritime Museum This delightful museum (☎ 962-12859) at Kauppatori 1, behind the library, displays a private collection of sea-related items collected by an old sea captain. If you call beforehand, you can get the captain himself to tell you about the collection. There are interesting stories to be heard. The sailboat *Fides*, while transporting metal pipes and taps from Kristinestad to Australia, was caught in a storm near South Australia in 1860. The boat sank. Ten of the sailors drowned immediately. A giant wave washed the remaining five onto rocks on the coast of Kangaroo Island, and they were saved. During the 1980s, a man from

Kristinestad, visiting relatives on Kangaroo Island, told the story of the *Fides* to locals. The site was found, over 100 years after the accident, and a memorial stone was sunk there. The musem has a copy of the memorial and pictures from Kangaroo Island in a photo album. The museum is open daily (except Mondays) from 1 May to 30 September from noon to 4 pm. Admission is 5 mk.

Ulrika Eleonora's Church This old church in the centre of Kristinestad was built in the 18th century. It's a typical coastal church, with votive ships hanging from the ceiling.

Kiili Museum On the island of Kiili is an open-air museum with old buildings and historical items. The most interesting building in the area is a wooden chapel by the sea. The museum is open from 10 am to 6 pm in June and the first half of August and from 10 am to 8 pm in July. It's closed on Mondays in August. Admission is 5 mk. On Wednesdays, Thursdays and Sundays, a cruise to Kiili departs at 11 am from a pier at the shore. You can stay in Kiili for 2½ hours, then take the same boat back.

Lappväärtti Church In the village of Lappväärtti there is a beautiful church, which is huge in relation to the size of this little village. All the inhabitants of Lappväärtti could easily fit into the church, which can seat 3000 people.

Activities
Canoeing Rowing boats are available at the camping ground for 20 mk per hour. For a longer canoe trip, rent a canoe for 80 mk at the BP petrol station (☎ 962-23771) on road No 8 at Tiukka and paddle the seven km along the Tiukka River to Kristinestad. There are a few rapids along the route. To get to the BP station, you can rent a bike at the camping ground and leave it at the BP. You can leave the canoe back at the camping ground.

Fishing There are lots of fish in the Tiukka River, so Kristinestad is also a good place for fishing. Ask for further details at the tourist office or the Tiukka petrol station. The service station sells fishing permits.

Swimming For swimming and sunbathing, go to the beach next to the camping ground.

Festivals
Traditional markets are held three times a year, in winter, autumn and summer. During the summer markets, which take place on the second weekend of July, there are musical performances, dancing, art exhibitions and a variety of programmes of all kinds. The 'Kreivin aikaan' ('On the Count's Days') is a 17th century-style party in which the people of Kristinestad receive Count Per Brahe, the founder of the town. The programme starts in Ulrika Eleonora's Church at 6 pm and, at this point, is open for everyone. A dinner party, with food prepared according to 17th century recipes, and old music, costs 190 mk. The event is held a few times each summer. For further information, call the Hotel Kristina (☎ 962-12555). The last weekend of July sees the 'Festival of the 1960s' in the Hotel Kristina, with music from that decade.

Places to Stay – bottom end
The cheapest place to stay in Kristinestad is *Bockholmen Camping* (☎ 962-11484) on Salantie, 1.3 km from the town centre. This pleasant place at a small beach is open from 1 June to 15 August. Cottages for two cost 90 to 110 mk and cottages for four are 130 to 200 mk. Camping is 55 mk per family, 30 mk if you are alone.

The *Kilstrands youth hostel* (☎ 962-25611) in Kiili is recommended. Its location, right next to the open-air museum at the seaside, is superb, and the hostel itself is of reasonable standard. Most of the rooms have four beds, but there are also some doubles. For members, dormitory beds cost 35 mk. Doubles are 45 mk per person. The hostel is open from 15 May to 15 August, and there are two buses a day to Kiili from both Pori and Kristinestad. The youth hostel has canoes for hire.

Places to Stay – middle
The *Gasthaus Kuivamäki* (☎ 962-12878) at Rautatiekatu 4, on the western side of the bay, has singles for 110 to 160 mk and doubles for 170 to 230 mk. Breakfast costs an extra 15 mk. The place is nothing special, though. A km away and run by the same family, the 'summer hotel' *Högåsen* is open in June and July. Reception is at the Gasthaus. Singles/doubles are 80/120 mk, not including breakfast and sheets, and a kitchen is available for guests.

Places to Stay – top end

The *Hotel Kristina* (☎ 962-12555), across the bridge from the town centre, offers comfortable accommodation with a great view over the bay. Singles are 350 to 420 mk and doubles cost 450 to 520 mk. There is dancing and live music in the evenings.

Places to Eat

The lunch restaurant *Ninette* at Merikatu 33, with good food and substantial portions, can be recommended for its excellent 'all you can eat' salad bar (20 mk), or its lunch (30 mk). The *Kissanpiiskaaja* at the market square has a buffet lunch for 45 mk Monday to Friday. The *Torikahvila*, a pleasant café at the market, has good pastries and snacks at reasonable prices.

Getting There & Away

There are five buses a day between Pori and Vaasa, which go via Kristinestad. The trip from either Vaasa or Pori takes approximately 1½ hours. There are two buses a day from Tampere, a trip of over five hours.

Getting Around

You can rent bicycles at the camping ground for 10 mk per hour. To get to Kiili, take the post bus, which departs twice a day. There is also a boat three times a week.

NÄRPES/NÄRPIÖ

Närpes ('Närpiö' in Finnish) has one of the highest rates of Swedish speakers in the country – 94% of the inhabitants speak Swedish as their native language, with a special local accent that is hard to understand. There are few attractions to see there, apart from the unique 150 church stables on the Kyrkbacken. Churchgoers attending the service would keep their horses in these stables. At the nearby Bengtsgården, there is an open-air museum with several old buildings. The old pharmacy is especially interesting.

Getting There & Away

You can get to Närpiö by taking a bus from Turku to Vaasa. There are four buses a day, and the same buses go via Kristinestad and Pori.

PORI/BJÖRNEBORG

Pori is one of the most important harbours in Finland, and industries are the town's major employers. However, Pori has more recently become very famous for its annual jazz festival, considered to be one of the most important jazz events in Europe, and this is the best time to visit Pori.

History

In 1558, Duke Juhana of Finland decided to establish a strong trading town on the eastern coast of the Gulf of Botnia. As a result, Pori was founded at the mouth of the Kokemäenjoki River. Since then, Pori has been a regional centre for trade, shipping and industry. The population is 77,000.

Orientation

Pori is divided into several parts by the Kokemäenjoki River, the railway and the main Helsinki to Vaasa road. Yrjönkatu, the main street, borders the market square in the north. Interesting old houses can be found between Rauhanpuisto, Maantiekatu and the railroad tracks, and between Vähälinnankatu, Itsenäisyydenkatu and Paanakedonkatu. The interesting seaside resorts of Yyteri and Reposaari are 20 to 30 km north-west of the town centre and can be reached by car, bicycle or bus.

Information

The tourist information office (☎ 939-335 780) in the town hall at Hallistuskatu 9A has an excellent collection of brochures, both of Pori and of nearby places. You can also borrow a bicycle here. The office is open from 1 June to 15 August from 8 am to 6 pm Monday to Friday and from 9 am to 1 pm on Saturdays. At other times, it's open on weekdays only, from 8 am to 4 pm.

Things to See & Do

Satakunta Museum This regional museum (☎ 939-338 141) at Hallituskatu 11 features the history of the area and also has temporary exhibitions. On the 2nd floor, there is an interesting miniature of Old Pori. The museum is open daily (except Mondays) from 11 am to 5 pm. Admission is free.

Pori Art Museum This is one of the most respected museums in Finland. The exhibits are based on a private collection of modern art owned by Ms Maire Gullichsen. The museum building on Eteläranta is an old warehouse, which was turned into a museum in 1981. It's open daily (except Mondays) from 11 am to 6 pm. Admission is free.

Poriginal Gallery This gallery (☎ 939-417 873) at Eteläranta 6, almost next door to the Pori Art Museum, is in the same place as the Pori Jazz office, hence the name – Poriginal is one of the slogans of the jazz festival. When there are exhibitions, the gallery is open daily (except Mondays) from 11 am to 6 pm. Admission is free.

Juselius Mausoleum This art gallery at the Käppänä Cemetery is the most famous sight in Pori. Mr F A Juselius, a rich businessman, had it built as a memorial to his daughter, who died at the age of 11. Mr Juselius was so distraught at the death of his only child that he wanted to build the most beautiful mausoleum money could buy. He also wanted to do anything possible to prevent other people from similar suffering, so he started a foundation that was to donate money for medical research. Today, this foundation is one of the most important sources of private funding in the country.

The frescoes in the mausoleum were originally painted by Akseli Gallen-Kallela, the most prominent Finnish artist of the National Romantic era. Mr Gallen-Kallela had just lost his own daughter, and he got deeply involved in the frescoes, working on them for three years. The original frescoes were later destroyed, and the ones you can see now were painted by Jorma Gallen-Kallela, Akseli's son, after his father's death. The mausoleum is open from 1 May to 15 September from noon to 3 pm daily. At other times, it's open on Sundays from noon to 2 pm.

Kirjurinluoto This island in the Kokemäenjoki River is a beautiful park and also the main site of the Pori jazz festival. You can play minigolf here on indoor or outdoor courses.

Yyteri This beach resort in Meri-Pori (Sea Pori) features a long beach with dunes, and there is plenty to do. You can play tennis, golf, badminton and volleyball, and there are also water slides. Yyteri is a nice place to spend time on the beach, if the weather is fine. Immediately after you turn off the main road to Yyteri, there is a observation tower with a café. It's open from noon to midnight Monday to Friday and from 10 am to midnight on weekends. There is a lift fee of 5 mk, which you don't have to pay if you buy something at the café. The view is nice, but unfortunately you can't see the Yyteri beach, which is behind trees. To get to Yyteri, take bus Nos 32 or 42 from the market square.

Reposaari Reposaari is at the end of the north-western peninsula of Pori. This interesting little fishing village is on an island which has only been connected to the mainland by a bridge since 1956. Reposaari still has its own unique character – it is probably the only place in Finland where people take a one-hour 'siesta' at noon. All the shops close, and people disappear from the streets to have their lunch. Reposaari is a picturesque place, with its wooden houses and well-kept parks, and it is hard to believe that, even today, it is primarily an industrial village. Reposaari has Finland's best natural harbour, and its fishing harbour is the most modern in Finland.

Festivals
Pori hosts the annual Pori Jazz Festival, one of the most popular festivals in the country. The festivals started in 1966, when some local musicians arranged a two-day festival with an audience of 1000 people. Nowadays, the festival is a nine-day event with 100

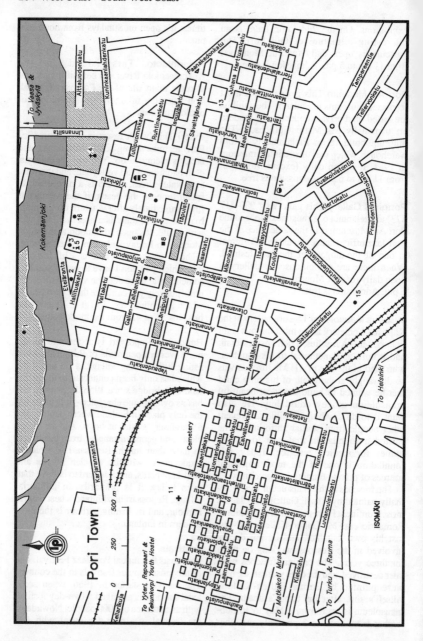

1	Kirjurinluoto
2	Satakunta Museum
3	Pori Art Museum
4	Church
5	Tourist Information Office
6	Hotel Vaakuna
7	Public Library
8	Matkakoti Keskus
9	Market Square
10	Post Office
11	Hospital
12	Old wooden buildings
13	Old wooden buildings
14	Bus Terminal
15	Railway Station
16	Poriginal Gallery
17	Town Hall

concerts, and Jazz Street (Eteläkatu) is full of stands. Some of the concerts are held in tents, outdoors or in old warehouses. Ticket prices range from 20 to 800 mk but most concerts cost about 80 mk. The popular open-air concerts on Kirjurinluoto cost 130 to 170 mk.

Even if you don't feel like paying to go to concerts, Pori is a fantastic place to visit during the Jazz Festival. There are a lot of visitors who come from everywhere, and there are also free performances every day on Jazz Street. The regular accommodation capacity of Pori is not enough to cope with the festival, so the tourist office arranges extra accommodation at homes and in school gyms. It is also possible to spend the whole night at a jam session, some of which last until 7 am.

Places to Stay – bottom end

Yyteri Camping (☎ 939-343 778) is a popular site, with access to the dunes and the beach. Camping costs 70 mk per family or 45 mk per individual traveller, and four-bed cottages cost 160 to 270 mk. Big cottages with a shower or a sauna are 350 to 400 mk. In Midsummer, Yyteri is noisy, crowded and filled with partying people. At other times, however, the users are mostly families. Yyteri is open from June to August. The

other camping ground at Reposaari, the *Siikarannan leirintäalue* (☎ 939-344 120), is smaller and quieter than Yyteri. The camping fee is 65 mk per family or 35 mk per individual camper, and there are two/four-person cottages for 175/190 mk.

The *Tekunkorpi* (☎ 939-28400) on Korventie, open from 15 May to 15 August, is a youth hostel and a summer hotel. The youth hostel rooms and the hotel rooms are rather similar, the main difference being that in the youth hostel, you have to bring your own sheets. In the summer hotel, singles/doubles cost 180/250 mk, including breakfast. The youth hostel costs 50 mk per person (35 mk for members). To get there, take bus Nos 32 or 42 towards Yyteri, get off at Ammatillinen kurssikeskus, walk across two streets and follow the signs. The Tekunkorpi is 200 metres away, in the woods.

During the jazz festival, there are several cheap accommodation options (from 55 mk). You can book a bed at the tourist office.

Places to Stay – middle

The *Matkakoti Keskus* (☎ 939-338 447), a simple guesthouse at Itäpuisto 13, in the town centre, has singles/doubles at 155/220 mk. Showers and toilets are in the corridors, and no breakfast is available. Some 3.5 km from the centre, in the Musa area, the *Matkakoti Musa* has pleasant singles/doubles for 180/270 mk. Still further away from town, in Mäntyluoto, there is the *Mäntyluodon Hotelli* (☎ 939-343 270), in the dull, industrial area. The location, between roads and railways, is not the best possible, but the hotel is in a nice old wooden building. Singles/doubles are 170/220 mk.

In the Yyteri area, there are several places to stay. The *Yyterin kievari* (☎ 939-343 922), a guesthouse on Santojentie, is run by a friendly family and is very close to the beach. Singles/doubles cost 240/290 mk; breakfast is not included. For cheaper accommodation, ask whether it is possible to sleep in the *aitta*.

Places to Stay – top end

If you want to stay in a hotel, the *Vaakuna* (☎ 939-820 100) at Gallen-Kallelankatu 7, right in the town centre, can be recommended. The rooms are tasteful and the hotel has popular bars and restaurants. Singles/doubles are 300/400 mk on weekends and in summer, 430/560 mk at other times. If you have Finncheques, use them here.

Places to Eat
You'll find an incredible number of grillis in the centre of Pori. A popular kebab place is on Itäpuisto, on the opposite side of the street from the Matkakoti Keskus. Another popular place is the *Hesburger*, which has a restaurant at the Bebop shopping centre on Yrjönkatu. For self-catering meals, use the food store on the ground floor of the Bebop and eat at one of the tables in front. The *Liisanpuisto* restaurant at Liisankatu 20 is run by the catering school and has good, cheap food. The food is also good at the *Raatihuoneen Kellari*, a cosy basement restaurant at Hallituskatu 9. The *Amado* at Keskusaukio, close to the bus terminal, has excellent Mediterranean-style food for 30 to 100 mk a meal. For excellent fish, try the *Reposaari* at Satamapuisto 34 in Reposaari. The buffet, with good fish dishes and several main courses, is 65 mk. The buffet is served daily in July and August, and on Sundays at other times. Many people drive to Reposaari just to dine here.

Entertainment
The lobby bar/restaurant of the Hotel Vaakuna is a popular place in the evenings, as is the nightclub Moriz in the same building. The Moriz has a cover charge of 40 mk on Wednesdays, Fridays and Saturdays. Both places have an age limit of 22, but this can be flexible. At the restaurant Punainen Kukko, there is dancing to all kinds of live music. Patrons are 20 to 50 years old. The Monttu, at the market square on Antinkatu, has live music daily and a singing night on Thursdays. There is no cover charge.

Getting There & Away
Air There are four flights a day between Pori and Helsinki on weekdays and one on weekends. There are also daily flights to/from Turku and Vaasa.

Bus There are 16 buses daily between Helsinki and Pori. There are 12 buses a day between Rauma and Pori on weekdays and seven on weekends. The trip takes approximately one hour. There are three buses from Turku, and a daily bus from Seinäjoki (travel time is approximately three hours, for either journey). A bus leaves Tampere in the morning and returns around noon, a 2½-hour journey each way. There is also a bus from Pori to Jyväskylä in the morning and from Jyväskylä to Pori in the afternoon. The trip takes four hours one-way.

Train All trains to Pori go via Tampere, where you often have to change trains. There are five or six trains a day between Tampere and Pori, all of which have good connections to trains from Helsinki.

Getting Around
Bus An extensive bus service operates in the town area; route maps are available at the tourist office. In addition to single tickets, you can buy 10-trip discounted tickets. Most buses pass the market square.

Bicycle The tourist office lends bicycles for up to one week. There is a 20 mk service charge. You have to leave a deposit of 100 mk, which will be refunded when you return the bicycle without damage.

RAUMA
Rauma (population 31,000) is one of the most interesting places to visit in Finland. Even if you are short of time, make sure you find a day or two to spend in Rauma – it has a character all its own. The main attraction, the old town, was recently placed on the UNESCO World Heritage List as Finland's first entry. Although it is the largest wooden town preserved in the Nordic countries, Rauma's old town is not a museum but a living town centre, with many artisans, lace makers and goldsmiths working in small studios. Yet another feature of Rauma is its

dialect, which is almost a separate language. The dialect is so different from Finnish that it is not easy for outsiders to understand – Finnish and Rauma are like English and pidgin English.

Orientation

More or less everything in Rauma is either in the old town or along the canal or Valtakatu, the main street. On the western side of town is a big harbour, which looks more like a modern industrial plant than a romantic port for vessels from all around the world. Pleasant recreational areas are to be found at Poroholma and Fåfänga.

Information

In summer, there are two municipal information offices in Rauma. The more accessible one, at the market square, is open from 15 June to 15 August from 10 am to 6 pm Monday to Friday and from 10 am to 3 pm on weekends. They have a lot of useful brochures, the best of which is a walking-tour guide of old Rauma which includes information on all the main sights. Ask also for the tourist map, which includes both old Rauma and the whole town. The main tourist office (☎ 938-344 551) at Valtakatu 2 is open from 1 June to 31 August from 8 am to 3 pm Monday to Friday, and until 4 pm from September to May.

Things to See

Old Rauma Old Rauma as a whole is worth taking some extra time to explore. Walk along the streets, visit shops and stop at cafeterias. Most of the buildings were erected in the 18th and 19th centuries. The old town covers 30 hectares, and there are 600 houses and 180 shops in this area. The oval signs on the buildings give the name of each house. There are guided walking tours on Tuesdays and Saturdays in July, departing from the Church of the Holy Cross at 5 pm. The tour costs 10 mk and takes 1½ hours. The walking route shown in the tourist office's brochure is also excellent. There are occasional sightseeing tours by bus; ask for details at the tourist office.

The market square is the heart of Old Rauma and a lively centre for commerce even today. At one end of the square, there are two wooden stalls which sell coffee and refreshments. They open at 7 am. The locals call them *pystcaffe* ('a coffee place'), where you stand while drinking.

Museums If you buy the 10 mk ticket to any of these museums, it is valid for the others during the same or the following day.

Marela This house museum at Kauppiaankatu 24 belonged to a rich trader. After his death, his two sons spent all their father's money on wine and women. In a few years, they were totally broke and had to sell everything from the house. The museum is open daily from 10 am to 5 pm. In winter, it's closed on Mondays.

Kirsti House Museum This house was once the home of a sailor, and people actually lived here as recently as 1972. Note the china dogs in the bedrooms. They were placed in a window and actually had an important function: when the dogs faced outside, the sailor was sailing; when they faced inside, the sailor was home and could be visited. The museum is open daily from 10 am to 5 pm in summer.

Potter's House This house at Nummenkatu 2 is the smallest of the town museums. Here you can watch how pottery is made and try making some for yourself. Children are particularly keen to make their own pottery. The house is open from 15 May to 15 August from 10 am to 1 pm daily.

Rauma Museum This museum on the market square exhibits old objects from the area and also various lace models. In the garden are the types of plants that people used to have years ago.

Lönnström Museum Another house museum is the home of Teresia and Rafael Lönnström, at Syväraumankatu 41. In addition to furniture, this museum exhibits old

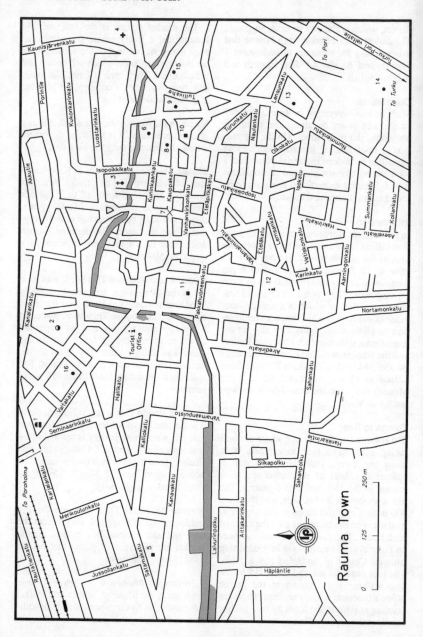

Rauma Town

1	Post Office
2	Bus Terminal
3	Church of the Holy Cross
4	Hospital
5	Summer Hotel Rauma
6	Kirsti Home Museum
7	Market Square, Town Hall & Rauma Museum
8	Marela Museum
9	Art Museum
10	Kalatorin Majatalo
11	Hotel Cityhovi
12	Tourist Information Office
13	Potter's House
14	Water Tower
15	Puppet Theatre Tiuku
16	Lönnström Art Museum

paintings. It's open from 3 to 6 pm on Wednesdays and from noon to 4 pm on Sundays. Opening hours are longer during lace week.

Art Museum The art museum (☎ 938-224 346) is conveniently located in Old Rauma, at Kuninkaankatu 37. There are temporary exhibitions all the time, and every other year, there is a major event called Biennale Balticum, featuring contemporary art from all the countries around the Baltic Sea, including Estonia, Latvia and Lithuania. The Biennale Balticum lasts from April to mid-July. The museum is open from 1 June to 31 August from 10 am to 6 pm Monday to Friday, 10 am to 4 pm on Saturdays and noon to 6 pm on Sundays. In winter, it's closed on Mondays. Admission is 10 to 15 mk during the Biennale and 2 mk at other times.

Church of the Holy Cross The Pyhän Ristin Kirkko at Luostarinkatu 1 is a 15th century Franciscan church. A Catholic monastery functioned here until 1538, when the Lutheran reform closed the monastery, forcing the monks out. The church can be visited from 1 June to 31 August from 9 am to 6 pm Monday to Friday, 9 am to 1 pm on Saturdays and noon to 6 pm on Sundays. In September, it is open from 10 am to 4 pm Monday to Friday, 9 am to noon on Saturdays and noon to 3 pm on Sundays.

Water Tower This tower, which also functions as an observation tower, is open daily in summer from 10 am to 8 pm. There is a lift fee of 2 mk.

Reksaari The holiday island of Reksaari is owned by the town of Rauma. You can get there by boat, leaving from Syväraumanlahti. The boat runs twice a day in summer, at 10 am and 5 pm, and the return trip costs 30 mk. If you want to take the same boat back, you'll have 30 minutes in Reksaari. You are allowed to camp on the island free of charge. There are also four-bed cottages at 140 mk and doubles at 55 mk. The facilities are meant for the local people (ie taxpayers), but if you like the place, it doesn't hurt to ask if you can stay there overnight.

Activities
There is a little beach and a nice pool at Fåfänga, where you can also hire windsurfing boards. Canoes and boats are available (15 mk per hour) at Poroholma Camping, where you can also play minigolf. On the island of Rekholms, you can hire rowing boats for 5 mk per hour or 30 mk per day.

Festivals
Rauma lace week is the town's biggest annual event. It starts on the last weekend of July and includes a host of exhibitions and events. Shops are open later than usual, and the whole weekend starts with the 'Night of Black Lace', a small-scale carnival, during which shops and restaurants are open till 3 am and there are masses of people on the streets. Another annual event is the Rauma Blues Festival, a one-day festival held in a big tent at the beach towards the end of July.

Places to Stay – bottom end
The best place to stay is at Poroholma, by the sea. At *Poroholma Camping*, camping costs 60 mk per family, 30 mk for individuals. Four-bed cottages are 170 mk. The youth

hostel (☎ 938-224 666) here is one of the most beautiful youth hostels in Finland. Reception is at the entrance of the camping ground, not inside the building. At the turn of the century, this old villa was the summer residence of a rich merchant. One of the rooms is especially attractive, since it has access to a tower. If you want this room, book beforehand. For YHA members, beds cost 30 mk in dormitories, 45 mk in doubles. Non-members pay 15 mk more. Both the camping ground and the youth hostel are open from 15 May to 31 August.

Places to Stay – middle

The *Summer Hotel Rauma* on Satamakatu is a student dormitory in winter and a hotel in June, July and August. The rooms are OK but not especially attractive. Singles/doubles cost 170/230 mk, including breakfast.

Places to Stay – top end

The *Kalatorin Majatalo* (☎ 938-227 111), at Kalatori 4 in Old Rauma, is the most pleasant hotel in town. It is in a beautifully renovated old warehouse – the architect responsible for the plans got a major international award for the work he has done in preserving buildings in Old Rauma. The owners are very friendly and know a lot about the history and sights of Rauma. If you want to stay in a hotel only once or twice during your stay in Finland, this is a good candidate. It is not luxurious, simply pleasant. Singles/doubles are 250/310 mk in summer, 340/450 mk in winter.

The *Hotelli Cityhovi* (☎ 938-222 811) at Nortamonkatu 18, right in the centre of Rauma, is another nice place to stay. The rooms are spacious and comfortable, and the hotel serves a good breakfast. Singles/doubles are 210/260 mk from Midsummer to mid-August, 300/390 mk at other times.

Places to Eat

A good way to have a cheap meal is to buy your own food at the market square and use the tables in the back yard of the museum for dining. Another option is the local student cafeteria *Kulinarium* on the corner of Semi-naarinkatu and Satamakatu. It's open for lunch Monday to Friday until 2 pm in summer and slightly longer in winter. If you're not a student in Finland, you can't get the special discount, but even without it, you pay only 15 mk for a full meal.

The *Kontion Kahvila-Konditoria* at Kuninkaankatu 9 serves pastries and other snacks. Even if you just want a cup of coffee, this wonderful café is worth a visit. It's strictly nonsmoking. The restaurant *Rosso* at Savilankatu 1 serves pizzas in a nice old building. The service is friendly and the pizzas cost 40 to 50 mk. The *Kalatorin majatalo* has good food, especially fish. Its prices start at 50 mk for a main course. The *Mustan Kissan kellari*, a basement restaurant at Anundilankatu 8, has a popular terrace, which has sunlight until quite late in summer.

Entertainment

The Pikku Ritari at Kauppakatu has live music, and often features bands playing Finnish rock music. The general style is rock/pop and the audience consists of relatively young people. The Kalliohovi at Kalliokatu 25 is a popular evening spot, with dancing every night, except Sundays. Wednesday is popular among younger people, and on Mondays there are 'Women's dances', where women ask men to dance. The cover charge varies from 10 to 35 mk, depending on the band. The Pigalle at Valtakatu 5, in the Hotel Raumanlinna, is another dancing spot. On Saturdays, it is crowded with young people; on other nights, most of the patrons are more mature. The disco at the Cumulus is popular among 18 to 25-year-olds.

Things to Buy

One of the things for which Rauma is famous is its bobbin lace. The skill was brought from abroad by sailors, who learnt how to make bobbin lace. Originally, laces were made only by men, but later, women adopted the trade, and today, only a few men make lace. The best place to buy lace is the Pits-Priia at Kauppakatu 29, where you can see the bobbin lace being made. The laces are not cheap – you can't really get anything for less than 200 mk – but the makers say that if they charged a decent hourly wage, the prices would at least double. For them, making lace is not a business but a hobby.

There are many other places selling handicrafts. For a current, complete list of the shops, ask for a brochure at the tourist office. Among the more interesting ones are the Ateljee Eila Minkkinen at Vanhankirkonkatu 20 (jewellery and metal reliefs) and the Lahjanavetta at Kulmakatu 6 (all kinds of souvenirs and traditional things, including stones that have been painted to look like cats). The Kultasuutari at Kalatori 4 is a goldsmith's shop where you can actually watch the goldsmith at work and where you can also buy conventional jewellery and some local specialities, such as gold jewellery that looks like lace.

Getting There & Away
Bus The daily direct bus between Helsinki and Rauma takes approximately 4½ hours. Between Rauma and Pori, a journey of approximately one hour, there are 12 buses a day each weekday and seven on weekends. There are more than 10 buses a day between Turku and Rauma. The travel time is 1½ hours.

Train Rauma can no longer be reached by train, but the Finnish state railway has three daily connections from Tampere via Kokemäki, where you have to change to a bus. The bus ticket to Rauma is included in the price of the train ticket.

VAMMALA
This small historic town offers the visitor a number of attractions. Most shops and restaurants are along or near the main street, Puistokatu.

Information
From 1 June to 15 August, the tourist information booth (☎ 932-198 255) on Rautavedenkatu, at the harbour, is open every day from 10 am to 5 pm. The staff is

helpful, and the place stocks a lot of useful brochures.

Things to See & Do
Tyrvää Museum This museum (☎ 932-42750) at Jaatsinkatu 2 has a collection of old objects from around Vammala. Because the area has been inhabited for a very long time, the museum also has some archaeological items. It's open from noon to 4 pm Sunday to Friday. Tickets cost 3 mk.

Tyrvää Church The church at the northern end of Puistokatu is the first church in Finland to have two towers. It's open in summer from 10 am to 6 pm every day.

St Olaf's Church This church is outside the town centre. It was built in the late 14th century and its current interior dates from the 18th century. The church is open in summer from 10 am to 4 pm Monday to Saturday and from 11 am to 6 pm on Sundays.

Jaatsi This old house (☎ 932-198 266) on Asemakatu is the childhood home of Akseli Gallen-Kallela, probably the most famous Finnish painter of all time. It houses the art collection of the town of Vammala, including a few small works by Gallen-Kallela. All the other works are by artists who have some kind of connection to Vammala. Jaatsi House is open from 10 am to 3 pm every day. Admission is free.

Tractor Exhibition This exhibition, open from 1 June to 15 August, is next to the camping ground. Tickets cost 10 mk for adults, 5 mk for children.

Ellivuori At Ellivuori, there is an interesting place called Pirunvuori ('mountain of the devil'). A painter, Emil Danielson, built a studio of grey rocks on top of the hill in 1906 and called it Kivilinna ('rock castle'). A good path will take you the 1.5 km up from the Hotel Ellivuori. You can get keys and further information on opening hours from the hotel reception desk, but the studio is also interesting from the outside. Ellivuori can be

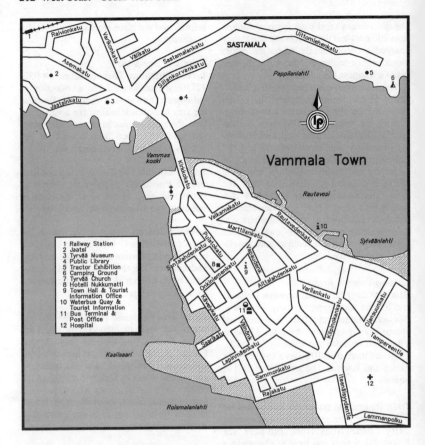

reached by bus. However, a more pleasant way to get there is by boat. The trip takes 80 minutes and costs 20 mk one-way. Boats run on Wednesdays and Saturdays from June to August; you can catch one at 8 am in Vammala and come back on the afternoon boat, which leaves Ellivuori at 4 pm.

Vehmaanniemi At Vehmaanniemi, three km east of the town centre along Tampereentie, there is a nature path along the little peninsula, protected by the World Wildlife Fund. The path runs through a preserved area in which, in addition to the natural beauty, Iron Age graves have been found. The path is approximately two km long and is marked by signs along the way.

Festivals

The most famous annual event in Vammala is its 'Vanhan kirjallisuuden päivät' ('Days of Old Literature'), held on the last weekend of June. During the event, there are various exhibitions, auctions and presentations of old books. The whole programme is in Finnish, but if you are interested in books, this is a good time to visit Vammala. The Satakunnan Kansansoutu, a popular rowing and paddling event, is held on the third weekend of July. The 109-km route takes the rowers from Vammala to Pori in three days. The Kansansoutu is not a competition, but everyone overnights in the same places and there are activities in the evenings. The participation fee of 120 mk covers insurance, transportation of the luggage from Vammala to Pori, and camping and sauna fees. You have to provide your own boat/canoe and a tent. For further information on borrowing/renting a boat, call Mr Markku Torpo (☎ 932- 33595).

Places to Stay

The camping ground at the end of Uittomiehenkatu is tiny and not especially pleasant. Pitching a tent costs 50 mk per family, 25 mk for an individual, and cottages for four cost 200 mk. The *Hotelli Nukkumatti* (☎ 932-42623) at Onkiniemenkatu 6 offers a quiet, homely place to stay. Some of the decoration is rather old-fashioned, but the rooms are neat and clean. Singles/doubles cost 240/350 mk. The *Hotelli Ellivuori*, several km from the town centre along road No 41, is more of a resort than a hotel. A host of activities is available, including tennis, golf, fishing, boating and hiking. Singles/doubles are 260/365 mk in summer and around Christmas, 470/600 mk at other times.

Places to Eat

The *Gasthaus Liekoranta* at Asemakatu 34 serves an 'all you can eat' buffet lunch for 34 mk. The restaurant of the *Hotelli Seurahuone* at Puistokatu 4 has a salad bar with a soup for 30 mk at lunch time. This hotel is also the most popular nightspot in town, with pop, rock and dancing. The *Herkku-Tuote* at Onkiniemenkatu 6, near the market square, is a pleasant place for coffee or snacks.

Getting There & Away

Bus The bus terminal is on Puistokatu. There is a daily connection between Vammala and Helsinki, a journey of approximately three hours. On weekdays, there are two additional buses. There are seven buses a day between Tampere and Vammala. The trip takes approximately one hour.

Train The railway station can be found on the other side of the bridge that crosses the Vammaskoski River. Trains between Tampere and Pori stop at Vammala, and there are five or six trains a day. If you come from Helsinki or the north, change trains in Tampere.

Getting Around

In the town centre, you can reach every place on foot. If you want to travel further away, catch a bus from the bus terminal. To get to the Ellivuori, take the twice-weekly boat. For more precise information, ask at the bus terminal.

Vaasa

Vaasa (population 54,000), the largest town on the West Coast, has a culture all its own. Some 30% of the people speak Swedish, but as the surrounding countryside is largely inhabited by Swedish speakers, Vaasa is the largest distinctively bilingual town in Finland. Consider this as one of its attractions. Vaasa is also one of the coastal towns that can be reached from Sweden by regular passenger ferry.

History

Vaasa started in the 14th century as a village called Korsholm, an important harbour around the present Old Vaasa, now in ruins. It gained town rights in 1606 to become the capital of Ostrobothnia, and was renamed after the royal Swedish Wasa family. The town was to become important for administrative and military reasons. During the civil war that followed Finnish independence, Vaasa was the capital of the 'Whites'.

Information

Tourist Office The tourist information office (☎ 961-325 1145) at Hovioikeudenpuistikko 11 has maps and brochures on Vaasa and

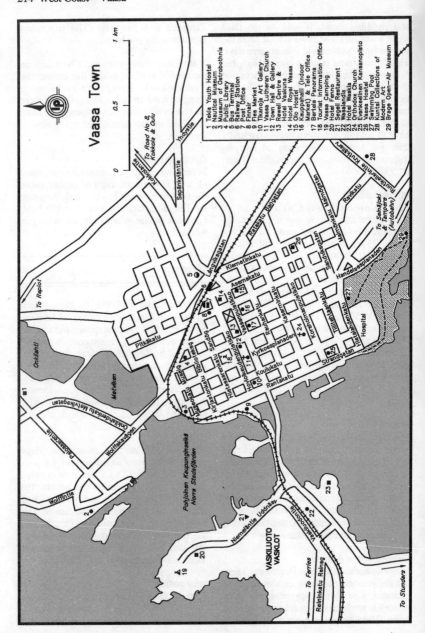

Vaasa Town

1 km   0.5   0

1 Tekla Youth Hostel
2 Nautical Museum
3 Museum of Ostrobothnia
4 Public Library
5 Bus Terminal
6 Railway Station
7 Post Office
8 Finnair
9 Flea Market
10 Tikanoja Art Gallery
11 Vaasa Lutheran Church
12 Town Hall & Gallery
13 Tourist Centre &
   Hotel Vaakuna
14 Hotel Royal Wassa
15 Olo Hostel
16 Kauppahalli (Indoor
   Market) & Tele Office
17 Bertels Panorama
18 Tourist Information Office
19 Vaasa Camping
20 Hotel Fenno
21 Segeli Restaurant
22 Wasalandia
23 Hotel Waskia
24 Orthodox Church
25 Evankeelinen Kansanopisto
26 Vaasa Hostel
27 Swimming Pool
28 Kuntsi Collections of
   Modern Art
29 Brage Open-Air Museum

Korsholm, and heaps of material from the rest of Finland. It is open from June to August from 8 am to 7 pm on weekdays and from 10 am to 7 pm on weekends. At other times, it's open from 8 am to 4 pm Monday to Friday.

Post & Telephone There are nine post offices in Vaasa. The main post office is opposite the train station, at Hovioikeudenpuistikko 23A. Tele has an office at Pitkäkatu 44.

Library The public library is at Kirjastonkatu 13, near the railroad tracks. It is also a provincial library, so you will find literature and maps relating to the entire Province of Vaasa. The library is open from 11 am to 8 pm Monday to Friday and from 10 am to 3 pm on Saturdays.

Things to See
Vaasa Lutheran Church This large red brick building, with an interior of beautifully carved wood, is open from June to August from 6 am to 3 pm Tuesday to Friday and from 6 to 8 pm on Saturdays. For the rest of the year, it's open from 1 to 3 pm Tuesday to Friday.

Orthodox Church This church has old icons, some of them brought from St Petersburg. It's open from late June to early August from 10 am to 2 pm daily.

Museum of Ostrobothnia The Pohjanmaan museo displays some of the cultural wealth for which Ostrobothnia is famous: decorations, traditional wedding items and colourful artefacts. The highlight is the Hedman collection upstairs. You need someone to open the door and show you the priceless collection of paintings and sculptures, donated to the museum by a wealthy collector. Don't miss this place. The museum is open from noon to 4 pm on Mondays, noon to 8 pm Tuesday to Friday and 1 to 6 pm on weekends. Admission is 10 mk, free for students and children.

Nautical Museum This museum exhibits old vessels and artefacts recovered from sunken boats. It's open from 21 May to 15 August from 11.30 am to 6.30 pm Tuesday to Saturday. Admission is 5 mk.

Brage This open-air museum has a dozen buildings, which feature an original farmyard from the Närpes municipality. The main building has a decorated Ostrobothnian wedding room, which is a mixture of, say, Mexican and Scandinavian styles. You have to ask the warden to show you the other houses, such as the Seal-Hunting Museum, and the old saunas. The museum is one km south of the town centre. It is open from 2 to 7 pm Tuesday to Friday and from noon to 4 pm on weekends. Entry is 10 mk, 5 mk for students.

Taidehalli The art gallery in the town hall has temporary exhibitions. Admission is free.

Tikanoja Art Gallery The Tikanojan taidekoti has a good collection of Finnish and foreign paintings. It is open from 11 am to 4 pm Tuesday to Saturday and from noon to 5 pm on Sundays. Entry is 5 mk, free for students.

Kuntsi Collections of Modern Art This museum at Ravikatu 9 is on the premises of a business school. It's open from 1 June to 1 August from 9 am to 3 pm Monday to Friday and from noon to 3 pm on weekends. Admission is free.

Wasalandia
This typical amusement park is open daily from 16 May to 12 August, and on weekends from 30 April till early September. Besides the 70 mk pass, valid for all park facilities, there is a small entry fee in the high season.

Festivals
During the Vaasa Carnival in early August, there is dancing, music and beer drinking. Many of the Korsholm Music Festival concerts are held in Vaasa.

Places to Stay – bottom end

Vaasa Camping (☎ 961-173 852) on the island of Vaskiluoto, some two km from the town centre, is open from 1 June to 31 August. The four-bed bungalows cost 190 mk (230 mk in July). The camping ground is well kept and has good kitchens, showers and toilets. They also rent bicycles and boats. The *Tekla* (☎ 961-177 850) at Palosaarentie 58 is the only youth hostel in Vaasa. Beds start at 65 mk, but this price is only from 1 June to 15 August. The Tekla is also open from 2 May to 31 August as a summer hotel, with singles/doubles from 175/230 mk.

Places to Stay – middle

The two central hotels in Vaasa are the *Olo* (☎ 961-174 558) at Asemakatu 12, with singles/doubles for 100/150 mk, and the *Vaasa* (☎ 961-175 778) at Tiilitehtaankatu 31, where singles/doubles cost 120/200 mk. The *Evankeelinen Kansanopisto* (Evangelical Folk School) at Rantakatu 21-22 has singles/doubles for 200/240 mk, but rooms have to be reserved in advance. It's open in June and August only.

Places to Stay – top end

Many of the more expensive hotels in Vaasa offer special discount rates in summer. Hotels in the top price bracket include:

Hotel Vaakuna (☎ 961-327 4111), in the Rewell Centre. This Sokos hotel has singles/doubles for 350/450 mk (Finncheques OK).
Hotel Royal Waasa (☎ 961-327 8111), Hovioikeudenpuistikko 18. Singles/doubles are 375/490 mk (Finncheques accepted).
Hotel Fenno (☎ 961-121 055), in Vaskiluoto. Singles/doubles cost 260/350 mk in summer.
Hotel Waskia (☎ 961-325 7111), Lemmenpolku 3. This hotel in Vaskiluoto has rooms from 450 mk (Finncheques OK, with a supplement).

Places to Eat

There are several grillis, pizzerias and hamburger restaurants near the market square and in the Rewell Centre. A recommended place for a discount lunch (30 mk, including all extras) is the *Bertels Panorama* at Vaasanpuistikko 16. It is open only on week-days, till 5 pm. Vaskiluoto has a few summer restaurants, such as the *Segeli* at Niemeläntie 14, towards the camping ground, which offers a buffet lunch for 34 mk from 11 am to 2 pm. Close to the camping ground is the more expensive *Merenkyntäjät*. The *Faros* boat restaurant, near the bridge that leads to Vaskiluoto, is quite special. Enquire at the hotels for a buffet breakfast.

Things to Buy

The market square is bustling till 5 pm on weekdays and till 2 pm on Saturdays. The old Kauppahalli sells foodstuffs, glassware and handicrafts, with similar opening hours to the market square. The Rewell Centre, the pride of Vaasa, is a modern shopping centre near the market square. There are some bargains here, if you look. A delightful flea market has been active lately in a park at the end of Hovioikeudenpuistikko, at the waterfront. People come to sell bric-a-brac, and interesting things can be found. You have to bargain. The market is in operation daily till the end of September. Hours are 11 am to 8 pm Monday to Friday, 9 am to 4 pm on Saturdays and noon to 6 pm on Sundays.

Getting There & Away

Air There are several flights a day from Helsinki to Vaasa. The cheapest return flight from Helsinki is currently 420 mk. There are also flights to/from Kokkola, Pietarsaari, Pori and Turku.

Bus There are daily bus services from all major western and central towns, and several express buses a day from Helsinki and Turku via Pori. Buses run along the west coast almost hourly on weekdays.

Train Vaasa is off the main railway lines, but there is a connecting line from Seinäjoki to Vaasa. There are half a dozen trains per day. The fastest IC train from Helsinki covers the 420 km in four hours.

Getting Around

Bus Although the town centre is small enough for you to walk around, local buses come in handy if you want to reach more distant places. Take bus No 10A/B to the harbour or to Old Vaasa, and bus No 2 to the youth hostel. Buses accept the 10-km Coach Holiday Ticket coupon for a journey.

Bicycle Bicycles can be rented at the tourist office for a bargain 10 mk per day. Tekla and Vaasa Camping rent bikes, too.

Central West Coast

SEINÄJOKI
Seinäjoki (population 27,500), the most important town in this part of Ostrobothnia, is known for the architecture of Alvar Aalto. There is also an unusually interesting museum area at the southern edge of town. So, even if you don't make it for the summer festivals, Seinäjoki offers an excellent excuse to interrupt an otherwise boring train trip.

History
There has been human settlement in the Seinäjoki region for some 4000 years. Seinäjoki started its slow growth with the founding of the ironworks in 1798, but it was not until 1960 that it was incorporated as a town. It is now the commercial centre of the region.

Orientation
Seinäjoki is almost flat. All shops and services are very near the railway/bus station. To the south is the suburb of Törnävä, which has several museums. The bus terminal is next to the railway station.

Information
Tourist Office The tourist information office (☎ 964-416 2184) is opposite the modern church, at Kirkkokatu 6.

Post & Telephone Seinäjoki has four post offices. The main post office is at the railway station, at Valtionkatu 1. It is open from 8 am to 5 pm.

Library The public library is opposite the church, next to the tourist office, at Koulukatu 21. It is open from 10 am to 7 pm Monday to Friday and from 11 am to 3 pm on Saturdays.

Things to See
Aalto Centre The Aalto Centre monumental buildings include the Lakeuden Risti Church, the town hall, the library and a few others. The massive church is the most famous building of them all, though its decorations are minimal.

Törnävä Museums Another notable area, several km south of the town centre, has a number of attractions. It is a very different area and looks almost idyllic, especially if the weather is fine. The small island is perfect for a picnic. The Provincial Museum includes an open-air museum, Pharmacy Museum, Gunpowder Museum, Agriculture Museum and other exhibitions. Set aside enough time for all these. From 15 May to 31 August, the museums are open from 11 am to 7 pm daily (except Mondays). The rest of the year, they're open from 9 am to 2.30 pm Monday to Friday.

Tradition Museum The exhibits at the Perinnemuseo feature some issues that were taboo just a few years ago. The wartime Lotta Organisation, a women's auxiliary defence service, was considered inappropriate by the Soviet Union after WW II, when the 'friendship' was being introduced. The Lotta Organisations were banned by the Paris Peace Conference in 1947. Entry is 5 mk.

Festivals
You may be interested in the Provinssirock Rock Festival, held in Törnävä in June, or the Tangomarkkinat ('Tango Fair'), held in July.

Places to Stay – bottom end
The cheapest place to stay is the *Marttilan Kortteeri* (☎ 964-414 4800) at Puskantie 38, the youth hostel of Seinäjoki. It is a student dormitory, so it is only open for travellers from 1 June to 31 August. You can get a bed

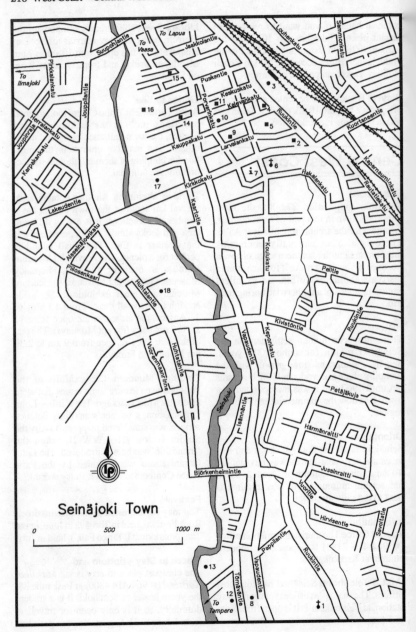

Seinäjoki Town

0   500   1000 m

1   Törnävä Church
2   Hotel Lakeus
3   Railway Station, Bus Terminal, Post
    Office & Taxis
4   Hotel Areena
5   Hotel Cumulus
6   Church
7   Tourist Information Office, Public
    Library & Town Hall
8   Törnävä Museum Area
9   Hotel Sokos Vaakuna
10 Suojeluskunnan Talo Museum
11 Hotel Seinäjoen Seurahuone
12 Törnävä Manor
13 Törnävä Island & Park
14 Hotelli Nurmela
15 Bothnia Centre Hostel
16 Marttilan Kortteeri Youth Hostel
17 Swimming Hall
18 Health Care Centre

for 75 mk, but most rooms are singles/
doubles, priced at 160/200 mk for YHA
members.

Places to Stay – middle

Reasonably priced hotels in Seinäjoki
include the *Vuorela* (☎ 964-423 2195) at
Kalevankatu 31, where singles/doubles start
at 160/200 mk, the *Hotelli Nurmela* (☎ 964-
414 1771) at Kalevankatu 29, with
singles/doubles start at 180/260 mk, and the
Seinäjoen Seurahuone (☎ 964-423 1944) at
Keskuskatu 12, which has singles/doubles
for 200/300 mk.

Places to Stay – top end

The rates in the best hotels reflect the significance of Seinäjoki as a regional business
centre, but you can save some money using
Finncheques as a means of payment. Choices
in this price bracket include:

Hotel Lakeus (☎ 964-419 0111), Larvalankatu 2.
    Singles/doubles start at 460/620 mk
Hotel Sokos Vaakuna (☎ 964-419 3111), Kauppakatu
    3. Singles/doubles are 460/620 mk
Hotel Areena (☎ 964-414 2111), Kalevankatu 2.
    Singles/doubles cost 360/550 mk
Cumulus (☎ 964-418 6111), Kauppakatu 10. Singles/
    doubles start at 425/570 mk

Places to Eat

There are several restaurant-cum-bars
around Seinäjoki where you could look for
special lunch prices. A few pizzerias, grillis
and hamburger kiosks come in handy for
budget travellers.

Getting There & Away

Bus There are excellent connections to
towns and villages, both near and distant.

Train Seinäjoki is the travel hub of
Ostrobothnia, with trains from all directions.
The fastest trains from Helsinki cover the
346 km in three hours.

Hitchhiking You will have to walk several
km out of Seinäjoki to hitchhike successfully.

Getting Around

The Seinäjoki town centre is small enough
for you to walk around. Local bus Nos 1, 2,
10 and 13 will take you to Törnävä in the
south. The tourist office has tours in town on
Wednesdays. On request, they will arrange
excursions further afield.

ILMAJOKI

The small village of Ilmajoki is a recommended side trip from Seinäjoki. It offers
fine museums, and a few interesting events
at the Kyrönjoki riverside.

Things to See

Yli-Laurosela Museum This large house,
built in 1849, has been carefully renovated
by the National Board of Antiquities. It now
houses exhibitions, including old furniture.
It is open from 2 May to 30 September from
11 am to 5 pm daily. The rest of the year, it's
open from 10 am to 4 pm Sunday to Friday.
Entry is 6 mk.

Ilmajoki Museum Across the 'Ilkka Field',
this church-shaped museum has 15,000
items on display. The museum is open from
June to August from 9 am to 5 pm daily.
Admission is 5 mk.

Festivals

The Ilmajoki Music Festival in June features song and opera. Further information is available from Ilmajoen Musiikkijuhlat (☎ 964-547 049, fax 964-547 171), Kahmankuja 6, 60800 Ilmajoki.

Places to Stay

There is no accommodation in Ilmajoki itself, but you can stay at the Viitala youth hostel in the village of Huissi, 10 km away. Beds cost 60 mk for YHA members, 75 mk for nonmembers.

Getting There & Away

The village is a few km off the main Seinäjoki to Kurikka road. There are regular buses from Seinäjoki, 15 km away.

ISOKYRÖ

Stop at this historical village if you want to look at the old church and the local museum. The population is 5300.

Information

Tourist information (☎ 964-470 1111) is available at Pohjakyröntie 136 from 8 am to 3 pm Monday to Friday.

Things to See

Church This old stone church was probably built in the late 14th century, but the exact date is uncertain. During the Catholic Era, it was one of the most important churches in the West Coast area. Its unique paintings, 114 in all, date from the 16th century and are the main reason for a visit. The church is open daily from 15 May to 31 August.

Local Museum Close to the church, this museum has more than 10 buildings and some 4000 artefacts. It's open from 1 May to 31 October from noon to 6 pm Tuesday to Friday and till 4 pm on weekends.

Pläkkyrimuseo Get off at the Tervajoki railway station to have a look at this unusual sheet-metal museum, open from 1 June to 15 August from 9 am to 8 pm Monday to Friday,

9 am to 4 pm on Saturdays and 11 am to 8 pm on Sundays.

Places to Stay

The *Sarin Trafteerikortteeli* (☎ 964-472 4808), near the Isokyrö station, offers accommodation for 130 mk per person, breakfast included.

Getting There & Away

Isokyrö is on the main Seinäjoki to Vaasa road; a bus from either end costs 22 to 25 mk. There are two railway stations for Isokyrö, both several km from the village. All trains stop at the Tervajoki station, and most stop at the Isokyrö station. You will have to hitch-hike, walk or catch a bus from the station to the village.

KORSHOLM/MUSTASAARI

This unusually shaped municipality surrounds Vaasa on almost all sides. Consequently, much of it can be seen on day trips from Vaasa, and all attractions in Korsholm can be conveniently reached by bus from Vaasa. Almost 75% of the population speak Swedish.

Stundars

This fantastic open-air museum comes alive in summer. There are several days when people dress up in national costume and celebrate, most notably during the 'Kalas' days (check dates at tourist offices) – don't miss this. The large museum has up to 50 different buildings, and there is always something going on inside the houses in summer; lots of handicrafts are available. Stundars is near the church of Solf ('Sulva' in Finnish), built in 1786. Buses from Vaasa make the 16-km trip to Stundars.

Replot

Replot ('Raippaluoto' in Finnish) is a large island off Vaasa and one of the possible day tours you can make from Vaasa. It is also worth some more serious research if you have a bicycle.

Bodbacka This fishing harbour at the end of

the old coastal road has a dozen old fisher's houses. In 1617, locals were given the responsibility of mail transport, in exchange for tax deductions and an exemption from military service.

Bullerås The small village of Bullerås is at the south-west corner of the island, some 10 km from the village of Replot. It has a fishing museum and a restaurant in a 1920s villa. There are cruises to Bullerås from Vaasa in summer.

Klobbskat Kalle's Inn (☎ 961-526 364), at the west end of the island of Replot, is in a Lappish-like setting. To get away from it all, you'll pay about 390/700 mk for singles/doubles.

Festivals

The Korsholm Music Festival, Finland's 'Swedish' summer festival, has a slightly different tone from other festivals. It usually takes place right after Midsummer, and is well worth a visit.

VÖRÅ/VÖYRI

The church of Vörå, built in 1627, is the oldest surviving wooden church in Finland, and its pulpit and wall paintings are worth the effort of getting there. The church can seat 1000 people. Vörå has 4000 inhabitants, 85% of whom speak Swedish. Vörå is 36 km from Vaasa, and there are several buses a day from Monday to Saturday.

North-West Coast

EVIJÄRVI

The Järviseudun museo, or 'Lake District Museum' (☎ 964-52836), some 10 km west of Evijärvi village, is one of the largest open-air museums in Finland. On display are several houses, dating from the 1600s to the mid-1800s, and thousands of artefacts. The museum is open in summer, or by appointment in winter.

Getting There & Away

Unless you have a vehicle, you will have to hitchhike. The buses from Pietarsaari depart at 4.10 pm on weekdays, and that may be too late. You can catch the 7 am bus from Vaasa to the village of Evijärvi (63 mk), and hitchhike from there.

KALAJOKI

Most Finns know Kalajoki for its sandy beaches. Over the years, as package charter flights to Spain have become cheaper than a holiday in Kalajoki, the region has sought new ways to attract Finnish tourists. Consequently, Kalajoki provides many services for tourists, including an amusement park and expensive hotels. Skip all this, if you like, but don't miss the autonomous Maakalla Islet.

Orientation

You'll find the bus terminal, supermarkets, banks, a post office and a pharmacy along the Kalajoki ('Fish River'), in Kalajoki village. The large Kalajoki Beach area is six km south of the village.

Information

The tourist information office is off the main road, at the southern end of the beach area. It's open in summer from 10 am to 6 pm Monday to Friday and from 11 am to 6 pm on weekends.

Things to See & Do

Plassi One km north of Kalajoki village, the Plassi area has old wooden houses and a small fishing museum (Kalastusmuseo), which displays fishing and seal-hunting equipment. It is open daily (except Mondays) from 10 am to 4 pm, with a lunch break at noon. Entry costs 2 mk. In the red house opposite the museum, you will find a guide who will show you around the area.

Museum The local museum, one km south of the bus terminal, is open from 21 June to 9 August from noon to 4 pm Tuesday to Sunday.

Kalajoki Särkät One of the most popular holiday spots for Finns is Kalajoki Beach, some six km south of Kalajoki village. It has a lot to offer: the JukuJuku Fun Park, a spa, a golf course, holiday villas, sandy beaches, good hotels and discos. If you want to have a Mediterranean-style holiday experience at a latitude of 64°, this is your ticket.

Maakalla This is recommended as a side trip from Kalajoki Beach. An isolated islet that has only existed since the 15th century, Maakalla has retained a genuine fishing-village image. There are no roads, shops or electricity, but you will find an interesting wooden church, abundant plant and bird life and some red fishing huts. Maakalla is protected and, in fact, has an autonomy of sorts, even though there aren't any permanent inhabitants. The owners of the tiny fishing huts gather regularly and vote to keep the islet as it is.

For the most isolated accommodation in Finland, ask the boat operator for rooms on the island of Ulkokalla, a rocky islet five km west of Maakalla. Rooms cost 200 mk and sleep four people. There is no electricity, and fresh water for the sauna stove is brought from the mainland! To get to Maakalla and Ulkokalla, book a return boat ride (60 mk) at Kallan Matkailu (☎ 983-465 223) or at the pier. From 5 June to 9 August, boats depart daily at 2 and 6 pm. In July, there is an extra departure, at 10 am.

Places to Stay & Eat
There are two places to look for accommodation: the village itself and the beach area six km south. In the village of Kalajoki, try the youth hostel (☎ 983-462 933) at Opintie 1. It is a student apartment building. Because the staff doesn't like to mix people, you get a whole room for 50 mk. The place usually fills up, partly because of this strange policy. It is not the cleanest place in Finland, but it's quite OK, with a common kitchen available free of charge.

Further south in the beach area is the *Tapion Tupa* (☎ 983-466 622), near the main road. It is open all year round and has a range of accommodation options, mostly in the top-end price category. Most popular are the old aitta houses with modern amenities (doubles from 140 mk). A superb buffet lunch is available, if you're looking to splurge. The top-end hotels at the beach are the *Sanifani*, sometimes referred to as 'Sunny funny' (☎ 983-466 613), and the *Hotelli Rantakalla* (☎ 983-466 642).

In the high season, you'll find grillis and restaurants. The village supermarkets sell foodstuffs for self-catering travellers.

Getting There & Away
There are several buses a day from Oulu, Raahe, Kokkola and other coastal places to Kalajoki and the beach. There are weekday bus connections from both Oulainen and Ylivieska railway stations.

KAUSTINEN
Kaustinen (population 4500) is a small village south-east of Kokkola. There isn't much to see in the village itself, but the Kaustinen Folk Music Festival changes the scene, so it is recommended that you visit then. Incidentally, the Peanuts cartoon character 'Woodstock' is called 'Kaustinen' in the Finnish version.

Orientation
The bus terminal and most shops and banks are along Kaustintie, within walking distance, in the village centre.

Information
The tourist information office (☎ 968-612 201) is close to the main road, at Kaustintie 1. During festivals, go straight to the festival office for free maps and accommodation reservations.

Things to See & Do
Folk Music Instrument Museum This small but interesting museum in the festival square, off the main street, is open from 10 am to 7 pm in summer. Admission is 5 mk. In winter, you can see the museum during office hours, if the warden is in his office.

There is also a small local museum at Siltatie 7, near the church.

Pauanne Don't miss this strange place on a small hill above Kaustinen. It is a weird, off-beat centre that combines shamanism, handicrafts and (apparently) weed that is secretly smoked. The architecture is also unique. Rock-bottom accommodation is available, and baths in the popular smoke sauna can sometimes be had for a mere 10 mk per person. Visit Pauanne and see what is currently going on. It's about three km from the centre of Kaustinen.

Festivals
The Kaustinen Folk Music Festival is one of the most loved summer festivals in Finland. It attracts huge crowds and many musicians from both Finland and abroad. At any time from 10 am to midnight and beyond, there are several official venues and half a dozen extempore jam sessions going on. Bring your own instrument if you would like to join in.

To enter the area, you have to purchase a festival pass which gives unlimited admission to the area for one day. Prices range through the week from 50 to 90 mk. Several concerts require additional admission tickets, but attending these is not essential to get into the mood. As well as the fiddle and accordion music that is performed in Kaustinen, you will also experience ethnic music and dance from all continents. New trends and fringe theatre shows are also featured, and there is definitely jazz in the air.

The festival lasts a full week (or more) in July. For details, contact Finland Festivals, or Kaustisen kulttuuritoimisto (☎ 968-611 701, fax 611 481), Kappelintie 13, 69600 Kaustinen.

Places to Stay & Eat
The festival office organises all accommodation during the busy periods. There are two hostel accommodation locations, offering beds for 60 mk per person, home accommodation at 110/160 mk for singles/doubles, and hotel-style rooms for 180 mk per person. Camping is expensive, at 80 mk. The

Koskelan Lomatalo (☎ 968-611 338) at Känsäläntie 123 is a youth hostel, open all year around. A top-end option, the *Motelli Marjaana* (☎ 968-611 211), across the main road, is also open all year around.

The festival area has a busy restaurant, which serves down-to-earth meals for around 40 mk. Kaustinen also has a grilli, a bar and a few restaurants.

Getting There & Away
To reach Kaustinen from Helsinki, you can take the biweekly Kokkola-bound express bus, which arrives in Kaustinen just after midnight. A preferable option is to catch a bus from Kokkola, which has a railway station and is just 47 km away. There are several buses every day. There are also daily express buses from Jyväskylä to Kokkola via Kaustinen.

KOKKOLA
Seen from the train station, Kokkola looks very boring, but an interesting old town is hidden behind the box-like supermarkets, and the seaside is quite scenic. Kokkola serves as a jumping-off point for train travellers who want to explore the West Coast by bus. Kokkola is also another of the coastal towns that can be reached from Sweden by regular passenger ferry. Twenty per cent of the town's 35,000 inhabitants speak Swedish.

History
In 1620, Kokkola was founded on the west coast of Finland. The importance of this village increased with the tar trade, which flourished in the 17th century. The uprise of land threatened Kokkola's excellent harbour, but dredging made seafaring possible. In the 1850s, during the Crimean War, the British attacked the harbour of Kokkola; they lost, and one barge was confiscated. This boat is still on display near the river, despite efforts by the British to buy it back.

Information
Tourist Office The tourist information office (☎ 968-311 902) is in the heart of Kokkola, on Mannerheiminaukio.

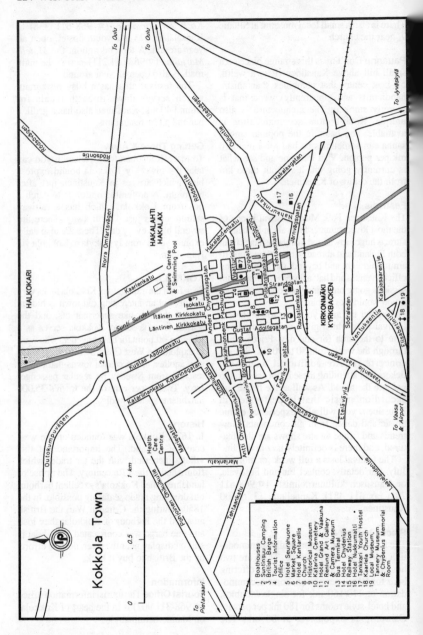

Kokkola Town

1 Boathouses
2 Suntinsuu Camping
3 British Barge
4 Tourist Information
   Office
5 Hotel Seurahuone
6 Market Square
7 Hotel Kantarellis
8 Church
9 Historical Museum
10 Hotel Grand & Vaakuna
11 Renlund Art Gallery
   & Camera Museum
12 Kattarine Centre
13 Bus Terminal
14 Hotel Chydenius
15 Railway Station
16 Hotel Nukkumatti
17 Tankkari Youth Hostel
18 Kaarlela Church
19 Local Museum,
   Tannery Museum
   & Chydenius Memorial
   Room

Top: The Youth Hostel, Rauma (VM)
Bottom: Market Square, Pori (VM)

Top: Boat shelters, Kaskinen Town (VM)
Bottom: The Skata (Old Town), Pietarsaari (ML)

Post & Telephone There are five post offices in the Kokkola municipal area. The main post office, at Rantakatu 4, is open from 8 am to 5 pm Monday to Friday.

Things to See

Old Town The entire old town, the 'Neristan', is worth a close look. It is a quiet, solitary place. The most interesting streets are Itäinen Kirkkokatu, Läntinen Kirkkokatu and Isokatu.

Kaarlela Church The oldest church in Kokkola is a long walk south of the railway station. The altar is of especially fine work. Hours are 10 am to 6 pm daily, and a guide is available in summer.

Museums All museums in Kokkola town centre have free admission. They are open from noon to 3 pm Tuesday to Friday and from noon to 5 pm on weekends. On Thursdays, museums also open from 6 to 8 pm.

The Historical Museum, in an old house at Pitkänsillankatu 28, has several exhibitions. The Renlund Art Gallery at Pitkänsillankatu 39 displays Finnish art, and adjacent to the gallery, the Camera Museum has an impressive collection of old cameras. If you don't find it, ask at the gallery.

The local museum, near the Kaarlela Church, exhibits local tools and artefacts. It is open from 15 May to 31 August from noon to 6 pm Tuesday to Sunday. Admission is 2 mk. There is also a small Tannery Museum in the area. The Chydenius Memorial Room can be seen only on request.

Tankari The island of Tankari is a pleasant place to visit from Kokkola harbour. It has a seal-hunting museum and an old chapel. Regular cruises will take you there in summer.

Other Sights There is an old British barge at the riverside, or for a nice walk, visit the row of old boathouses north of the town centre. The historic Katarina Cemetery, to the west of the old town, is an old park.

Places to Stay – bottom end

The cheapest place in Kokkola, the *Tankkari youth hostel* (☎ 968-18274) at Vidnäsinkatu 2, is open from 1 June to 20 August. Dormitory beds cost 65 mk, sheets included.

Places to Stay – middle

Suntinsuu Camping (☎ 968-314006), not far from the old town, has cottages from 135 mk. The *Turisti hostel* (☎ 968-18968) at Isokatu 22 has singles/doubles at 125/250 mk.

Places to Stay – top end

Kokkola has several top-end hotels. Most are expensive, but there are often special prices in summer:

Nukkumatti (☎ 968-310 890), adjacent to the 'K' petrol station. This hotel, to your right from the railway station, has singles/doubles from 200/250 mk.
Chydenius (☎ 968-314 044), Rautatienkatu 6. Just opposite the railway station, this place has singles/doubles for mk.
Grand (☎ 968-313 411), Pitkänsillankatu 20B
Kantarellis (☎ 968-25000), Kauppatori 4. Singles/doubles are 410/520 mk.
Seurahuone (☎ 968-12811), Torikatu 24. Singles/doubles cost 300/400 mk.
Hotel Sokos Vaakuna (☎ 968-28711), Rantakatu 16. Singles/doubles are 410/520 mk.

Places to Eat

There are quite a few restaurants in town, most of which offer a discount lunch at noon. Many hotels serve an inexpensive buffet breakfast. The *Pikantti* at the city market, to your right from the railway station, has lunch specials available.

Getting There & Away

Air The nearest airport serves both Kokkola and Pietarsaari. There are several flights a day from Helsinki, the cheapest return flight currently costing 435 mk.

Bus Regular buses run to/from all coastal towns, especially Vaasa and Pietarsaari.

Train There is a major railway station in Kokkola, and all trains using the main western railway line stop here. The journey from Helsinki takes less than five hours in daytime.

Ferry Kokkola has ferry connections with the Swedish towns of Skellefteå and Umeå, both of which have bus transport to the harbour. In Kokkola, buses to the harbour leave from the market square 45 minutes prior to each departure.

Getting Around
The Tankkari youth hostel rents bicycles for 50 mk per day or 180 mk per week.

LOHTAJA
Most visitors to this quiet village (population 3000) come to see the old church, built in 1768. There are several paintings by Mikael Toppelius inside the church. The belfry dates from 1732. The nearby museum is also worth a look, if it is open. The Vexila Regis Church Music Festival takes place during the second week of July. To get to Lohtaja, catch one of the daily buses from Kokkola, 33 km away.

NYKARLEBY/UUSIKAARLEPYY
Nykarleby is a small old town south of Pietarsaari. It is a pleasant place to stay for a day, exploring the streets and museums. Some 7800 people live here, and 91% of them speak Swedish.

Orientation
The town centre is on the left bank of the Nykarleby River, which divides the town into two parts. The bus terminal, post office, banks, pharmacies, shops and library are all on the small central square, which is bisected by the main street, Topeliusesplanaden.

Information
In summer, you can get tourist information and excellent maps at the Brostugan café (☎ 967-220 139), opposite the church, across the bridge. It is open from noon to 8 or 9 pm.

Things to See
Church The church has 18th century paintings and a beautiful pulpit. It's open daily in summer from 9 am to 6 pm.

Herlers Museum This old red house, to the north along the main street, has plenty of character, with its bric-a-brac, old costumes and furniture. It is open from noon to 5 pm Sunday to Friday.

Kuddnäs Museum This museum is located at the birthplace of Zacharias Topelius. Born in 1818, his fairy tales are much loved. The exhibits are not all that interesting, but you can visit several houses and walk in the garden. The place is open daily (except Mondays) from May to August from 10 am to 5 pm, but times vary a bit, so check at the tourist office first. Admission is 3 mk.

Water Tower There are good views from the café up the tower. It's open till 6 pm; pay the 2 mk admission fee to the cashier at the café.

Places to Stay & Eat
The only place to stay in Nykarleby is the *Juthbacka* (☎ 967-220 677), one km south of the town centre along the main street; it has a hotel, huts and camping. Camping costs 35 mk for one person, or ask for the budget double, or for a four-bed hut, each costing 95 mk. For greater comfort, there are better cottages and singles/doubles for 315/415 mk. The place also rents bicycles (50 mk per day).

The restaurant at the Juthbacka has a fish and salad buffet for 39 mk, but beware the exorbitant prices for drinking water! The daily lunch includes drink, bread and coffee and costs 38 mk. The town centre has a few grillis, and the *Ravintola von Döbeln* at Pankkikatu 7 has inexpensive lunch specials. The *Brostugan*, across the river, opposite the church, is a historical building. Good våfflor, with plenty of cream and strawberry jam, is the speciality.

Getting There & Away
Kokkola, Pietarsaari and Vaasa are the main gateways to Nykarleby; there is a regular bus service from all these towns. Nykarleby is seven km off the main road, which makes hitchhiking slightly difficult.

AROUND NYKARLEBY

The Nykarleby municipality includes the villages of Jeppo, Munsala and Kovjoki, which have their own churches and local museums. The museums are usually only open on Sundays. The churches in Jeppo and Munsala are open in summer from 9 am to 6 pm daily.

PIETARSAARI/JAKOBSTAD

Pietarsaari would be one of the most pleasant of all coastal towns in Finland, if it were not for the huge pulp factory that gives the town its distinctive bad smell. This shouldn't put you off visiting Pietarsaari, or Jakobstad as it is called in Swedish. Over 55% of the 20,000 inhabitants speak Swedish. Pietarsaari can be reached from Sweden by regular passenger ferry.

History

Pietarsaari was a Swedish town, founded by Ebba Brahe, wife of the war hero Jacob de la Gardie. The national poet of Finland, J L Runeberg, was born here in 1804, and many memorabilia remain. The harbour has always been important; Finland's first round-the-world sailing expedition started here, in 1844.

Orientation

Pietarsaari is a large town. Fortunately, you'll find both the town centre and the old town handy if you arrive by bus.

Information

Tourist Office The tourist information office (☎ 967-723 1796) is near the market square. It is open from 8 am to 6 pm Monday to Friday and from 9 am to 3 pm on Saturdays. In winter it is open Monday to Friday from 8 am to 4 pm.

Post & Telephone The main post office is at Asematie 4.

Things to See

Skata The old town is the foremost sight in Pietarsaari and should not be missed. This large section of town has been beautifully preserved. Most of the 300 houses were built in the 19th century; the 18th century houses along Hamngatan are the oldest in town.

Museums There are several museums in Pietarsaari. They generally open at noon and close four or five hours later, so you have to plan ahead if you only come for a day.

Malm. House Malmin talo at Isokatu 2 has exhibitions relating to local and maritime culture. It is open from noon to 4 pm daily, and also from 6 to 8 pm on Tuesdays and Thursdays.

Tobacco Museum Associated with the local industry, this museum (☎ 967-723 0333) displays old products and techniques. Call ahead for admission.

Jacobstads Wapen This new vessel was constructed according to a 17th century design. It is open for visitors, when in dock.

Places to Stay – bottom end

A good place to stay is the *Svanen* (☎ 967-723 0660). Known as 'Joutsen' in Finnish, this place is six km north of town, in Nissasörn. You pass the factory as you get there. Two old houses make up the youth hostel, with dormitory beds for 30 mk. You may have to negotiate to be accepted, if it is already 'full'. Two-bed huts start at 80 mk. You can hire bicycles (25 mk per day), boats and canoes. Camping costs 25 mk. To get to Svanen, take a local bus from the station. It runs infrequently, but you can catch it around 4, 5 and 7 pm each weekday.

One km south of the town centre is the *Bodgärdet* on Pitäjäntie, near the old church. Beds in double rooms cost just 65 mk, if you have your own sheets. There are also more expensive hotel rooms. It is only open from 1 June to 31 July.

Places to Stay – middle

For accommodation in old Pietarsaari, try the *Westerlund resandehem* (☎ 967-723 0440) at Norrmalmsgatan 8. This homely, spotlessly clean place is run by a friendly

Swedish-speaking lady. Singles/doubles are 120/200 mk. Breakfast costs 25 mk, or you can use the kitchen.

Places to Stay – top end
Top-end possibilities include the small *Park Hotel Vanadis* (☎ 967-723 4700) at Skolgatan 23, just at the edge of the old town, which has singles/doubles for 430/530 mk. There is also the *Hotel Fontell* (☎ 967-786 4111) at Kanalesplanaden 13, one block from the central square, where singles/doubles cost 470/590 mk. The *Hotel Pool* (☎ 967-723 5235) at Alholmsvägen, north from Gamla Hamn, is not a very attractive place to stay, but it has a quiet location and singles/doubles from 370/470 mk.

Places to Eat
There are quite a few grillis and restaurants to choose from. Before you order, it is worth checking the water prices, as some places charge even for ice cubes! The *Pizzeria Hambis* at the market square has a large pizza special (35 mk) from 11 am to 2 pm. The price includes a drink, salad and coffee. The *Saigon* at Alholminkatu 6 has similar prices. The *Old Skipper* at Alholminkatu 1 has a bargain salad bar for 18 mk; lunch starts at 26 mk. The *Sesam*, run by an Indian couple, used to be a vegetarian restaurant. It is rather expensive these days.

Getting There & Away
Bus There is a night bus from the Turku harbour to Oulu via Pietarsaari, but the arrival time in Pietarsaari is unpleasant. There are regular express and ordinary buses to Pietarsaari from Kokkola, Vaasa and other coastal towns.

Train Pännäinen, 11 km away, is the closest railway station to Pietarsaari. A shuttle bus meets most arriving trains.

Ferry Jakob Lines (☎ 967-723 5011) shares an office with the tourist office. There are a few regular ferry connections from Skellefteå and Umeå (in Sweden) to Pietarsaari. In both Swedish towns, bus transport to the harbour is available. The Pietarsaari harbour is six km north of the town centre, and buses to each departing ferry leave the market square 30 minutes prior to departure.

Getting Around
The tourist office rents bicycles for a bargain 20 mk per day.

PYHÄJOKI
The river-mouth village of Pyhäjoki, along the coast road, once had more significance than it does today. There is a new town centre, where essential services are available. The **Annala open-air museum** (☎ 983-439 0246), a little way off the main road, opposite the commercial centre, has been an important estate since the 17th century; it now has 17 houses, with exhibits. In summer, the museum is open from noon to 6 pm daily. In winter, call ahead to get someone to show you the place. Entry costs 5 mk.

PÄNNÄINEN/BENNÄS
There is a bus service to Pietarsaari, 11 km away, from the old train station of Pännäinen. Most trains stop at this tiny village, which has several beautiful wooden houses, a bank and a post office.

RAAHE
Raahe used to be an important port, and you will still see evidence of its glorious past. Founded in 1649 by Count Per Brahe (hence the name), Raahe is now a sleepy little town with 18,500 inhabitants. Not many travellers go there, but it is actually the most interesting place along the coast between Kokkola and Oulu.

Orientation
Raahe is divided into an old and a new town. The bus terminal and most of the shops are in the new town.

Information
Tourist Office The tourist information office (☎ 982-299 2268) at Rantakatu 51 is in the

tallest building in town. There is a nice view from the top. The office is open in summer from 9 am to 5 pm Monday to Friday and till 1 pm on Saturdays. In winter, hours are 8 am to 3.30 pm.

Post & Telephone Raahe has three post offices. The main post office is at Fellmaninpuistokatu 2.

Library The public library at Rantakatu 49 also has a café.

Things to See & Do
Old Town Many wooden houses have been restored in the old town, which remains quiet and attractive. Two houses, at Rantakatu 33 and 36, have been opened to the public as museums.

Museum The local museum, at the waterfront, is mostly devoted to maritime and religious paraphernalia. Highlights include the world's oldest diving suit and some old wooden religious sculptures. It is open from noon to 6 pm daily. Entry is 10 mk, 5 mk for students.

Island Cruises Boats to islands outside Raahe depart from behind the museum. The summer cruises are available daily (except Mondays) at 1 and 5 pm.

Places to Stay
The camping ground is just north of the youth hostel. The youth hostel (☎ 982-38448) itself, north of the old town at Seminaarinkatu 2-4, is hard to beat. It is open from 1 June to 15 August. Dormitory beds cost 30 mk and small rooms are 65 to 90 mk. It is a student apartment building and is seldom full. There are also two expensive hotels in Raahe: the *Nätterpori* (☎ 982-37881), in the new centre, and the *Tiiranlinna* (☎ 982-38701), one km south of the centre towards Kokkola.

Places to Eat
There aren't that many restaurants in Raahe, but grillis and cafés may keep your hunger at bay. The *Alto Mare* at Kirkkokatu 27 has set weekly pizzas at a discount (around 35 mk). The popular *Klubi Ravintola*, near the museum, has good live music on Friday and Saturday evenings all year round.

Things to Buy
Hiirenkorva at Koulukatu 3 is a 'green' shop with a flea market. It is open from 11 am to 5 pm Monday to Friday. For bicycle spare parts, go to Urheilunurkka at Kauppakatu 31.

Getting There & Away
Bus There are a few useful bus connections from regional travel hubs, and bus traffic connects Raahe to more central villages. Hitchhiking to/from Raahe is not difficult, but Raahe is three km off the main road, so you may have to walk.

Train Vihanti, 36 km away, is the closest train station to Raahe. A shuttle bus meets most arriving trains. Railway tickets, including train passes, are valid on the bus.

VIHANTI
If you have time to spend, see the old red church, which is a good example of the region's architecture. Buses to Raahe depart from outside the Vihanti railway station.

YLIVIESKA
This railway junction can come in handy for those who wish to visit Kalajoki from here. The bus and taxi stations are near the train station, and a few buses are always waiting when the train arrives. There is a restaurant at the bus terminal and a left-luggage office at the railway station. Misto and other supermarkets are to be found close to the river.

Savo

If asked to nominate one region of Finland as their favourite for travelling, few travellers would have second thoughts in choosing Savo, also known as the Lakeland. Savo officially comprises the provinces of Mikkeli and Kuopio. It epitomises the isolation of Finns – this is where you'll find the numerous lakes, islands, narrow straits, canals and isolated beaches. Here, too, are the most popular steamer routes. But this water-blessed area would not be what it is without its people, the *savolaiset*. No other group in Finland seems to make so much fuss about themselves, but with good reason: these are witty, open-hearted and easy-going people. Outsiders joke about the Savo dialect, but perhaps they just envy the locals their beautiful country.

The Savo region is one of the largest single areas covered in this book. We include in South Savo the eastern part of the Province of Mikkeli and the municipality of Parikkala from the Province of Kymi. In North Savo, we cover the entire Province of Kuopio, including Ylä-Savo ('Upper Savo'), as the Iisalmi region is called. The *Saimaa* topographical sheet, in 1:250,000 scale, covers the entire area of Savo, and is available in bookshops for 47 mk.

ACTIVITIES

Canoeing

The Oravareitti ('Squirrel Route') is 52 km long and runs from Juva to Sulkava. A free map is available from most tourist offices in the region. Consult the Sulkava section for further information. Sulkava is also a place to hire rowing boats, not to mention the unique church longboats.

In North Savo, you'll have several routes to choose from, many of them predominantly on larger lakes. For a one-day excursion, the Nurmijoki River to the west from Iisalmi offers relatively easy rapids along a 25-km route. The Kahvila Ruukin Tupa (☎ 977-65677) in the village of Ruukki rents canoes.

Lake Cruises

Savo is *the* region to do lake cruises, as this is where lakes dominate the landscape. Both Kuopio and Savonlinna are regional centres for short and long-haul trips, and the 'Heinävesi route' runs between these two places. Roll Line operates ferries from 9 June to 8 August, Tuesday to Sunday, between Kuopio and Savonlinna. A one-way trip in either direction costs 240 mk.

Savonlinna

Savonlinna (population nearly 29,000) would be your first choice if you wanted to see just one place outside Helsinki. It has some of the best lake scenery in Savo, the most dramatic medieval castle in Finland and a number of other superlative attractions in the vicinity. Consequently, Savonlinna is extremely busy in summer, especially during the one-month Opera Festival. Prices vary considerably with the season, and rise sky-high during the Opera Festival in July.

History

The slow growth of Savonlinna began in

1475 with the building of Olavinlinna Castle on islands between two large lakes. In 1639, Savonlinna was incorporated as a town, by an initiative of Count Per Brahe, founder of quite a number of towns around Finland. In 1743, this small market town was joined to Russia; it was returned to the Finnish grand duchy in 1812. By the 1920s, Savonlinna was important as the major hub for steamboat traffic in the Lakeland, and this image remains, even today.

Orientation

Savonlinna is one of Finland's most beautifully situated towns. Lake Haapavesi and Lake Pihlajavesi surround the town on both sides, and the town centre is on two islands.

Information

Tourist Office Busy but helpful, the tourist information office (☎ 957-273 492/3, fax 957-514 449) at Puistokatu 1 is across the river, near the market. The staff can help you with information about most places in the Savonlinna region, sell you tickets for cruises, passenger ships, operas and concerts, reserve accommodation, and organise tours to Retretti and other places in the vicinity. The office is open daily from 8 am to 6 pm, except in July, when hours are 8 am to 10 pm. In winter, the office is open from 9 am to 4 pm Monday to Friday.

Post & Telephone There are seven post offices in Savonlinna. The main post office is next to the bus terminal, at Olavinkatu 61, and is open from 9 am to 5 pm Monday to Friday. Telephones are in the bus terminal building across the street. The post office branch in the town centre, at Koulukatu 10, has similar opening hours.

Library The town library is on a small hill on Tottinkatu. It's open from 11 am to 7 pm Monday to Friday. There is a music branch library at Olavinkatu 24, open from 10 am to 3 pm on Fridays and from 1 to 7 pm on other weekdays. You can listen to operas on compact disc there.

Bookshops The Suomalainen Kirjakauppa at Pilkkakoskenkatu 3 stocks the best selection of English magazines and paperbacks.

Laundry Try to find inexpensive laundromats in hostels, but if you insist on using laundrettes, the Savonlinnan Pika-Pesu at Satamakatu 3 is right in the town centre.

Things to See

Olavinlinna Castle Olavinlinna Castle is the principal sight of Savonlinna, and probably of eastern Finland; it should not be missed. Founded in 1475 by E A Tott, Governor of Vyborg and the Eastern Provinces, Olavinlinna was meant to protect the eastern border of the Swedish-Finnish empire. It got its name from Olof, a 10th century Norwegian Catholic saint. Russians occupied the castle in the 1710s, and kept it for almost 200 years, adding the red towers and a yellow house inside its walls. Two small museums in the castle are also worth seeing. You are not allowed to visit the castle without a guide, but there are hourly guided tours every day, all year round, from 10 am to 5 pm between June and mid-August and from 10 am to 3 pm at other times of year. Guides speak English, Swedish, French, German or Italian. Entry is 14 mk, 7 mk for children. A motorised floating bridge to the castle is removed when ships pass.

Savonlinna Province Museum The Savonlinnan maakuntamuseo, in an old Russian warehouse near the castle, has a well-displayed collection highlighting traditional living in Savo and local artefacts and tools. There are free English-language leaflets available. Don't miss the old boats behind the main building; the MS *Salama* houses an exhibition. The museum is open in July from 10 am to 8 pm daily. The rest of the year, it's open from 11 am to 5 pm Tuesday to Sunday. Admission is 10 mk.

Suruton Villa This old villa, literally 'one without sorrow', was originally built to accommodate guests of the nearby spa. The permanent doll museum may not be of particular interest, unless you are an enthusiast, but they have other exhibitions, too, and it is a nice house. To get there, walk along the road beyond the Vuorilinna Hotel. Suruton Villa is open daily in summer from noon to 6 pm; in winter, enquire at the tourist office. Entry is 10 mk, 5 mk for students and children.

Pyrri Art Exhibition Paying 30 or 35 mk to see an art exhibition may sound a bit expensive, but Pyrri has been good value in the last couple of years. It has different exhibitions every summer, so enquire at the tourist office for details of current paintings. Pyrri is in Piispanmäen koulu (school), 300 metres north of the tourist office, and is open from 14 June to 2 August from 10 am to 7 pm daily.

Cathedral The beautifully renovated Lutheran church was reopened in November 1991. Concerts are held there in July. The church is open from 1 June to 18 August from 10 am to 6 pm daily.

Rauhalinna This romantic Moorish-style wooden villa was built in 1900 by Nils Weckman, an officer in the tsar's army, as a wedding anniversary present for his wife. Now owned by the government and protected by the Museums Department, it has beautifully decorated rooms, and the view from the tower is good. Rauhalinna is open from 1 June to 9 August. For a real treat, try the excellent herkkupöytä buffet (145 mk in July, 80 mk on June and August weekends). There is also a café. Upstairs, the Hotelli Rauhanlinna (☎ 957-523 119) has fine rooms for rent. Singles/doubles cost 290/380 mk and suites are 900 mk. To get there, take a motor boat from Savonlinna harbour. From Monday to Saturday, there are also a few buses from the Savonlinna bus terminal to a school near Rauhalinna. It is a half-km walk from there.

Harbour Cruises
In summer, Savonlinna pier is one of the busiest in Finland. In addition to scheduled passenger ferries to/from Kuopio and Lappeenranta and beyond, a number of short-range boat transport services are available. These may come in handy if you want to combine some lake scenery with bicycle touring, or if you want to see Savonlinna from a different angle. This is a list of regular boat tours around Savonlinna:

The SS *Heinävesi* sails daily at 11 am (6 June to 19 August) to Retretti in Punkaharju. A ticket costs 80 mk one-way, 120 mk return.

The MS *Princess of Saimaa* has daily cruises (6 June to 23 August) at 11 am and 1, 3 and 5 pm. The one-hour cruise costs 30 mk.

The MS *Salmetar* sails to Rauhalinna and back at 10.30 am and 12.30 pm from 1 June to 20 August; in July, there are also departures at 4.30 and 6.30 pm. The fare is 30 mk.

The SS *Figaro* departs for 75-minute cruises at 10 am, noon and 2 and 4 pm daily (17 June to 16 August); on weekends, there are also 6 and 8 pm cruises. The fare is 35 mk.

The MS *Faust* has five one-hour cruises every day in July. Tickets are 30 mk per person.

The MS *Fidelio* has hourly cruises from 9 am to 6 pm in July. The tour takes 45 minutes and costs 20 mk.

The *Timppa* and the *Timppa II* have nine cruises a day from 1 June to 31 August, at 30 mk per person.

Festivals
The Savonlinna Opera Festival is probably the most famous and appreciated of all summer festivals in Finland, offering four weeks of high-class opera performances in the most dramatic location in Finland: Olavinlinna Castle. It is quite a scene, as 100 trained singers enter through eight gates in the medieval walls while the sound of a good orchestra echoes around the historic castle, and swifts fly and scream outside. The sun shines till 10 pm; alternatively, raindrops can be felt, despite the light ceiling construction that protects the open-air stage.

The Opera Festival usually takes place in July. Generally, there is one opera or ballet performance in the castle every evening, and concerts at various locations in Savonlinna. Kerimäki Church and Retretti Art Centre also have a few excellent concerts during the Festival weeks.

For details of exact dates and programmes, contact Savonlinna Opera

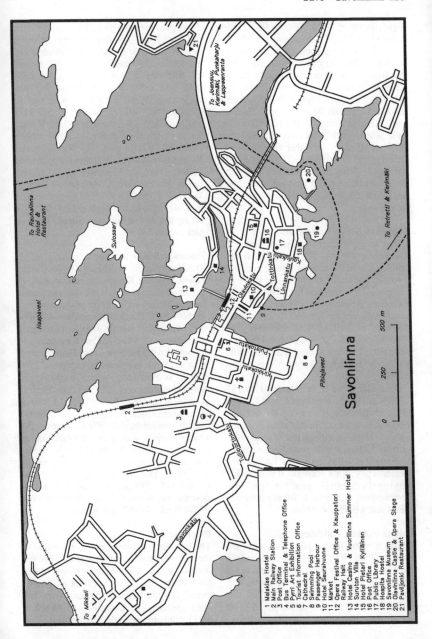

Savonlinna

1 Malakias Hostel
2 Main Railway Station
3 Post Office
4 Bus Terminal & Telephone Office
5 Pyrl Art Exhibition
6 Tourist Information Office
7 Cathedral
8 Swimming Pool
9 Passenger Harbour
10 Hotel Seurahuone
11 Market
12 Opera Festival Office & Kauppatori
   Railway Halt
13 Hotel Casino & Vuorilinna Summer Hotel
14 Suruton Villa
15 Hotel Pietari Kylläinen
16 Post Office
17 Public Library
18 Hospits Hostel
19 Savonlinna Museum
20 Olavinlinna Castle & Opera Stage
21 Pavlljonki Restaurant

Festivals (☎ 957-514 700, fax 957-21866), Olavinkatu 35, 57130 Savonlinna. The box office is open from 9 am to 4 pm Monday to Friday. Tickets for that night are sold after 6 pm from the booth near the bridge. No last-minute discounts are available. The Savonlinna Tourist Service also sells tickets, as does Lippupalvelu in Helsinki. There are only 50 or so tickets of the 100 mk variety available for each show, so book ahead; over 80% of all seats are either first or second quality, and expensive (300 to 400 mk, on average). Bring warm clothes and some food, and be prepared for hard seats. There are kids selling seat covers, but you can bring your own.

Places to Stay – bottom end

Close to the market on Casino Island, the *Vuorilinna* (☎ 957-575 0494) at Kylpy-laitoksentie functions as a youth hostel from 1 to 29 June and 9 to 31 August, when you can get a dormitory bed for 55 mk for YHA members. At other times in summer, it is a hotel, with singles for 240 to 290 mk and doubles at 340 to 400 mk. Use your Finncheques then, as you get breakfast at no extra cost. This is a student apartment build-ing, with a kitchen for each one or two rooms.

A similar place is the *Malakias* (☎ 957-23283) at Pihlajavedenkuja 6, two km west of the town centre. It's a nice walk, but there are local buses, too. The Malakias is open in summer when Vuorilinna has its hotel prices (ie from 29 June to 9 August). Each room has cooking facilities and two beds. YHA members pay 55 mk per night. If you feel like staying in a hotel, you can use your Finncheques, or pay cash, for the luxury of sheets and a buffet breakfast.

Places to Stay – middle

The best value in this price bracket is the *Hospits Hotel* (☎ 957-22443) at Linnankatu 20. There is a nice garden, with access to the beach, and its proximity to the castle is a bonus. Singles/doubles start at 130/220 mk.

The SS *Heinävesi* has cabins for 65 to 80 mk during the summer sailing season.

Enquire at the harbour in the evenings, after the last sailing. The ship has 30 beds and is seldom full. The experience is worthwhile, but facilities are basic and the traffic around the harbour is a bit noisy. Some other ships also have cabin accommodation, but you may have to sail with them next day to qualify. The *Nätkin Hostel* (☎ 957-557 912) at Kaarnatie 3-5 is open only in July. It is six km from the town centre, in Nätki suburb (take the eastbound bus No 2 to the Koivukatu bus stop). Reception is open until 10 pm. There are 35 rooms, all at 180 mk. Seven km outside Savonlinna, *Camping Vuohimäki* (☎ 957-537 353) has cottages from 410 mk in the high season, 295 mk during the rest of summer. Simple quadru-ples start at 235 mk.

Places to Stay – top end

The *Hotel Casino* (☎ 957-57500) on Casino Island, near the Kauppatori railway halt, is not a bad place to stay. It is a spa, and guests have unlimited access to the pool, sauna and Turkish bath. Singles/doubles are 430/690 mk (480/540 mk in July). The *Hotel Seurahuone* (☎ 957-5731) at Kauppatori 4-6, opposite the harbour, takes Finncheques, with a 75 mk supplement, except in July, when rooms are more expensive. Singles/doubles cost 420/570 mk. Singles/doubles at the *Hotel Tott* (☎ 957-514 500) at Satamakatu 1, near the harbour, cost 280/400 mk on weekends, 500/700 mk during the Opera Festival season and 400/550 mk at other times. Room prices include breakfast and morning sauna, and no Finncheques are accepted. The *Hotel Pietari Kylliäinen* (☎ 957-575 0500) at Olavinkatu 15 is a non-descript town hotel. Singles/doubles cost 290/400 mk (360/520 mk in July).

Places to Eat

The best place to have a lörtsy and coffee is the colourful market at the harbour. There are several grilli or kahvila (café) places in the town centre that serve fast food or simple meals. See also the *City Sokos kahvio* for lunch specials. The *Lounaskahvila Annukka* on Olavinkatu, near the market, offers a home-made lunch for 30 to 40 mk. The restaurant on the 2nd floor of the Hotel Tott has a lunch for 38 mk. A nice place to eat or just have a beer is the *Linnankrouvi* on Linnankatu, near the castle. It is an old wooden house with a garden bar. A popular evening pub is the *Majakka*, opposite the harbour. It also serves lunch from 32 mk; ask for the kotiruoka (home food). The *Snellman* on Olavinkatu is the town's top-end restaurant. For the best value, cross the long bridge east from Savonlinna and stop at the *Paviljonki* on your left, just over the bridge. They serve cheap meals, which are every bit as good as they *ought* to be. This is a restaurant school.

Things to Buy

The market at the harbour is open daily in July, and from Monday to Saturday the rest of the year, with handicrafts and souvenirs for sale. On Linnankatu, near the castle, there are several renovated old wooden houses. At No 10, Markun savipaja sells local pottery and Marja Putus has fine clothes made of wool, linen and silk. The Käsityöläismyymälä in the building opposite has more variety but perhaps less of real interest. Closer to the castle is the Linnankadun näyttelytilat, with handmade dolls. It is open from 11 am to 7 pm daily. Near the museum is a somewhat tacky Finndecor shop, but many tourists do buy these things.

Getting There & Away

Air There are two to three flights a day from Helsinki to Savonlinna. The cheapest return ticket from Helsinki currently costs around 370 mk.

Bus Savonlinna is the major travel hub of the south-eastern Savo bus network. There are three express buses a day from Helsinki to Savonlinna, and buses run almost hourly from Mikkeli.

Train Savonlinna is off the main railway lines, so you'll need to get off in Parikkala and catch either another train or a bus to Savonlinna, 59 km away. Train tickets and passes are valid on buses, too, but this may change, so it's best to enquire beforehand. There is also a bus service from the Pieksämäki railway station, but the journey is twice as long and you will have to pay the bus fare. The main Savonlinna railway station is a bit far from the town centre, but trains also stop at the small Kauppatori railway halt.

Ferry You can reach Savonlinna from as far away as Kuopio in the north or Lappeenranta in the south. The scenic 'Heinävesi route' is probably the most recommendable in Finland. There are also several ferries a day to/from Punkaharju.

Getting Around

Using the city bus service costs 7 to 8 mk per ride within the Savonlinna area, or use your 10-km Coach Holiday Ticket coupon. Taxis depart from opposite the tourist office but are expensive. Kesport, above the harbour at Olavinkatu 44, has the best selection of rental bikes – they even rent new bicycles if they run out of used ones. The charge is 40 mk per day or 380 mk per month. Bikes can also be rented for 40 mk per day at Polkupyöräkorjaamo Koponen Ky at Olavinkatu 42, near the tourist office. Boats of any kind can be rented for 90 mk per day or 400 mk per week at the Reissuvene Niskanen; enquire at the Savonlinna Tourist Service.

Around Savonlinna

ENONKOSKI

The large municipality of Enonkoski (population 2250) is blessed with much water. On their own initiative, local farmers have put up several 'off the beaten track' options for activitity holidays. You can stay at quiet farmhouses, visit a sheep farm, try herb and honey sauna baths or taste home-made food. Accommodation is available in several locations (from 130 mk, breakfast included). The best deal is Norppa-Veneet (☎ 957-381 076), which rents rowing boats for excursions into some of the most spectacular lake scenery in Savo: Kolovesi National Park. You can pick up the keys either at the Union petrol station in Enonkoski or at the T-shop Sairanen in the village of Ihamaniemi. The 24-hour rental fee of 100 mk includes a map of the park. Contact the Savonlinna tourist office for further information.

Getting There & Away

There are regular buses to the village of Enonkoski from Savonlinna. To tour the area, you will need a bicycle or a private vehicle.

JUVA

The village of Juva is midway between Mikkeli and Varkaus. There is a short walk from the bus terminal to the town's attractions, which include a church and the local museum, for those who get excited about these things. The 52-km Oravareitti canoeing route to Sulkava starts here.

Places to Stay

Juva Camping (☎ 955-51930) has cottages starting at 170 mk. You can also rent rowing boats and canoes here. The *Toivio youth hostel* (☎ 955-59622) is approximately 10 km from the village, on the Sulkava road. Dormitory beds start at 35 mk. It's open from 1 May to 30 September. In the village, the *Hotelli Juva* (☎ 955-51650) provides top-end accommodation.

Getting There & Away

Juva is most conveniently reached by regular northbound express bus from Mikkeli. The village itself is three km from the main road, so hitchhikers will probably have to walk all the way.

KERIMÄKI

The first thing that strikes you in Kerimäki is the huge church. Kerimäki is a small place (population 6500), yet it has the largest wooden church in the world. The small tourist information booth, open daily, sells souvenirs rather than giving information.

Things to See

Kerimäki Church Dominating the entire village, this wooden church was built in 1847 to seat 3300 people, a congregation larger than that of Kerimäki today. People would come to church in their *kirkkovene* longboats, across the lake. The ugly grey paint, the original colour, is supposed to resemble marble. For 5 mk, you can climb the *tapuli* (belfry), but you need a 24 mm lens to capture the entire church on film. Coffee and handmade woollen socks can be bought in the tapuli. The church is open from 1 June to 31 August until 8 pm Sunday to Friday and till 6 pm on Saturdays. There are free concerts on some summer Thursday evenings, but this may change from year to year. The Opera Festival-related concerts have admission fees.

Museum of Freshwater Fishing The Järvikalastusmuseo near the church is open from 1 June to 31 August from noon to 3 pm; in the high season, the opening hours are 11 am to 6 pm. Admission is 5 mk. If you don't find this interesting enough, cross the back yard to an open-air museum featuring old grey buildings and a windmill. Behind this area, visible from the main road, is a row of wooden boat shelters. They make a good photo.

War Exhibition The Hotel Herttua has a collection of old guns, and there is also a renovated bunker and a stretch of a WW II trench line behind the hotel. No battle was fought here, however. For 15 mk you can see the exhibition of war history inside the hotel. This small *sotahistoriallinen näyttely* has no English text.

Hytermä This protected island celebrates one of the weirdest of human achievements: it is the monument of Romu-Heikki ('Junk Heikki'), the man who piled millstones into large structures. The island is also quite beautiful, so you should try to find a way to visit it. Getting there is not easy, though. A regular boat service leaves the Hotel Herttua at 2 pm on Sundays, but then you won't have

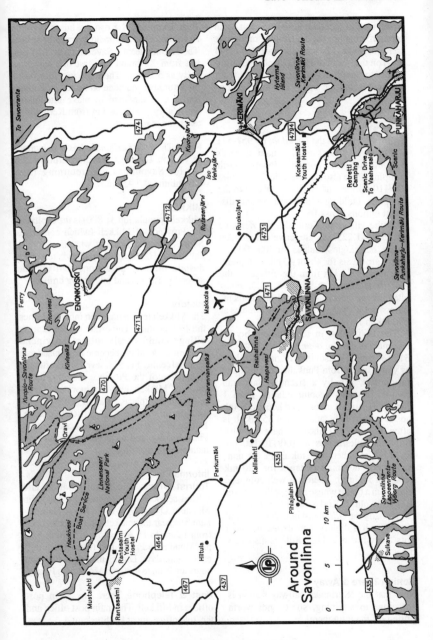

Around
Savonlinna

much time to spend on the island. You could hire a rowing boat at the Herttua, or arrange transport with Mr Karjalainen (☎ 957-544 920) on the island of Hälvä (itself a beautiful place to visit, accessible by road from Kerimäki), but the price (250 mk) is a rip-off.

Places to Stay

Worth checking is the *Lomalohi* (☎ 957-541 771), seven km from Kerimäki towards Savonlinna. This popular, down-to-earth camping place also has a few doubles/triples (90/110 mk) in a house 300 metres from the reception building. There are several discount options to ask for.

In the village of Kerimäki, the *Kerihovi* (☎ 957-541 225), an attractive old wooden house, has singles/doubles for 200/300 mk. There are meals for about 40 mk. A top-end alternative, 1½ km from the village, is the *Hotelli Herttua* (☎ 957-575 501). Finn-cheques are accepted, with a supplement; otherwise, it's very expensive (eg doubles at 690 mk in July).

The best value in the municipality of Kerimäki is the *Korkeamäki Hostel* (☎ 957-312 186), eight km south of Kerimäki village as you drive to/from Punkaharju. This quiet farmhouse, run by a friendly Savonian couple, provides accommodation from 1 June to 31 August in three old houses. Youth hostel prices apply, and start at 35 mk. It is often full, so call ahead. There are also singles/doubles/triples at 100/110/120 mk for YHA members (15 mk extra for non-members) and small cottages for 120 mk (200 mk in July). There's a well-equipped kitchen in a house whose stone walls are over 100 years old. If Korkeamäki is not for you or is full, try the *Ollila*, just next door by rural standards. It is slightly more expensive, with huts from 120 mk. The Ollila is also very quiet.

Getting There & Away

Note that the 'Kerimäki' railway station is not close to anything, so it's not worth getting off the train there!

Bus There are S Kosonen buses between Savonlinna and Kerimäki every hour or two. The last bus leaves Savonlinna at 8.15 pm, but from Kerimäki, the last one leaves as early as 5.20 pm. There are just four buses on Saturdays and none on Sundays. Enough traffic uses the road to make hitchhiking worth a try; walk one km from Kerimäki to reach the main road.

Ferry The MS *Kerilandia* has a passenger service on Tuesdays, leaving Kerimäki at 8 am for Savonlinna and returning from Savonlinna at 3.45 pm.

MIKKELI

Mikkeli (population 31,800) is the capital of the Province of Mikkeli (which comprises South Savo and a part of what is generally called East Häme). It is an undervisited town, despite offering attractions that include several museums and interesting cruises.

History

The Mikkeli region has been inhabited since the 14th century. The original 18th century village could barely attract provincial authorities, let alone become recognised as a regional centre. In 1838, seven years after the foundation of the Province of Mikkeli, the town of Mikkeli was incorporated. Originally a marketplace, Mikkeli soon grew as an administrative and military centre. During WW II, it was the headquarters of the Finnish army, and local museums preserve memories of that time.

Information

Tourist Office Tourist information and related services are provided by Mikkelin Matkailu Oy (☎ 955-151 444) at Hallituskatu 3A, near the market. The office is open from 1 June to 15 August from 9 am to 5.30 pm Monday to Friday and from 10 am to 3 pm on Saturdays. During the rest of the year, hours are 9 am to 4.30 pm Monday to Friday.

Post & Telephone There are seven post offices in Mikkeli. The main post office and the Tele office are at Hallituskatu 4.

Library For 1:20,000 topographical sheets of the entire Province of Mikkeli, go to the public library off the market square, at Raatihuoneenkatu 6. Upstairs in the *opintolukusali*, the warden will open the locked drawers in the *maakuntakokoelma*, where the maps are kept.

Things to See & Do

Infantry Museum Probably the best museum in Mikkeli, with its extensive weaponry and WW II exhibitions, the Infantry Museum is inside old barracks in the town centre. You may need at least a slight interest in these things to find the museum worth the 10 mk ticket. It's open in summer from 10 am to 5 pm daily; at other times of year, it's usually open on Wednesdays and weekends only.

Suur-Savo Museum Another good museum, the provincial museum of Greater Savo, is in an attractive building. It features several mysterious artefacts, and items tracing Mikkeli's proud history. The museum is open daily (except Mondays) from April to August from 11 am to 3 pm. Entry is free.

Headquarters Museum The Päämajamuseo, in a primary school at Päämajankatu 1-3, is in the very room where the Finnish army had its headquarters during WW II. This is a small museum, but everything is clearly explained in English. It's open from mid-May to August from 10 am to 5 pm daily. Entry is 5 mk.

Church Museum The oldest building in Mikkeli, Kivisakasti is easy to see, at the northern end of Porrassalmenkatu. Earlier in the 20th century, it was possible to see mummies of corpses that had been buried under the church. Kivisakasti is open in summer from 11 am to 5 pm daily. Admission is free.

Kenkävero Kenkävero means 'shoe tax', and probably refers to the old custom of changing into better shoes as you stepped out of your longboat at the lakeside on your way to attend the Sunday church service. The Kenkävero estate, the largest *pappila* ('pastor's residence') in Finland, was left uninhabited for years before being reopened in 1990 as a handicrafts centre. Visitors can make their own handicrafts here – you can use a loom, paint on silk or work with wood. Admission costs 10 mk. You pay extra for the materials you use, but the instruction is given for free. Avoid the boring bilingual tour.

Orthodox Church This church is generally not open to the public, so enquire at the tourist information office for admittance.

Tuomiokirkko The cathedral in the town centre is open from 10 am to 6 pm daily in summer only. It has a notable altar painting and is a majestic building overall. See the crypt, also.

Maaseurakunnan Kirkko A short distance to the west, this rural parish church is one of the largest wooden churches in Finland, with 1900 seats. It is open in summer only, from 11 am to 5 pm Monday to Thursday.

Naisvuori Hill There is a tower on Naisvuori Hill, in the middle of Mikkeli. The view isn't that great, and you have to pay 5 mk to walk up, but the tower is still something of a must. It's only open is summer. Taste the waffles with jam and ice cream for which the tower café is famous.

Urpola Nature Trail Just south of the Infantry Museum in Urpola, beyond the railway line, is a recently opened Luontokeskus ('Nature Centre'). There is a small information building with maps, but the major attraction is a jungle-like (in late summer) river valley with an old mill. Note that few of the animals shown in the pictures actually live here. East of Urpola, you can take a nice walk on a ridge and, if the weather is fine, swim with locals. Further south-east, in an ugly industrial area at the lakeside, you'll find a *hiidenkirnu* ('devil's churn') which, at

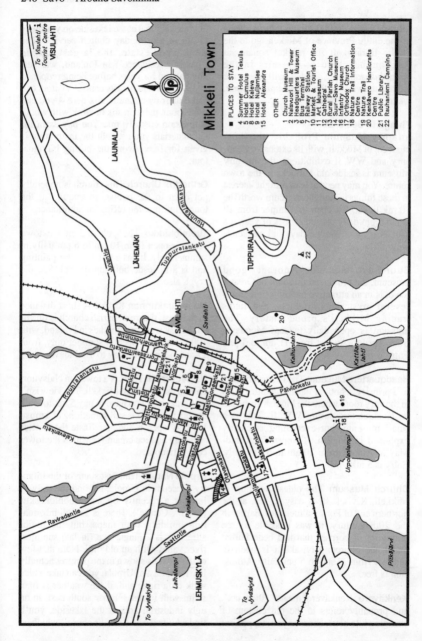

Mikkeli Town

PLACES TO STAY

- 4 Summer Hotel Tekulla
- 5 Hotel Cumulus
- 8 Hotel Kenva
- 9 Hotel Nuljamies
- 15 Hotel Alexandra

OTHER

- 1 Church Museum & Tower
- 2 Naisvuori Hill & Tower
- 3 Headquarters Museum
- 6 Bus Terminal
- 7 Railway Station
- 10 Market & Tourist Office
- 11 Art Museum
- 12 Cathedral
- 13 Rural Parish Church
- 14 Suur-Savo Museum
- 16 Infantry Museum
- 17 Orthodox Church
- 18 Nature Trail Information Centre
- 19 Nature Trail
- 20 Kenkävero Handicrafts Centre
- 21 Public Library
- 22 Rauhaniemi Camping

eight metres deep, is the third largest in Finland.

Visulahti If you have plenty of money to spend, you can see Mini-Finland, the Dinosauria Park, the Wax Museum and the Vintage Car Museum, in Visulahti, some six km from Mikkeli. It's only open in summer.

Places to Stay – bottom end
Rauhaniemi Camping (☎ 955-211 416), open from 1 June to 25 August, has cottages for rent. The *Summer Hotel Tekuila* (☎ 955-366 542) at Raviradantie 1, one km from the train station, is the cheapest place to stay in Mikkeli. This large student dormitory, run by the student body of the technical institute, is open for travellers from 1 June to 15 August. Prices start at 60 mk for YHA members.

Places to Stay – top end
Expensive hotels in Mikkeli include the following:

Hotel Cumulus Mikkeli (☎ 955-20511), Mikonkatu 9.
  Singles/doubles cost 425/570 mk (Finncheques OK).
Hotel Kaleva (☎ 955-206 1500), Hallituskatu 5. All rooms cost 350 mk (Finncheques OK).
Hotel Nuijamies (☎ 955-363 111), Porrassalmenkatu 21. Singles/doubles start at 300/350 mk.
Hotel Alexandra (☎ 955-20201), Porrassalmenkatu 9. From 13 June to 15 August, singles/doubles are 290/380 mk (Finncheques OK).

Places to Eat
Mikkeli's marketplace is busy till 2 pm. See also the Kauppahalli for fresh bread, vegetables and fruit. It makes sense to hunt for lunch offers on Maaherrankatu – the *Fernando* at No 17 is not a bad place to start.

Getting There & Away
Air Between them, Finnair and Air Botnia have three flights from Helsinki to Mikkeli each weekday. The cheapest return flight from Helsinki is currently 335 mk.

Bus The bus terminal is right in the centre of town. Plenty of express buses stop here on their way from Helsinki to towns further north.

Train The railway station is also in the town centre. Mikkeli is the main station between Kouvola and Pieksamäki, or along the Helsinki to Kajaani route.

Getting Around
Local buses can come in handy if you want to visit Visulahti or other places further afield. It is not possible to rent bicycles in Mikkeli, but for repairs and spare parts, enquire at Mikkelin Pyörä ja Kone at Mikonkatu 14, just below Naisvuori Hill.

PARIKKALA
When travelling through the municipality of Parikkala (population 4600), the train almost reaches the Finnish-Russian border. This is the jumping-off point for trains to Savonlinna, 60 km away. There are a number of attractions around Parikkala which you may want to see. The bus terminal is the cheapest place to eat, and the Siwa sells the cheapest tuna fish for self-catering meals.

Things to See
Siikalahti Among the freshwater bird-watching lakes in Finland, Siikalahti Bay is second to none, as far as we know. Some 40 species nest in the area. In the 1960s, the bay was threatened by local efforts to transform it into farmland, but environmentalists have been able to save it as a protected area. The World Wildlife Fund has also contributed. The best time to visit the area is May to June, and there's an information centre, a nature trail, a causeway and a bird-watching tower to help you. The information centre is three km from the village; consult the information map for the shortest walking route.

Church The church, built in 1817, is open Monday to Saturday.

Dairy Museum Several km north of Parikkala, in the village of Särkisalmi (where the road turns west to Savonlinna), you'll find the only dairy museum in Finland, open on weekends in summer.

Koitsanlahti Manor. This historic house, over 10 km south of the village, is administered by the National Board of Antiquities. To get there, catch the Simpele-bound bus from Parikkala.

Getting There & Away
There are regular trains from Helsinki and Joensuu, and trains and buses from Savonlinna. It is a short walk from the train to the bus terminal for connections.

PUNKAHARJU
You may have seen spectacular photos of a long ridge spanning the Savo Lakeland. Punkaharju Ridge offers a lot of scenic value for visitors, whether you drive through it or spend more time walking there. The village of Punkaharju has little to recommend it, unless you get off the train there and walk along the seven-km ridge road to the Retretti train station. In the village, there is a tourist office, a post office, bus and railway stations, and several shops.

Things to See
Punkaharju The long sand-ridge formation is one of the remaining signs of the long Ice Age that produced similar ridges all over the country. Few are as notable as this one. Because the ridge crosses a large lake, it has always been an important travelling route. There is less traffic on the scenic old road, the Harjualue, but the new highway and the railway tracks, connected by a causeway, don't offer good views. If you don't have a vehicle, get off at the Retretti train station, walk towards Punkaharju village and turn right. The best views are along the first couple of km after the Finlandia crossing. For superb views, take one of the paths up on the ridge top. The train travels through the less picturesque half of the ridge, but buses cross the entire Harjualue and even make a visit to the island of Vaahersalo.

Retretti An unusual but popular tourist attraction, Retretti is an art exhibition inside a cave, complete with waterfalls and a concert hall. There are different exhibitions every summer, so enquire at regional tourist offices for details of the current ones. Entry is a hefty 60 mk (5 mk less for students), but this is good value if you set aside half a day for it. There is much to see and explore. Retretti is open from 23 May to 30 August from 10 am to 7 pm daily. You can get there by bus, by train (get off at Retretti station) or on the daily steamer from Savonlinna. The Retretti area also has the enormously popular Kesämaa, a large fun and water park. Entry is 50 mk for everyone, but this place is only recommended for bored children.

Asema-Ateljee The old railway station studio might be closed by now, but you may meet the artist, Mr Niilo Lehikoinen, and see his woodcarvings in the house nearby; follow the 'Finlandia' sign off the ridge road.

Cruises
For something special, the SS *Heinävesi* sails daily in summer from Savonlinna to Retretti and to Valtionhotelli, departing at 11 am and returning at 3.40 pm. The MS *Princess* has daily cruises around the Punkaharju area every two hours from noon to 8 pm.

Places to Stay
You can't find bottom-end accommodation in Punkaharju. The *Punkaharjun Lomakeskus Retretti* (☎ 957-311 761) is a popular camping ground among Finns, so it is often crowded. The cheapest huts sleep two people and cost 215 mk in the high season, 190 mk in early June and in August. Pitching a tent is rather expensive. There is a regular steamer service from Savonlinna to Punkaharju by the SS *Heinävesi*.

The cheapest place to stay is the *Punkaharjun Kurssi ja leirikeskus* (☎ 957-314 189), on the island of Vaahersalo. Dormitory beds cost 100 mk in summer, but it is often full. Also on the island, a short walk from where the bus turns back, the *Kansanopisto* (☎ 957-311 471) has singles/doubles from 220/240 mk. It is open from 22

May to 22 August. Much easier to find, the romantic *Valtiohotelli* (☎ 957-311 761) is the oldest hotel in Finland. Singles/doubles start at 310/385 mk (360/445 mk in the high season).

The *Gasthaus* (☎ 957-311 371) is one km from the village of Punkaharju, at Palomäentie 18, but it is not very pleasant. You'll see it from the train as you come from Parikkala. Singles/doubles start at 230/300 mk. The train will stop on request at the *Kultakivi Holiday Village* (☎ 957-315 151), nine km south of Punkaharju village. It has cottages from 230 mk.

Places to Eat
For a splurge, a good buffet is available daily in the *Finlandia*, a beautiful house built in 1914, one km from the ridge road. The home-made lunch is served daily from noon to 4 pm for 65 mk (45 mk in winter). There is also a good buffet lunch (80 mk) at the *Valtiohotelli*.

Getting There & Away
All trains between Parikkala and Savonlinna stop in the village of Punkaharju, and at Retretti. There are buses from Savonlinna and Parikkala, too. If you drive from Kerimäki, road No 4794 is now sealed and is highly recommended.

RANTASALMI
Rantasalmi is the place to catch boats to Linnansaari National Park, on the Lake Haukivesi islands. Over 5000 people live inside the municipal area, 40% of which is water. The tourist information office (☎ 957-81478) in the village centre features the Geological Stone Exhibition. It's open daily, from 9 am to 9 pm from 8 June to 16 August and from 9 am to 4 pm at other times of year. The large church and the local museum can also be visited in summer.

Places to Stay & Eat
Cottages at *Myllyranta Camping* (☎ 957-81478) house up to four people and start at 160 mk. The cheapest place to stay in Rantasalmi, the *Rantapyyvilä youth hostel*

(☎ 957-81124), gets mixed reports. Some say it is not very pleasant. Its lakeside location is some four km from the village of Rantasalmi, but not close to the national park. The hostel is open all year round, with dormitory beds from 45 mk. You can rent bikes here; enquire at the Savonlinna tourist office.

In the village itself, the *Hotel Rinssieversti* (☎ 957-81761) has singles/doubles from 200/300 mk (360/450 mk in July). There are also several bungalow villages in or near the village of Rantasalmi.

Getting There & Away
There are regular buses between Savonlinna and Pieksamäki, via Rantasalmi.

LINNANSAARI NATIONAL PARK
One of the main attractions in the Savonlinna region, Linnansaari National Park is entirely on islands. The rare Saimaa Marble Seal is known to live there, though few visitors have actually seen it. Several rare birds can be seen and heard. The park centre is on the large island, Linnansaari, which derives its name from the Linnavuori ('Fortress Hill'). Many hills in Finland have had strategic significance for local people, even if no fortifications have ever been constructed. The view from the hill is spectacular.

Information
The main park information centre is in Savonlinna, at Linnankatu 10. You can also obtain information in the villages of Rantasalmi, Oravi and Mustalahti. Get a copy of the free map which is widely available in information offices.

Places to Stay
If you want to stay on the island of Linnansaari, go to *Sammakkoniemi Camping* (☎ 949-275 458). Beds in the cottage there cost 50 mk. You can camp for free, use the sauna for 30 mk and rent a boat for 50 mk per day. There are several camp sites on smaller islands, including the one near Linnavuori Hill.

Getting There & Away

The two most convenient access piers are Mustalahti (near Rantasalmi) and Oravi. The MS *Linnansaari* departs from Mustalahti at 12.30 pm on Sundays, Mondays and Wednesdays, 11 am on Tuesdays and Thursdays and 10 am on Saturdays. Return tickets cost 70 mk. On Saturdays, the boat leaves Oravi at 11.20 am, and the fare is 40 mk.

RISTIINA

Ristiina (population 5400), one of Savo's historic villages, was founded by Count Per Brahe and named after his wife Kristiina. Little remains of the village's glorious past, though the village church (1775) is worth a look. The old Brahenlinna (Brahe Castle) is in ruins, but the new Brahenlinna preserves Savonian traditions. The main attractions are several km from the village, reached also by lake cruises from Mikkeli.

Things to See

Rock Paintings Some of the finest prehistoric rock paintings are to be seen in Astuvanniemi, more than 15 km east of Ristiina village. There is a walking track from the road, and regular cruises from Mikkeli harbour in summer.

Pien-Toijola House This open-air museum contains almost 30 old houses, some of them from the 17th century. A visit to this place should be combined with a look at the rock paintings; there is a marked trail from here. The museum is open daily in summer.

Places to Stay

The *Löydön kartano* (☎ 955-44101), several km north of Ristiina, is a youth hostel, with dormitory beds from 35 mk. Singles cost 80 mk for YHA members, 95 mk for nonmembers.

Getting There & Away

There are regular buses from Mikkeli to Ristiina. For cruises, enquire at the Mikkeli tourist office.

SULKAVA

Sulkava (population nearly 4000) is known as the end point of the Oravareitti canoeing route, as well as for its rowing-boat competitions – it's water sports that count here. The village of Sulkava is a sleepy little place, with many attractive wooden houses around the small commercial centre near the bridge.

Information

Tourist information is available at the boat pier (☎ 957-71568), open from 1 June to 31 August.

Things to See & Do

Lake Pöllälampi With some determination, you can walk along Vilkaharju Ridge past highway No 438 to Lake Pöllälampi. You can rent boats there, and fish, if you've already purchased your fishing permit (30 mk per day) in Sulkava.

Rauhaniemi Museum Area Not far from the lake, the museum area features a logging museum and a 'smoke cabin'. It's open from 16 June to 16 August from noon to 3 pm daily (except Mondays). Entry is 5 mk.

Lake Cruises The MS *Tuulikki* offers evening cruises on Sundays and Wednesdays from 10 June to 12 August. The Sunday cruise takes you to a prehistoric fortress on a hill. The trip costs 40 mk.

Places to Stay

In Vilkaharju, the *camping ground*, open from 5 June to 9 August, has inexpensive four-bed cottages. The *Motel Muikkukukko* (☎ 957-71651) on Alanteentie, north of the village centre, has singles/doubles for 260/390 mk. This is also the best place to hire a canoe or a boat.

Getting There & Away

There are regular buses to Sulkava from Savonlinna, 39 km away.

Heinävesi Route

The most beautiful lake route in Finland passes by the large municipality of Heinävesi (population 5400), and ferries and boats stop at several canals. These canals also serve as ferry piers, where you can get on or off, which means that ferries can be used as local transport. Several attractions around Heinävesi make it one of the most rewarding areas to explore in Finland.

HEINÄVESI VILLAGE

The main village lies in hilly country. Few travellers actually stay in Heinävesi village, but it can be used as a stepping stone to the outlying accommodation of your choice. It's the services, including shops and the tourist office, that make a visit worthwhile.

Information

The friendly tourist information office (☎ 972-61458) is on the main street, at Kermanrannantie 10. It's open daily from early morning to 5 pm in summer; after 1 August, it's open from 9 am to 4 pm Monday to Friday. The staff will tell you about the private cottages that can be rented around Heinävesi.

Things to See & Do

Church Climb up to the church for views over Lake Kermajärvi. The church, built in 1892, seats 2000 people and is open from 10 am to 4 pm daily.

Local Museum Down the hill from the church, the local museum has a large collection of old tools and somewhat worn-out furniture. It's open from noon to 4 pm on weekdays and an hour earlier on weekends. Entry is 5 mk.

Handicrafts Sales Exhibition There is a handicrafts centre opposite the museum. Even if you don't want to buy anything, it is possible to make your own rug here. Renting a loom costs 10 mk per day, and materials a bit more, but instruction is provided free of charge.

Places to Stay & Eat

There is just one place to stay in the village of Heinävesi, and it is often full. The *Gasthaus* (☎ 972-62411) opposite the bus terminal has singles/doubles from 200/300 mk. The hotel and the *Kukkopilli*, a little way up the road, are good places to eat, but cheaper meals are available at petrol stations and at the *Brunssi* along the main road, east of the village crossing; the Brunssi's lunch specials start at 26 mk, extras included.

Things to Buy

The Yrttipaja shop down at the Heinävesi pier sells herbs and tea. It's open from 10 am to 7 pm Monday to Friday and from 10 am to 3 pm on Saturdays. Several km south of the village, the Kerman Savi is a factory sales exhibition, with a large variety of local pottery.

Getting There & Away

The bus terminal is conveniently located in the village centre, and bus services include local buses around the lake. The train station is five km to the south, and you may have to hitchhike from there. From 15 June to 17 August, passenger ferries from Kuopio or Savonlinna on Tuesdays, Thursdays and Saturdays call at the Heinävesi pier, just below the village. The trip costs 115 mk from Kuopio, 145 mk from Savonlinna. For about 50 mk, you can cross Lake Kerma to Karvio.

AROUND HEINÄVESI

Karvio

Karvio is an attractive canal. The area offers several opportunities for sleep, food and relaxation: the rapids are good for fishing (permits can be bought in camping grounds) and there are three choices of accommodation.

Places to Stay & Eat *Karvio Camping* (☎ 972-63603) is a clean place with good four-bed cottages starting at 170 mk. Bicycles and canoes can be rented for 30 mk per day. Across the road is the *Uittotupa* (☎ 972-63519). It has small bungalows (doubles) for 100 mk and large cottages for 300 mk. There are also boats for hire. The Uittotupa is known for its home-made bread, which can be tasted at lunch (35 mk, including salad and drink) or purchased by the loaf. Across the bridge is the *Karvion Kievari* (☎ 972-63504), a pleasant old manor house with singles/doubles for 150/250 mk. Room No 8 has a good view of the rapids. For a splurge, try the excellent buffet lunch for 45 mk (75 mk on Sundays).

Getting There & Away You can get to Karvio by bus or by ferry, and there is plenty of traffic for hitchhikers.

Kerma

You can use the Kerma canal as a jumping-off point from the ferry or bus, and proceed from here to the Savenaho, also called Wirran Wietävä (☎ 972-66251), which rents rooms and saunas. This place has a private pier, so you can get on/off the ferry right here. Rooms start at 100 mk per person, and the smoke sauna is available every night in July for a mere 30 mk per person.

Kolovesi National Park

This rugged island offers little in terms of accommodation, but it is one of the ultimate experiences for those willing to explore the Lakeland. You can rent or borrow a rowing boat or canoe at Pohjataipale, Säynämö or the Norppa-Veneet in Enonkoski. There is accommodation in an open hut, outside the park to the west.

Palokki

Palokki used to have a busy sawmill, but after a power station was built upriver, the river almost ran out of water and the population dwindled.

Things to See Palokki has little to offer in the way of sights, but there are a couple of attractions.

Lintula Monastery The only convent in Finland, Lintula is much quieter than Valamo. There isn't much to see, but you can visit in June, July and August from 8.30 am to 6 pm daily. Sometimes you do get the feeling, however, that the nuns are not at all interested in seeing tourists. Places you can visit include the new church, a shop and a café. To get there, follow the 'Lintulan luostari' signs north from Palokki, just before the municipality border.

Brontosaur Park This park features ugly iron creatures, popular with children, and several small private museums. In an exhibition downstairs in the main building, you can see the work of five generations of smiths. It's open all day in summer, and admission is 5 mk. Behind the garden are two houses – the Paja has ironsmith's tools and the Perinneaitta displays other old objects.

Places to Stay & Eat For attractive accommodation, the nearby *Ronttopuisto* (☎ 972-63188) has a few pleasant cottages. If you have a group of any size, try to reserve the unusual Mummula house. You go back 50 years in time, as well as getting two rooms and a kitchen with real peace and quiet. The house easily accommodates 10 people for a mere 250 mk per day. Small bungalows cost 120 mk and sleep three people. The smoke sauna costs just 30 mk per person (150 mk minimum). You can use the rowing boat for free. Fresh bread is baked daily, and meals are available, but you can also bring your own food and prepare it under a cooking shelter at the riverside.

Getting There & Away To get to Palokki, get off at the ferry pier of the same name.

Pohjataipale

The best place to stay around Heinävesi is the Pohjataipaleen kartano (☎ 972-66419), the youth hostel some 13 km south of the railway station and 18 km from the village of Heinävesi. The old sauna and the rowing boat can often be used free of charge, as many travellers have been happy to discover. There are only 24 beds available, at 45 to 65

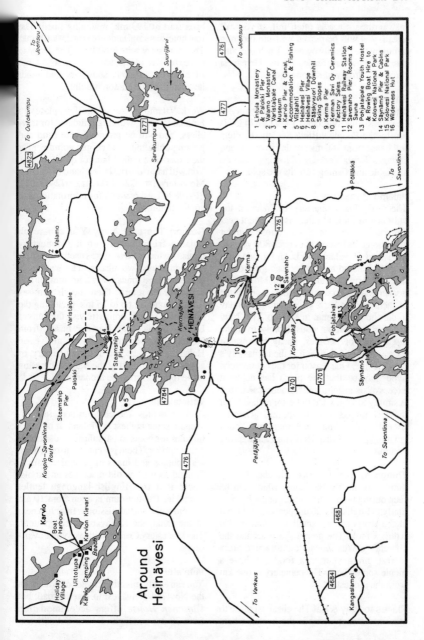

Around Heinävesi

1 Lintula Monastery & Palokki Pier
2 Valamo Monastery
3 Varistaipale Canal Museum
4 Karvio Pier & Canal, Accommodation & Fishing
5 Viitalahti
6 Heinävesi Pier
7 Heinävesi Village
8 Pääskyvuori Downhill Skiing Slopes
9 Kerma Pier
10 Kerman Savi Oy Ceramics Factory Sales
11 Heinävesi Railway Station
12 Savenaho Pier, Rooms & Sauna
13 Pohjalaipale Youth Hostel & Rowing Boat Hire to Kolovesi National Park
14 Säynämö Pier & Cabins
15 Kolovesi National Park
16 Wilderness Hut

mk, and the place is often full. If you call ahead, you will be picked up from the train or bus by the friendly owners. The hostel also has a pier, where ferries on the Heinävesi route will drop you off on request.

Säynämö

The last ferry stop inside the municipality of Heinävesi, the Säynämö (☎ 972-67435) is run by the People's Bible Society. It offers full board from 180 mk per day in rooms and cottages. Rental canoes and rowing boats are available and fishing permits are sold.

Valamo Monastery

The Orthodox monastery of Valamo, the only one in Finland (there is a convent near Palokki), is one of Savo's most popular attractions. Its history goes back 800 years to the island of Valamo on Lake Lagoda. The original Valamo monastery was annexed by the Red Army during WW II. Most of its treasures were brought to Finland, and some of them remain here. Others are on display in the church museum in Kuopio. The 'New Valamo' has grown considerably over the last couple of decades, partly because of increased tourism, which is the monastery's only income. One reason for the commercial hype may be that the place has debts in excess of six million mk! Sometimes Valamo is simply too crowded to be appreciated, but the few monks you do see are generally friendly and willing to communicate. You'll get more peace and quiet if you visit in spring or autumn.

Things to See The two churches have a number of invaluable icons, which can be seen during monastery tours, conducted regularly in English for 20 mk per person. Down at the riverside, the small tsasouna is also worth a look. The ample space around the churches makes Valamo an attractive place to rest; bring your own food and have a picnic somewhere. The cemetery is one km from the monastery.

Places to Stay & Eat The cheapest place to stay in the monastery is the hostel, where beds start at 100 mk, including linen. The fine hotel has singles/doubles at 250/400 mk. The monastery suite is 600 mk. The *Trapesa* has expensive meals, and Tuohus sells large supplies of religious souvenirs and other items in the information building.

Work Valamo is one of the few places in Finland to offer 'working holidays' for travellers. You will be provided with food and lodging only, and most people volunteer for the experience rather than for quick money. You will have to write beforehand to Valamo Monastery (☎ 972-61911, fax 972-62301), SF-79850 Uusi-Valamo for information and application forms.

Getting There & Away You can reach Valamo from Kuopio on a 'Monastery Cruise', which also serves as useful transport between these two places. The service is available three times a week in summer and costs 240 mk return. There are also cruises from Valamo for 65 to 75 mk, including the interesting Lintula cruise (to visit the nuns of Lintula Monastery). Regular buses, from Heinävesi, Joensuu, Mikkeli and even Helsinki, will take you to the monastery, or at least drop you off at the Valamo crossing some four km from the monastery.

Varistaipale

At 14.5 metres, the canal system in Varistaipale is the highest in Finland. It takes 45 minutes for boats to pass through the canal, going upriver. There is a canal museum here, with photos and maps of several canals in Finland as well as old machines and tools. There is a free English-language leaflet available. The museum is open from 10 am to 6 pm daily, and admission is free. Just next to the canal, the Kanavapaja sells pottery. The Monastery Cruises will take you to Varistaipale.

Viitalahti

You can easily miss this cluster of houses on the No 4784 Heinävesi to Karvio road, but *Vänttinen House* offers accommodation from 30 mk per night. Dearer but still reasonably priced is the *Viitalahden lomakylä*. Enquire at the Heinävesi tourist office about the availability of rooms. The large Lipokasverstas House sells honey and hand-made leather products.

North Savo

KUOPIO

Kuopio is the undisputed centre of North Savo, and one of the major lake shipping centres in Finland. Views from Puijo Hill are as unforgettable as the bustling Kuopio Market or the treasures of the Orthodox Church Museum. With a population of 80,000, the town is large enough to have a culture of its own and plenty of attractions. Accommodation is available in all price categories, and you could spend several days here.

History

The earliest discoveries indicate that there has been habitation in the Kuopio region for at least 1000 years. The first Savonian people entered the area at the end of the 15th century. In 1552 the first church was built on the peninsula, which probably got its present name from the Skopa family, who were local priests. In 1652 the ambitious Count Per Brahe founded the 'church village' of Kuopio, which had little significance until 1775, when Gustavus III of Sweden incorporated Kuopio as a provincial capital. Several important figures of the National Romantic era lived here from the 1850s, but the main growth of Kuopio has occurred during the 20th century.

Orientation

Kuopio spans an extensive area around Puijo Hill. Train and bus stations are at the northern edge of the town centre, within walking distance of anywhere in the centre.

Information

Tourist Office The tourist information office (☎ 971-182 586) at Haapaniemenkatu 17 is easy to find, next to the town hall. It is open in summer from 8 am to 5 pm Monday to Friday and from 9 am to 1 pm on Saturdays, and in winter from 8.30 am to 4 pm Monday to Friday.

Post & Telephone The main post office is at Kuninkaankatu 19, and there are at least 10 other offices around Kuopio. The market post office is open from 9 am to 6 pm Monday to Friday, and there are telephones here.

Library The public library (☎ 971-182 318) at Maaherrankatu 12 has a large collection of records to listen to, and plenty of travel books upstairs. For 1:20,000 topographical sheets of the region, go upstairs to the Opintolukusali room and enquire at the *neuvonta* desk; you will be taken to a small room where the maps can be studied. The library is open from 10 am to 7 pm Monday to Friday and till 3 pm on Saturdays.

Things to See

Puijo The symbol and pride of Kuopio, Puijo Hill and its observation tower should not be missed. The Puijo has one of the best-preserved spruce forests in the region, partly due to early conservation policies, but there is now more pressure for the development of the hill region into an international winter-sports centre. It is a large forest, however, and the area has been divided into several areas of activity to keep everyone happy. There are several walks, including a marked nature trail, and even a golf course. Puijo Tower can be seen from most points in the Kuopio area. The lift up to the top costs 15 mk and can be taken until midnight in June and July, until 10 pm in August. There are excellent views of Lake Kallavesi and beyond. To get there, follow the road past the bus terminal. It is not impossible to walk or ride a bicycle, if you're fit, but taxi bus No 6 goes up occasionally, too.

Orthodox Church Museum This is one of the most interesting museums in Finland. Its

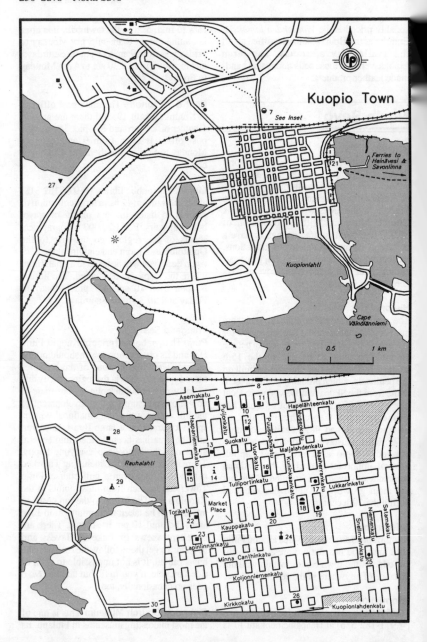

Kuopio Town

See Inset

Ferries to Heinävesi & Savonlinna

Kuopionlahti

Cape Väinölänniemi

0   0.5   1 km

Rauhalahti

Asemakatu

Haapaniemenkatu

Puijonkatu

Suokatu

Vuorikatu

Puistokatu

Museokatu

Hapelähteenkatu

Maljalahdenkatu

Maaherrankatu

Kuninkaankatu

Tulliportinkatu

Lukkarinkatu

Market Place

Torikatu

Kauppakatu

Lapinlinnankatu

Minna Canthinkatu

Koljonniemenkatu

Niemenkatu

Snellmaninkatu

Satamakatu

Kirkkokatu

Kuopionlahdenkatu

■ PLACES TO STAY

1   Sport Hotel Puijo
3   Tekma Youth Hostel
4   Hotel Savonia
9   Hotel Cumulus
11 Puijo-Hovi Hostel
12 Matkustajakoti Souvari
13 Hospitsi Hostel
16 Hotel Martina
22 Hotel Atlas
23 Hotel Kuopion Hovi
28 Rauhalahti Hotel &
    Youth Hostel
29 Rauhalahti Camping
30 Jynkkä Youth Hostel

▼ PLACES TO EAT

27 University Main Building & Restaurant

    OTHER

2   Puijo Tower
5   Orthodox Church Museum
6   Swimming Pool
7   Bus Terminal
8   Railway Station
10 Finnair
14 Tourist Information Office
15 Post Office & Telephone
17 Public Library
18 Main Post Office
19 Kuopio Museum
20 Art Museum
21 Kuopio Passenger Harbour
24 Cathedral
25 Snellman Home Museum
26 Old Kuopio Museum
27 University Main Building

collections were brought to the present territory of Finland from monasteries, churches and tsasounas in Karelia, occupied by the former Soviet Union. With artefacts dating from the 10th century, this is the most notable collection of Eastern Orthodox icons, textiles and religious objects outside Russia. The museum is one km west from the train station, at Karjalankatu 1. It's open from May to August from 10 am to 4 pm daily (except Mondays), and in winter from 10 am to 2 pm Monday to Friday and from noon to 5 pm on weekends. Entry is 15 mk, 10 mk for students.

Kuopio Museum This museum at Kauppakatu 23 is a beautiful Jugend building and is recommended for its archaeological and cultural displays. Probably the most delightful section is an old village shop. The 2nd floor has an extensive collection of stuffed animals (birds and mammals which you could expect to see in the Finnish wilderness). It's open daily from 9 am to 8 pm on Wednesdays, 11 am to 6 pm on Sundays and 9 am to 4 pm on other days. Entry is free. You can borrow the English guidebook to the museum.

Art Museum Nearby, at Kauppakatu 35, the Art Museum features a collection of Finnish art but often has special exhibitions, too. It is open daily, and entry is free.

Old Kuopio Museum This Korttelimuseo ('Block Museum') at Kirkkokatu 22 is another of Kuopio's delightful museums. It consists of several old houses, with appropriate furniture and décor, five of which are open at present. There is also a nice museum café, where you can have coffee and taste the delicious rahkapiirakka. The museum is open from 15 May to 15 September from 10 am to 5 pm daily. In winter, it's open from 10 am to 3 pm daily (except Mondays).

Snellman Home Museum This old house at Snellmaninkatu 19 is where Mr J V Snellman, the politician and an important cultural figure during the National Romantic era of the 19th century, used to live. The museum is similar to the Old Kuopio Museum, but less interesting. It's open from 10 am to 5 pm daily from mid-May to August. Admission is free.

Lake Cruises
There are several departures a day from Kuopio. The MS *Ukko* sails four times a day from 29 May to 23 August, and the SS *Lokki*

has three cruises a day from 12 June to 9 August. These cruises cost 40 to 50 mk.

Festivals

Of the several events in Kuopio, the 'Kuopio tanssii ja soi' Dance Festival in June is the most international and the most interesting. For information, contact Kuopio Tanssii ja Soi (☎ 971-221 541, fax 971-261 1990), Tulliportinkatu 27, 70100 Kuopio.

Places to Stay – bottom end

You can find cheap accommodation in cottages at *Rauhalahti Camping* (☎ 971-312 244), from 150 mk. Four people can stay in cottages that cost 210 mk per night. The *Tekma* (☎ 971-222925) at Taivaanpankontie 14B, on a hill above the university area, is the youth hostel nearest to town. Take bus No 5, unless you want to walk more than two km, partly uphill, to get there. The Tekma's youth hostel prices start at 45 mk, and they mix people in rooms. The place opens at 4 pm on weekdays, 5 pm on weekends. The *Jynkkä* (☎ 971-312 361) is a pleasant youth hostel several km south of Kuopio. It is open from May to mid-October and has dormitory beds from 35 mk.

Places to Stay – middle

There are three matkustajakoti hostels near the train station. The nearest is the *Puijo-Hovi* (☎ 971-114 943) at Vuorikatu 35, where singles/doubles cost 160/210 mk. Bargain on weekends. A much cleaner option is the *Matkustajakoti Souvari*, also called *Nurmi Ky* (☎ 971-122 144), at Vuorikatu 42, almost across the street. Singles/doubles are 170/250 mk. The best value is the *Hospitsi* (☎ 971-114 501) at Myllykatu 4, a bit closer to the market square. It is an old house with a certain character, and singles/doubles start at 90/180 mk. To the south from Kuopio, the *Rauhalahti* (☎ 971-311 700) at Katiskaniementie 8 has two kinds of accommodation for YHA members. The Finnhostel, open all year round, has rooms for 160 mk. Apartementos Rauhalahti offers student apartments from June to mid-August; doubles are 270 mk.

Places to Stay – top end

There are quite a number of good hotels in Kuopio. Most of them accept Finncheques as means of payment:

Atlas (☎ 971-152 611). This old, sad place is the most central, at the market square. Its rooms have been refurbished. Singles/doubles cost 390/490 mk.

Cumulus (☎ 971-154 111), Puijonkatu 32. Singles/doubles in this large hotel are 370/455 mk.

Savonia (☎ 971-225 333), Sammakkolammentie 2. Doubles cost 330 mk.

Sport-Hotel Puijo (☎ 971-114 841). This hotel on top of Puijo Hill was originally built in the 1920s, but its rooms were refurbished in 1985. Ask for their larger rooms. There are special prices every summer, but recent prices for singles/doubles were 250/300 mk, including breakfast, sauna and free entry to the tower.

Kievari Matias (☎ 971-228 333). Outside the town centre, this hotel has modern, clean singles/doubles for 230/280 mk, breakfast and morning sauna included.

Places to Eat

Kuopio has more than 50 restaurants and quite a few other places to eat. The tourist office hands out a city map, with a complete list of addresses and phone numbers. The *Kotiruoka Reetta* at Käsityökatu 19 serves Finnish home-style food at lunch time only, from 10.30 am to 3 pm Monday to Friday. *Zorbas* at Puijonkatu 37 could be described as a Savonian-Greek restaurant. It offers weekday lunch specials at 34 mk, salad, bread and coffee included. If you want to try something authentically local, go to the *Vapaasatama Sampo* at Kauppakatu 13, the oldest restaurant in Kuopio (over 60 years old, in fact). It is a smoky place, and not the friendliest one I have visited, but it serves muikku (whitefish) in various forms, charging 42 to 55 mk for a meal. The *Ankanpoika* in the Hotel Cumulus, near the train station, is one of the most popular restaurants in Kuopio. There are no lunch specials but the food is not particularly expensive. On Puijo Hill, both the tower and the hotel have special weekday lunch prices (45 mk, all extras included).

For beer, check *Foggy's* at Maljalahdenkatu 35, behind the town hall. Its unusual décor includes an aeroplane, a Triumph sports car and an elephant's head. Foggy's is also one of the cheapest places, if you like your beer in self-service glasses. Also popular is the *Kummisetä* at Minna Canthinkatu 44. It is more expensive, but on sunny summer days, its terrace is really packed.

Things to Buy

A trip to Kuopio would not be complete without a visit to the Kauppahalli and the market square. The building is open from 8 am to 5 pm Monday to Friday; on Saturdays it closes at 1 pm. The market opens at 7 am daily (except Sundays) and stays busy until 2 pm. Kalakukko (fish pie) is the thing to buy in Kuopio.

Getting There & Away

Air There are half a dozen direct flights from Helsinki to Kuopio every day. The cheapest return flight is currently 410 mk.

Bus The busy bus terminal just next to the railway station serves the entire southern half of Finland, with regular departures to all major towns and villages in the vicinity. Each destination has its own platform. Hitchhiking from Kuopio may require catching a local bus out of town.

Train Five trains a day run to Kuopio from Helsinki, 465 km away. The fastest connection takes just 4½ hours.

Ship Passenger and cruise ships depart from the passenger harbour, 500 metres east of the cathedral. Kuopio is one of the main harbours for passenger ships. Roll Line operates several cruises and a few interesting routes, all of which originate in Kuopio. From Tuesday to Sunday, ships depart at 10 am for Savonlinna, with stops along the way. This trip, 12 hours in total, is recommended, as it goes through practically virgin countryside, traversing narrow straits and several canals. For 18 mk, you can bring your bicycle. The trip costs 105 mk to Karvio (for Valamo Monastery), 240 mk to Savonlinna.

It is also possible to stay overnight before or after the journey. Cabin bunks start at 85 mk per person (not bad, considering the hotel prices). Lunch and dinner are available, but meals are expensive, and the food is not good either, so bring your own. A bar is open throughout the journey. Another possibility is a Monastery Cruise with Roll Line. You travel on two ships, with bus transport to/from Valamo and Lintula monasteries. This cruise operates from early June to early August and leaves at 10 am Tuesday to Sunday, returning at 9.30 pm. The price is 180 mk per person.

Getting Around

To/From the Airport Finnair runs airport buses that depart after each arrival.

Bus The extensive local bus network comes in handy for excursions in and around Kuopio. There are timetables available.

IISALMI

Iisalmi (population 24,000), 85 km north of Kuopio, is the regional centre for Upper Savo. It is known for its Olvi Brewery and its annual beer festival, but there are also several historic places around Iisalmi. During the 18th century, the area became known for the Runni 'health springs', and in 1808 one of the successful (for Finland, that is) battles against the Russians was fought in Koljonvirta, near Iisalmi.

Information

Tourist Office The tourist information office (☎ 977-150 1223, fax 977-26760) at Kauppakatu 14 is open in summer from 8 am to 6 pm Monday to Friday, and in winter from 8 am to 3.30 pm Monday to Friday. For special group requests, contact Ms Johanna Ehnquist (☎ 977-14433, fax 977-14698), Savonkatu 21, 74100 Iisalmi. For special group requests contact Congress & Travel Services Johanna (☎ 977-18411) or Iisalmi Ditsrict Tourist Service (☎ 977-22346, fax 977-26 760).

Post & Telephone The main post office is at Riistakatu 5.

Things to See
Evakkokeskus This exhibition at Kirkkopuistonkatu 28 displays icons and miniature models of Orthodox churches and tsasounas from (Russian) Karelia. The name translates roughly as 'Refugee Centre', and the place concentrates on the Orthodox heritage of the Karelian areas, lost to the former Soviet Union after WW II. It's open daily (except Mondays) all year round; hours in summer are noon to 6 pm. Admission is 8 mk, 5 mk for students.

Local Museum This small museum in the town centre is open from noon to 8 pm daily.

Brewery Museum This museum at the harbour was the first brewery museum in the Nordic countries. It's open daily from 10 am to 9 pm from 1 May to 30 September, and entry is free.

Festivals
The most famous of Iisalmi events is the four-day Oluset Beer Festival, which usually takes place on the second weekend of July.

Places to Stay
The cheapest place to stay in Iisalmi is the *NNKY retkeilymaja*, or YWCA youth hostel (☎ 977-13586), at Sarvikatu 4C, open from 1 June to 8 August. Accommodation costs 55 mk per person in doubles, and you can use the sauna for 30 mk. There is a common kitchen and a bathroom for every three rooms. The cheapest hotel is the *Artos* (☎ 977-12244) at Kyllikinkatu 8, with singles/doubles at 200/300 mk in summer (60 mk more at other times). The *Koljonvirta* (☎ 977-23511) at Savonkatu 18 costs 350 mk per room, and the *Seurahuone* (☎ 977-15501) at Savonkatu 24 has singles/doubles for 250/350 mk in summer.

In Koljonvirta, five km to the north, *Koljonvirran Camping* (☎ 977-49161) has two-bed huts for 135 mk and four-bed ones from 180 mk. In the spa village of Runni, the *Runnin terveyskylpylä* (☎ 977-41601) has rooms for 385/550.

Places to Eat
The cheapest meals are available at the *Eveliina* in the EKA Market at Satamakatu 8; lunch starts at 27 mk, including bread, nonalcoholic drink, salad and dessert. The *Blue Moon* at Savonkatu 17 is the cheapest restaurant, with a home-style lunch at 30 mk, including all extras. Game and smoked food are the specialities. Good value for money is the *Kultainen Peura* at Pohjolankatu 5, with an 'all you can eat' lunch for 40 mk. The *Olutmestari* at the harbour is not very cheap, but its terrace seats 300 people, and the brewery museum is upstairs. The *Timosaurus* at Kilpivirrantie 1, one km north of the town centre, is open 24 hours a day. It serves a fish lunch for 29 mk and dinner from 29 mk.

Getting There & Away
Bus Iisalmi is the hub for bus traffic in Upper Savo, and a link between West Coast and North Karelia, so you can catch buses from Joensuu in the east or from Kokkola, Raahe or Oulu in the west.

Train There are five trains a day from Helsinki to Iisalmi, via Lahti, Mikkeli and Kuopio. Coming from the north, you can reach Iisalmi from Oulu, Kajaani or even Ylivieska in the west.

AROUND IISALMI
Koljonvirta
The riverside village of Koljonvirta was the scene of a battle between Finland and Russia on 27 October 1808. Apparently, the Finns defeated the Russians here, killing or injuring almost 1000 Russians and losing just 33 men. There are several war memorials in the area. Koljonvirta has a camping ground, and you can walk the 2.5-km Mansikkaniemi track.

Things to See
Juhani Aho Museum This museum honours the local author, who was born in 1861 and lived here as a child. There are old

houses and 500 items on display. The museum is open from 1 May to 31 August from 9 am to 1 pm and 2 to 6 pm daily. Admission is 10 mk.

Church The old church, a 1.5-km walk from Koljonvirta, was built in 1779 and features 20 paintings by Mikael Toppelius. The belfry dates to the 1650s. The church is open daily in summer from 11 am to 6 pm.

Paloisvuori

There's a six-km walking track around Paloisvuori Hill, five km east of Iisalmi. Get a copy of a walking guide which has a few maps of the area.

Runni

This village, 23 km west of Iisalmi, has a spa, and a 1.3-km walking track which will take you to the Kiurujoki River and to the spring from which the place derives its name *(brunn* is Swedish for a natural spring). The MS *Pepsi* will take you to Runni and back on Wednesdays, Fridays and Sundays for 50 mk, and there are cruises on Lake Iisjärvi on Tuesdays and Thursdays for 45 mk.

LAPINLAHTI

You can visit the Eemil Halosen Museo (☎ 977-32288), which displays the sculpture of Eemil Halonen, one of the most notable Finnish sculptors of the early 20th century. The museum is on Suistamontie, not far from the village of Lapinlahti, and is open daily except Mondays from 1 June to 31 August from 10 am to 6 pm, until 4 pm on Saturdays. Admission is 15 mk, and there is a 50% discount for students. The nearby art museum has similar opening hours and an admission fee of 10 mk. All trains stop at the railway station in Lapinlahti.

LEPPÄVIRTA

Soisalo, the largest island in Finland, is surrounded by lakes, canals and rivers. Leppävirta is one of the canal towns that make the trip around Soisalo possible. This is the 'Heinävesi route', the most beautiful

ferry route in Finland. You have two choices; the western route takes you via Leppävirta.

Things to See

Stop at both churches along the main street. There is also the tourist-oriented Unnukka centre, just off the main road. This is the place for discounted (low-quality?) factory products, which make good souvenirs for those driving their own vehicles. The historic Konnus canal, six km from the village along the ferry route, has an exhibition and offers fishing opportunities.

Places to Stay

Mansikkaharju Camping (☎ 972-41383), 500 metres south of Unnukka House, has cottages for 100 to 200 mk. There is a *youth hostel* (☎ 972-42061) at Tuikkalantie 6, near the bus terminal, but it is open only seven weeks of the year, from 15 June to 5 August. There are 70 dormitory beds, all in double rooms, for 60 mk. Much more expensive is the *Linnunlaulu* (☎ 972-41511), where singles/doubles cost 230/390 mk.

Getting There & Away

Bus Buses between Varkaus and Kuopio call at the Leppävirta bus terminal; there are several buses daily. Hitchhiking along the highway is no problem.

Ferry A couple of times per week, Roll Line sails from Kuopio to Savonlinna via Varkaus and Leppävirta, or vice versa. This beautiful route passes through some old canals. Boats dock at the Unnukka pier.

SUONENJOKI

'Strawberry Town', home to 8800 people, attracts crowds of strawberry pickers every summer, and travellers should be able to earn some extra cash if there is a labour shortage. There is a local museum and a church near the railway station.

Information

Suonenjoki has all the essential services, located around the railway station. Tourist information is available at Herralantie 6, opposite the bus terminal.

Work

Suonenjoki is known for its strawberries and, consequently, for employment opportunities in the strawberry fields. The local employment office (☎ 979-512 698) at Ainonkatu 2 would be your best bet, but paperwork should be arranged in advance.

Places to Stay & Eat

The cheapest place to stay is the *youth hostel* (☎ 979-510 545) at Koulukatu 23, one km from the railway station, which has dormitory beds for 50 mk. The hostel is open in July only. The *Matkustajakoti Aula* (☎ 979-510 127) at Asemakatu 5 has a few inexpensive rooms. The *Mansikkapaikka*, or 'Strawberry Place' (☎ 979-511 761), at Koulukatu 2 has singles/doubles for 300/400 mk.

Getting There & Away

There are several Kuopio-bound trains that stop at Suonenjoki. Catching a suitable bus from Mikkeli, Kuopio or Pieksamäki is not a problem either.

VARKAUS

The town of Varkaus has a superb location, surrounded by water, but its centre is rather depressing, due to the several huge factories that dominate the view. There is a bad smell and some pollution, too. Almost 25,000 people have made their home in Varkaus, many of them working for local paper and pulp industries. Although *varkaus* means 'stealth', Varkaus is not a dangerous place to visit! In fact, there are several reasons to come here, most notably the good museums. From 4 to 8 pm on summer Tuesdays, there is an evening market in the square.

Information

Tourist Office The tourist information office (☎ 972-27311) is along the main street, at Kauppatori 6. It's open from 9 am to 6 pm Monday to Friday, till 2 pm on Saturdays, and has a good supply of leaflets from Varkaus and the rest of Finland.

Post & Telephone There are post offices near the railway station, and near the tourist office, at Ahlströminkatu 18.

Things to See

Museum of Mechanical Music If you have a vehicle, it is well worth driving the two km from the town centre to the Mekaanisen musiikin museo (☎ 972-162 611). A Finnish-German couple runs this delightful collection of unusual musical instruments. It has been voted the best museum in Finland, but I would rather call it the funniest show. The two floors of old, carefully renovated mechanical instruments from the USA and Europe are presented in a hilarious way, especially by Dimitri Akimoff, who speaks fluent Finnish, English, German and Russian. This place is highly recommended. There are guided tours every half hour, if there is demand, and admission is 30 mk. The museum is open from 19 February to December from 11 am to 7 pm Tuesday to Sunday; in July, opening hours are 9 am to 9 pm.

Taipale Two km east of the town centre is a canal museum featuring the ruins of an old canal, but even the new canal is worth a look, especially when logs are floated through it. The museum is open from 11 am to 6 pm daily. Admission is free. Cruises on the SS *Paul Wahl* leave from the northern pier at the canal at 2 pm on Sundays and Saturdays.

Local Museum The Varkauden museo at Wredenkatu 5, in the town centre, has displays relating to local history, from archaeological finds to items from the more recent phases of industrial development. There are also temporary exhibitions upstairs. Admission is 2 mk.

Handicrafts Centre If you only stop at the station, take a short walk to the Kotiteollisuusasema, a handicrafts centre, which is now in the old railway station.

Top: Kerimäki Village (ML)
Left: Pauper Statue in Larsmo Church (ML)
Right: Pauanne Shamanistic Community, Kaustinen Commune (ML)

Top: Steamship harbour, Kuopio (ML)
Left: Taipale Canal & logs being floated, Varkaus Town (ML)
Right: Late night in the Ruunaa area, Lieksa (ML)

Places to Stay & Eat

The youth hostel being closed, there is no cheap accommodation available, unless you go to *Camping Taipale* (☎ 972-26644) and rent a cottage for three to four people, from 180 mk. The nearby *Hotelli Taipale* has discounted singles/doubles (200/300 mk) in June. The *Keskus-Hotelli* (☎ 972-22501) at Ahlströminkatu 18 has singles/doubles for 300/400 mk, and the nearby *Hotel Oscar* (☎ 972-2901) is slightly more expensive.

Getting There & Away

There are several flights a day from Helsinki to Varkaus; the cheapest return flight currently costs 355 mk. Buses run from Helsinki, Joensuu and Kuopio and from many other cities along these routes. Trains between Joensuu and Turku stop in Varkaus five times daily in each direction. You can also sail from Kuopio to Varkaus on one of the Roll Line ferries.

Getting Around

Bus and train stations share the *keskusliikenneasema* building, so changing between trains and buses is easy. Taxis also have their station here.

North Karelia

There is no area in Finland like North Karelia, or Karjala ('Place of Cattle') as it is called in Finnish. When Finland lost the Karelian Isthmus and the Salla region after WW II, this province was the only corner of Karelia to remain part of Finnish territory. Some 500,000 Karelian refugees had to be settled around Finland after WW II. Under the shadow of the Soviet Union, Karjala was a taboo subject, and starting a conversation about how and when Karelia should be returned to Finland was a definite end to any political career.

All nations have their symbols and their nationalistic dawn. For Finns, Karelia provided both. The wild Karelian 'outback' inspired artists during the National Romantic era, from Sibelius, the composer, to Gallén-Kallela, the painter. This sparsely populated frontier area (just 177,000 people live in the province these days) does its best to cater to all Karelian aspirations. For the traveller, it is a unique region in which you can meet friendly people, visit beautiful Orthodox churches and take advantage of the good facilities provided along trekking paths.

ACTIVITIES
Trekking
There are established trails, with clear signs, in the national parks and recreational areas of North Karelia (free sketch maps are available in tourist and park offices). These include the areas of Patvinsuo, Petkeljärvi and Ruunaa. There are four established trails you can take:

Susitaival ('Wolf trail') in Ilomantsi. This 90-km trail starts at Möhkö and ends at Patvinsuo National Park. From there, it continues as the Bear's Path.
Taitajan taival ('Expert trail') in Ilomantsi. This 26-km trail follows beautiful ridges. The starting point is in the village of Putkela, a few km north of Ilomantsi, and the trail ends in Petkeljärvi National Park.

Tapion taival ('Tapio trail') in Ilomantsi. This 21-km trail covers some of the best scenery in the area.
Karhunpolku ('Bear's Path') in Lieksa. This 120-km trail covers the entire Lieksa municipal area, and the best attractions are along the route.

Canoeing
In addition to the tough Ruunaa waterways, and the other excellent routes around Lieksa, the Vaikkojoki River between Juuka and Kaavi has been promoted as a good canoeing route.

Lake Cruises
There are several routes on Lake Pielinen, and ferries operate between Koli, Lieksa and Nurmes. There are also ferries between Joensuu and Lake Pielinen.

Driving
Right along the border, the Runon ja rajantie ('Road of the poem and frontier') takes you through very quiet landscape. As such, this is a recommended driving route. The provincial tourist office has printed a leaflet, *Karjalan kirkkotie*, which guides drivers along the 'Karelian church route', from the Heinävesi monasteries to the municipality of Ilomantsi.

Joensuu

Joensuu (population 47,000) is both the capital of the Province of North Karelia and its major travel centre. With a university and a lively cultural life, it tries to compensate for the lack of any major tourist attraction. It does have a good market and plenty of services. The Pielisjoki River and adjacent parks are some of the town's main attractions.

History
Joensuu was founded in 1848 at the mouth of the Pielisjoki River (whence the name), which flows through town. Joensuu became an important trading post for the region, and an international port, after the completion of the Saimaa Canal in the 1850s. Forest products have been shipped from Joensuu ever since. Sawmills and plywood industries developed in the eastern part of Joensuu.

Orientation
The Pielisjoki rapids divide Joensuu into two parts. Train and bus stations are to the east, the town centre to the west. The market square is the heart of Joensuu. If you come by bus, you can also get off at a bus stop in the town centre.

Information
Tourist Office The city and regional tourist information offices (☎ 973-167 5300) are both at Koskikatu 1, in an decorative old wooden house close to the market. The friendly staff (in Karelian costume) hands out good maps and brochures.

Post & Telephone The main post office at Rantakatu 6 is open on weekdays only. There are telephone booths inside.

Library The new public library, with a good collection of magazines and handbooks, is near the university, on Koskikatu. In summer, it is open from 10 am to 7 pm

Monday to Friday, 9 am to 2 pm on Saturdays and 11 am to 3 pm on Sundays. In winter, opening hours are slightly longer. Carelia House, at the university, also has an excellent library.

Things to See & Do
North Karelian Museum A small museum on an island in the Pielisjoki River features old furniture and artefacts from Russian and Finnish Karelia. It's open from noon to 4 pm on Tuesdays, Thursdays and Fridays, 4 to 8 pm on Wednesdays, 10 am to 4 pm on Saturdays and 10 am to 6 pm on Sundays. Admission is 5 mk.

Joensuu Art Museum The Joensuun taidemuseo has art from Finland, Greece and Egypt, including a few old icons. Among the Finnish paintings, see *Pariisitar* by Edelfelt, in room No 23. Opening hours are as above. Admission is free on Wednesdays; at other times, it costs 15 mk, 10 mk for students.

Orthodox Church The most interesting church in Joensuu is the wooden Orthodox Church of Sankt Nikolaos (☎ 973-122 564), built in 1887. The icons were painted in St Petersburg in the late 1880s. The church is open to the public from 1 June to 15 August from 10 am to 8 pm Monday to Friday. The church is at the northern end of Kirkkokatu ('Church Street').

Lutheran Church Symbolically at the other end of Kirkkokatu is the Lutheran Church, whose windows are worth a look. It's open from 1 June to 11 August from 10 am to 6 pm daily.

Tropical Butterfly Garden The world's northernmost butterfly garden is at Avainkuja 2, in industrial quarters a little to the north of Joensuu. It's open from 10 am to 7 pm Monday to Friday, 9 am to 4 pm on Saturdays and 11 am to 4 pm on Sundays. Admission is 40 mk.

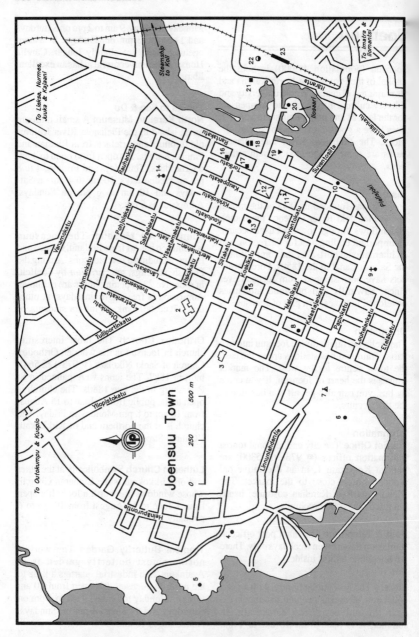

Joensuu Town

■ PLACES TO STAY

1   Partiotalo Youth Hostel
7   Linnunlahden Camping Ground &
    Cabins
8   Joensuun Elli Summer Hotel &
    Youth Hostel
16 Hotel Vanha Jokela
17 Hotel Vaakuna
18 Hotel Atrium
21 Hotel Kimmel &
    Restaurant Fransmanni

▼ PLACES TO EAT

2   Student Restaurant & Carelia Hall
16 Hotel Vanha Jokela Restaurant
19 Teatteriravintola Restaurant

    OTHER

2   University Main Building &
    Carelia Hall
3   Swimming Pool
4   Botanical Garden
5   Vainoniemi Art Nouveau Villa
6   Song Festival and Concert Stage
9   Lutheran Church
10 Boat Pier & Handicraft Exhibition
11 Tourist Information Office
12 Market Square
13 Joensuu Art Museum
14 Orthodox Church
15 Public Library
18 Post Office
19 Town Hall & Pilettipuoti Ticket Office
20 North Karelian Museum
22 Bus Terminal
23 Railway Station

Botanical Garden The greenhouses of
Joensuu University contain 700 plants. They
are at Heinäpurontie 70, near the camping
ground, and are open daily (except Tuesdays) from 10 am to 6 pm, closing earlier in
winter. Admission is 15 mk.

Swimming & Sauna Of the three indoor
swimming pools in Joensuu, at least one
stays open in the summer low season. Swimming and sauna costs 15 mk, and there is a
50% discount for ISIC cardholders. Swimming gear and towels can be rented.

Festivals
The Joensuu Song Festival really changes
the street scene, and is by far the best reason
to visit Joensuu in June. There are always
free concerts, or something happening at the
market. High-class concerts are held in the
modern Carelia Hall, at the university. Check
the dates in the current *Finland Festivals*
brochure, and get your tickets a few days in
advance, as concerts are often sold out.
Tickets are sold at Pilettipuoti in the town
hall, normally open from 10 am to 5 pm
Monday to Friday but open a bit longer
during the festival.

Places to Stay – bottom end
There are two youth hostels in Joensuu. The
dilapidated boy scouts' house, *Partiotalo*
(☎ 973-123 381) at Vanamokatu 25, open
from 1 June to 31 August, certainly has character. Dormitory beds start at 28 mk. Another
option, the *Joensuun Elli* (☎ 973-25927) at
Länsikatu 18, is a student apartment building, open for travellers from 1 June to 31
August. It has clean four-bed dormitories,
with a bathroom and a kitchen in each room.
Beds are good value, at 45 mk for YHA
members. Summer hostel rooms cost 145
mk, with a 15 mk discount available for YHA
members.

Places to Stay – middle
Linnunlahden Camping (☎ 973-126 272)
has a superb location at the lakeside, near a
vast open-air stage, so expect occasional free
concerts and lost sleep! There are huts for
160 to 200 mk, with at least four beds in each.
In July, make reservations in advance. Pitching a tent is expensive. A sauna bath costs 50
mk but is free for lodgers from 7 to 10 am.
The *Apartementos Eden* (☎ 973-24886) at
Torikatu 47 has singles/doubles for 140/220
mk. Also, the tourist office arranges accommodation in private homes, at 120 mk per
night.

Places to Stay – top end
There are six expensive hotels in Joensuu:

Hotelli Kimmel (☎ 973-1771). With 500 beds, this is the largest hotel in Joensuu. It is most conveniently located opposite the railway and bus stations. All rooms are 400 mk (Finncheques OK, with a supplement).

Atrium (☎ 973-126 911), Siltakatu 4. Singles/doubles cost 320/400 mk (Finncheques accepted, with a supplement).

Karelia (☎ 973-24391), Kauppakatu 25. This hotel, right in the town centre, has singles/doubles for 320/400 mk.

Vaakuna (☎ 973-27311), Torikatu 20. Rooms in this recently renovated hotel cost 350 mk (Finncheques accepted).

Vanha Jokela (☎ 973-122 891), Torikatu 26. A small private hotel, it has singles/doubles for 180/250 mk.

Viehka (☎ 973-29531), Kauppakatu 32. Singles/doubles cost 300/400 mk (Finncheques not accepted).

Places to Eat

For snacks and local specialities, lörtsy and karjalanpiirakka pies at the market are something of a must. Pastries cost 3 to 7 mk a piece, and you can even bargain a bit. Junk food at the market grilli stands is all domestic.

The University of Joensuu has five student cafés. The student restaurant in the main building is open in July only. Go there at noon for lunch, Monday to Friday. A decent meal costs less than 20 mk, milk, bread and salad included, but no discount is available for ISIC holders.

Lunch is served in restaurants from 11 am to 2 pm. The *Vanha Jokela* at Torikatu 26 is probably the most attractive budget restaurant. For ISIC holders, there is a 10% discount on the price of the filling buffet lunch. The *Gold Finger* at Kauppakatu 26 serves lunch for 35 mk. For good atmosphere, fresh pastries and a soup lunch, go to the *Trube* on Torikatu, opposite the Hotel Vaakuna. The best place to wine and dine is reputedly the *Fransmanni* in the Hotel Kimmel, opposite the railway station. The menu is in English but there are no discount lunch specials. The *Teatteriravintola* in the town hall building, snobbish yet popular, may be a bit overpriced.

Things to Buy

For an interesting collection of the work of local artists, check the sales exhibition at Kirkkokatu 27. The tourist office provides information on other handicrafts exhibitions and shops. Handicrafts are also sold at the market – bargaining may help you get prices down a bit. See Lampukka for Orthodox icons and other artefacts, and Rihmankiertämä at Wahlforssinkatu 18 (open Tuesday to Saturday afternoons) for secondhand clothes. A similar place is Lähetyksen Kehitysapu at Koskikatu 5.

For bicycle repairs or spare parts, check Joensuun Sportman at Torikatu 37B, or J Pesonen at Merimiehenkatu 27. Joensuun Retki ja Pyörä at Koskikatu 9 sells bicycles and trekking gear.

Getting There & Away

Air Finnair, Karair and Finnaviation operate up to five flights a day between Helsinki and Joensuu, with departures from Helsinki between 6.30 am and 7.45 pm. The cheapest return flight from Helsinki is currently 420 mk.

Bus Regular buses to all destinations in North Karelia and Savo depart from the modern bus terminal, where there is a 24-hour restaurant. Tickets are sold from 8 am to 4 pm Monday to Friday, but you can pay the fare on the bus.

Train There are five trains a day to Joensuu from Helsinki, and four trains from Turku. There is also one direct train daily from Oulu, and another with a change in Nurmes. There are 3 mk lockers in the Matkatavara office in the beautifully renovated old railway station. You'll find a VR Matkapalvelu 'travel service' booth at the ticket office.

Getting Around

The Joensuu town centre is small enough to walk around. Local buses run infrequently and taxis are expensive. The Matkatavara left-luggage office at the railway station, open all day, rents bicycles and mountain bikes. There is a Finnair bus to the airport 40 minutes prior to each departure.

Around Joensuu

OUTOKUMPU

Outokumpu (population 9300) was a wealthy mining town until the 1980s, when all three mining locations were permanently closed. With little else to do, Outokumpu was on the verge of becoming a ghost town. Its property prices plunged to the lowest level in Finland, and with an unemployment rate exceeding the national average, Outokumpu had a neglected look of depression and poverty. A new industrial area attracted several companies to the town, and employment figures are now close to the national average. The excellent mining museum is certainly worth a visit.

Information

Outokummun Matkailu (☎ 973-54793) at Sepänkatu 6 is the tourist information office of Outokumpu.

Things to See & Do

Vuorenpeikonmaa On a hill above the town centre lies an abandoned mine, which was reopened to the public in 1985 as a 'mountain troll's land'. There is an extensive mining museum and an adjacent tunnel with mining equipment. You can climb the tower for a superb view, or watch the hourly slide show. For children, there is a fun park down at the bottom of the valley. There is an underground restaurant, and a café with a good view. The entire area takes several hours to explore. It's open daily from 10 am to 6 pm. Admission to the museum is 5 mk, or 35 mk for all attractions. Discounts are available for children and students.

Sysmäjärvi One of the best bird-nesting lakes in Finland lies south of the Outokumpu centre. Sysmäjärvi was declared dead in the 1950s, due to the polluted mining deposits that flowed freely into the lake. Since recov-

ered, Sysmäjärvi is now surrounded by lush vegetation, and birds have returned here in numbers: a recent study found 72 species and unusual density figures. There are plans to construct two observation towers that would be accessible from the main road; enquire at Outokummun Matkailu for the exact locations. From the youth hostel, you have to go through a real jungle to reach the lake. May and June are the best months to visit.

Places to Stay & Eat

One of the best places to get away from it all is the Outokumpu youth hostel, the *Muurajan kartano* (☎ 973-552 309), in a beautiful rural setting near Lake Sysmäjärvi, six km from Outokumpu. It is a nice 1.5-km walk/ride past farms and forests along a gravel road from the Kuopio to Joensuu highway. Beds and common rooms are in old houses, and there is little that is modern. Even the houses themselves are worth a closer look. A bed costs 30 mk for YHA members, but bring your own sheets and all food. The hostel is open from 1 May to 30 September.

The only hotel in Outokumpu, the *Malmikumpu* (☎ 973-550 333) at Asemakatu 1, is easy to find in the town centre. Its rates start at 150 mk in summer but approach the ordinary Finnish hotel prices on winter weekdays.

The hotel also serves the best food in town. Go downstairs for a cheap lunch on weekdays, or upstairs for a good daily buffet lunch. Apart from a few economical grillis, the rest of Outokumpu's eateries are quite depressing beer-drinking joints.

Getting There & Away

Viinijärvi has the train station nearest to Outokumpu. All buses between Kuopio and Joensuu call at the Outokumpu bus terminal.

LAKE VIINIJÄRVI LOOP

Roads around Lake Viinijärvi are scenic, with beautiful churches and old houses. In August, you can find blueberries in nearby forests. If you have a bicycle, you can bring it to Viinijärvi by train or by bus from

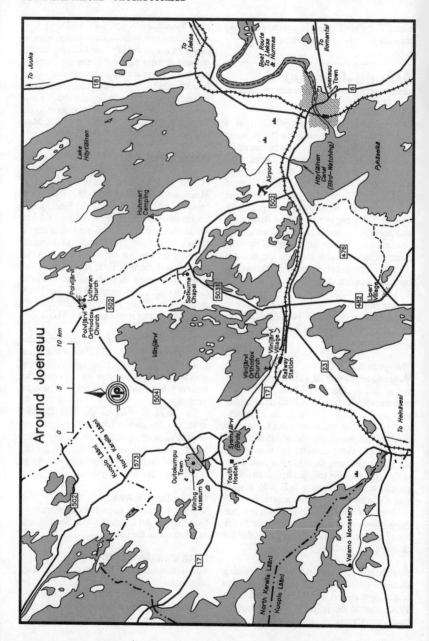

Joensuu, Varkaus or Kuopio, and ride the 60-km loop between Viinijärvi, Sotkuma, Polvijärvi and Outokumpu in one day. Another option is to take a bus from Joensuu to Polvijärvi, seeing Outokumpu and Viinijärvi only.

Viinijärvi

There are a few banks, many shops and a post office in the village of Viinijärvi. Viinijärvi is actually quite famous domestically, as its women's *pesäpallo* (baseball) team was Finland champion in 1990. Viinijärvi is really packed on Sundays during matches. A colourful Praasniekka Festival is held on 26 June each year.

Things to See The beautiful Orthodox church is west of the village centre. The church is open from 11 am to 3 pm Tuesday to Saturday, but few services are held. The 19th century icons are copies of those in Kiev Cathedral.

Getting There & Away Viinijärvi has a train station, and all buses between Joensuu and Kuopio stop here. In the bus terminal, the Kahvila Matkaeväs serves meals every day.

Sotkuma

The narrow road from Viinijärvi to Sotkuma is scenic. Follow the 'Ort rukoushuone' sign just before you hit the main road. Sotkuma is not much of a village, but the small tsasouna (☎ 973-638 522), built in 1914, has interesting 19th century icons inside; note the large ones on side walls. If you want to go in, phone ahead to get the warden to open the door for you. The Praasniekka Festival is held here on 20 July each year.

Polvijärvi

Polvijärvi has an interesting history. When a canal was being constructed at the southern end of Lake Höytiäinen in 1859, the embankment collapsed, with the result that the water level sank 10 metres, revealing 170 sq km of fertile land. Polvijärvi was soon incorporated as a municipality, and its population soared to the current figure of almost 6000. The village has a bus terminal, a few banks, a post office, several food stores and a taxi (☎ 973-631 066).

Things to See The beautiful **Orthodox church**, built in 1914, is not far from the village centre. Coming from Joensuu or Outokumpu, turn right as you see the 'Haavikonmäki' sign, and left at the 'Ort kirkko' sign. The Mutakatti restaurant keeps the key for the church, so go there first. Someone will then show you around, if they have time, but the church is also interesting from outside. Its icons are from St Petersburg and were probably painted in the early 20th century. The church has its Praasniekka Festival on 24 June each year.

Don't mistake the Orthodox church for the less appealing Lutheran church in the centre of the village. Polvijärvi also has a local **museum**, north of the village centre.

Places to Stay & Eat The only hotel in Polvijärvi village is the *Mutakatti*, with six rooms; singles/doubles cost 155/225 mk. The place also serves lunch on weekdays for 35 mk, salad, bread and coffee included. The *Huhmari Holiday Village* is about 20 km from Polvijärvi village, though the sign doesn't indicate the distance.

Getting There & Away There are several buses a day from Joensuu and a few others from Kuopio and Juuka. Surprisingly, buses from Outokumpu run on school days only.

Lieksa

LIEKSA TOWN

If you're looking for wilderness, Lieksa has more to offer than any other place in North Karelia. This vast area (administratively, a city) boasts such natural attractions as Ruunaa, Jongunjoki, the Koli and Patvinsuo National Park. Lieksa is probably the only city in the world to have 100 km of common border with Russia, and to have a city ferry service across a 30-km lake. A 1:50,000

Lieksa map, printed in 1985, covers the area. Over the last 30 years, the population has dwindled by 10,000, to 17,000, half of them engaged in services.

History

Saame people inhabited Lieksa over 500 years ago, but immigrant Karelians pushed them further north. Count Per Brahe founded the town of Brahea in 1653, but it didn't survive long. Lieksa township was refounded in 1936 and was incorporated as a town in 1972.

Orientation

The town of Lieksa is at Lake Pielinen. The main street, Pielisentie, has most shops, banks and restaurants, and a post office. Train and bus stations are towards the lake, and the harbour is one km from the main road.

Information

Tourist Office Tourist information services are provided by Lieksan Matkailu at Pielisentie 7. In summer, the office is open from 8 am to 6 pm on weekdays, 9 am to 2 pm on Saturdays and 11 am to 3 pm on Sundays. There are a few useful English-language leaflets and several excellent maps available, and the staff, wearing Karelian *feresi* dress, speaks good English and is helpful. You can get advice and practical assistance for most of your trekking itineraries. Mari Palosaari, the wilderness guide, is eager to take groups on treks or for other activities.

Post & Telephone The post office is at the northern end of the main street.

Library There is a good public library at the market square, near the post office, open Monday to Friday from 10 am to 7 pm. A section upstairs contains travel books, and if you would like to listen to music, there is a large compact disc collection to choose from.

Things to See

Pielisen Museum The best open-air museum in Finland, this place has more than 70 traditional houses, each containing appropriate tools and artefacts. Get yourself an English-language guide map, as there are almost 100 distinctive attractions in the area. The museum area has been divided into several sections, according to the century or trade they feature. The new building has a large indoor museum, with artefacts organised along similar divisions. The museum is open from mid-May to mid-September from 9 am to 6 pm daily. In winter, only the Exhibition Hall stays open, from 10 am to 3 pm Tuesday to Sunday.

Lutheran Church The Pielisen kirkko was built in 1982 to replace the old wooden church that burned down on a freezing New Year's night in 1979. Designed by Reima and Raili Pietilä, it has huge cross-shaped roof windows, and wood sculptures by Eva Ryynänen (see the Vuonislahti section). The church is open from 11 am to 7 pm daily from June to mid-August.

Sarkkila Manor The privately owned Sarkkilan hovi has been renovated with care. Lieksan Matkailu has more details.

Festivals

The Lieksa Brass Festival, held in late July, attracts quite a number of international players to Lieksa. There are several concerts each day, with prices ranging from 30 to 60 mk. There are also free concerts, and a few concert cruises to the Koli Hill on the car ferry *Pielinen*. For further details, contact Lieksan Vaskiviikko (☎ 975-23134), Koski-Jaakonkatu 4, 81700 Lieksa, or ticket offices in Helsinki.

Places to Stay

Lieksa is not known for its variety in budget accommodation. For camping and bungalows, go to *Timitra Camping* (☎ 975-21780), three km from the town centre. It is off the main road, south of Lieksajoki bridge. This place is open from 1 June to 31 August and

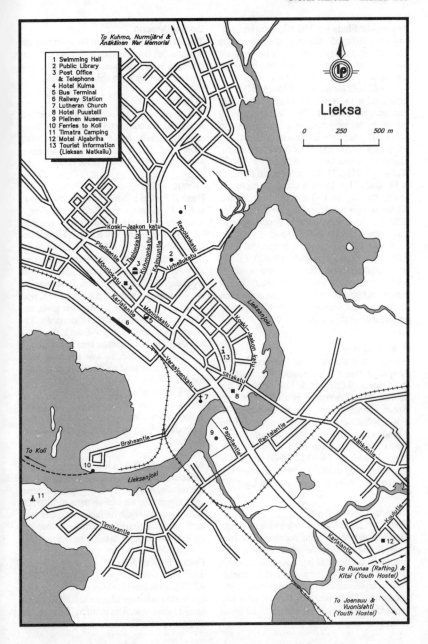

To Kuhmo, Nurmijärvi &
Änäkäinen War Memorial

1 Swimming Hall
2 Public Library
3 Post Office
  & Telephone
4 Hotel Kulma
5 Bus Terminal
6 Railway Station
7 Lutheran Church
8 Hotel Puustelli
9 Pielinen Museum
10 Ferries to Koli
11 Timatra Camping
12 Motel Algabriha
13 Tourist Information
   (Lieksan Matkailu)

Lieksa

0   250   500 m

Koski–Jaakon katu

Repolankatu

Pielisentie

Tapionkatu

Mönninkatu

Kuhmonkatu

Kainuuntie

Urhellukatu

Karjalantie

Mönninkatu

Lieksanjoki

Koski–Jaakon katu

Varaslonkatu

Siltakatu

Braheantie

Peplantie

Rantalantie

Mähköntie

To Koli

Lieksanjoki

Timitrantie

Karjalantie

Koylutie

To Ruunaa (Rafting) &
Kitsi (Youth Hostel)

To Joensuu &
Vuonislahti
(Youth Hostel)

has two-bed huts for 150 mk, four-bed cottages for 210 to 350 mk and eight-bed houses for 420 mk, but prices are lower before mid-June and after mid-August. Camping costs 25 mk per person.

The *Hotelli Puustelli* (☎ 975-25544) is the best hotel in the town of Lieksa. Modern and convenient, it accepts Finncheques and has generally lower prices in summer than in winter. If you pay with cash or card, accommodation costs 300 to 380 mk per night, including sauna and breakfast. The *Hotelli Kulma* (☎ 975-22112), on the main street, is a bit sleazy but has the cheapest rooms in town, starting at 150 mk for one person. There is also the *Motel Aigabriha* (☎ 975-22922), three km towards Joensuu, with singles/doubles for 260/320 mk.

If you have a car or a bicycle, try the *Lieksan kotitalousoppilaitos* (☎ 975-35211) at Märäjälahdentie 19, seven km south of Lieksa (turn right towards Tiensuu). It is a household school, open to guests from June to August. Singles/doubles are 120/140 mk, sheets included.

Things to Buy

Along the main street are several budget shops, such as the Tokmanni. For trekking gear, see Lieksan Ase & Erä, opposite the tourist office, though it is a bit expensive. Spare parts for bicycles can be bought at Polkupyöräliike, at the market square, open Monday to Friday from 9 am to 5 pm. Sometimes, they also have used bikes for sale. Matkakaverit Oy (☎ 975-22069), at the bus terminal, rents trekking gear. It's open from 7.30 am to 5.30 pm Monday to Friday.

Getting There & Away

There are three trains a day to Lieksa from Helsinki and three from Joensuu. The first one leaves Joensuu at 7.20 am and Vuonislahti one hour later, so you'll have a full day to cover all the sights and to arrange further connections to the wilderness accommodation. There are also two buses a day from the Joensuu airport and up to 10 buses from Joensuu.

Getting Around

The taxi station is between the train and bus stations, but taxis are expensive, so you may prefer to walk. You can hitchhike along the highway, not far from the town centre.

VUONISLAHTI

Often referred to as southern Lieksa, Vuonislahti, a completely rural village, has a railway station and a host of interesting attractions. This is where one of the Lieksa area's two youth hostels is located.

Things to See

Paateri Paateri is best known as the gallery of Eva Ryynänen, a respected woodcarver. A sculptor since her teens, she is now well over 70 years of age, and still active. This isolated spot, surrounded by pine trees, is the childhood home of her husband, Paavo. Together, they have embellished their residence with woodcarvings. The latest work is an impressive wilderness church, opened in 1991, with walls and floor made of Russian pine, and huge doors carved from Canadian cedar. The altar was created using a stump that once belonged to the largest fir tree in Finland.

To get to Paateri, follow the road signs from the main road or from the secondary road north from Vuonislahti. You can also rent a bicycle at the Herranniemi youth hostel, or ask for the raft journey. The gallery is open from June to August from 11 am to 6 pm daily. Entry is a hefty 20 mk, 5 mk for children.

War Memorial There is a war memorial on a small hill across the road, as you come from the railway station. This is where Russians were stopped by Finnish soldiers in 1808. On Saturdays in July, a village market is held here, and the nearby *tanssilava* house has dancing on summer Saturday evenings.

Places to Stay & Eat

The *Herranniemi youth hostel* (☎ 975-42110), open from 20 May to 30 September, is a good choice for those wanting to stay in an old farmhouse. The main building is over 200 years old. There are cheap dormitories

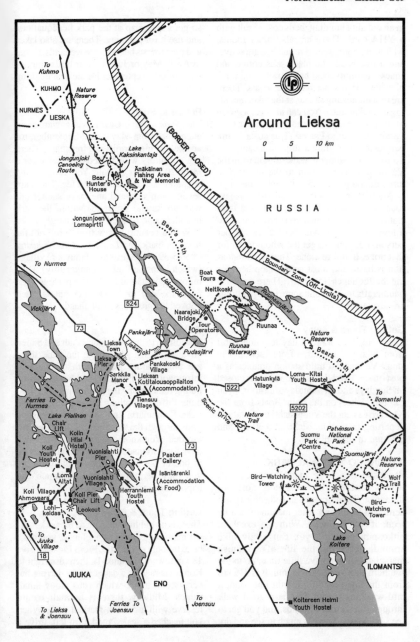

Around Lieksa

0   5   10 km

(BORDER CLOSED)

To Kuhmo

KUHMO
Nature
Reserve

NURMES   LIEKSA

Jongunjoki
Canoeing
Route

Lake
Kaksinkantaja

RUSSIA

Bear
Hunter's
House

Änäkäinen
Fishing Area
& War Memorial

Jongunjoen
Lomapirtti

Bear's Path

To Nurmes

Boundary Zone (Off-Limits)

Vieki järvi

Boat
Tours

Neitikoski

Ruunaanjärvi

524

73

Naarajoki
Bridge

Pankajärvi

Tour
Operators

Ruunaa

Nature
Reserve

Bear's Path

To
Ilomantsi

Lieksa
Town

Lieksanjoki

Pudasjärvi

Ruunaa
Waterways

Lieksa
Pier

Sarkkila
Manor

Pankakoski
Village

Lieksan
Kotitalousoppilaitos
(Accommodation)

Hatunkylä
Village

Loma–Kitsi
Youth Hostel

Ferries To
Nurmes

Tiensuu
Village

522

Scenic Drive

Nature
Trail

5202

Lake Pielinen

Chair
Lift

Kolin
Hiisi
(Hotel)

Vuonislahti
Pier

73

Suomu
Park
Centre

Patvinsuo
National
Park

Koli
Youth
Hostel

Paateri
Gallery

Suomujärvi

Nature
Reserve

Loma
Altat

Vuonislahti
Village

Isäntärenki
(Accommodation
& Food)

Bird–Watching
Tower

Wolf
Trail

Koli Village
Ahmovaara

Koli Pier
Chair Lift

Herranniemi
Youth
Hostel

Bird–
Watching
Tower

Lohi-
keidas

Lookout

To Juuka
Village

18

Lake
Koitere

JUUKA

ENO

ILOMANTSI

To Lieksa
& Joensuu

Ferries To
Joensuu

To
Joensuu

Koitereen Helmi
Youth Hostel

in an old aitta building; beds cost 35 mk with a YHA card. There are also hotel rooms, which are more expensive and less attractive, and a few huts. The place sells coffee and snacks, exhibits local handicrafts, and rents bicycles (35 mk per day) and boats. There are two interesting saunas at the lake, including a smoke sauna. You can also get a group of 10 people together and sail upriver on a *laituri* raft boat to Paateri. This costs 20 mk per person, including a stop for a campfire. To get to Herranniemi, walk straight from the Vuonislahti train station to the main road, turn left and proceed 500 metres to the sign.

Another option is the *Isäntärenki* on main road No 73, a bit far away from the train station but convenient if you drive. There are a few aitta rooms, with beds at 95 mk per person, but you can get the whole room for that price, if you're alone. The accommodation is basic, but most people stop here for the buffet lunch (50 mk). There are also handicrafts for sale, and some local paintings are displayed.

Getting There & Away

There are three trains a day to Vuonislahti from Joensuu, and three from Lieksa. The small Vuonislahti train station doubles as a post office. Even though the station is closed on Sundays and on Saturday afternoons, you can buy tickets on the train. Boats from the Koli arrive near the Vuonislahti train station, departing from Vuonislahti at 9.30 am and 3.30 pm in July only.

PATVINSUO NATIONAL PARK

Patvinsuo is a large marshland area, just where southern Lieksa meets northern Ilomantsi. Swans, cranes and other birds nest here, and bears and other mammals can be seen, if you're lucky. With the excellent pitkospuu network, you can easily hike around, observing the life of a Finnish marshland. If you have little time, go to the southern shore of Lake Suomu. It is 3½ km from the main road to Teretin lintutorni, a bird-watching tower. This is a good walk through forests and wetlands, and you get to see some birds. There is much to see and do,

so get a free map at the park headquarters, and use it for planning. There are also lakes and pine forests between the wetlands. Come in April, May or June to hear birds sing, or from June to September for the best trekking conditions.

Places to Stay

The *Suomu Park Centre* has a warden in attendance from May to mid-September, for advice, fishing permits and free maps. There is a dormitory with 10 beds, available for a mere 20 mk per person. You can use the telephone and the sauna for a fee. There are seven camp sites and one laavu shelter (all with toilets and firewood) within the park boundaries, to be used free of charge.

With a beautiful view from a hill not far from the park, the *Loma-Kitsi youth hostel* (☎ 975-39114) is near the Hattuvaara village (which is inside Lieksa municipality). Dormitory beds start at 5 mk. The place is open from 15 May to 15 October but is often booked for groups, so call ahead.

Trekking

In addition to the long Bear's Path and Suden taival trails that go through the park, there are three nature trails (with educational information in Finnish), and several good hiking routes along the pitkospuu paths. Two quite different options are walking around Lake Suomujärvi and following pitkospuu trails through the wetlands. Both are recommended. You should set aside at least two days for Patvinsuo. Spend several hours up in one of the two bird-observation towers; you may be surprised at how much can happen once you stop to look.

Getting There & Away

There is no public transport, as the park is off the main routes, and to hitchhike, you must be extremely optimistic. From Lieksa, drive 18 km towards Hatunkylä, then turn right to Kontiovaara. It is a dangerously narrow but very scenic road, which runs along small ridges. Midway, there is a small nature reserve with a 5.2-km marked path. When you reached a sealed road, turn left, drive a few hundred metres and turn right. This park road should be sealed by now. If you drive along the eastern Runon ja rajantie route, turn west as you see the small 'Uimaharju' sign, just south of the Lieksa-Ilomantsi border. If you are trekking, Bear's Path and Suden taival both lead there, as the park is where these trails meet.

RUUNAA

Ruunaa boasts 38 km of waterways, five relatively difficult rapids, reputedly the least polluted wilderness in Europe, excellent trekking paths and good fishing. The area is run by the government, which puts over 6000 kg of fish into the waters every year. Campfire sites are provided and maintained, and several commercial services provide many options for activities.

Activities

Ruunaa is actually busy all year round, as it is used for skiing and motor-sledge sports in the winter.

Boating & Canoeing In summer, people shoot the rapids in wooden motorboats. Canoeing is also possible. The rapids aren't really that bad, but beware: in 1990, four people died, in two accidents, because none of them wore a life jacket while canoeing in Ruunaa. Get one, and a helmet, too, if you plan to try your canoeing skills here.

Fishing Ruunaa, run by the National Board of Forestry, is one of the most popular fishing spots in North Karelia. Those using a wheelchair can reach the water along a long wooden road. One-day fishing permits cost 40 mk and are available in Lieksa town from R-kiosks and Kesport, and in many Ruunaa area locations. There is also a fishing permit machine near the Neitijoki rapids. Fishing is allowed from 1 June to 10 September and from 16 November to 31 December.

Trekking There are basically two trekking routes in the Ruunaa area. Bear's Path, a longer trekking route, runs across Ruunaa. You will find it just 50 metres north of the Naarajoki bridge. The path is marked with round orange symbols on trees. Around the river system and over two beautiful suspension bridges runs Ruunaan koskikierros, a 29-km loop along good pitkospuu paths, with good signs along the way and beige paint on trees. If you have more time, there are another 20 km of side trips you can make.

If you start at the Naarajoki bridge, you have to walk some five km along the Bear's Path to reach the Ruunaan koskikierros trail. Another 3.3 km brings you to the Neitikoski rapids, where you'll find commercial services. You can also drive there, if you have a vehicle.

Organised Tours At least four operators run long wooden motorboats along the Ruunaa waterways. The boats are safe, unlike small canoes. Operators provide participants with waterproof jackets and pants, life jackets and food. There are daily morning and afternoon departures in summer, but times vary; enquire at Lieksan Matkailu or go to the Naarajoki bridge, where all tours start. You can join practically any departure, if there is space in the boat. Prices range from 120 to 195 mk, depending on the quality and quantity of the food provided. The easiest way to organise a tour is to go to Lieksan Matkailu, as they can bargain a bit for you. Transport is available from Lieksa to Naarajoki bridge, and on to the boat launch, and if you would like to return to Lieksa, that can be arranged, too.

For both the cheapest and the costliest tours, the most established operator is the *Pielisen Erämatkat* (☎ 975-33166), with several departures daily in summer. There is a café and an information centre near the bridge. Highly recommended is Ismo Räsänen (☎ 975-33111), who is something of a Crocodile Dundee of the Karelian wilderness. He is flexible, according to your needs, and has a picturesque island for the meal stop. His family prepares lanttukukko and karjalanpiirakka pies, and other food, and he catches his own salmon. He also manufactures his boats. Other operators are the Ruunaan Matkailu (☎ 975-33130), which has a kiosk near the bridge, and Kari Sainio (☎ 975-31583), with two daily departures.

Places to Stay

There are at least 10 laavu shelters and another 10 camp sites in the area. Camping, and sleeping in laavu, is free of charge. Get the free *Ruunaa Government Hiking Area* map and guide, for accommodation information. You will need a lightweight mattress, a sleeping bag and some mosquito repellent. Lighting a fire is allowed, except during fire alerts.

Near the Neitikoski rapids, the Pielisen Erämatkat Company runs the *Ruunaan retkeilykeskus* (☎ 975-33170), which has several deluxe bungalows, each with six beds, air-conditioning, designer crockery and a sauna. They can be rented for 390 mk in the low season, 520 mk in July and something in between in summer and in February. You can pitch your tent there for 35 mk. This is a modern place, with public telephones and a TV available, and you can use the kitchen, laundry machines and showers at no extra cost. Use of the sauna costs 35 mk per person. There are mountain bikes and rowing boats for hire (95 mk per day). Canoes and kayaks cost a hefty 125 mk per day, but free transportation is provided within 10 km. Pielisen Erämatkat also rents three large huts at the eastern end of Ruunaa area. The huts take eight people and cost 350 mk per night.

Ruunaan Matkailu has several huts five km east of Naarajoki bridge; enquire at the kiosk near the bridge.

Getting There & Away

There is no public transport to Ruunaa, but on weekdays, you can take a bus to Pankakoski, eight km from Lieksa, and hitchhike from there. If you drive, follow the 'Ruunaa 27' sign east from the Union petrol station, two km south of the town centre. This is also the place to start hitchhiking, with a likely change of vehicle right after Pankakoski, six km away. Lieksan Matkailu can get the boat operators to take you to Naarajoki bridge, if you make the arrangements at their office in Lieksa.

NURMIJÄRVI AREA

Generally called northern Lieksa, the Nurmijärvi area is wild and remote, with quite a few interesting places to visit. Nurmijärvi village has enough services to get you to the Jongunjoki River or Lieksa River canoeing routes, or to the Änäkäinen area for fishing, trekking and exploring WW II ruins.

Things to See
Änäkäinen War Memorial & Fishing Area

Änäkäinen saw fierce fighting during the early weeks of the 'Winter War' in December 1939. Finnish soldiers held their positions here, and left a large number of Russian soldiers dead. In order to stop enemy tanks, the Finns used horses to bring large rocks, and when the war erupted again in 1940, even larger ones were added. The area is now a government fishing area, with the Bear's Path trek running through it. To get there, turn right as you drive north from Nurmijärvi, and proceed six km. To your left is the fishing area, with a korsu, a rebuilt underground bunker used by Finnish soldiers during WW II, and the Korsukierros area, with *juoksuhauta* trenches opposite the korsu.

Probably the best place to see in Änäkäinen is a cave that has been dug on the other side of the main road. Rocks from the cave were brought in 1940 to block the tanks. Follow the 'korsukierros' sign to the entrance, up on a hill. Bring your torch, as it is totally dark and you will have to climb two ladders inside. The exit is narrow, so your clothes are likely to get a bit dirty.

Bear Hunter's House (Kaksinkantaja)

Väinö Heikkinen has killed almost 40 bears since July 1948, and his collection of bear skulls is the largest in Finland. Situated just 10 km from the Russian border, his old house is one of the most isolated in Lieksa, as the nearest house is one km away, and abandoned. Pay him 5 mk when you come, but don't expect any stories, except in Finnish. His farm is quite an authentic piece of traditional Finnish life, and a visit is well worth the effort. To get there, follow the signs along gravel roads before the Änäkäinen area. If you want to trek or ride your mountain bike, you can reach Änäkäinen and the Bear Hunter's House by following the Bear's Path, starting either from Teljo in the north or from Naarajoki in Ruunaa. If you decide to travel by canoe, you can reach the house easily by landing when you see the 'Kaksinkantaja, Karhunkaatajan koti' signs halfway along the Jongunjoki route.

Activities

Canoeing There are two main routes in this area, both of which are rewarding.

Lieksajoki Route While in Nurmijärvi, rent a canoe at the Räsänen K-Kyläkauppa store (350 mk for three days, or 700 mk a week). The route starts across the road. Get yourself a free copy of a route guide, which is widely available in brochure outlets, or at Lieksan Matkailu. The route follows the Lieksajoki River downriver to Lake Pankajärvi. From there, you paddle south-east under a road bridge to Lake Pudasjärvi. Avoid the dangerous Pankakoski power station in the south, and paddle upriver to the upper part of the Lieksajoki River. Heading north-west from this point, you first reach Naarajoki at Ruunaa and then pass a few tricky rapids, especially Käpykoski (pull the canoe with a rope here, unless you are experienced), before returning to Nurmijärvi.

Jongunjoki Route This beautiful wilderness river has over 40 small rapids, but none is very tricky. Lieksan Matkailu has a good English-language guide to the route. You can start at Jonkeri up north (in the municipality of Kuhmo), or further south at Teljo bridge, or at Aittokoski, or even at Kaksinkantaja. Allow four days if you start at Jonkeri and one day from the last point. The Räsänen shop in Nurmijärvi will take your group and up to 10 canoes to Jonkeri for 250 mk, to

Teljo for 200 mk or to Kaksinkantaja for 150 mk. Rental charges are 200 mk per day.

Fishing The National Board of Forestry controls fish quantities in three lakes in the area. Fishing is allowed all year round, except in May. The Aunen kahvila, the Karjalan Eräkeskus and the Jongunjoen Lomapirtti have boats and fishing permits for 40 mk per day. Permits are also available in Lieksa.

Places to Stay & Eat

If you come by bus, you can walk from the main road to the *Jongunjoen Lomapirtti* (☎ 975-56131), two km from the main road towards Änäkäinen and the Russian border. There is also a connecting five-km path from the Bear's Path to the Lomapirtti. This is reputedly the best place to stay and eat along the trekking route. Try the green fir jelly (havuneulashyytelö), which is best with beaver meat, another speciality. The overnight charge is 100 mk per person in spotlessly clean four-bed rooms, even if you have the room alone. For groups, it is possible to negotiate a price. You can camp for 20 mk, with use of showers and toilets. There are two smoke saunas available; the small WW II-style one is quiet and isolated and can be rented for 300 mk by up to six people, while the big sauna can easily take over 15 people in an evening. There are bicycles, canoes and boats for rent. The nearby *Karjalan Eräkeskus* (☎ 975-56141) used to be overpriced, judging by its standards and atmosphere, but now has lower prices.

If you trek along the Bear's Path to the bear hunter's house, ask if the double room in the aitta is available – the rent is a mere 20 mk per person. The bear hunter will heat his sauna (10 mk) or prepare game food, if you let him know you're coming (Lieksan Matkailu can make the phone call for you).

The Änäkäinen area has free accommodation for trekkers. It is possible to stay overnight in one of the three laavu shelters, or inside a *luppokota* cabin, which can take up to five people for one night. Camping is also possible there. If you find it attractive enough, you can even stay overnight inside the korsu, but clean it first, as it is usually filthy. If it is wet, burn some wood in the stove.

Nurmijärvi village has no place to sleep, but check the *Aunen kahvila*, a remote but enormously popular roadside café. It is 15 km from the Russian border and is visited by local authorities as well as by accidental tourists. Aune offers home-made meals (30 mk), sells fishing permits and has keys for the Änäkäinen fishing boats that she rents. The Aunen kahvila is open every day till 7 pm.

Getting There & Away

There is a bus from Lieksa to Kuhmo at 2 pm each weekday. It passes Nurmijärvi and the Änäkäinen crossing, and continues past Teljo and Jonkeri villages. To hitchhike there from Lieksa, walk two km towards Nurmes to the road crossing. While in Nurmijärvi, you can arrange a taxi ride at Räsänen shop (50 mk to Änäkäinen, 70 mk to Kaksinkantaja). If you have a vehicle or bicycle, proceed slowly, as roads are not sealed.

KOLI

Koli Hill is dubbed the first tourist attraction of Finland. Several Finnish artists of the National Romantic era draw their inspiration from this place. Jean Sibelius, the composer, is said to have brought a grand piano to the top of the hill to celebrate his honeymoon. In 1991, the Koli was declared a national park, after hot debate between environmentalists and landowners. Owners agreed to sell their land, and environmentalists dropped their demand that the Koli Hotel, up on the hill, be closed down and demolished. Most of the area is still untouched, and there are many walking tracks on the hill.

Information

Most travel-related institutions stock brochures and maps. Koli village has a tourist information office (☎ 9800-5600), 'Program service of the National Park of Koli', which is open daily from 10 am to 4 pm in winter and from 9 am to 7 pm in summer. There is

also a bank, a shop and postal services in the village.

Kelvänsaari

The MS *Tuula* has cruises to this beautiful Lake Pielinen island, nine km from the Koli pier, for 100 mk. The price includes dinner, smoke sauna, accommodation, morning sauna and breakfast. Enquire at the Koli (☎ 973-672 212) or Vuonislahti (☎ 975-42212) for more information.

Places to Stay – bottom end

The youth hostel, the *Kolin retkeilymaja* (☎ 973-673 131), is in an old school building. This is one hostel that stays open all year round. It is five km from the main road and the bus, so you have to hitchhike or walk. The trip is slightly uphill, for those riding a bicycle, but the road is scenic. Once you arrive, you will forget the trouble of getting there. This magnificently quiet youth hostel must be one of the most relaxing places to stay in Finland. A bed costs 35 mk for YHA cardholders; sheets are extra. Bring food to prepare in the kitchen, or buy sausages (from the family that runs the place) to cook over a campfire; firewood is in the *liiteri* building. You can walk to the nearby Käränkävaara hills. See the map on the wall for routes.

For near rock-bottom prices, the *Lohikeidas*, three km out of Koli village towards Ahmovaara, is a tasteless salmon-fishing business and a very nonurban place. It has four huts, at 50 to 80 mk each. You can try to catch salmon there for 35 mk per kg. Another bargain place is the *Loma-Aitat*, in the back yard of a farmhouse a few km further from the harbour crossing. The elderly couple doesn't speak much English, and although their daughter does, she's not always there. You can get a two-bed aitta room for 80 mk, 50 mk if you are alone and bargain a bit. If there are four of you, it will cost 120 mk for the big room. You have to clean the room before you go.

Places to Stay – top end

The *Kolin Hiisi* (☎ 973-673 211), near Koli Hill, is the best place to stay in the Koli. It has excellent singles/doubles for 250/360 mk and four-bed apartments at 600 mk, with drying facilities and car shelters. Four-bed cottages cost 230 mk. The place also runs the nearby downhill skiing slopes.

Getting There & Away

Bus The Koli is served by regular buses from Joensuu, Juuka and Nurmes. If you drive, the village of Koli is some 10 km east of Ahmovaara village, which is near the main Joensuu to Nurmes road.

Ferry There are four ferry or boat connections each day. The most convenient is the twice-daily car ferry from the Lieksa pier. The MF *Pielinen* is a Norwegian car ferry, which sails across Lake Pielinen. The journey takes 100 minutes and costs 50 mk, plus 10 mk for a bicycle or 30 mk for a car. The return trip is cheaper. There are also boats from Joensuu, Nurmes and the Vuonislahti railway station.

Getting Around

Bus If you arrive at the Koli pier from Lieksa (11.45 am and 4.45 pm), a bus will be waiting to take you to the Koli hilltop, via Koli village, for 7 mk. Buses leave from the hill at 11.20 am and 4.20 pm, and all buses go via the Koli Hiisi.

Bicycle The camping ground near the Koli Hiisi rents mountain bikes on an hourly or daily basis (50 mk per day).

Ferry Cruises in the Koli region depart from the passenger harbour.

JUUKA

The municipality of Juuka (population 7400) covers an area of 1503 sq km on the western side of Lake Pielinen. This area has probably the most beautiful natural scenery in the region, but you have to look around for it. Famous for its soapstone mining and handicrafts, Juuka is a little way off the tourist routes but is still worth a visit. It has two excellent museums and a small wooden old town. Juuan kirkonkylä, the village itself, is

off main road No 18, equidistant from Nurmes and the Koli. The best views can be enjoyed from a narrow parallel road that runs from Nunnanlahti village north to Juuka, and along the Vuokko road north of Juuka.

Information

The tourist information office (☎ 976-70650) is at Poikolantie 1. There is a tourist centre 'Kolinportti' (☎ 976-671333) near the village of Ahmovaara along road No 18. The place is slightly commercial, and it also serves visitors to the nearby Koli area. It's open daily in summer until 6 pm. Juukeli House, in the Puu-Juuka quarters, also has information available. There are a few banks, a post office, a pharmacy and several supermarkets in the village. The public library at Poikolantie 6 is open on weekday afternoons. For a good village map, get a copy of *Juuan palvelukartta* from any of the regional tourist offices.

Things to See

Puu-Juuka There are at least 60 wooden houses in Juuka village, some of which are over 100 years old. Largely through the efforts of individuals, they were preserved from demolition. Many have been beautifully renovated. See Rikas Rouwa for handicrafts sales and coffee, Juukeli for information and an art exhibition, and Tuulian tupa for handmade dolls.

Mill Museum The Myllymuseo's beautiful natural setting, behind Puu-Juuka, includes an old grain mill, which has served the villagers since 1870. There are four buildings, with old tools and machines, including a genuine smoke sauna. The Juuka River runs through the lush vegetation, and in the old days, logs were floated downriver past the rapids, through the *uittoränni* on the other side. The museum is open from 1 June to 31 August daily (except Mondays) from 10 am to 5 pm. Entry is free.

Pitäjänmuseo Visible from the main road, a big red wooden house with 'Museo' written on it houses the Juuka village museum. An interesting construction, built in 1825 with double walls to prevent thieves from stealing the grain that was stored inside, the museum has an impressive collection of local and regional artefacts, some up to 200 years old. Each room features a distinctive person or profession. The museum has similar opening hours to the mill museum, and entry is free.

Paalasmaa The largest island on Lake Pielinen is connected to the mainland by a free lossi ferry and a causeway through small islands. Noted for its scenery and peaceful atmosphere, the island was isolated until a few decades ago, when the road was constructed. Two km from the main road, Mustikkapaikka ('Blueberry Place') sells *savipitsi* ceramics by Sinikka Häyrinen. Press the doorbell of the small house and wait for her to come. A bit further down, the Rantakioski sells snacks and, on Sunday afternoon, delicious muurinpohjalettuja. On the island itself is a shop, open every day in summer. There are no restaurants.

To get to Paalasmaa, drive two km north of Juuka village and turn right. It is 15 km to the end of the island, where you will find Paalasmaan Lomamajat Camping (☎ 976-79516); two/four-bed cottages cost 120/220 mk. A modern sauna can be rented for 40 mk per hour. The road continues to Toinensaari ('Second Island'), which has a few farmhouses.

Nunnanlahti Nunnanlahti, south of the village of Juuka, is known for its soapstone production. The small village along the narrow parallel road has a few attractive wooden buildings. The restaurant Sinikko (☎ 976-78190) has an interesting semi-Oriental décor, and factory sales of stone items. It's open from 9 am to 7 pm Monday to Friday and from noon to 10 pm on Saturdays. Try the whitefish dish, Tillinen muikkupata. There are also a few singles/doubles at 200/300 mk.

Canoeing
The 50-km Vaikkojoki route has been restored to its original state and is no longer used for floating logs. It is promoted as a canoeing route from Juuka to the municipal-

ity of Kaavi. There are 40 rapids, of varying difficulty, and a few accommodation options along the route. Get a free copy of the *Vaikkojoki* brochure (English and German text) or buy a waterproof route map (25 mk) at the Juuka tourist office. The route starts 25 km west of Juuka, at the Ahmonkoski rapids, and ends near the village of Kaavi. You can rent canoes at two downriver holiday villages in Kaavi, Kaavin lomakeskus (☎ 971-675 333) and Luikonlahden lomakylä (☎ 971-671 589), or upriver at Vaikon kanoottimajat (☎ 976-70507) in Juuka.

Places to Stay & Eat
For pleasant accommodation on the shore of Lake Pielinen, go to the *Piitteri* (☎ 976-72000). It is run by Paavo Tuononen, who also arranges fishing trips to what is reputedly one of the best salmon-fishing areas in Finland. Piitteri has simple but clean two-bed huts at 180 mk, four-bed cottages at 220 mk and camping at typical prices. If you would like to take part in a fishing safari, organise a group of five to seven people and call one week ahead. If you come alone, ask whether you can join a group. Four-hour trips cost 150 mk and include one salmon, all gear and a local fishing permit.

Paavo has a laavu and a smoke sauna on an island, where he takes people to eat the fish. It is possible to arrange an overnight stay at the laavu, in a superb, quiet location. Because a guide has to tend the campfire, expect to pay 250 mk for the night, including transportation, two meals and a sauna bath. There are excellent views from the hill above Piitteri. There is also a typical Finnish *huvilava* (dancing stage), where some minor Finnish celebrities sometimes sing on Saturday nights. Tickets cost about 50 mk. The place is not recommended for music, but rather for observing rural nightlife. For further information on Piitteri tours, write to Piitteri Oy, SF-83900 Juuka.

In the village of Juuka, the *Rikas Rouwa* (☎ 976-72010) has a few large rooms for rent, but they are a bit overpriced, at 320 mk for two. Food is available. The place arranges home accommodation, too. Also in the village, the

Hotel Petra (☎ 976-72700) has singles/ doubles for 250/320 mk. The *Juuan Elli* (☎ 976-70360), along road No 18, has singles/doubles for 180/230 mk. Many private cottages around Juuka are available for weekly rental; enquire at the Juuka tourist office.

In addition to hotel restaurants, there are grillis, petrol station cafés and many supermarkets in Juuka.

Getting There & Away
The regular buses between Joensuu and Nurmes will drop you off in Juuka. Hitchhiking along the main road is relatively easy, as there is a lot of traffic.

Nurmes

Nurmes (population 11,000) is probably the most pleasant of those eastern towns that claim to embody the Karelian heritage. The terraced old town is attractive, with its beautiful wooden houses and views of two surrounding lakes. Nurmes was founded in 1876 by Tsar Alexander II of Russia, and the old town still has the character approved by the 19th century Russian emperor. The small town of Nurmes is overshadowed by a sawmill, but the municipality area of 1605 sq km features genuine wilderness and good fishing waters.

Orientation
Train and bus stations are in the town centre, opposite the Kauppatori market square. Car ferries and cruise ships dock near the train station. The main street is Kirkkokatu, with its beautiful birches; most banks, shops, a pharmacy and an Alko store are located here. Old Nurmes is north-west from Kauppatori. The Bomba (a Karelian theme village) and most places to stay are a few km to the east.

Information
Tourist Office The excellent tourist information services, and most of the commercial tourist services for that matter, are run by the semiprivate Loma Nurmes company (☎ 976-21770). The railway station has an information

booth, open from 1 June to 10 August from 9 am to 9 pm daily, but the main tourist office is actually at Hyvärilä, four km east of the town centre. The place is open from 8 am to 10 pm. You can also get tourist information from Nurmes Marina (☎ 976-21244), the local shipping company. The office, at Kirkkokatu 16, is open from 9 am to 4 pm Monday to Friday.

Post & Telephone The post office is at Torikatu 14 and is open from 9 am to 4.30 pm Monday to Friday. There is a telephone service at Kirkkokatu 14.

Library Officially called the Nurmes-talo, and designed by Mr Helasvuo, a well-known architect in North Karelia, the public library at Kötsintie 2 has a good range of travel books and maps, including regional 1:20,000 topographical sheets in the käsikirjasto section, as well as a local museum.

Things to See
Puu-Nurmes In the old wooden town northwest of the train station, there are idyllic wooden houses, surrounded by birch trees and now protected by law. Proceed beyond the main street, past the library, and continue to the low Kirkkoharju Ridge, which has an old red belfry and good views of both lakes.

Kötsin Museo There is a local museum in the public library. It's open daily (except Mondays), and admission is 5 mk.

Orthodox Church This small church, east of the town centre, is open only during services. It offers little of interest.

Bomba Bomba House, two km east of the centre of Nurmes, is by far the most important attraction in Nurmes. It was constructed in 1978 and now houses a traditional Karelian restaurant. It is a copy of a family house built in 1855 by Jegor Bombin, a farmer from Suojärvi (now in Russian Karelia), but the original house was demolished some 80 years later. This area is by no means another Disneyland – rather, it is a genuine village, complete with an Orthodox tsasouna, that can be reached by a pitkospuu path. The small church was donated to the congregation in 1991. In the area, you will also find an exhibition house, Kalevanhovi, a summer theatre and the Jarmanka shop yard.

Festivals

Bomba Festival Week, from late June to early August, is held as part of the Bomba summer theatre season. In the mid-1980s, the *Kalevala* drama established the festival's popularity, which nowadays depends largely on the success of the yearly show (performed in Finnish). A few concerts are held at other locations, so check with the tourist office.

Places to Stay

The best place to stay is the *Hyvärilä* (☎ 976-21770), four km east of Nurmes, with a hotel, a youth hostel, a camping ground and over 30 bungalows. Hyvärilä staff will also help you arrange to rent a private cottage in the Nurmes area. The superbly quiet Finnish lakeside scene is perfect, with a beach, tennis courts, minigolf and golf courses, and other activities. You can walk from here to Bomba along jogging routes. A dormitory bed in the old youth hostel building starts at 55 mk, with a YHA card. The Pehtoori Hotel has singles/doubles for 200/300 mk each. The bungalows, hidden in a forest, house three to four people and cost 180 to 280 mk per day. You can rent saunas, and also hire bicycles, canoes and boats for 20 mk per hour or 100 mk per day. Hyvärilä is open all year round.

The *Bomba* (☎ 976-22260) rents attractive rooms in Karelian cabins, from 370 mk. They may lack sophistication but not character, as they are built of dark, round logs. Each room has a TV and telephone. The modern spa *Sotka* (☎ 976-22520), east of Bomba, was opened in 1991, and has the best accommodation in Nurmes. A double room costs 580 mk, including a buffet breakfast and use of the spa. Non-guests can use the saunas, Turkish steam rooms and swimming pools for 50 mk. There are also special physiological treatment programmes available.

In the town centre, the student dormitory building *Pompannappi* (☎ 976-21770) at Koulukatu 16 is open from 1 June to 10 August. It is associated with the YHA, so there are discounts for cardholders. Singles/doubles start at 135/170 mk. The *Nurmeshovi* (☎ 976-20750) at Kirkkokatu 21, in the town centre, is a bit of a travelling salesperson's joint, with a smoky bar and exorbitant prices, but the rooms are good. Singles/doubles start at 310/360 mk.

Places to Eat

In the town centre, you can rely on the nearest grilli, or do your grocery shopping at the reasonably priced Misto supermarket at the market square. For a splurge, the *Bomba* has a Karelian smorgasbord abounding in Karelian pies, fried muikku (whitefish) and varieties of karjalanpaisti (stew). The buffet (80 mk) is served all day. The *Hyvärilä* centre has a restaurant with home-made meals from 26 mk, which includes milk, bread and coffee.

Getting There & Away

Bus Buses run regularly to Nurmes from Joensuu, Juuka, Kuhmo, Kuopio and Lieksa, but there are fewer buses on weekends.

Train There is a scenic train journey from Oulu to Nurmes twice a day, and from Joensuu three times a day. There are no lockers at the station, but many people keep their luggage in one of the rooms there; it is free, if you ask politely.

Taxi The taxi stand is opposite the train station.

Ferry Nurmes Marina runs car ferries from the Koli once a week from 23 May to 23 August. The MS *Vinkeri II* arrives in Nurmes from the Koli on Saturdays, sails three cruises a day in northern Lake Pielinen waters until Tuesday, then sails back to the Koli on Wednesday mornings. Timetables are available from most local tourist offices in Finland. Cruise prices range from 50 to 70 mk, depending on whether a beer or lunch is included. A one-way ticket between the Koli and Nurmes costs 70 mk.

Getting Around

Local buses run from the market to the Hyvärilä crossing a few times each morning on weekdays. Timetables are available.

AROUND NURMES

Saramo

This remote small village, 24 km north of Nurmes, is where the Korpikylien Tie ('Road of Wilderness Villages') begins. At the far end of the village, the Kalastajatalo, or 'Fisher's House' (☎ 976-34066), owned and run by three energetic women, serves as an information centre and restaurant. The menu includes loimulohi (salmon prepared at an open fire) and perunakukko (brown bread stuffed with potatoes), and a malt drink spiced with juniper branches. Kalastajatalo is open from 1 June to 20 August from 10 am to 9 pm daily. It is open on weekends from 10 am to 6 pm during the rest of the year. The place rents canoes for 100 mk, which includes transportation of two people and a canoe upriver, and even assistance past the difficult rapids. There is a shop and a post office in Saramo.

Kourukosken Tervaslohi

Some six km further north, in a totally isolated spot, is a small-scale business (☎ 976-34050) with a salmon-fishing pond, smoke sauna and free accommodation. The proprietor, Mr Kauko Timonen, speaks hardly any English, so you should ask someone to call at least one day in advance if you want to arrange heating of the smoke sauna. To fully enjoy the place, fish for salmon (40 mk per kg) and get Kauko to prepare it on the campfire, then rent the sauna (about 200 mk for the entire evening) and sleep for free under an open-air laavu at the riverside. This is a very informal place, so you should negotiate all prices. Get a group together to make it more economical.

Peurajärvi Fishing Area

Carefully planned and well kept, this area has good, economical services to keep you busy for days, and peace and quiet to keep you relaxed for weeks. Go first to the service cabin (☎ 976-53011), which has an informa-

tion booth, open from noon to 9 pm every day from 1 June to 18 August. Fishing is not allowed in May. Three-hour fishing permits (20 mk) allow you to catch one salmon and unlimited numbers of other species, or get a one-day permit for 40 mk. Stores in the region sell permits, and there is also a machine for the 20 mk permits. The service cabin rents rowing boats (30 mk per day) and the sauna at the lakeside (35 mk per hour). The fishing area is managed by the National Board of Forestry, which puts 5000 kg of salmon into the waters every spring, to be caught by licensed amateur fishers.

Apart from the fishing, a trekking route (marked by orange paint on the trees) runs west to Hiidenportti National Park and east to the main road, and further to the Mujejärvi trekking area. This is a new area being developed for wilderness trekking, and it may have a few campfire sites by now.

Places to Stay Camping is allowed in many places – get a free map that shows the locations. The *Peurajärvi centre* has two rental cabins (200 mk per day) for whoever comes first. The larger one, in the main building, has eight beds, so even if it's already occupied, you may still be able to sleep there if you negotiate a price with the guests. Two km west of the main building is a luppokota, a Lappish-style small house, with room for three trekkers. It can be used for free all year round and is always open.

Getting There & Away Saramo and Peurajärvi can be reached from the Nurmes to Kuhmo highway. Some 17 km north of Nurmes, turn left and hitchhike or walk the seven km to Saramo village. There is also a bus (19 mk), leaving Nurmes at 9.40 am and 2 pm on Mondays, Wednesdays and Fridays. The one-way taxi ride would cost 120 mk. Kalastajatalo can arrange a taxi to Peurajärvi, 14 km further afield. The trip costs a fixed 50 mk, which is relatively cheap for a group of four people. From Peurajärvi, a marked trail due east crosses the highway; from there, you can hitchhike or catch a bus to Nurmes or Kuhmo. The only sealed road is road No 75.

Ilomantsi

Ilomantsi is Finland's most Karelian, Orthodox and eastern municipality. Its inhabitants are probably the friendliest people in Finland, and its forests contain bears and other big animals. The large land area (2770 sq km) is home to some 8000 people.

Information

The tourist information office (☎ 974-21833/707), right in the village centre at Mantsintie 8, 82900 Ilomantsi, is managed by Ilomantsin Matkailu Oy. The office is open from 8 am to 4 pm Monday to Friday. From 26 June to 2 August, hours are 8 am to 6 pm Monday to Friday and 9 am to 2 pm on Saturdays. There are several banks in the village centre. The post office is open from 9 am to 4.30 pm Monday to Friday. The excellent *Ilomantsi* 1:100,000 map shows all trekking and canoeing routes around Ilomantsi. You can have your clothes washed in the laundry at Teollisuustie 7.

Things to See

Parppeinvaara One of the most famous of Ilomantsi's historical characters was Jaakko Parppei (1792-1885), a bard and a *kantele* player. Named after its previous inhabitant and owner, Parppeinvaara Hill now features a Karelian village with several attractions. Built since the 1960s, it is the oldest of the Karelian theme villages in Finland, and probably the most attractive. To qualify for their job, feresi-wearing guides must know how to play kantele and be fluent in several languages. Runonlaulajan pirtti, the main building, has exhibitions on the *Kalevala* epic, and Orthodox arts.

A copy of the Tolvajärvi tsasouna, appropriately created at the government TV studios, stands behind the Matelin museoaitta, a tiny museum commemorating female rune singer Mateli Kuivalatar. In 1838, while sitting on the steps of this building, she sang a third of all the poetry of the *Kanteletar* epic.

Finally, down the hill a bit, stands Rajakenraalin maja, which was used as a command centre by General Raappana, of WW II fame. Part of this house is original, first built in Rukajärvi (east of Kuhmo in Russian Karelia), where Finnish troops advanced on 15 September 1941. It now houses memorabilia from the war.

To get to Parppeinvaara, leave Ilomantsi village and proceed towards Joensuu. Turn left and follow the 'Runonlaulajan pirtti' sign. The place is open from June to August from 9 am to 8 pm daily. Tickets are 15 mk and include admission to all buildings.

Pyhän Elian Kirkko This beautiful Orthodox church is one km from the village centre, towards Lake Ilomantsinjärvi. It's open from 11 am to 6 pm Monday to Friday and from noon to 6 pm on Sundays. The 'kalmisto' sign near the church will lead you to the old graveyard at the waterfront. It is a silent place, where old trees give shade to a few old graves.

Festivals

As Ilomantsi has so many (Russian) Orthodox believers, several Praasniekka festivals are held. Originally, these were strictly religious events, but these days, they also attract tourists. Sometimes, there is dancing afterwards. Ilomantsi village celebrates Petru Praasniekka on 28 to 29 June, and Ilja Praasniekka on 19 to 20 July every year.

Places to Stay

Ruhkarannan Camping (☎ 974-43161) offers clean cottages at the lakeside and a smoke sauna for hire. A large restaurant is open daily. The *Retkeilyhotelli Haapakallio* (☎ 974-43107) has cheap dormitory beds all year round. Prices for YHA members range from 40 to 120 mk, and bicycle rental costs 40 mk per day. The house is eight km from the village of Ilomantsi, or two km from the Möhkö road. Views from the hill are superb, and you can see some Russian territory, too.

On a hill a few km from the village centre towards Joensuu, 500 metres off the main road, is the *Maatilamajoitus Anssilan Monola*

(☎ 974-21181), where a very friendly family rents rooms in their farmhouse. Singles/doubles are 125/165 mk (bring your own sheets). There are cows, so fresh milk is served at breakfast for 25 mk per person. Bicycles can be rented for 30 mk per day.

There are two expensive places to stay in the village itself. The *Hotelli Ilomantsi* (☎ 974-22533), in the main street, has singles/doubles for 345/425 mk. The *Pääskynpesä* (☎ 974-26311) at Henrikintie 4 is on the lakeside. It has similar prices, and also has a public swimming pool.

Places to Eat

There are a few restaurants in the village of Ilomantsi. For a real Karelian buffet, called *pitopöytä*, go to the *Parppeinpirtti* on Parppeinvaara Hill. The buffet is a bit expensive, at 68 mk, but it is filling. Taste the excellent mushroom salad and vatruska pies, and the slightly sweet vuašša malt drink. The *Kelopirtti* on the main highway, just outside the village, offers a similar buffet. For self-catering, there are several budget food stores along the main street in the village.

Getting There & Away

Buses run throughout the day, Monday to Friday, from Joensuu to Ilomantsi village. There are fewer buses on weekends, so plan ahead. Some trips involve a change of bus in Eno village. The bus terminal in Ilomantsi is right in the village centre. From here, there are several connections to Möhkö, Hattuvaara and Naarva villages, but most buses run only on school days; during the summer holidays, there is usually just one daily departure, Monday to Friday. Taxis depart from near the bus terminal.

HATTUVAARA

Hattuvaara is a small village along the little-travelled Runon ja rajantie route. As the easternmost village in Finland, after Möhkö, it is a definite must.

Things to See

Orthodox Tsasouna Hattuvaara has the oldest Orthodox tsasouna in Finland. Built in the 1720s, it has several old Russian icons inside, and its small tower was used as a watchtower during WW II. In summer, it is open from noon to 6 pm Tuesday to Sunday. On 29 June, a colourful Praasniekka festival takes place here, with a *ristinsaatto* from the tsasouna to the nearby graveyard.

Taistelijan Talo The 'Fighter's House' is down the road from the tsasouna. Designed by Joensuu architect Erkki Helasvuo, who has done a lot of work in the region, this house symbolises the meeting of East and West. There is a WW II museum downstairs, with interesting photos, guns, and handicrafts *(puhde-esineitä)* made by Finnish soldiers in moments of wartime stalemate. There is more to see in the back yard. The house serves food, and is open daily from 10 am to 6 pm Monday to Friday, till 5 pm on weekends. Entry to the museum costs 20 mk.

Activities

Trekking A few km north of the village, at the 'Hoikka' sign, a gravel road follows the northern boundary of Koivusuo Nature Protection Area. An old road leads through some impressive pine forest. There wouldn't be much reason to come here, except that the path is part of a longer trekking route, Tapio trail, which takes you through some of the most beautiful and remote wilderness scenery in the municipality of Ilomantsi.

Fishing For fishing, try Lake Hoikan Kylkeinen, a bit further north. Salmon are added to this lake. The Hatun Puoti and the Taistelijan Talo sell fishing permits.

Places to Stay & Eat

The *Arhipanpirtti* (☎ 974-30138) is the only place to stay in Hattuvaara. Built by its energetic owner, Jouni Puruskainen, this superb cottage accommodates at least six people and costs 400 mk per night. For individuals, Jouni can provide a bed in his house, for 60 mk per night. Jouni has his own photos of bears, and if you're lucky, he will show you around the area, where bears abound.

For a good buffet, go to the *Taistelijan*

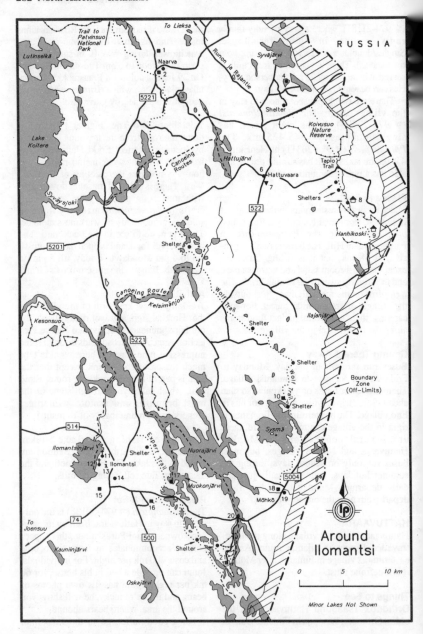

To Lieksa

RUSSIA

Trail to
Patvinsuo
National
Park

Lutinselkä

Naarva

5221

Lake
Koitere

Syväysjoki

5201

Kesonsuo

5221

514

Ilomantsinjärvi

Ilomantsi

To
Joensuu

74

Kauniinjärvi

500

Oskajärvi

Rumon ja Rajantie

Syväjärvi

Shelter

Koivusuo
Nature
Reserve

Canoeing
Routes

Hattujärvi

Tapio
Trail

Hattuvaara

Shelters

Hanhikoski

522

Shelter

Canoeing Route
Kelsimänjoki

Wolf Trail

Shelter

Ilajanjärvi

Shelter

Wolf Trail

Boundary
Zone
(Off–Limits)

Shelter

Sysmä

Expert Trail

Nuorajärvi

Shelter

Muokonjärvi

Möhkö

5004

Shelter

Around
Ilomantsi

0   5   10 km

Minor Lakes Not Shown

1	Salhola Farm Accommodation
2	Hirvola Farm Accommodation & Gunsmith's Museum
3	Aittosenjärvi (Bird-Nesting)
4	Hoikan Kylkeinen Lake
5	Harkkojärvi Wilderness Hut, Laavu & Ferries Puoti
6	Hattuvaara Tsasouna & Hatun Puoti
7	Taistelijan Talo Museum & Restaurant
8	Niemipuro Hut
9	Hanhikoski Hut
10	Pohjoinen Pitkäjärvi Hut
11	Ilomantsi Orthodox Church
12	Lutheran Church
13	Commercial Centre & Tourist Office
14	Parppeinvaara Hill
15	Anssilan Monola Farm Accommodation
16	Haapakallio Youth Hostel
17	Ruhkarannan Camping & Cabins
18	Möhkö Holiday Village & Manta Café
19	Ruukki Museum
20	Oinassalmi War Memorial
21	Petkeljärvi Park Centre, Accommodation & War Remains

Talo; for 65 mk, you can eat as much as you like. In summer, the place serves food all day. You can get food supplies at the only shop in the village, Hatun Puoti, near the tsasouna.

Getting There & Away
Hattuvaara is by far the largest village between Ilomantsi and Lieksa along the Runon ja rajantie route. There are two buses from Ilomantsi village each afternoon, Monday to Friday, and a few more buses on school days.

MÖHKÖ
One hundred years ago, Möhkö was a busy village with an ironworks. Ludvig von Arppe, a clever industrialist, employed 2000 people in his plants, and even printed his own money to pay his employees. Local shops, also owned by Mr Arppe, accepted only his money. Russian soldiers destroyed most of the town during WW II, but an interesting museum and a few other sights remain.

Möhkö, two km from the Russian border, has just 200 inhabitants today. Möhkö is a Saame word for a river curve – the Koitajoki River, flowing from Russian territory, curves here.

Things to See & Do
Renovations are currently underway in the ironworks area, so there will be more to see in the near future. **Ruukki Museum**, the museum of Möhkö, is in an old Pytinki house, built in 1849. It has old furniture, and exhibitions illustrating old techniques used in the iron and paper industries. There is also a two-km *lemmenpolku* ('romantic trail') around the area. Well worth a visit, the museum is open from June to mid-August from 11 am to 7 pm Sunday to Friday and from 11 am to 4 pm on Saturdays. Entry is 8 mk.

Places to Stay & Eat
The *Möhkön lomakylä* (☎ 974-44180) is the easternmost holiday village in Finland. It has good huts for rent, and camping is possible. Although the service is not especially good, the location is definitely something special. The cheapest doubles start at 140 mk. There are boats for rent, and you can buy fishing permits here.

The *Manta-kahvila*, near the bridge, is a must. An old barge that was once used to accommodate factory workers, it is now renovated and serves coffee and real Karelian vatruska and kukkonen pies.

Getting There & Away
Möhkö is well connected by sealed road to Ilomantsi. In summer, there are buses twice daily on Mondays, Wednesdays and Fridays, with several buses on school days. If you have a good car, an interesting loop route is a possibility: Ilomantsi to Möhkö to Hattuvaara.

NAARVA
This tiny village can be visited as a side trip from the quiet Runon ja rajantie route. Naarva has a bank, and a K-shop where you can buy petrol.

Things to See

From Naarva village, there are good views of the surrounding wilderness. As you drive along the road, an 'asepajamuseo' sign indicates a Gunsmith's Museum. The grey building was built in 1790 and looks as if it's about to collapse. It is normally closed, but you can see through the windows, or ring the bell in the hope that someone might come from the house nearby to open the door. Admission is 5 mk.

Places to Stay & Eat

One reason to visit Naarva is to relax for a day or two, staying in an old farmhouse. The *Hirvolan maatilamajoitus*, a short distance past the village shop, has a few rooms. It is run by an elderly Karelian couple, who prepare excellent rye bread and traditional food. Prices are negotiable, but expect to pay 50 mk per person, sauna included. Another place, two km off the main road, is the *Salhola*. There are two four-bed houses, at 60 mk per person. Try to get the red *mummonmökki* house behind the spruce trees – it is very quiet. Views from both places are splendid.

Getting There & Away

Naarva is seven km from the Runon ja rajantie route. There is a bus from Ilomantsi village each afternoon, Monday to Friday. If you trek on the Susitaival trail, you'll pass Naarva.

PETKELJÄRVI NATIONAL PARK

Petkeljärvi park is one of the smallest national parks in Finland. Founded in 1956 to protect an attractive piece of ridge and lake scenery, the emphasis is more on recreation than nature preservation. There is a sealed road through the park, and many clearly marked trails. To appreciate Petkeljärvi, take

mosquito repellent, walk to an isolated spot, sit down and listen to what nature has to say. There are a few wilderness bird species, such as the black-throated diver and some owls, that you may see as you walk. To see birds, the best time to visit is April to June, but all summer is fine.

Things to See

There are renovated WW II sites at the southern tip of Petraniemi, near the park headquarters. The korsu bunker was where soldiers were supposed to sleep while their comrades guarded the other side of the lake, crawling in *taisteluhauta* trenches. No fighting took place here, however, and most of what you see has been rebuilt. A large war monument is along the main road at Oinassalmi, close to the Petkeljärvi crossing.

Places to Stay & Eat

The *National Park Centre* (☎ 974-44199), six km from the main road, has accommodation in superbly modern rooms. Prices range from 54 to 145 mk per person, according to the size of the room. Camping costs 25 mk for one person, 40 mk for two or more. You can hire boats and canoes, buy fishing permits or rent the sauna (55 mk per hour). Buffet breakfast is available, by order, but it may be cheaper to bring your own food and prepare it in the kitchen that is provided free of charge for guests.

Getting There & Away

Möhkö buses run along the good road from Ilomantsi. A sealed road takes you the six km from the main road to the park headquarters. If you want to trek, follow the 22-km Taitajan taival ('Expert trail') from Putkela village, five km north of Ilomantsi village, or join the path from the Möhkö road, a 13-km hike from the main road.

Oulu

The large Province of Oulu can easily be divided into three different regions. The area around the town of Oulu is flat and of little interest in terms of landscape. It was a seabed after the Ice Age, until a few thousand years ago. These days, it is relatively fertile farmland, which is still rising one cm every year. There are several historical museums and churches scattered around the area. The town of Oulu is the centre of the region.

OULU

Oulu (population 105,000) is the largest town in North Finland. The real capital of northern Finland, it is a busy place, with a large university campus and a host of high-technology industries. Unfortunately, the stinking pulp factory nearby is too visible to be ignored. Despite this, Oulu is a pleasant town to visit in summer, with good parks, lively markets and a host of attractions. In June and July, it never gets dark in Oulu, even at night.

Locals often tell you that Oulu is the only town with 'a university built on a swamp, a theatre on the sea, a ship on the marketplace or a science centre in a factory', which gives you an idea of the sense of humour of the people of Oulu, who may not be joking at all. Locals also tell you about recent 'unexplained' fires, which may pave the way for new architecture. Building companies own some of the finest wooden houses in the town centre. The Oulu School of Architecture is a regional version of postmodern architecture (featuring small towers, porticoes and combinations of various elements), many examples of which can be seen around Oulu.

Oulu has a long history in the busy tar business. Hard-working pioneers of the Kainuu forests floated barrels of tar to Oulu, where this essential raw material (used in the building of wooden ships) was traded.

Orientation

Oulu is situated at the mouth of the Oulujoki River, with bridges connecting the riverbanks and several islands. You can easily walk from the railway and bus stations to most places in the town centre.

Information

Tourist Office The tourist information office (☎ 981-314 1295) at Torikatu 10 has a good selection of brochures for most parts of Finland, and local information is especially good. The office is open from 9 am to 4 pm Monday to Friday. From July to mid-August, it's open daily till 6 pm, except on Sundays, when it closes at 4 pm.

Post & Telephone The main post office, near the train station, is open from 9 am to 5 pm Monday to Friday. The Tele office is next door. The poste restante address is 90101 Oulu.

Library The new public library building was erected on reclaimed land at the market. There is an excellent choice of magazines on the 1st floor, travel books on the 2nd floor and the käsikirjasto section on the 3rd floor, with 1:20,000 maps of the entire Province of Oulu. The library is open from 10 am to 8 pm Monday to Friday, with shorter hours on Saturdays and Sundays.

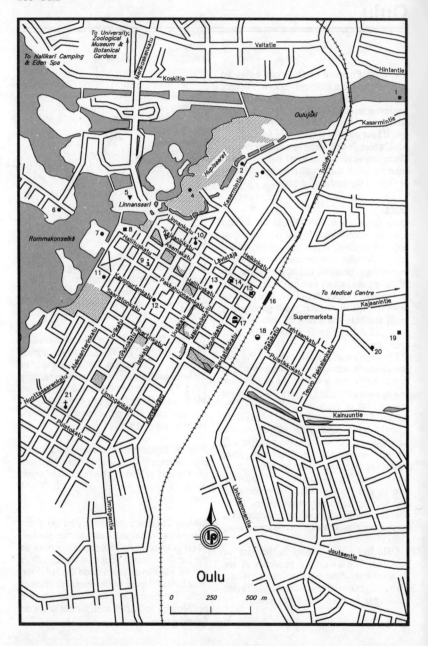

Oulu

0   250   500 m

Travel Agencies Oulu has the northernmost Kilroy student travel bureau (☎ 981-372 720), at Pakkahuoneenkatu 8. It's open on weekdays only.

Bookshops The Akateeminen is at Kirkkokatu 29.

Things to See & Do

Tori The market now has its *Toripolliisi* statue, a funny representation of local police. There's just something special about the police of Oulu! The old red storehouses at one end, and the slightly newer houses at the other (notably the Hirvosen Vanha Makasiini), are inspirational places to see, even if you don't want to buy anything. The market is surrounded by attractively renovated houses, and nearby are two of the abovementioned Oulu oddities: the ship and the theatre.

Tietomaa This is the oldest Science Centre in Finland. It's not particularly special in terms of scientific discoveries, but its location, in an old factory building, makes Tietomaa a worthwhile place to visit. Entry is 50 mk and includes the big-screen film (shown at noon, 2 and 4 pm daily).

Ainola Provincial Museum This is the best museum in Oulu, and can be found in the area of Hupisaaret. The four floors house well-displayed local trade and industry exhibitions, plus a Lappish section. Don't miss this place, and set aside several hours to see everything. No English-language presentation is provided. The museum is open from 10 am to 8 pm Sunday to Thursday and from 10 am to 3 pm on Saturdays. Entry is 5 mk, 2 mk for students.

Oulu Art Museum This modern museum at Kasarmintie 7, near Tietomaa, is well worth a look. It's open from 11 am to late afternoon daily (except Mondays). Admission is 5 mk, sometimes more during special exhibitions.

Turkansaari This island in the Oulujoki River has an open-air museum that should not be missed. If the weather is fine, and you have the time to spend getting there, Turkansaari makes an excellent day trip from Oulu. Originally a trading post for Russians and Swedes, it has a 17th century church and quite a number of old houses, with various items on display. Bring some mosquito repellent on hot summer days. There is a Sunday Lutheran service on the island at noon, and cultural shows at 3 pm. On Saturdays, you may see a local wedding in the little church.

To get there, drive about 10 km towards Muhos, and follow the 'Turkansaari' signs. Hourly buses from Oulu will drop you off at the crossing 1.7 km from the museum, and three buses a day pass close by. You can make the trip by boat, along the Oulujoki River. This costs 60 mk return, museum admission included. Otherwise, entry to the museum costs 10 mk, 3 mk for students.

Walking Tour The islands on the Oulujoki River are connected by bicycle bridges, and there is a lot to explore. Linnansaari ('Fortress Island') has an historical exhibition in the basement of the tower. The nearby Hupisaaret ('Fun Islands') is a pleasant place to relax.

Festivals

Among the relatively few festivals held in Oulu, the Kuusrock weekend in late July may be worth checking, as there are several good bands playing, though it days may be numbered. Expect to pay about 100 mk for a one-day ticket if it is still happening. The pedestrian street Rotuaari is where most other activities take place in Oulu.

Places to Stay – bottom end

Oulu is notorious for its lack of budget accommodation. If you don't want to camp, you should form a group and rent a hut at *Camping Nallikari*, open May to September. It is a busy, well-established camping ground five km from the town centre. To get there, take bus No 5 ('Eden' bus) or the more expensive Potnapekka bus. There are 50 huts, with two-bed huts costing 150 to 200 mk. In July, four-bed huts cost 290 mk. Camping charges are 30 mk per person.

Places to Stay – middle

The *Välkkylä* (☎ 981-377 707) at Kajaanintie 36, the only official youth hostel in Oulu, is open only from 2 June to 30 August. Dormitory beds are expensive (65 mk per person in four-bed rooms) but comfortable. The Välkkylä is also a summer hotel, with student apartment rooms from 160 mk a double. Each room has a kitchen, but you can get a buffet breakfast for 25 mk.

Places to Stay – top end

Oulu has an excellent choice of expensive accommodation:

Turisti (☎ 981-375 233). This hotel, opposite the railway station, has singles/doubles at 265/345 mk, and sometimes offers special prices.

Lanamäki (☎ 981-379 555). Next door to the Turisti, the Lanamäki has singles/doubles from 250/340 mk (Finncheques OK), and a few unusual bars downstairs.

Apollo (☎ 981-374 344), Asemakatu 31-33. Also near the station, this hotel has singles/doubles from 210/290 mk.

Vaakuna (☎ 981-372 666), Hallituskatu 1. The Vaakuna is ugly but is located right at the waterfront, with good views from rooms. Prices start at 490 mk (Finncheques accepted).

Arina (☎ 981-311 4221), Pakkahuoneenkatu 16. This is the most central hotel in Oulu. Singles/doubles cost 430/540 mk (Finncheques OK).

Rantasipi (☎ 981-313 9111), Kirkkokatu 3. The most modern hotel in Oulu, the Rivoli has singles/doubles from 550/690 mk (Finncheques OK).

Eden (☎ 981-550 4100). This modern spa, several km away in Nallikari, has saunas, pools, water slides and physical treatment programmes. Singles/doubles are 420/610 mk, but there are special two-day offers, especially from Sunday to Tuesday. All prices include unlimited use of pools and saunas.

Places to Eat

Snacks For nice pastries, go to the *Bisketti*, along Rotuaari. They are proud of their rahkaviineri and mansikkakori, and also have good fresh bread. Another place to have a cup of coffee or a warm lohikeitto is the traditional *Tähtitornin kahvio*, a wooden tower on Linnansaari island. It is hard to miss, and is recommended more for the atmosphere and the view than for the quality or the prices.

Main Dishes The best value 'all you can eat' breakfast (21 mk) is served in the *Hotel Vaakuna* from 6.30 to 10 am daily (one hour later on Sundays). You'll find good, cheap pizza at the *Koti Pizza* at Torikatu 9, or at *Da Mario*. The *Jumpru* bar at Kauppurienkatu 6 serves lunch for 36 mk, including salad, drink, bread and coffee. Opposite, the *Döner Kebab* offers a substantial 28 mk plate. The daily lunch at the *Botnia Emigrants*, along Rotuaari, is more expensive. The *Neptunus* ship at the market is recommended for its

Top: Vuonislahti Youth Hostel, Southern Lieksa (ML)
Left: Coffee being prepared, Ruunaa area, Lieksa (ML)
Right: Logs waiting to be transported along river, Lieksa (ML)

Top: Petkeljärvi National Park, Ilomantsi Commune (ML)
Left: A small sauna on a lakeshore, Northern Karelia (ML)
Right: The Orthodox Church, Ilomantsi (ML)

food and service, but be warned: a proper meal costs well over 100 mk.

Self-Catering Oulu specialties include rieska (thin chappati-like bread), leipäjuusto (large baked cheese loaf), and lohikeitto (salmon soup). These food items can best be found at the marketplace or the Kauppahalli.

Bars The people of Oulu enjoy their cold beer sitting out on the patio in good 'patio weather'. The *Jumpru Patio* is the most popular of them all, though the beer is a bit dearer here than elsewhere. The *Mosel* near the railway station is cheaper.

Entertainment
The *45 Special* has live Finnish rock music on Wednesdays and Sundays.

Things to Buy
Rotuaari, off Kirkkokatu, is a short walking street, where many shops can be found. It is a nice area, with street musicians and several events in summer. Look for handicrafts and souvenirs at the tori. For cheap food and bargains, try the three large, competitive supermarkets in Raksila, just next to the bus terminal.

Getting There & Away
Air Oulu airport is the second busiest in Finland. The cheapest return flight from Helsinki is currently 510 mk.

Bus Buses depart from near the railway station, and each destination has its own platform. There are seven buses to Kuusamo each day. Local Koskilinjat buses, departing from the town centre, take you to nearby villages.

Train Trains take you directly to the town centre. Six to 10 trains a day run from Helsinki to Oulu, the fastest trains covering the 680 km in a little over six hours. There are also trains via Joensuu and Kajaani.

Getting Around
To/From the Airport Each arriving flight is met by a Finnair bus to Oulu.

Bus Local buses have a large network. Each ride costs about 8 mk, and route maps are displayed at bus stops.

Bicycle The cheapest rental bicycles (30 mk per day) can be found at Nallikari Camping. The only place in the town itself is the Laatupyörä at Saaristonkatu 27, where bicycles cost 45 mk per day. Oulu is said to have the best local bicycle routes in Finland.

HAILUOTO
Hailuoto (population 950) didn't even exist 2000 years ago – it is a product of the uprise of land in western Finland. This flat island has a fragile yet well-preserved natural environment. Its population, mainly fishers, has been isolated for centuries, and these days, Hailuoto's main appeal is its peace and quiet, as its traffic is effectively regulated by ferries. Many artists come here to seek inspiration – the island's old rural scenes have escaped the bulldozers that have changed most of Finland over the last couple of decades.

Orientation & Information
The island is 30 km long, from one end to the other, and there is just one main road. Hailuoto village has shops, a bank and a library. There is no official tourist information office, but brochures are available at both ferry harbours.

Things to See & Do
Church The modern church near Hailuoto village was built in 1972 after a fire, probably deliberately lit, destroyed the 300-year-old wooden church. It is a bit of a disappointment, with its concrete walls, but there is an exhibit of old religious artefacts inside. The church is open on Mondays, Wednesdays and Fridays from 11 am to 3 pm.

Kniivilä Museum This open-air museum, a

little to the west of the church, is an interesting collection of old houses, complete with furniture, lots of rusty tools and the like. It's open in June and July only, from 10 am to 3 pm (one hour later on Sundays). Admission is 5 mk.

Marjaniemi The westernmost point of Hailuoto has a lighthouse and a cluster of old fisher's houses. There is also a *luontopolku* trail, if you want to see more of the countryside. In fact, most of Hailuoto can be explored only on foot. April, May and September are the most rewarding times for seeing the great bird migration.

Places to Stay & Eat

Ranta-Sumppu Camping has the largest capacity on Hailuoto. It is at the far end of the island, 30 km from the ferry. There are 17 huts for rent, and camping is possible too. A buffet lunch is available for 50 mk.

The *Ailasto* is the first place along the road. Run by a Polish man who plays his keyboards on weekends, the Ailasto has five modern, four-bed cabins at 300 mk per day. Rather expensive meals are available. The *Maatilamajoitus Heikkinen* is a few km further on. This farmhouse has been an inn since 1766, and the half dozen rooms for rent have plenty of character. Accommodation costs a mere 55 mk per person in three-bed rooms. The kitchen and other facilities are in an old cowshed. Bring your own food.

You may save a bit by buying food at stores in the main village. *Saaren leipä*, a few km west of the church, sells fresh bread.

Getting There & Away

There are two or three buses (No 18) a day from Oulu to Marjaniemi and Sumppu. A free lossi makes the 6.8-km journey from the mainland to Hailuoto. It takes 60 cars and is seldom full, but expect delays when returning on weekends.

HAUKIPUDAS

Haukipudas (population 13,500) is a small place north of Oulu. The main attraction is the particularly interesting church, one of the most notable 'picture churches' in Finland. It has superb naive frescoes on the walls and a small vaivaisukko figure outside, begging for alms. It's open from 10 am to 6 pm Monday to Friday.

Places to Stay & Eat

The *Virpiniemi* (☎ 981-401 222), at the seashore in Kello village, is five km from Haukipudas village and 23 km from Oulu. It is classified as a Finnhostel and is open all year round. There are large dormitories, with beds available from 35 mk for YHA members.

The restaurant *Särkyneen pyörän karjatila* is hard to find, even though it is just near the main road. It is a 150-year-old cowshed, now wonderfully transformed into a cosy restaurant. There is a special lunch menu (34 mk, including salad, bread and coffee) from 11 am to 2 pm.

Getting There & Away

Trains no longer stop at the Haukipudas railway station, but buses run almost hourly from Oulu to Haukipudas. Hitchhiking from Haukipudas is easy.

II

Ii is a small village along the Ii River. The unusual name may come from a Saame word for 'night'. If you are passing by, it may be worth stopping to see the Iin Hamina, a historical area with a handful of attractive old houses. The village of Ii offers all kinds of services, if you need anything. Trains stop at Ii railway station, and buses run almost hourly from Oulu to Ii.

KEMPELE

The village of Kempele, to the south of Oulu, is almost like a suburb of Oulu. The unusual church, built in the 1680s, has some of the most colourful works of Mikael Toppelius, painted between 1785 and 1795. The belfry was built in 1733. The hourly bus No 9 will take you to Kempele from Oulu.

KIIMINKI

Kiiminki village has one of Finland's most

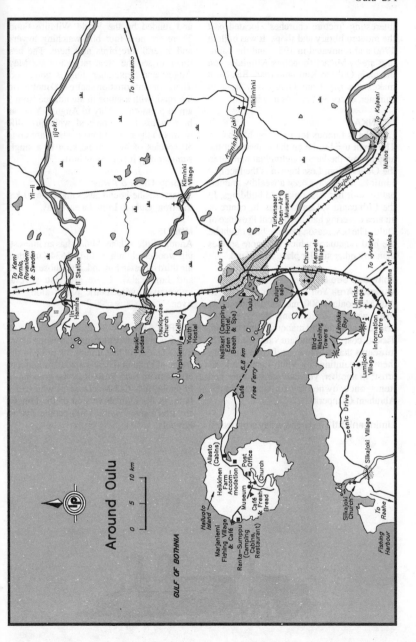

Around Oulu

0 5 10 km

GULF OF BOTHNIA

To Kuusamo

Iijoki

To Kemi, Tornio, Rovaniemi & Sweden

Yli-Ii

Ii

Iin Hamina II Station

II

Kiiminki-joki

Kiiminki Village

Ylikiiminki

Oulujoki

To Kajaani

Muhos

Turkansaari Open-Air Museum

Church

Kempele Village

To Jyväskylä

Oulu Town

Oulunsalo

Oulu

To Liminka

Four Museums of Liminka

Liminka Village

Information Centre

Liminka Bay

Bird-Watching Towers

Lumijoki Village

Haukipudas Church

Kello

Youth Hostel

Virpiniemi

Nallikari (Camping, Eden Hotel, Beach & Spa)

6.8 km

Café

Free Ferry

Scenic Drive

Siikajoki Village

Hailuoto Island

Ailasto (Cabins)

Heikkinen Farm Accommodation

Post Office

Museum

Church

Café & Fresh Bread

Marjaniemi Fishing Village & Café

Rante-Sumppu (Camping Cabins, Restaurant)

Siikajoki Church

To Raahe

Fishing Harbour

interesting 'picture churches', located past the modern library and shops. It was built in 1760 and renovated in 1954, and the paintings are by Mikael Toppelius. Kiiminki is on the main Oulu to Kuusamo road. Bus No 8 makes the trip from Oulu every hour in summer, every 30 minutes in winter.

LIMINKA

Liminka is famous for its many hay barns. The town used to be on the seabed, but the area is now the largest individual plateau in the Oulu region. Less known is the fact that Liminka has always been a wealthy municipality, so it has many nice old buildings. In the 17th century, Liminka was the centre of an area covering half the present Province of Oulu. The best reason to come here might be the bird sanctuary, which has more species than any other similar place in Finland.

Things to See & Do

Museum Area You'll find four museums in this Museoalue, 500 metres off the main road; walking there along the river, past bridges and beautiful manors, is half the fun. Tickets cost 10 mk and are valid for the two museums that charge a fee. In one museum, there are paintings by Vilho Lampi, a local artist; in another, you can see furniture and items once owned by an opera singer, Abraham Ojanperä.

Liminganlahti The large sea bay is protected and funded by the World Wildlife Fund. There are now four bird-watching towers, and several rare birds nest here. The best times to see the great migration are May, August and September. June is good, too. There's an information centre 600 metres off the road, with a guide in attendance from 9 am to 5 pm daily, May to August. You can borrow his telescope and walk just 400 metres to the nearest tower. There are up to 50 species of birds to be seen in a single summer day, if you know birds.

Getting There & Away

Several Raahe-bound buses make the 30-km trip from Oulu to Liminka each day.

MUHOS

Another little village, Muhos has an interesting wooden church, built in 1634 (and thus the third oldest in Finland, after those in Vörå and Janakkala). There are also several impressive hydroelectric plants along the river.

PIIPPOLA

There is absolutely nothing interesting about Piippola, except that it happens to be in the centre of Finland. There's a small monument off the main road. Also, it is 'the grandpa of Piippola' (not Old MacDonald) who had a farm, in the Finnish version of the famous children's song. Some 1500 people live in Piippola.

Kainuu

The large wilderness area to the east of the flat Oulu region has been exploited over the centuries as a source of timber and tar. It boasts extensive forests and several stories of heroic survival. Kainuu, possibly an independent province of the future, is changing, from a poor backwater to a more developed region in modern Finland. As one of the least known areas among travellers, Kainuu offers much to explore, both in its small towns and villages and in its desolate wilderness.

ACTIVITIES
Trekking
Walking tracks in Kainuu are little travelled but well established. The common name for these tracks is UKK-Reitti ('UKK route'), after Mr Urho Kaleva Kekkonen, who was the president of Finland from 1956 to 1981. There are trails through Sotkamo via Vuokatti, but we haven't heard from many trekkers who have done that path. The track inside the municipality of Kuhmo can be reached either from the Peurajärvi area in northern Nurmes or from the village of Lentiira in northern Kuhmo, both ends leading to the town of Kuhmo. See the Kuhmo section for more detailed information.

Canoeing
A most demanding (and rewarding?) canoeing route, between Kuhmo and Kajaani, follows the historic tar route through lakes, rivers and rapids. No longer used for floating tar barrels, the river has been restored to its 'original' state, which has also made water transport more difficult. There is an excellent route guide in English, which may still be available at the Kuhmo tourist office or at other information offices around Kainuu. The detailed route map by Karttakeskus costs about 50 mk.

Another canoeing route runs from Lentiira in the north to the town of Kuhmo in the south.

Driving
Some of the smallest, most remote villages along the easternmost roads have been lumped together to create the Korpikylien tie ('Road of Wilderness Villages'). This route starts from the village of Saramo in northern Nurmes and ends in Hossa, in the north-east of Suomussalmi.

Snowmobile Safaris
As in other areas in North Finland, there are established routes for snowmobiles. Kuhmo and Sotkamo are good places to rent snowmobiles. In Kuhmo alone, you'll find 350 km of marked routes. Enquire at the Hotel Kalevala in Kuhmo.

KAJAANI
Kajaani (population 36,000) is the undisputed centre of the Kainuu region, and home of 'secessionist' ideas about the establishment of an independent Province of Kainuu. As far as tourism is concerned, Kajaani has little to recommend it, except that it is a good starting point for visits to other places in the area. It is, however, an interesting town for at least half a day, as you run through the sights. Locals are proud of their town, which boasts good fishing in the town centre, as well as the only tar-boat canal in the world.

History
In the late 16th century, Kainuu witnessed

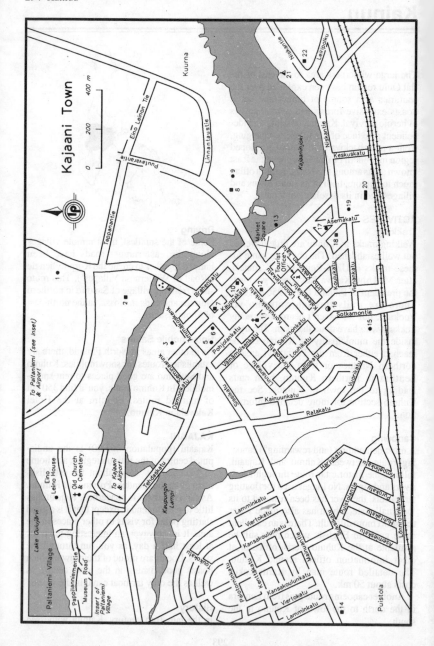

Kajaani Town

Eino Leinon Tie

Kuurna

Linnansilta

Puutavarantie

Teppanantie

Kajaaninjoki

Niskantie

Niskantie

Leirinpolku

22

21

Keskuskatu

20

9

8

19

13

Market Square

17

Asemakatu

18

Koulukatu

Tourist Office

Väinämöisenkatu

Kirkkokatu

Kauppakatu

Brahenkatu

Kauppakatu

10

Kalliokatu

Sammonkatu

Linnankatu

12

11

7

6

5

4

3

2

1

Pohjolankatu

Väinämöisenkatu

Sissikatu

Osmonkatu

Asemakatu

Sampokatu

Antinkoskentie

Kainuunkatu

Ratakatu

Louhikatu

Kalliokatu

Vuorikatu

Sotkamontie

16

15

Vienankatu

0   200   400 m

To Paltaniemi (see inset)
& Airport

Insert of Paltaniemi Village

Lake Oulujärvi

Paltaniemi Village

Eino
Leino House

Old Church
& Cemetery

Papinniemenemetie

'Museum Road'

To Kajaani & Airport

Tehdaskatu

Kaupungin
Lampi

14

Lamminkatu

Viertokatu

Kansakoulunkatu

Kansakoulunkatu

Viertokatu

Lamminkatu

Toukokatu

Pelotiminkatu

Kenttäkatu

Nahankatu

Puistokatu

Asemiekatu

Harjukatu

Purotokatu

Hurttakatu

Lönnrotinkatu

Puistola

Väinämöentie

1	Nature Trail
2	Hotel Karolineburg
3	Public Library
4	Kajaani Castle Ruins & Tar Canal
5	Finnair
6	Old Town Hall
7	Sokos-Hotelli Vanha Välskäri
8	Arctia Hotel Kajanus
9	Congress & Cultural Centre
10	Hotel Seurahuone
11	Lutheran Church
12	Sokos-Hotelli Valjus
13	Boat Pier
14	Kajaani Youth Hostel
15	Swimming Pool
16	Bus Terminal
17	Kainuu Museum
18	Nevalainen Hostel
19	Taxis
20	Railway Station
21	Onnelan Camping
22	Hotel Kajaani

fierce frontier wars between Russians and the coastal inhabitants, then citizens of the Swedish empire. King Carl IX had the castle built on an island in the Kajaaninjoki River. Later in 1651, when the castle was still being constructed, Count Per Brahe founded the town of Kajaani. Russians attacked in 1716, and destroyed the castle after five weeks of fighting. The town has since been an important link in the Oulu-based tar-transporting business.

Orientation
Kajaani was founded at rapids on the Kajaaninjoki River. It is an easy town to find your way around. The railway station, with its beautiful décor, is at the southern edge of the town centre. The bus terminal is practically in the middle of town.

Information
Vuokatin Matkailukeskus Oy (☎ 986-155 845) at Pohjolankatu 16 gives information, arranges hotel reservations and sells fishing permits.

Things to See & Do
Church The wooden cathedral is worth a look, both from outside and inside. It's open daily in summer from 10 am to 8 pm, and there is a guide inside.

Riverside The Kajaaninjoki River drops 15 metres in Kajaani. The lower Ämmäkoski waterfall has a unique tar-boat canal. Shows explaining its function are held on Tuesdays and Sundays in summer, usually at 5 pm. The old wooden Lussitupa house has exhibitions. Under the river bridge stands Kajaani Castle, built in the 17th century. Damaged by wars, time and some more recent mischief, it can be explored at all times. Admission is free.

Kainuu Museum The Kainuun museo at Asemakatu 4, near the railway station, is a nice place to visit. There is an extensive exhibition featuring the old tar trade. There are also displays of WW II and traditional living. The museum is open daily (except Mondays) from noon to 3 pm. It closes at 8 pm on Wednesdays, 6 pm on Sundays. Admission is 2 mk, 1 mk for students. There is no information available in English.

Nature Trail Walking tracks (with Finnish comments) can be found around Pöllyvaara Hill, just above Karolineburg Manor.

Places to Stay – bottom end
There are no rock-bottom accommodation options in Kajaani, unless you take advantage of the 'everyman's right', and pitch your tent in any forest *outside* the inhabited town area. For groups, *Onnelan Camping* (☎ 986-22703) is the best value in Kajaani. Not far from the train station, it has huts for two/six people (145/270 mk). There are also four-bed rooms for 220 mk. The place rents boats, canoes and bikes.

The youth hostel, *Retkeilyhotelli Kajaani* (☎ 986-25704) at Oravantie 1-3, quite a distance from the town centre, is a student apartment and, consequently, is only open from 1 June to 31 August. Beds in double rooms start at 60 mk.

Places to Stay – middle
The *Matkustajakoti Nevalainen* (☎ 986-22254) at Pohjolankatu 4, near the railway station, has singles/doubles for 160/215 mk. Lower prices are available on weekends.

Places to Stay – top end
There are six top-end hotels in Kajaani:

Arctia Hotel Kajanus (☎ 986-1641), Koskikatu 3. Across the river, this is the largest and one of the best hotels in North Finland. It has singles/doubles at 515/720 mk (Finncheques accepted).

Kartanohotelli Karolineburg. This expensive hotel provides accommodation for groups, and for individuals on request. Its elegant rooms reflect the historical ambience of this old manor.

Kajaanin Seurahuone (☎ 986-23076), Kauppakatu 11. Singles/doubles start at 390/520 mk (Finncheques OK).

Sokos-Hotelli Valjus (☎ 986-150 200), Kauppakatu 20. This is the finest hotel in the town centre, with refurbished rooms and a noisy disco. Rooms start at 395 mk. With Finncheques, this hotel is a good deal.

Sokos-Hotelli Vanha Välskäri (☎ 986-150 200), Kauppakatu 21. Rooms cost 250 mk (Finncheques accepted).

Asuntohotelli Vanha Kulkuri (☎ 986-29151), on Reissumiehentie. This hotel, two km west of the railway station, has singles/doubles for 230/290 mk.

Places to Eat
Kajaani market is not very special, but you can find a few kukko varieties and good smoked fish there. For those on a budget, the cheapest options are the several grilli kiosks and fuel station cafés, or try the *Kissburger* on Kauppakatu for fast food.

Most restaurants are on Kauppakatu. They include the *Rosso*, which offers a 50 mk lunch with four options (all extras included). The best value is the *Pikantti*, not far from the market. There is a 35 mk buffet lunch all day, Monday to Saturday, and for this price, you'll get vegetable soup and a main course, many salads to choose from, bread, milk, dessert and coffee. Most hotels have a buffet breakfast (20 mk). The *Seurahuone* is recommended for its superb choice of food.

For something different, look for the 'Kainuu à la carte' restaurants, which serve local specialities.

Getting There & Away
Air Finnair and Karair have daily flights from Helsinki to Kajaani at 6.45 am and 12.50 and 6.30 pm. The lowest return fare available is 480 mk.

Bus Kajaani is the major travel hub in Kainuu, or the central Province of Oulu. There are frequent departures for Kuhmo and Suomussalmi, but on weekends, there is little traffic. The bus terminal has timetables.

Train Four daily trains from Helsinki (via Riihimäki, Kouvola, Mikkeli and Kuopio) take you to Kajaani. The fastest train takes less than seven hours. A night train takes over nine hours, enough time for a good rest. The same trains return from Oulu. If you are coming from North Karelia, change trains at Kontiomäki.

Ferry The MS *Sininen Ajatus* sails between Kajaani and Sotkamo, usually on Wednesdays and Sundays.

Getting Around
The local bus service is only useful if you want to visit Paltaniemi. Taxis depart from near the bus terminal but are expensive.

PALTANIEMI
Although the village of Paltaniemi is now part of the town of Kajaani, it has a distinctive history. Paltaniemi carved its independence from the then-strong Liminka centre, becoming the regional centre for the Lutheran Church, and the first church here was built as early as 1599. You'll see some of the most exciting church paintings in Finland here.

Things to See
Church The old wooden church was built in 1726, and its belfry dates from 1776. This wonderful masterpiece is known for its paintings. Unfortunately, some of them were altered and repainted in 1940. The *Hell* scene

has been partly covered, apparently to avoid disturbing the locals. The church is open from 10 am to 6 pm daily. There is an information tape in English, to which you can listen on request.

Leino House This house was built in 1978 to commemorate the centenary of the birth of Finland's famous poet Eino Leino, who was born in Paltaniemi. There is little to see, but the house has the only café in the village. It's open from 14 June to 2 August from 11 am to 6 pm daily. Admission is free.

Tsar's Stable This wooden house was used as a boarding house for Tsar Alexander I when he toured Finland in 1819. This simple building was actually the best available for the visitor. The keys to the stable are kept at the church.

Museotie An old three-km road has been declared a museum road; it runs west from Paltaniemi. There are old trees, some of them over 500 years old, and nice views at the end of the road.

Getting There & Away
There is a regular town bus service from Kajaani to Paltaniemi (bus No 4), leaving hourly on weekdays. There are half a dozen buses on Saturdays and four on Sundays.

SOTKAMO
Sotkamo, a long-time rival of Kuhmo, is famous for its Vuokatti sports and tourist centre, and also for its pesäpallo (baseball) team, 'Sotkamon Jymy'. Unlike Kuhmo, Sotkamo now has traffic lights, which is another reason for local pride. The village centre is modern but offers little of interest. It is the setting that makes Sotkamo so special. Surrounded by lakes on all sides, this is a beautiful area to travel through, between Kajaani and Kuhmo. There are good beaches around the village, which are quite popular when the weather is fine. All shops, banks, the post office and the bus terminal are in the village centre. Over 11,000 people live in the municipality.

Information
There is a tourist information office (☎ 986-60055) on your right as you arrive in the village from Kajaani. The place stocks quite a number of brochures detailing Sotkamo's services.

Things to See
The tiny local museum, just off the main Kuhmo road, has few interesting things; you'll have to decide whether you want to pay 5 mk to see them. The wooden church east of the village centre can seat 1500 people, and has large paintings. It is open daily in June, July and August.

There is also a recently erected elk sculpture on an island along the Kajaani road. It honours Mr Veikko Huovinen, the famous Sotkamo author. A quote from his best-known book is carved into the rock: 'Man has the authority of an ant in this universe'.

Places to Stay & Eat
The youth hostel, *Matkakoti Tikkanen* (☎ 986-60541), is at Kainuuntie 31. It has dormitory beds for 40 mk in triples, but there are also singles/doubles at 100/110 mk for members (15 mk extra for nonmembers). Bring your own sheets, or pay 25 mk more. The 'bed without breakfast' at *Duo-asunnot* (☎ 986-61651) means suites for up to four people, with prices starting at 350 mk per night.

There are a few lunch restaurants in Sotkamo offering inexpensive meals around noon.

Getting There & Away
Buses between Kajaani and Kuhmo pass through the village of Sotkamo. It's also easy to hitchhike along this road.

VUOKATTI
Vuokatti is becoming a better-known part of the municipality of Sotkamo. There is not really anything to see here, but the sports facilities have brought fame to this small place. Vuokatti Hill has now several downhill skiing slopes, and the whole area is crisscrossed by jogging and skiing trails.

Recent developments include a spa and an international time-sharing village, the Katinkulta. The area caters mostly to professional and amateur Finnish athletes, but you can rent a room or a cottage anywhere. The unpolluted environment and good facilities make this a pleasant place to stay and to engage in sports. Vuokatti village is small, with a post office, banks and shops next to the train station.

Places to Stay – bottom end
The *Vuokatinranta* (☎ 986-640 261) is a Lutheran holiday centre, and religious events are held here. The summer bungalows (ie without heating) are available from 180 mk per night and sleep three people, but they are often full, so ask early. The *Vuokatinhovi* (☎ 986-640 211), surrounded by pine forests, is in a quiet lakeside location. The cheapest rates for singles/doubles are 180/260 mk, but there are also more expensive hotel rooms and cottages. If you come in the low season, ask for three-day full-board prices. You can rent practically any sports or fishing equipment here. Bicycles cost 20 mk per day or 70 mk per week.

Places to Stay – middle
The *Vuokatin urheiluopisto* (☎ 986-64911), the sports institute of Vuokatti, has singles/doubles from 250/340 mk, including breakfast and use of facilities. The place rents canoes, boats and any other equipment you might need.

Places to Stay – top end
Off the Vuokatinranta road is the *Suvikas* (☎ 986-640 401). This place is recommended if you are looking for high-quality Swiss-style family accommodation. Singles/doubles cost 350/450 mk, but there are lower summer rates that are worth checking on arrival. There is a good restaurant here. The *Katinkulta* (☎ 986-647 711) includes a holiday village, sports facilities and a spa. Opened in late 1991 in the midst of the recession, the resort has a rather yuppie flavour, with superb facilities.

Getting There & Away
Bus Buses run frequently from Kajaani, but you have to get off along the main road and walk to the place of your choice. If you hitchhike, choose any bus stop along the main road, but be warned: cars drive fast here.

Train There is a daily train from Helsinki and one from Oulu. Trains stop at Vuokatti village and at the small Latu station near the sports institute.

Bicycle Vuokatti is also easy to reach by bicycle from Kajaani, but note that there is no place to buy food or drink between these two places.

KUHMO
Kuhmo, with an area of 5458 sq km, is the largest city in Finland. Of course, this is just a technical definition, as there could hardly be an area more remote than the 'suburbs' of Kuhmo, along the Russian border. Kuhmo is famous for its annual Chamber Music Festival and for several WW II battlefields, as well as for its indigenous forest reindeer population, which reaches 600 head in winter and 400 in summer. The population of Kuhmo is 13,000, 7500 of whom live in the town of Kuhmo.

Information
The helpful tourist information office (☎ 986-561 382) is right in the town centre, on the main street. It's open in summer from 8 am to 6 pm Monday to Friday and from 8 am to 4 pm on Saturdays, and in winter from 8 am to 5 pm Monday to Friday. The office stocks good maps and walking guides to the region. The post office is at the market, and the pharmacy is opposite the Hotel Kainuu.

Things to See
Lutheran Church The large wooden Lutheran church in the town centre has been beautifully repainted. Concerts are held there during the Chamber Music Festival, but at other times, admission is free. It is open from daily from 1 June to 15 August.

Orthodox Church More interesting is the Orthodox church, one km outside town towards the suburb of Kalevala. There are several 18th century icons, which were painted in the Valamo Monastery, annexed by the former Soviet Union, and a 300-year-old Madonna icon in the inner sanctuary. The church is open on request only; enquire at the tourist office.

Tuupala Museum This homestead museum at Tervatie 1 was originally a wealthy farmhouse. The main building is open daily from 1 May to 15 September from 10 am to 4 pm, at other times of the year Tuesday to Friday from noon to 2 pm. Admission is 5 mk.

War Museum There is a 'Winter War' exhibit in the Yritystalo house at Kainuuntie 126, though it will move (check with the tourist office). Many of the artefacts were found in the Kuhmo wilderness. Another attraction is a model of the village of Kuhmo as it was in 1939, right before WW II. The museum is open from 10 am to 6 pm daily. Admission is 20 mk, 10 mk for students.

Library Don't miss the beautiful library at Pajakkakatu 2. Opened in 1988, it represents some of the most inspirational modern Finnish architecture. There are magazines and travel books to be read, and you can listen to compact discs featuring similar music to the current Chamber Music Festival programme. It's open from 10 am to 7 pm Monday to Friday and from 9 am to 3 pm on Saturdays.

Kalevala This Kalevala-epic theme park shows how Finns used to live and work in Karelia. It is not only a museum – there is always something going on. Three km from the centre of Kuhmo, the Kalevala area also has a hotel, a camping ground, sports facilities and a children's playground. If you insist, you can pay a 30 mk admission fee and skip the guided tour. A guide costs an extra 20 mk. The park, marked by a sign that says 'Kalevalakierros', is open daily from May to September. Hours in June-August are

9 am to 6 pm; at other times, the park is open from 8 am to 4 pm.

Festivals
Of the several annual events held in Kuhmo, the international Kuhmo Chamber Festival stands out. Over 100 acclaimed international musicians make the long journey to Kuhmo for the two weeks of music. Estonians play with Americans, and Finns tune their instruments alongside international guests. In addition to this symbolism, the event displays a real 'Kuhmo spirit'. Many players dress casually to perform in informal venues, such as local schools, using bicycles to zoom between places in the sleepy Kuhmo centre. In 1992, some female German violinists caused a sensation by playing Bach in bikinis on a local beach.

From 1993 or 1994 on, concerts will be held in the new concert hall. There is usually just one concert at any one time between 11 am and 11 pm, so you can actually hear everything, unlike in Kaustinen. Tickets cost 20 to 75 mk, with student discounts available. There are also free concerts every day. Some call Kuhmo a music factory, because musicians mix, concerts are relatively short and several groups can play together in one venue. Weekly passes are available. For further information, contact the Kuhmon Kamarimusiikki in Helsinki (☎ 90-493 902), Frederikinkatu 77A 2-4, 00100 Helsinki, or in Kuhmo (☎ 986-520 936), Torikatu 39, 88900 Kuhmo.

Places to Stay – bottom end
For those on a budget, *Kalevala Camping* (☎ 986-561 388) offers the cheapest dormitory beds in Finland. It is three km from the town centre, behind the Kalevala park. Ask for the 'Tervapirtti'. There are 24 beds available, at 16 mk, and two/four-bed huts for 135/170 mk. Camping costs 25 mk for one person. You can rent a rowing boat or a canoe for 20 mk per hour, but they are a bit lax about this, so you may be able to negotiate the price.

The *youth hostel* (☎ 986-561 245) in the Piilola school is open from 10 June to 10

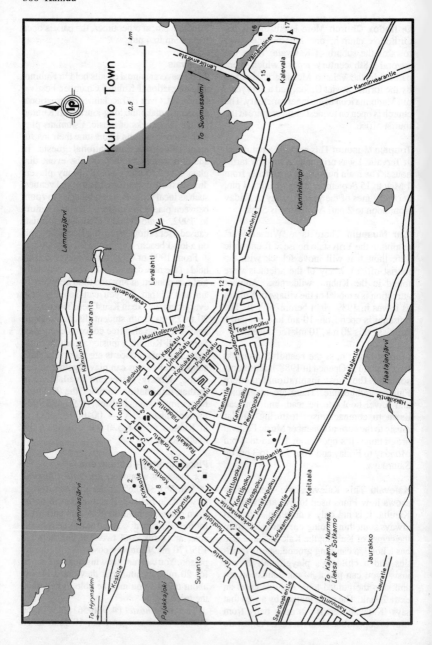

Kuhmo Town

0   0.5   1 km

To Suomussalmi

Lentiiravirista

Väinämöinen

Kalevala

Kanninvaarantie

Kanninlampi

Kanninlahti

Kanninlie

Lammasjärvi

Levälahti

Hankaranta

Kainuntie

Lentiäsuontie

Muuttolinnuntie

Käpykatu
Urheilukatu
Koulukatu

Sudenpolku

Teerenpolku

Puistokatu

Pallokuja

Kontio

Tapiolantie

Pallotie

Viientie

Karhunpolku

Peuranpolku

Lammasjärvi

Torikatu

Raejelentie

Kontionlahti

Kirkkotie

Hyyyntie

Huoltotie

Kittupolku
Lonttipolku
Prikoapolku
Konstanpolku

Pillolantie

Keitaala

Haatajantie

Haatajanjärvi

Hakkiläntie

To Hyrynsalmi

Koskitie

Pajakkajoki

Suvanto

Terkatie

Saarikoskentie

Kannuntie

Riihimäentie

Korkeamäentie

Kirkosmäentie

Jaurakko

Jauratie

To Kajaani, Nurmes,
Lieksa & Sotkamo

1	Tourist Information Office
2	Health Care Centre
3	Hotel Kainuu
4	Market & Taxis
5	Post Office & Tele Office
6	Bus Terminal
7	Public Library
8	Lutheran Church
9	Tuupala Museum
10	Kuhmon Matkakievari
11	Youth Hostel
12	Orthodox Church
13	War Museum & Sales Exhibitions
14	Swimming Pool
15	Kalevala Theme Park
16	Hotel Kalevala
17	Kalevala Camping & Cabins

August. Dormitory beds start at 45 mk, and double rooms are 100 mk for members. A sauna will cost you a mere 10 mk.

Places to Stay – middle
The *Kuhmon Matkakievari* (☎ 986-50271) is not really pleasant but isn't bad either. Singles/doubles cost 150/200 mk, breakfast included, but prices are a bit higher in July. Rooms don't have their own toilets.

Places to Stay – top end
The *Hotel Kainuu* (☎ 986-51711) is the best place to stay in the town centre, with singles/doubles from 360/450 mk. The *Hotel Kalevala* (☎ 986-564 411) looks better in reality than it does in photos. Comfortable, modern singles/doubles are 425/570 mk. This place handles most of the rental services, including canoes. For bicycles, though, there are better options in the town centre.

Places to Eat
The small market is busy all summer, until the first snow comes; there are stalls till late afternoon. This is the place to bargain for fresh karjalanpiirakka pies or rönttönen, if you happen to like them. Look for strawberries, and lakka (Arctic cloudberry) berries in late summer.

Cheap food is available from cafés at petrol stations, or from the *Sirkan Grilli* or the *Matkapysäkki*, near the bus terminal. If this is not your style, there are a few typical restaurants in Kuhmo. The *Pizz Burger* on the main road serves a good buffet-style set lunch from 11 am to 4 pm. You can choose soup (27 mk) or a full meal (32 mk), salad, bread, drink and coffee included. There is also a traditional buffet lunch/dinner (70/90 mk) at the *Hotel Kalevala*. Several fish and kukko varieties make this splurge something special.

Things to Buy
For handicrafts, see what is currently on sale in the Kalevala village locations. You can talk to many artists in the Pohjolan talo or at Taidepaja, and the smith in the Ilmarisen paja sells what he makes. The Yritystalo has a sales exhibition, which has similar opening hours to the war museum there. The Kuhmo market has some handicrafts, especially items made of birch bark.

Getting There & Away
Kajaani is the main gateway to Kuhmo. A minibus runs from Kajaani airport to Kuhmo village after the arrival of each flight. The fare is 100 mk per person. Many trains are met by a bus from Kajaani station to Kuhmo. There are 12 buses a day from Kajaani to Kuhmo, and a few buses from Nurmes and Oulu. Hitchhiking is easier if you walk out of town, regardless of your direction.

Getting Around
There are several bicycle rental places in Kuhmo.

AROUND KUHMO
Trekking
Kuhmo has pockets of the now-rare Finnish wilderness, best preserved along the eastern border of Finland. There are over 230 km of trekking trails around Kuhmo. The recommended options, starting from the town of Kuhmo, are the two legs of the enormously long UKK route. In the Kuhmo area, the trail is well maintained. Every 10 to 20 km, you

will find a waterfront laavu shelter area. Carry a sleeping bag and mosquito repellent to take advantage of this free open-air accommodation. Each laavu has an established campfire place, firewood and a simple toilet. The trail is marked with occasional blue plastic ribbons on trees, and there are clear signs when the path forks. Get a free copy of the route map at the tourist office in Kuhmo, or other brochure outlets in the region.

Kuhmo to Lentiira This long route first heads east, almost to the frontier, then continues north-west to Lentiira village. The trek takes at least four days, but you can spend eight days on this route, if you stay at each shelter along the way. The scenery is better here than along the south-western leg of the UKK route. Highlights include the two pockets of the Finno-Russian Friendship Park. To shorten the route (and to avoid walking along the main road), hitchhike or catch a bus to the northern entry point on highway No 912.

Elimyssalo This park has an indigenous deer population. There is a parking place off the unsealed Juntti road, and a laavu shelter and a few campfire sites inside the park.

Iso-Palonen To the north from Elimyssalo, this government trekking area has several walking tracks, shelters and campfire places. There is also the *Ryti-Palonen* (☎ 986-577128), with accommodation from 50 mk in simple rooms.

Kuhmo to Hiidenportti This interesting route follows the small park trails in the nature reserves through which it passes. It is recommended that you add the Hiidenportti National Park, the Peurajärvi fishing area and even the Mujejärvi area to this route (see the Nurmes section for details of these areas).

Jauhovaara This hill (253 metres) is a nature reserve. It has a three-km trail, with a campfire place and a shelter. Many of the

trees were brought from abroad and planted in the 1930s.

Road of Wilderness Villages – Kuhmo loop Recommended for vehicles and cyclists alike, this route features some interesting WW II battlefields, desolate farmhouses and real wilderness. It is also possible to combine hitchhiking or trekking with travel on the twice-weekly bus that runs through Saunajärvi and Korkea.

Sivakka The old school building near the road crossing has accommodation (☎ 986-535 107) from 50 mk per person.

Saunajärvi 'Village' This place has several WW II sites. The old korsu (bunker) has been refurbished; take matches from the letter box and light a candle downstairs. It is legal, but cold and unpleasant to sleep inside the korsu, but that is what Finnish soldiers did during the war. See also the watermill, marked by a 'Vesimylly' sign, at the river. It is still used sometimes for making flour. The small kiosk at the bridge rents boats for use on the lake, where you can fish, with a permit (5 mk per week).

Kilpelänkangas Some 10 km off the Korpikylien Tie, towards the border, is the largest WW II memorial on this route. There is also a three-km trail, Retkeilypolku, with renovated log-floating constructions along the river.

Korkea Follow the road north. The Perukan kauppa (shop) sells petrol and probably the cheapest doughnuts in Finland.

Kiekinkoski The large house (☎ 986-538 019) rents cabins on a weekly basis, but you have to call ahead. Rates for four-bed cottages start at 1500 mk per week. The place also rents boats and sells fishing permits.

Elimyssalo Follow the 'Juntti' sign north along a gravel road. See the Trekking section earlier in this chapter for park information. It is one km from the road to the parking area

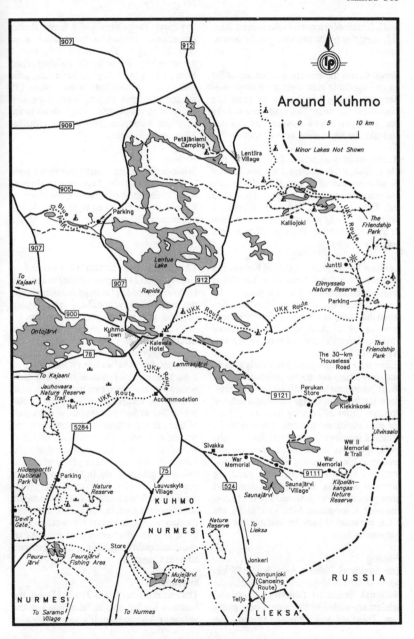

Around Kuhmo

0   5   10 km

Minor Lakes Not Shown

and a further 600 metres to the nearest lakeside campfire place, or five km to the nearest laavu.

Juntti Climb the fire observation tower for an unforgettable view over the Kainuu wilderness. Bring binoculars to scan the marshland for deer. The road here is very bad, so if you have a camper, skip this one and take the alternative western route.

Kalliojoki If you blink, you'll miss this place. The road crossing area has several farmhouses that offer commercial services, but there are no signs. You can rent boats and buy fishing permits. The fuel tanks a bit further on belong to a shop which is hidden in the house behind. You can fill your tank here at any time.

Lentiira The biggest 'suburb' of Kuhmo is a side trip from the Kuhmo loop. Lentiira is known as a centre of the 'axe people'; the term refers to the skilful builders who finished the fourth consecutive wooden church here in 1992. Although the first three churches have all burned down, the new one is made of local wood.

See the Punainen tupa (open daily in June and July only) for travel information and local handicrafts. Petäjäniemi camping, three km from the village crossing, has good cottages (from 270 mk for two, plus 30 mk for each additional person). There is also a seasonal supplement from mid-June to July.

Petäjäniemi rents boats, canoes and mountain bikes. Lentiira is actually a good location from which to start paddling towards Kuhmo, so negotiate transport arrangements at Petäjäniemi. You could also consider a mountain bike tour along the UKK route, as it may be suitable for that purpose by now.

Fishing

The Syväjärvi Fishing Area, some 17 km north-west from Kuhmo, is controlled by the National Board of Forestry. Trout and salmon are added to the waters here every year. There are walking tracks around Lake

Syväjärvi; camp sites and a laavu shelter provide rock-bottom accommodation at no cost. Fishing is allowed all year round, except in May. The reception building (open from 25 May to 31 August) has a café, sells fishing permits and hires rowing boats (35 mk for 12 hours). Fishing permits are also available at petrol stations in Kuhmo town, from the Intersport shop and at Urheilu-Tikkanen in Sotkamo.

Rafting

White-water rafting is arranged from 1 June to 20 August at the Lentuakoski Rapids, some 15 km north of Kuhmo, from 10 am to 8 pm daily. Prices range from 25 to 40 mk per person, depending on the size of the group.

PUOLANKA

The highest waterfall in Finland is Hepoköngäs (24 metres), off the Puolanka to Hyrynsalmi road. This large municipality is the most sparsely populated area outside Lapland, with just two people per sq km.

SUOMUSSALMI

One of the largest municipalities in Finland, Suomussalmi has always been something of a backwater. Many people have left their homes here and emigrated to the south, or to Sweden, to escape poverty. Some 12,500 people live in Suomussalmi these days, half of them in the village of Ämmänsaari, the commercial centre. The area has a number of attractions, scattered around the wilderness, but you need either a car or plenty of time to tour the region properly. In addition to Hossa (covered in the Kuusamo chapter), Suomussalmi has some WW II monuments and one of the most isolated youth hostels in the country. Suomussalmi's only other claim to fame is its proclamation of itself as an *eko*-municipality, signifying its concern with all things 'green'.

Information

The tourist office (☎ 986-719 1243) is in the Kiannon Kuohut spa, at Jalonkatu 1 in the village of Ämmänsaari. It's open in summer from 8 am to 6 pm Monday to Friday, from noon to 6 pm on Saturdays and till 4 pm on Sundays. All other services are near the bus terminal, as is the tourist office.

Things to See & Do

Raate Road Almost 40,000 Russian soldiers attacked the Suomussalmi area along the Raate road in early December 1939. In a week, they advanced to the village of Suomussalmi. The Russians apparently tried to cut Finland in two, and started here, but by the end of January, they had been defeated. Some 22,500 Russians were buried along the road by the summer of 1940, and 6500 Finns were left dead or wounded. There are still a few places to visit along this dramatic route. Don't miss the **Raatteen Portti**, 24 km east of Ämmänsaari. There is a war exhibition and a restaurant here. It's open from 1 May to 27 September from 9 am to 4 pm daily, and in summer from 10 am to 8 pm. Admission is 15 mk.

Cruises From 22 June to 16 August, there are daily cruises to Turjanlinna House, departing at 11 am and 3 pm. The two-hour cruise costs 40 mk.

Places to Stay

The cheapest place to stay in Ämmänsaari is the *Matkakoti-Kianta-Baari* (☎ 986-711 173) at Ämmänkatu 4, with singles/doubles for 130/210 mk. The *Kiannon Kuohut* has singles/doubles at 440/550 mk, and the price includes breakfast and swimming. Several bungalow villages around Ämmänsaari offer accommodation from 120 mk per night.

One of the most recommendable 'off the beaten track' places to stay anywhere in Finland is the *Domnan Pirtti* (☎ 987-23179), not far from the village of Kuivajärvi, 75 km from Ämmänsaari. It is named after Ms Domna Huovinen (1878-1963), a native Viena-Karelian and mother of 11 children, who was one of the most notable singers of traditional Kalevala-inspired poems and of *itkuvirsi* ('cry psalm') songs. Dormitory beds cost 55 mk, and singles/doubles are 125/200 mk. There are good walks nearby.

Places to Eat

For a simple meal from 8.30 am to 3 pm Monday to Friday, try the *Retrika* at Kauppakatu 2-4. A similar place is the nearby *Kahvila Sirkka Matero*, also on Kauppakatu, open all day Monday to Saturday. For some better food, the *Tervereitti* at Keskuskatu 24 and the *Hotel Kiannon Kuohut* at Jalonkatu 1 have higher prices and better service.

Esso, Shell and Teboil all have cafeterias, but they are outside the town centre. Eight km north of Ämmänsaari on road No 5, the *Ryysyranta* has a fish pond (you can catch and prepare the fish), and a licensed restaurant (if you can afford the alcohol prices). There is also a dance stage for elderly people.

Getting There & Away

Up to 10 buses from Kajaani, four from Kuusamo and one from Oulu travel to Ämmänsaari each weekday, and there are several buses on weekends.

AROUND SUOMUSSALMI
Road of Wilderness Villages – Suomussalmi Loop

The distant gravel roads along the border area lead you to several isolated villages.

Kuivajärvi You'll find the Domnan Pirtti (see the Suomussalmi Places to Stay section) and a tsasouna in this village of about 10 houses.

Ala-Vuokki Some 60 km from Kuivajärvi, this village has grown on both sides of Lake Vuokkijärvi. Several farms rent rooms and serve home-made food.

Raate In addition to WW II monuments, there are a few inexpensive accommodation possibilities here.

Puras The Villa-Puras (☎ 986-738 100) has singles/doubles at 220/360 mk. The place rents boats for use on nearby lakes, and there are walks in the area's forests.

Juntusranta This local centre has many WW II sites to visit. The nearby Martinselkonen area offers walking tracks, with several wilderness huts for free accommodation. The area may become a national park in the future.

Kuusamo & Koillismaa

The Kuusamo area is unique. All regional elements meet here: the fells and reindeer of Lapland, the Lakeland, the Kainuu-type wilderness and the Karelian scenery. This region is blessed with an abundance of water and rugged landscape, and records the 'worst' earthquakes in (geologically stable) Finland. Rivers from the many lakes run in all directions: Kuusamo is a watershed area. This is also where the northern and southern fauna meet, and there are more species to be found in Kuusamo than almost anywhere else. Add to this the fierce local pride and excellent services, and you have a most interesting region to explore. Consequently, Kuusamo ranks high on the list of popular holiday destinations among Finns.

The distinctive Koillismaa region, literally 'Land of North-East', is a transitional region between Oulu and Kuusamo, and buses run through it. Koillismaa is traditionally one of the poorest areas in Finland. Without the busy winter sports activity and the related services, there would be little reason to go there.

ACTIVITIES
Trekking
The 75-km Karhunkierros is one of the most popular treks in Finland, and can be recommended as the first one to undertake. Another trekking region can be found in the south, near the border between the municipalities of Kuusamo and Suomussalmi. Several areas, including Hossa, the 'fisher's paradise', can be toured there. The entire municipality is covered by the 1:100,000 *Kuusamo* topographical sheet.

Canoeing
The two magnificent rivers in Kuusamo, the Kitkajoki and the Oulankajoki, have several dangerous waterfalls. Despite (or because of) that, they are very rewarding routes to take. For anyone not feeling secure about their paddling skills, several operators offer white-water rafting along both rivers. This option may come in handy, if you just want to experience the thrill and the beauty. AJP Safaris, at the Karhuntassu tourist office in the village of Kuusamo, might be your best bet, but Rukapalvelu and Ruka Safaris, located in Ruka, offer similar services and prices.

Kuusamo

KUUSAMO VILLAGE
Locals consider Kuusamo a town rather than a village, and indeed, it has grown considerably over the last couple of years. There is little to see, but the place serves as an excellent base for obtaining information and planning treks in the large municipality of Kuusamo.

History
A Lutheran parish for over 300 years, Kuusamo was incorporated as a municipality in 1868. By 1900, its population had grown to 10,000, and relations with nearby Russia were close. During WW II, the village was a command centre for German troops, who also supervised the construction of the 'Death Railway' that operated for just 242 days. When the Soviet army marched into

Kuusamo on 15 September 1944, the Germans burned down the entire village and blew up the railway. The Soviets retreated, after occupying Kuusamo for about two months, and the inhabitants of Kuusamo returned to their destroyed village. A large number of refugees from the annexed Salla region were settled around Kuusamo after WW II, and the last phase of the Finnish land reform was carried out in Kuusamo.

Information

Tourist Office Excellent tourist services are available at the Karhuntassu Tourist Centre (☎ 989-850 2910, fax 989-850 2901) at Torangintaival 2, two km from the village, on main highway No 5. It's open in summer from 9 am to 8 pm, and in winter from 9 am to 5 pm Monday to Friday. Get a copy of the *Kuusamo: a Green Adventure* leaflet; it is probably the best free guide ever produced in Finland, with plenty of useful information and glossy photos. The staff will arrange reservations at any of over 600 accommodation units scattered around Kuusamo. The Centre also has a café, souvenirs for sale and offices of tour operators.

Money Several banks in the village centre change money during banking hours, Monday to Friday.

Post & Telephone The post office is right in the village centre. The telephone office, near the Hotel Kuusamo, is open from 8 am to 5 pm Monday to Friday.

Library The public library is opposite the bus terminal, at Kaiterantie 22. It has 1:20,000 maps of the Kuusamo area, available in self-service drawers in the käsikirjasto section.

Local Museum

Some 500 metres beyond the church is the museum, featuring several old grey buildings and some artefacts. It's open from 14 June to 15 August from noon to 6 pm daily, and from 15 to 31 August from 9 am to 3 pm Monday to Friday. Admission is free.

Festivals

The annual Kuusamo Natura festival offers concerts, theatre and art exhibitions, focusing on the interaction between human beings and their natural environment. For further information, contact Kuusamo Natura (☎ 989-850 6024), Culture Office, Kaiterantie 22, 93600 Kuusamo.

Places to Stay – bottom end

The *Kuusamon Kansanopisto* (☎ 989-852 2132) at Kitkantie 35 is a youth hostel, open from 1 June to 31 August. Conveniently located across the street from the bus terminal, it has dormitory beds from 40 mk. There is a kitchen, and a satellite TV in the common room.

Places to Stay – middle

There is a cluster of three camping areas five km north of Kuusamo village. The *Rantatropiikki* is by far the most comfortable of these. Associated with the neighbouring spa, its cottage rates include use of the spa facilities. Rates for bungalows are lower at the *Matkajoen leirintä* and at the *Petäjälammen leirintäalue*. The latter also has cottages available close to the main road; the camping area is 500 metres from the road.

Places to Stay – top end

The *Hotelli Kuusamo* (☎ 989-85920) is a concrete box-like structure but is, in fact, the best hotel in Kuusamo; the *kota* (traditional Lappish hut) is quite impressive. This is also where you'll find the most interesting nightlife in Kuusamo. Singles/doubles start at 400/620 mk, and Finncheques are accepted, with a supplement. Some five km north of Kuusamo is the *Kuusamon Tropiikki* (☎ 989-85960), a superb modern spa and hotel. There are singles/doubles from 400/550 mk, including breakfast and use of the pool and saunas. For nonguests, a two-hour visit to the spa costs 60 mk.

Places to Eat

The best deal in Kuusamo is the 30 mk lunch offer at the *Koillispohja* – there are five

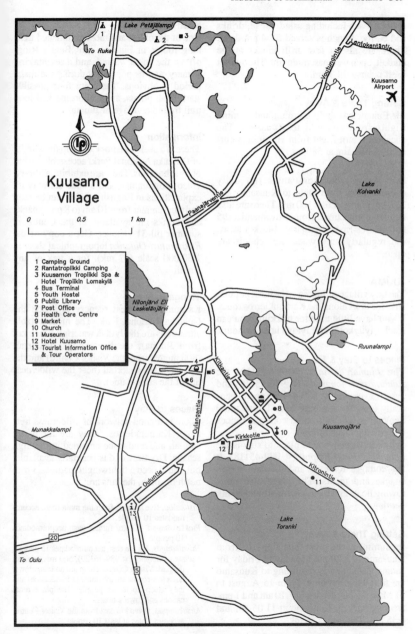

Kuusamo
Village

0   0.5   1 km

1 Camping Ground
2 Rantatropiikki Camping
3 Kuusamon Tropiikki Spa &
   Hotel Tropiikin Lomakylä
4 Bus Terminal
5 Youth Hostel
6 Public Library
7 Post Office
8 Health Care Centre
9 Market
10 Church
11 Museum
12 Hotel Kuusamo
13 Tourist Information Office
   & Tour Operators

options, each including salad, bread, drinks and coffee. Lunch is served till 4 pm daily. There are also a few grilli kiosks at the market, open well past midnight. The market itself is busy till 3 pm.

Getting There & Away

Air Finnair has daily morning and evening flights from Helsinki to Kuusamo. The cheapest return flight from Helsinki is currently a bargain, at 580 mk.

Bus Several bus companies run daily express buses from Oulu to Kuusamo; the 217-km journey costs 100 mk. There are also regular connections from Rovaniemi (195 km). Buses from Kemijärvi, 145 km away, run regularly only when the schools are open.

JUUMA

The tiny village of Juuma is the most popular base for treks along the Karhunkierros route. If you have little time for trekking, you can reach Myllykoski and Jyrävä in a few hours.

Places to Stay & Eat

The *Juuman leirintä* (☎ 989-45112), the *Juumajärven lomakylä* (☎ 989-45113) and *Jyrävä Camping* (☎ 989-45136) are all generally open for camping from 1 June to 30 September. They also offer cottages, canoes and rowing boats for rent.

The most convenient place to stay is the *Lomakylä Retki-Etappi* (☎ 989-45118). It has cottages for rent, and the café serves snacks and meals. The place also rents rowing boats and bicycles, for around 50 mk per day.

Getting There & Away

In summer, the post bus departs from Kuusamo at 2.20 pm Monday to Friday for Juuma, 50 km away, returning to Kuusamo the following morning. From 15 August to 31 May, the bus departs at 7.10 am and 1 pm, arriving back in Kuusamo at 11.05 am and 4.35 pm. The fare is 56 mk.

KARHUNKIERROS

One of the oldest and most established trekking routes in Finland, the 'Bear's Ring' offers the most varied and breathtaking scenery, and its popularity during the ruska period is obvious. There are four possible start/finish points, and a short marked loop trail from the village of Juuma.

Information

There is a useful Visitor Centre in the middle of Oulanka National Park, accessible by car or by school bus. There are exhibits, a library, video programmes, and a slide show (with explanations in English), which can be seen daily in summer from 10 am to 8 pm. Snacks and drinks are available at the Centre in summer till 31 October. Get a copy of the *Rukatunturi-Oulanka* topographical sheet in 1:50,000 scale (47 mk), for a trek of any length.

Things to See

Karhunkierros' best scenery is inside the Oulanka National Park. The most notable attractions are the Jyrävä waterfall (three km from Juuma), the Kiutaköngäs waterfall (800 metres from the Visitor Centre) and the Taivalköngäs waterfall (near the wilderness hut of the same name).

Places to Stay

There is a good network of wilderness huts along Karhunkierros. They are all pretty similar, and tend to be crowded in the high season. Dry firewood is generally available, but you'll need a lightweight mattress. From north to south, the huts are:

Ristikallio, five km east from the main road, accommodates 10 people.
Puikkokämppä, 2.7 km further east, accommodates 10 people.
Taivalköngäs, 1.3 km east, accommodates 15 people.
Oulanka Camping (☎ 989-46129), 500 metres from the park Visitor Centre. There are no bungalows, but a few rooms are available (150 mk each) and they sleep up to six people. The place rents canoes and rowing boats.
Ansakämppä, seven km east from the Visitor Centre, accommodates at least 10 people.

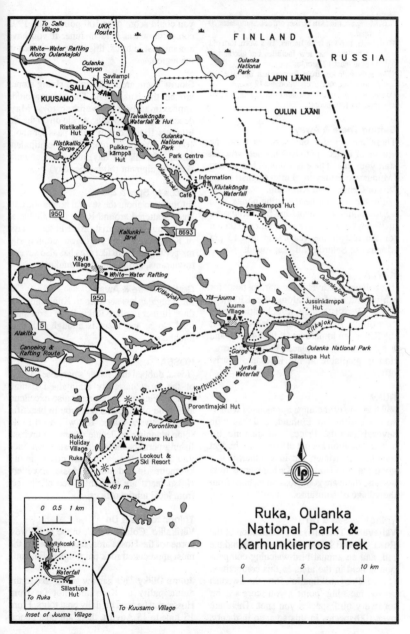

Ruka, Oulanka
National Park &
Karhunkierros Trek

Jussinkämppä, nine km further on, accommodates 20 people.

Myllykoski, two km from Juuma. This worn, torn old mill building has few facilities but accommodates at least 10 people.

Siilastupa, four km from Juuma, just opposite the Jyrävä waterfall, accommodates 12 people.

Porontimajoki, eight km south from Juuma, accommodates four people.

Getting There & Away

There are regular bus services from the village of Kuusamo to Ruka, where you can start your trek. There is a school bus service (Monday to Friday from mid-August) to the Visitor Centre from Kuusamo.

For the two northern starting points, take a Salla-bound bus, departing from Kuusamo at 10 am on weekdays in summer (6.05 am for the rest of the year), and at 2.15 pm Monday to Saturday all year round.

KÄYLÄ

The village of Käylä is the starting point for white-water rafting along the Kitkajoki River. There is a shop, a fuel station and a post office. Accommodation is available at the Kitkajoen lomatuvat (☎ 989-41149) and in a handful of other places. Further information is available at the Kuusamo tourist office.

RUKA

Ruka is one of the most appreciated wintersports centres in Finland, and has won several awards. Prices and demand for accommodation keep it off-limits for budget travellers in winter, but in summer, it is a good place to start the Karhunkierros trek, because there are good bus connections from the village of Kuusamo.

Things to See & Do

Valtavaara This hill is a continuation of the Ruka. Several unusual birds nest around the hill, and an annual bird-watching competition is held in the area. In this competition (called 'Pongauskilpailu', from the Swedish *poeng*, meaning 'point'), you score a point for every bird species you spot. There are over 100 species in this area, so in theory,

you could score over 100 points. The 1992 competition was held in June. If you have any interest in birds, this is the best place in the region.

Skiing There are 25 downhill skiing slopes around the Ruka Fell. The ski season is approximately 1 November to 2 May, depending on snowfalls. A ride up on the ski lift costs 10 mk, or buy a day pass for about 100 mk. You can rent slalom equipment (about 100 mk per day) and cross-country skiing equipment (50 mk per day).

Places to Stay & Eat

Information about the several hotels and cottages scattered around Ruka is available at the Karhuntassu tourist office in the village of Kuusamo. Prices start from around 100 mk per night. The Ruka area has also several restaurants, grillis and supermarkets.

Getting There & Away

Most regular bus services to Kuusamo continue further north to Ruka. Ruka is on main road No 5, and there is enough traffic to hitchhike.

HOSSA

Hossa, dubbed the 'fisher's paradise', is one of the most carefully maintained fishing areas in Finland. Trekking is also excellent, and some of the paths take you to beautiful ridges between lakes. You will need to do some planning, to decide where to purchase fishing permits and where to stay, but once you get started, you can cover many kilometres in and around Hossa. Excellent *Hossa* maps are available, free of charge, from local tourist offices.

Things to See & Do

Värikallio 'Colour Rock', in the north-west corner of the Hossa area, features one of the most appreciated rock paintings in Finland.

Julma Ölkky This narrow gorge lake in the municipality of Kuusamo, not far from Hossa, can be seen on daily boat tours. From 15 June to 15 August, there are boat opera-

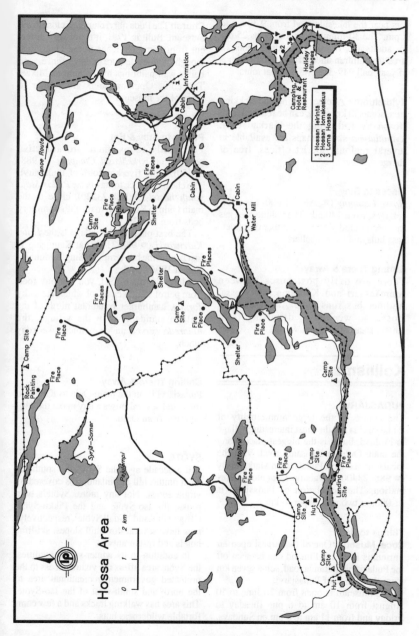

tors near the lakeside road from 9.30 am to 8 pm. The 30-minute boat tour costs 25 mk for adults and 10 mk for children under 12 (free for children under five). At other times of year, call 949-389 345 for boat tours.

Kylmäluoma Another fishing and trekking area, some 30 km away, can be reached from Hossa by following the marked trail. *Kylmäluoma* sketch maps are available in several regional tourist offices, free of charge.

Places to Stay
Hossa Camping (☎ 986-711 600) has a few cottages, from 140 mk. The fishing area has free accommodation in a number of wilderness huts and laavu shelters.

Getting There & Away
There are daily post buses between Ämmänsaari and Kuusamo, via Hossa. Another bus runs from Ämmänsaari to Hossa on weekdays, departing from Ämmänsaari at 2.45 pm.

Koillismaa

PUDASJÄRVI
The centre of the large municipality of Pudasjärvi is not the most interesting village in Finland, but it is the biggest place along the main Oulu to Kuusamo road. Visit the local tourist office, Pudasjärven Matkailu Oy (☎ 988- 23400) at Varsitie 7, for more information. The population of Pudasjärvi is 11,000, or two people per sq km.

Things to See
Local Museum One of the largest open-air museums in North Finland can be seen off the Pudasjärvi to Ranua road, some seven km from the village of Pudasjärvi.

The museum is open from 20 June to 10 August from 10 am to 6 pm Tuesday to Friday and from 11 am to 6 pm on Sundays.

Church The Pudasjärvi church is close to the museum. Built in 1781, it is not very different from many churches in the Oulu area, though it does feature a long fence, and belfry wall paintings by the famous Mikael Toppelius. Opening hours are similar to those of the museum.

Places to Stay & Eat
For small groups, there are attractive cottages at *Jyrkkäkoski Camping* (☎ 988-22550), some five km north of Pudasjärvi. The cheapest place to stay is the *Pudas-Maja youth hostel* (☎ 988-23220), close to the main Oulu to Kuusamo road, with dormitory beds from 55 mk.

The best place in the village is the *Hotel Kurenkoski* (☎ 988-21400) at Kauppatie 7, just behind the bus terminal. Singles/doubles start at 190/250 mk.

Along the main road, you can buy food from petrol station cafés, of which the tacky *Tornick* hamburger restaurant north of the village stands out. In the village, the *Amaretto* serves an economical weekday lunch.

Getting There & Away
Pudasjärvi is on the main Oulu to Kuusamo road, and several buses a day make the 1½-hour trip from Oulu.

SYÖTE
Just a decade ago, the Syöte, the southernmost tunturi hill in Finland, was covered by virgin forest. Not any more. Syöte's twin peaks, the Iso-Syöte and the Pikku-Syöte ('Big Syöte' and 'Small Syöte', respectively) now have several downhill slopes, ski lifts, hotels and restaurants.

In addition to its winter-sports facilities, the Syöte area offers the visitor access to the protected government recreational area to the north and south-west of the Iso-Syöte. This area has walking tracks and a few comfortable wilderness huts.

Information

Get yourself a copy of the excellent *Syöte* brochure. It is available free of charge at most tourist establishments in Syöte, and from tourist offices around Finland.

Activities

Trekking Only a few trekkers a week seem to take advantage of the excellent facilities along the walking tracks around Syöte, provided free of charge by the National Board of Forestry. There are a number of possible walking routes in the area. Most trekkers use the Ahmatupa hut as a base, and do a loop around the northern pocket of the trekking area.

Another route, indicated by yellow markings on trees, makes a loop around Iso-Syöte Hill. Also, the long UKK Route, marked with blue paint on trees, runs from Puolanka to Posio, via Syöte. New shelters and pitkospuu paths are being constructed all along this route.

Fishing There are three fishing areas around Syöte, and the National Board of Forestry adds fish to all of them. Along the Pärjänjoki and Livojoki rivers, fishing is allowed from 1 June to 10 September. In lakes Hanhilampi, Kellarilampi and Lauttalampi, near the Iso-Syöte, you can fish all year round, except May.

There are three laavu shelters around these lakes. Several places sell fishing permits (20 to 35 mk per day, or 50 to 60 mk per week), including the Kuksa kiosk on the main Oulu to Kuusamo road. A map is provided to buyers of a permit.

Skiing There are some 90 km of skiing tracks that are regularly carved with a snow-mobile. Getting lost is practically impossible, and there are good signs when tracks fork.

The best place to start is the Ski Stadium, at the foot of Iso-Syöte Hill. For downhill skiing, the more popular Iso Syöte has an elevation of 195 metres. You can rent skiing equipment and purchase a three-hour lift pass at the Romekievari station.

Places to Stay

Practically all accommodation in the Syöte region can and should be arranged by Pudasjärven Matkailu Oy (☎ 988-23400, fax 988-23453). If you plan to stay, you can choose either a daily or a weekly rate. Groups can get lower prices, especially in summer, which is definitely the low season. The *Syöte* brochure features about 50 individual lodging options.

The cheapest place to stay is the *Kuntosyöte*, in the village of Syötekylä. In summer, rooms and cabins cost 120 to 130 mk per night for one or two people, plus 30 mk for each additional person.

Some of the most luxurious *kelo* log cabins on top of Syöte Hill have microwave ovens and TV sets. In the spring high season, these cabins cost 500 to 640 mk per night, or 2900 to 3700 mk per week (900 to 1350 mk per week in summer). They accommodate six people.

Wilderness Huts There are three huts and several kota or laavu shelters around the Syöte area. One of the best wilderness huts in Finland, the *Ahmatupa* hut, takes at least six people. It has gas, comfortable mattresses and a stove.

During the winter high season, there is a café, open till 4 pm. Just 50 metres away is the *Ahmakota*, which gives shelter when the hut is fully occupied. Outside the 'official' trekking area, there is the *Toraslampi* hut, at the lakeside, and the *Romesuvanto* hut, near the Pärjänjoki River, popular among fishers. All these facilities can be used free of charge.

Places to Eat

You should bring supplies of food with you in summer. A few restaurants around the downhill slopes are busy in winter, and there are grillis and a few grocery stores in the village of Syötekylä.

Getting There & Away

Buses for Syöte depart from Oulu, 140 km away, at 2.40 pm on weekdays. The trip takes about 2½ hours and costs 63 mk.

Getting Around

In winter, snowmobiles can be rented near the Iso-Syöte slopes. You will have to use established routes. A taxi is available (☎ 988-23333, 949-287 080).

West Lapland

Lapland is the great adventure in Finland, whether you just drive through it or do extensive trekking around the region. Both options are rewarding, but if you set aside enough time to get off the main roads and into the wilderness, Lapland will provide unforgettable experiences, and some of the best free accommodation available anywhere in the world.

West Lapland is characterised by its high fells and its proximity to Sweden; this is the busiest border area in Finland. Although there are fewer trekking opportunities here than in East Lapland, the 'arm of Finland' should be seriously considered as a trekking region by the first-time visitor to Finnish Lapland.

The Province of Lapland has a population of 200,000, or 2.1 people per sq km. Much of the population lives in towns in South Lapland.

WARNING

When the German troops withdrew from Lapland during the latter days of WW II, they practically destroyed Lapland, burning houses and entire villages. Since then, Lapps have had reasons not to love all foreign tourists. Even though Finnish trekkers may cause more harm, it is always foreigners that are accused. With this in mind, visitors to Lapland should be on guard – both the people and the environment are sensitive to the influx of the masses. This applies throughout Lapland. Don't exploit the availability of free accommodation, be careful with fire, and replace all wood and food you take from open huts. Remember that all rubbish must be carried out from the wilderness. And don't tease the reindeer.

ACTIVITIES
Trekking

Almost the entire north-west of Lapland can be covered on foot, taking advantage of free or cheap wilderness accommodation along

the way. The most popular areas for trekking are the Pallastunturi and the Kilpisjärvi region.

Canoeing

See the individual sections for details of river routes in West Lapland.

Rovaniemi

The capital of Finnish Lapland is both a northern and a southern city: for most Finns, Rovaniemi is as far north as they will ever go, but for the people of Lapland, Rovaniemi is part of 'the south'. Rovaniemi is not an incredibly exciting city, but it has many good sources of information and is the best stepping stone for practically all trips to Lapland. Reserve at least one full day for Rovaniemi, and more time if you need to make preparations for trips or treks further into Lapland.

History

Most of Rovaniemi was burned down by German soldiers as they left Lapland towards the end of WW II. Consequently, most of what you see has been built in the last five decades.

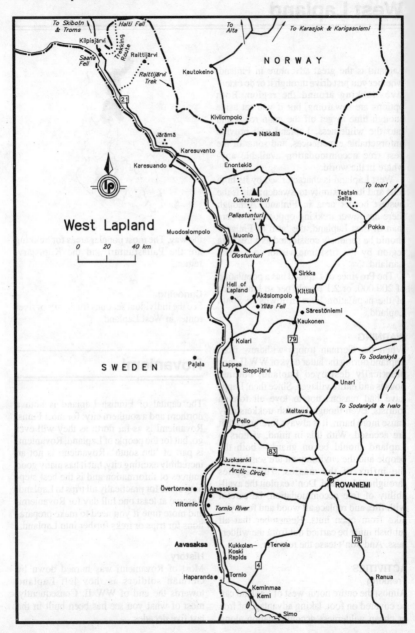

West Lapland

Map showing:

To Skibotn & Troms, Halti Fell, *To Alta*, *To Karasjok & Karigasniemi*

Kilpisjärvi, Raittijärvi, Trekking Route, Saana Fell, *Raittijärvi Trek*, Kautokeino, **NORWAY**, 21, Järämä, Kivilompolo, Näkkälä, Karesuvanto, Karesuando, Enontekiö, *To Inari*, Taatsin Selta, *Ounastunturi*, *Pallastunturi*, Pokka, Muodoslompolo, Muonio, *Olostunturi*, Sirkka, Kittilä, Hell of Lapland, Äkäslompolo, *Ylläs Fell*, Särestöniemi, Kaukonen, Kolari, 79, Pajala, Lappea, Sieppijärvi, Unari, **SWEDEN**, *To Sodankylä*, Meltaus, *To Sodankylä & Ivalo*, Pello, 83, Juoksenki, Arctic Circle, **ROVANIEMI**, Övertornea, Aavasaksa, Ylitornio, *Tornio River*, **Aavasaksa**, 78, Kukkolan-Koski Rapids, Tervola, 4, Haparanda, Tornio, Ranua, Keminmaa, Kemi, Simo

0   20   40 km

Orientation

Rovaniemi is built along the Ounasjoki River. The town centre is on the western bank of the river. The eastern bank of the river is dominated by the Ounasvaara Hill, from which there is a good view. The railway station is situated to the west of the town centre. Administratively, Rovaniemi is divided into two municipalities: the town of Rovaniemi (Rovaniemen kaupunki) and Rovaniemi county (Rovaniemen maalaiskunta).

Information

Tourist Offices Few places offer better tourist information services than Rovaniemi. The tourist office (☎ 960-346270, 960-322 2279) at Aallonkatu 1 has a lot of useful information on both Rovaniemi itself and the rest of Lapland. In addition to the normal brochures, the office publishes the weekly *This Week in Rovaniemi*. From 1 June to 31 August, the office is open from 8 am to 6 pm Monday to Friday and from 9 am to 6 pm on Saturdays and Sundays. From 1 September to 31 May, it's open from 8 am to 4 pm Monday to Friday only.

An information booth (☎ 960-62096) is at the Santa Claus Village. It's open from 8 am to 8 pm every day in June, July and August, from 9 am to 5 pm at other times.

Post Office & Telephone The post office and the Tele office are in the same building, between the railway station and the bus terminal and easily seen from both.

Library The public library (☎ 960-3222466) at Hallituskatu 9 is an excellent source of information. In the Lapland section, you can find books about Lapland and the Saame people, works by Lappish authors, literature on Christmas and old travel sketches of Lapland from as early as the 16th century. The department also has a collection of guidebooks to Lapland and detailed maps of the area. The necessary maps can also be bought at the nearby Karttakeskus shop.

Travel Agencies Lapin Matkailu Oy (☎ 960-346052) at Maakuntakatu 10 is a marketing organisation for tourist services in Lapland. You can book hotel rooms and arrange tours there.

Things to See

Church The main church of the Rovaniemi parish, at Kirkkotie 1, is worth seeing for the interesting fresco above the altar. It depicts a Christ figure emerging from the Lappish scenery, together with various representations of men and women. The church was completed in 1950, replacing the one destroyed during WW II. Donations from abroad helped in financing the new building. It's open from 1 June to 15 September from 9 am to 8 pm daily. On Sundays, there is a service at 10 am.

Lapland Provincial Museum The Cultural History Department of the Lapland Provincial Museum is, despite its name, a museum worth visiting. The collections have recently been moved to the new Arctic Centre 'Arktikum', itself an interesting place to visit. There are two main exhibitions in the museum, featuring the history of Rovaniemi and the Saame culture. The Rovaniemi exhibition includes two miniatures of the city: one showing Rovaniemi before it was destroyed in the war and the other showing the city immediately after. The museum is open from 15 June to 31 August from 10 am to 8 pm Tuesday to Sunday, and from 1 September to 14 June from 10 am to 6 pm Tuesday to Sunday. Admission is 30 mk, children 10 mk.

Lapland Forestry Museum An open-air museum (☎ 960-182 083) at Metsämuseontie 7 exhibits old buildings and objects used by lumberjacks during the first half of the 20th century. It's open from 1 June to 15 September from noon to 6 pm Tuesday to Sunday. Entry costs 5 mk for adults, 2 mk for children.

Ethnographical Museum of Pöykkölä This museum (☎ 960-181 095) is situated on the eastern bank of the Kemijoki River, 3.5

km south of the town centre. It consist of 18 buildings, most of which have been brought here from various parts of Rovaniemi. Objects connected with salmon fishing, cattle raising and reindeer husbandry form the focus of the collection. The museum is open from 1 June to 31 August from noon to 4 pm daily. Entry costs 5 mk for adults, 2 mk for children.

Rovaniemi Art Museum The art museum (☎ 960-322 2822) at Lapinkävijäntie 4 has temporary art exhibitions. It is open from noon to 6 pm Tuesday to Friday and on Sundays, and from 10 am to 4 pm on Saturdays. Admission is free.

Norvajärvi Chapel Three thousand German soldiers who died in Lapland during WW II are buried in the cellar of Norvajärvi Chapel, 22 km from Rovaniemi. The chapel is open in summer.

Arctic Circle The Arctic Circle, nine km north of Rovaniemi on the main Rovaniemi to Sodankylä road, is the home of the **Santa Claus Village**. It consists of several buildings, including Santa's Office and some shops. All letters sent to Finland for Santa Claus are answered here – in 1990, almost 500,000 letters were received from 150 different countries; the Japanese alone sent over 80,000 letters. Many of the children also send pictures of themselves, and these are all kept in photo albums. Santa's Office is a nice place and there is no entry fee. The village is open daily, from 8 am to 8 pm in summer and from 9 am to 5 pm at other times. To get there, take local bus No 8, or one of the long-distance buses from platform Nos 3 or 4 at the central bus terminal.

Contrary to common belief, the Arctic Circle is not a fixed line. By definition, the Arctic Circle is a line around the North Pole whose angular distance is the same as the elliptic inclination. In practice, this means that the Arctic Circle is the southernmost line where the midnight sun can be seen. Since all celestial bodies affect each other, the Arctic Circle can shift several metres daily.

Thus, the signs along the road do not mark the exact location of the Arctic Circle, though they do make good spots for tourists' photos.

Administrative Buildings The administrative buildings on Hallituskatu were designed by Alvar Aalto, the world-famous Finnish architect. There are guided tours of Lappiatalo, a conference centre and theatre, at 10 am and 1 and 4 pm Monday to Friday from 24 June to 15 August.

Reindeer Farm If you are interested in seeing a reindeer farm and learning how to ride a reindeer, contact the Napapiirin porofarmi (☎ 960-384 150/048) in Nivankylä. It is probably better to phone beforehand to make arrangements, as they usually receive groups. To get there, drive seven km towards Pello along road No 79 and turn to the right.

Activities
Trekking For a one-day trek, try the 27-km Rovaniemi to Pohtimolampi route. Maps for this trek can be obtained from the tourist office.

Skiing The Ounasvaara offers both cross-country and downhill skiing. There is a good five-km skiing track, which can be used free of charge. The slope is 750 metres long and 110 metres high. Skiing equipment can be rented at the Sky Hotel Ounasvaara, downhill equipment at the Ounasvaara slalom centre.

Canoeing Canoes can be rented at the EP-Muovi (☎ 960-369050) at Pallarintie 14.

Bobsleigh Rides There are summer bobsleigh rides at Ounasvaara, available daily from 1 June to 18 August from noon to 6 pm. A chairlift ride up and a bobsleigh ride down costs 10 mk.

Organised Tours Plenty of entrepreneurs arrange tours ranging from canoe trips to reindeer safaris. Prices start at 200 to 300 mk

Top: Rotuaari pedestrian street, Oulu Town (ML)
Left: The Museum, Kuusamo Village (ML)
Right: Jyrävä Rapids, Karhunkierros Trek, Kuusamo Commune (ML)

Top: Kilpisjärvi Lake, Lapland (VM)
Middle: Autumn colours in Lapland (ML)
Bottom: Lemmenjoki National Park, Lapland (ML)

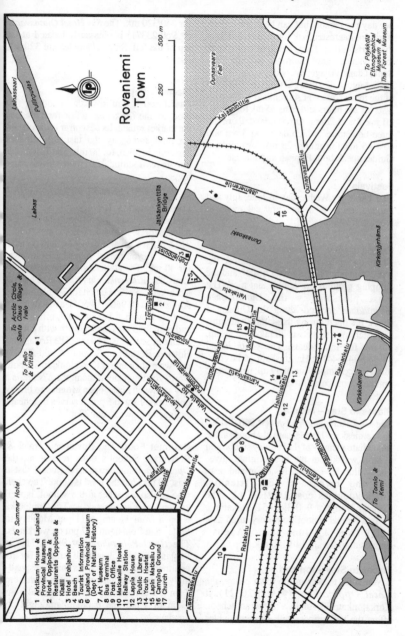

Rovaniemi Town

0   250   500 m

1   Arktikum House & Lapland
    Provincial Museum
2   Hotel Oppipoika &
    Restaurants Oppipoika &
    Kisälli
3   Hotel Pohjanhovi
4   Beach
5   Tourist Information
6   Lapland Provincial Museum
    (Dept of Natural History)
7   Art Museum
8   Bus Terminal
9   Post Office
10 Matkakoti Hostel
11 Railway Station
12 Lappia House
13 Public Library
14 Youth Hostel
15 Lapin Matkailu Oy
16 Camping Ground
17 Church

per day per person, but can be much higher. If you're interested, ask for further details at the tourist office. There are sightseeing tours to Rovanieni and environs, including the Santa Claus Village, every day from 11 June to 18 August, departing at 6 pm from in front of the tourist office at Aallonkatu 1. The tour lasts for 2½ hours and costs 35 mk for adults, 20 mk for children. On Sundays, there are three-hour tours, which depart at 3 pm and cost 45 mk for adults, 25 mk for children. Guides speak both English and Finnish.

Festivals
At 7 pm every Wednesday in June, July and August, there is a free musical event at Konttisen kenttä.

Places to Stay – bottom end
Camping at Rovaniemi costs almost the same as staying in the youth hostel, and the camping grounds are not all that nice. The most pleasant is the *Ounaskosken leirintäalue*, located along the Ounasjoki River. It's open during the summer months, and pitching a tent costs 70 mk for a group, 35 mk for individuals. The *youth hostel* (☎ 960-344644) at Hallituskatu 16 has dormitory accommodation at 39 mk per person; double rooms cost 100 mk.

Places to Stay – middle
The *Matkakalle youth hostel* (☎ 960-20130) at Asemieskatu 1, a pleasant old house in the immediate vicinity of the railway station and a short walk from the bus terminal, gives good value for money. It's clean and neat, and the owner is very friendly. Singles/doubles cost 150/180 mk. The *Summer Hotel* (☎ 960-392 651) at Kairatie 75 is a typical school dormitory, used as a hotel from 15 June to 15 August. Singles/doubles are 140/180 mk.

Places to Stay – top end
If you want to stay in the town centre, the *Hotel Oppipoika* (☎ 960-20321) at Korkalonkatu 33, run by a restaurant school, offers the best prices, with singles/doubles

for 250/320 mk. The *Sky Hotel Ounasvaara* (☎ 960-23371) is pleasantly located at the top of the fell. Singles/doubles are 320/400 mk.

Places to Eat
Fast Food If you're in the mood for fast food, try the *Torikeidas*, a fast-food place at the market square. Its best offer is the cheapest (and some say the tastiest) reindeer casserole in town, for 30 mk. The Torikeidas also serves traditional fast food, such as hamburgers.

Lunch Eateries Rovaniemi has a fair number of restaurants offering buffet-type lunches for 30 to 35 mk. The *Sampo* (☎ 960-312 574) at Korkalonkatu 32 offers perhaps the best 'all you can eat' lunch buffet in town, for 40 mk. The starters are especially delicious. The *Rinteenkulma* (☎ 960-318 822) at Koskikatu 25 offers lunch for 34 mk, and the *Monte Rosa* (☎ 960-314 501), a restaurant in the City Hotelli at Pekankatu 9, offers salad and soup for 33 mk, and a lunch with a warm main course for 39 to 60 mk. The Rovaniemi Hotel & Restaurant School (☎ 960-20321) has two restaurants at Korkalonkatu 33, both worth visiting. One of them, the *Kisälli*, is a tiny sandwich place, open Monday to Friday only, from 9 am to 5 pm. It serves the cheapest lunch in town, from 20 mk.

Gourmet Food The Rovaniemi Hotel & Restaurant School's other restaurant, the *Oppipoika*, is more expensive (meals cost at least 50 mk) but the food is good. The chef, who is also a teacher at the school, is well known for his gourmet skills. The Oppipoika is open from 11 am to 11 pm Monday to Friday and from noon to 7 pm on weekends. The *Hotel Pohjanhovi* (☎ 960-33711) at Pohjanpuistikko 2 is well known for its gourmet food, and its prices are correspondingly high. The main restaurant is open from 7 am to 2 am Monday to Saturday and from 7 am to 3 pm and 6 pm to midnight on Sundays.

Entertainment

Rovaniemi has few nightspots, and if you want to get in on weekends without queuing, you should go early, around 8 pm. On weekdays, it is quieter. All places with dancing have cover charges. In the Lapinportti at Kairatie 2, you can dance typical Finnish humppa. The average age of the crowd is likely to be over 30, though there are people of all ages. The Pohjanhovi at Pohjanpuistikko 2 is the fanciest nightspot in town, and rather expensive. To get in, you will have to be well dressed. The Sampo at Korkalonkatu 32 is a popular dancing place for younger people, but most of the local students go to the Kantakrouvi at Kansankatu 8, a pub with no dancing and, consequently, no cover charge.

Things to Buy

The most popular souvenirs are traditional Saame handicrafts made of reindeer skin and horns, or of arctic birch. Whole reindeer skins are also a popular buy, but they are hard to transport and may cause troubles with some countries' customs services. If you don't intend to go further north than Rovaniemi, this is a good place to do your shopping. Otherwise, it may pay to wait until you get out of town.

Lauri-tuotteet (☎ 960-22501) at Pohjolankatu 25 sells handicrafts from 9 am to 5 pm Monday to Friday. J Marttiinin puukkotehdas (☎ 960-21751) at Marttiinintie 6 is the most famous knife manufacturer in Finland. The shop is connected to the factory. You can buy puukkos cheaper here than in other places, but the same items are available in stores throughout the country. The shop is open from 8 am to 3.30 pm Monday to Friday.

Getting There & Away

Air There five flights a day between Helsinki and Rovaniemi. Some of them are nonstop, and others go via Oulu or Kemi.

Bus There is a daily bus between Oulu and Rovaniemi. The trip takes 3½ hours. From Kemi, buses run Monday to Saturday.

Train There are four trains a day to/from Helsinki via Tampere, Seinäjoki, Oulu and Kemi, two of which are night trains. The trip from Helsinki takes approximately 12 hours.

Getting Around

Bus maps and timetables can be obtained from the tourist office. The Urheilypyörä (☎ 960-312 444) at Valtakatu 17 rents bicycles for 40 mk per day.

South-West Lapland

KEMI

Kemi is an industrial town that grew around saw and paper mills. Today, a large proportion of the population is still employed in the wood-processing industries.

Information

Tourist Office The tourist office (☎ 9698-199 465, fax 9698-199 468) at Kauppakatu 22 is open from 8 am to 4 pm Monday to Friday.

Library There is a well-stocked public library near the market square, opposite the tourist office.

Things to See & Do

Gemstone Gallery The most famous sight in Kemi is the Gemstone Gallery (☎ 9698-20300), in an old seaside customs house. It has a collection of over 3000 items, including a crown that was meant for the king of Finland. The crown was made in the 1980s, from the original drawings. As there has never been a king in Finland, the crown was never made, until the gallery's owner, Mr Ypyä, found the drawings and created the 'first and only' crown of the king of Finland. The gallery is open from 10 am to 6 pm Monday to Saturday and from noon to 6 pm on Sundays. Admission is 30 mk.

Keminmaa The old church in the village of Keminmaa, several km north of Kemi across the Kemijoki River, is a must! You'll see a mummified reverend in this church, dating from 1521.

Icebreaker Cruises In winter, you can take the only icebreaker cruise in the world, from Ajos harbour, 15 km from Kemi. The icebreaker *Sampo* sails at 4 pm on Thursdays, Fridays and Saturdays from January to April. The cruise costs a hefty 630 mk per person.

Places to Stay
Kemi has no youth hostel, but there are several hotels to choose from, the cheapest of which is the *Summer Hotel Relletti*.

TORNIO & HAPARANDA
The twin towns of Tornio and Haparanda are the best known pair of the Finnish-Swedish towns along the long border. The border does exist on the map, but in many respects, the towns function as one.

Orientation
The centre of Tornio is located on the island of Suensaari, in the middle of the Tornio River. There are two crossing points to Haparanda: the busy crossing point is from the south of Suensaari to the north of Haparanda, and the other is across the international golf course. The bus terminal is in Suensaari, and everything is within easy walking distance of the station. The railway station is on the mainland, but no passenger trains leave from here. To get to the suburb of Alatornio, you have to cross to the mainland, then head south.

Information
Tourist Offices Tornio's tourist information office (☎ 9698-40048) is located at Lukiokatu 10. It's open from 1 June to 15 August from 8 am to 6 pm Monday to Friday and from 11 am to 6 pm on weekends. At other times, it is open from 8 am to 4 pm Monday to Friday only. The Green Line Welcome Centre at the border also provides information and money exchange facilities.

The Haparanda tourist information office is located at Storgatan 92 (☎ 0922-15045) from 15 June to 15 August; at other times,

it's at Företaggsvägen 3 (☎ 0922-11480). In summer, the office is open from 8 am to 7 pm Monday to Friday and from 10 am to 4 pm on weekends. At other times, it's open during normal office hours. Note that Swedish time is one hour behind Finnish time.

Library The public library is in the same building as the Aine Art Museum, at Torikatu 2.

Things to See
Church The old church of Tornio is considered to be one of the most beautiful wooden churches still in use in Finland, and should not be missed. It was completed in 1686 and is dedicated to the Swedish Queen Eleonora. The church is open in summer from 9 am to 5 pm Monday to Friday.

Alatornio Church The church in the suburb of Alatornio was completed in 1797 and is the largest church in North Finland, seating 1450 people. It is open from 1 June to 15 August from 9 am to 3 pm Monday to Friday.

Orthodox Church The Orthodox church of Tornio was constructed when Tsar Aleksander I of Russia ordered the building of a military church in Tornio. The church is near the border station. It's open from 10 am to 2 pm Monday to Friday in May, and from 11 am to 6 pm daily in June, July and August.

Historical Museum The Tornio River Valley Historical Museum (☎ 9698-432 451) at Keskikatu 22 has displays relating to the history of West Lapland. It is a good place to visit at the beginning of a trip. The museum is open from noon to 7 pm Tuesday to Friday and from noon to 5 pm on weekends.

Aine Art Museum The art museum (☎ 9698-432 438) at Torikatu 2 features a private collection of Finnish art from the 19th and 20th centuries. It also has temporary exhibitions. The museum is located next to the Historical Museum and has the same opening hours. There is a voluntary admission charge of 5 mk.

Alatornio Village Museum This museum, a two-storey grain storage building beside the church of Alatornio, exhibits everyday domestic and practical items. The museum is open from 15 June to 15 August from noon to 4 pm Monday to Friday and from 11 am to 1 pm on Sundays.

Kukkolankoski Rapids These rapids on the Torniojoki River, some 15 km north of Tornio along road No 21, are the longest free-flowing rapids in Finland. In the Middle Ages, Kukkolankoski was already a well-known fishing place, and today, it is visited for its natural beauty. The annual whitefish festival is celebrated on the last weekend of July. At other times, you can eat whitefish in one of the two restaurants, on either side of the river. White-water rafting can also be arranged. On the Swedish side of Kukkolankoski is a **Fishing Museum**, open from 25 June to 12 August from 11 am to 8 pm daily.

Water Tower For a view over Tornio, take a lift (5 mk) to the top of the water tower at Seminaarikatu.

Other Attractions At Kalliopudas, the three-hectare Arboretum Park has about 500 different plants. There is a public beach on the island of Pikisaari, connected to the mainland by a bridge.

Places to Stay
Tornio Camping on Matkailijantie, 2.5 km from the town centre, is open from 1 June to 31 August. Camping costs 60 to 70 mk per tent, and four/six-bed cottages are 200/240 mk.

The *Suensaari youth hostel* (☎ 9698-41682) at Kirkkokatu 1, one km from the railway station, is open from 3 June to 11 August and has dormitory beds for 50 mk. During school terms, the building is used as a dormitory. In the Swedish town of Haparanda, there is a *youth hostel* (☎ 0922-

11117) at Strandgatan 26. Dormitory beds cost 85 kroner for members. The hostel is conveniently located in the centre of town, close to the Finnish border.

The *Hospice Kaivopuisto* (☎ 9698-41316) at Saarenpäänkatu 21 is in the centre of Tornio. It is a nice, clean place, with singles/doubles for 120/210 mk, plus 50 mk for an additional bed. Prices include breakfast.

Places to Eat
There are very few places to eat in Tornio. You may have to rely on grillis and local bars, or check out the supermarkets. You can cook food at the youth hostel. If you feel you must eat out, try one of the restaurants in the town's only large hotel, the *Kaupunginhotelli*. The *Haparanda Stadtshotel* has live music and dancing.

Getting There & Away
There are two buses a day from Rovaniemi, and buses from Kemi to Tornio run almost hourly. Most of the buses continue to Haparanda in Sweden. There are also frequent buses between Haparanda and Tornio.

Getting Around
Bicycles can be rented at the Suensaari youth hostel.

YLITORNIO
Ylitornio (population 6350) is a small township at the Swedish border. On the Swedish side of the Torniojoki River is Övertorneå, Ylitornio's twin town. The main attraction is the Aavasaksa Fell, which has been a popular holiday spot since the turn of the century.

Places to Stay
Close to the railway station is a cosy *youth hostel*, with singles/doubles for 100/150 mk. Cottages at the top of the Aavasaksa Fell can be rented for 100 mk in summer.

Getting There & Away
To get to Ylitornio, take one of the two daily buses from Kemi to/from Pallastunturi via Tornio, Ylitornio, Pello, Kolari, Äkäslompolo

and Muonio. During the winter holiday season, trains from Helsinki to Kolari stop at Ylitornio.

Central West Lapland

KITTILÄ
Kittilä (population 6000) is a large municipality north of Rovaniemi. According to one story, the place was named after Kitti, a daughter of the mighty witch Päiviö, who appears in old fairy tales.

Orientation
The centre of Kittilä has 3000 inhabitants and is still one of the main centres of Lapland. The airport is served by regular flights and road connections are good. Most of the places of interest are either in the centre of Kittilä or at the nearby village of Sirkka, 20 km to the north. Sirkka is near Levitunturi Hill, where most of the area's outdoor activities are centred.

Information
Tourist information (☎ 9694-28510) is available in Kittilä not far from the southern end of the village.

Things to See
Church The old wooden church of Kittilä was designed by C L Engel, one of the most famous Finnish architects, and completed in 1831. It's open from 1 June to 15 August from noon to 8 pm Monday to Friday.

Kittilä Museum The Kittilä open-air museum features old buildings. It's open from 1 June to 15 September daily (except Mondays) from 11 am to 6 pm.

Särestöniemi Museum Visiting this unusual museum (☎ 9694-84480) is a must for everyone visiting Kittilä. Mr Reidar Särestöniemi, who died in 1981, is the best known painter from Lapland. Except for the years when he studied painting in Helsinki and in Leningrad (St Petersburg), he always

lived in Särestö in Kittilä. Today, his home has been converted into a museum, where his big, colourful paintings are exhibited, together with some drawings and graphic works. Reidar Särestöniemi's brother Anton still lives in the area. The museum is hard to reach, as it is off the main road. Follow the signs from the main road, some 20 km south of the Kittilä town centre, and you should find your way. It's nine km from the main road to the museum; although the road is in bad shape, it is passable, even for a bus. The museum is open daily, from 10 am to 8 pm from 15 February to 15 October and from noon to 4 pm at other times of year. Tickets cost 30 mk for adults, 15 mk for students.

Pöntsö Gallery Another interesting place is the Pöntsön galleria (☎ 9694-77122), home of Reijo Raekallio, an artist in the village of Pöntsö. Unlike Särestöniemi, Mr Raekallio is alive and well, and if you are lucky, he will tell you about his painting and about the house he has designed himself. To get to the Pöntsön galleria, take road No 79 west of Kittilä and drive some 18 km. The gallery is open Tuesday to Sunday from 10 am to 6 pm. Admission costs 15 mk. It may also be possible to stay there overnight, as the family has some rooms to rent out.

Taatsin Seita This pillar-shaped stone god, worshipped by the ancient Saame people, is situated at Lake Taatsi, 13 km from the village of Pokka.

Activities
In winter, Kittilä is a major skiing centre. In summer and autumn, trekking and canoeing are the main outdoor activities. Skiing is possible until May.

Trekking For trekkers, Kittilä offers only some minor attractions. Climbing all the way up to the Levitunturi is a rewarding experience. The top of the fell (where you'll find the Tuikku Restaurant), can also be reached by car. Alternatively, you can walk around the fell. The 1:50,000 *Ylläs-Levi* map is available for 47 mk. For a slightly longer and more interesting trip, walk from Sirkka to Pyhätunturi, on the northern side of Kätkätunturi. The one-way trip is 12 km long, and there is a wilderness hut at the Pyhätunturi end.

Skiing Downhill-skiing tickets at the Levitunturi are 95 mk per day or 455 per week. Equipment rental costs 80 mk per day or 350 per week. Ask at the Levin Hissit (☎ 9694-81246). Opportunities for cross-country skiing are better. There are routes to the Aakenustunturi, Särestöniemi (for the museum) and other places. The length of marked walking tracks varies from a few km to several hundred km. On longer ski treks, you can stay overnight in wilderness huts, which have supplies of firewood. Always take a good map and a compass, and listen to weather forecasts before departing.

Canoeing A few good canoeing routes along the Ounasjoki River start from Kittilä. Equipment can be rented at the Levin Safarit (☎ 9694-81484, 949-398 427) for 150 mk per day or 800 mk per week. The Levin Safarit also arranges safaris by snowmobile, dogsleigh or canoe. The company has a good reputation and can arrange English-speaking guides. The tour prices start at 200 mk per person for half-day tours and go up to 4000 mk per person for extensive snowmobile safaris. If you want to try snowmobiling on your own, Levin Safarit also rents equipment (from 100 mk per hour or 2500 mk per week).

Dogsleigh Safaris For a dogsleigh safari, contact Mr Reijo Jääskeläinen (☎ 9694-81565). He arranges one-day trips (500 mk per person), and longer trips with camping in cottages or tents.

Mountain Biking If you are interested in bicycle trekking, you can rent a mountain bike (90 mk per day) at the Levi Racing Camp (☎ 9694-81618) at the Levitunturi. The place is open from 9 am to 1 pm in summer.

Swimming & Sauna At the Hotel Levitunturi, there is a spa with Finnish and Turkish saunas and a big swimming pool. Admission is 48 to 56 mk, depending on the season.

Festivals
Since the 18th century, Kittilä has been the site of the biggest market in West Lapland. These days, the traditional market has turned into a summer fair, which takes place at the beginning of July and attracts people from all over Lapland. Local entrepreneurs sell their products, and there is entertainment for both young and old. For further information, call ☎ 9694-28418.

Early September sees a marathon race, which is probably the northernmost regularly organised such event in the world.

Places to Stay
For the cheapest accommodation in Kittilä, try one of the two youth hostels. The *Sillankorvan maja* (☎ 9694-83428), the better one, is situated north of the village of Sirkka. The standard is as high as in most of the holiday cottages, but the prices are far lower. The only negative is that you really need a car or a good bicycle to get there. The *Kittilän retkeilymaja* (☎ 9694-12238) is conveniently situated in the centre of Kittilä. A school dormitory in winter, it is not very pleasant.

In the small centre of Kittilä, the *Gasthaus Kultaisen Ahman Majatalo* has nice, clean singles/doubles for 180/300 mk. In the low season, the price of doubles goes down to 200 mk.

Kittilä has plenty of hotels and holiday cottages, most of which are of high quality and price. If you arrive in town without a reservation, shop around for the best deal. In summer, this should be easy, but in winter, everything may be booked well in advance. A typical holiday cottage has beds for four to six people, plus a kitchen and a sauna. Do not pay more than 600 mk per day during the high season, 350 mk per day in summer. Prices may be considerably lower than this, especially in summer.

Places to Eat

The *Kittilän Hotelli* serves a good cheap lunch. You can get a soup and salad buffet for 24 mk, or add a main course and pay 40 mk. At the Levitunturi, the restaurant *Hullu Poro* ('Crazy Reindeer') offers good food, a nice atmosphere and reasonable prices (40 to 50 mk for lunch). There is also a pub.

Getting There & Away

There is a daily flight between Helsinki and Kittilä. Four buses a day run between Rovaniemi and Kittilä, a 2½ to three-hour trip, depending on the route. Buses depart at the K petrol station.

KOLARI

The municipality of Kolari (population 5000) is best known for its busy skiing centre at the Ylläs Fell. The village of Kolari, close to the Swedish border, is the municipality centre, and the village of Äkäslompolo is another commercial centre.

Kolari is the last stop for the northbound train, so you may end up there on your way north or south. The village itself is rather boring, with few sights, but take your time to explore some of the interesting natural sights scattered around the area. It is also easy to make a trip to Sweden by crossing the bridge over the Torniojoki River. The nearest village in Sweden, Pajala, is 30 km south of Kolari.

Information

The municipal tourist information office (☎ 9695-61713/471) is in the centre of Kolari.

Things to See

Church The old church of Kolari was built in 1818 on an island in the Muoniojoki River. To get to the island, take a bridge across the river. The church is open daily during the summer months.

Local Museum The local open-air museum is situated at Sieppijärvi, some 30 km south of Kolari along road No 21. It's open from 1 June to 31 August from 2 to 6 pm Monday to Friday and from noon to 6 pm on weekends.

Hell of Lapland Pakasaivo, or Lapin helvetti, is a deep forest lake, where ancient Lapps used to make sacrifices to the gods. The surface of the lake is some 50 metres below ground level. To get there, drive 25 km from Kolari towards Äkäslompolo, then turn left and continue 11 km along a forest road. The road to Pakasaivo has signs and can be driven by car all the way to the end.

Lappea There are rapids worth seeing in Lappea, where the Torniojoki and Muoniojoki rivers meet. Take the small road along the river and drive 30 km south from Kolari. This road will eventually take you to Pello.

Activities

Skiing In winter, the Yllästunturi Fell, 35 km north-east of Kolari, is one of Finland's most popular skiing centres. In summer, the village of Äkäslompolo is like a ghost town. There are empty holiday cottages everywhere, restaurants are closed until October and few people can be seen on the road. The Ylläs has the longest slopes in Finland (up to three km), and skiing is possible from November to May. Lift passes cost 80 mk per day or 360 mk per week. Renting equipment also costs 80 mk per day or 350 mk per week.

Mountain Biking Mountain biking is a popular summer activity in the Ylläs. Special biking trails have been designed, with maps available from the big hotels in the area. The car rental company Varaporo, which has an office in Äkäslompolo, rents mountain bikes.

Festivals

Every year in late July, there is a music festival in the Ylläs. The music is mostly Finnish pop. Some of the concerts are free; tickets for others cost 30 to 100 mk.

Places to Stay

The *youth hostel* (☎ 9695-61086) has singles

for 80 mk and doubles for 130 to 150 mk. The hostel is located south of the centre and is well signposted. In Äkäslompolo, close to the Yllästunturi Fell, there are plenty of empty hotel rooms and cottages in summer, so you should be able to find reasonably priced accommodation. Many of the cottages, however, are privately or cooperatively owned, and not for hire. In winter, accommodation is more expensive, starting at 2500 mk per week in four-bed cottages.

Places to Eat

In the village of Kolari, the *Nuuskakairan baari* along the main road serves a good lunch, including a warm main course, for 32 mk. Pizzas start at 40 mk and hamburgers cost 15 to 20 mk. The *Restaurant Lydia* (☎ 9695-69320) at Äkäslompolo has good food and bakery products. It is not always open, so phone and check before travelling any distance to get there.

Getting There & Away

Bus A bus runs between Kolari and Rovaniemi each weekday. There are also two buses a day between Kemi and Kolari, travelling via Tornio, Ylitornio and Pello.

Train During the winter holiday season, from mid-February to mid-April, there are trains to Kolari from Helsinki.

PELLO

Pello is another border village with a twin village on the other side of the river. The municipal tourist information point is close to the bridge from Sweden.

Green Stop

The most advertised sight in Pello is one of the Santa Claus Land attractions, the Green Stop. This fairly artificial place sells pottery, handicrafts and, above all, plants. Downstairs is an excellent playroom for children. The Green Stop is open daily between 9 am and 6 pm.

Fishing

Lake Miekkojärvi, 30 km south-east of Pello, is teeming with fish. At the northern end of the lake is a little fish harbour for fishers. The National Board of Forestry has also built some laavu shelters and a wilderness hut, which can be used free of charge. The village store at Sirkankoski, six km from the lake, sells fishing permits for 20 mk per day, 40 mk per week or 60 mk per month.

Festivals

The biggest annual event in Pello is the Poikkinainti Festival, held to celebrate the fact that people marry across the border. The festival takes place in July and lasts from Friday to Monday. A real wedding ceremony, conducted in the middle of the river, is part of the festival, followed by dancing in several locations on the Saturday, Sunday and Monday nights.

Places to Stay & Eat

Pello has a youth hostel called *Kittisvaaran hiihto- ja leirikeskus* (☎ 9695-86155), open from 15 June to 15 August. Dormitory beds cost 32 to 35 mk. If you prefer cottage accommodation, there are some pleasant cottages just around the corner from the youth hostel, at 150 to 250 mk per cottage. Midway between Pello and Ylitornio, at the Arctic Circle, there is the *Tuomaan Paja*, a snack bar and souvenir shop which sells handicrafts, art and kitsch.

Getting There & Away

To get to Pello, take one of the two daily buses between Kemi and Pallastunturi via Tornio, Ylitornio, Pello, Kolari, Äkäslompolo and Muonio.

North-West Lapland

Enontekiö is the northernmost municipality in West Lapland. The four municipal centres are Hetta (also known as Enontekiö), Ylikyrö, Karesuvanto and Kilpisjärvi. In addition, there are some Saame villages.

Reindeer herding provides employment for many – there are over 20,000 reindeer in Enontekiö. The population of Enontekiö is 2500, of which 300 are Saame.

Enontekiö borders both Sweden and Norway. A road north from Hetta leads to Kautokeino and Alta in Norway, and is also the quick way to get to Nordkapp, the northernmost point in Continental Europe. From Kilpisjärvi, there is a short route to Tromsø in Norway, and the Swedish village of Karesuando is just across the river from the Finnish village of Karesuvanto.

HETTA

Hetta, previously known as Enontekiö, is the centre of the municipality of Enontekiö, and a good place to start trekking and exploration of the surrounding area. Connections to Norway are good, too. Hetta is not a big place, with just a few dozen houses on either side of the road, but travel services are good. The popular Pallas to Hetta trekking route brings many travellers to the village.

Information

There is a municipal tourist information booth in a little 'shopping centre' at the crossroads of the Hetta main road and the road to Norway. The place stocks a lot of useful material, including information on the most popular trekking routes. It's open in June, July and August from 9 am to 8 pm Monday to Saturday and from 9 am to 6 pm on Sundays. In September, it is open from 9 am to 6 pm every day. At other times, tourist information can be obtained at the municipal office building in the centre of Hetta.

Things to See

Church Enontekiö Church, in the centre of Hetta, was built in 1952 with the financial help of American churches. The organ was a gift from Germany. The church has a very special altar mosaic, which pictures Christ blessing Lapland and its people.

Saame Museum On the eastern side of Hetta, some three km from the church, there is an interesting Saame museum. It's open every day between Midsummer and the end of August from noon to 8 pm.

Näkkälä This Saame village is situated approximately 40 km north-east of Hetta. You can drive all the way to Näkkäläjärvi, where the Saame people live in winter. If you want to go on to the summer place at Pöyrisjärvi, 16 km further west, you will have to leave your car in Näkkälä and walk the rest of the way. The 26-km route from Hetta to Näkkälä is itself a popular trek; you will need the 1:50,000 *Topografinen kartta* topographical sheet for Enontekiö and Näkkälä.

Activities

Canoeing The Ounasjoki River runs through Hetta. It is ideal for canoeing; trips, from one day to a week or more, can be arranged. A good route for a week-long trip is from Hetta to Särestöniemi, or to Kaukonen near Kittilä. Canoes (including paddles and life vests) can be rented at Fell Guiding Bureau Haldi (☎ 9696-51230), on the eastern side of Hetta, for 140 mk per day or 600 mk per week, and must be returned at your own expense. Haldi also arranges guided tours (about 2000 mk per week). To take part in a tour, no previous experience is necessary.

Fishing There are good fishing waters around Hetta. The Hetan aitta, in the centre of Hetta, sells fishing permits and maps.

UpSki This form of skiing has been described as 'sailing on snow'. The skier has a parachute, and is pulled by windpower up a mountain. Descending the slope can be done either on skis or with the parachute. For further information, call the UpSki-Club of Enontekiö (☎ 9696-51358) or Ohjelmapalvelut Esko Mäntylä (☎ 9696-51432).

Places to Stay

The *Hetan Pysäkki*, at the western end of the village, has cottages and a camping ground. Cottages come in various sizes and standards and cost 120 to 600 mk. The cheapest four-bed cottage is 190 mk. Camping costs 60 mk per tent. The *Paavontalo*, on the eastern side of the village, hires two/four-bed cottages for 150/200 mk. The *Hetan majatalo* is a comfortable, inn-type establishment in the centre of the village. Singles/doubles cost 250/320 mk with facilities, 160/220 mk without facilities.

Places to Eat

The *Hetan pysäkki* offers 'the dish of the day' for 27 mk between 11 am and 8 pm. The *Karhuntassu* between the tourist office and the church prepares large pizzas and has set lunch at reasonable rates. The *Jussan Tupa* has a 35 to 45 mk lunch between 11 am and 1 pm. Dinner is expensive, at 80 mk.

Getting There & Away

There are two buses a day from Rovaniemi to Hetta, one of which continues in summer to Kautokeino in Norway. To get to Kilpisjärvi from Hetta, you have to change buses at Palojoensuu.

KARESUVANTO

Karesuvanto and its twin town, the Swedish village of Karesuando across the Ounasjoki River, form an 'international' centre of 1000 inhabitants. There is a bridge between the two villages, and locals cross it daily to go shopping or to visit friends and relatives. Payments can be made in either currency, and Finnish, Swedish and Saame are spoken on both sides of the river.

Information

The Karesuvanto tourist information point is located just across the bridge from Sweden. It stocks information on the Enontekiö area and other parts of Finnish Lapland, as well as for North Sweden and Norway.

Things to See

Churches There is a church on the Finnish side of the border and one on the Swedish side. The Karesuando church was built in 1905 to replace a wooden church destroyed by the weather. It was here that the famous preacher L L Laestadius preached. His teach-ings led to the foundation of the strictest Lutheran sect in Finland. Next to the vicarage is the small cottage of L L Laestadius, which serves as a museum and religious shrine.

Järämä On the way to Kilpisjärvi, about 25 km north of Karesuvanto, there is a fortification area constructed during the war fought against the Germans in Lapland in 1944. After Finland had negotiated a ceasefire with the Soviets, the withdrawal of German troops from Lapland turned into a full-scale war. The Järämä fortification was built during the last phase of the 'Lapland War' and is known as Sturmbock-Stellung. A substantial area has now been renovated. Some of the korsu bunkers offer shelter from the weather, and you can actually stay overnight, though you should not light fires in the korsus. There is a river nearby.

Places to Stay

Close to Karesuvanto, in the village of Markkina, the pleasant *Lätäsenon majat* offers accommodation for 110 to 140 mk in cottages that accommodate two to four people. For 40 mk per day, you can also pitch your tent and use the cooking and washing facilities.

The *Hotel Ratkin* (☎ 9696-42101) has cottages for three to four people, starting at 180 mk in summer and 260 mk in winter. These cottages have good facilities, including a kitchen. Cottages with a sauna cost more. The *Rantamökit* (☎ 9696-42079) is a group of cottages pleasantly located at the riverside. The friendly owner charges 120/130/140 mk for two/three/four-bed cottages.

The most interesting deal is a cottage in the wilderness, five km away along the river, for 250 mk per day. This place can accommodate six people, and the price includes the use of a sauna and a boat. The surrounding waters are supposed to be good for fishing.

Getting There & Away

The bus from Rovaniemi to Kilpisjärvi will take you to Karesuvanto.

KILPISJÄRVI

The village of Kilpisjärvi, the northernmost place in the 'arm' of Finland, is situated right in the 'thumb'. It is a tiny place between Lake Kilpisjärvi and the magnificent surrounding fells. The highest fells of Finland can be seen here. Both Norway and Sweden are next door, and one of the most popular treks reaches the joint border of these three countries. There is nothing else to see in Kilpisjärvi besides the beauty of the countryside, but it is well worth visiting just for that.

Note that Kilpisjärvi consists of two 'villages' – one has two hotels and a shop, and the other has the Kilpisjärvi trekking centre and a fuel station. The distance between the two villages is several km.

Information

The Kilpisjärven retkeilykeskus (Kilpisjärvi trekking centre) (☎ 9696-77771) is a central place for all trekkers. There, you can meet up with people, get advice on routes, and buy maps and other equipment. The centre also sells fishing permits and rents those huts that can be rented (35 mk per night per person).

All trekking routes and wilderness huts around the Kilpisjärvi area are clearly displayed on the 1:100,000 *Käsivarsi* map (47 mk). The 1:50,000 *Kilpisjärvi* topographical sheet (25 mk) covers a small area.

Activities

Trekking The area around Kilpisjärvi offers a fantastic setting for trekking. Routes range from easy day treks to demanding two-week treks to the mountains.

A marked loop route to the Saana Fell starts right behind the Kilpisjärven retkeilykeskus. This route takes one full day. Another very popular day trek is the 15-km route through the Malla nature park to the joint border post of Finland, Sweden and Norway. A boat will take you there from the Kilpisjärvi trekking centre, across the lake, with departures at 10 am and 2 and 6 pm. Boats wait for three hours, for the return journey. The fare is 50 mk for adults, 10 mk for children. The trek starts from the main road, just before the customs point on the

way to Norway – the beginning of the trail is clearly marked. At the border is a wilderness hut, if you want to stay overnight.

If you are interested in learning more about the Saame people, make a trek to Raittijärvi, a traditional Saame village. There is no road, so walking is the only way to get there. A path starts at the village of Saarikoski, some 35 km south of Kilpisjärvi, and is approximately 40 km long.

For more experienced trekkers, a one to two-week trip from the Saana Fell to the Halti Fell, the highest point in Finland (there is snow in June), is a demanding but rewarding trip. The scenery is magnificient, and there are excellent fishing possibilities on the way. You will find wilderness huts at Saarijärvi (to accommodate 10 people), Kuonjarjohka (six people), Meekonjärvi (six people), Pihtsusjärvi (12 people) and Halti (five people). Between the Meekonjärvi and Pihtsusjärvi huts, you will have to cross rivers. If you are interested in this trek but are not quite sure of your capabilities, join one of the groups organised by Kilpisjärven retkeilykeskus – there are a few departures every year.

Canoeing Canoes can be rented at Kilpisjärven retkeilykeskus (☎ 9696-77771).

Scenic Flights There is a heliport at the southern end of the village of Kilpisjärvi. Helicopter flights cost a minimum of 200 mk per person. For information, call 9696-77743 or 949-394 594. There are also hovercraft flights, from 100 mk per person (minimum of four people).

Places to Stay

Best value for money is the youth hostel *Peeran retkeilykeskus* (☎ 9696-2659), some 25 km south of the village of Kilpisjärvi. It is a pleasant place by the fell, kept by an older lady. English may not be spoken well, but the place is charming. It's open from 25 February to 15 May and from 22 June to 30 September. Dormitory beds cost 35 mk for YHA members.

The *Saanan maja* is on the right-hand side of the road on the way to Kilpisjärvi. The place is pleasant, if rather quiet. Four-bed rooms cost 320 mk, and cottages for two are 180 mk. The *Kilpisjärven retkeilykeskus* (☎ 9696-77771) has hotel accommodation at hotel prices. A less-expensive alternative is staying in the four-person cottages (280 to 340 mk). If you have your own tent, you can pitch it for 60 mk.

Places to Eat
At the *Saanan maja*, you can get lunch for 43 to 55 mk and meat pies, hamburgers and other small dishes for 10 to 15 mk. The *Kilpisjärven retkeilykeskus* serves an 'all you can eat' buffet lunch for 45 mk in the high season.

Whether or not you need to go shopping, visit the local supermarket. All the prices are in both Finnish and Norwegian currencies (sometimes more in Norwegian), and you can pay in either currency. Most of the customers come from Norway to buy discounted food.

Getting There & Away
There is a daily bus connection between Rovaniemi and Kilpisjärvi via Kittilä, Muonio and Karesuvanto. To get from Hetta to Kilpisjärvi, you have to change buses at Palojoensuu. The road to Kilpisjärvi is excellent, so driving is no problem. Just make sure your car is in reasonably good shape and that you have enough petrol; in the wilderness between Karesuvanto and Kilpisjärvi, you certainly won't find a place to get your car fixed.

MUONIO
This northern municipality (population 2850) is not a bad place to start an excursion to Lapland. For trekkers, the Pallas-Ounastunturi National Park offers one of the most popular treks in West Lapland.

Things to See & Do
Church There is an old wooden church in Muonio. When the Germans burned the village during WW II, the church was among the few buildings to escape the fire.

Keimiöniemi At Keimiöniemi, on the northern shores of Lake Jerisjärvi, you will find some fisher's cottages dating from the 18th century. To get there, drive 10 km from Muonio towards Pallas, then turn towards Jerismaja. The lakeside cottages are four km from the Jerismaja crossing.

Canoeing & Rafting
The Muoniojoki River is excellent for canoeing and rafting. The Harrinivan lomakylä (☎ 9696-2491), south of the village of Muonio, rents out canoes (120 mk per day) and kayaks (60 mk per day). Weekly rates are negotiable, and all prices include equipment. A white-water rafting trip takes approximately one hour and costs 85 mk. After rafting, you will get a 'diploma' and coffee. There are two departures a day in summer. The owner is a lot of fun and speaks good English.

Places to Stay
There are two youth hostels in Muonio. The *Lomamaja Pekonen* (☎ 9696-2237) is in the centre of Muonio. Accommodation costs 50 mk per person in double rooms, 40 mk per person in four-bed cottages. The other hostel (☎ 9696-8504) is located along Lake Jerisjärvi, on the way to Pallastunturi. Accommodation starts at 70 mk for YHA members. Both hostels are open all year round. There are also dozens of holiday cottages in the Muonio area.

Places to Eat
Muonio does not have many places to eat, especially at night time. Try one of the petrol station *cafeterias*, which serve decent food at reasonable prices. Your only other eating-out alternative is to try the hotels, which are outside the town centre and are expensive. Self-catering is the best option.

Getting There & Away
There are two buses a day between Rovaniemi and Muonio. The trip takes approximately four hours, and the bus

travels via Kittilä and Olostunturi. From Kemi and Tornio, there are two buses each weekday and one on Saturdays, via Ylitornio, Pello and Kolari.

PALLASTUNTURI

The Pallastunturi Fell is in the middle of the Pallas-Ounastunturi National Park. The park, established in 1938, is one of the first national parks in the country. The main attraction is the excellent 60-km trekking route through the park to the village of Hetta in Enontekiö. The trek takes three to four days, though many people spend longer.

Information

At the Pallastunturi, there is a good information centre (☎ 9696-2451) for trekkers. The information centre sells maps, makes reservations for locked huts (20 mk per night) and provides slide presentations about the area, its flora and its fauna. It also has slide presentations about the national park, in several languages. The centre is open from 1 June to 30 September from 9 am to 8 pm Monday to Friday and from 9 am to 4.30 pm on weekends. The two 1:50,000 maps for the area, *Pallas-Olos* and *Hetta-Outtakka*, cost 47 mk per copy.

Activities

Trekking This route is probably the easiest in the country. One reason for this is that much of the route is treeless – you can see several km ahead. The route is also easy because it is well marked, with poles every 50 metres or so. There are several wilderness huts along the way. The larger huts have a 1:50,000 map on the wall, so carrying a map is not necessary. Unfortunately, the trek is so popular that in some huts (especially the Hannukuru hut), there may be up to 60 people there at one time.

At the Hetta end of the trek, you have to cross the lake to get to/from the national park. There is a boat-taxi system, and you pay according to a fixed tariff (approximately 40 mk). If you come from Pallastunturi, there is a flagpole at the riverside. Raise the flag, and someone from the Hetta side will come to pick you up.

Skiing In winter, the Pallastunturi is a popular place for both cross-country and slalom skiing. The longest slope is two km long, and lift passes cost 85 mk per day or 360 mk per week.

Places to Stay

For trekkers in the Pallas-Ounastunturi National Park, free accommodation is available in wilderness huts. From north to south, these are:

Taukota – This tepee-style kota right at the lakeshore, across from the village of Hetta, gives you shelter from the rain, and you can make a campfire inside. You can even sleep on the floor, if necessary.

Pyhäkero – This hut is five km from the lake. You cannot sleep here, except on the floor, but there is a gas stove, a toilet and a café, open in March and April only.

Sioskuru – A further seven km away, this hut accommodates up to 16 people. There are a few mattresses, a gas stove, a telephone and dry firewood.

Tappuri – A nice hut one km off the main path, this place is visible from both directions, because of the red roof. The hut accommodates six people, and has a gas stove and good water, from a nearby creek.

Pahakuru – This hut is 10 km from Sioskuru. It sleeps up to 10 people, and has a gas stove and a toilet. You'll need to walk a few hundred metres to get water.

Hannukuru – Just two km from Pahakuru, this hut has room for 16 people, but is often full. There are a few mattresses, a gas stove and a telephone here, as well as plenty of firewood. You can use the lakeside sauna.

Laavu – Some five km further on, this shelter is useful if it rains, and you can make a campfire here.

Montellin autiotupa – Some nine km further, across high fells, this nice hut has just a fireplace, and room for five people.

Nammalankuru – Just one km beyond the Montellin autiotupa, this large hut accommodates 16 people. There is a gas stove, a telephone, excellent scenery across the fells and a café, open in March and April.

Laavu – This shelter, just two km further on, is the last place to rest before the hotel, 10 km away across high fells. The scenery between here and the hotel is probably the best along the entire route.

If you arrive too late to catch a bus or start a trek, or just want to make shorter day trips, try the *Hotelli Pallas*, just 50 metres from the

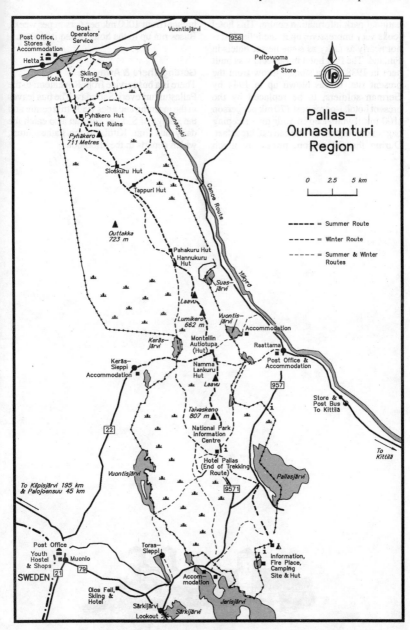

Pallas–
Ounastunturi
Region

0   2.5   5 km

------ = Summer Route

------ = Winter Route

------ = Summer & Winter Routes

national park information centre. This hotel looks very impressive, up in the fells, and is not nearly as tacky as some newer hotels in Finland. The first hotel in Lapland was built here in 1938, just a stone's throw from the present site. It was blown up in 1944 by German soldiers, to be replaced by the present hotel. Rooms cost 170 mk per person (100 mk if you sleep in your own sleeping bag), including an 'all you can eat' breakfast. During the ski season, prices are much higher (from 1000 mk per person per week). Buses run up to the hotel, when it is open.

Getting There & Away

There is a bus service from Rovaniemi to the Pallastunturi every Saturday. The bus leaves in the morning and goes via Kittilä centre and the village of Sirkka. You can also catch the daily bus from Kittilä to the Pallastunturi, which departs in the afternoon.

East Lapland

East Lapland offers some of Finland's most rewarding and demanding treks. Here, as in other areas of eastern Finland, the mysterious, virtually sealed Russian border has retained a frontier character. This is the region of the Saame people, the gold rush and the famous Arctic Road, taken every summer by thousands of Europeans on their way to the midnight sun of Nordkapp, the northernmost point in Continental Europe.

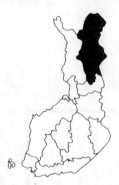

ACTIVITIES

Trekking

East Lapland is *the* place for some serious trekking. In fact, much of the area can be covered on foot, taking advantage of free accommodation in wilderness huts. This list gives some idea of the route possibilities in East Lapland, from Kemihaara in the east to Lemmenjoki in the west:

Kemihaara to Raja-Jooseppi, crossing the popular Saariselkä region

Raja-Jooseppi to Nellim (few facilities, no trekking maps available)

Nellim to Näätämö or Sevettijärvi, crossing the Kessi wilderness (few facilities, except in the north)

Näätämö or Sevettijärvi to Nuorgam (several huts along the way)

Kevo Nature Park, from Utsjoki to the Karigasniemi road

Muotkan Ruoktu to Angeli (little trekked, several huts)

Angeli to Lemmenjoki National Park

Fishing

Several good fishing areas are to be found in East Lapland, quite a few of them around Inari. Get a copy of the free *Kalassa Inarissa* guidebook, which has basic information in English.

Canoeing

One of the most interesting canoeing routes starts from the village of Kuttura and finishes in Ivalo, 70 km away. The river is passable all summer, but there are rocks along the route. Of the 30 rapids, the Saarnaköngäs and the Toloskoski rapids are the trickiest. There are free leaflets available in Ivalo for this route. Another good place for canoeing is the Lemmenjoki River.

South-East Lapland

KEMIJÄRVI

Kemijärvi gets a steady flow of travellers, as it is the northernmost town in Finland with a railway station. It is definitely a disappointment to anyone expecting to see genuine Lappish life, complete with reindeer and so on, but there are attractions to visit, and Kemijärvi is a gateway to the north-eastern part of Lapland. The municipality is large (3568 sq km) and has a population of 12,300.

Information

Tourist Office The tourist information office (☎ 9692-13777) is near the train station, at Rovaniementie 6. The office stocks a good selection of maps and brochures for Kemijärvi and all Finland.

Post & Telephone The post office is at Hallituskatu 5. It's open from 9 am to 5.30 pm Monday to Friday.

Library The interesting public library at

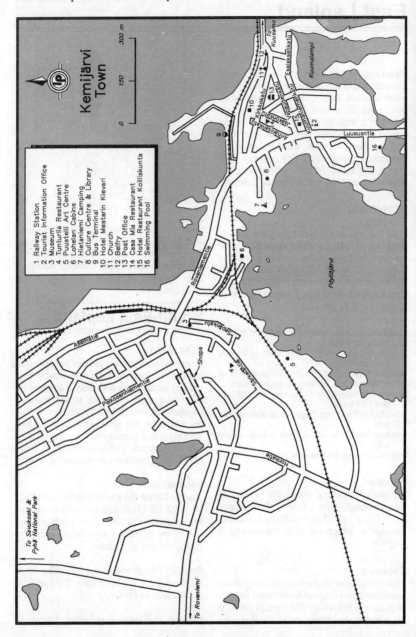

Kemijärvi Town

1 Railway Station
2 Tourist Information Office
3 Museum
4 Tunturila Restaurant
5 Puustelli Art Centre
6 Lohelan Cabins
7 Hietaniemi Camping
8 Culture Centre & Library
9 Bus Terminal
10 Hotel Mestarin Kievari
11 Church
12 Belfry
13 Post Office
14 Casa Mia Restaurant
15 Hotel Restaurant Kolliskunta
16 Swimming Pool

To Savukoski &
Pyhä National Park

To Rovaniemi

Asemtie
Pelkosenniementie
Honkatie
Sairaalatie
Seppäxatu
Shops

Rovaniementie

Luusuantie

Kirkkokatu
Esaläksenkatu
Uusikoskentie
Nummelantie
Vapaudenkatu

To Kuusamo

Pöyliöjärvi
Kuumalampi

Hietaniemenkatu 3, near the camping ground, is worth a look for its architecture. You can read there, too.

Things to See & Do

Local Museum The Kotiseutumuseo features several old houses from various time periods. In the main building, there is dried rye bread that was baked in 1977! The museum is open from 10 June to 31 August from 10 am to 6 pm daily. Admission is 6 mk, 4 mk for students.

Church The attractive church was built in 1951, but the old belfry (1774) remains. The church is open from 10 am to 8 pm daily in summer (till 15 August).

Puustelli The most interesting event in Kemijärvi is the annual week of woodcarving. Artists from all over the world attend, and the results from previous years are on display in this exhibition, not far from the youth hostel. It's open daily from 15 June to 15 August.

Suomu The downhill skiing slopes 42 km from Kemijärvi have had fewer visitors of late, because of the recent recession, but if you come in winter or early spring, you can ski there.

Places to Stay

The cheapest place to stay in Kemijärvi is the *Matkatupa youth hostel* (☎ 9692-88517). There are 56 beds (bunk prices start at 30 mk), a good kitchen and a superb common room with a TV. This is a good place to meet other travellers. The hostel is open from 1 April to 30 October. The best hotel is the *Mestarin Kievari* (☎ 9692-13577) at Kirkkokatu 9, with singles/doubles from 250/300 mk.

Places to Eat

For cheap home-style food, see the daily lunch menu at the *Tunturila* in the youth hostel building (open Monday to Friday only), or at the *Kahvio* in the Volvo building, not far from the tourist office. A meal costs 30 mk and includes bread, milk and coffee. Fresh berries are used for desserts. The best place to dine is reputedly the *Mestarin Kievari*. The place serves Lappish specialities and gives 10% discounts to Interrail passholders. Their special lunch prices start at 34 mk with salad, bread, nonalcoholic drink and coffee included.

Getting There & Away

Bus The bus terminal is right in the centre of town. There are several buses each weekday to Pyhä (50 km), Sodankylä (110 km), Savukoski (95 km), Salla (71 km) and Kuusamo (160 km). On weekends, buses run infrequently. All trains from Helsinki to Rovaniemi are met by a bus to Kemijärvi. (There is also a bus from Kemijärvi to Rovaniemi prior to train departures for Helsinki.)

Train A direct daily train makes the 14-hour journey from Helsinki to Kemijärvi, arriving in the morning and leaving again after 7 pm.

KOROUOMA

This impressive gorge makes a natural short cut between the two main roads to the west from the village of Posio. A path follows the steep valley from north to south. In between are a few open huts and several laavu shelters, for free accommodation. In winter, Korouoma is famous for its *paannejää* (spectacular ice walls on cliffs). If you have the money to spend, ice-climbing tours can be arranged in the village of Posio.

Trekking

The typical trek takes you from Pernu in the north to Lapiosalmi in the south. The Lapiosalmi centre, the retreat of a Lutheran mission, has accommodation available on request. For good fishing, the National Board of Forestry puts salmon into the lakes along the southern part of the route. Fishing in lakes, springs and rivers is allowed from 1 June to 10 September. One-day permits (25 mk) are available at petrol stations in Posio, and from the shop in Pernu.

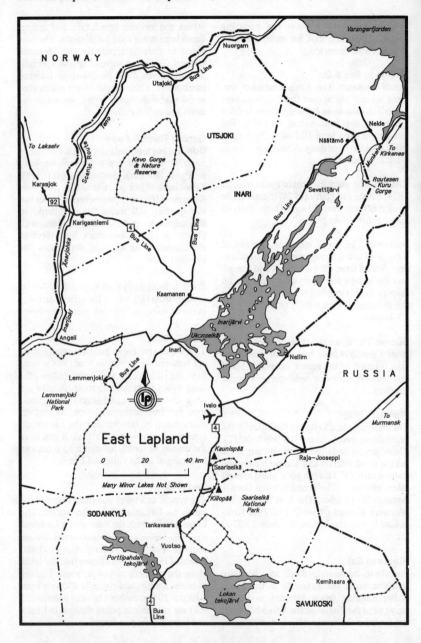

Getting There & Away

Several buses a day between Rovaniemi and Posio will take you to the northern starting point. There is just one bus daily from Ranua to Posio, stopping at Lapiosalmi around 4 pm Monday to Friday, so plan ahead.

PYHÄ/LUOSTO REGION

Pyhätunturi National Park, one of the oldest in Finland, is a popular winter-sports centre these days, so prices and demand are high from February to May. Summer hikes are recommended, as there are fewer people around and less demand for free accommodation in wilderness huts. Some of the walks in the area are day trips, so even those without proper equipment can reach many of the points of interest.

Information

For accommodation information, you can't beat Pyhä-Luosto Matkailu (☎ 9693-15200, fax 9693-13478) at Jäämerentie 9 in the village of Sodankylä. For information on the national park, there is a superb park centre (☎ 9692-82773) near the Hotel Pyhä. There is a free English-language slide show to be seen. For an overnight trek, a good map is highly recommended. Karttakeskus has a 1:40,000 *Luosto-Pyhätunturi* map, which can also be purchased in local hotels and resorts for 47 mk. Shorter walks are possible without a map, as signs and paths are clearly displayed inside the park.

Pyhäkuru

The most notable sight in Pyhätunturi National Park is this steep gorge between the Kultakero and Ukonhattu peaks. If you have only a little time to spend, the 10-km gorge loop is a good hike to choose. There are good signs and paths, and an impressive wooden staircase from the bottom of the gorge to higher slopes. According to a legend, the small Lake Pyhänkasteenlampi (Lake of Holy Baptism) down the gorge was where E M Fellman, the 'Apostle of Lapland', performed the first baptisms of Sompio Lapps to Christianity.

Places to Stay & Eat

Cottages As a result of the economic upswing of the late 1980s, a lot of new accommodation was constructed around Pyhä and Luosto. The best guide to rental cottages is the excellent *Pyhä-Luosto Majoitusopas* leaflet, which features over 80 individual options. Prices range from 100 mk per day (four beds) to over 1000 mk per day (up to 18 beds). Call (☎ 9693-15200 for reservations.

Wilderness Huts It is perfectly possible to arrive at the Pyhä Tourist Centre late on a summer afternoon and walk to the nearest designated sleeping place (laavu or wilderness hut). The morning bus allows you plenty of time for preparations and sightseeing. You are not allowed to stay at the *Karhunjuomalampi hut*, some five km from the tourist centre and four km from the Asteli. Nevertheless, this well-equipped hut, with a gas stove and a telephone, is a popular place for preparing a meal. Some two km west, in a gorge, there is a small *Annikinlampi laavu*, with water and dry wood available.

The only hut where you can sleep inside the national park is the clean, modern *Huttuloma hut*. Six people can sleep here, and there are mattresses. Further west towards Luosto is the simple *Porontahtoma laavu*, where there is dry wood but no water available. About four km north-west, the *Rykimäkuru hut* has two beds but half a dozen mattresses, which can also be used by trekkers sleeping under the nearby shelter. There is a gas stove in the hut, and river water is available nearby. This hut has little appeal, and the visitor's book is full of complaints that fellow travellers have failed to meet their wilderness hut obligations and clean up the hut before leaving! A highly recommended place for staying a few nights is the *Kuukkeli*. It is a well-equipped two-room cabin run by the Asteli resort. You can have either room for a mere 20 mk per person, and using the sauna is free of charge. The Kuukkeli is two km from Rykimäkuru along a river, one km from the main road. Some five km from

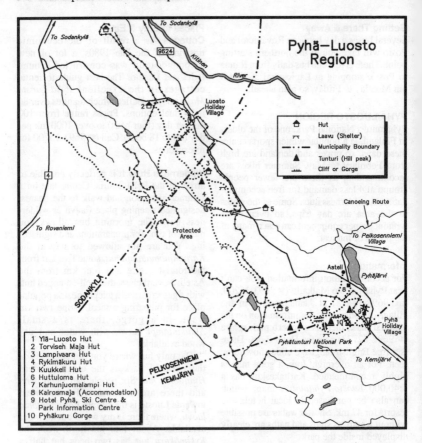

Pyhä–Luosto Region

To Sodankylä

To Sodankylä

9624

Kitinen River

Luosto Holiday Village

	Hut
	Laavu (Shelter)
	Municipality Boundary
	Tunturi (Hill peak)
	Cliff or Gorge

To Rovaniemi

Protected Area

Canoeing Route

To Pelkosenniemi Village

Asteli

Pyhäjärvi

SODANKYLÄ

PELKOSENNIEMI

KEMIJÄRVI

Pyhä Holiday Village

To Kemijärvi

Pyhätunturi National Park

1 Ylä–Luosto Hut
2 Torviseh Maja Hut
3 Lampivaara Hut
4 Rykimäkuru Hut
5 Kuukkeli Hut
6 Huttuloma Hut
7 Karhunjuomalampi Hut
8 Kairosmaja (Accommodation)
9 Hotel Pyhä, Ski Centre &
   Park Information Centre
10 Pyhäkuru Gorge

Luosto resort is the *Lampivaara hut*, which is only for day use. There are two other huts available, if you plan to walk from Luosto to the main highway, a rough 25-km hike along the Luosto ridges. It is five km from the Luosto resort to the *Torvisen maja* and a further eight km north-west to the *Ylä-Luosto hut*, which houses eight people.

Hotels The *Pyhä Hotel* (☎ 9692-12081) is the best hotel in Pyhä, and is worth a look even if you don't stay there. Singles/doubles start at 270/340 mk. There is a good view from the hotel's *Bistro* restaurant, which has

lunch at 40 mk. Down the hill and along the road, the *Kairosmaja* (☎ 9692-52134) has rooms at 110 to 160 mk, including breakfast (200 to 275 mk with full board). The nearby Revontulikappeli is the first 'tourist church' in Finland, open daily from 7 am to 10 pm. A very charming place to stay is the *Asteli* (☎ 9692-52141). The Lapinkenttä field has half a dozen Lapp houses as an open-air museum; sometimes you can sleep in one of them free of charge. A dormitory bed costs 95 mk, sauna, sheets and breakfast included. There are also several cottages, of varying quality, size and price. If you stay here, you get one night at the Kuukkeli hut for free. You can rent bicycles (15 mk per day), and canoes for the nearby Pyhäjoki River. You can also arrange treks to the nearby national park.

In Luosto, the superb *Hotelli Kantakievari Luosto* (☎ 9693-13681) has the largest kelo log restaurant in the world. Singles/doubles start at 280/360 mk. Some of the best cottages in Lapland can be found around the hotel. The nearby Tupasvilla shop sells groceries.

Getting There & Away
The easiest connection to the Pyhä Tourist Centre is the 10 am (2.25 pm on Saturdays) bus from Kemijärvi. There are buses between Luosto and Sodankylä on school days only (ie Monday to Friday, from mid-August till end of May). Hitchhiking can be easy, but there aren't that many cars.

POSIO
The village of Posio has supermarkets, four banks, an Alko store, a post office and a laundry. It is a one-km walk from the bus terminal to the main highway.

Information
The tourist information office (☎ 960-421 412) is on Pentikmäki.

Things to See & Do
Pentikmäki A bit off the village centre, along the main road, is Pentikmäki, a low hill. It was named after Ms Anu Pentik, a designer of ceramics and clothes. The Pentik factory shop is located on Pentikmäki. There is also a unique Coffee Cup Museum there.

Riisitunturi National Park This park features unusual sloped bogs. There is one wilderness hut available for free accommodation, but few trekkers cover the walking track that leads across the park. The Posio tourist office has produced a simple map to hand out.

Places to Stay & Eat
There is a hotel in the village with rooms for around 300 mk in summer. There is a café and ice-cream factory on Pentimäki.

Getting There & Away
Buses run regularly from Rovaniemi to Posio, and you can also reach Posio from Oulu and Kuusamo.

SALLA
This large municipality (population 6300) lost quite a piece of territory after WW II, and consequently, its centre has been rebuilt on its present site. The unusual church (1951) is an attractive example of postwar architecture. Locals are watching the border and waiting for it to be opened to travellers. That would increase interest in visits to the Kola Peninsula in north-west Russia. There are railroad tracks across Salla, all the way to the Russian border, and even now, trips can be arranged. Meanwhile, Salla offers large areas of untouched wilderness and a host of tourist services. The Sallatunturi Hill Tourist Centre, 10 km from the village, has downhill skiing slopes, and the Sallan Poropuisto (☎ 9692-37771) has exhibitions, reindeer rides and inexpensive wilderness accommodation for small groups.

Information
The tourist office (☎ 9692-32141) is called Yrityspalvelukeskus and is located on the Sallatunturi road.

Getting There & Away
Buses from Kemijärvi are your best bet, or try hitchhiking, crossing the long causeway from the town of Kemijärvi.

North-East Lapland

ANGELI
This remote village of 70 inhabitants can be used as a base between the Lemmenjoki

National Park and the Muotkatunturi region. No buses run here, and hitchhiking can be slow, but accommodation is available at *Hello Holidays* (☎ 9697-58134), run by an English-speaking couple.

INARI

At 17,321 sq km, Inari is the largest municipality in Finland. The small village of Inari, inhabited by 550 people, is the main Saame community in the region, which is why it has more of interest than Ivalo, the centre of commercial activity for the municipality of Inari. Once voted the ugliest village in Finland, Inari has supermarkets, banks and tacky souvenir shops scattered along the scenic road which follows Lake Inari, but it does have three not-to-be-missed, world-class attractions. You will need at least one full day to cover the Inari village attractions. The village can also be used as a base for exploring the northern part of the municipality.

Information

The Inari Info tourist office is open daily in summer from 8 am to 8 pm. Several maps are available for the large municipality of Inari. The 1:100,000 *Inarijärvi* map covers the entire Lake Inari area.

Things to See & Do

The Inari day-trip itinerary includes a morning trek to the wilderness church, a two-hour lake cruise at 2 pm and a visit to the Saame Museum in the evening.

Saame Museum Also called Saamelaismuseo, this museum should not be missed: it is one of the best open-air museums in Finland with unique Saame handicrafts, old buildings and local artefacts on display. For a few mk, you can get a map which might be useful for finding your way through the thick pine forest. It's open daily from 8 am to 8 pm. Admission is 12 mk, with discounts available for children.

Pielpajärven Wilderness Church The *erämaakirkko* of Lake Pielpajärvi can be reached by walking seven km from Inari. The hike itself serves as an introduction to trekking in Lapland. The track, marked by yellow paint on tree trunks, is of medium difficulty, with several desolate lakes along the route. The church area has been an important marketplace for the Saame over the centuries, with the first church erected here in 1646. The present church was built in 1760, and careful work in 1973 to 1976 restored the original subtle paint of the pulpit. To get to the path, follow the 'Kansanopisto' sign near the Saamenmuseo. It is a 4.5-km walk from the parking place.

Karhunpesäkivi If you have a vehicle, it may be a good idea to stop at the souvenir

Lap Hunter in traditional dress

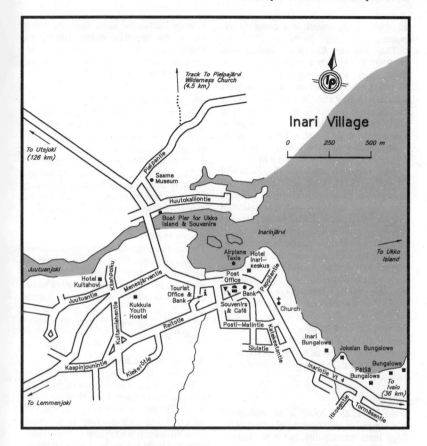

shop midway between Inari and Ivalo. This large hollow rock, 200 metres from the main road, is called the 'Bear's Den Stone'. The legend goes that a hunter, while looking for a shelter, found a bear under this stone.

Lake Cruises There are regular departures for Lake Inari as soon as the ice melts from the lake, usually by mid-June. There are daily cruises until the end of August, at 2 pm, with two extra departures in July (10 am and 6 pm). The destination is the island of Ukko (*Äjjih* in Saame), sacred to the Saame for at least 1000 years. During the brief (20-

minute) stop, most people climb to the top, but the northern side (on your left on arrival) has several cave formations worth exploring. An interesting burial island is seen from a distance during the cruise.

Places to Stay & Eat
For those on a tight budget, the Pielpajärvi church area has a wilderness hut which can be used by visitors. The sign above the door reads '1966'. The hut has four beds with mattresses but seems to get few overnight visitors. There is also a self-service sauna at the lakeside. Note that lighting an open fire

anywhere in the church area is strictly forbidden.

The simple *Kukkula youth hostel* (☎ 9697-51244), open from 1 June to 30 September, is a popular place among Nordkapp-bound drivers and travellers alike, but finding a bed (from 30 mk for YHA members) is normally no problem. The hostel has a small kitchen. Several bungalow villages are to be found to the south of the village, such as the *Pätilä* (from 110 mk) and *Uruniemi Camping* (from 120 mk).

The top-end choice, the *Kultahovi* (☎ 9697-51221), a bit off the main road along the Lemmenjoki road, accepts Finncheques. It has the only real restaurant in Inari village, with a 25 mk buffet breakfast that keeps you full till afternoon. The restaurant also serves three-course lunches (55 to 70 mk), but the offer does not include the normal extras. The *Koskikrouvi* hotel bar serves siika (whitefish) to weight, from 15 mk. This slightly salted fish is excellent with cold Lapin Kulta beer.

Getting There & Away
Inari is the next stop after Ivalo along the much-travelled 'Arctic Road'. Several buses a day make the 40-km trip between the two villages.

IVALO
Ivalo (population 3500) is the undisputed administrative and commercial centre of the huge Inari municipality, but it has little to recommend it. Even its unusually designed church is bleak from inside. With daily flights from Helsinki, Ivalo is the major transport hub in East Lapland, and it has the services you would expect in a small Finnish town.

Information
Tourist Office The tourist information office (☎ 9697-12521) at the bus terminal is open in summer from 8 am to 8 pm Monday to Friday and from noon to 7 pm on weekends. In winter, it closes at 3 pm. The office has an excellent choice of tourist literature for Lapland, including northern Norway.

Library Across the street from the tourist office, the beautiful public library has English magazines in the reading room and 1:20,000 maps of the entire Inari municipality in the käsikirjasto section.

Places to Stay
There are no bottom-end accommodation options in Ivalo. The *Matkakoti* (☎ 9697-21106), 500 metres off the main road towards Nellim, has singles/doubles at 175/250 mk. The *Hotelli Ivalo* (☎ 9697-21911) in the south and the *Kultahippu* (☎ 9697-21825) to the north of the village centre are both luxurious top-end hotels, but they sometimes have summer discounts.

Places to Eat
The *Lauran grilli*, the most popular eatery in Ivalo, stays open till 3 am – its kebabs and poronkäristys taste excellent after a one-week diet of trekkers' food. There is a branch of the *Nouto-Pizza* opposite the Lauran grilli. The K-Halli Ylävaara, one of several supermarkets in Ivalo, is open daily from 9 am to 9 pm.

Getting There & Away
There is a daily morning flight from Helsinki to Ivalo, and a few others on weekends. The cheapest return flight from Helsinki is currently 630 mk. A connecting bus from the airport meets each arriving flight. Buses from Rovaniemi always stop in Ivalo. Hitchhiking to Ivalo is easy, but I found it hard to hitchhike south from Ivalo – start by walking out of the village centre.

KAAMANEN
Kaamanen has none of the characteristics of a typical village but is worth noting because it lies at the crossroads of three northern roads. All post buses call at the Kaamasen Kievari, a few km north from the Sevettijärvi crossing, with connections available between various villages in the north. There are huts (120 mk) and meals (40 mk). The Kotipuoti shop has postal services and a fuel station. Some five km north is the

Karigasniemi crossing, where the Jouni Nuorgam shop sells reindeer-horn powder.

KARIGASNIEMI

This small village (population 470) is a crossing point from Finland to Norway along the popular Nordkapp Route. There are several shops and a few banks in Karigasniemi, and the post office is open from 10 am to 4.30 pm Monday to Friday. The village itself can be totally missed, as the border crossing seldom involves a stop. Fell Saame, the language of the local people, is a dialect spoken largely in Norway, across the border.

Places to Stay & Eat

The *Välimäen youth hostel* (☎ 9697-61188) dominates the village scene, as its restaurant, the *Välimäen baari*, is the most popular bar for the locals. An excellent lunch is served from 11 am to 2 pm daily (30 mk, including salad bar, bread, milk and coffee). The youth hostel prices start at 30 mk per bed, but there are also doubles from 80 mk and four-bed huts at 130 mk. An inexpensive sauna bath is available.

Getting There & Away

Two buses a day travel from Ivalo to Karigasniemi, continuing on to the Norwegian town of Karasjok. Eskelinen even drives to/from Lakselv in summer. An interesting drive along the Teno River is taken twice on Tuesdays and Fridays by a shared taxi, serving the little Saame villages along this beautiful route. Prices are similar to those charged by buses.

KEVO NATURAL PARK

Probably the most breathtaking sights in Finland (though they are nothing spectacular if you've spent your life in Norway or near the Grand Canyon) can be enjoyed by following the splendid gorge of the Kevo River, which also has some spectacular waterfalls. The rough 70-km (one-way) trek takes about four days. The 1:100,000 *Kevo* topographical sheet is rather overpriced at 47 mk.

Places to Stay

The *Kenestupa* (☎ 9697-72531), near the eastern starting point, next to the main road rents cabins from 110 mk per day. Use of the sauna costs 40 mk.

There also are four free wilderness huts along the north-western path between the two main roads, and a few other shelters. If you plan to walk from hut to hut, up in the fells, you won't have a chance to walk down in the gorge. If you want to cover the entire riverside, you'll need a tent, which you can pitch at designated camp sites. The huts along the north-western route, from south to north, are:

Ruktajärvi hut, at the south end of the gorge route (accommodates eight people and has a telephone and an oven)
Njavgoaivi hut (10 people, telephone)
Kuivi, inside the park (10 people, oven)
Madjoki ('Mad River'), inside the park (eight people)

Getting There & Away

If you start from the Kenestupa, catch a Nuorgam-bound bus from Inari. It is easier to start from the other end, as the Kenestupa and its sauna can come in handy after a rough trek; you have to catch the Karigasniemi-bound bus from Inari, and get off at the starting point (ask the driver to drop you off at the right place). Those with a car can leave their vehicle at the Kenestupa, catch the afternoon bus to Kaamanen and change to the Karigasniemi-bound bus. Plan ahead, as there is apparently just one connection that works!

KIILOPÄÄ

Kiilopää, the major trekking centre for the Saariselkä region, is the best place to start your trek. If you've made the preparations for your trek beforehand, you will probably spend no more than an hour in Kiilopää, but you can also make most arrangements there and stay overnight. Buy food elsewhere, though, as it is not that cheap in Kiilopää.

Places to Stay & Eat

All accommodation and services are taken

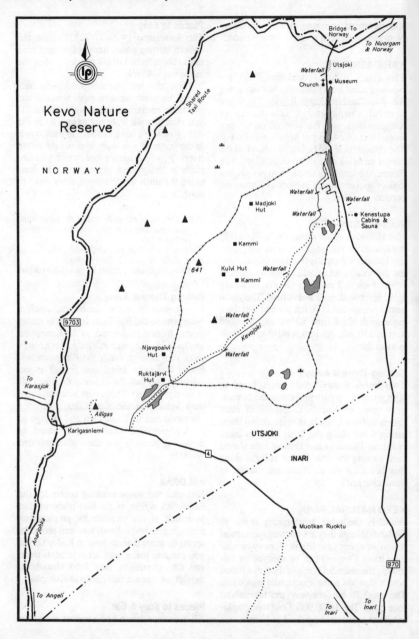

care of by the same company, Tunturikeskus Kiilopää (☎ 9697-87101). The cheapest place to sleep is the *Niilanpää* dormitory, very similar to wilderness huts, with beds for 40 mk. At the *Ahopää youth hostel*, dormitory beds cost 65 mk, singles/doubles are 190/300 mk and superb cottages cost 280 to 435 mk. The place rents mountain bikes, rucksacks, sleeping bags, skiing equipment and much more, sells fishing permits, rents the *varaustupa* huts inside the park and provides trekkers with advice. The left-luggage service costs 5 mk per day. Write your name and trekking route in the trekkers' book, and don't forget to inform the place as soon as you've completed the trek.

The *Kakslauttanen* (☎ 9697-87100) on the main Rovaniemi to Ivalo road has luxurious cottages from 290 mk per day. Meals are also available (from 42 mk).

Getting There & Away

Kiilopää is six km from the main road. I tried to hitchhike, with little success, until I was picked up by Matti Malm company, which has several buses for the one-hour trip between Ivalo and Kiilopää. Buses run only when schools are open. Arriving by bus from Rovaniemi, you have to ask whether the bus actually goes all the way to Kiilopää: some do and some don't.

LEMMENJOKI NATIONAL PARK

The largest national park in Finland, Lemmenjoki offers some of the most exciting trekking in Lapland. Some people say Lemmenjoki has less appeal than the more popular Saariselkä, but the Lemmenjoki experience is more diverse: zoom through desolate wilderness rivers, explore the rough Arctic landscape and bump into a lonely gold panner in the middle of nowhere. True, there are fewer wilderness huts, facilities are scantier and even the tunturis are not as high and spectacular as those in Saariselkä. However, if you want to do just one trek in Finland, keep Lemmenjoki on your list. For any serious trekking, you will need the 1:100,000 *Lemmenjoki* topographical sheet, available in bookshops for 47 mk.

Things to See

The Lemmenjoki River is scenic, with its steep slopes. The Ravadasköngäs waterfall can be seen from the river. You can walk there, and climb the staircase, from the Ravadasköngäs hut. The Morgamjoki River is the main gold-panning area, and there are several old huts where gold panners still sleep in summer.

Activities

Trekking All logical trekking routes are within the relatively small area between the Lemmenjoki and the Vaskojoki rivers. The shorter 18-km loop between the Kultala and Ravadasjärvi huts takes you to some of the most interesting gold-prospecting areas. As you can do this in two days, many trekkers head over the Ladnjoaivi Fell to the Vaskojoki hut and back, which extends the trek to four to five days.

Fishing Much of the Lemmenjoki River and beyond is good for fishing. You can buy permits (20 mk per day or 60 mk per week) and rent canoes and boats at the Ahkun Tupa in Njurgulahti, and cover the beautiful river route by yourself.

Places to Stay

You can either stay in the village of Njurgulahti, or head straight to the free huts inside the park. The *Ahkun Tupa* (☎ 9697-57135), which arranges river transport, has accommodation in rooms (70 mk) and superb cottages (230 mk).

Inside the park, half a dozen wilderness huts along the most popular trekking routes provide free accommodation. The *Härkäkoski* hut and the *Ravadasköngäs* hut, with 20 bunks and mattresses, are both along the river, visible from the river boat. At the end of the river-boat route, there are three options: the *Kultala* hut (four simple bunks), the kota shelter (space for five) and a camp site, up the steep staircase. The Kultala hut is owned by gold prospectors but can be used by trekkers. Some 4.5 km from the Kultala, the *Pellinen* hut has room for six people. Outside the smaller loop, there is another

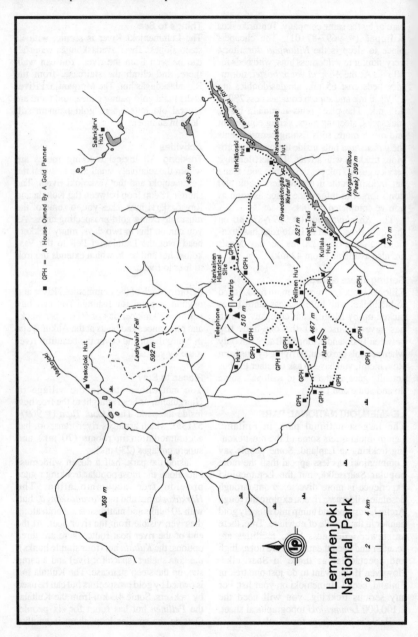

■ GPH = A House Owned By A Gold Panner

Saánkijärvi Hut

Lemmenjoki River

480 m

Härkäkoski Hut

Ravadasköngäs Hut

Ravadasköngäs Waterfall

Morgam–Viibus (Peak) 599 m

Boat–Taxi Pier

521 m

Kultala Hut

470 m

Kankainen Historical Site

GPH

GPH

GPH

Pellinen Hut

GPH

GPH

Airstrip

Telephone

510 m

GPH

GPH

467 m

Airstrip

GPH

Ladnjoaivi Fell 592 m

Hut

GPH

GPH

GPH

GPH

GPH

GPH

GPH

GPH

Vaskojoki Hut

Vaskojoki

369 m

Lemmenjoki National Park

0   2   4 km

hut, about eight km north-west from the Pellinen hut. Finally, the *Vaskojoki* hut, at the Vaskojoki River, has room for eight people, though there are not that many visitors there.

If you have a great deal of time and stamina, and want to walk from the Kultala to the village of Ivalo, head first to the *Oahojoki* hut, midway between the river and the main Inari to Kittilä road.

Getting There & Away

There are usually one or two post buses daily from Inari to the Njurgulahti village, or Lemmenjoki. If you have very little time, and want to use the river taxi, the afternoon bus in the village waits until the boat has made the return trip, then drives back to Inari. The scenic boat tour along the Lemmenjoki River is quite worth the fare (50 mk one-way, 100 mk return). There are daily departures at 10 am and 5.15 pm from 14 June to 15 September, with an extra departure at 10 am from 21 June to 18 August. Departures from Kultala are at 11.40 am and 6.40 pm. You can get on/off the boat at other piers along the route.

MUOTKAN RUOKTU

The *Muotkan Ruoktu* (☎ 9697-64100), midway between Kaamanen and Karigasniemi, has cottages from 200 mk per night. This is a possible starting point for the little-travelled trekking route across the Muotkatunturi Fells. You can reach the village of Angeli, staying in a few wilderness huts along the way.

NELLIM

This small village of 260 people has become a meeting point for two distinctive Saame groups of people, and there is a tsasouna of the Orthodox Scolt Lapps that can be seen. Nellim has a shop and a café, and the Koskela Nellim (☎ 9697-86925) offers rooms from 60 mk.

Nellim is also a gateway to the controversial Kessi wilderness, seriously threatened by overzealous loggers. If Kessi remains virgin forest, Nellim will be an interesting starting point for exploring one of the most isolated trekking regions in Finland. With some careful planning and good maps, it is possible to follow old roads and walking routes through the wilderness, all the way from Nellim in the south to Näätämö in the north. Consult the *Inarijärvi* map for routes.

Getting There & Away

On weekdays, there are morning and afternoon post buses from Ivalo to Nellim, 43 km away, and Virtaniemi, eight km further on.

NUORGAM

Nuorgam (population 210) is the John O'Groats of Finland, and that may be its only appeal. You easily miss the whole village when heading to north-eastern Norway. The commercial services, which include a bank, shops and a mail box, are scattered along the narrow main road. The Nuorgamin lomakeskus (☎ 9697-74312) has rooms from 100 mk, huts from 150 mk and a café. The last houses in Finland are tacky discount shops that sell cheap clothes to Norwegians. Further south, the beautiful riverside road towards Utsjoki has several choices of cabin accommodation, including the Alaköngäs, the Ala-Jalven Tuvat, the Lohiranta, the Vetsituvat and the Vetsikon lomamökit. These places have similar prices and services, and cater mostly to people fishing the Teno River.

There are a few minor tourist attractions, such as the Kuninkaan kivi ('King's stone') a royal signature from 1766, carved on a rock by the king of Sweden, and the Museotie (Museum Road), a narrow dirt road along the riverside.

Getting There & Away

A daily post bus serves Nuorgam from Rovaniemi, with an earlier bus on weekdays. It is a two-km walk from the Norwegian village of Polmak to the border, and another four km to the village of Nuorgam.

NÄÄTÄMÖ

Näätämö (population 70) is the last village before the Norwegian border along the Sevettijärvi route, and a popular Sunday shopping spot for Norwegians from across the border. The village is situated on a bare altiplano. You can start your trek south from Näätämö (see the Sevettijärvi section for details).

Places to Stay

The only place to stay is the Loma-Näätämö (☎ 9697-55511). The very helpful young Lappish warden rents boats (35 mk per day) and organises snowmobile tours in winter (a hefty 500 mk per day). Camping costs 10 mk per day and 5 mk per person, and two/four-bed cottages are 130/170 mk. There is a fee for using the shower or the sauna.

RAJA-JOOSEPPI

This border station is a crossing point to Russia for travellers to Murmansk, 250 km away. Many trekkers enter the Saariselkä region from here. If you don't feel like trying to hitchhike, a post taxi departs from Ivalo at 1.55 pm.

SAARISELKÄ

The village of Saariselkä, with good down-hill skiing facilities on nearby slopes, has become synonymous with the entire trekking region, so beware: the village is now one of the busiest yuppie resorts in the whole of Lapland. Real-estate prices here are second only to those in Helsinki, big companies have luxurious log houses in the village and hotels are expensive. However, this is not a bad place to start hiking, partly because of the good transport connections and partly because of the good supplies of trekking goodies available in local supermarkets.

Places to Stay & Eat

Finnair sometimes has special package tours from Helsinki that include a few nights in the comfortable Saariselkä hotels. Without such arrangements, most budget travellers could not afford to stay in these hotels. The *Saariselän Tunturihotelli* (☎ 9697-8111) is the oldest (and, incidentally, the least expensive), with singles/doubles from 340/450 mk. The *Riekonlinna*, the *Riekonkieppi* and the *Saariselkä Spa* are all very luxurious, but

you can't get a room for under 400 mk. A few km to the south in Laanila, the *Laanihovi* (☎ 9697-81816) is one of the older hotels, and is not a bad place to begin a trek. Singles/doubles start at 330/450 mk.

For an unusual place to eat, climb or drive to the top of Kaunispää Hill. Several stuffed birds decorate the restaurant. There are also several gourmet restaurants in the village of Saariselkä.

Getting There & Away

Each aeroplane arriving in Ivalo is met by a bus to Saariselkä. All northbound buses from Rovaniemi can drop you off at Saariselkä, and some buses make a loop through the village. Timetables in shops give departure times.

SAARISELKÄ NATIONAL PARK

The most popular trekking region in Finland has recently become slightly overcrowded, partly due to the yuppie presence in the village of Saariselkä. But the further you trek, the more natural beauty you will find and the fewer people you are likely to meet. I walked for three days in the eastern part of the park and saw no-one. The large hut network is one reason for the area's popularity; another is the sheer beauty of the low tunturi hills. Saariselkä may be tough going for the less experienced. Enter your route information in the Kiilopää Centre trekkers' book, or wherever your starting point is, and write your name and next destination in visitors' books in each hut. It is easier to locate and rescue trekkers whose routes can be traced through the information they have provided. Always call the starting point to advise that you have finished your trek.

Information

Due to the size of the park area, you are likely to visit the information centre that is closest to your starting point. The most established is the Tankavaara information centre (☎ 9693-45251). There are exhibitions, a slide show (available on request, in English, German, Swedish and Russian) and fishing permits for sale. There are also short nature trails in the vicinity, for those who have no time for longer treks. In Savukoski village, there is another modern information centre, catering mostly to those visiting the eastern part of the park. Ask to see the English-language slide show, with excellent photos. The Kiilopää Trekking Centre has a trekkers' book, in which departing trekkers enter route plans before departure. This place is likely to give the most valuable practical information on trekking.

Maps You should not enter the park area without a good map and a compass. There are three maps available for the area. For short treks around the village of Saariselkä, the 1:50,000 *Kaunispää-Kiilopää* map (25 mk) will do. The 1:50,000 *Kiilopää-Sokosti* map (47 mk) will take you beyond Lake Luirojärvi. The entire park is shown on the 1:100,000 *Koilliskaira* topographical sheet (47 mk). You should have at least some basic orienteering skills to enter the eastern area of the park.

Zone Division The park has been divided into four zones, with different rules for each zone. The basic zone is the area closest to main roads. Camping and fires are only allowed in designated places. In the wilderness zones of Saariselkä (in the Saariselkä Hill area) and Nuortti (the south-eastern area at the Nuortti River), camping is allowed everywhere except in certain gorges and on treeless areas. The Kemi-Sompio wilderness zone is in the eastern part of the park. Camping is allowed in all places, and fires can be lit anywhere, using dead wood from the ground.

Things to See

Few trekkers visit the Saariselkä area to see a particular sight. It is the sheer vastness of the virgin wilderness and the physical exercise that make this such a popular area. There are two historical **Scolt fields**, with restored old houses, two km south of Raja-Jooseppi, and two km west from the Snelmanninmaja hut, respectively. Another sight near Raja-

Jooseppi is a museum farm, inside the border zone. Entry is restricted.

There are several natural attractions within the park boundaries, of which the Rumakuru Gorge, near the huts of the same name, is closest to the main road. Lake Luirojärvi is the most popular destination for any trek, and a hike up the nearby Sokosti summit (718 metres, the highest in the park) is something of a must. Paratiisikuru ('Paradise Gorge'), a steep descent from the 698-metre Ukselmapää summit, and the nearby Lumikuru ('Snow Gorge') are also popular day trips between the Sarvioja and Muorravaarakka huts.

Trekking

There are a large number of possible walking routes in the Saariselkä area. Use wilderness huts as bases and destinations, and improvise according to your ability: it is possible to cover three to four km per hour, and up to 25 km per day, but even 20 km on the first day may be too tough. You'll enjoy it more if you walk just a few hours daily and spend more time preparing food and enjoying the quiet and solitude of the wilderness.

A four to six-day loop from the main road to Lake Luirojärvi and back is about the most popular route, and you can extend it further, beyond the lake. To reach areas where very few have been, take a one-week walk from Kiilopää to Kemihaara, or do the most remote route; with some careful planning and a good map, it is possible to follow old roads and walking routes through the fells all the way from Raja-Jooseppi in the north to Kemihaara or even Tulppio in the south-east. Carry all the food you need and ration it carefully.

Places to Stay – the basic zone

It is generally possible to arrive at any starting point during the day and walk to the nearest wilderness hut within hours. Note that there is daylight 24 hours a day in June and July. Most huts near the main road have been declared huts for day use only, but I found staying overnight no problem, as there

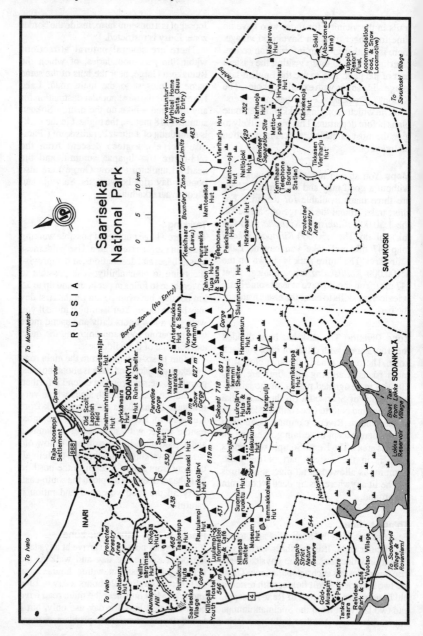

are still bunks inside most of them. On the other hand, more distant huts have comfortable mattresses and better amenities for an overnight stay. There are a number of wilderness huts in the basic zone:

Rumakuru – Some six km from Saariselkä village, this is the most popular day cabin in Saariselkä, with over 200 skiing visitors on busy April days. There are bunks for four (no mattresses) and a gas stove, but staying overnight is not encouraged. Some 500 metres east is the old Rumakuru hut, which dates from the turn of the century. With similar facilities, it easily accommodates two, and has character.

Luulampi – Four km from Rumakuru, this is an information centre for tourists. There is even a café in the high season. No sleeping is allowed here, except in an emergency.

Taajostupa – This cosy hut near a river, with two open sides available, accommodates up to 10 people, and has several mattresses to soften the sleep. There are normal facilities, but the sauna burned down in 1990.

Vellinsärpimä – This hut, seven km from Kaunispää/Saariselkä, is supposedly a day cabin, but sleeping is OK. There is space for four. There are normal facilities, with good water available from the river.

Kivipää – Five km from Vellinsärpimä at a small lake, this hut accommodates four people. It's open to anyone from May until the winter comes; at other times, it must be reserved. Even though it is off the beaten path, it gets lots of praise for its thick foam mattresses.

Niilanpää – This Lappish kota-style shelter for five people, only four km from Kiilopää, is seldom used for sleeping. For water, follow the reindeer fence down to a nearby river.

Rautulampi – A popular hut at the northern end of a lake of the same name, Rautulampi hut is for day use only (sleeping is OK, but not encouraged). There is a telephone available, if it's not out of order.

Suomunruoktu – Fifteen km from Kiilopää, at a creek, this hut is usually busy in the high season. It accommodates 10 people in the open side and 10 in the reserved section, with mattresses in both rooms. If the place is full, walk 200 metres upriver and cross the river to the old hut, which gets few overnight visitors. There are no amenities, as it has been declared a wilderness museum, but sleeping is OK.

Tammakkolampi – This small kammi three km south of the Suomunruoktu hut accommodates only three people, and you have to reserve it in advance. Getting there is not worth it.

Lankojärvi – This hut on the western shore of the Suomujoki River has two sides, with 10 places in each. There is a crossing point across the river, to the south of the hut.

Porttikoski – This northern hut is one km from the bridge over the Suomujoki River. The hut sleeps 10 people and has a popular sauna.

Snellmanninmaja – This small hut is on the northern shore of the wide Suomujoki River. It sleeps five people but is out of bounds for most trekkers, due to its location.

Places to Stay – Saariselkä wilderness zone

The hilly Saariselkä region is quite busy during the winter holidays, in August before school starts and during the ruska weeks in late September. Most trekkers visit this area, where superb wilderness huts abound:

Tuiskukuru – This popular hut near a creek has two sides, with space for 10 people in the open side and mattresses in both rooms. There is gas and firewood available.

Luirojärvi – There are three lakeside huts, each with good facilities (including a gas stove), and a popular sauna. The largest hut was built in 1991. It has space for 12 people in both rooms, but there are no mattresses in the open one. The smaller *porokämppä* accommodates six people. The third hut has to be reserved in advance. Many groups pitch tents near the huts during the summer high season.

Hammaskuru – This hut has two sides. One side is always open, with room for 12 people (but no mattresses). The hut has normal facilities, and good drinking water is available from the nearby creek..

Hammaskammi – Two km south along a good road, this primitive lakeside shelter for two has a stove inside, and dry firewood.

Siulanruoktu – The dramatic position of this hut, halfway up a ridge, makes it an unforgettable place to stay. Steep stairs lead from the path to the hut, and further down to the river. There is room for six people, a few mattresses, gas and a stove.

Tahvon tupa – Six km east of the Siulanruoktu hut is this gem among wilderness huts, in a small river valley. There is a good self-service sauna, plenty of firewood and half a dozen mattresses, but relatively few visitors. The small *niliaitta* is used to store empty bottles; take one for extra water if you are heading further east to the riverless region.

Peuraselkä – This lonely hut, seven km north-east from Tahvon tupa, and just eight km from the Russian border, has few visitors. It is easy to find with a map and a compass, but getting there is hard, as there are plenty of fallen trees in the area. There is no bridge across the river, but crossing it with long rubber boots is generally OK. The hut accommodates four people, and has mattresses and a gas stove.

Jyrkkävaara – This two-room hut sleeps 10 people in each room. Located at a small lake, it serves mainly those heading south-west from the Raja-Jooseppi starting point. There is a telephone in the hut.

Kiertämäjärvi – This small hut for five people, at the northern shore of a lake, is the first sleeping place for many of those who start their trek from Raja-Jooseppi.

Sarvioja – This hut has two rooms, with 10 places in the open side. Slightly off the beaten track, the hut nevertheless serves as a base for several side trips.

Muorravaarakka – There is a good two-room hut (with 10 beds in the open side, and a telephone) and a small kammi, both of which must be reserved in advance. These huts are in a river valley at the junction of a few paths. There are several popular hikes in the neigbourhood, so expect a few other trekkers to show up by night time.

Anterinmukka – This beautiful hut (also called Keskon mökki) is one of the most liked huts in the whole park, with a good sauna available for trekkers. The hut accommodates up to 15 people, but its isolated location makes it hard to predict its nightly usage.

Karapulju – An isolated hut south of Lake Luirojärvi, it has room for five trekkers, but there are few reasons to come to this place surrounded by hostile bogs.

Vongoiva – This kammi in an upper river valley has room for two people only, and it has to be reserved in advance. Many trekkers stop here en route between Anterinmukka and Siulanruoktu.

Places to Stay – Kemi-Sompio wilderness zone

This area gets few trekkers – it is a transitional region between two popular areas, the Saariselkä hill region and the Nuortti fishing area. The terrain is flatter than that of Saariselkä, and there is little water available in summer. The narrow spruces are typical of the wilderness which Finns call *kaira*. It is easy walking country, though, and large bogs can be crossed on *pitkospuu* paths (if you

follow trails, that is). There are several wilderness accommodation options:

Keskihaara – This *laavu* shelter marks the crossroad of paths between Peuraselkä and Manto-oja huts, and the Kemihaara border station. It is a good place to stop and get water. If it is late, try to sleep under the shelter.

Peskihaara – This small hut, previously a border guard's hut, takes five people. It is a side trip from the main path leading to Kemihaara.

Manto-oja – This hut, a one-day hike from Peuraselkä, is an essential stop along a transpark route. There is room for eight people, and a telephone.

Mantoselkä – If the Manto-oja hut happens to be full, this hut, one km north, has six beds in the open side. The Tulppio holiday village has keys for the other side.

Vieriharju – Five km east from Manto-oja, this hut has room for six people, and a sauna.

Other – Very distant huts in this zone include *Härkävaara*, which has a sauna, and *Tammikämppä*, which can be reached if you arrange boat transport from Lokka village across the Lokka reservoir, and enter the park from that side.

Places to Stay – Nuortti wilderness zone

The Nuortti region is popular for fishing, and most visitors come for this reason. Tulppio is used as a starting point for exploring the area. If you plan to trek from here, negotiate a ride from Tulppio to one of three places: Kärekeoja, Tikkasen vieriharju or the Kemihaara border station. Wilderness huts in the area include:

Kärkekeoja – This hut is the closest to Tulppio, with a gravel road across the river. It is possible to cross the river on foot.

Mettopalo – There are bunks for four people in this hut, a dozen km further downriver.

Karhuoja – Six people can stay here for free, and there is room for another six in the reserved side.

Naltiojoki – This hut, not far from Kemihaara, accommodates 10 people.

Hirvashauta – There are two rooms in this hut, with room for six people in each. The hut is on the other side of the river, a few km south of the Karhuoja hut.

Tikkasen vieriharju – This hut, close to the park boundary and a gravel road, can be reserved in Tulppio for up to four people. There is a sauna, and a natural well nearby provides fresh water.

Getting There & Away

As the park is so vast, it is possible to start the trek from several points.

To/From Kiilopää There is a regular bus service from Ivalo village, and the morning post bus from Rovaniemi makes the side trip to Kiilopää. You should head first either to the Luulampi information centre or to Niilanpää kota.

To/From Saariselkä See the Saariselkä section for information on getting to Saariselkä. Start the trek from the southeastern corner of the village. The first leg will take you to Rumakuru.

To/From Tankavaara This is not a good starting point, unless you want to visit the Sompio Nature Reserve.

To/From Kaunispää You have to hitchhike up to this hill, then descend the downhill skiing slope to a valley. Follow the path down there to your left. The nearest hut is Vellinsärpimä.

To/From Raja-Jooseppi On weekdays, there is a regular post taxi to Raja-Jooseppi. Otherwise, you'll have to hitchhike. This is a good starting point for a trek, as it takes you directly into the real wilderness. The first huts are Kiertämäjärvi and Jyrkkävaara.

To/From Kemihaara There is no public transport to this border station, so you'll have to negotiate transport at Sotajoki or Tulppio. The park boundary is just one km from Kemihaara. The nearest hut is Peskihaara, but the path leads directly to Keskihaara, where there is a laavu.

To/From Tulppio See the Tulppio section for information on getting to Tulppio. Negotiate a ride closer to the park boundary, or follow gravel roads to Kärekeoja.

To/From Lokka Villagers will take trekkers across the large Lokka reservoir by boat. The nearest hut will then be Tammikämppä.

SAVUKOSKI

Savukoski is a genuine wilderness municipality with a declining population, currently 1800, or 0.3 people per sq km. The village of Savukoski serves as a base for visits to the isolated attractions around the region, including the eastern part of the Saariselk area.

Things to See

Joulupukin Muorin Tupa One of the Santa Claus Land attractions, this place has local handicrafts, and paraphernalia of Santa Claus' wife.

National Park Centre At the hotel is a superb wilderness exhibition, especially of the Savukoski side of Saariselkä National Park. Ask to see the English slide show, with excellent photos. The centre is open daily from 10 am to 6 pm. Admission and the slide show are free.

Martti The small village of Martti is the last stop for buses running north from Savukoski. In Martti, you will find the K-market Mulari (open daily in summer), a bar that sells snacks only, a fuel station and a telephone booth. There are no fuel sales north of here, until you reach Tulppio.

Places to Stay & Eat

The *camping ground* has two huts, with six beds in each. The minimum charge for two people is 160 mk, and additional people pay 50 mk. Pitching a tent costs 40 mk for up to three people. The café sells snacks only.

The top-end choice in Savukoski village is the *Samperin Savotta*, a suberb modern hotel at the Kemijoki River waterfront. Singles/doubles are 300/400 mk.

Getting There & Away

Post buses and Möllärin Linjat buses run daily from Kemijärvi to Savukoski, 94 km away, via Pelkosenniemi. Buses from Salla run only on school days.

SEVETTIJÄRVI

One of the roads from Kaamanen heads

eastwards to Sevettijärvi, on the shores of Lake Inari in the north-east of the 'head' of Finland. It is mostly inhabited by a distinctive Lappish group called Scolt Lapps (kolttalappalaiset). The women wear typical Russian scarfs, and on special occasions, a hat is worn under the scarf. Some of the Scolts speak Scoltish, Finnish and Russian. The Sevettijärvi region has more lakes per square km than any other region in Finland. Very few trekkers explore this desolate wilderness, yet it is worth any effort you put into it.

Things to See

The orthodox tsasouna, built in 1951, is dedicated to Father Trifon from Petsamo (now part of Russia). The altar has several beautiful icons, some of which were brought from the Soviet-occupied monastery of Valamo. In front of the church is a wooden memorial to the dead who were left in Petsamo. The oldest graves have a wooden grobu above them, with a wooden bird attached. The church is open from 10 am to 3 pm Monday to Friday, but you may have to knock first at the warden's door.

Places to Stay

The Sevettijärven Lomamajat (☎ 9697-54215) is right behind the church – follow the sign. The reception is in the private home. There's a lake, with clear water, but the area is inhabited and not that quiet. Doubles are 120 mk, and four-bed huts with cooking facilities are 150 mk. The Café Siitapirtti (☎ 9697-54211) and the K-Valinta Nykänen each have one or two rooms for rent.

Further south from Sevettijärvi are several holiday villages. The modern Nili-Tuvat (☎ 9697-54240), four km to the south, has several huts but is close to the road. There is a food kiosk there. Some 26 km south of Sevettijärvi, the modern Kolttamajat (☎ 9697-53531) has several huts (from 200 mk). There is good fishing in the nearby lake. Further south, in the village of Partakko, the Siuttajoen lomamökit (☎ 9697-53116) has huts from 100 mk. The place rents boats for

50 mk per day. A sauna costs 20 mk per person.

Places to Eat

It is advisable to buy your own food and prepare it either in your hut or while you trek. The Café Siitapirtti is the only place that offers meals, snacks and coffee. The only shop in the village, the K-Valinta Nykänen, has the usual selection of the less-expensive Pirkka products. They even sell bananas cheaper than in Helsinki!

Activities

Trekking Three major treks can be done in the Sevettijärvi region:

Sevettijärvi to Kirakkajärvi This is the shortest route, and there are two huts along the way. You can walk the route in two days, or set a more leisurely pace and do it in three days. The route takes you across the rocky, hilly region on the other side of Lake Sevetti. Cross the narrow strait just south of the Siitapirtti. Follow the route north-east, and you'll end up on the other side of Lake Sevetti. Use the 1:20,000 map No 4911 for this route. At the other end, preferably at the western side of Lake Kirakka, you'll come to a minor road that will take you to the main road. Buses pass Monday to Friday at 8.30 am (south) and 7.45 pm (north) on weekdays.

Näätämö to Sevettijärvi This exciting route starts at Näätämö and goes via Jankkila, Routasenkuru, Vätsäri, Tuulijärvi and Sollomisjärvi to Sevettijärvi, taking you to an area where very few people go. Be careful not to cross the border to Norway by accident – it is illegal! There are a few huts along the way, all clearly marked on major trekking maps. First head for Näätämö, right at the border. There is a marked path from there south to Jankkila house (14 km). The path is marked on the 1:20,000 map No 4913, as well as on the nature trail (stones piled on rocks, wood nailed on trunks of trees, etc). The marked path will take you to a very interesting Scolt Lappish reindeer farmhouse, which must be one of the most isolated houses in the whole of Europe! It is still occasionally inhabited, so you have no right to enter the main house. You may ask for shelter, though, if there is someone in, or just stay overnight in one of the barns if you are desperate. There is no electricity. If it is not too late in the day, it is better to go on, east from Jankkila house, along the Pakanajoki River. There is a path to a large lake, and you have the choice of two routes around the lake. The northern one is easier.

The next destination is a very beautiful gorge, Routasenkuru. It is easy to find, as it extends north-south for over five km. There are a few campfire places on the eastern side of the gorge, and you may camp near these, or stay at the border guards' hut, which has shelter for two to three trekkers. The following day, trek south along the Routasen Gorge to the Vätsäri fells, then turn west again. There is no path, so have your compass ready. You'll find a mountain hut to the west of Vätsäri, and another at Tuulijärvi – one route has a path, the other does not. Further west is the Lake Sollomis hut. From the hut, there is another short walk through the wilderness or a slightly longer trek along a path. The last stage takes you to the Sevettijärvi village.

Sevettijärvi to Nuorgam This is an established trekking route, and the most popular from Sevettijärvi. There are six mountain huts along the route, and you'll need the 1:20,000 map Nos 4911, 3933, 3934, 3943 and 3941. Also available are 1:100,000 topographical sheets, which will be cheaper to purchase. There are two places to start the trek, the better one just north of Sevettijärvi, at Saunaranta. You'll see a sign reading 'Ahvenjärvi 5', and a trekking sign – 12 km to Opukasjärvi, 69 km to Pulmankijärvi. The mountain huts and their distances are Opukasjärvi (12 km), Iisakkijärvi (five km), a nameless hut (14 km), Tsarajavrrik (13 km), a nameless hut close to the border (20 km) and Pulmankijärvi (five km). From Pulmankijärvi, you can walk to Nuorgam

along a road, or make a phone call from a local home for a taxi to Nuorgam village.

Organised Tours The only person who takes tourists on guided tours is a Dutch man, Ernest Dixon. He has guided his 'Lapland Pulka Tours' and 'Lapland Ruska Tours' for almost 30 years, and has the best local knowledge in the region. Ernest takes trekkers to local Lappish homes, will locate reindeer herds for photographers and provides food that he prepares over an open fire – he buys fresh salmon from the Lapps! Write well beforehand to J Ernest Dixon, SF-99930 Sevettijärvi, Finland, or contact representing tour agencies: Waymark (☎ 0753-516 477, fax 0753-517 016), 44 Windsor Rd, Slough SL1 2EJ, United Kingdom, or Dixon Nature Holidays (☎ 020-110 762), De Sneeuwlopers, Postbus 5772 – 1007 AT, Amsterdam, Holland.

Getting There & Away
The nearest airport to Sevettijärvi is Kirkenes in Norway. From the airport, take a bus to Kirkenes (no hitchhiking, as the airport is in a military area). From Kirkenes, you can catch a bus to the Finnish border. The nearest Finnish airport is in Ivalo, and there are Finnair buses and post buses to the Ivalo bus terminal. You can hitchhike from Ivalo, but traffic is sparse beyond the Kaamanen crossing. Many Norwegians drive north on Sunday evenings and south on Friday afternoons. In summer, there is more traffic but the cars are usually full with families on their holidays. There is a post-bus connection on weekdays, leaving Ivalo at 4.15 pm and arriving in Sevettijärvi at 7.35 pm. You can catch the bus at any post box or post office along the road. From the Norwegian border village of Neiden, buses leave at 7.40 pm but don't go any further than Näätämö. Buses from Näätämö to Sevettijärvi leave at 8 am and arrive at 8.45 am.

SODANKYLÄ
The village of Sodankylä is a busy commercial centre for the large Sodankylä

municipality, which has a population of 10,500, or 0.9 people per sq km. Buses stop here regularly, but the village itself has little of interest. The bus terminal is slightly off the main road, and taxis depart from the same square.

Things to See
Church Built in 1689, the old church near the Kitinen riverside stands out as one of the few buildings in Lapland to survive the German troops in WW II. It's open daily in summer, from 9 am to 8 pm.

Alariesto-Galleria Not far from the church, near the main road, the gallery displays paintings by this famous Lapp painter. It's open from 10 am to 5 pm Monday to Saturday and from noon to 6 pm on Sundays.

Museum The local museum is several km south of the village. It's open from 1 June to 30 August from 10 am to 4 pm Monday to Saturday and from noon to 6 pm on Sundays.

Places to Stay & Eat
The cheapest place in Sodankylä is the *Lapin Opisto youth hostel* (☎ 9693-21960), across the river, with dormitory beds from 40 mk. It's open from 5 June to 11 August. The two hotels in Sodankylä, the *Kantakievari* (☎ 9693-21924) and the *Gasthaus* (☎ 9693-13801), have rooms from 300 mk.

There are two eateries along the main road. The *Nouto-Pizza*, north of the bus terminal, has pizzas from 28 mk. Very different is the *Seita Baari*, almost in the village centre. Open daily till 10 pm, it offers a selection of home-made food, including Lappish specialities.

Getting There & Away
Sodankylä is on the main Rovaniemi to Ivalo road, and a bus from either end costs 60 mk to 80 mk. Buses from the Rovaniemi railway station depart on the two-hour journey to Sodankylä soon after the train arrives. Walk out of the village if you want to hitchhike.

TANKAVAARA
Famous for its gold museum and for the annual Gold Panning Competition, Tankavaara, in the northern part of the Sodankylä municipality, is quite a good place to stop during a trans-Lapland tour.

Things to See & Do
Gold Museum The Kultamuseo of Tankavaara displays tools and other paraphernalia from Lapland's crazy goldfever years, explained with good English text. The museum can be found behind the hotel and restaurant. It's open daily from 9 am to 5.30 pm, and admission is 20 mk.

National Park Centre The large information centre (☎ 9693-46251) for the Saariselkä National Park is worth a look, even if you're not planning to visit the park itself. The centre is open from 10 am to 7 pm in summer and from 10 am to 4 pm in winter.

Walking Several nature trails around Tankavaara are suitable for short walks. Some routes require waterproof boots.

Festivals
Several gold-related events are held during the summer, and early August sees the Gold Panning Finnish Open, which should not be missed. It is totally unique, with much activity. The competition itself is short-lived: each competitor's bucket holds a certain number of gold chips (two to 10). Finding the chips quickly also means the risk of losing a chip or two, and for each missing chip, five minutes is added. Entry to the area during the competition is 50 mk per day.

Places to Stay & Eat
The *Kultakylä* (☎ 9693-46158) has cottages for 160 to 210 mk, depending on the season, and doubles for 270 to 360 mk. Of the two restaurants, the *Nugget* ('the only III class restaurant beyond the Arctic Circle)' is the more economical.

Getting There & Away
Tankavaara is on the main Rovaniemi to

Ivalo road. All northbound buses pass the village, stopping on request.

TULPPIO

Tulppio has significance mostly as a stepping stone to one of the most interesting natural fishing rivers in Finland, the Nuorttijoki River, which is inside the Saariselkä National Park. Tulppio used to be a busy logging station before WW I, but little of this legacy remains, as Finnish troops burned down the houses during the 'Winter War' of 1939-40 to prevent the Russians making bases in them. As the Savukoski wilderness is attracting more visitors these days, Tulppio is becoming more popular.

Steam Locomotive

The old steam locomotive behind the cottages has plenty of historical significance. As the economic value of the Savukoski forests was discovered in the late 19th century, research was done to find ways to exploit the area. In 1911, a Finnish mechanic was sent to Minnesota to learn how Americans solved the problems of transporting logs. As a result, two steam locomotives were brought to Tulppio via Hanko and Rovaniemi in January 1913. Both locomotives were brought in pieces to Rovaniemi, transported in horse sledges over frozen bogs and forests, with temperatures reaching -30°C. One locomotive is in Rovaniemi, and the other one is here.

Places to Stay & Eat

The *Tulppio* (☎ 9692-44101) has 19 rooms in cottages with few amenities, but the rooms are clean and can be heated. Doubles start at 180 mk. The café is a popular beer-drinking bar for locals, but there are also meals available (from 37 mk). Poronkäristys can be had for 56 mk.

Getting There & Away

A private vehicle is the easiest way to reach Tulppio, but there are other options. You could take a bus to Martti, then call the Sotajoki for free transport. The Tulppio and the Kairiver charge 1.50 to 2 mk per km.

There is also a daily post taxi to Tulppio, leaving the village of Savukoski at 4 pm Monday to Friday. It is also possible to trek to Tulppio from the Saariselkä National Park. Hitchhiking is easiest on weekend afternoons, when people drive to Tulppio for the Tisko, a sort of lumberjacks' disco.

AROUND TULPPIO
Korvatunturi Fishing Area

The Kairijoki River has become a popular place for fishing, partly because of the good services provided by the Kairiver (☎ 9692-41482). It has excellent cottages for 400 mk and comfortable laavu dormitory beds for 70 mk. The Kairiver also rents canoes and fishing gear, and helps with trekking plans. In winter, snowmobile safaris are arranged. Several places around the Savukoski and Kemijärvi municipalities, including the Kairiver itself, sell fishing permits (about 30 mk per day or 90 mk per week). You'll get a map of the area when you buy the permit. The riverside has several kota and laavu shelters, for free accommodation. The problem with the Kairiver is its remote location. Unless you have a vehicle, prepare to stand for several hours when hitchhiking. You can try the unusual *kapulalossi* ferry across the Kemihaara River, from the village of Ruuvaoja, halfway between Martti and Tulppio, then proceed along the bad gravel roads from there.

Sotajoki

The desolate area between Martti and Tulppio has always been a source of timber. A few logging cabins have been converted into hostels. The Sotajoen kämppäkartano (☎ 9692-43468, 949-291 898), some 20 km north of the small village of Ruuvaoja, stands out because free transport is provided for overnight guests. Expect to pay 100 mk for sauna, bed and breakfast. The transport comes in handy if you start/end your trek at the Kemihaara border guards' station. This place, as well as the toutist office in Savukoski village, also keeps keys for the Reutuvaara loggers' house, some 10 km south from Sotajoki. Beds are just 25 mk per night, but a minimum of four people is required (you pay 100 mk if you're alone). This large house has an open room as an *autiotupa*, so staying for free is possible. This place is difficult to find, so enquire at the Savukoski tourist office.

UTSJOKI/OHCEJOHKA

It would be misleading to call the village of Utsjoki (population 630) an attractive place, but as the northernmost municipality in Finland and with a relatively large Saame population, it has certain interest. The most notable sight is Kevo Gorge.

Information

In the village of Utsjoki, there is a tourist information office (☎ 9697-71111), open from 9 am to 3 pm Monday to Friday. There are two banks, a post office and several shops in the village.

Things to See & Do

Church The Utsjoki church, six km south from the village, and the *kirkkotuvat* (church huts), across the main road, are worth a look. The huts, old lodging facilities for long-distance visitors to the church, have been restored. In summer, there is a café for the many visitors that stop here.

Swimming & Sauna The indoor swimming pool is generally open in the afternoon, Tuesday to Saturday. Swimming and sauna costs 15 mk.

Places to Stay & Eat

Utsjoki Camping (☎ 9697-71213), at the southern end of the village, has huts for 150 mk, and they accommodate four to five people each. Little English is spoken by the friendly warden, who closes at 10 pm to go fishing. There is a kitchen and coin-operated showers. If you have little money, ask for permission to sleep in the old sauna. The top-end *Utsjoki Tourist Hotel* (☎ 9697-71121), behind the post office, takes Finncheques. Lunch is available from 45 mk, all extras included. For cheaper meals, check lunch prices at the *Tenohelmi*.

Getting There & Away

The daily post bus leaves Rovaniemi each morning (with later departures from Ivalo, Inari and Kaamanen) and reaches Utsjoki by 5 pm. There is an earlier bus on weekdays. The same bus returns from Polmak (Norway) and Nuorgam to Utsjoki. There is also a new bridge crossing from Norway at Utsjoki, and occasional shared-taxi transport from Karigasniemi village.

VUOTSO

Vuotso is another stop along main road No 4 to the north. There is a somewhat commercial reindeer village, where buses stop for 10 or 15 minutes for passengers to have a cup of coffee. If you want to see the pitiful reindeer, ask at the counter for someone to open the door (there is a 15 mk admission fee). The restaurant serves meals.

Glossary

aapa – open bog
aitta – small wooden storage shed in a traditional farmhouse, used for accommodating guests
ämpäri – bucket

erämaa – wilderness

feresi – old Karelian dress used daily by working women, now used in Northern Karelia for entertaining the tourists

hämärä – twilight
halla – soil frost, typically a night frost in early summer that often destroys crops or berries
hankikanto – springtime snow cover that you can walk on without breaking it
harju – ridge or esker, one of the legacies of the Ice Age
havupuu – evergreen coniferous tree. Pine is the main raw material for Finland's pulp and paper industries.
heinä – hay
hiidenkirnu – literally 'devil's churn', a round-shaped well, caused by water and small rocks and the dramatic force of moving ice during the latter years of the Ice Age
hilla – highly appreciated orange Arctic cloudberry, which grows on marshlands (also *lakka* or *suomuurain)*
honka – pine

ilmavoimat – Air Force

jää – ice
jääkausi – Ice Age. Prehistoric period, some 10,000 years ago, when all of Finland was covered by a thick ice layer. Moving and melting ice has shaped the Finnish geography.
jäätie – ice road. A road across a lake in winter
jäkälä – lichen

järvi – lake
joiku – sung lyric poem
joki – river
joulu – Christmas
joulupukki – Santa Claus
juhannus – Midsummer
juoksuhauta – trench, used during wars

kämppä – wilderness hut, cabin
köngäs – rapids, waterfall
kaamos – twilight time, the period of darkness over the Arctic Circle when sun doesn't rise at all
kaira – wilderness
kala – fish
Kalevala – The national epic of Finland. Kalevala combines poetry, runes and folk tales with various personalities and biblical themes, such as creation and the fight between good and evil. Originally, Kalevala village was located in northern Russian Karelia.
kalmisto – old graveyard, especially pre-Christian or Orthodox
kansallispuisto – national park
kantele – traditional Karelian string instrument, similar to a harp (also *kannel)*
kaupunki – town or city
kaura – oats
kelirikko – season of bad roads after the snow has melted
kelo – dead, standing, barkless tree, usually pine
kirkonkylä – any village that has a church
kokko – bonfire, lit during Midsummer festivals
korpi – wilderness
koski – rapids
kota – traditional Lappish hut, resembling a tepee or wigwam (from the Finnish *koti)*
kotimaa – 'home country'
koulu – school
kruunu – crown, krone (Scandinavian currency)
kuksa – Lappish cup, carved from a burl/gnarl/burr

kunta – commune or municipality, the smallest administrative unit in Finland

kuntopolku – 'fitness path' (jogging track in summer, skiing track in winter)

kuusi – spruce

kylä – village, as opposed to town

lääni – province

laakso – valley

laavu – permanent or temporary open-air shelter, used by trekkers for sleeping

laituri – pier

lakka – cloudberry

lama – recession

lampi – pond, small lake

lappalainen – member of the Saame community

Lappi – Lapland

lappilainen – inhabitant of Lapland, either Finn or Saame

lehtipuu – deciduous tree

lestadiolaisuus – a strict Lutheran sect in North Finland

liiteri – shelter for firewood

lintu – bird

lohi – salmon

luppokota – see *kota*

mänty – pine tree, the most common of Finnish trees

mökki – cottage

maa – country, earth, land

majoitus – accommodation

makuupussi – sleeping bag

marja – berry

matkustajakoti – hostel, inn

metsä – forest

Midsummer – (or *Juhannus*) the most important annual event when Finns celebrate the longest day of the year. It is celebrated on the Saturday between 20 and 26 July, but the most important time is the Friday night.

mono – skiing shoe (plural *monot)*

muikku – vendace, a typical lake fish

mummonmökki – 'grandma's cottage'

museo – museum

mustikka – blueberry

nähtävyys – tourist attraction

Neuvostoliitto – the Soviet Union (now 'IVY')

niliaitta – a small store on a pole

nuoska – wet snow

nuotio – campfire

ohra – barley

opas – guide (person) or guidebook

opiskelija – student

öljy – oil

pää – head, end

paja – workshop

pakkanen – below-freezing weather

pelto – cultivated field

petäjä – pine

peura – deer

pihlaja – rowan (tree)

pikkujoulu – 'Little Christmas', an often hilarious and easy-going party arranged by companies or schools for employees/students

pirtti – small room in a traditional Finnish farmhouse

pitäjä – see *kunta*

pitkospuu – easily walkable log (lumber) path constructed on wetlands or swamps, usually for recreational purposes

pitopöytä – large buffet table

polku – path

polttopuu – firewood

poro – reindeer

poroerotus – reindeer roundup, held annually in designated places around Lapland

poronhoitoalue – reindeer herding area

poronkusema – Lappish (slightly vulgar) definition of distance: how far a reindeer urinates

Praasniekka – Prazniek, Orthodox religious festival that includes a *ristisaatto* to a lake, where a water sermon takes place

pulkka – boat sledge

puomi – boom

puro – stream

puu – tree, wood

puukko – sheath knife (a useful tool on treks)

räntä – wet snow (snowing)

rakovalkea – log fire

rauhoitettu – protected
reppu – backpack
retkeilymaja – youth hostel, hostel
retki – excursion
revontulet – Northern lights, 'fires of the fox'
riista – game
rinkka – rucksack
ristinsaatto – an Orthodox procession of the cross, an annual festival to commemorate a regional saint
roskakori – rubbish bin
rotko – gorge
routa – ground frost, causes *kelirikko*
ruis – rye
Ruotsi – Sweden
rupla – (Russian) rouble
ruska – period in autumn (fall) when leaves turn red, yellow, etc. Ruska is especially aesthetic in Lapland. It is most beautiful with the right combination of night frost and rain.

sää – weather (also *säätila)*
sääski – mosquito (in Lapland)
sähkö – electricity
Saksa – Germany
sauva – skiing pole
savotta – logging site
savusauna – traditional Finnish sauna, smoke sauna. There is no chimney, just a small outlet for smoke.
seita – holy idol or shrine in Lapland
sieni – mushroom
sora – gravel
sota – war
sotilasalue – military area
suo – swamp, bog, marsh
suomalainen – Finnish, Finn
Suomi – Finland
suomu – gill

taajama – a modern village centre, or any densely populated area

taisteluhauta – trench
takka – fireplace (inside a house)
talo – house or building
tanssilava – dance floor or stage
Tapaninpäivä – Boxing Day
teltta – tent
tervas – old pine tree stump with a high tar content and a distinctive smell. Because it burns well, Finnish trekkers use it to light fires, even in wet weather conditions (also *tervaskanto).*
tsasouna – small prayer hall, which is used by the Orthodox congregation in Eastern Finland (also *tšasouna)*
tukki – log
tulva – spring flood
tunturi – fell, a hill in Lapland
tuohi – birch bark
tupa – the largest room of the main building in a traditional farm
turve – peat
työvoimatoimisto – employment office
tykkylumi – crown snow load

uistin – lure (in fishing)
uitto – log floating

vaara – danger, or wooded hill (typical in North Karelia)
vaellus – trek (verb *vaeltaa)*
valaistu latu – illuminated skiing track
valtio – state, or government
vehnä – wheat
Venäjä – Russia
vesi – water, sometimes lake
vilja – grain
virasto – state or local government office building
vyöhyke – zone

yö – night
yliopisto – university

Index

MAPS

TEXT

Map references are in **bold** type

Aavasaksa Fell 325
Åbo 126-132
Accommodation 48-50
Agricola, Mikael 24
Ähtäri 196
Air travel
  air passes 61
  to Finland 55-57
  within Finland 61-62
Äkäslompolo 328
Ala-Vuokki 305
Åland Islands 139-155, **141**
Alatornio 324
Änäkäinen Area 272
Angeli 343-344
Annoyances 46
Architecture 23
Arts 23-26
Asikkala 165
Asterholma 152
Aurajoki River 126

Bennäs 228
Bicycle 65
Billnäs 104-105

Björkö 153
Björneborg 202-206
Bodbacka 220-221
Bomarsund Fortress 150
Books 41-42
Borgboda Castle 149
Bovik 147
Brändö 152
Bromarv 108
Bullerås 221
Buses
  bus passes 63
  to Finland 58
  within Finland 62-63
Business Hours 38
Busking 46-47

Camping 48
Canoeing 120, 151, 156-157,
  169, 188, 197, 201, 230, 258,
  271, 273, 276, 293, 307, 317,
  327, 330, 333, 337
Car Rental 65
Christianity 27-28
Cinema 26
Climate 17-18, 37
Costs 35-36

Count Per Brahe 12
Culture 26-27
Customs Regulations 35
Cycling 139, 144-145, 149, 152,
  156

Dalsbruk 134
Dance 24
Dangers 46
Degerby 152, 153
Dragsfjärd 134
Drinks 53-54

East Lapland 337-362
Eckerö 145-146
Economy 19-21
Education 22-23
Ekenäs 105-108
Electricity 41
Elimäki 109
Embassies 33-34
Enklinge 152, 153, 154
Enonkoski 235-236
Enontekiö 329
Eräjärvi 180
Eräpyhä Hill 180
Espoo 88

368 Index

Keep in touch!

We love hearing from you and think you'd like to hear from us.

The Lonely Planet Newsletter covers the when, where, how and what of travel. (AND it's free!)

When...is the right time to see reindeer in Finland?
Where...can you hear the best palm-wine music in Ghana?
How...do you get from Asunción to Areguá by steam train?
What...should you leave behind to avoid hassles with customs in Iran?

To join our mailing list just contact us at any of our offices. (details below)

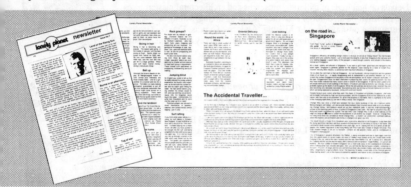

Every issue includes:

- a letter from Lonely Planet founders Tony and Maureen Wheeler
- travel diary from a Lonely Planet author - find out what it's really like out on the road
- feature article on an important and topical travel issue
- a selection of recent letters from our readers
- the latest travel news from all over the world
- details on Lonely Planet's new and forthcoming releases

Also available Lonely Planet t-shirts. 100% heavy weight cotton (S, M, L, XL)

LONELY PLANET PUBLICATIONS

Australia: PO Box 617, Hawthorn, 3122, Victoria (tel: 03-819 1877)
USA: Embarcadero West, 155 Filbert Street, Suite 251, Oakland, CA 94607 (tel: 510-893 8555)
UK: Devonshire House, 12 Barley Mow Passage, Chiswick, London W4 4PH (tel: 081-742 3161)

Lonely Planet guides to Europe

Eastern Europe on a shoestring
This guide has opened up a whole new world for travellers – Albania, Bulgaria, Czechoslovakia, eastern Germany, Hungary, Poland, Romania and Yugoslavia.
'...a thorough, well-researched book. Only a fool would go East without it.' – *Great Expeditions*

Mediterranean Europe on a shoestring
Details on hundreds of galleries, museums and architectural masterpieces and information on outdoor activities including hiking, sailing and skiing. Information on travelling in Albania, Andorra, Cyprus, France, Greece, Italy, Malta, Morocco, Portugal, Spain, Tunisia, Turkey and former republics of Yugoslavia.

Scandinavian & Baltic Europe on a shoestring
A comprehensive guide to travelling in this region including details on galleries, festivals and museums, as well as outdoor activities, national parks and wildlife. Countries featured are Denmark, Estonia, the Faroe Islands, Finland, Iceland, Latvia, Lithuania, Norway and Sweden.

Western Europe on a shoestring
This long-awaited guide covers all of Western Europe's well-loved sights and provides routes for cycling and driving tours, plus details on hiking, climbing and skiing. All the travel facts on Andorra, Austria, Belgium, Britain, France, Germany, Ireland, Italy, Liechtenstein, Luxembourg, Netherlands, Portugal, Spain and Switzerland.

Iceland, Greenland & the Faroe Islands – a travel survival kit
Iceland, Greenland & the Faroe Islands contain some of the most beautiful wilderness areas in the world. This practical guidebook will help travellers discover the dramatic beauty of this region, no matter what their budget.

USSR – a travel survival kit
Invaluable advice on getting around and beating red tape for individual and group travellers alike. This comprehensive guide includes an unsanitised historical background and complete information on art and culture. Over 130 reliable maps, and all place names are given in Cyrillic script. (includes the independent states)

Trekking in Spain
Aimed at both overnight trekkers and day hikers, this guidebook includes useful maps and full details on hikes in some of Spain's most beautiful wilderness areas.

Trekking in Turkey
Few people are aware that Turkey boasts mountains with walks to rival those found in Nepal. This book gives details on treks that are destined to become as popular as those further east.

Also available:
Eastern Europe phrasebook
Discover the most enjoyable way to get around and make friends in Bulgarian, Czech, Hungarian, Polish, Romanian and Slovak.

Mediterranean Europe phrasebook
Ask for directions to the galleries and museums in Albanian, Greek, Italian, Macedonian, Maltese, Serbian & Croatian and Slovene.

Scandinavian Europe phrasebook
Find your way around the ski trails and enjoy the local festivals Danish, Finnish, Icelandic, Norwegian and Swedish.

Western Europe phrasebook
Show your appreciation for the great masters in Basque, Catalan, Dutch, French, German, Irish, Portuguese and Spanish (Castilian).

Moroccan Arabic phrasebook
Essential words and phrases for everything from finding a hotel room in Casablanca to asking for a meal of *tajine* in Marrakesh. Includes Arabic script and pronunciation guide.

Turkish phrasebook
Practical words and phrases that will help you to communicate effectively with local people in almost every situation. Includes pronunciation guide.

Russian phrasebook
This indispensable phrasebook will help you get information, read signs and menus, and make friends along the way. Includes phonetic transcriptions and Cyrillic script.

Also:
Look out for **Lonely Planet travel survival kits** to the Baltic states, France, Greece, Hungary, Ireland, Italy, Poland and Switzerland.

Lonely Planet Guidebooks

Lonely Planet guidebooks cover every accessible part of Asia as well as Australia, the Pacific, South America, Africa, the Middle East, Europe and parts of North America. There are five series: *travel survival kits*, covering a country for a range of budgets; *shoestring guides* with compact information for low-budget travel in a major region; *walking guides*; *city guides* and *phrasebooks*.

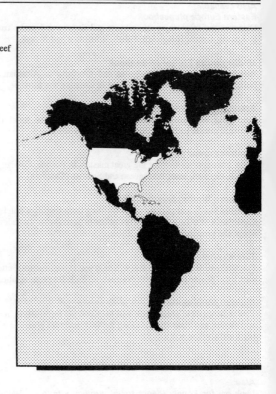

Australia & the Pacific
Australia
Bushwalking in Australia
Islands of Australia's Great Barrier Reef
Fiji
Micronesia
New Caledonia
New Zealand
Tramping in New Zealand
Papua New Guinea
Papua New Guinea phrasebook
Rarotonga & the Cook Islands
Samoa
Solomon Islands
Sydney
Tahiti & French Polynesia
Tonga
Vanuatu

South-East Asia
Bali & Lombok
Bangkok
Burma
Burmese phrasebook
Cambodia
Indonesia
Indonesia phrasebook
Malaysia, Singapore & Brunei
Philippines
Pilipino phrasebook
Singapore
South-East Asia on a shoestring
Thailand
Thai phrasebook
Vietnam, Laos & Cambodia

North-East Asia
China
Mandarin Chinese phrasebook
Hong Kong, Macau & Canton
Japan
Japanese phrasebook
Korea
Korean phrasebook
North-East Asia on a shoestring
Taiwan
Tibet
Tibet phrasebook

West Asia
Trekking in Turkey
Turkey
Turkish phrasebook
West Asia on a shoestring

Middle East
Egypt & the Sudan
Egyptian Arabic phrasebook
Iran
Israel
Jordan & Syria
Yemen

Indian Ocean
Madagascar & Comoros
Maldives & Islands of the East Indian Ocean
Mauritius, Réunion & Seychelles

Mail Order

Lonely Planet guidebooks are distributed worldwide. They are also available by mail order from Lonely Planet, so if you have difficulty finding a title please write to us. US and Canadian residents should write to Embarcadero West, 155 Filbert St, Suite 251, Oakland CA 94607, USA; European residents should write to Devonshire House, 12 Barley Mow Passage, Chiswick, London W4 4PH; and residents of other countries to PO Box 617, Hawthorn, Victoria 3122, Australia.

Indian Subcontinent
Bangladesh
India
Hindi/Urdu phrasebook
Trekking in the Indian Himalaya
Karakoram Highway
Kashmir, Ladakh & Zanskar
Nepal
Trekking in the Nepal Himalaya
Nepal phrasebook
Pakistan
Sri Lanka
Sri Lanka phrasebook

Africa
Africa on a shoestring
Central Africa
East Africa
Kenya
Swahili phrasebook
Morocco, Algeria & Tunisia
Moroccan Arabic phrasebook
Zimbabwe, Botswana & Namibia
West Africa

Mexico
Baja California
Mexico

Central America
Central America on a shoestring
Costa Rica
La Ruta Maya

North America
Alaska
Canada
Hawaii

Europe
Eastern Europe on a shoestring
Eastern Europe phrasebook
Finland
Iceland, Greenland & the Faroe Islands
Mediterranean Europe on a shoestring
Mediterranean Europe phrasebook
Scandinavian & Baltic Europe on a shoestring
Scandinavian Europe phrasebook
Trekking in Spain
USSR
Russian phrasebook
Western Europe on a shoestring
Western Europe phrasebook

South America
Argentina, Uruguay & Paraguay
Bolivia
Brazil
Brazilian phrasebook
Chile & Easter Island
Colombia
Ecuador & the Galápagos Islands
Latin American Spanish phrasebook
Peru
Quechua phrasebook
South America on a shoestring
Trekking in the Patagonian Andes

The Lonely Planet Story

Lonely Planet published its first book in 1973 in response to the numerous 'How did you do it?' questions Maureen and Tony Wheeler were asked after driving, bussing, hitching, sailing and railing their way from England to Australia.

Written at a kitchen table and hand collated, trimmed and stapled, *Across Asia on the Cheap* became an instant local bestseller, inspiring thoughts of another book.

Eighteen months in South-East Asia resulted in their second guide, *South-East Asia on a shoestring*, which they put together in a backstreet Chinese hotel in Singapore in 1975. The 'yellow bible' as it quickly became known to backpackers around the world, soon became *the* guide to the region. It has sold well over half a million copies and is now in its 7th edition, still retaining its familiar yellow cover.

Today there are over 100 Lonely Planet titles – books that have that same adventurous approach to travel as those early guides; books that 'assume you know how to get your luggage off the carousel' as one reviewer put it.

Although Lonely Planet initially specialised in guides to Asia, they now cover most regions of the world, including the Pacific, South America, Africa, the Middle East and Europe. The list of *walking guides* and *phrasebooks* (for 'unusual' languages such as Quechua, Swahili, Nepalese and Egyptian Arabic) is also growing rapidly.

The emphasis continues to be on travel for independent travellers. Tony and Maureen still travel for several months of each year and play an active part in the writing, updating and quality control of Lonely Planet's guides.

They have been joined by over 50 authors, 48 staff – mainly editors, cartographers, & designers – at our office in Melbourne, Australia and another 10 at our US office in Oakland, California. In 1991 Lonely Planet opened a London office to handle sales for Britain, Europe and Africa. Travellers themselves also make a valuable contribution to the guides through the feedback we receive in thousands of letters each year.

The people at Lonely Planet strongly believe that travellers can make a positive contribution to the countries they visit, both through their appreciation of the countries' culture, wildlife and natural features, and through the money they spend. In addition, the company makes a direct contribution to the countries and regions it covers. Since 1986 a percentage of the income from each book has been donated to ventures such as famine relief in Africa; aid projects in India; agricultural projects in Central America; Greenpeace's efforts to halt French nuclear testing in the Pacific and Amnesty International. In 1991 $68,000 was donated to these causes.

Lonely Planet's basic travel philosophy is summed up in Tony Wheeler's comment, 'Don't worry about whether your trip will work out. Just go!'